MANY PASTS:

Readings in
American Social History

Volume two / 1865–the present

MANY PASTS:

Readings in
American Social History

Volume two | 1865–the present

Edited by
HERBERT G. GUTMAN
City College of the City University of New York

GREGORY S. KEALEY
University of Rochester

Prentice-Hall, Inc., Englewood Cliffs, New Jersey

Library of Congress Cataloging in Publication Data

GUTMAN, HERBERT GEORGE, COMP.
    Many pasts.

    Includes bibliographies.
    CONTENTS: v. 1. 1600-1876.—v. 2. 1865-1973.
    1. United States—Social conditions—Addresses,
essays, lectures. I. Kealey, Gregory S.,
joint comp. II. Title.
HN57.G85   309.1'73   72-12861
ISBN   0-13-555938-3   (v. 2)

PRENTICE-HALL INTERNATIONAL, INC., *London*
PRENTICE-HALL OF AUSTRALIA, PTY. LTD., *Sydney*
PRENTICE-HALL OF CANADA, LTD., *Toronto*
PRENTICE-HALL OF INDIA PRIVATE LIMITED, *New Delhi*
PRENTICE-HALL OF JAPAN, INC., *Tokyo*

Contents

MANY PASTS:

Readings in
American Social History

Volume two / 1865–the present

Introduction

"The mystery of the human condition," anthropologist Sidney W. Mintz has written, "is not in what man has, but what he does with what he has." This question applies both to the contemporary world and to the world of the past. One of the important questions in the new social history, it is equally applicable to a colonial indentured servant (or slave) and to a colonial merchant, to an early-nineteenth-century New England mill girl and to her Yankee employer, to a mid-nineteenth-century Irish immigrant and to an early-twentieth-century Italian or Jewish immigrant, to an unskilled Gilded Age factory worker and to a rural tenant farmer, to a resident of a contemporary inner-city ghetto and to a third-generation American who has moved from a ghetto to a suburban setting. This two-volume collection of historical writings in United States social history explores the many dimensions of that "mystery" over time. It spans the entire American experience, reaching back into early-colonial society and then returning to the present day. The readings have been selected to satisfy three objectives: first, to acquaint readers with some of those historians whose writings in American social history directly or indirectly focus on the critical intersections between culture and society; second, to supplement in essential ways the traditional political emphasis in most general American history courses; and, third, to illustrate how diverse methods of historical inquiry have been (and are being) used by a range of historians to shed light on important, but often neglected, aspects of the American past.

These unusual principles of selection are meant to give a distinctive quality to these volumes. Most collections of readings often either lack a clear central focus or are organized to illuminate, nearly exclusively, powerful political processes central to our national history. By intent, the emphasis in these pages is quite different. Here we emphasize the structure of American society, how that structure changed, and especially how those changes were experienced, interpreted, and responded to by those men and women who are part of Michael Harrington's "other America." These groups, of course, have varied in composition over time and behaved in quite dissimilar ways, but all have shared unequally in both the material rewards available to them as contrasted with their better situated *contemporaries,* and in the attention devoted to them by historians. A library wall can be filled with studies of the careers of men like Abraham Lincoln, Theodore Roosevelt, or Woodrow Wilson, but a library shelf with books on either colonial indentured servants or early-twentieth century East- and South-European immigrants would remain half empty. Such groups deserve attention for many reasons. We do not study them to "expose" their conditions. Others have done that in great detail. Nor is there reason to idealize or romanticize their life-style or behavior. Put simply, they, too, have a past, and that past deserves to be fully understood. Their everyday lives and common beliefs were subtle and complex in texture, and often distinctive. It is that distinctiveness in historical experiences, and even in behavior and thought, which allows us to talk of many American pasts, not "the American past" or "the American experience." Moreover, only the study of these experiences makes possible comparisons over time and within a particular time period between persons of different social classes, sexes, and ethnic origins. But such comparisons—comparisons that explore similarities and differences— require first that we examine the interior histories of the groups and their relationships to other segments in a society. "The daily job of living did not end with enslavement," Mintz writes of the seventeenth- and eighteenth-century Afro-Americans, "and the slaves could and did create viable patterns of life, for which their pasts were pools of available symbolic and material resources." This was as true for other oppressed and dependent classes and social groups as for the slaves, and the first concern of their historian is to recreate those "viable patterns of life" and to explain how and why they changed over time.

These groups deserve attention for yet other compelling reasons. Their perceptions of the larger society cast a light on it that is often unavailable elsewhere. More than this, just as the changing structure of American society affected them in important ways, their behavior also helped to shape the larger social system. In studying such groups, we therefore gain insight into the larger society and its changing class and social structure. This is not a trivial point. The distinguished French historian Fernand Braudel said it well:

> Victorious events come about as the result of many possibilities, among which life has finally made its choices. For one possibility which actually is realized, innumerable others have been drowned. These are the ones which have left little trace for the historian. And yet it is necessary to give them their place because the losing movements are forces which have at every moment affected the final outcome.

Clearly (with concrete examples from the American experience), it is not possible to understand fully the behavior of slave owners without first studying the behavior of slaves. It is not possible to grasp the sources of middle- and upper-class reform movements in the late-nineteenth and early-twentieth centuries without first understanding the behavior of farmers and of native and immigrant urban workers. It is not possible to assess the significance of the New Deal without first examining the ways in which countless Americans expressed their discontents in the 1930s outside the settled political process. Part of the excitment of the new social history is that in retrieving the past experiences of the neglected groups, we enrich our understanding of other groups and of large, long-term historical processes.

American social history is still in its infancy as a branch of historical inquiry. As the sociologist Norman Birnbaum has written, "insofar as major aspects of its past are concerned" the United States "remains an unknown country." Birnbaum nevertheless predicts "a voyage of self-discovery that may yet revise some of our notions of social provenance." He is right. More, however, is involved in such a "voyage" than the social historian shifting the focus of attention to lower-class groups or, as is quite fashionable, to the "certitude" found in "quantitative data." The readings in these volumes should make that clear. Good social history of the lower-classes (and other classes as well) demands a conceptual clarity and rigor no less severe than, say, the study of Florentine paintings, demographic movements in medieval Europe, land tenure systems in Latin America, or business cycles in nineteenth-century America. Nothing of importance is gained by shifting the focus of historical interest and then asking of a new subject narrow or restricting questions.

The conceptual framework—that is, the ways in which historians frame questions about particular aspects of the past and go about answering them—is critical. For that reason, the conceptual apparatus used in these two volumes deserves brief attention.

The volumes have been organized and the readings chosen to focus on the interaction over time between *society and culture.* The emphasis is on how the two interacted to shape the behavior and thought of neglected social classes, but again we should note that this interaction also shaped the behavior and thought of the better-advantaged social classes. *American society* has changed greatly in the past three centuries and so has *American culture.* The two sets of changes are closely related but *not* similar, and the distinction between them is essential to studying and understanding lower-class groups. "There is no such thing," the British social historian E. P. Thompson has written, "as economic growth which is not, at the same time, growth or change of a culture." Nevertheless Thompson warns, "We should not assume any automatic or over-direct correspondence between the dynamic of economic growth and the dynamic of social or cultural life."

Broadly described, in its essential structure American society has passed through three distinctive stages of development. Until the 1830s and 1840s, nearly all Americans lived in a *preindustrial society,* that is, a society in which everyday behavior (work, family life, leisure patterns, etc.) are not yet affected by machinery and the new technological and organizational imperatives associated with the Industrial Revolution. Old America was not simply an "agrarian" society; it was a preindustrial society similar to, but also different from, the more settled and traditional pre-modern societies in other parts of the world. (Preindustrial cultures, it should be emphasized, varied greatly in their interior structure. Slaves and their owners, Indians and the pioneer farmers who helped drive them to the West, and artisans and the merchants who marketed their goods, for example, all lived in a pre-modern world but experienced it and responded to it in quite distinctive ways.) Between the 1840s and the end of the nineteenth century, preindustrial American society *became* industrial American society. Here was a profound and radical shift that took half a century, and directly or indirectly transformed work and leisure, politics and ideology, family life and associational activities. Not all social classes and distinctive groups were affected similarly by this process. All brought to the process itself distinctive historical experiences. The central tension in this rapidly changing world was between the Old and the New America. Twentieth-century American social history differs radically from either of these two earlier "stages." By the end of the nineteenth century, the United States had *become* an industrial society, and much of twentieth-century American social history has centered about the processes and problems particular to a *maturing* industrial society.

So much, in brief, for the larger structural changes in American society. But what of *American culture?* Here, the writings of the Polish sociologist Zygmunt Bauman and certain contemporary American anthropologists will help. Bauman writes:

Human behavior, whether individual or collective, is invariably the resultant of two factors: the cognitive systems as well as the goals and patterns of behavior as defined by culture system(s), on the one hand, and the system of real contingencies as defined by the social structure on the other. A complete interpretation of social processes can only be achieved when both systems, as well as their interaction, are taken into consideration.

Bauman's distinction between *culture* and *society* is profoundly important to the study of social history. Altogether too often, American social historians have emphasized "society" at the expense of "culture" in describing historical patterns of lower-class life and behavior. It is essential, of course, to define the particular "real contingencies" in a given society and for a particular social class, sex, or ethnic community. However, it should not be assumed, as some habitually do, that these were the only determinants of behavior. Scant attention is given to the ways in which accumulated past experiences ("culture") in the different strata of particular societies affected the choices made by men and women. But it is precisely this cultural-societal interaction that helps to begin the unravelling of the "mystery" posed by Sidney Mintz.

Another anthropologist, Eric Wolf, sharpens our understanding of the critical differences between culture and society:

> By culture, I mean the historically developed forms through which the members of a given society relate to each other. By society, I mean the element of action, of human manoeuver within the field provided by cultural forms, human manoeuver which aims either at preserving a given balance of life-chances and life-risks or at changing it.

Mintz himself expands on this distinction in a manner especially useful to the student of social history:

> . . . We see culture depicted as a kind of resource, and society as a kind of arena—the distribution is between sets of historically available alternatives or forms on the one hand, and the societal circumstances or setting within which these forms may be employed, on the other. . . . Culture is *used;* and any analysis of its use immediately brings into view the arrangements of persons in social groups for whom cultural forms confirm, reinforce, maintain, change, or deny particular arrangements of status, power, and identity.

Brief concrete examples help illustrate the theoretical point. When machinery or new technology displaced the traditional skills of an artisan, the "real contingencies" available to him altered radically. But in dealing with them, he was affected by the accumulated historical experiences related to his older craft life. Emancipation radically altered the slaves' status by expanding the "arena" (society) within which southern blacks could make choices, but their particular choices were also shaped by the patterns of work and life (culture) they had known as slaves. A similar analysis allows us to examine in new ways the behavior of migrant and immigrant groups, native and foreign-born, white and non-white.

Careful attention to the critical intersection between culture and society in the past contributes to the examination of particular patterns of human behavior and processes of social change in new ways. Not all the historians included in this collection of readings explicitly make these distinctions, but nearly all use evidence in critical or imaginative ways tending toward this view. For each period, where available, readings have been chosen that emphasize in different ways the cultural-societal interaction and thereby, at quite different times in our past, describe the determinants of such important historical "facts" as family behavior, work habits, ethnic identity and self-assertion, collective self-protection, and peaceful and violent conflict. A subtle awareness of how past (culture) and present (society) have shaped, and continue to shape, human behavior also permits us to go beyond the increasingly sterile disputes between so-called "consensus" historians and so-called "conflict" historians. "There is no more need for romances," Walt Whitman insisted nearly a century ago. "Let facts and history be properly told."

section **1**

Industrializing America: The South and the West 1865-1900

For two centuries before the Civil War, American society and its economy had rested primarily on agricultural enterprise of all sorts. Settled but distinctive social structures had characterized farm production and life in the South and in the North and West. The plantation system in the South and the freehold farms in the North and the West had produced surpluses which, in turn, had made possible the transformation of Old American society into an industrial society. The consequences for the rural population—those who owned the land and those who worked it, as well as those who grew the crops and those who marketed them—were profound and complex. Industrial development and the power associated with it altered the place of the agrarian social structure in American life. Farm production and the life-styles it sustained grew relatively less important as greater numbers of Americans (native and foreign in birth) were drawn to the cities and to the new industrial "sector." Industrial development, however, did not mean the absolute decline of the agricultural "sector." Put simply, agricultural employment increased 50 percent between 1860 and 1890, but non-agricultural employment went up 300 percent.

The key to this seeming paradox was the impact of industrial and urban development on the agricultural "sector." In 1860, for example, farmers produced 800,000,000 bushels of corn. By 1915, they turned out nearly three billion bushels of corn. In these same years, wheat production went up from 173,000,000 bushels to just over one billion bushels. Technological improvements and increased labor efficiency helped explain these increases in production. The value of farm implements rose from $246 million in 1860 to $750 million in 1900 and to $1,265 million in 1910. Uniform prosperity, however, did not follow from such increases. "The more industrialism advanced," one historian has written, "the more did the fortunes of an agricultural America become affected by forces beyond its control." Such "forces," though, were not that distant. The power associated with industrial wealth and values found expression in the South and West themselves.

Rural America underwent a profound crisis in the post-Civil War decades and responded to its changing place in the New America in diverse ways. Farm protest movements of great importance occurred in both regions. But these movements were significantly shaped by the particular historical experiences of farmers and farm workers. The West and the South had known different pre-modern social experiences and at the core of these differences was the plantation and slave experience.

1.1

Mudsills and Bottom Rails

C. VANN WOODWARD

The "New South" was not the utopia its promoters had promised when "redeeming" southern state governments from white and black Radical Republicans. Poverty remained endemic in the region for most blacks and large numbers of whites. Sharecropping, cash tenantry, and farm labor did not discriminate between blacks and whites. A credit system (the crop-lien system) added to the depressed condition of both groups. Northern capital helped to diversify the southern economy, but the region still remained predominantly agricultural or produced industrial raw materials for northern mills and factories. Textile mills, mostly in the Carolinas and Georgia, were an exception. Assuring investors of its pliant and cheap labor force, southern whites anxiously pleaded for northern capital to build the "New South." Southern white workers and farmers had two quite distinct choices: to remove blacks from all areas of the economy where whites had established some control, or to encourage blacks to resist being used either as

C. Vann Woodward, *Origins of the New South* (Baton Rouge, La.: Louisiana State University Press, 1971), pp. 205–9, 211–34. Reprinted and footnotes omitted by permission of the publisher.

strikebreakers or as competitive cheap labor. After Reconstruction, both choices were acted upon by southern whites, as C. Vann Woodward ably shows.

If Reconstruction ever set the bottom rail on top, it was not for long and never securely. Redemption seemed to leave little doubt that the bottom rail was again on the bottom—whatever its temporary dislocation. It remained for the New South to find what Reconstruction had failed to find: the measure of the emancipated slave's freedom and a definition of free labor, both black and white; for the white worker's place in the New Order would be vitally conditioned by the place assigned the free black worker.

Much discussion about the Negro's civil rights, his political significance, his social status, and his aspirations can be shortened and simplified by a clear understanding of the economic status assigned him in the New Order. Emancipation and Reconstruction had done little to change that picture. The lives of the overwhelming majority of Negroes were still circumscribed by the farm and plantation. The same was true of the white people, but the Negroes, with few exceptions, were farmers without land. Questionnaires from the census of 1880 revealed that in thirty-three counties of Georgia where Negro population was thick, "not more than one in one hundred" Negro farmers owned land; the same proportion was reported from seventeen black Mississippi counties; twelve others reported not one in twenty, and many not one in fifty. From Tennessee as a whole the report was that only "a very small part of the Negroes own land or even the houses in which they live"; also from Louisiana and Alabama came report of "very few" owners.

More specific information is provided for one state by the report of the Comptroller General of Georgia for the year ending October 1, 1880. Of a total of some $88,000,000 in land value, the Negroes, who made up nearly half the state's population, owned around $1,500,000. Of a total of some $23,000,000 value put upon cattle and farm animals, the Negroes owned about $2,000,000, and of some $3,200,000 in agricultural tools, the Negroes reported a little more than $163,000. It is pretty clear that as a rule the Negro farmer not only worked the white man's land but worked it with a white man's plow drawn by a white man's mule. In the next two decades the race's landholdings improved slightly, but in 1900 black Georgians had taxable titles to only one twenty-fifth of the land; only 14 per cent of the Negro farmers owned their farms, and in 1910 only 13 per cent. In the South as a whole, by 1900, 75.3 per cent of the Negro farmers were croppers or tenants.

The landless Negro farmers, like the landless whites, worked either for wages or for shares, under any of several arrangements. When the Alabama planter furnished tools, animals, and feed, as well as the land, his share was one half of all crops; when he furnished only the land he took one fourth of the cotton and one third of the corn. There were numerous variations, including the "two-day system" on Edisto Island, where the tenant worked two days of the week for the landlord in the feudal manner. The impression of uniformity in the labor system that replaced slavery would seem to have been exaggerated. As late as 1881 it was reported that in Alabama "you can hardly find any two farmers in a community who are carrying on their business alike," and frequently one planter might use several methods at once: "To one he rents, to another he gives a contract for working on shares, to another he pays wages in money, and with another he swaps work, and so *ad infinitum.*" Whatever system was used "there follows the same failure, or partial failure."

The share system called forth especially severe criticism from all sides as being "ruinous to the soil" and "a disgrace to farming." A large proportion of landlords preferred and used the wage system. From Tennessee in 1880 it was reported that "advocates for shares and wages are about equally divided in number." Census reports of wages paid for labor in cotton production in 1880 make no distinction between white and black workers, and there probably was little difference. Prevalent monthly wages for a man's work "from sun to sun" were $8.00 to $14.00 in Alabama; $8.00 to $15.00 in Arkansas; $6.00 to $10.00 in Florida; $5.00 to $10.00 in Georgia ($4.00 to $6.00 per month for women); $6.00 to $15.00 in Louisiana; $8.00 to $12.00 in Mississippi, South Carolina, and Tennessee; $8.00 to $15.00 in Texas. Daily wages were usually 50 cents with board, or 75 cents without. A year's wages for a man in the central cotton belt of Georgia were $60.00 to $100.00; in Tennessee they were $100.00 to $125.00. Both yearly and monthly wages included rations. In 1888 it was estimated by an authority that "the regular allowance of an ordinary hand is 12 pounds of bacon and 5 pecks of meal by the month," which "would cost him twenty-three dollars in the course of twelve months."

It should be noted that the year 1880, for which the wage rates are quoted, was a relatively "good" year for cotton prices. When the price fell to half that in the nineties the wages could not have been nearly so high. If a yield of only three to six bales per hand could be expected, as estimated in Arkansas in 1880, the product of a year's labor would likely bring little more than $100.00 on the market in the middle nineties. Working on shares, the cropper at that rate received about $50.00 for his year's work. Neither he nor his landlord was likely to see or handle any cash, since both were in all probability deeply enmeshed in the toils of the crop lien. They received instead meager supplies at the prices demanded of credit customers.

The tides of Negro migration that had set in during Reconstruction, as the first and most characteristic expression of freedom, continued to move in the same general directions for some years after Redemption. These movements were of three kinds: from the country to the towns; from the poorer lands to the delta, bottom, and richer lands; and from the older states to the newer states of the Southwest. Intermittent complaint and a few laws against "enticing" labor persisted through the eighties. With one striking exception, however, the Negro migrations were largely from one part of the South to another. The great exodus northward did not begin until a half century after freedom.

A census survey of the relation of land and labor in the cotton state of Alabama in 1880 revealed that the Negroes were most thickly concentrated upon the most fertile soil in the state, and the whites, upon the poorest soil; that the most fertile land, where the sharecropping system was most prevalent, yielded the least product, and was rapidly being exhausted; that poorer lands under cultivation by owners produced greater yield per capita and per acre; and that the white farmer was rapidly gaining on the black in the proportion of cotton produced.

In spite of these facts, there was an almost universal preference among Black-Belt landlords for Negro tenants and workers. "White labor is totally unsuited to our methods, our manners, and our accommodations," declared an Alabama planter in 1888. "No other laborer [than the Negro] of whom I have any knowledge, would be as cheerful, or so contented on four pounds of meat and a peck of meal a week, in a little log cabin 14 × 16 feet, with cracks in it large enough to afford free passage to a large sized cat." "Give me the nigger every time," echoed a Mississippi planter. "The nigger will never 'strike' as long as you give him plenty to eat and half clothe him: He will live on less and do more hard work, when properly managed, than any other class, or race of people. As Arp truthfully says 'we can boss him' and that is what we southern folks like."

The writer who estimated the cash value of freedom for the Negro thirty years after emancipation at a little less than one dollar a year to the individual overstated his point, though not so grossly as it might seem. At least such expensive luxuries as civil liberties and political franchises were beyond his reach. He knew very well that immediate, daily necessities came first—land, mules, plows, food, and clothes, all of which had to be got from a white man who oftener than not had too little himself.

In the working out of a new code of civil rights and social status for the freedman—in the definition of the Negro's "place"—Reconstruction had been only an interruption, the importance of which varied from state to state, but which was nowhere decisive. The transition from slavery to caste as a system of controlling race relations went forward gradually and tediously. Slavery had been vastly more than a labor system, and the gap that its removal left in manners, mores, and ritual of behavior could not be filled overnight. The so-called "Black Codes" were soon overthrown, as were the laws imported by the Carpetbaggers. Redemption and Hayes's policy of *laissez faire* left the code to be worked out by Southern white men. It has already been pointed out that there was no unity of opinion among them concerning the Negro's political rights. There also existed a roughly comparable division with reference to his civil rights. . . .

It is one of the paradoxes of Southern history that political democracy for the white man and racial discrimination for the black were often products of the same dynamics. As the Negroes invaded the new mining and industrial towns of the uplands in greater numbers, and the hill-country whites were driven into more frequent and closer association with them, and as the two races were brought into rivalry for subsistence wages in the cotton fields, mines, and wharves, the lower-class white man's demand for Jim Crow laws became more insistent. It took a lot of ritual and Jim Crow to bolster the creed of white supremacy in the bosom of a white man working for a black man's wages. The Negro pretty well understood these forces, and his grasp of them was one reason for his growing alliance with the most conservative and politically reactionary class of whites against the insurgent white democracy. A North Carolina Negro wrote: "The best people of the South do not demand this separate car business . . . and, when they do, it is only to cater to those of their race who, in order to get a big man's smile, will elevate them [*sic*] to place and power." He believed that "this whole thing is but a pandering to the lower instincts of the worst class of whites in the South."

The barriers of racial discrimination mounted in direct ratio with the tide of political democracy among whites. In fact, an increase of Jim Crow laws upon the statute books of a state is almost an accurate index of the decline of the reactionary regimes of the Redeemers and triumph of white democratic movements. Take, for example, the law requiring separate accommodations for the races in trains, said to be "the most typical Southern law." No state enacted such a law for more than twenty years after 1865. Yet in the five years beginning in 1887 one after another adopted some variation of the law: Florida in 1887, Mississippi in 1888, Texas in 1889, Louisiana in 1890, Alabama, Arkansas, Kentucky, and Georgia in 1891. These were the years when the Farmers' Alliance was first making itself felt in the legislatures of these states. Mississippi, in 1888, was the first state to adopt a law providing for the separation of the races in railway stations, and Georgia, in 1891, the first to adopt the law for streetcars. These laws, though significant in themselves, were often only enactments of codes already in practice. Whether by state law or local law, or by the more pervasive coercion of sovereign white opinion, "the Negro's place" was gradually defined—in the courts, schools, and libraries, in parks, theaters, hotels, and residential districts, in hospitals, insane asylums—everywhere, including on sidewalks and in cemeteries. When complete, the new codes of White Supremacy were vastly more complex than the ante-bellum slave codes or the Black Codes of 1865–1866, and, if anything, they were stronger and more rigidly enforced.

Among the institutions of the Old Order that strained to meet the needs of the New, none proved more hopelessly inadequate than the old penitentiaries. The state was suddenly called upon to take over the plantation's penal functions at a time when crime was enormously increasing. The strain was too great. One after another of the states adopted the expedient of leasing the convicts to private corporations or individuals. In Louisiana the convict-lease system had an ante-bellum origin; in the other Southern states it was introduced by the provisional or military governments and retained by the Carpetbaggers and Redeemers.

For a number of reasons the lease system took firm roots in the New Order and grew to greater proportions. For one thing, it fitted perfectly the program of retrenchment, for under it the penitentiary not only ceased to be a heavy burden on the taxpayer but became a source of revenue to the state—sometimes a very lucrative source. The system also fitted conveniently the needs occasioned by the new criminal codes of the Redemption regimes, which piled up heavy penalties for petty offenses against property, while at the same time they weakened the protection afforded the Negro in the courts. The so-called "pig law" of Mississippi defined the theft of any property over ten dollars in value, or any cattle or swine of whatever value, as grand larceny, with a sentence up to five years. After its adoption the number of state convicts increased from 272 in 1874 to 1,072 by the end of 1877. The number in Georgia increased from 432 in 1872 to 1,441 in 1877. Additional convictions meant additional revenue instead of additional taxes. The system quickly became a large-scale and sinister business. Leases of ten, twenty, and thirty years were granted by legislatures to powerful politicians, Northern syndicates, mining corporations, and individual planters. Laws limiting hours of labor and types of work for convicts were nonexistent in some states and negligible in others, and in two states protective laws were later removed or modified. Responsibility of lessees for the health and lives of convicts was extremely loose. Some states had no inspectors and in others inspection was highly perfunctory if not corrupt. Where the law permitted, the large lessees subleased convicts in small or large gangs for short periods, thus rendering responsibility to the state even more fictitious and protection of the state's prisoners all but impossible. County prisons in many cases adopted the system and in Alabama had twice as many convicts leased as the state. The South's "penitentiaries" were great rolling cages that followed construction camps and railroad building, hastily built stockades deep in forest or swamp or mining fields, or windowless log forts in turpentine flats.

The degradation and brutality produced by this system would be incredible but for the amount of evidence from official sources. A report of the inspectors of the Alabama penitentiary revealed that the prisons were packed with several times the number of convicts they could reasonably hold. "They are as filthy, as a rule, as dirt could make them, and both prisons and prisoners were infested with vermin. The bedding was totally unfit for use. . . . [It was found] that convicts were excessively and sometimes cruelly punished; that they were poorly clothed and fed; that the sick were neglected, insomuch as no hospitals had been provided, that they were confined with the well convicts." A grand-jury investigation of the penitentiary hospital in Mississippi reported that inmates were "all bearing on their persons marks of the most inhuman and brutal treatments. Most of them have their backs cut in great wales, scars and blisters, some with the skin peeling off in pieces as the result of severe beatings. . . . They were lying there dying, some of them on bare boards, so poor and emaciated that their bones almost came through their skin, many complaining for want of food. . . . We actually saw live vermin crawling over their faces, and the little bedding and clothing they have is in tatters and stiff with filth." In mining camps of Arkansas and Alabama convicts were worked through the winter without shoes, standing in water much of the time. In both states the task system was used, whereby a squad of three was compelled to mine a certain amount of coal per day on penalty of a severe flogging for the whole squad. Convicts in the turpentine camps of Florida, with "stride-chains" and "waist-chains" riveted on their bodies, were compelled to work at a trot. "They kept this gait up all day long, from tree to tree," reported the warden. The average annual death rate among Negro convicts in Mississippi from 1880 to 1885 was almost 11 per cent, for white convicts about half that, and in 1887 the general average was 16 per cent. The death rate among the prisoners of Arkansas was reported in 1881 to be 25 per cent annually. An indication of what was called "moral conditions" is provided in a report of the Committee on the Penitentiary of the Georgia Legislature: "We find in some of the camps men and women chained together and occupying the same sleeping bunks. The result is that there are now in the Penitentiary twenty-five bastard children, ranging from three months to five years of age, and many of the women are now far advanced in pregnancy." For the Southern convict-lease system a modern scholar can "find parallel only in the persecutions of the Middle Ages or in the prison camps of Nazi Germany."

The lease system was under bitter attack, especially from the various independent parties, and repeated attempts were made to abolish or reform it. Julia Tutwiler of Alabama was a moving spirit in the reform movement. Almost everywhere, however, the reformers were opposed by vested interests within the Redemption party—sometimes by the foremost leaders of that party. Senator Brown of Georgia was guaranteed by his twenty-year lease "three hundred able-bodied, long-term men" to work in his Dade Coal Mines, for which he paid the state about eight cents per hand per day. Senator Gordon was also a member of a firm leasing convicts. Colonel Colyar, leader of one wing of the Redemption party in Tennessee, leased that state's prisoners at $101,000 a year for the Tennessee Coal and Iron Company. Control over these Southern state "slaves" was the foundation of several large fortunes, and in one case, of a great political dynasty. Robert McKee, who was in a position to know all the workings of the system, wrote that the state warden of Alabama, John H. Bankhead, "grew rich in a few years on $2000 a year," and manipulated the legislature at will. "The 'penitentiary ring' is a power in the party," he wrote privately, "and it is a corrupt power. One of the State officers is a lessee of convicts, and has a brother who is a deputy warden." Former Secretary of State Rufus K. Boyd believed that the convict-lease ring was "as unscrupulous as any radical in the days of their power. . . . Are we all thieves? What is it leading to? Who can submit to these things patiently?" Yet the party continued to submit.

The convict-lease system did greater violence to the moral authority of the Redeemers than did anything else. For it was upon the tradition of paternalism that the Redeemer regimes claimed authority to settle the race problem and "deal with the Negro."

The abandonment of the Negro by his Northern champions after the Compromise of 1877 was as quixotic as their previous crusade in his behalf had been romantic and unrealistic. The *Nation* thought the government should "have nothing more to do with him," and Godkin could not see how the Negro could ever "be worked into a system of government for which you and I would have much respect." The New York *Tribune,* with a logic all its own, stated that the Negroes, after having been given "ample opportunity to develop their own latent capacities," had only succeeded in proving that "as a race they are idle, ignorant, and vicious."

The Supreme Court's decision in October, 1883, declaring the Civil Rights Act unconstitutional was only the juristic fulfillment of the Compromise of 1877, and was, in fact, handed down by Justice Joseph P. Bradley, Grant's appointee, who had been a member of the Electoral Commission of 1877. "The calm with which the country receives the news," observed the editor of the New York *Evening Post,* "shows how completely the extravagant expectations . . . of the war have died out." A Republican who held repudiated bonds of South Carolina wrote from

New York that the Civil Rights decision came "as a just retribution to the colored people for their infamous conduct" in assisting in the repudiation of the bonds; "if they expect the people of the North to fight their battles for them they can wait until doomsday," he added.

It has already been pointed out that the wing of the Republican party that raised the loudest outcry against Hayes's policy of deserting the Negro promptly abandoned him itself as soon as it came to power under Garfield and Arthur and threw support to white Republicans in alliance with any white independent organization available. Repeated warnings from the South that the Negro voters were "getting demoralized," that they would "make terms with their adversaries," and that the Republican party was "losing its hold on the younger generation" were ignored.

Political leaders of his own race furnished guidance of doubtful value to the Negro in his political quandary. For one thing the average cotton-field Negro voter had little more in common with the outstanding Negro politicians of the South than he had with the corporation lawyers who ran the Republican party in the North. Former Senator Blanche K. Bruce of Mississippi owned "a handsome plantation of 1,000 acres," which he operated as absentee landlord, much as had his predecessor, Senator Jefferson Davis. Former Congressman James T. Rapier of Alabama was "the possessor of extensive landed interests" in that state in which he employed more than a hundred people. Former Congressmen Josiah T. Walls of Florida and John R. Lynch of Mississippi were reported to be "proprietors of vast acres under cultivation and employers of large numbers of men," and Norris Wright Cuney, Negro boss in Galveston, Texas, was the employer of some five hundred stevedores. Former Senator Bruce was quoted in 1883 as saying that his party represented "the brains, the wealth, the intelligence" of the land, and that "the moneyed interests of this country would be seriously affected" by a Republican defeat.

The more successful of the Negro politicians were maintained in some Federal office "of high sounding titles and little importance" in Washington. At home they often came to an understanding with Democratic leaders of the Black Belt called "fusion," which served the interests of both by diminishing the power of the white counties in the white man's party and the authority of white leaders in the black man's party. The confusion in which this policy resulted for the average Negro voter may be imagined from the nature of the instruction Lynch gave Mississippi Republicans at a meeting in 1883. It made no difference whether the county machines decided "to fuse with the Independents instead of the Democrats, or with the Democrats instead of the Independents, or to make straight [Republican] party nomination instead of fusing with either"; it was the duty of all good party men, whatever the decision, to follow the machine, "although they may honestly believe the decision to be unwise." Such instructions would not have sounded unfamiliar to followers of the white man's party.

Soon after the war Negroes began to break up into differentiated social and economic classes that eventually reproduced on a rough scale the stratified white society. Enough of a Negro middle class had emerged in the eighties to reflect faithfully the New-South romanticism of the white middle class, with its gospel of progress and wealth. A Negro paper named the *New South* made its appearance in Charleston. It warned the race against "following the *ignis fatuus* of politics," and urged the gospel of "real progress"—money-making. The class of 1886 at Tuskegee adopted the motto "There is Room at the Top," and freshman W. E. B. Du Bois found his classmates at Fisk in 1885 of the same blithe turn of mind. No American success story could match the Master of Tuskegee's *Up From Slavery!*

Another considerable Negro element saw nothing better than to take refuge under the paternalism of the old masters, who offered some protection against the extreme race doctrines of the upland whites and sometimes more tangible rewards than the Republican bosses. Cleveland's administration and its Southern lieutenants encouraged this tendency among Negroes. The *Nation,* a Cleveland supporter, rejoiced that "Thousands of them" had discovered "that their true interests are bound up with the interests of their old masters."

Although the majority of the Negro masses remained Republican or potentially Republican voters, suspicion and criticism of the party of liberation were on the increase during the eighties. The Compromise of 1877 was described as "disillusioning"; the Civil Rights decision as "infamous," a "baptism in ice water"; Chandler's politics as "fatuous" and "degrading." There was also a growing tendency to look upon Republican tariff, railroad, and financial legislation more critically. "The colored people are consumers," said the chairman of a Colored People's Convention in Richmond. "The Republicans have deserted them and undertaken to protect the capitalist and manufacturer of the North." "Neither of these parties," wrote a Negro editor, "cares a tinker snap for the poor man. They are run in the interest of capital, monopoly and repression." The defeat of the Blair bill was a bitter disappointment. Professor J. C. Price, editor of a Negro journal in Salisbury, North Carolina, pointed out that "the Republican party was committed to the enactment of national legislation for the education of the masses," yet the Blair bill had been "voted down and owed its death in the Senate to Republican opposition." Under the circumstances the Negro was not impressed by the Lodge bill to re-enact Reconstruction election laws, and was more disillusioned when it was defeated. "He is beginning to distinguish between real friendship and demagoguery."

In the meanwhile, the movement to make the party "respectable" was gaining ground among "Lily-white" Republicans in the South. A party leader addressing the Lincoln Club of Arkansas on the problem of attracting "persons who have heretofore acted with the Democratic party," announced that he was seeking "a way by which they could act with the Republican party without being dominated over by the negro." The Republican White League of Texas believed that "the union is only safe in the hands of the Anglo-Saxon race, and that a Republican party in Texas to merit the respect of mankind must be in the hands of that race." A New England traveler was grieved to report to the "kinsmen and friends of John Brown, Wendell Phillips, and William Lloyd Garrison" the words of a Southern white Republican who said, "I will not vote to make a negro my ruler. . . . I was a white man before I was a Republican." Even the Northern churches in the South, stoutest proponents of the missionary phase of Northern policy, had drawn the color line by the end of the eighties.

Not long after the inauguration of President Benjamin Harrison in 1889, the Negro press began to accuse him of throwing his support to the Lily-white faction of his party in the South and of not giving the Negroes their fair reward in patronage. The protest soon became bitterly critical. In January, 1890, delegates from twenty-one states met at Chicago and organized the National Afro-American League. Professor Price was elected president and T. Thomas Fortune, who was easily the foremost Negro editor of his day, was chosen secretary. In a militant speech Fortune said of the old parties that "none of them cares a fig for the Afro-American" and that "another party may rise to finish the uncompleted work" of liberation. Inspired by the Chicago meeting, which established numerous branch leagues, other Negro conventions were held. In Raleigh a "Negroes' 'Declaration of Independence' " was proclaimed, declaring that "The white Republicans have been traitors to us," and the Negroes, "the backbone of the Republican party, got nothing" in the way of patronage. Joseph T. Wilson, chairman of a Negro convention in Richmond, protested that his race had been "treated as orphan children, apprenticed to the rice-, cotton-, and tobacco-growers at the South." As for the Negro's political plight, "The Republican party does not know what to do with us and the Democratic party wants to get rid of us, and we are at sea without sail or anchor drifting with the tide." Five such conventions were held in 1890, and all of them were said to have "declared their disaffection with existing political parties." The black man was beginning to feel toward his party much the same as the Southern white man was feeling toward his—that his vote was taken for granted and his needs were ignored.

By 1890 a million Negroes were reported to have joined the Colored Farmers' Alliance. At their annual convention, held at the same time and place as the convention of the white Alliance, the black farmers took a more radical position than their white brethren, substantially affirming the single-tax philosophy that "land is not property; can never be made property. . . . The land belongs to the sovereign people." They also leaned even more toward political independence. Their leader reminded them: "You are a race of farmers, seven-eighths of the colored people being engaged in agriculture," and there was "little hope of the reformation of either of the existing political parties."

As the Populist rift in the ranks of white solidarity approached, the Negro race was more prepared for insurgency than at any time since enfranchisement. Leaders shrewdly calculated their opportunities. For some it was the chance to "teach the White Republicans a lesson"; for others, to strike a blow against "our old, ancient and constant enemy—the Democracy"; for still others, an experiment in joint action with white Southerners on a platform of agrarian radicalism. The general temper was perhaps best expressed in the slogan offered by one Negro: "Let the vote be divided; it will be appreciated by the party who succeeds to power."

The appeal that the proslavery argument had for the poorer class of whites had been grounded on the fear of being leveled, economically as well as socially, with a mass of liberated Negroes. Social leveling after emancipation was scotched by sundry expedients, but the menace of economic leveling still remained. The rituals and laws that exempted the white worker from the penalties of caste did not exempt him from competition with black labor, nor did they carry assurance that the penalties of black labor might not be extended to white.

The propagandists of the New-South order, in advertising the famed cheap labor of their region, were not meticulous in distinguishing between the color of their wares. If they stressed the "large body of strong, hearty, active, docile and easily contented negro laborers" who conformed to "the apostolic maxim of being 'contented with their wages,' and [having] no disposition to 'strike,' " they claimed the same virtues for the "hardy native Anglo-Saxon stock." The pledge of the *Manufacturers' Record,* for example, that "long hours of labor and moderate wages will continue to be the rule for many years to come," amounted almost to a clause of security in the promissory note by which the New South got capital to set up business. Additional security was not lacking. "The white laboring classes here," wrote an Alabama booster, "are separated from the Negroes, working all day side by side with them, by an innate consciousness of race superiority. This sentiment dignifies the character of white labor. It excites a sentiment of sympathy and equality on their part with the classes above them, and in this way becomes a wholesome social leaven."

It was an entirely safe assumption that for a long time to come race consciousness would divide, more than class consciousness would unite, Southern labor. Fifty strikes against the employment of Negro labor in the period from 1882 to 1900 testify to white labor's determination to draw a color line of its own. It is clear that in its effort to relegate to the Negro the less desirable, unskilled jobs, and to exclude him entirely from some industries, white labor did not always have the co-operation of white employers.

In the cotton mills, at least, racial solidarity between employer and employee held fairly firm. By a combination of pressures and prejudices, a tacit understanding was reached that the cotton-mill villages were reserved for whites only. Probably no class of Southerners responded to the vision of the New South more hopefully than those who almost overnight left the old farm for the new factory. The cotton-mill millennium had been proclaimed as the salvation of "the necessitous masses of the poor whites." One enthusiastic promoter promised that "for the operative it would be Elysium itself." Historians have placed the "philanthropic incentive," undoubtedly present in some cases, high on the list of motives behind the whole mill campaign.

The transition from cotton field to cotton mill was not nearly so drastic as that which accompanied the change from primitive agriculture to modern factory in England and New England. For one thing, the mill families usually moved directly from farm to factory, and usually came from the vicinity of the mill. For another, the ex-farmer mill hand found himself in a mill community made up almost entirely of ex-farmers, where a foreigner, a Northerner, or even a city-bred Southerner was a curiosity. As late as 1907 a study revealed that 75.8 per cent of the women and children in Southern cotton mills had spent their childhood on the farm, and the 20.2 per cent who came from villages usually came from mill villages.

The company-owned shanties into which they moved differed little from the planter- or merchant-owned shanties they had evacuated, except that the arrangement of the houses was a reversion to the "quarters" of the ante-bellum plantation instead of the dispersed cropper system. As pictured by an investigator in Georgia in 1890, "rows of loosely built, weather-stained frame houses, all of the same ugly pattern and buttressed by clumsy chimneys," lined a dusty road. "No porch, no doorstep even, admits to these barrack-like quarters." Outside, in the bald, hard-packed earth was planted, like some forlorn standard, the inevitable martin pole with its pendant gourds. Inside were heaped the miserable belongings that had furnished the cropper's cabin: "a shackling bed, tricked out in gaudy patchwork, a few defunct 'split-bottom' chairs, a rickety table, and a jumble of battered crockery," and on the walls the same string of red peppers, gourd dipper, and bellows. In certain mill villages of Georgia in

1890 not a watch or clock was to be found. "Life is regulated by the sun and the factory bell"—just as it had once been by the sun and farm bell. The seasons in the vocabulary of the cracker proletariat were still "hog-killin'," "cotton-choppin'," and " 'tween crops." The church was still the focus of social life, and the mill family was almost as migratory as the cropper family. The whole of this rustic industrialism moved to a rural rhythm.

Mill-village paternalism was cut from the same pattern of poverty and makeshift necessity that had served for plantation and crop-lien paternalism. In place of the country supply store that advanced goods against a crop lien there was the company store that advanced them against wages, and since the weaver was as rarely able to add and multiply as was the plowman, accounts were highly informal. Mill-village workers were sometimes little further advanced toward a money economy than were cotton croppers, and payday might bring word from the company store that the family had not "paid out" that week. Pay was often scrip, good only at the company store, or redeemable in cash at intervals. Company-owned houses were usually provided at low rent and sometimes rent free. "Lint-head" fealty often carried with it certain feudal privileges like those of gathering wood from company lands and pasturing cows on company fields. The unincorporated company town, in which everything was owned by the mill corporation, was the most completely paternalistic. Here company schools and company churches were frequently subsidized by the corporation, which of course controlled employment of preacher and teacher. In the smaller mills the relationship between owner and employees was highly personal and intimate, with a large degree of dependency on the part of the workers. "Not only are relations more friendly and intimate than at the North," found a Northern writer, "but there is conspicuous freedom from the spirit of drive and despotism. Even New England super-intendents and overseers in their Southern mills soon glide into prevailing *laissez-faire* or else leave in despair."

After all allowance has been made for the manna of paternalism, the "family wage," and the greater purchasing power of money in the South, the wages of Southern textile workers remained miserably low. The very fact that the wages of the head of a family combined with those of the other adult members were inadequate to support dependents makes the "family wage" a curious apology for the system. Wages of adult male workers of North Carolina in the nineties were 40 to 50 cents a day. Men constituted a minority of the workers, about 35 per cent in the four leading textile states in 1890; women, 40 per cent; and children between the ages of ten and fifteen years, 25 per cent. The wages of children, who entered into degrading competition with their parents, varied considerably, but there is record of mills in North Carolina that paid 10 and 12 cents a day for child labor. The work week averaged about seventy hours for men, women, and children. Wages were slow to improve, and did not keep pace with mounting capitalization and profits. Adult male spinners in representative mills of North Carolina who had received $2.53 a week in 1885 were getting $2.52 in 1895, and adult female spinners in Alabama got $2.76 a week in the former and $2.38 in the latter year. Hourly wages for adult male spinners in the South Atlantic states were not quite 3 cents in 1890, only 2.3 cents in 1895, and a little over 3 cents in 1900; for female spinners in the same section the rate declined from about 4.5 cents an hour in 1890 to 4 cents in 1900. Yet with these wages and conditions, there seems to have been no trouble in filling the company houses to over-flowing. Few workers ever returned to farming permanently, and strikes were almost unheard of.

The glimpses one gets of life among this sunbonneted, wool-hatted proletariat raise doubts about the sense of *noblesse oblige* and the "philanthropic incentives" with which their employers have been credited. If paternalism sheltered them from the most ruthless winds of industrial conflict, it was a paternalism that could send its ten-year-old children off to the mills at dawn and see them come home with a lantern at night. It could watch its daughters come to marriageable age with "a dull heavy eye, yellow, blotched complexion, dead-looking hair," its "unmarried women of thirty . . . wrinkled, bent, and haggard," while the lot of them approached old age as illiterate as Negro field hands. If white solidarity between employees and employer was to save the white worker from the living standard of the Negro, the results in the cotton mills were not very reassuring.

The extent to which labor in other industries shared in the prosperity of the New South is indicated by the level of wages maintained. In few industries or crafts did wages rise appreciably, and in many they were actually reduced. In the tobacco industry of the South Atlantic states, for example, cigar makers got 26 cents an hour in 1890 and 25 cents in 1900, while stemmers' wages remained at about 10 cents; in representative leather industries of the same states tanners remained on 11-cent wages, while in the South Central states their wages fell from 12.75 cents in 1890 to 11.5 cents in 1900; compositors' wages in the printing industry advanced from about 24 cents to nearly 26 cents in the South Atlantic states over the decade, from 28 cents to 29 cents in the South Central states; machinists did little better than hold their own in this period; bricklayers' wages declined from 45 cents to 43 cents in the South Central states and rose from 35 cents to about 37 cents in the South Atlantic states; carpenters in the former section got nearly 26 cents in 1890 and over 27 cents in 1900, while in the latter section their wages were raised from about 24 cents to about 26 cents; and wages of unskilled labor in the building trades varied from 8 cents to 12 cents an hour in the nineties.

To a large extent the expanding industrialization of the New South was based upon the labor of women and children who were driven into the mills and shops to supplement the low wages earned by their men. In several states they were being drawn into industry much more rapidly than men. In representative establishments studied in Alabama the number of men increased 31 per cent between 1885 and 1895, that of women increased 75 per cent; girls under eighteen, 158 per cent; and boys under eighteen, 81 per cent. The increases over the same period in Kentucky were 3 per cent for men, 70 per cent for women, 65 per cent for girls, and 76 per cent for boys. Of the 400,586 male children between the ages of ten and fourteen gainfully employed in the United States in 1890, the two census divisions of the Southern states accounted for 256,502, and of the 202,427 girls of that age at work they listed 130,546. The great majority in each case were employed in agriculture, fisheries, and mining. Thousands of women who went to work in the cities lived on subsistence wages. In Charleston shops, where the average weekly earnings for women were $4.22, were "well-born, well-educated girl[s] side by side in the least attractive pursuits with the 'cracker.' " In Richmond, where women's wages averaged $3.93 a week, there was an "almost universal pallor and sallowness of countenance" among working women. In Atlanta "great illiteracy exists among the working girls. Their moral condition also leaves much to be desired. The cost of living is comparatively high."

In spite of the contributions of women and children, the working family in the South seemed less able to own a house than that of any other section. Of the eighteen cities in the whole country with a percentage of home tenancy above 80, eleven were in the South. Birmingham, with 89.84 per cent of tenancy had the highest rate in the United States; the percentage in Norfolk was 85.62, and in Macon, 84.66. In the South Atlantic states as a whole, over 75 per cent of home dwellers were tenants. Interlarded with the long, shady boulevards of the "best sections" of Nashville, Norfolk, Macon, Memphis, and Montgomery were alleys lined with one- and two-room shanties of colored domestics. In the "worst sections" of every city sprawled the jungle of a darktown with its own business streets and uproarious, crime-infested "amusement" streets. Beyond, in suburban squalor and isolation, were the gaunt barracks of white industrial workers, huddled around the factories.

Conditions of public health and sanitation under which the urban working classes lived cannot be grasped from general descriptions, since health improvements and safeguards were highly discriminatory within the cities. Richmond justly boasted in 1887 of her relatively high expenditures for municipal improvements, of being "the best-paved city of her population in the Union," and of the splendor of Broad, Main, and Cary streets, "yearly improved by elegant houses built for merchants and manufacturers." Yet in 1888 the United States Commissioner of Labor blamed "bad drainage of the city, bad drinking water, and unsanitary homes" for the appalling conditions of health among the working girls of Richmond. New Orleans, with a long start over her sisters, easily achieved preeminence among unsanitary cities by the filth and squalor of her slums. The president of the State Board of Health of Louisiana reported in 1881 that "The gutters of the 472 miles of dirt streets are in foul condition, being at various points choked up with garbage, filth and mud, and consequently may be regarded simply as receptacles for putrid matters and stagnant waters. The street crossings are in like manner more or less obstructed with filth and black, stinking mud."

"We have awakened, or are fast awakening, from our dream," commented a Southern editor. "We have pauperism, crime, ignorance, discontent in as large a measure as a people need. Every question that has knocked at European doors for solution will in turn knock at ours." When work relief was offered at twenty cents a week by private charity in Alexandria, Virginia, "poor women were more than glad to get the work, and came from far and near, and many had to be sent away disappointed every week." In New Orleans "a multitude of people, white and black alike," lived on a dole of thirteen cents a day in the nineties.

Labor in the Southern textile mills, largely unorganized, has claimed a disproportionate share of the attention of scholars. The result has been a neglect of the history of labor in other industries and in the crafts, as well as an encouragement of the impression that no labor movement existed in the region at this period.

A study of the labor movement in the largest Southern city concludes that "the South, to judge by New Orleans, had craft labor movements smaller but similar to those in Northern cities," and that they were growing in power and influence in the eighties and nineties. It was a period of testing unknown strength and challenging tentatively the Old-South labor philosophy of the New-South doctrinaires and their pledge to Northern investors that long hours, low wages, and docile labor were assured.

However appealing white Southern labor found the doctrine of white supremacy, it realized pretty early that "In nearly all the trades, the rates of compensation for the whites is [*sic*] governed more or less by the rates at which the blacks can be hired," and that the final appeal in a strike was "the Southern employer's ability to hold the great mass of negro mechanics *in terrorem* over the heads of the white." Agreement upon the nature of their central problem did not bring agreement upon the proper means of dealing with it. Two possible but contradictory policies could be used:

eliminate the Negro as a competitor by excluding him from the skilled trades either as an apprentice or a worker, or take him in as an organized worker committed to the defense of a common standard of wages. Southern labor wavered between these antithetical policies from the seventies into the nineties, sometimes adopting one, sometimes the other.

The rising aristocracy of labor, the railway brotherhoods, drew a strict color line. On the other hand, the Brotherhood of Carpenters and Joiners claimed fourteen Negro locals in the South in 1886. The coopers', the cigar makers', the bricklayers', the steel workers', and the carpenters' unions had by the eighties adopted the practice of "issuing . . . separate charters to Negro craftsmen wherever existing locals debarred them." The federations of dock workers in the cotton ports of New Orleans, Savannah, and Galveston overrode race barriers and admitted, equally, white and black longshoremen, draymen, yardmen, cotton classers, and screwmen. Especially successful were the efforts to organize the Negroes in New Orleans. The Central Trades and Labor Assembly of that city was said "to have done more to break the color line in New Orleans than any other thing . . . since emancipation of the slaves."

Much of this temporary "era of good feeling" between black and white workingmen has been credited to the guidance of the Knights of Labor. The Knights' doctrine of interracial solidarity and democratic idealism makes the history of the order of particular significance for the central problem of Southern labor. The history of the Knights also confutes the legend of the Southern worker's indifference to unionism. As soon as the national organization of the Knights was established in 1878 it dispatched 15 organizers to the South. A quickening of Southern interest was evident in 1884, and by 1886 there were in ten states 21,208 members attached to the Southern District assembly and perhaps 10,000 more members of locals attached to national trade assemblies or directly to the General Assembly of the Knights. An incomplete list places 487 locals in the South in 1888, but there were many more. Concentrated around such cities as Birmingham, Knoxville, Louisville, New Orleans, and Richmond, locals were also scattered over rural areas and embraced cotton hands and sugar workers, black as well as white. The national convention of the Knights in 1886, the year of their greatest strength, met in Richmond and was attended by delegates of both races from many parts of the South. The convention heard reports that "colored people of the South are flocking to us" and that "rapid strides" have been made in the South.

The Knights were involved in numerous strikes in the South during the latter years of the eighties. These conflicts broke out in the coal mines of Alabama and Tennessee, in the cotton mills of Augusta, Georgia, and Cottondale, Alabama, among the sugar workers of Louisiana and the lumber workers in Alabama. The Knights' greatest strike victory, that against the Missouri Pacific system and Jay Gould in 1885, was won in considerable part in the shops of Texas and Arkansas. The Southwestern strike of 1886, which marked the climax and greatest failure of the order, broke out in Texas, and some of its most violent phases occurred there. The Knights experimented with co-operative enterprises of various kinds, though on no such scale as did the Farmers' Alliance. The order figured conspicuously in the politics of several cities. In 1886 the Workingman's Reform party, backed by the Knights, elected two blacksmiths, a cobbler, and a tanner to the city council of Richmond, and took control of nearly all departments of the government. In 1887 the Knights claimed that they had elected a Congressman and eleven of the fifteen city council members in Lynchburg, a majority of the city and county officers in Macon, and several officers in Mobile. The following year they asserted that they had elected the mayors of Jacksonville, Vicksburg, and Anniston. The mayor of Anniston was a carpenter and the council included two molders, a brick-maker, a butcher, a watchmaker, and a shoemaker. Their reforms were mild enough, but their experimental defiance of the color line was bitterly attacked in the Southern press. Under these burdens and the additional ones of lost strikes, the Knights passed into a decline in the South as in the nation. Co-operation with the Farmers' Alliance gave the order a de-cided agrarian color by the end of the eighties.

A second peak of activity in the Southern labor movement came in 1892. It therefore coincided with the outburst of the Populist revolt and, like it, was symptomatic of popular discontent with the New Order of the Redeemers. It may be illustrated by two unrelated outbreaks of contrasting character—the general strike in New Orleans and the violent insurrection of Tennessee coal miners against the employment of convict labor.

The general strike in New Orleans, which followed the Homestead strike in Pennsylvania and preceded the Pullman strike in Chicago, has been described as "the first general strike in American history to enlist both skilled and unskilled labor, black and white, and to paralyze the life of a great city." It came as "the climax of the strongest labor movement in the South." New Orleans was about as well unionized as any city in the country when the American Federation of Labor began a success-ful drive early in 1892 that added thirty new chartered associations, thus bringing the total up to ninety-five. A new unity was achieved in the Workingmen's Amalgamated Council, a centralized but democratically elected body made up of two delegates from each of the forty-nine unions affiliated with the A. F. of L. The New Orleans Board of Trade, an organization of the merchants of the city, was as determined to maintain traditional prerogatives of hiring and firing as the labor council was to establish the right of collective bargaining.

Inspired by a victory of the city streetcar drivers that put an end to a sixteen-hour day and gained a closed-shop agreement, the so-called "Triple-Alliance," consisting of the unions of the teamsters, scalesmen, and packers (which included Negro members), struck for a ten-hour day, overtime pay, and the preferential closed shop. The Workingmen's Amalgamated Council appointed a committee of five workers, including a Negro, to conduct the strike. The Board of Trade refused to recognize the unions or to deal with them in any way. The workers' committee first threatened, and finally, on November 8, called a general strike in support of the unions of unskilled workers. Forty-two union locals, with over 20,000 members, who with their families made up nearly half of the population of the city, stopped work. Each union on strike demanded recognition and a closed shop. Business came to a virtual standstill; bank clearings were cut in half. The employers openly declared that it was "a war to the knife" and that they would resort to extreme measures, including violence. Yet in spite of the hysteria kept up by the newspapers, the importation of strikebreakers, and the threat of military intervention, the strikers refrained from violence and there was no bloodshed. On the third day of the strike the governor of the state came to the aid of the capitalists with a proclamation that, in effect, set up martial law and implied that the militia would be called unless the strike was ended. The labor committee, never very aggressive, accepted a compromise which, though gaining the original demands of the Triple Alliance concerning hours and wages, forfeited the fight for collective bargaining and the closed shop. The Board of Trade, confident that labor, like the Negro, had been put in its "place," boasted that New Orleans was an open-shop city, and that the old philosophy of labor had been vindicated.

The second labor struggle was fought upon a more primitive level, for the most elemental rights, and fought with savage violence. Competition with convict labor leased by corporations had been a long-standing and often-voiced grievance of labor all over the South. As a conservative paper stated the case in Alabama, "Employers of convicts pay so little for their labor that it makes it next to impossible for those who give work to free labor to compete with them in any line of business. As a result, the price paid for labor is based upon the price paid convicts."

In 1883 the Tennessee Coal, Iron, and Railroad Company leased the Tennessee penitentiary, containing some 1,300 convicts. Thomas Collier Platt, the New York Republican leader, was president of the company and Colonel Colyar, the Tennessee Democratic leader, was general counsel. "For some years after we began the convict labor system," said Colyar, "we found that we were right in calculating that free laborers would be loath to enter upon strikes when they saw that the company was amply provided with convict labor."

Tennessee labor protested, and the legislature occasionally investigated, once reporting that the branch prisons were "hell holes of rage, cruelty, despair and vice." But nothing was done. In 1891, the miners of Briceville, Anderson County, were presented by the Tennessee Coal Mine Company with an "iron-clad" contract relinquishing employees' right to a check weigher, agreeing to "scrip" pay, and pledging no strikes. When they turned down the contract the company ordered convicts to tear down their houses and build stockades for the convicts who were to replace free labor. The evicted miners then marched in force on the stockades and, without bloodshed, compelled guards, officers, and convicts to board a train for Knoxville. Governor John P. Buchanan, with three companies of militia, promptly returned the convicts to the stockades. A few days later more than a thousand armed miners packed the guards and convicts off to Knoxville a second time, and those of another company along with them, again without bloodshed. Only after the Governor had promised to call a special session of the legislature were the miners pacified. Labor demonstrations in Chattanooga, Memphis, Nashville, and other towns demanded an end to convict labor and sent aid to the miners. Kentucky and Alabama labor, afflicted with the same evil, also became aroused. The Tennessee state convention of the Farmers' Alliance, which the Governor attended, demanded the repeal of the convict-lease law. In spite of the official position of the Alliance, the fact that there were fifty-four Alliance members of the legislature, and that Governor Buchanan owed his election to the order, the special session of the legislature took no satisfactory action. After a futile appeal to the courts, the miners took the law into their own hands. On the night of October 31, 1891, they forcibly freed the convicts of the Tennessee Coal Mine Company, allowed them all to escape, and burned down the stockades. They repeated the same tactics later at two other mining companies, releasing in all some five hundred convicts. The mine operators of the area then employed free labor, gave up the "iron-clad" contract, and granted a check weigher.

The insurrections of the following year made those of 1891 seem tame by comparison. The Tennessee struggles involved more men and deeper issues than the contemporary Homestead strike, but they got little attention then or later. These insurrections broke out in Middle Tennessee at the mines of the Tennessee Coal and Iron Company, which had put its free labor on half time and employed 360 convicts full time. Miners overcame the Tracy City guards, burned the stockades, and shipped the convicts to Nashville. Inspired by this example, miners of one of the Tennessee Coal, Iron, and Railroad Company mines in Anderson County, at which convict labor had been reinstated, burned the stockades, renewed their war, and laid siege to Fort Anderson, which was occupied by militia and civil guards paid jointly by the company and the state to guard the convicts. Although the miners killed a few of the troops sent to relieve the besieged fort, the convicts were again reinstated. The final insurrection spelled the doom of the convict lease, however, for the following year the system was abolished by the legislature.

By their actions the Tennessee miners, the New Orleans trade unions, and workers in the mines and foundries of Alabama, Georgia, and Virginia gave notice in 1892 that Southern labor was not going to accept the Old-South labor philosophy of the New-South leaders—not without a fight, anyway. The militancy of Southern labor also gave notice to the insurgent Southern farmer that he might seek recruits for the Populist revolt in the mines and factories as well as in the fields.

1.2

Black Protest and White Power

WILLIAM IVY HAIR

After Reconstruction ended, "order" did not return to the South. The planters, merchants, and bankers who dominated the region's economy and its powerful Democratic Party still had their southern critics, whites as well as blacks. Initially, such critics identified with the small Greenback movement, and their protest culminated in two larger, more significant movements: the Knights of Labor in the economic sphere and, later, the People's (or Populist) Party in the political sphere.

Drawing on well-entrenched republican and egalitarian traditions, the Knights of Labor briefly but successfully organized rural and urban southern workers, black and white. The reform union had its greatest strength among black farm laborers and coal miners and white textile workers and coal miners. That former slaves—defeated politically during Reconstruction and dependent upon powerful whites for their livelihood—turned so quickly to reform trade unionism on the Louisiana sugar plantations receives

William Ivy Hair, *Bourbonism and Agrarian Protest: Louisiana Politics, 1877–1900* (Baton Rouge, La.: Louisiana State University Press, 1969), pp. 170–97. Reprinted and footnotes omitted by permission of the publisher.

pioneering attention from William Ivy Hair. The violence resorted to by Bourbon political authorities to cope with the rural Knights of Labor in such places measures the significant political potential of that organization in the South.

Yet another aspect of what Hair analyzes deserves special attention. All too often anti-black violence is just associated with "poor whites," not the better off and more powerful southern elite. That was not the case here in Louisiana in the 1880s.

Why was it, wondered a Bourbon leader of Opelousas, that Negroes kept on trying to rise above their station in life. He knew of some who were "scared to death" of visits from white vigilantes and yet, paradoxically, even the most frightened of them persisted in taking an interest in politics and other matters which did not concern them. This was odd behavior for a sub-human species. All he could surmise was that "niggers are strange animals any way you take them."

This view of the black caste as something outside the pale of humanity was heard all too frequently in post-Reconstruction Louisiana. The fierce Negrophobia of Hearsey's *Daily States* became the standard response of a predominant portion of the political and journalistic elite; and the supposed horrors of "rapine and robbery" of Reconstruction's "negro rule" were constantly recalled, although the state had never at any time been under the control of blacks. During the 1880's and 1890's individual instances of paternalism toward the Negro were still discoverable, but the ruling classes' public attitude, being one of contempt and cruelty, militated against the humane instincts of *noblesse oblige.* Sometimes even acts of presumed kindness revealed racial discrimination in its shabbiest forms. In a typical example, the Shreveport *Times,* in offering to give away mutilated coins to local children, thought it necessary to add: "the white babies can have the large pieces and the colored ones the nickels."

Not many Louisiana Negroes of the time were able to leave written evidence of their reaction to the increasingly hostile environment in which they lived. There was, to be sure, an articulate and relatively well-to-do black minority in and near New Orleans; their recorded opinions show a grim cognizance of what was happening and a helpless rage against Bourbonism. While on occasion, the actions of the poverty-stricken black majority spoke as loudly as words. The "Kansas Fever" of 1879 gave strong proof of their discontent. In the decade which followed, although few attempted emigration, mass black protests against conditions within the state by no means ceased.

In 1880 and again in 1887, Negro wage earners in the sugar parishes engaged in strikes which brought down upon them the wrath of their employers and the state government. Upstate, the blacks appeared more docile. The sharecropping system prevalent in the cotton parishes held out less hope for economic advancement than did the meager wages paid cane field workers, but the decentralized nature of cotton plantations limited the possibility of unified protests by Negro families. In the sugar country, on the other hand, the gang labor system and the existence of an active (though white-run) Republican Party encouraged cohesion among Negroes; they were allowed a modicum of choice in politics as well as in place of employment. Blacks in the cotton parishes generally had little free will in anything.

The 1880 sugar strikes commenced in the fields of St. Charles Parish on March 17. Plantation owners immediately accused the Negro ringleaders of trespassing upon private property "and inciting the laborers to stop work in the fields." According to the parish judge, the instigators were armed with weapons and had been "forcing workers to join their band by assaults and threats." Judge James D'Augustin admitted, however, that most of the black population of St. Charles was in sympathy with the "rioters." For that reason, D'Augustin claimed that local authorities could not handle the disturbance, and so he called upon the state for militia.

Richard Gooseberry, spokesman for the St. Charles strikers, denied the allegations of violence. The colored people, he said, "had simply struck for one dollar a day, as they could no longer work for seventy-five cents." Nevertheless, the planters maintained that Gooseberry's followers threatened to kill white people, burn down dwellings, and seize control of the entire parish. As it turned out, there were no specific acts of violence against the white minority of St. Charles. It must also be said that the strikers displayed remarkable forbearance when they gathered, on March 19, to listen to speeches by Judge D'Augustin and others who "expounded the law to them." One official passed this compliment on to the black audience: "The great arm of the great wheel of agriculture is the nigger. Next is the mule."

A battalion of state militia presently arrived in St. Charles. No resistance was met. Twelve strikers were arrested, sent to New Orleans, and sentenced to jail terms. Ostensibly they were guilty of trespass; but more to the point, they had run afoul of the Bourbon position that "all strikes are wrong, criminally wrong, both in theory and act." The trouble in St. Charles appeared to be over, and as yet there had been no outbreaks reported elsewhere.

But labor discontent soon extended to other parishes along the lower delta. By March 29, the situation in St. John the Baptist Parish looked more serious than had the previous disturbance in neighboring St. Charles. The same demand was voiced: daily wages must be raised from the present level of seventy-five cents. But the St. John Negroes struck a more militant pose. They proclaimed that "the colored people are a nation and must stand together." Indeed, the ringleaders set up a governing council, complete with a a constitution. All strikers in the parish took an oath to obey this constitution, which stated that none would work for less than one dollar a day, and any who violated the oath "shall be punished with a severe thrashing." A correspondent for the *Daily Picayune,* though hostile to the strike, was impressed by the earnestness of the blacks. "Strange to say," he wrote, "they have kept sober."

Governor Wiltz responded to the pleas of the St. John landowners with a warning to "these evil doers and mischievous persons to desist from their evil doings." He also sent in state troops. The militia, it was explained, was being used to "protect the laborers" from harm. Despite a number of arrests, the disturbance in St. John continued for several days. Blacks paraded along the dusty parish roads, carrying banners which read: "A DOLLAR A DAY OR KANSAS," and "PEACE—ONE DOLLAR A DAY." But no violence, outside of the whipping of Negroes by Negroes, was reported. One of the instigators of the strike, when arrested, remarked that he was "glad to go to jail," for at least there he would get "enough to eat."

It was not entirely a coincidence that the St. John strike occurred during the same week that ex-President Ulysses S. Grant paid a visit to Louisiana. The strike leaders knew of it, and apparently timed their activities accordingly. Grant arrived in New Orleans at the peak of the trouble in nearby St. John. "The deluded laborers," one report noted, anticipate that "Grant will come up and make the planters pay extra wages." As the *Weekly Louisianian* rather sadly put it, the unlettered black masses viewed Grant as a kind of superman. At the opposite extreme, his visit touched off a predictable editorial tirade in the *Daily States.*

The hero of Appomattox was, in one sense, concerned with Negro affairs in Louisiana. During his stay in New Orleans, he attended a reception at the home of P. B. S. Pinchback, where he met "the cream of Negro society." Pinchback and a number of his guests were scheduled to be delegates to the upcoming Republican national convention. And Grant hoped to return to the White House in 1881. Other than that, he demonstrated no interest in local matters except when he said that "I think the South is better suited [for the black man] than any other place. . . . I want him to have the right to stay where the climate suits him."

Shortly after Grant's departure from New Orleans, the strike in St. John was broken. Later in the month of April, however, sporadic strikes by cane field laborers were reported in Ascension, St. James, St. Bernard, Jefferson, and Plaquemines parishes. But in these instances the presence of the militia was not required. Local authorities broke up the disturbances by summary arrests of the ringleaders. Thus the strikes of 1880 had totally failed. During the next few years, wages generally remained at seventy to seventy-five cents a day for "first class" adult males. Only in the busy harvest and grinding season (from around late October to the end of the year) was there a wage raise, usually to ninety cents or one dollar.

Localized labor disturbances, poorly organized and barren of results, sprang up at intervals in the sugar country during the years from 1881 through 1886. Until the latter year, black workers were not affiliated with any recognizable labor organization. Even in the relatively serious strikes of 1880, there seems to have been no effort to unify the laborers of the several parishes. Those in one locality may have taken their cue from events elsewhere, but no attempt at interparish coordination was observed by correspondents on the scene.

In New Orleans, meanwhile, a degree of cooperation among laboring groups was slowly being achieved—including some unity between black and white—but as yet there were no tangible benefits from it. Late in 1880 a vague "Association" of thirteen city unions was formed, embracing whites and Negroes, skilled and unskilled. In September of the following year the various orders within the Association all threatened to strike for higher wages; and the more than ten thousand dockworkers, of whom 30 percent were Negro, carried the threat into action. Negro strikebreakers were hired and brought in from as far away as Savannah, but for once the local dockworkers of both colors stood together in demonstrations and attacks against the "scabs." The strike eventually subsided without significant concessions to the laborers, but even so an unprecedented degree of biracial harmony had been revealed. When a black demonstrator was killed by police, "it was a source of satisfaction" to the Negro press to see great numbers of white workers march in his funeral procession.

In 1883 the Knights of Labor entered Louisiana. One of the most ambitious and visionary associations in American labor history, the Knights advocated a uniting of all working people, of whatever skill, color, or sex, into one gigantic order. At the same time, however, the Knights shunned the Marxist and anarchistic radicalism of the time; their national leaders did not seek the extinction of capitalism. But the very fact that the Knights promoted class consciousness and organized Negroes along with whites made the order, in the eyes of Southern Bourbons, a dangerous disturber of the status quo.

At first confined to New Orleans, and inconsequential there, the Knights drew little attention in the Pelican State until 1886. Nationally, the order reached its peak membership that year, then began to decline.

Yet contrary to the trend elsewhere, the Knights developed new strength in the rural South; losses in Northern cities during the late 1880's were partially offset by fresh adherents from the Southern towns and countryside. Particularly was it growing in North Carolina and Louisiana. New Orleans provided most of the leadership for the Knights' plan of expansion in the Pelican State. At least five thousand urbanites joined it by mid 1887, and a Knights newspaper, *Southern Industry,* had commenced weekly publication.*

It was from the city that Knights organizers fanned out into the lower delta parishes in 1886, to impress upon cane field Negroes the need for unity in obtaining concessions from their landlord-employers. Higher wages and payment in regular currency "instead of commissary paste board" were the prime rallying points. The Knights simultaneously recruited artisans of both races in South Louisiana's towns. Early in 1887 the Knights were potent enough in Morgan City to run a slate of candidates in the municipal election, and every man on the labor ticket won office. Conservative planters and businessmen were beginning to take alarm.

Louisiana's sugar growers, after experiencing a bad crop in 1886, reduced wages for the following year to sixty-five cents per day, without rations. Most workers averaged twenty days out of every month in the fields. The larger planters paid wages in commissary script, redeemable only at the plantation stores. Actually, a Negro family with one employed member would receive what amounted to six or seven dollars in real wages per month during the ten-month growing season. Workers without rations had to feed and clothe their families out of this small amount, although usually no rent was charged for the cramped living quarters. Pay for the grinding season of 1887 was set at rates varying from seventy-five cents to $1.15 per day for "first class" adult males; and for six hours of overtime night work, called a "watch," the planters offered fifty cents.

During August of 1887, ten weeks before harvest, the Knights leadership requested a conference with local branches of the Louisiana Sugar Planters' Association. They wanted to discuss wages for the approaching busy season. Association officials sent no reply. Later, on October 24, the Knights District Assembly 194 addressed a circular letter to planters in Iberia, Lafourche, St. Martin, St. Mary and Terrebonne parishes, insisting that wages be raised for the November-December months of harvesting and grinding. The scale drawn up by the Knights proposed $1.25 per day without rations, or $1.00 per day with rations. For a night watch, no less than sixty cents would be accepted. Furthermore, instead of monthly pay-

---

* New Orleans *Southern Industry* was edited by William I. O'Donnell. It was one of twenty-one Knights newspapers published at that time in the United States. Philadelphia *Journal of United Labor,* April 9, 1887; New Orleans *Weekly Pelican,* July 9, 1887.

ments, the Knights demanded that wages for day work be received every two weeks, and "watch" money each week. The District Assembly of the Knights comprised about forty locals in the five parishes. Planters were informed that they must meet the terms by November 1, or face a general strike.

An estimated six thousand to ten thousand laborers went on strike when the deadline date arrived with no sign of acquiescence from the planters. Nine-tenths of the strikers were Negroes. All were said to be members of the Knights of Labor. The planters, although refusing to negotiate, were visibly disturbed; the growing season of 1887 had been one of near-perfect weather, and a large crop yield was in prospect. Conservative newspapers depicted the strikers' demands as "unreasonable" and "reprehensible," and insisted that the current market price of sugar precluded any increase in wages. As for biweekly or weekly paydays, the planters claimed that this "would demoralize labor." Because it was "a well known fact that as long as the average laborer has money he will not work."

The local officials of the Knights, who were white men and literate blacks, received the brunt of landowner wrath. Special bitterness was expressed toward J. R. Foote and D. Monnier, white laborers of the town of Thibodaux, in Lafourche Parish. Other leaders among the Lafourche Knights included Henry Cox, George Cox and P. O. Rousseau. The Cox brothers were Negro artisans. Rousseau, a white man, had once been a planter but "times [had] changed" for him. In Terrebonne Parish, a light-skinned Negro named Jim Brown led the strike, while in St. Mary, black men took the lead in labor agitation among the sugar workers. They, together with Negroes who urged the strike in other parishes, were categorized by Major Burke's *Times-Democrat* as "bad and dangerous . . . relic[s] of Radical days."

Planter spokesmen also vented anger upon the New Orleans Knights who had first organized the lower sugar country. These urban "communists," as the *Daily States* termed them, were blamed for arousing "passions" among the usually tractable Negroes. Concerning the attitude of rank-and-file laborers, it was obvious that they placed great faith in the Knights of Labor. One wealthy planter, W. W. Pugh, used the word "veneration" to describe Negro attitudes toward the labor society. When directives came down from Knights headquarters, said Pugh, the workers "generally obey at whatever sacrifice it may prove to their own welfare." A leader of the strike remarked, when the trouble began, that the white employers "had never met the negroes united before," and he predicted that every one of the four hundred laborers in his group would lay down their lives before giving in to the planters.

On the morning of the first day of the strike a battery of state militia arrived in Lafourche Parish. Members of the Sugar Planters' Association—not the local government—had asked for the troops. For the landowners perceived that "serious trouble" would result from their announcement that all laborers who refused to work must vacate the plantation cabins. By November 10, Governor McEnery had ordered ten companies and two batteries of state militia into the troubled parishes. At least one unit brought along a Gatling gun. These militiamen were assigned the work of eviction.

Some critics of Governor McEnery asserted that he "had acted hastily" in sending out the militia; the New Orleans *Mascot* suggested that His Excellency's action "was caused by his eagerness to curry favor with the . . . wealthy sugar planters in the hopes that he can transfer their allegiance from Nicholls to himself." Major Burke's newspaper, on the other hand, dwelt upon McEnery's alleged knowledge "of the negro character," which allowed the Governor "to appreciate the danger." The trouble in the sugar country, philosophized this administration organ, was not a mere labor dispute. It was a racial matter.

The first report of bloodshed came on November 2, from Terrebonne Parish. According to pro-planter sources, the blacks shot down four of their race who refused to join the strike. More severe was the disturbance which followed in St. Mary Parish: near the town of Berwick, on the night of November 4, Negroes fired upon and wounded four unidentified white men; the next day, militiamen killed "four or five" strikers outside of Pattersonville community. Each side had its own version of the St. Mary shootings. Spokesmen for the Knights claimed the militia shot without provocation; other reports said the troops were forced to act in self-defense. A St. Mary newspaper accused "leading colored men" in the Pattersonville area of making "incendiary speeches . . . that would put the Chicago anarchists to shame," and it quoted one Negro Knight as saying that "if the planters do not come to our terms we will burn the damn sugar houses." Elsewhere, by November 20, at least one black laborer was killed and several wounded in Lafourche Parish.

The sugar strike reached its violent climax during the last week of November. As some had feared, the town of Thibodaux then was the scene of a bloody riot. For Thibodaux had become a refugee center for the strikers; hundreds of Negro families, evicted from the plantations where they refused to work, were crowding into its dingy backstreets. A *Daily Picayune* correspondent described the spectacle: "Every vacant room in town tonight is filled with penniless and ragged negroes. All day long a stream of black humanity poured in, some on foot and others in wagons, bringing in all their earthly possessions which never amounted to more than a frontyard full of babies, dogs and ragged bed clothing. . . . On many of the plantations old gray-headed negroes, who were born and have lived continually upon them, left today."

Residents of Thibodaux who were members of the Knights of Labor attempted to provide food and shelter for the homeless blacks. One observer, sympathetic to the refugees, said they behaved peaceably and tried to avoid incidents with local whites. But an opponent of the strike wrote that a number of the incoming male Negroes were armed and that the women "made threats to burn the town down." By late November the atmosphere was growing more tense each day.

Judge Taylor Beattie, who had once been a defender of Negro rights —at least voting rights—when he ran for governor on the Republican ticket in 1879, took the lead in setting up a committee of local planters and Thibodaux property owners for the purpose of keeping the town's new residents under control. Beattie described the black refugees as "ignorant and degraded barbarians." He said flatly that "the question of the supremacy of the whites over the blacks" had become the paramount issue.

Actually, from the planters' point of view the situation was becoming desperate, but for another reason. The entire sugar crop was in immediate danger of ruin. On November 21, the first ice of the season formed in the puddles and ponds around Thibodaux; cane in the fields showed considerable damage and it was feared that the remainder of the crop would soon "be lost through the senseless . . . strike of laborers." The day of the freeze Judge Beattie declared martial law in the town. The militia had recently been withdrawn. In place of the troops were armed bands of white vigilantes, composed of local "organized citizens" plus a number of grim-visaged strangers to the community. These newly arrived men were alleged to be "Shreveport guerrillas, well versed in killing niggers."

Reports of the gruesome events that followed are conflicting. All dispatches agreed that the shooting began on the night of November 22. But the planters' and the Knights' versions of who commenced it were, as might be expected, quite different. Each blamed the other. For what it may be worth, the conservative *Iberville South,* which sided with the planters, in later years accused Judge Beattie of having "instigated" the riot "which resulted in the death of so many sons of Africa." There is no question that many were killed.

When the firing ceased at noon the next day at least thirty Negroes lay dead or dying in Thibodaux. The injured list ran into the hundreds, of which only two people were white. One planter journal stated that "quite a number of darkies" were unaccounted for and might also have been killed. The *Daily Picayune's* reporter told of additional bodies being found in nearby swamps, and related an ugly story about a large, dark canine which one vigilante supposedly shot by mistake, because it "looked like a negro lying down." A member of one prominent planter family, Lavina Gay, cryptically wrote in a letter that "they say the half has not been published."

The massacre at Thibodaux virtually ended the sugar strike of 1887. As a sequel, the two Cox brothers were taken from jail a day or so later and they "disappeared." By the beginning of December, most Negroes were back at work, harvesting and grinding the cane at wages previously set by the planters. Yet the violent repression of the strike appeared to stimulate a shortlived revival of Exodus talk among Louisiana's black population. One group did leave the state to seek, they said, more humane surroundings. Their destination was the state of Mississippi.

Having dealt with the strike, planter interests now gave attention to what was considered the root of the trouble, the Knights of Labor. During the subsequent year a determined effort was made to eradicate the order from the sugar region. As the Jeanerette *Teche Pilot* made plain: "The darkey who steers clear of that organization will always find himself better off in this section." Those who persisted in holding membership in the Knights were likely to find their household goods unceremoniously dumped on the levees and themselves blacklisted. In 1888 minor strikes broke out in four sugar parishes, but were quickly put down. Whites there and elsewhere in the state had meantime put into motion a new "Regulating Movement" aimed at discouraging economic or political assertiveness on the part of Negroes. And so failed the attempt to unionize the field hands of rural South Louisiana. By 1891, state membership in the Knights of Labor was not of any size outside of its original base in New Orleans.

Viewed in perspective, the Thibodaux bloodletting was simply a deadlier-than-usual example of a much broader phenomenon. The lot of the Louisiana Negro, although never good, was growing harder. Indeed throughout the South, during the late 1880's and the 1890's, repression and discrimination against the black race was on the rise. Nor was this unlovely trend confined to the states of the late Confederacy. As the American nation took up imperialistic adventures in the Pacific and the Caribbean, the Northern public came increasingly to accept the doctrine of the natural superiority of Anglo-Saxons over dark-skinned peoples. Doubtless the expatriate Louisianian George W. Cable was grieved to discover that his pleadings on behalf of the black man, which had fallen upon deaf ears in his native state, now received little better attention in the North.

But it is unlikely that Negroes in any other state suffered more than those in Louisiana. That they received less in the way of education has already been demonstrated. Available evidence also points to the conclusion that Pelican State blacks were subjected to a greater degree of violence than Negroes in other parts of the South during the late nineteenth century. Why was this so? The answer lies partially hidden in the labyrinthine social history of antebellum and colonial Louisiana. Somehow, the commingling of English-speaking and Creole-Cajun cultures had resulted in a milieu of political instability and unusual insensitivity to human rights. Long before the Civil War, the state had been notorious for its lawlessness and for its maltreatment of slaves. When Harriet Beecher Stowe tried to portray the cruelest side of slavery in *Uncle Tom's Cabin,* it was not by chance that she located Simon Legree's plantation up the Red River, near Shreveport.

Upper class conservatives in the post-Reconstruction South have been regarded as being, relatively speaking, the black man's best friends among the white population. Presumably they believed that he was due some protection; that though an inferior, he should not be deliberately hurt or degraded. This generalization, whatever its worth elsewhere, was hardly valid for Louisiana. The ruling class of the Pelican State continued, as in the days of slavery, to hold an extraordinarily circumscribed view of Negro "rights." The most rabid Negrophobes in the state were as consistently vehement in defense of upper class white privileges. Some of the white elite did, to be sure, sincerely try to uphold the ideals of *noblesse oblige.* But, as Daniel Dennett once remarked about honest politicians in the state, "they [were] lonesome."

Editorial diatribes and mob outrages against the black people grew to such proportions by 1890, that at least a few whites thought the time for a moratorium had arrived. "Heavens," exclaimed the Welsh *Crescent,* "how we would enjoy a rest on the 'nigger' question! It seems that four-fifths of the State [newspapers] can't come out without a long-winded article . . . with the negro as their target; and what's more, they have been at it for the Lord only knows how long." Many Negroes, however, bore the brunt of something more hurtful than mere words.

Lynchings not only occurred with growing frequency, but those who died at the hands of mobs might consider themselves fortunate if they expired quickly by a bullet or the rope. For some reason, 1881 marked a turning point toward extreme cruelty; several of the sixteen reported lynchings in the state that year involved brutal tortures. One of the dead had been accused of only stealing a chicken. Another victim, a Negro woman of Claiborne Parish named Jane Campbell, was burned at the stake. At the same time, a mob in Morehouse Parish was congratulated for discovering a "new and original mode" of punishment for a black man guilty of cattle theft. He was trussed up inside the carcass of a cow, "leaving only his head sticking out," so that buzzards and crows would pick out his eyes. The Rayville *Beacon* joked that this amounted to "COW-PITAL punishment," but added that "a great many worse things are . . . being done in our vicinity."

Between 1882 and 1903, according to a Chicago *Tribune* survey, Louisiana lynchings accounted for 285 deaths. Of this number, 232 victims were black. Records kept by Tuskegee Institute corroborate the

Tribune figures. Not included are the numerous deaths resulting from the sugar country riot of 1887, but even without these Louisiana ranked third in the nation in total lynchings for the period. The two states with higher totals had larger populations. Also, the above statistics failed to include many cases reported by the local press. For example, the Tuskegee records for 1888 list seven lynchings for the state, but a contemporary account from just one parish, Iberia, told of no less than ten blacks murdered by vigilantes. The Negroes were described as "vagrant and lewd." Some instances were probably not reported anywhere. The Monroe *Bulletin* refused to print any stories about lynchings in Ouachita Parish because white citizens in the area regarded such matters "not only with indifference but with levity."

Blacks were usually, but not always, the victims of lynch law. Notable among the white sufferers were the eleven Italians murdered by a mob in downtown New Orleans in 1891; this event was praised by much of the leadership of the state, including the editor of the *St. Mary Banner,* who hailed "the killing of the Dagoes" as "the greatest event of the year." Three others of that nationality were strung up in Hahnville in 1896. In reply to the protests of the Italian government over these murders, the *Times-Democrat* thought it well to point out that residence in the Pelican State entailed, for anybody, a certain amount of danger, and that "foreigners who come to this country must take the same risk with natives."

More often than not, serious acts of violence against Negroes in Louisiana were committed by men of some substance in the white community. Contemporary sources make it clear that the poorer whites were not involved in a majority of cases reported. To cite one of the most notorious instances of persecution, a reign of terror was conducted in 1890 against "industrious, reliable" Negroes near Baton Rouge by certain white landowners; only those blacks who had managed to accumulate property were shot, whipped, or otherwise molested. The black farmers were told to sell their property cheaply or be killed. The Bourbon *Daily Advocate* strongly condemned the whites responsible. But almost never did conservatives publicly criticize the many lynchings in which the black victims had been accused of some crime. Often they praised such events, and demurred only if a trivial offense had been involved. "Lynch law," said a prudent gentleman of the town of Arcadia, "should not be resorted to except in very aggravated cases."

"A crowd of the most worthy citizens of our Parish . . . took charge of the prisoner, and in a short time he was launched into eternity." This report from Abbeville in the summer of 1881 would be repeated, like a dreary refrain, by other localities in the years which followed. As one example among many, in 1898 "hundreds of the most prominent citizens in Bossier Parish" conducted a dual lynching near the town of Benton. A Tangipahoa Parish group known as the "Phantom Riders" molested Negro families without fear of the law because, it was stated, "good" citizens rode with the band. And upper class participation was most obvious in the lynching which attracted the greatest notice outside Louisiana: the killing of the eleven Italians in New Orleans in 1891. Included among the prominent citizens who headed that mob was none other than the District Attorney. The *Nation* was forced to conclude that New Orleans was unique among American cities in that "even the more respectable and sober-minded portion of the community are in a constant state of readiness for remedial violence."

At least one Bourbon spokesman seemed to fear that the murder of the Italians had momentarily diverted attention away from the more pressing need for lynching Negroes. The *Morehouse Clarion,* which posed as an aristocratic journal, advised its readers shortly after the New Orleans massacre that more "little 'neck tie' parties" would "do a lot of good" among the black population around Bastrop. Years earlier it had similarly urged an increase in "swingings." But it took a Shreveport newspaper to describe a lynching as "beautiful." This was "the right way," the *Evening Judge* decided, "to deal with every such black brute. Before the war they kept their places like the other beasts of the field."

Shreveport advertised itself as a city of New South "energy, push, and vim." Yet at the same time its businessman elite, together with the planters around the town, supported or condoned the most pitiless forms of social injustice to be found anywhere in the state. The "Shreveport Plan" of 1889 was a representative specimen. Conceived by a local publication, the *Daily Caucasian,* the proposal revolved around the old concept that the Negro was a sub-human species and should be treated accordingly. Specifically, Negroes were not to hold "easy jobs." Under this heading were listed the occupations of bootblacks, waiters, porters, cooks, clerks and teachers. But the plan also implied intimidation of whites. For "no white man" was to "be permitted to employ a colored man . . . in any other manner than at the hardest and most degrading tasks." Apparently an exception could be made for the staff of Shreveport's Negro newspaper, *Bailey's Free South,* because they were supposed to be conservative Democrats.

One New Orleans Negro leader, hearing of the plan, described it as "an old mummy" exhumed from "the Shreveport pyramids." He added: "The pernicious idea must be limited to the mean locality in which it had its origin. It would not live in more generous soil, and there are few places in this wide world so sterile in noble sentiments as that which immediately surrounds the publication office of the *Caucasian.*"

The extent to which the "Shreveport Plan" was actually practiced in the area is problematical. Almost certainly, many residents of the city continued to hire blacks for tasks which were proscribed by the *Daily Caucasian*. But that "white supremacy" was "always . . . the motto" of Shreveport there was never any doubt. Of course "we are kindly disposed to the negro race," said one prominent citizen in 1896, "wherever and whenever they properly demean themselves." The indications are that the city's gentry often acted in a barbarous fashion toward the less fortunate of both races. This must have been the impression of two white men who once appeared in municipal court on a charge of vagrancy. Both were one-legged. The judge, who was also the mayor of Shreveport, enjoyed a grotesque sense of humor. He gave the crippled derelicts a sporting chance. If they could hop outside the city limits within twenty-five minutes, they would not have to serve one hundred days in jail.

In other parts of Louisiana, well-to-do conservatives such as Howard G. Goodwyn of Colfax, occasionally complained that Negroes "were shamefully and needlessly bulldozed, and could hope for no legal redress." But the most explicit plea for racial justice was voiced by a man who represented lower class whites. He was Aurel Arnaud, a legislator from St. Landry Parish. Arnaud was a political independent and of poor Cajun ancestry.

One day in 1886, Representative Arnaud stood up in the State House to speak on the unfairness of the method by which Louisiana maintained her public roads. His opening remarks were aimed at a statute of 1880 which instructed parish officials to impose twelve days of "road work," or a stipulated cash assessment, upon all adult males. He pointed out that this law worked a special hardship upon Negro tenants and laborers, since most black families seldom had as much as forty dollars a year to spend on clothes, medicine, and fresh meat. Arnaud expanded on his theme with blunt language: "Can you not see that this amount is not sufficient to support the laborer? And every day you divest him from a chance of earning something is a robbery of his daily bread? Should any one familiar with these facts, be surprised to hear that the negroes steal? *I am only surprised that they do not steal more.*"

Arnaud raised the possibility of another, more serious, Kansas Exodus of the state's black population, if their sufferings continued. He hastened to add that he was not a "leveller"; he offered no socialistic proposals. He merely believed that Negroes "must be treated with as much consideration as we treat our mules." That, he indicated, would be a vast improvement over present conditions. Finally, in what must stand as among the most candid words ever uttered by a white Louisiana official, Arnaud said:

> I have treated the subject entirely as from a . . . negro standpoint. But are there only negroes involved . . . ? And if there were only

negroes involved, would I be here defending their cause? That is a question I have often asked myself, but I have never dared to probe my heart sufficiently to answer it, for fear I would perhaps find myself selfish enough to answer: no, because they are negroes. . . . But in what way is the white laborer treated with more consideration? Does the law give him any more protection? Is he paid better wages? Does he get more or better goods for his money? Do his children get more schooling? Yes, there is an immense difference between the two classes; but this difference exists only in the fancy of unscrupulous and rascally politicians: in every respect the white laborer stands exactly on the same footing with the negro. . . .

Not quite so frank, but to the same point, were statements made by leaders of the more liberal element in the Louisiana Farmers' Union. Especially, John A. Tetts and Thomas J. Guice spoke up for the Negro. "What we want distributed to all men, 'regardless of race, color, or previous condition of servitude,' " Tetts wrote, "is the opportunity for the pursuit of happiness." Tetts believed that the Alliance movement was doing what "the sword, the press and the pulpit" had failed to do: it was forcing the "half Ku Klux and half desperado" white cotton farmer of the South out of his provincial shell, and into an awareness of class interest which transcended racial or regional boundaries. In his typically quaint style, Tetts optimistically reported that "the horns of the Ku Klux were knocked off . . . and the [bloody] shirt that has been waved so faithfully has been torn up . . . and cast into the Mississippi, and by this time no doubt [is] in the maw of some cat-fish, or making a nest for some mud-turtle of a politician who will have to crawl into his shell when he sees the result of the next election."

Guice, the state Lecturer of the Farmers' Union, agreed with Tetts on the need for biracial unity and joint protest. According to Guice, the "spirit of fairness," if nothing else, required that white agrarians include poor blacks in their drive to ameliorate economic and political evils. He believed that working people, "be they white or black," must act together because the "liberties and happiness" of both were at stake. The old agrarian activist from Winn and Grant parishes, the Reverend Benjamin Brian, who was now prominent in the Farmers' Union, had been proposing the same thing since the latter days of Reconstruction.

The Louisiana Farmers' Union was, however, exclusively a white organization. Neither were Negroes admitted to the interstate Alliance proper. But there was a subsidiary association, the Colored Farmers' Alliance, which existed as a means of bringing the South's black agriculturists into the movement. It was founded in Houston County, Texas, in 1886. Spreading across the South with the white Alliance, the Negro order claimed 1,200,000 members by 1890. Though separate, the white and colored Alliances pledged "fraternal regard" for each other. Both orders held their annual national conventions at the same date and in the same city, beginning at St. Louis in December of 1889. The following December, both met at Ocala, Florida.

Fifty thousand Louisiana Negroes were reported on the membership rolls of the Colored Farmers' Alliance by the time of the Ocala convention. In 1891, at the peak of activity, the state's Negro Alliance claimed to be organized in twenty-seven parishes. Detailed information regarding it is lacking, but the alleged fifty thousand membership was probably far above the actual number. The Colored Alliance may have entered the state as early as 1887; but the first report discoverable tells of a Grant Parish lodge which was set up in October of 1889. Black Alliancemen were most numerous in the cotton parishes along the Red River. Apparently, few if any Negroes in the Mississippi River delta joined the order. Neither was there much activity in the sugar country; the recent suppression of the Knights of Labor, and the weakness of even the white Alliance there, must have negated organizational efforts among the Negroes. Below the Red River, the Colored Farmers' Alliance was strongest in St. Landry Parish, where it did not take root until 1891.

L. D. Laurent, an Alexandria Negro, was the first superintendent of the state's Colored Alliance. He held the post until succeeded by Isaac Keys of Catahoula Parish in 1891. Another significant black Allianceman was state secretary J. B. Lafargue. These men were rather circumspect in their activities; conservative whites seldom noticed anything they said or did. The mass of Louisiana Negroes, in or out of the Alliance, tended toward caution in their dealings with local whites, and Laurent, Keys, and Lafargue were probably no exceptions. Certainly, the rising racial bitterness of the late 1880's hampered attempts at biracial agrarian protest. White Alliancemen who came to offer advice at Negro farmers' meetings were said to be received "with great courtesy," but were likely received with suspicion as well. Many blacks in St. Landry Parish refused to join the Colored Alliance because they believed that the white Farmers' Union included men who were anti-Negro "regulators."

Race relations within the Alliance movement were not helped by the fact that the Farmers' Union president, Thomas S. Adams, in 1889, selected the Shreveport *Weekly Caucasian* as the official state organ of the white agrarians. From the Negroes' standpoint, a more insulting choice could scarcely have been made. Equally inauspicious was the fact that in 1890, most of the Democratic state legislators who happened to be members of the Farmers' Union (including ex-president John M. Stallings and G. L. P. Wren) voted for a bill which made racial segregation compulsory on all railroad coaches within the state. Upper class Bourbons were, as a Negro legislator pointed out, the prime movers behind this bill; but the Farmers' Union solons had, with few exceptions, quietly supported it.

Even so, the possibility of white and Negro agrarian unity was still alive. During the year 1890, a third-party revolt against the conservative leadership of both the Democratic Party and the Farmers' Union began to reverberate among the hills of North Louisiana, and the white farmers who led the protest immediately sought the support of the Colored Alliance. The Negro Alliancemen were more than willing to help. At the Ocala gathering of the Alliances in December, three of the seven Louisianians present signed a call for a national third-party convention, scheduled to meet the next year at Cincinnati: they were L. D. Laurent, J. B. Lafargue and I. Miller. All three were Negroes. The state's white delegation at Ocala, dominated by Thomas S. Adams, refused to sign this birth certificate of the Populist Party.

1.3

Populist Dreams and Negro Rights:
East Texas as a Case Study

LAWRENCE C. GOODWYN

For a brief but powerful moment, southern blacks and whites turned to
politics to deal with their region-wide discontents. The Populist movement and
the varied farm protest organizations that emerged in the late 1880s and the
early 1890s drew upon past experiences and attitudes to build a fragile
movement cutting across racial and class lines and directly challenging the
political authority symbolized in 1877 by the "marriage" between southern
and northern conservatives. This was not a simple movement. Relations between
black and white Populists and between these two groups and their white
opponents reflected profoundly important patterns of political behavior in
the post-Reconstruction South. In response to these movements, a one-party
South emerged, as did political disfranchisement and a widened separation
in law of blacks and whites.

In his finely textured study of the Grimes County, Texas Populists and

Lawrence C. Goodwyn, "Populist Dreams and Negro Rights: East Texas as a Case Study,"
American Historical Review, 76 (December, 1971), 1435–56. Copyright Lawrence C.
Goodwyn. Reprinted, omitting figure on p. 1445 and all footnotes except fn. 10, by
permission of the author.

their opponents, Lawrence Goodwyn describes the persistence of "an indigenous black political structure for thirty-five years following the Civil War." The strength and success of such a tradition in an East Texas county tells us little about the presence of similar patterns of behavior in other parts of the Deep South, but for this one county Goodwyn reveals a great deal. Once again, the sources of violence are quite different from those usually associated with southern disorders. The author's unusual use of both black and white oral sources together with his strictures against relying on "one" such oral tradition (in this instance, the dominant white oral tradition) add greatly to the value of his study.

The following book is suggested for further reading:

C. VANN WOODWARD, *Tom Watson: Agrarian Rebel,* New York: The Macmillan Company, 1938.

Nearly a century later the Populist decade lingers in historical memory as an increasingly dim abstraction. The very word "Populism" no longer carries specific political meaning. It is now invoked to explain George Wallace, as it was used to explain Lyndon Johnson in the sixties, Joe McCarthy in the fifties, and Claude Pepper in the forties. Though afflicting principally the popular mind, this confusion is at least partly traceable to those historians who have insisted on concentrating on Populism as exhortation, so that Ignatius Donnelly's utopian novels or Mary Lease's pronouncements on the respective uses of corn and hell become the explanatory keys to agrarian radicalism. For scholars who mine political movements with a view to extracting cultural nuggets, the focus has been chiefly upon the word, not the deed; in the process the agrarian crusade has become increasingly obscure.

Much of the difficulty centers on the subject of race. There is essential agreement that, on economic issues, Populists were men of the Left, primitive to some, prophetic to others, but leftists to all. But did their banner indicate a highly selective nativist radicalism for whites only, or did they grapple with the inherited legacies of the caste system as part of an effort to create what they considered a more rational social and economic order? The analysis of Populist rhetoric has left us with contradictory answers.

While party platforms can be useful tools in determining professed attitudes, the gap between asserted ideals and performance is sufficiently large to defeat any analysis resting on the implicit assumption that political manifestos have an intrinsic value apart from the milieu in which they existed. In America the distance between assertion and performance is especially evident in matters of race; as a result, on this issue above all, the context of public assertions is central to the task of their political evaluation. An inquiry into the murkiest corner of Populism, interracial politics, should begin not merely with what Populists said but what they did in the course of bidding for power at the local level. What was the stuff of daily life under Populist rule in the rural enclaves where the third party came to exercise all the authority of public office, including police authority? What can we learn not only about Populist insurgency but also about the orthodoxy the third party opposed?

Grimes County, Texas, was one of many counties scattered across the South and West where the People's party achieved a continuing political presence in the latter part of the nineteenth century. Located some sixty miles north of Houston in the heart of what the natives call the Old South part of Texas, Grimes County displayed the cotton-centered economy typical of rural East Texas in 1880. Its largest town, Navasota, contained 1,800 persons in 1890 and its second largest town, Anderson, the county seat, only 574 persons as late as 1900. Farms in Grimes County ranged from plantation size in the rich bottomland country of the Brazos River on the county's western border to small, single-family agricultural units on the poorer land of the northern part of the county. The 1890 census revealed a county population of 21,312, of which 11,664 were black.

Populism in Grimes County is the story of a black-white coalition that had its genesis in Reconstruction and endured for more than a generation. In time this coalition came to be symbolized by its most enduring elected public official, Garrett Scott. The Scotts had roots in Grimes County dating back before the Civil War. Their sons fought for the Confederacy and returned to face a postwar reality by no means unique in the South; possessing moderately large holdings of land but lacking necessary capital to make it productive, the Scotts did not achieve great affluence. During the hard times that continued to afflict undercapitalized Southern agriculture through the 1870s Garrett Scott became a soft-money agrarian radical. His stance was significant in the political climate of Grimes County in the early 1880s. During Reconstruction Negroes in the county had achieved a remarkably stable local Republican organization, headed by a number of resourceful black leaders. When Reconstruction ended and white Democrats regained control of the state governmental machinery in Texas, Grimes County blacks retained local power and sent a succession of black legislators to Austin for the next decade. The local effort to end this Republican rule took the usual postwar Southern form of a political movement of white solidarity under the label of the Democratic party. In supporting the

Greenback party Garrett Scott not only was disassociating himself from the politics of white racial solidarity, he was undermining it.

In 1882 a mass meeting of various non-Democratic elements in Grimes County nominated a variegated slate for county offices. Among the candidates were black Republicans, "lily-white" Republicans, and Independent Greenbackers. Garrett Scott was on the ticket as the Independent Greenback candidate for sheriff. Not much is known about the racial climate in Grimes County in 1882, but it must not have been wholly serene, because the "lily-white" nominee for county judge, Lock Mac-Daniel, withdrew from the ticket rather than publicly associate with black candidates. Garrett Scott did not withdraw, and in November he was elected. Also elected, as district clerk, was a black man who became a lifelong political ally of Scott, Jim Kennard. Thus began an interracial coalition that endured through the years of propagandizing in Texas by the increasingly radical Farmers Alliance and through the ensuing period of the People's party. The success of the coalition varied with the degree of white participation. After the collapse of the Greenback party in the mid-eighties visible white opposition to the Democratic party declined for several years before Grimes County farmers, organized by the Alliance, broke with the Democracy to form the nucleus of the local People's party in 1892. Scott and Kennard were the most visible symbols of the revitalized coalition, but there were others as well. Among them were Morris Carrington, a Negro school principal, and Jack Haynes, both staunch advocates of Populism in the black community, as well as J. W. H. Davis and J. H. Teague, white Populist leaders. These men led the People's party to victory in the county elections of 1896 and again in 1898.*

A subtle duality creeps into the narrative of events at this point. To

---

* Carrington and Haynes as well as Kennard had been active in the county Republican organization prior to the emergence of the third party. The information from contemporary sources on the political lives of Negro leaders in Grimes County that was used in this paper was augmented by oral interviews with their descendants. The author wishes to express his gratitude to Maurice Lyons and B. T. Bonner, both former students at the University of Texas, for their assistance in the conduct of oral interviews in the black communities of Navasota, Anderson, Plantersville, and Richards in Grimes County. Largely through the efforts of Mr. Lyons and Mr. Bonner, the author was able to locate the descendants of every known black leader of the People's party in Grimes County. With respect to the third party's white leadership, the political histories of Teague, Davis, and Scott, traced through both oral interviews and contemporary sources, stand as examples of the diverse sources of Southern Populism. Teague, like Scott, spent his entire political life in opposition to the Democratic party—but as a Republican rather than as an agrarian radical. Quietly progressive on the race issue, Teague possessed considerable administrative talents and eventually became chairman of the third party for the first congressional district of Texas. He was elected county judge in 1896 and was reelected in the local third-party sweep of 1898. Davis, a Democrat, became quite radical on economic issues, broke with his party, and became a third-party editor. He displayed an ambivalent stance on the race issue and was not prominent in the events described in this paper.

the world outside Grimes County in the 1890s, to both Populists and Democrats, Garrett Scott was simply another Populist officeholder, distinguished for his antimonopoly views and his generally radical approach to monetary policy. To his white supporters within Grimes County he was doubtless respected for the same reasons. But to the Democrats of Grimes County the sheriff symbolized all that was un-Southern and unpatriotic about the third party. Under Populist rule, it was charged, Negro school teachers were paid too much money; furthermore, in Scott's hands the sheriff's office hired Negro deputies. The two Democratic newspapers in Navasota were fond of equating Populist rule with Negro rule and of attributing both evils to Scott. The Navasota *Daily Examiner* asserted that "the Negro has been looking too much to political agitation and legislative enactment. . . . So long as he looks to political agitation for relief, so long will he be simply the means of other men's ambition." To the Navasota *Tablet* Scott was simply "the originator of all the political trouble in Grimes County for years." Both these explanations oversimplify Grimes County politics. The political presence and goals of blacks were definite elements of local Populism, as was, presumably, the personal ambition of Garrett Scott. But the Populists' proposed economic remedies had gained a significant following among the county's white farmers, and this was of crucial importance in inducing white Populists to break with Democrats and ally themselves with blacks. Garrett Scott was a living embodiment of white radicalism; he did not cause it. Beyond this the political cohesion of blacks was a local phenomenon that had preceded Scott's entry into Grimes County politics and had remained relatively stable since the end of the war. The ease with which Democratic partisans saw the fine hand of Garrett Scott in Negro voting was more a reflection of their own racial presumptions than an accurate description of the political dynamics at work in the county.

Through the election of 1898 Democrats in Grimes County had labored in vain to cope with the disease of Populism among the county's white farmers. Finally, in the spring of 1899, the Democrats moved in a new direction. The defeated Democratic candidate for county judge, J. G. McDonald, organized a clandestine meeting with other prominent local citizens and defeated Democratic office seekers. At this meeting a new and—for the time being—covert political institution was created: the White Man's Union. A charter was drawn providing machinery through which the Union could nominate candidates for county offices in elections in which only White Man's Union members could vote. No person could be nominated who was not a member; no person could be a member who did not subscribe to these exclusionary bylaws; in effect, to participate in the organization's activities, so adequately expressed in its formal title, one had to support, as a policy matter, black disfranchisement. Throughout the summer and fall of 1899 the White Man's Union quietly organized. Writing years later McDonald explained that care was taken not to launch the organization publicly "until the public attitude could be sounded." By January 1900 the covert organizing had been deemed sufficiently successful to permit the public unveiling of the White Man's Union through a long story in the *Examiner*. During the spring the *Examiner's* political reporting began to reflect a significant change of tone. In April, for example, the *Examiner's* report of a "quiet election" in nearby Bryan noted that friends of the two mayoral candidates "made a display of force and permitted no Negroes to vote. All white citizens went to the polls, quietly deposited their ballots for whom they pleased and went on about their business." The *Examiner* had progressed from vague suggestions for disfranchisement to approval of its forcible imposition without cover of law.

The first public meetings of the White Man's Union, duly announced in the local press, occupied the spring months of 1900 and were soon augmented by some not-quite-so-public night riding. The chronology of these events may be traced through the denials in the local Democratic press of their occurrence. In July the *Examiner* angrily defended the county's honor against charges by the Negro Baptist State Sunday School Conference that the county had become unsafe for Negroes. The Austin *Herald* reported from the state's capital that the Sunday School Board, "after mature thought and philosophical deliberation," had decided to cancel its annual meeting scheduled for Navasota. The *Examiner* cited as "irresponsible slush" the charge that Negroes were being threatened and told to leave the county, but within weeks reports of just such events began cropping up in the *Examiner* itself. One example of terrorism left no one in doubt, for it occurred in broad daylight on the main street of the county seat: in July Jim Kennard was shot and killed within one hundred yards of the courthouse. His assailant was alleged to be J. G. McDonald.

Intimidation and murder constituted an even more decisive assault on the People's party than had the ominous bylaws of the White Man's Union. The Populist leadership recognized this clearly enough, and Scott went so far as to attempt to persuade Southern white farmers to shoulder arms in defense of the right of Negroes to vote. Beyond this we know little of the measures attempted by the local Populist constabulary to contain the spreading terrorism. A well-informed member of the Scott family wrote a detailed account of these turbulent months, but the manuscript was subsequently destroyed. In the early autumn of 1900 members of the White Man's Union felt sufficiently strong to initiate visits to white farmers with a known allegiance to the People's party. Under such duress some of these farmers joined the White Man's Union.

In August the Union, aided by a not inconsiderable amount of free publicity in the local press, announced "the Grandest Barbecue of the

Year," at which the "workings of the White Man's Union" would be explained to all. The leadership of the People's party objected to announced plans to include the local state guard unit, the Shaw Rifles, in the program. After some discussion the Texas adjutant general, Thomas Scurry, placed at the discretion of the local commander the question of the attendance of the Shaw Rifles in a body. The commander, Captain Hammond Norwood, a leading Navasota Democrat and a member of the White Man's Union, exercised his option, and the Shaw Rifles appeared en masse at the function. Populist objections were brushed aside.

Shortly after this well-attended barbecue had revealed the growing prestige of the White Man's Union as well as the inability of the People's party to cope with the changing power relationships within the county, a black exodus began. People left by train, by horse and cart, by day and by night. The *Examiner,* with obvious respect for the new political climate its own columns had helped engender, suggested elliptically that the exodus could produce complications. Some citizens, said the *Examiner,* "are beginning to feel a little nervous as the thing progresses, and lean to the idea that the action will bring on detrimental complications in the labor market."

The next day, however, the paper printed a public address that it said had been "ordered published by the executive committee of the White Man's Union in order to combat the many reports that are calculated to injure the Union." After reaffirming the Union's intent to end "Negro rule" in the county, the report concluded with a message "to the Negroes":

> Being the weaker race, it is our desire to protect you from the schemes of those men who are now seeking to place you before them. . . . Therefore, the White Man's Union kindly and earnestly requests you to keep hands off in the coming struggle. Do not let impudent men influence you in that pathway which certainly leads to trouble. . . . In the future, permit us to show you, and convince you by our action, that we are truly your best friends.

Fourteen days later a black Populist leader, Jack Haynes, was riddled with a shotgun blast by unknown assailants. He died instantly in the fields of his cotton farm.

The White Man's Union held a rally in Navasota two nights later that featured a reading of original poetry by one of the Union's candidates, L. M. Bragg. The verse concluded:

> Twas nature's laws that drew the lines
> Between the Anglo-Saxon and African races,
> And we, the Anglo-Saxons of Grand Old Grimes,
> Must force the African to keep his place.

Another White Man's Union rally held in Plantersville the same week displayed other Union candidates whose conduct won the *Examiner*'s editorial approval: "They are a solid looking body of men and mean business straight from the shoulder." Apparently this characterization of the Plantersville speakers was not restricted to approving Democrats; Populists, too, responded to events initiated by the men who "meant business." In October the Plantersville school superintendent reported that only five white families remained in his school district and that all the Negroes were gone. The superintendent stated that twelve white families had left that week, and "the end is not in sight."

Amid this wave of mounting terror the People's party attempted to go about its business, announcing its nominating conventions in the local press and moving forward with the business of naming election judges and poll watchers. But there were already signs of a fatal crack in Populist morale. The People's party nominee for county commissioner suddenly withdrew from the race. His withdrawal was announced in the *Examiner,* and no explanation was offered.

Throughout the late summer and autumn of 1900 the demonstrated power of the White Man's Union had protected McDonald from prosecution in the Kennard slaying. Nothing short of a war between the Populist police authority and the White Man's Union could break that extralegal shield. An exasperated and perhaps desperate Garrett Scott angrily challenged a White Man's Union official in October to "go and get your Union force, every damn one of them, put them behind rock fences and trees and I'll fight the whole damn set of cowards." That Scott had to use the first person singular to describe the visible opposition to the Union underscores the extent to which terror had triumphed over the institutions of law in Grimes County. By election eve it was clear that the Populist ticket faced certain defeat. The third party had failed to protect its constituency. White Populists as well as black were intimidated. Many would not vote; indeed, many were no longer in the county.

Over 4,500 votes had been cast in Grimes in 1898. On November 6, 1900, only 1,800 persons ventured to the polls. The People's party received exactly 366 votes. The Populist vote in Plantersville fell from 256 in 1898 to 5 in 1900. In the racially mixed, lower-income precinct of south Navasota the Populist vote declined from 636 to 23. The sole exception to this pattern came in a geographically isolated, lower-income precinct in the extreme northern part of the county that contained few Negroes and thus, presumably, fewer acts of terrorism. The Populist vote in this precinct actually increased from 108 to 122 and accounted for one-third of the countywide vote of 366. In north Navasota, also almost all white but not geographically isolated from the terror, the Populist vote declined from 120 to 3. An additional element, nonstatistical in nature, stamped the election as unusual. The underlying philosophy of the South's dominant political institution, the Democratic party, has perhaps never been expressed more nakedly than it was in Grimes County in 1900 when "the party of white supremacy," as C. Vann Woodward has called the Southern Democracy, appeared on the official ballot as the White Man's Union.

On the way to its landslide victory the Union had grown more self-confident in its willingness to carry out acts of intimidation and terrorism in defiance of the local Populist police authority. Now that that authority had been deposed and a sheriff friendly to the White Man's Union had been elected, would terrorism become even more public?

On November 7, 1900, the morning after the election, a strange tableau unfolded on the streets of Anderson, the tiny county seat. Horsemen began arriving in town from every section of the county, tied their horses all along the main street, and occupied the second floor of the courthouse. In a nearby house Garrett Scott's sister, Cornelia, and her husband, John Kelly, watched the buildup of Union supporters on the courthouse square, not fifty yards from the sheriff's official residence on the second floor of the county jail. They decided the situation was too dangerous to permit an adult Populist to venture forth, so the Kellys sent their nine-year-old son with a note to warn Scott not to appear on the street.

At about the same time that this mission was carried out Garrett Scott's younger brother, Emmett Scott, came into town from the family farm, rode past the growing clusters of armed men, and reined up in front of the store belonging to John Bradley, his closest friend in town. Bradley was a Populist but, as befitting a man of trade, a quiet one. His store was adjacent to the courthouse.

Cornelia Kelly's son found the sheriff at Abercrombie's store across the street from the jail and delivered the warning note. As Scott read it an outbreak of gunfire sounded from the direction of Bradley's store. Scott stepped to the street and peered in the direction of the fusillade. Rifle fire from the second floor of the courthouse immediately cut him down. Upon hearing the gunfire Cornelia Kelly ran out of her house and down the long street toward the courthouse. The gunsights of scores of men tracked her progress. Seeing her brother's body in the street she turned and confronted his attackers. "Why don't you shoot me, too," she yelled, "I'm a Scott." She ran to her brother and, with the assistance of her son, dragged him across the street to the county jail. He was, she found, not dead, though he did have an ugly wound in his hip. Inside Bradley's store, however, three men were dead—Emmett Scott, Bradley, and Will McDonald, the son of a Presbyterian minister and a prominent member of the White Man's Union. McDonald had shot Scott shortly after the latter had entered the store; the two men grappled for the gun, and the fatally wounded Scott fired one shot, killing McDonald. Bradley was killed either by a shot fired from outside the store where Union forces had gathered near the courthouse or by a stray bullet during the struggle inside.

The siege of Anderson continued for five days, with the wounded sheriff and his deputies—black and white—in the jail and the White Man's Union forces in the courthouse. Shots crossed the fifty yards between the two buildings intermittently over the next several days. On the evening of the fatal shooting another member of the Scott clan, Mrs. W. T. Neblett, had left Navasota for Austin to plead with the governor, Joseph D. Sayers, for troops. On Friday she returned, accompanied by the adjutant general of the State of Texas, Thomas Scurry—the same official who had earlier acquiesced in the participation of the state guard in the White Man's Union barbecue. After conferring with the contending forces Scurry pondered various methods to get the wounded Scott out of town and into a hospital; gangrene had set in. For protection, Scurry suggested that he be authorized to select a group of twenty prominent citizens of Navasota to escort the sheriff from the jail to the railroad station. Since most of the "prominent citizens" of Navasota were members of the White Man's Union, it is perhaps understandable that Scott declined this offer. The adjutant general then suggested that the Shaw Rifles be employed as an escort. This idea was respectfully declined for the same reason. Asked what he would consider a trustworthy escort, the wounded sheriff suggested a state guard unit from outside the county.

On Saturday, four days after the shooting, a company of Houston light infantry of the Texas Volunteer State Guard detrained at Navasota and marched the eleven miles to Anderson. On Sunday morning Garrett Scott was placed on a mattress, the mattress put in a wagon, and the procession began. In the wagon train were most of the members of the large Scott clan—Emmett Scott's widow and children, the Kelly family, and the Nebletts, all with their household belongings piled in wagons. A file of infantrymen marched on either side as the procession formed in front of the jail, moved past hundreds of armed men at the courthouse and onto the highway to Navasota, and then boarded a special train bound for Houston.

Thus did Populism leave Grimes County. From that day in 1900 until well after mid-century Negroes were not a factor in Grimes County politics. J. G. McDonald regained his judgeship and served for many years. The White Man's Union continued into the 1950s as the dominant political institution in the county. None of its nominees, selected in advance of the Democratic primary, was ever defeated. The census of 1910 revealed the extent of the Negro exodus. It showed that Grimes County's Negro population had declined by almost thirty per cent from the 1900 total. School census figures for 1901 suggest an even greater exodus.

To this day the White Man's Union, as a memory if no longer as an institution, enjoys an uncontested reputation among Grimes County whites as a civic enterprise for governmental reform. In this white oral tradition the general events of 1900 are vividly recounted. Specific events are, however, remembered selectively. The exodus of Negroes from the county is not part of this oral tradition, nor is the night riding of the White Man's Union or the assassination of the Negro Populist leaders.

As for Garrett Scott, he endured a long convalescence in a San Antonio hospital, regained his health, married his nurse, and moved to a farm near Houston. He retired from politics and died in his bed. He is remembered in the oral tradition of the black community as the "best sheriff the county ever had." Kennard and Haynes were killed because they "vouched" for Scott among Negroes. In this black oral tradition the Negro exodus plays a central role. It is perhaps an accurate measure of the distance between the races in Grimes County today that two such contradictory versions of famous events could exist side by side without cross-influence.

To these two oral traditions a third must be added—the Scott tradition. The Scotts were, and are, a proud family. One by one, as they died, they were brought home to be buried in the family plot in the Anderson cemetery, little more than a mile from the site of the bloody events of 1900. Tombstones of female members of the clan bear the Scott middle name, defiantly emblazoned in marble. Edith Hamilton of Richards, Grimes County, was ten years old in November 1900 and remembers vividly the day her nine-year-old brother carried her mother's message to Garrett Scott. She remembers the defiance of her mother, the political commitment of her father, the acts of intimidation by the White Man's Union, the Negro exodus, and what she calls the "intelligence of Uncle Garrett." "They said that Uncle Garrett was a nigger-lover," recalls Mrs. Hamilton. "He wasn't a nigger-lover, or a white-lover, he just believed in being fair to all, in justice."

The Scott oral tradition—similar to the black oral tradition and at odds with the white tradition—is virtually the only legacy of the long years of interracial cooperation in Grimes County. Beyond this the substance of political life that came to an end in Grimes County in 1900 cannot be measured precisely from the available evidence. Very little survives to provide insight into the nature of the personal relationship that existed between Garrett Scott and Jim Kennard, between any of the other Populist leaders of both races, or between their respective constituencies. Scott and his third-party colleagues may have been motivated solely by personal ambition, as the White Man's Union charged; on the other hand, the impulses that made them Populists in the first place may have led them toward public coalition with blacks. It is clear that such stridently white supremacist voices as the Navasota *Tablet* were unable to project any reason other than personal ambition to explain the phenomenon of white men willingly associating themselves politically with black men. To what extent this attitude reflected Populist presumptions is another question. White Populists and black Republicans shared an animosity toward the Southern Democracy that grew in intensity during the bitter election campaigns of the 1890s. Democratic persistence in raising the cry of "Negro domination" to lure Populist-leaning voters back to the "party of the fathers" was effective enough to keep white Populists on the defensive about the race issue throughout the agrarian revolt in the South. The circumstance of a common political foe nevertheless provided Populists and Republicans with a basis for political coalition that was consummated in a bewildering variety of ways—and sometimes not consummated at all. The stability of local black organizations and their demonstrated capacity to withstand Democratic blandishments or acts of intimidation were only two of the factors governing the complex equation of post-Reconstruction interracial politics. A stable, local black political institution existed in Grimes County, and its enduring qualities obviously simplified the organizational task confronting Garrett Scott. What might be regarded as "normal" Bourbon efforts to split blacks from the Populist coalition—mild intimidation, petty bribery, campaign assertions that the Democrats were the Negroes' "best friends," or a combination of all three—failed to achieve the desired results in Grimes County in the 1890s. The precise reasons are not easily specified. The Navasota *Tablet,* seeing the world through lenses tinted with its own racial presumptions, ascribed the credit for Negro political cohesion solely to the white sheriff. In the face of all Democratic stratagems, the third party's continuing appeal to Negroes was, in the *Tablet*'s view, a thing of "magic." A white supremacist view does not automatically exclude its holder from rendering correct political analyses on occasion, and it is possible that the *Tablet*'s assessment of the cause of Negro political solidarity was correct; however, such an analysis does not explain how the Negro Republican organization was able to send a succession of black legislators to Austin in the 1870s and 1880s, before Garrett Scott became politically active. It seems relevant that when Grimes County Democrats decided upon an overt campaign of terrorism, the men they went after first were the leading black spokesmen of Populism in the county rather than the third party's white leadership. To this extent the actions of Democratic leaders contradicted their public analysis of the causal relationships inherent in the continuing Populist majorities.

Before they indulged in terrorism the Democrats already possessed another method of splitting the Populist coalition: regaining the loyalty of white Populists. Against the historic Democratic campaign cry of white supremacy, the People's party had as its most effective defense the economic appeal of its own platform. The persuasiveness of Populism to white farmers in Grimes County was confirmed by newspaper accounts of the public reaction to the Populist-Democratic debates that occurred during the years of the agrarian uprising. While the reports in the *Examiner* were uniformly partisan and invariably concluded that Democratic spokesmen "won" such debates hands down, the papers conceded that Populist speakers also drew enthusiastic responses from white residents. The absence of reliable racial data by precincts renders a statistical analysis of the Populist vote in Grimes County impossible; however, the fragmentary available evidence suggests that the People's party was generally able to hold a minimum of approximately thirty per cent of the county's white voters in the four elections from 1892 to 1898 while at the same time polling approximately eighty to ninety per cent of the Negro electorate. The inability of the Democratic party to "bloc vote" the county's white citizenry, coupled with the party's failure to win black voters by various means or, alternatively, to diminish the size of the Negro electorate, combined to ensure Democratic defeat at the polls. The fact merits emphasis: both the cohesion of black support for the People's party and the maintenance of substantial white support were essential to the local ascendancy of Populism.

This largely deductive analysis, however, reveals little about the internal environment within the third-party coalition during the bitter struggle for power that characterized the decade of Populist-Democratic rivalry. However scrutinized, the bare bones of voting totals do not flesh out the human relationships through which black and white men came together politically in this rural Southern county. In the absence of such crucial evidence, it seems prudent to measure the meaning of 1900 in the most conservative possible terms. Even by this standard, however, a simple recitation of those elements of Grimes County politics that are beyond dispute isolates significant and lasting ramifications.

An indigenous black political structure persisted in Grimes County for thirty-five years following the Civil War. Out of his own needs as a political insurgent against the dominant Southern Democratic party, Garrett Scott decided in 1882 to identify his Greenback cause with the existing local Republican constituency. Once in office as sheriff he found, among other possible motives, that it was in his own self-interest to preserve the coalition that elected him. It is clear that the style of law enforcement in Grimes County under Scott became a persuasive ingredient in the preservation of black support for the People's party. The presence of black deputy sheriffs and Scott's reputation within the black community seem adequate confirmation of both the existence of this style and its practical effect. The salaries paid Negro school teachers constituted another element of third-party appeal. Comparisons with white salaries are not available, but whatever black teachers received, partisans of the White Man's Union publicly denounced it as "too much." It is evident that Grimes County Negroes supported the People's party for reasons that were grounded in legitimate self-interest—an incontestable basis for political conduct. The point is not so much that the county's Negroes had certain needs, but that they possessed the political means to address at least a part of those needs.

From this perspective the decisive political event of 1900 in Grimes County was not the overwhelming defeat of the local People's party but the political elimination of that part of its constituency that was black. Scott was valuable to Negroes in short-run terms because he helped to translate a minority black vote into a majority coalition that possessed the administrative authority to improve the way black people lived in Grimes County. In the long run, however, it was the presence of this black constituency—not the conduct of a single white sheriff nor even the professed principles of his political party—that provided the Negroes of the county with what protection they had from a resurgent caste system. As long as Negroes retained the right to cast ballots in proportion to their numbers they possessed bargaining power that became particularly meaningful on all occasions when whites divided their votes over economic issues. Disfranchisement destroyed the bargaining power essential to this elementary level of protection. Arrayed against these overriding imperatives for Negroes such questions as the sincerity of Garrett Scott's motives fade in importance. Whatever the sheriff's motives, both the political realities that undergirded the majority coalition and Scott's ability to respond to those realities shaped a course of government conduct under the People's party that was demonstrably of more benefit to Negroes than was the conduct of other administrations before or since. The permanent alteration of those realities through black disfranchisement ensured that no other white administration, whether radical, moderate, or opportunistic, would be able to achieve the patterns in education and law enforcement that had come to exist in the county under Populism. Stated as starkly as possible, after 1900 it was no longer in the interest of white politicians to provide minimal guarantees for people who could not help elect them.

Beyond this crucial significance for the county's black people, disfranchisement also institutionalized a fundamental change in the political environment of whites. More than a third party passed from Grimes County in 1900; in real political terms an idea died. Though a new political idea invariably materializes in democratic societies as an expression of the self-interest of a portion of the electorate, the party that adopts the idea in the course of appealing for the votes of that sector of the electorate inevitably is placed in the position of having to rationalize, defend, explain, and eventually promote the idea. If the concept has substance, this process eventually results in the insinuation of the idea into the culture itself. In this sense it is not necessary to know the precise depth of the commitment to Negro rights of the Grimes County People's party to know that the *idea* of Negro rights had a potential constituency among white people in the county as long as black people were able to project its presence through their votes. Given the endurance of this real and potential constituency, one could reasonably intuit that twentieth-century politics in Grimes County would have contained one, or a dozen, or a thousand Garrett Scotts—each more, or less, "sincere" or "ambitious" than the Populist sheriff. Disfranchisement destroyed the political base of this probability. A political party can survive electoral defeat, even continuing defeat, and remain a conveyor of ideas from one generation to the next. But it cannot survive the destruction of its constituency, for the party itself then dies, taking with it the possibility of transmitting its political concepts to those as yet unborn. It is therefore no longer possible to speak of two white political traditions in Grimes County, for the White Man's Union succeeded in establishing a most effective philosophical suzerainty. Seventy years after disfranchisement Mrs. Hamilton can recall the racial unorthodoxy of Uncle Garrett; she cannot participate in such activity herself. "The Negro people here don't want this school integration any more than the whites do," she now says. "They're not ready for it. They don't feel comfortable in the school with white children. I've talked to my maid. I know."

While Garrett Scott's memory has been preserved, the local presence of the creed of his political party died with the destruction of that party. There has been literally no political place to go for subsequent generations of Scotts and Teagues, or Kennards and Carringtons. This absence of an alternative political institution to the Democratic party, the party of white supremacy, has been a continuing and unique factor in Southern politics. The circumstance is based on the race issue, but in its long-term political and social implications it actually transcends that issue.

The Populist era raises a number of questions about the interaction of the two races in the South, both within the third party and in the larger society. It is widely believed, by no means merely by laymen, that after the failure of Reconstruction meaningful experiments with the social order were finished in the South and that the aspirations of blacks were decisively thwarted. The example of Grimes County suggests, however, the existence of a period of time—a decade perhaps, or a generation—when nascent forms of indigenous interracial activity struggled for life in at least parts of the old Confederacy. Was some opportunity missed and, if so, how? How widespread through the South, and the nation, was this opportunity?

The White Man's Union was organized and led by men who considered themselves the "best people" of the South. If this attitude was typical, major adjustments must be made in our understanding of precisely how, and for what reasons, the antebellum caste system, in altered form, was reinstitutionalized in Southern society a generation after the formal ending of slavery. Was the "red-neck" the source of atrocity, or was he swept along by other stronger currents? And what of the Populist role? To what extent was agrarian racial liberalism in Texas traceable to an overall philosophy within the third-party leadership? Through what intuition of self-interest did the radical organizers of the Farmers Alliance, the parent institution of the People's party, accept the political risks of public coalition with blacks? What were their hopes and fears, and where did they falter? And, finally, what does the substance of their effort tell us about the Democrats in the South and the Republicans in the North who opposed them?

Answers to these questions rest, in part, on detailed knowledge of such events as those in Grimes County, but they require more than compilations of local histories, just as they assuredly require more than cultural assessments based on novels, speeches, and party manifestoes considered apart from their organic milieu. These answers will not provide much of a synthesis—Populism was too diverse, too congregational, and too ideologically thin—but they should tell us more about the larger society that, along with the Populists, failed to erect the foundations for a multiracial society in the nineteenth century. As the inquiry proceeds, it should be remembered that Populism perished before developing a mature philosophy—on race, on money, or on socialism. One must generalize, therefore, not only from contradictory evidence but, more important, from incomplete evidence. An analogy, doubtless unfair, could be made with the plight that would face modern historians of Marxism had that movement been abruptly truncated at the time, say, of the Brussels Conference in 1903. Who could have predicted on the evidence available to that date the Stalinist reign of terror that evolved from the mature, victorious revolutionary party of 1917? By the same token sweeping generalizations about what Populist radicalism could have become are not only romantic but historically unsound.

It should be sufficient to observe that in the long post-Reconstruction period—a period not yet ended—during which the social order has been organized hierarchically along racial lines, Populism intruded as a brief, flickering light in parts of the South. For a time some white Southerners threw off the romanticism that has historically been a cover for the region's pessimism and ventured a larger, more hopeful view about the possibilities of man in a free society. Under duress and intimidation this public hope failed of persuasion at the ballot box; under terrorism it vanished completely.

The Grimes County story dramatically illustrates this failure, but in the insight it provides into the underlying politics of black disfranchisement and the achievement of a monolithic one-party political environment in the American South it is not unique. Other Populists in East Texas and across the South—white as well as black—died during the terrorism that preceded formal disfranchisement. In Texas the extraparliamentary institutions formed by white Democrats to help create the political climate for disfranchisement bore a variety of local names: the Citizens White Primary of Marion County; the Tax-Payers Union of Brazoria County; the Jaybird Democratic Association of Fort Bend County; and the White Man's Union of Wharton, Washington, Austin, Matagorda, Grimes, and other counties. The available historical material concerning each of these organizations comes largely from the founders themselves, or their descendants, reflecting an incipient or a mature oral tradition—one oral tradition. The secondary literature based on these accounts, including scholarly works used in graduate schools as well as primary and secondary textbooks, is correspondingly inadequate.

A surprising amount of uninterpreted material from violently partisan white supremacist sources has found its way into scholarly literature. One example from the Grimes experience pertains directly to the scholarly characterization of Negro political meetings during the Populist era. It is worth attention as an illustration of the impact of white supremacist modes of thought on modern scholarship. The sunup-to-sundown work routine of Southern farm labor obviously precluded daytime political meetings. Accordingly, Kennard, Haynes, and Carrington campaigned among their black constituents by holding political meetings in each of the towns and hamlets of the county at night. Democratic partisans termed these rallies "Owl Meetings" and characterized black Populist leaders as " 'fluence men." Drawing upon their own party's time-honored campaign technique with Negroes, Democrats further asserted that owl meetings were more concerned with sumptuous banquets and whisky than with politics. If partisans of white supremacy had difficulty finding reasons for white acceptance of political coalition with blacks, they were culturally incapable of ascribing reasons for Negro support of the third party to causes other than short-run benefits in terms of money and alcohol. The point is not that Democrats were always insincere in their descriptions (as white supremacists they were quite sincere), but that scholars have subsequently accepted such violently partisan accounts at face value. The darkly sinister picture of " 'fluence men" corrupting innocent blacks with whisky at surreptitious owl meetings served to justify, at least to outsiders, the use of terrorism as the ultimate campaign technique of Democratic interracial politics. This sequential recording of events has found its way into scholarly monographs that otherwise demonstrate no inherent hostility to the Populistic inclinations of Southern farmers, black or white. In *The People's Party in Texas* Roscoe Martin precedes his brief allusion to the White Man's Union with a resumé of owl meetings and " 'fluence men" that reflects in detail the bias of white supremacist sources. Other scholars writing broadly about Gilded Age politics have routinely drawn upon such monographs as Martin's, and by this process " 'fluence men" have materialized as an explanation of Negro political insurgency in the nineties. In the heat of local political combat, however, Democratic leaders often were able to face a wholly different set of facts in the course of persuading their followers, and the citizenry as a whole, to adjust to the necessity of terrorism. As the time approached for actual precinct campaigning in Grimes County in the autumn of 1900, the executive board of the White Man's Union published a notice of the Union's intentions, climaxed by a "fair distinct warning" to the county's Negro leadership. The statement is revealing—not only of the transformation visited upon normal campaign practices when they were viewed through the cultural presumptions of white supremacy but also of the dangers of uncritical acceptance of such perspectives by scholars relying upon monoracial sources. The notice read in part:

> The Union is largely composed of the best citizens of the county. . . .
> They are the tax payers, representing the worth, the patriotism, the intelligence, and the virtues of the county. . . . We are not fighting any political party or individuals, but only those who band together under any name, who seek to perpetuate negro rule in Grimes County. [Good citizens] are astounded at the manner in which the children's money has been expended. Colored teachers with fat salaries and totally incompetent have been appointed for political "fluence." Our white teachers, male and female, enjoy no such fat salaries as these colored politicians or these sweet colored girls. . . . One of the most corrupting practices in the past has been the system of Owl Meetings whicn has been in vogue for years. . . . This is the school and hot bed where the negro politician received his inspiration, and riding from one end of the county to the other as an apostle of his race, corrupting his own people who may be in the honest pathway of duty. We give fair warning that any effort to continue these Owl Meetings—by the appointment of special deputies sheriffs to organize and carry them on—will be prevented. No threat of shotguns will deter us from the discharge of this duty.

Even without recourse to other perspectives this view of the existing political situation in Grimes County contains serious internal contradictions. Black Populist leaders were "incompetent" but as "apostles of their race" they had been so effective that their efforts needed to be stopped. Black teachers were paid "fat salaries" solely for political reasons, but among those receiving such gross patronage were "sweet colored girls," who obviously were not conducting owl meetings. The assertion that black teachers were actually paid more than white teachers must be rejected out of hand. In addition to the compelling fact that such an arrangement would have constituted poor political behavior on the part of a third party strenuously endeavoring to hold a substantial portion of the white vote and the further reality that such expenditures were unnecessary since parity for blacks in itself would have represented a notable accomplishment in the eyes of

Negro leaders, Democrats had access to the records of all county expenditures and no such charge was ever leveled, much less documented, at any other time during the Populist decade. Whites complained that Negro teachers received "too much," not that they received more than white teachers. In any case, it seems necessary only to observe that American political parties have routinely utilized night gatherings without having their opponents characterize them as owl meetings and that persons who benefited from incumbency were not presumed to be acting in sinister ways when they campaigned for their party's re-election. The only thing "special" about Garrett Scott's deputies was that some of them were black. Viewed as some sort of black abstraction Jim Kennard might appear convincing as a shadowy " 'fluence man," but as an intelligent and determined voice of the aspirations of Negro people he merits scholarly attention from perspectives not bounded by the horizons of those who murdered him. To an extent that is perhaps not fully appreciated, decades of monoracial scholarship in the South have left a number of Jim Kennards buried under stereotypes of one kind or another. They sometimes intrude anonymously as " 'fluence men," but they simply do not appear as people in books on Southern politics.

This circumstance suggests that not only the broad topic of interracial life and tension but the entire Southern experience culminated by disfranchisement needs to be tested by a methodology that brings both black and white sources to bear on the admittedly intricate problem of interpreting a free society that was not free. At all events, evidence continues to mount that monoracial scholarship, Northern and Southern, has exhausted whatever merit it possessed as an instrument of investigating the variegated past of the American people. The obvious rejoinder—that written black sources do not exist in meaningful quantity—cannot, of course, be explained away; at the same time, this condition suggests the utility of fresh attempts to devise investigatory techniques that offer the possibility of extracting usable historical material from oral sources. The example of the erroneous report in the Navasota *Examiner* of Morris Carrington's death illustrates, perhaps as well as any single piece of evidence, not only the dangers inherent in relying on such "primary sources" for details of interracial tension in the post-Reconstruction South but also the value of received oral traditions in correcting contemporary accounts. Nevertheless, the problem of evaluating such source material remains; white and black versions of the details of racial conflicts are widely contradictory. When they are measured against other contemporary evidence, however, the interpretive problem becomes considerably less formidable; indeed, the task of penetrating the substance behind partisan contemporary accounts may be lessened through recourse to available oral sources, as I have attempted to demonstrate.

Since much of the *Realpolitik* of the South, from Reconstruction through the modern civil rights movement, rests on legal institutions that, in turn, rest on extralegal methods of intimidation, the sources of political reality may be found less in public debate than in the various forms of intimidation that matured in the region. However determined a historian may be to penetrate the legal forms to reach this extralegal underside of the political culture of the South he is, in our contemporary climate, blocked off from part of his sources by his skin color. For black scholars there are limits to the availability both of courthouse records in the rural South and of responsive white oral sources. There are corresponding limits to the information white scholars can gain from interviews in black communities. Here, then, is fertile ground for scholarly cooperation. Methods of achieving this cooperation need to be explored. In its fullest utilization the subject is not black history or Southern history but American history.

1.4

Western Radicalism, 1865-1901: Concepts and Origins

CHESTER McARTHUR DESTLER

Chester McArthur Destler uses numerous illustrations to enlarge upon a significant social process: the ways in which culture and ideology moved from the East to the West and helped shape the ideological content of farm protest movements after the Civil War. Rejecting the geographic determinism explicit in Frederick Jackson Turner's classic and profoundly influential essays on the meaning of the frontier in American history, Destler suggests instead a far more subtle interplay and interaction between "urban" and "rural" patterns of thought. The ideas men and women brought with them to a newly settled region (even a "frontier" area) were as important in explaining their behavior as the challenge of new material conditions of life.

The following books are suggested for further reading:

JOHN HICKS, *Populist Revolt*, Lincoln: The University of Nebraska Press, 1961.

Chester McArthur Destler, *American Radicalism, 1865–1901* (New York: Quadrangle/ The New York Times Book Co., 1966), pp. 2–31. Reprinted, omitting figures and footnotes, by permission of Connecticut College, New London, Connecticut.

RICHARD HOFSTADTER, *The Age of Reform,* New York: Random House, Inc., Vintage Books, 1955.

WALTER NUGENT, *The Tolerant Populists,* Chicago: The University of Chicago Press, 1963.

MICHAEL ROGIN, *McCarthy and the Intellectuals: The Radical Spectre,* Boston: The M.I.T. Press, 1967.

Although students of western history have long contended for the existence of a unique agrarianism in the West after 1865, they . . . have failed to establish the existence there of a distinctive school of radical thought. Insulated by the continued influence of the frontier hypothesis from the records of contemporary or preceding urban movements within or without the region, and preoccupied largely with local sources of information, they have based the traditional story of western radicalism upon the assumption of an isolated, rural development undisturbed by external influences other than those affecting the marketing of farm surpluses. The singularly barren result, so far as knowledge of fundamental tenets or their implications is concerned, must be attributed to the conviction that radicalism in the American West was exclusively the product of repetitive sociological and economic processes at work on the frontier, which found expression in a somewhat emotional discontent or in a patchwork of remedial proposals that lacked any philosophical basis other than a desire to restore the working prosperity of a small entrepreneur, rural economy.

An escape from this *cul de sac* has been suggested by the new emphasis upon the region's participation in the technological, urban, and intellectual movements of the late nineteenth century that was urged upon historians nearly a decade ago. The late Marcus L. Hansen stressed particularly the need for study of the processes of cultural importation and acclimatization that were intensified in the West by the quickened communication and huge population movements of the period. The implied suggestion that historians take advantage of the familiar approach of the social anthropologist to the study of cultural diffusion is especially fruitful when applied to the study of western radical thought. It suggests the possibility of ideological transmission between rural and urban areas in both directions, not only of single concepts as culture traits, but of an entire complex of ideas, the limitation upon the process being the suitability of an imported thought cluster for inclusion within the prevailing ideology of the region after modification of one or both of the patterns of thought involved so as to produce, finally, an integrated product.

Applied to the task in hand, this approach involves, first, identification of the fields of significant intercourse between western agrarians and preceding or contemporary urban movements; second, analysis of the basic concepts of the resulting system of radical thought; and third, demonstration of the identity of these concepts with those of the contributing radical and liberal movements. The indigenous character of the product, its radical deviation from the accepted canons of the period, and its significance for subsequent eras can be indicated in the course of the analysis. . .

The existence in the Upper Mississippi Valley, in 1865, of a system of democratic thought derived from an earlier integration of urban radicalism with the coonskin democracy of the hardwood frontier, suggests that subsequent intercourse between urban and agrarian radicals occurred within a conceptual pattern common to both. William Trimble has shown how the working-class Locofocoism of the Jacksonian era was transplanted by the westward movement to the rich soil of the Middle West in the forties and fifties. There it fused with the similar but less well-defined conceptions of the Benton Democracy in neighboring upland southern areas of settlement. It was reproduced so completely by wheat farmers on the prairies and oak openings farther to the north that insistence upon "equal rights" and intense hostility to monopoly, chartered corporations, banks, and the "money power" are to this day frequently regarded as peculiar to the rural mind. The great emphasis placed upon natural rights and the social compact by the Locofocos served in the North Central States only to reemphasize the still dominant Lockean psychology and political theory that the region had received with its population from the Atlantic seaboard. Insistence that "Democracy is the cause of Humanity" quickened there and in the Old Northwest alike the humanitarian impulse that Charles Grandison Finney and the Second Great Awakening had aroused in American Protestantism. Although much of the older liberal heritage had been institutionalized by the establishment of constitutional democracy and the development of democratic churches, it had been vitalized anew by the evangelical movement, the temperance and anti-slavery agitations, the homestead movement, and the continuous struggle against chartered banks and special privilege in the prairie states until the appeal to arms imposed an ill-kept truce upon domestic quarrels. Shared by western farmers and the laborers of East and West alike, the radical democracy of the Locofocos and Free Democrats was Abraham Lincoln's mainstay in 1860.

The revival of the democratic movement in the trans-Allegheny states after the Civil War was more than the resurgence of ante-bellum quarrels provoked by exclusively western impulses. It offers the first clear illustrations in this period of the effect of intercourse and co-operation between eastern and western, urban-born and agrarian movements upon the development of western radical thought and action. This is notably true of the antimonopoly sentiment that flourished in the western states in the half dozen years before the panic of 1873. Although rural grievances against a railroad and steamboat combination in the Upper Mississippi Valley furnished the initial impetus, and the Locofoco heritage supplied the intellectual foundation, the continuing antimonopoly movement of these years cannot be fully understood without reference to mercantile interests, the National Labor Union, and the activities of several propaganda organizations that operated from central offices on the eastern seaboard. Resentment against the extortions and monopolistic practices of the railroads was not peculiar to western farmers. It was shared by western merchants, eastern importers and shippers, the producers and refiners of the Pennsylvania oil region, and laboring men as well.

It is not surprising to find in 1867 a National Anti-Monopoly Cheap Freight Railway League with headquarters in New York City. Although not much is known of this interesting organization, the private papers of its secretary reveal a far-flung agitation in behalf of cheaper railroad and telegraph rates that was directed from the eastern metropolis. Distribution of pamphlet literature and a "Monthly Circular," and attempts to influence the press and bring pressure to bear upon state governors, such as Reuben E. Fenton of New York, were accompanied by successful efforts to stimulate antimonopoly conventions and recruit supporters in the East, the Middle West, and as far away as Houston, Texas. The interested support that these efforts received from John A. Gano, president of the Cincinnati Chamber of Commerce, documents the mercantile aspect of the cheap freight movement.

The propaganda stimulus to the western antimonopoly movement was even more noteworthy in the case of the American Free-Trade League, whose headquarters were also in New York City. It was financed there largely by New York importers and by manufacturers' and shipping agents dealing with Great Britain, who had an immediate interest in the reduction of the war tariff. Although its technique bore a striking resemblance to that of the Anti-Corn Law movement, the leaders of the Free-Trade League were avowedly disciples of "the peculiar Free Trade doctrines of William Leggett," the prophet of Locofocoism. Chief of these was William Cullen Bryant, editor of the New York *Evening Post* and persistent champion of the Locofoco creed, who was president of the League during its formative years. By 1869 the free traders had expanded their activities into an intensive, far-flung propaganda campaign among the wage earners of the seaboard and westward in the interior towns and farming districts of Ohio, Illinois, Missouri, Iowa, Wisconsin, Minnesota, and California. Its numerous tracts, circulated by over half a million annually by *colporteurs* and voluntary workers, the numerous public meetings stimulated in all the important towns of the West, and tariff reform copy supplied gratis to an extensive list of western newspapers that were supported by paid advertisements, were reenforced by branch leagues in Cincinnati, Chicago, St. Louis, and San Francisco, which were financed in part by eastern funds.

The central theme of this propaganda was "equal rights" and "no monopoly." This was a deliberate, intensive appeal to the antimonopoly stereotypes of urban wage earners and the agrarian West, upon which the changes were rung by Bryant's *Evening Post,* Horace White's Chicago *Tribune,* and by paid lecturers and the monthly organ of the movement, the *Free-Trader.* It was the theme of William M. Grosvenor's *Does Protection Protect?,* the preparation of which was subsidized by the League and circulated as a more popular reply to the arguments of Horace Greeley and Henry C. Carey than the technical reports of David A. Wells. Colonel Grosvenor, it should be noted, was at the same time a paid agent of the Free-Trade League, and, as chairman of the Missouri Liberal Republican State Committee, the lieutenant of Carl Schurz.

The synchronism of the propaganda of the Cheap Freight Railway League and the Free-Trade League with the continuing antimonopoly movement in the West, is in itself highly suggestive. It is obvious that the revival of Locofoco stereotypes in the Mississippi Valley was but part of a nation-wide development that was shared by all the elements that suffered from the high tariff and the abuses of railroad and telegraph management.

The central role of the tariff reformers in the Liberal Republican movement illustrates both the intersectional character of the antimonopoly revival and the role of nonagrarian elements in it. At the outset the Liberal Republican revolt in Missouri was itself an urban movement, initiated and sustained as it was by the liberals of St. Louis of whom Colonel Grosvenor, then editor of the *Democrat,* was a leading figure. In the original Missouri movement, as in its larger extension to the Old Northwest, the urban free traders were the most active and influential single element. They were encouraged by the branch Free-Trade Leagues in the region and by the home office in New York, which was deliberately stimulating a widespread movement against special legislation and the corrupt, pressure politics of the period. In Ohio the merchants and lawyers prominent in the free-trade movement furnished the leadership of the Liberal Republicans and the closely allied Reunion and Reform movement. In Illinois Horace White's Chicago *Tribune* gave the main impulse to the Liberal Republican revolt from Grantism. He was ably seconded by the president of the Chicago Tribune Company, ex-Lieutenant Governor William Bross, a free trader and railroad antimonopolist. In San Francisco the branch of the American Free-Trade League was the means of bringing Henry George and Governor Henry H. Haight together in a state-wide crusade against tariff, railroad, telegraph, and land monopoly.

The fiasco of the Cincinnati Convention of May, 1872, must be attributed to the New York free traders who, over the strenuous protests of their western allies, bowed to Carl Schurz's demand that the Greeley-Fenton high tariff faction be admitted through compromise of the all-important tariff issue. Thus the rise and decline of free-trade propaganda from 1865–1872 and of the closely related Liberal Republican movement furnish well-defined examples of interaction between the agricultural West and urban centers within and outside the region that occurred on the ideological plane and through political organization and action. Re-enforcing earlier low tariff and Locofoco sentiment, they clearly identified protectionism with the rise of monopoly in western democratic thought.

Most students of western radicalism had overlooked the dual character of the Greenback agitation that spread so rapidly after the panic of 1873. Judged by its origins, Greebackism was at once a western inflationist proposal and an eastern radical philosophy by means of which its urban working-class adherents sought to substitute a co-operative economy for the mercantile and industrial capitalism of the day. In its former capacity it originated with Henry Clay Dean, the bitter end Iowa "Copperhead," who urged greenback inflation upon a depressed, indebted West as a means of liquidating the war debt, overthrowing Radical rule, and emancipating the region from eastern financial and economic controls. It was taken up by the Cincinnati *Enquirer* in 1867 as a means of wresting control of the Democratic party from August Belmont and Tammany Hall. Toned down by George H. Pendleton into a currency stabilization, debt reduction scheme involving little or no inflation, it continued to attract support in the West for nearly a decade under the title of the "Ohio rag baby."

Some of the support enjoyed by the *Enquirer's* brand of Greenbackism came from the trades unions of Cincinnati. The political spokesman of this element was Congressman General Samuel F. Cary. Along with the wage earners of Cincinnati, Chicago, and the Atlantic seaboard, he adhered to a much more elaborate economic and monetary theory. This, for want of a more distinguishing name, must be termed Kelloggism. Its author, Edward Kellogg, had been a New York merchant during the Locofoco period. Forced into assignment by the panic of 1837, he had found in the usurious manipulation of currency and credit by privately owned banks the cause of periodic depressions and of the concentration of wealth. Arguing that monetary policy and banking were strictly governmental functions, he sought to supplant private and state banks with a national banking and currency system to be operated exclusively by the central government. Its outstanding features were to be a flexible currency, loans on real estate at low rates, and interchangeability of the paper currency with government bonds. Such a system with its low interest rates, Kellogg taught, would destroy money monopoly, secure to labor its just reward, lower rents, and promote the development of rural society. His book, *Labor and Other*

Capital, was republished in successive editions after 1860 and became a classic of American radicalism, the "Bible" of currency reformers until shunted aside by the free-silver craze of the nineties.

Kelloggism won wide support among wage earners and western anti-monopolists after the Civil War. Alexander Campbell disseminated its doctrines among the discontented farmers of the Mississippi Valley and urged them to institute the new monetary and banking system by adapting it to the greenback currency and public debt of the day. While Campbell and another Illinois Congressman seconded the efforts of General Cary in pressing Kellogg's system upon the national legislature, the Illinois Anti-Monopoly Association joined hands with noted labor leaders, A. C. Cameron of Chicago and William L. Sylvis. Together they wrote the Kellogg program into the platform adopted by the National Labor Union at Chicago in 1867, the same year in which the "Pendleton plan" emerged from the inflationary agitation initiated by Henry Clay Dean and the Cincinnati *Enquirer.*

Space is lacking to trace in detail the interaction of the two currency agitations upon each other and of both upon the agricultural West through the next three decades. It should be noted, however, that after the failure of the Labor Party in 1872, the labor reformers secured endorsement of Kellogg's monetary system from the Illinois State Farmers Association in 1874–1875. They persuaded it and the Indiana farmers to join them in the organization of an independent political party representing both laborers and farmers, a movement that culminated in the National Greenback Party of 1876. Revived in the eighties by the Knights of Labor, Kellogg's familiar monetary and land banking proposals were taken up by farm journals such as the Chicago *Express* and the *Western Rural,* and championed by W. D. Vincent, the future journalistic exponent of Populism in Kansas. Eventually the National Farmers' Alliance, led by Jay Burrows, a disciple of Kellogg's, embodied the land loan plan in its platform while the southern Alliance advanced from this to the noted "subtreasury" scheme as an adaptation more attractive to staple farming. Government loans of greenbacks to farmers on land or crop mortgage security became the central feature in the platforms of farm organizations from 1886–1892, of the Union Labor Party in 1888, and of the Populists in 1892. Faith in the far-reaching efficacy of such a program was a common and distinguishing feature of working-class and western agrarian radicalism until the decline of the Knights of Labor and the rising free-silver crusade pushed its advocates into the "middle-of-the-road" during the "Battle of the Standards."

The co-operative movement is another example of the alacrity with which western agrarians borrowed urban formulas ready-made in their attempts to solve agricultural problems. In this case European experience was clearly drawn upon, while the influence of organized labor in America upon the farming co-operative movements seems almost indubitable. Although ante-bellum *Arbeiterbund* experiments and agitation by Horace Greeley may have suggested the feasibility of a co-operative movement, the first vigorous development of productive and distributive co-operation in the United States occurred after Appomattox in the urban centers of the East and the Ohio Valley. There workmen in all leading trades experimented with co-operative workshops and patronized co-operative stores. This movement was vigorously espoused by William L. Sylvis and the National Labor Union as "a sure and lasting remedy for the abuses of the present industrial system." The need of these co-operative experiments for adequate credit was one reason why the laborers espoused Kellogg's monetary and banking system. Western antimonopolists, whose delegates attended the congresses of the National Labor Union, learned there of the co-operative plans of the wage earners. By 1871, in the same region where Kelloggism was propagated by Alexander Campbell and the railroads and war tariff were attacked by the antimonopolists, the farmers turned also to "Co-operation" as a sovereign remedy for rural ills. Eventually the Grangers adopted the Rochdale plan of consumers' co-operation and made direct contact with the English Co-operative Union. The revival of interest in co-operation among western and southern farmers during the eighties followed hard upon the renewed agitation of the idea by the Knights of Labor who were the greatest agency then propagating knowledge of European and American co-operative experiments in the United States. Its contact with the farmers increased rather than diminished after its catastrophic defeats in 1886 since it deliberately penetrated the country towns and rural areas of the East in search of recruits. Thus, while the ideological impulse to the co-operative experiments of the Farmers' Alliance movement was partially derived from surviving Granger experiments or drawn directly from British experience, a portion at least came from the American labor movement. In this period, also, co-operative creameries were introduced into the Middle West from Scandinavia by Danish immigrants.

During the same period midwestern farmers made an original and important contribution to the theory and method of democratic control over corporate enterprise. Individualistic and with no previous experience in the eastern states or Great Britain to guide them, they sought a practicable remedy for the vicious practices of railroads and grain elevators. Inspired by the antimonopoly movement and by the Locofoco tradition of using the power of the democratic state to eliminate special privilege, their demands ranged from legislative rate-fixing to construction and operation of a transcontinental railroad by the national government. Eventually, they secured the adoption in a number of states of the novel method of controlling railroads and warehouses by means of independent regulatory commissions with rate-fixing powers. Although the originality of this Granger device has been called into question as recently as 1940, the most careful research reveals that in neither the Atlantic seaboard nor Great Britain were strong regulatory commissions placed in control of railroads or other utilities until Illinois had led the way in 1871–1873. Furthermore, the establishment of the Illinois Board of Railroad and Warehouse Commissioners and the vindication of the state police power in Munn *v.* Illinois by the Supreme Court was so radical a departure from the dominant theories of Herbert Spencer and Judge Thomas M. Cooley that Associate Justice Stephen J. Field delivered an indignant dissent and expressed his views privately as follows:

> I send you by today's mail a copy of my dissenting opinion in the Chicago Elevator case and in the so-called Granger cases. I think that the doctrine announced by the majority of the Court practically destroys the guarantees of the Constitution intended for the protection of the rights of private property.

In this instance western agrarian radicalism perfected a governmental agency and an addition to democratic constitutional theory that were accepted eventually by eastern states and the national government as well. Yet, lest the interaction here be thought to have been exclusively from west to east, it should be observed that the legal theory upon which the power of the regulatory commission rested was first championed in the Illinois constitutional convention of 1869–1870 by Reuben M. Benjamin, a New York graduate of the Harvard Law School, who had migrated to Bloomington, Illinois, on the eve of the Civil War.

Western cities made significant contributions to the radical movements of the rural West and urban East in the seventies and eighties. The wider antimonopoly movement that was directed against industrial combinations and speculative manipulation of commodity prices received its initial impetus from Henry Demarest Lloyd. His antimonopolism was derived from a Locofoco family background. It was confirmed by four years' work as assistant secretary of the American Free-Trade League. After this he joined the staff of the Chicago *Tribune*. First as financial editor and then as chief editorial writer, he campaigned for over a decade for reform of the Chicago Board of Trade, exposed the looting of western mining companies by rings of insiders, described the daily misdeeds and monopolistic practices of the railroads, and attacked the Standard Oil Company and other trusts as they emerged into public view. He lent vigorous support, also, to the agrarian demand that Congress establish a strong, national rate-fixing commission in control of the railroads and a postal telegraph to be operated by the national government in competition with the Western Union. He then turned to a wider public in a series of impressive magazine articles that laid bare the implications of the combination movement for democracy in America and demanded its control through further extension of the regulatory powers of the state. These articles with his editorials and other contributions in the *Tribune* initiated the antitrust movement that was superimposed upon the continuing struggle with the railroads in the West. Diverted from journalism to a career of social reform, Lloyd continued the fight against monopoly by publication of his great work, *Wealth against Commonwealth,* and by participation in the Populist revolt. Until after its collapse he was regarded by the western agrarians as one of their chief inspirers.

An equally notable contribution to American radicalism came from San Francisco and Oakland, California, urban centers developing within a few hundred miles of the mining and agricultural frontier of the Far West. There Henry George, another journalist, but onetime Philadelphia printer's devil, perfected the single-tax theory in the midst of a prolonged struggle with the West Coast monopolies. An admirer of Jefferson, a Jacksonian Democrat of the Locofoco tradition, he saw in land monopoly the cause of poverty. By taxing away the unearned increment in land values, or virtually confiscating ground rents, he would break up the great speculative holdings in the West, check the dissipation of the national domain, and weaken franchise monopolies of all kinds. Abolition of all other taxes would destroy the monopolies dependent upon the protective tariff. Thus a single, decisive use of taxing power would restore both liberty and equality of opportunity to American economic life while at the same time it would check the urban movement, revive agriculture, and enrich rural life. After leading a fruitless land reform movement on the West Coast during the depressed seventies, Henry George moved to New York City where he published *Progress and Poverty* in 1880. Its appeal to natural rights, its indictment of the existing business system, its moral overtones and moving appeal to the traditions of humanitarian democracy, and its utopian panacea all exerted a profound influence upon public opinion in Ireland, Great Britain, and the United States.

In a crusade for social justice that continued until his dramatic death in 1897, George exercised an unprecedented influence upon the American labor movement. He awakened journalists, intellectuals, small capitalists, and young lawyers to a comprehension of the grave economic and social problems of the rising urban world. His system of democratic economics dealt the first shattering blow to the economic determinism derived from the "Manchester School" and to the Social Darwinism that discouraged all attempts to remedy social evils or shackle the anarchic business of the day. Independent labor politics, municipal reform, and the development of a more public-spirited political leadership received direct and powerful impetus from the single-tax movement in eastern and midwestern cities between 1880 and 1900, while the single-tax panacea offered to discontented

workers, farmers, small capitalists, and intellectuals an alternative to
Marxian Socialism that promised social justice while preserving the old
individualism. Most leaders of the Farmers' Alliance movement refused to
accept the single tax as "the universal solvent that will melt away the
social and industrial ills that afflict our nation." The agitation for the single
tax, nevertheless, did much to increase agrarian interest in the land question, while "Sockless Jerry" Simpson, Populist Congressman from Kansas
in the nineties, was an earnest disciple of Henry George. In this decade,
also, the support given by George A. Schilling and the powerful single-tax
bloc in the Illinois Federation of Labor was an important factor in the
election and progressive administration of John P. Altgeld. Although the
exact extent of Henry George's influence upon the rural West remains to
be determined, the single-tax movement is an outstanding illustration of
the far-flung influence of a western but urban-born school of thought upon
proletarian movements and middle class liberalism in regions as far distant
as the Atlantic seaboard, the British Isles and Australasia.

During the late eighties an urban, eastern, American-born socialist
movement attracted interest in the cities and farming areas of the West.
Known as Nationalism it developed spontaneously from enthusiasm provoked by Edward Bellamy's *Looking Backward*. Converts to Bellamy's
utopia of a highly centralized, almost militarized socialist commonwealth
organized Nationalist Clubs as far west as California. Members and officials
of the Farmers' Alliances, trades unions, the Knights of Labor, and a few
outstanding railroad executives joined the movement. The earlier antimonopoly movements and the propaganda of the Knights of Labor had prepared
the soil well for sowing Nationalist principles among western agrarians. It
is not surprising, therefore, to find N. B. Ashby, lecturer of the National
Farmers' Alliance, endorsing Nationalism "as the only true and effectual
cure" for "the social question," and as the logical, evolutionary fulfillment
of the nation's destiny. With Nationalist clubs active in fourteen Middle
and Far Western states the organizers of the People's Party were almost
compelled to invite them to send delegates to the Cincinnati Conference
of May, 1891, where five Nationalists helped to frame the first national
manifesto of the Populist revolt. At the subsequent conventions at St. Louis
and Omaha in 1892, the Nationalists joined with the Knights in giving
effective support to the "transportation plank" in the revised platform.
So gratified were they at its adoption that the Nationalists gave Populism
such wholehearted support that Nationalism lost its identity in the People's
Party. To its strength Bellamy's followers contributed especially in the
eastern states, although he continued to enjoy considerable influence with
the older antimonopoly element in the West.

The examples of effective intercourse between the rural West and the
urban world, whether within or outside the region, could be increased still

further by reference to the agitation for reform of the nation's land policy, led by George W. Julian, and the free-silver movement. They are sufficient, however, to indicate something of the diverse origins and composite character of the western radicalism that burgeoned beyond the Alleghenies in the last third of the century. Western agrarian movements were influenced by at least five schools of reform or radical agitation originating from without the region before 1890. In at least one important field the farmers' movements of the region made a major contribution to democratic thought and action in the same period, while publicists in two western cities initiated the important antitrust and single-tax movements. Such cross-fertilization between eastern and western, urban and rural movements was but one aspect of the larger development of the West, which on intellectual, technological, business, and artistic planes was subject to similar processes of acculturation. In each field the result was a mosaic of indigenous and imported elements, all adapted in greater or lesser degree to the regional *milieu*.

This analysis suggests that in Populism may be found the system of radical thought that emerged in the West from three decades of recurring unrest, agitation, and intercourse with radical and reform movements in the urban world. Although scholars have studied it as a political movement or as the product of social and economic conditions, as a school of thought Populism has been rarely, if ever, subjected to the careful analysis that Socialism, Anarchism, or Communism have received. Yet the Populists themselves regarded Populism as a faith and a creed as well as a program. They exhibited, furthermore, a clear sense of continuity with preceding radical movements. This was illustrated at the Omaha convention by the wild cheering that greeted Alexander Campbell, the aged prophet of Kelloggism to midwestern farmers in the sixties. Further continuity between Populism and its forerunners was exhibited by the leadership of the People's Party. Not only were General James B. Weaver and Ignatius Donnelly representatives of the older Greenback and Anti-Monopoly traditions in the West, but the chairman of the national executive committee, Herman E. Taubeneck, was a former Greenbacker, while the first secretary of the committee was Robert Schilling, veteran labor reformer and labor leader. As secretary of the platform committee in the Cincinnati conference of May, 1891, Schilling reported and together with Colonel S. F. Norton of the Chicago *Express* undoubtedly induced the committee to base its manifesto on Edward Kellogg's economic philosophy. Further evidence of continuity between Populism and earlier radical movements is found in the long series of conferences that began with the organization of the Union Labor Party in Cincinnati in 1887 and culminated at Omaha on July 4, 1892. There Kelloggism, Nationalism, the more limited program of government ownership proposed by the Knights, the single tax, land reform, woman suffrage, the liquor question, and the cause of organized labor were urged upon successive platform committees by reformers who had grown gray in the service of each particular "cause."

At first glance the program that emerged from this process seemed like a "crazy-quilt" of unrelated and "crackpot" proposals. Yet it produced a fairly durable synthesis, judging from the tenacity with which the Populists reiterated their Omaha platform on all and sundry occasions, until an era of unemployment, mortgage foreclosures, Coxey's armies, and industrial conflict had so heightened the emotional overtones of the movement that the least well-ballasted agrarians and the professional politicians in control of the party machinery sought quick relief and easy victory through free silver. It was this synthesis, under the name of Populism, which received such intense loyalty from its adherents and provoked an emotional opposition from conservative elements. Proclaimed in the Omaha platform as the official version of the Populist creed, it must now be analyzed in an attempt to identify the basic concepts that it shared with its progenitors and to determine the extent to which it presented a well-defined system of radical thought.

The continuing vitality of the equalitarian tradition among the radical movements that produced the Populist "revolt" will be apparent from the foregoing narrative. Examination of the Omaha platform, also, indicates beyond doubt that Populism, too, was consciously cast in the mold of "equal rights." Inherent in its thought lay the traditional Jeffersonian hostility to special privilege, to gross inequality in economic possessions, to concentrated economic power, and a preference for human rights when opposed by overshadowing property rights. All of this had motivated American democratic radicalism since the days of Thomas Paine and the Democratic Republican Clubs of 1793–1800. So oriented it is not surprising to find the preamble of the Omaha platform declaring in 1892 that the purpose of a government freed from corporate control would be to establish "equal rights and equal privileges . . . for all the men and women of this country." Coupled with this is the clearly expressed, traditional faith of American liberals in "civilization" as a liberating, elevating process, which, like human rights, must be saved from the machinations of the money power. Thus, Populism was but an extreme projection of the Jeffersonian creed.

Antimonopolism was the dynamic element in Populism. It sprang directly from the equalitarian tradition. The preamble and planks of the Omaha platform demonstrate this beyond question. The preamble denounced the corruption of democratic government by privileged business, and the abuses by which a buccaneering capitalism exploited the people and created a new class of millionaires. Rather than the "sham battle over the tariff," the real issue, it declared, lay "in the formation of combines and rings," in the power of "capitalists, corporations, and national banks," "the oppression of the usurers." The dominant antimonopoly bias of Populism was even more clearly expressed in the platform itself. This was devoted entirely to the three great fields of monopoly that had been the butt of agrarian agitation for decades: money and banking, railroads and communication, and land. The remedies proposed show clearly how far the Populists were committed to government intervention in business and to limited experiments with state socialism as a means of combating the great movement toward monopoly and economic concentration then under way in the business world. To destroy "the money power" and to solve the "financial question," to use terms employed by the presidential nominee of the party, the platform proposed an exclusively governmental currency and a combination of government operated postal savings banks and "subtreasuries." The latter "or a better system" was to loan money to farmers on crops or land at no more than two per cent interest, while the volume of the currency was to fluctuate with the demand for agricultural credits. Irrespective of the obvious indebtedness of this financial program to the earlier agitation of Kelloggism, it is plain that money monopoly was the evil for which such a drastic extension of government activity into banking was proposed. Monopoly on the railroads and in communications was dealt with in the same manner. Here again government ownership and operation was the remedy, a solution derived from the Knights of Labor and Nationalism. Land monopoly, the third great problem dealt with, was to be remedied by government action also, in this case by restoration to the national domain of alien holdings and land held by railroads and other corporations in excess of their actual needs. The graduated income tax was proposed by the Omaha convention as the proper means of dealing with the giant fortunes accumulated through government favoritism to capitalists and usurers. Considered apart from the supplemental resolutions adopted at the convention, the Omaha platform, therefore, was directed almost entirely at destroying monopoly and at correcting the economic evils that it had produced.

In taking antimonopolism as its central principle Populism revealed its fundamental identity with all the varied "isms" that had agitated the West during the "Thirty Years' War," as one veteran of radical movements termed the preceding decades of agitation. Populism was laid on foundations quarried from Lockean thought and evangelical Protestantism. Upon this substratum and in the *milieu* supplied by frontier opportunities and corporate repressions Locofocoism had erected the frame of prairie radicalism and built into it an abiding hostility to monopoly. Buttressed and strengthened by the controversies of the postwar decades, the antimonopoly spirit had attacked railroads, the protective tariff, money monopoly, and the trusts. Kellogg's program had re-enforced the demand of

Granger legislators that the machinery of the state be turned to positive use in breaking monopolies as the only way in which a just economy could be achieved. In the eighties this novel program of state intervention in business had developed to a point where some farmers joined the Knights of Labor in demanding a postal telegraph and a government owned and operated railroad system. Thus in its platform, Populism fulfilled the promise of Locofocism and successive antimonopoly movements although, unlike the earlier working class champions of equal rights, the Populists sought relief through the extension of governmental action into economic life.

Populism was more than antimonopolism, therefore. It advocated a program of economic collectivism which it urged upon the American people as the only remedy adequate to solve the problem of monopoly. Not only did the Populists propose to employ government power through actual ownership and operation of banks, railroads, means of communication, and the monetary system, but in the preamble of their Omaha platform they promised to remedy "falling prices, the formation of combines and rings, the impoverishment of the producing class . . . by wise and reasonable legislation, in accordance with the terms of our platform." But, as if this might prove insufficient, they went on to declare:

> We believe that the powers of government—in other words of the people —should be expanded (as in the case of the postal service) as rapidly and as far as the good sense of an intelligent people and the teachings of experience shall justify, to the end that oppression, injustice, and poverty shall eventually cease in the land.

The full implications of this declaration were revealed two years later when, in St. Louis after the autumn election, a great conference of party leaders under the leadership of Lyman Trumbull and Henry Demarest Lloyd advanced to the extreme position of advocating government ownership of all monopolies that affected the "public interest."

Collectivist though the Populist philosophy was in its demand for state intervention and ownership in the field of monopoly enterprise, it would be a mistake to conclude that it was socialistic either in purpose or spirit. The object of government ownership, as desired by the Populists, just as in the case of the independent regulatory commission championed by the Grangers two decades earlier, was the strengthening of comeptitive capitalism and the salvation of small enterprise. As the Populists saw it, the chief danger to the American system lay in the threatened destruction of free enterprise by the rise of an irresponsible, unsocial monopoly system which rested in last analysis upon legislative, executive, and judicial favoritism.

As H. S. Person has written recently of the midtwentieth-century problems of cartels and monopoly:

> Strategic regulation of basic industries through ownership and yardstick operation of a fraction of the national plant would prevent monopolies and provide basic services and materials at the lowest possible prices on equal terms to all private competitors in industry and would strengthen competition under fair conditions, promote private enterprise and eventually be the salvation of small enterprises.

Such appears to have been the object of Populist collectivism, which was what was to be expected from small enterprisers engaged in wheat and cotton farming. Their economic position would have been strengthened immeasurably by the low cost of land and manufactured products that they hoped to secure as a result of government ownership and operation in the limited fields of economic activity that they designated. Their economic independence and political importance might well have been enhanced by means of it.

Populism's kinship with preceding radical movements in the rural and urban West and East was indicated, also, by the sympathy which its adherents gave to the co-operative idea. Now and then, as in Illinois, the State Purchasing Agent of the Farmers' Alliance was active in organizing the new party, while the Nationalists in its ranks were eager to hasten the coming of a co-operative utopia. Despite the havoc wrought by the depression upon the underfinanced co-operative organizations of the farmers, and perhaps because of the widespread distress, interest in co-operation continued among the Populists and their sympathizers. Utopian novels such as *Altruria* by William Dean Howells and *Equality* by Edward Bellamy were expressions in literature of an attitude in Populist ranks that led to the projection or establishment of a series of co-operative communities. Such was Mrs. Annie L. Diggs' proposed "Colorado Co-operative Colony," the Ruskin Co-operative Colony in Tennessee, whose *Coming Nation* had such a wide circulation in Populist ranks, or the Christian Commonwealth Colony established in Georgia after the collapse of the People's Party by the former editor of the *Wealth Makers* of Lincoln, Nebraska. The American Co-operative Union was the product, in 1896, of a Congress convened at St. Louis by the co-operative elements within the People's Party simultaneously with its last great national convention. The shattered remnants of the American Railway Union, which for two years had supported Populism, organized the Brotherhood of the Co-operative Commonwealth, a few months later, by means of which they planned to colonize a western state so thoroughly with co-operative communities that they could control it politically and use the power of the state to aid them in establishing a "co-operative common-wealth." These same elements in the St. Louis convention of 1896 were part of the "middle-of-the-road" faction that remained loyal to the anti-monopolism and economic collectivism of the Omaha platform. Thus in supporting the co-operative movement, whether of producers or of consumers or in especially organized communities, the Populists were seeking through private, voluntary organization in the economic field to diminish "the power of the industrial empire." This might well have been accomplished by means of "a great co-operative movement in America" as much as by government ownership of monopolies.

How radical the Populist advocacy of a democratic collectivism was in the light of the contemporary historical situation can be determined easily. The emotional reaction that it provoked among conservatives was so extreme that in propertied circles it made "Populists" more "a term of reproach than was 'Red' a generation later." A comparison of Populism with the contemporary single-tax and tariff reform movements makes the point even clearer. Henry George advised his followers not to enter the People's Party, while the Populists rejected his single tax as inadequate to the task in hand. Although Henry George's gospel resembled Populism in its appeal to natural rights, its hatred of monopoly and special privilege, and to a limited extent in its proposal to right economic injustice by use of the taxing power, the Populists rejected as unrealistic the assertion that the single tax alone would destroy all monopolies, eliminate poverty, and make land available once more to the masses. Henry George was seeking to turn the hands of the clock back to the full opportunity of the frontier and to the unrestrained individualism of the competitive system. The Populists, on the other hand, believed that such liberty gave strength only to the strong, who in turn oppressed the weak.

> The Triumphant Plutocrats . . . believe in a civilization whose fitting coat of arms would show a hog and tiger rampant, slaying and rending, devouring and gorging, while on the shield's bar sinister . . . would be such legends as "supply and demand"; "devil take the hindmost"; . . .

It was the obligation of democratic government, the Populists asserted, to extend its fostering care to the weak and to protect them from the strong lest the "producing masses" be enslaved. Only through state intervention, control, and expropriation of the greatest economic aggregations of the day, could the problem of monopoly be solved. Thus, over the issue of individualism versus collectivism Henry George and the Populists were in direct antagonism. It is not surprising to find the single taxers on the side of Grover Cleveland in 1892.

That the Populists regarded tariff reform as a mere palliative is indicative of their determination to embark upon a revolutionary use of governmental power in subjecting the corporate business system to democratic controls. Although the free trade agitation had been an important factor in the revival of antimonopolism in the West from 1867–1872, the eastern free traders from the outset had advocated specie payments and laissez faire. Such outstanding tariff reformers of the eighties and nineties as Carl Schurz, David A. Wells, E. L. Godkin, and Grover Cleveland adhered to this position. In basic interests and sympathy they were far closer to the national banks and the existing business system than they were to the western agrarians and the Knights of Labor. In 1896 the tariff reformers were found along with William McKinley and Marcus A. Hanna on the side of the railroads, the protected industries, and high finance. Men of such stamp had little to offer to western radicals who were bent upon a drastic reorganization of American economic life through collective action by the democratic state.

If more evidence were wanted to establish the radical character of Populist collectivism it could be found in a study of the contemporary schools of law and constitutional interpretation. In the late nineteenth century, as Roscoe Pound has shown, the courts and legal profession were dominated by the natural rights and historical schools of jurisprudence with their emphasis upon individual liberty. Guided by such publicists as Judge Thomas M. Cooley and Christopher G. Tiedeman, and by the leaders of the American bar, federal and state courts reduced the police power to a minimum and imposed judge-made restraints upon the legislative power. The fate of the federal income tax in the Pollock case, the emasculation of the authority of the Interstate Commerce Commission, and the failure of the first important antitrust suit in the Knight case show how far removed the courts and bar were from the Populist conception of the welfare state.

It is apparent that as a radical system. Populism was primarily economic in character. Its contributions to political theory and constitutional practice were secondary and derivative rather than of primary importance to the Populists. In order to attack monopoly, to break its hold on the government, and to apply the collectivist program, it was necessary that the government be fully and continually responsive to the public will. To accomplish this the Populists elaborated a program of direct democracy, which they offered as a corrective for the then feebly functioning system of representative government. The initiative and referendum, the Australian ballot, honest elections, and the popular election of United States Senators were accepted and endorsed at Omaha in a series of supplemental resolutions that were attached to but not made an integral part of the platform. Although they were regarded undoubtedly as desirable in themselves, they were linked in Populist eyes with the larger objective of subjecting corporate capitalism to the control of the democratic state.

If Populism as a radical system was primarily economic in character, was any concept other than antimonopolism and the desirability of a semicollectivist economy fundamental to its economic theory? Careful study of the St. Louis and Omaha platforms of 1892 indicates that there was. Closely linked with declarations in favor of an alliance with urban labor is found the statement, identical in both documents: "Wealth belongs to him who creates it. Every dollar taken from industry without an equivalent is robbery. If any one will not work, neither shall he eat." This statement furnishes the second key to Populist economic thought. Its origins can be found in the early antimonopoly and Granger movements. The *Prairie Farmer's* famous cartoon of the early seventies, showing the farmer, who pays for all, surrounded by a clergyman, merchant, lawyer, legislator, soldier, railroad magnate, and doctor, expressed this theory of wealth. It had been shared by the National Labor Union, the Industrial Congress, and the Knights of Labor. More remotely, the same view had been postulated by Edward Kellogg as fundamental to his new monetary system. It was basic to the ante-bellum labor movements.

This third fundamental concept in Populist economic theory, which it inherited from earlier labor and agrarian movements, was none other than the "labor-cost theory of value" as the economists term it. Although it was derived ulitmately from classical economics, it had been widely accepted in Europe and America in the sixties by radicals opposed to the machine age. In it the European anarchists and American labor reformers and agrarian leaders had found justification for their struggle against merchant capitalists and the great corporations.

The labor-cost theory was derived from the conceptions of a pre-industrial age. By its application small producers, whether wheat growers and cotton farmers, or skilled laborers and small shopkeepers, sought to regain or bulwark an economic position that was being undermined by the factory age, the middleman, and monopoly capitalism. The adherents of this theory regarded capital as the product of labor alone, possessing "no independent power of production" of its own. As such, they thought that it deserved little or no reward. The whole value of the product should go to the producer, although a nominal interest might be allowed to the possessors of idle funds who loaned them to productive workers. Consumers' and producers' co-operation, the independent regulatory commissions, a government operated banking and monetary system, government owned railroads, telegraphs, and telephones had been regarded by labor reformers and agrarian leaders as the means, not only of combating monopoly, but also of establishing an economic system in harmony with the labor-cost theory. Loyal to this philosophy of wealth the Populists at Omaha asserted that the middleman, the financier, the railroad promoters with their watered stock and monopoly rates, the bankers and mortgage holders, and the organizers of "trusts and combines" were all nonproducers. They were profiting from bad laws and the perversion of democratic government at the expense of the producing masses who, by this process, were being so impoverished that they were "degenerating into European conditions."

Since urban labor suffered from these evils as much as the farmers, since it was denied the right to organize and, in addition, was assailed by hired bands of Pinkerton detectives, the Omaha convention urged it to join the agrarians in an independent political alliance. By means of the ballot box, they could promote a peaceful revolution in American government and economic life. "[T]he union of the labor forces of the United States this day accomplished shall be permanent and perpetual. . . . The interests of rural and civic labor are the same; their enemies are identical." Antimonopolism and the labor-cost theory of value, twin foundations in the economic theory of Populism, were thus offered to urban labor as the ideological basis of an independent farmer-labor alliance in politics.

The desirability and practicability of such a coalition had long been an article of faith for both labor reformers and leading agrarians. Their adherence to this view explains the persistence with which the consummation of the alliance had been sought over three decades. Attention has already been directed to repeated instances of co-operation between organized labor and the farmers' movements. At least two attempts had been made to organize such a political party before the Populist period. Even earlier, labor reformers had appealed to antimonopolism in order to induce their followers to ally themselves with the farmers, as did Francis A. Hoffman, Jr., in his address to the Workingmen's Party in Chicago, January 25, 1874:

> I hope, however, that you will enlarge the sphere of your labors beyond this narrow field, and extend an invitation to the laborers and workers of all other cities and towns to form similar organizations, harmonizing in spirit and action with your own; more particularly with a view of joining hands with the farmers, the laborers of the country, your natural allies, in one common, united effort to free this country from the shackles of monopoly . . . extend a helping hand to the farmers, the laborers of the field. They are your vanguard. . . . Aid them in their brave warfare with your common enemy, hydraheaded monopoly. Workingmen, laborers, come in solid phalanx, unite with your brethern [*sic*] in the country, . . .

The kindred interests of laborers and farmers as producers, and their common hostility to monopoly were emphasized by Ethelbert Stewart, editor of the Chicago *Knights of Labor,* in 1888, in his attempt to unite the labor movement with the farmers in support of the Union Labor party. Alson J. Streeter, the presidential nominee, appealed to the same concepts when he justified the campaign of the party in his letter of acceptance. The Populist invitation to urban labor, extended in the heated preamble of the Omaha platform, was little more than a repetition of these earlier pleas for a united front. It was based on identical concepts.

The effectiveness of the Populist appeal to urban labor depended on the degree to which the labor movement still adhered to the producers' economic philosophy which its labor-cost theory and antimonopolist creed. From 1825 until the late eighties, together with the concept of self-help through co-operatives, they had furnished the ideological foundation of working-class movements in the United States. This economic philosophy, which represented the outlook of the lower middle class, instead of that of a job-conscious proletariat, made it possible for labor reformers to support the farmers in radical movements that were based upon a similar philosophy derived originally from working-class Locofocoism and elaborated on the basis of rural experience and subsequent intercourse with urban centers. Perhaps, as Henry David contends, anti-monopolism was the peculiar program offered by the American workingman as his contribution to the realization of the "American dream." Only with the rise of modern trades unions after 1880 did wage earners come gradually to the view that they should work for their own craft interests independently of the farmers or the middle class. The story of the labor movement in the late eighties and early nineties centers upon the struggle between the new trades unionism and the older school of labor reform with its producers' philosophy that had united wage earner and farmer in a common faith over six decades.

It was entirely normal, therefore, for the leaders of the farmers' alliances and for agrarian advocates of a third party to confer with Terence V. Powderly, rather than with Samuel Gompers, between 1889 and 1892. Unfortunately for the Populists, the swift decline of the Knights of Labor, champions of the older philosophy of American wage earners, made them an insufficient recruiting ground. The trades union leaders, on the other hand, apart from their job-conscious, autonomous outlook, were hardly conciliated by Populist preference for the leaders of the rival labor movement. Both factors, undoubtedly, motivated Samuel Gompers to write for the *North American Review,* just before the Omaha convention, that although labor would be friendlier to the People's Party than to any other, there could be no hope of a complete "unification of labor's forces in the field, farm, factory, and workshop." Because the Populists were largely *"employing* farmers" in contrast with the *"employed* farmers of the country districts or the mechanics and laborers of the industrial centers," Gompers persuaded his followers and the public that complete "coöperation or amalgamation of the wage-workers' organizations with the People's Party" was "impossible, because it is unnatural."

The success of the Populists in recruiting a following from the ranks of organized labor depended, therefore, upon whether the wage earners' attachment for the older and more distinctively American philosophy of labor reform was greater than its loyalty to the newer, imported trades unionism. In 1892 the hold of the latter seems to have been stronger. After the panic of the following year had plunged labor into unemployment and acute distress, however, even Gompers wavered in his devotion to a strictly job-conscious, craft program. The American Federation of Labor actually moved toward a *de facto* alliance with Populism. The depression years, therefore, tended to force organized labor back into the older philosophy and justified making one more attempt to form a common front with the agrarian movement. This presented the Populists with their long-sought opportunity to recruit heavily from urban labor. It furnished the acid test of a radical creed based upon antimonopolism, the labor-cost theory of wealth, and belief in the common interests of all producers, which offered a limited but clearly defined economic collectivism as the goal of the farmer-labor alliance.

Perhaps because they have been preoccupied with interpretations derived from the older Turnerism, historians are just beginning to inquire into this neglected aspect of the Populist movement. When it is given full attention it will be found that the greatest problem of ideological conflict and adaptation produced by the attempted coalition did not develop out of a clash between Populism and the half-formulated philosophy of a shattered trades unionism. It sprang, instead, from the clash of indigenous Populism, produced by decades of cross-fertilization between urban and agrarian radical movements, with an imported, proletarian Socialism which made its first appeal to English-speaking wage earners in America in the depression-ridden nineties. At least some of the zeal with which the Populist national headquarters and Congressional delegation turned to free silver in 1895–1896 was the result of this far more irreconcilable conflict. The tendency of the strong antimonopoly bloc within the party to come to provisional terms with the Socialists on the basis of government ownership of all monopolies which Henry D. Lloyd and the Nationalists supported, motivated some of the steamroller tactics with which Herman E. Taubeneck and Senator William V. Allen deprived the powerful antimonopolist-Nationalist-labor-and-Socialist element at the St. Louis convention of effective expression in 1896 and delivered the People's Party into the hands of the free-silver Democracy. This precipitated the withdrawal of the labor and left wing elements from all association with the Populists.

Leaderless, lacking a separate party organization after the turn of the century, the antimonopolist radicalism of the West survived as a vital force in American thought and politics. The Populist demand for an effective, but restricted, democratic collectivism had been the American counterpart of the "new liberalism" in Great Britain that had arisen under the stimulus of Irish land reform agitation, Henry George, and Socialism, in response to the problems of an even more mature industrialism. Like the "Newcastle Program" of 1891, which enjoyed a temporary vogue before defeat by the conservative reaction in 1895 only to re-emerge a decade later as the foundation of the program of Campbell-Bannerman, Asquith, and Lloyd George, Populist antimonopolist collectivism was re-enforced in the new century in America by the social awakening of the middle class and continued as the central feature of the neo-democratic movement. Essentially American still, somewhat less extreme in the devices that it advocated as the means of governing the economic forces of the day, it produced nevertheless a new crop of "American radicals" that escaped the notice of President James B. Conant in his plea for an indigenous radical movement. Led by Robert M. La-Follette, Hiram Johnson, George W. Norris, and the Bryan brothers, they continued the old fight against the railroads, tariff, trusts, "Wall Street," and corporate exploitation of the public domain. Less extreme in their collectivism than the Populists had been, they borrowed the agrarian conception of the democratic welfare state and employed the independent regulatory commission as their chief agency in subjecting American capitalism to a system of government regulation and control that has expanded with each revival of the democratic movement. . .

Industrializing America: The Urban North 1865-1900

American society was radically transformed in the few decades following the Civil War. Fundamental economic changes associated with the machine and a new industrial technology which had started in the 1830s and the 1840s accelerated in the postwar decades. Essential statistics suggest the ways in which industrial capitalism came of age in these latter decades. In 1860, the United States ranked behind Great Britain, France, and Germany in the value of its manufactured product. Less than forty years later, the American manufactured product nearly equalled in value that of these three industrial nations combined. Between 1860 and 1890, investment in industry increased from one billion to 6.5 billion dollars and the value of industrial goods went up from 1.8 billion to 10 billion dollars. By 1890 no fewer than 4.6 million Americans labored in factories and another three million persons worked in the transportation and construction industries. At the century's end, 17 million men, women, and children earned wages but no more than 500,000 belonged to trade unions.

Profound changes in the social structure accompanied but did not precisely mirror these economic changes. Work-styles changed as greater numbers of Americans came to know the large factory and a new technology. Life-style changed as greater numbers of Americans were drawn to expanding towns and cities. In 1820, about six percent of Americans lived in towns of 2500 or more. Nearly 20 percent did in 1860, but most then did not work in factories. About five million Americans lived in cities of more than 8000 persons in 1860; nearly 25 million did so in 1900. Nevertheless urban-industrial development retained a regional character. In 1890, more than 80 percent of all urban dwellers still lived in the North Atlantic and North Central states, and 39 of the 50 largest American cities were located there.

Internal migration but especially foreign immigration fed these new factories and cities. The post-Civil War decades were the great moment of northern and western European immigration to the United States. Lesser numbers of immigrants came from China and Canada. Not surprisingly, in 1880 more than 75 of every 100 persons in Chicago (87), Milwaukee (84), Detroit (84), New York (80), Cleveland (80), St. Louis (78), and San Francisco (78) was of foreign birth or the child of an immigrant parent. In 1890, New York and Brooklyn together had more foreign-born residents than any other city in the world.

Old America and the cultures and traditions of rural and pre-modern Americans but especially northern and western European immigrants were tested in the northern and western cities and factory towns of Gilded Age America.

2.1

Old Ways and New Ties

ROWLAND T. BERTHOFF

Rowland Berthoff studied the most assimilable of all immigrant groups: the English, the Welsh, and the Scots. They, too, he found, formed viable and distinctive ethnic communities after migrating to the United States. It is often assumed that such communities—ethnic "enclaves"—had as their reason for existence mere self-protection from a hostile and alien outside world. English-speaking immigrants, however, were seldom the targets of steady nativist prejudices and protest. Still, ethnic self-identification and distinctive cultural institutions—deeply flavored by the fact that most Gilded Age British immigrants were skilled and unskilled industrial workers and farm laborers— thrived among them as among the "less desirable" contemporary and later immigrant groups.

Reprinted, omitting all footnotes, by permission of the publishers from pp. 143–53, 154– 63, and 164 of British Immigrants in Industrial America, by Rowland Berthoff (Cambridge, Mass.: Harvard University Press). Copyright 1953 by the President and Fellows of Harvard College.

The following book is suggested for further reading:

CHARLOTTE ERICKSON, *American Industry and the European Immigrant,* Cambridge, Mass.: The Harvard University Press, 1957.

Like all other immigrants whose hearts were still at home, British-Americans strove to preserve what they could of the familiar ways of the old country. At whatever points America seemed lacking they banded together in their own social institutions. Thus linked, they were an autonomous community like those Irish-American or Polish-American enclaves which native Americans thought so insidious. But while the strange and unfriendly environment helped drive Irish or Polish newcomers in upon themselves, the British were quite free to enter American affairs. Nor did their voluntary banding together cut off either English, Scots, or Welsh from the broader society about them. Yet even they, prizing their peculiar cultural identity in the midst of the new world, could hardly live without social institutions of their own.

What the British could not bring with them to the United States they at least remembered fondly. British public personages still seemed more real than the ludicrous statesmen of Yankeeland. Apart from that ostentatious republican Andrew Carnegie, a few radicals, and a handful of eccentric Boston Jacobites, Englishmen and Scotsmen of every class revered the Queen and her family. In 1900 one observed, "Nothing . . . develops the loyalty of an Englishman to his Sovereign to such an extent as expatriation." Schism rent an English club in Philadelphia during the 1850's after a banquet toastmaster dared to pledge the President of the United States before the Queen.

When Victoria was married in 1840, the British of New York celebrated for two days, regaling several hundred poor English, Scottish, and Irish widows of the city with a roast ox and a thousand-pound wedding cake. The Queen's subject and former subjects throughout the country annually banqueted on her birthday, May 24, and perpetuated it after her death as Empire Day. To commemorate her Jubilees in 1887 and 1897 every town with enough British-Americans to form a committee had its special church services, processions, outings, and banquets. During the 1887 festivities in New York two thousand persons attended services at Trinity Church, four thousand packed the Metropolitan Opera House for a musical program, and twenty thousand went to Staten Island for games and fireworks.

When the old Queen died in 1901, British-Americans thronged churches all across the North and West. They turned out again the next year to mark her son's coronation and thereafter to commemorate his birthdays, his death in 1910, and the crowning of George V. Other joyful milestones in the royal family's course, such as the marriage of Princess Louise in 1871, they marked with dinners and balls; unhappy events, like the death of the Prince Consort in 1861 and of the Duke of Clarence in 1892, with condoling messages. When Prince Arthur visited the United States in 1870, the British residents of New York, Boston, and other cities offered addresses of welcome. Other notables likewise got warm greetings from deputations such as the Scots who honored the Duke of Argyll in 1879 or those who sailed to New Brunswick in 1901 to see the future King George and Queen Mary.

During most of the nineteenth century the reigning house reminded the Welsh only of their long-lost independence; they had small love for the "scandalous" Albert Edward—"Prince of Wales, indeed!" But the ceremony at Caernarvon castle in 1911, when a boyish and more winning prince assumed the title, fired their hearts.

From across the ocean British politicians' struggles appeared more titanic than ever. What were paltry Yankee politics alongside the battles which Gladstone waged with Disraeli or Chamberlain? After Disraeli in 1878 plucked Peace with Honor out of the Eastern Question, the California British rewarded him with another trophy, "a silver brick adorned with quartz specimens." In later years the fondest dream of Welsh-Americans was a visit by the—to them—incomparable Lloyd George. So too when British squadrons put into American ports, their officers could count on a banquet with their expatriate countrymen. The leading British residents of Boston entertained the band of the Grenadier Guards in 1872 and the Honourable Artillery Company of London in 1903.

British tavern-keepers in American cities catered to their fellow exiles' home thoughts under such signboards as the "Robin Hood," the "Dog and Partridge," the "St. George's and Cambrian," and the "Carnarvon Castle." In New York in the 1830's Luke Shaw's Eagle Porter House advertised —besides its skittle alley—that "a *free and easy* takes place every Tuesday evening in the old English style," and for the Welsh the Owain Glyndŵr Tavern kept a harp to accompany its weekly "harmonic meeting." At such houses an immigrant, free from Yankee censure, could "enjoy himself in the true 'Old Country' fashion, taking his pipe instead of cigar, his jug of ale or beer, sitting also to regale himself instead of standing." The host dispensed "the best of malt liquors" and served up "a variety of English relishes in first-rate style, as Welch rare-bits, chops, steaks, ham and beef" —a good English supper—hours after American boardinghouse mistresses had doled out their last meal for the day. In Chicago the Round of Beef

House announced in 1870 that it would mark the Queen's birthday with "a match at quoits for a silver goblet" and then provide "a mammoth English Round of Beef." Scots in Chicago could play shuffleboard and quoits at the Caledonian or in later years in New York savor the "musty ale and mutton pie" of the Old Grapevine. In Boston the landlord of the Park House in 1882 regaled his British friends with an "old style English Christmas lunch" for which he had imported a quarter of English beef. Boston Scots met at the Breadalbane Dining Rooms.

In the large cities Scottish-American households relied on grocers who imported Edinburgh oatmeal, Glasgow peasemeal, Lochfyne herrings, finnan haddies, and Dundee marmalade and on bakers who made "oat cakes, soda scones, Abernethy biscuits, shortbread, mutton pies, and other national dainties." As for drink, though Bourbon might be tolerated, Scotch and Irish whiskies were preferred; importers also advertised Scotch ale and Dublin porter. A party of Scots who toured the States in 1883 could find nothing worthy of the name of usquebaugh except in their countrymen's homes; at Milwaukee they complained, "We had nae whiskey since we landed—only something ca'd 'rye'." The eventual American popularity of Scotch may have begun among the immigrants. "Some say," a British consul observed in 1901, "that it came into fashion with golf."

With such tastes British workingmen seemed to Americans to be sots who "just filled up their time betwixt the workshop and the beershop." At Paterson an American asserted in 1832 that the English mill hands, usually drunken and unruly, were "the most beastly people I have seen." The first Staffordshire potters to come to Trenton appeared to include "hardly a sober man." In New Bedford the English cotton operatives, an eye out for the police, brewed their bitter in the company tenements. During the 1870's it was not alone the high wages of the hand-jack spinners which led the woolen mills to adopt automatic machinery instead; they still had "the disorderly habits of English workmen. Often on a Monday morning half of them would be absent from the mill in consequence of the Sunday's dissipation."

Pennsylvania anthracite towns in the 1870's had dozens of "saloons *Cymreig*." The preoccupation of Welsh-American communities with the temperance movement only reflected the fact that the miners and mill hands "had learned in Aberdare, Merthyr, Rhymney, &c., to drink beer like water, to get as drunk as tinkers, to swear and curse worse than the demons of the bottomless pit."

Some excused their drinking as an antidote to the exhausting labor in American mines and factories. Others on Middle Western farms thought beer prevented the ague. But, unlike Americans' reckless whiskey guzzling, most of the immigrants' beer drinking was harmless enough—"an old English custom introduced by old-country people like myself," a respectable Fall River Englishman said in 1885:

In England, where I was reared, the habit was for a man, when he drew his pay every Saturday night, to go in and enjoy himself. He was not considered a drunkard; neither do I consider the people of Fall River drunkards. They go in and get their glass of beer as they do in the old country. In this country there has perhaps been some spirits introduced, but the people are not anything like drunkards.

The immigrant artisans to whom beer was so essential long held that America could never hope to make steel to match the English—she " 'adn't the 'ops, you know."

Though tastes in drink differed, Americans shared most of the chief holidays of the British calendar. But Christmas, struggling free from Calvinist inhibitions, lacked the English Yuletide traditions. Among the English-speaking Protestants of New York as late as the 1860's only the Episcopalians held Christmas services. When a party of English farmers celebrated their first Wisconsin Christmas Eve in 1843 by midnight caroling through the village, some startled Americans rushed out in their night-shirts, sure the Indians were attacking. Such ignorance bothered the im-migrants not a bit. During the 1870's Fall River stores offered them "your Christmas beef and goose" and "the genuine English plum pudding," and the operatives decked the mill halls with evergreen boughs, ate oranges and apples, and sang, danced, and feasted. In later years an American noted:

> The English trim their churches with their own hands—it is no mean-ingless ceremony with them; they gather the greens and wreathe the holly to welcome the coming of the Christ Child. On Christmas Eve the candles are lighted in many homes and shine a welcome through the windows to the wayfarers; and, best of all, after the midnight service in the church, the waits go about the sleeping city—no whir of spindles or clatter of looms is heard—singing carols.

Early in the twentieth century a party of Fall River Lancashire folk yearly came to Boston to carol through the Back Bay, accept the hospitality of its mansions, and collect money for their parish fund. But while Americans were assimilating such customs, Boxing Day and the rest of the English season fell before the exigencies of American jobs.

Although in Scotland as in New England dour Calvinists long had ignored Christmas, during the late nineteenth century the Scots gradually softened. But the real holiday of their season was Hogmanay—New Year's Eve. Then in the old country the people gathered at village and town cross-roads to consign the old year to "Auld Lang Syne" while guizards, like English waits, went about singing for gifts. The next day brought the "first fittin'," somewhat like the New Year's calls which mid-nineteenth-century Americans paid each other. While Scottish-Americans gradually dropped the old drunkenness of the day, Hogmanay remained their chief festival.

Some English immigrants observed the tradition of sweeping out the old year and carrying the new over the threshold. Until late in the century Scots also celebrated Auld Handsel Monday, about ten days after the "new style" New Year's Day.

Scottish immigrants' Hallowe'en traditions probably helped fix that night's American form, though it had long been known in some parts of the country. In 1891 a Scottish-American editor called it

> a festival about which, outside Scottish circles, comparatively little is known in the New World, but . . . if it could only be celebrated in regular old-fashioned style with a blazing fire in the open grate, and on the fire a big pot full of potatoes, and round the fire a wheen lads and lasses trying their fortunes by putting nuts on the live coals, with the younger members of the family dookin' for apples in the dimly lighted background, and all the other accompaniments of covered looking-glasses, turnip lanterns and flickering shadows, we fancy it would be a popular entertainment with other nationalities besides the Scotch.

While Americans did not take up such other British holidays as Whitsuntide, the immigrants soon added American festivals to their calendar. A Waterbury cutler in 1850 explained to friends back in Sheffield, "We have a day that they call thanksgiving & if there is any person that has not a turkey that day they are thought nothing of. That day is on the 29 november so you see we was forced to have one." But the most warmly enjoyed days were those which awakened memories of the homeland.

However America may have won its battles, it was not upon any playing fields. The United Kingdom, however, was swept during the mid-nineteenth century by a gospel of sport preaching the moral virtues of cricket, football, and other games of villagers and public school boys. To Americans, however, such play was a waste of God-given time. In 1840 an emigrant guidebook warned the English workingman that Americans knew

> none of those sports, pastimes, amusements, and recreations such as he has been accustomed to in his own country, as cricket, quoits, rackets, five, &c., although many attempts have been made on the part of 'old country' people to establish them; to walk much about the city is contrary to general custom and therefore only renders him singular; few, if any, Americans doing so for mere pleasure, Sundays perhaps excepted, and then only for a few hours in the middle of the day, never in the latter part of it.

Americans might be all business, but English newcomers preferred an afternoon of cricket. During the 1830's the knitters and weavers of Philadelphia mills organized cricket clubs; mill proprietors played alongside their workmen. As in England, cricket was equally a game of "gentle-men" amateurs; in Philadelphia, New York, Brooklyn, Boston, Lawrence, and Lowell certain cricket clubs were begun in the 1840's and 1850's by well-to-do English merchants and professional men, and others by work-ingmen. Fascinated, young Americans soon took the field. Before long a cricket team might include either English veterans or American novices, or both. After the 1840's baseball seduced all Americans except a few snobs and Anglophiles. But on any summer's Saturday afternoon from the 1850's through the 1890's the anthracite miners of Schuylkill county, the English hotelkeepers of New York and Brooklyn, the textile operatives of half a dozen Massachusetts and Rhode Island mill towns, and almost any twenty-two Englishmen in the East, the Middle West, or on the Pacific coast were likely to be found on some level piece of ground with bat, ball, and wickets. "Gentlemen's" clubs, both English and American, also carried on in several cities.

Now and then an "All-England," Irish, Canadian, Australian, or West Indian team thought matches with these cricketers worth a tour of the States. An All-American team which paid a return visit necessarily included several English-born players. Sometimes an American club hired an English expert for the season; eleven such professionals played eleven "gentlemen" of Philadelphia in 1880. But cricket remained an exotic. As British immigration slackened after 1890, each year saw fewer matches. Furthermore, English, Irish, and Welsh immigrants and their children eventually turned to baseball. In fact, the organizer of the first professional baseball team, the Cincinnati Red Stockings, was Sheffield-born Harry Wright, who had been professional bowler of the St. George's Cricket Club of New York.

British football ran a similar course. The United States saw its first rugby and association football during the 1870's. Though American college boys soon adopted a form of the rib-smashing rugger, immigrant working-men, only part-time athletes, preferred soccer. Since by this time soccer was as well known in Scotland, Wales, and Ireland as in England, men from all corners of the United Kingdom played it. No sooner did a new mill go up than the English or Scottish operatives organized an eleven. During the 1880's clubs took the field in New York and in Fall River, Newark, Paterson, and other textile centers; they battled annually for the championship of the American Football Association. In 1890 there were about twenty-five soccer clubs in Fall River, where two thousand persons might turn out to see a game, and Philadelphia had seven clubs made up almost entirely of British immigrants. Miners, steelworkers, and stone-cutters across the country organized football clubs and leagues. Their sons, eyes on the famous personages who played for American colleges, gradually drifted away from soccer. But since it was becoming a European favorite, by 1910 the leagues included teams of Scandinavians, Hungarians, and Czechs as well as British immigrants. Thus the game continued to thrive.

American athletes appropriated the favorite sport of the Scottish immigrants. In Scotland each year many a rural community held its day of "games"—a rudimentary track and field meet—and the best men competed at the great Highland gatherings. In 1836 the Highland Society of New York held its "First Sportive Meeting." Within the next thirty years Scots in Boston, Philadelphia, and several other cities likewise staged Highland games. Caledonian clubs sprang up to manage these patriotic and profitable field days, with all the old contests: "throwing the heavy hammer," "putting the heavy stone," "tossing the caber," "vaulting with the pole," "the running high leap," "the long jump," "the hitch and kick," "the hop, step, and leap," "hurdle races," the tug o' war, and races of 100 yards to a mile. Americans as well as Scots soon flocked by the thousands to Caledonian games in cities the country over. If the Scots frowned on these motley crowds, they welcomed the flood of silver at the gates and soon threw the competitions open to all athletes, be they Scots, Americans, Irish, Germans, or Negroes. Down to the 1870's, however, practiced Scotsmen won most of the prizes. After the Philadelphia games of 1866, they could boast that in the hammer throw "a number of robust men entered, but their awkward style of throwing showed clearly that they had no experience in the art of throwing. Scotland beat the field." The champions of Scotland itself, those braw lads Donald Dinnie and James Fleming, came over in the 1870's for a triumphant and profitable circuit of the Scottish-American games.

By this time the Caledonian clubs had to compete for public favor with American imitators. In fact, the modern American track and field meet evolved directly from the games of the immigrants. The New York Athletic Club ("athletics" then meaning only track and field events) started "handicap Scottish games" in 1868, and Princeton, a Presbyterian college with a Scottish president, held its first "Caledonian Games" in 1873 with a Scottish athlete from Montreal, George Goldie, as gymnastics instructor. Americans abandoned some too peculiarly Scottish events like caber-tossing and—more suitable for picnics—the three-legged and sack races. Objecting to American semiprofessionalism and preoccupation with "records," the young Scottish workingmen of the Caledonian clubs kept up their games in the old tradition, in several cities to this day. English and Welsh immigrants sponsored less variegated field days.

Scotsmen's "ain game," however, was curling. On many a frozen American pond broom-wielding Scots and Canadians could be seen frantically sweeping the way before a granite "hog" which their skip had sent skimming down the ice. Regular matches between the stonecutters and stonesetters of New York or Chicago suggested the forgotten origins of the game. Nearly every Scottish settlement in the North had its curling club. In New York and the Middle West their leagues held annual bonspiels and challenged visiting rinks from Ontario. The Grand National Curling Club, formed in 1867, during the next fifty years included as many as thirty local clubs. When a mild winter south of the Canadian border gave them only a few days of the sport, curlers nevertheless sat down to a supper of beef and greens and recounted the deeds of skips and sweeps of the past. Though others occasionally joined them in the "roarin' game," curling remained a Scottish and Canadian crotchet. During the summer the Scots played quoits, bowls, and shuffleboard, outdoor games with some elements of curling; they organized a few quoiting and bowling clubs.

On the American copper and iron ranges Cornish miners in rope-trimmed canvas jackets enjoyed their old-style wrestling. A few Scots had shinty teams. During the 1870's in the West, hunting and shooting were popular alike among English gentlemen farmers and coal miners. At the fashionable Illinois shooting resort of Wilmington, where "a tough wiry Englishman" kept bird dogs, there were "so many Britishers about that the place [was] called Little Britain."

In 1873 a Chicago Scot "returned from a visit to Scotland with a knobby set of golf sticks and commenced knocking the 'gutty' balls around a field . . . to the amusement of his neighbors and the joyous sneers of the hoodlums." Shortly after a few Scotsmen started playing golf in a vacant Yonkers lot in 1887, the first club in the country was formed there under the august name of St. Andrew's. In ten years more than a hundred clubs —most òf their members wealthy Americans—sprang up; Scots started a few, and many employed Scottish professionals.

Other British sports such as lawn tennis, polo, and yachting were likewise fads of the rich and not of immigrants, and only college boys rowed four- or eight-oared shells. The blue-blooded Englishmen of Le-Mars did play polo. But British workingmen were at least vicarious sportsmen. The *Labor Standard* kept Fall River mill operatives abreast of New Bedford yachting; the hopes of all the Scots in America sailed with the Clyde-built *Thistle* when she raced for the *America's* cup in 1887. After Harvard oarsmen unsuccessfully challenged Oxford on the Thames in 1869, immigrants in New York—especially "the frequenters of the English alehouses in Bleecker and Houston streets"—pocketed wagers on their countrymen.

Some newcomers were glad to find that horse racing on the English model was already popular in the States. English bookies in 1879 "almost monopolized the straight book-betting business" at Saratoga. The young English gentlemen riders of LeMars formed a Jockey Club before their first year there was out; those of Fairmont, clad in homemade pinks, introduced hurdle jumping to the Minnesota state fair; and even Lancashire colliers wasted no time in clearing Wyoming sage brush for a quarter-mile track.

As mid-nineteenth-century English magistrates suppressed the old prize ring, bare-knuckle fighters—"lusty, low-browed, short-cropped, broken-nosed"—emigrated to America. But the day of the disciples of Bendigo and Gentleman John Jackson was done even there. After the 1880's, when American pugilism adopted the Marquess of Queensberry's boxing rules and gloves, the hardest hitters were generally Americans. In 1897, Cornish–New Zealander Bob Fitzsimmons won the heavyweight championship in the United States. . . .

To many British-Americans Saturday afternoon's pastimes mattered less than Sunday's institutions. To be sure, during the nineteenth century few emigrants left Great Britain for religious reasons. Parliament freed even Roman Catholics and Jews from their old civil disabilities, and, though the Anglican establishment offended Nonconformists, old and new forms of dissent flowered as freely in Britain as in America. A few tiny groups did hope to set up their own Bible commonwealths on American soil, among them John Alexander Dowie's disciples at Zion City, Illinois, and some Scottish families who went to Maine in 1904 to establish "the Corporation of the Kingdom." But other British-inspired religious movements in the United States, such as the Y.M.C.A. and the Salvation Army, involved at most only a few immigrant missionaries. Although American Mormons between 1840 and the 1880's persuaded tens of thousands of converts in England, Wales, and Scotland to come to Utah, the vision of land ownership probably moved these immigrants no less than spiritual faith.

If few British came to America expressly to plant their faith, most did wish to worship as they had in the homeland. Since American sects rested on the same doctrinal and ecclesiastical foundation as British churches and chapels, immigrants were likely to find their particular denominations wherever they settled. Nevertheless, in places where they did not or where they swamped the existing congregation, they created their own churches—"immigrant churches" no less than the Irish Catholic, Swedish Lutheran, and other national groups even stranger to native Americans.

Most English immigrants were, if anything, either Anglicans or Methodists. Although the Church of England had long neglected the growing industrial population, many workingmen held to the faith and forms which their village forebears had known. Other Protestant Episcopalians emigrated from Ireland and Canada. But the Episcopal church which they found in the United States, though the well-to-do often patronized it, was a minor sect unprepared for so many new communicants.

When Lancashire cotton workers started to come to Fall River, the town had only one Episcopal church. In the 1870's most English operatives there had no church to which to go. Even if they could find a pew, they "were made to feel the difference between a good coat and a poor one." One explained:

> I was brought up to go to Sunday school and to church, and went in England, but after I got here, folks were different. I suppose if I was going to die, I should have to own to some kind of belief, but as churches run here, I don't like to go. If working people were always treated kindly by those above them, they would go; but as it is these folks that run the churches take no pains whatever to elevate us in any way.

Some operatives joined other Protestant denominations. But old ties were strong. Between 1878 and 1900 Episcopal authorities responded to the Fall River mill hands' desires by creating six new churches or missions; even the original one became known as "the church of the English operatives."

Many Gloucester fishermen from the Maritime Provinces were Anglicans, and towns and villages in mining or farming districts where British people settled soon had their Episcopal churches. In many an American industrial center the spread of this faith was far more the work of English workingmen than of the fashionable newly rich. In a mill town with no Episcopal church a new cricket club was a signal to diocesan authorities that an "English remnant" awaited rescue. If many immigrant Episcopalians resorted to their churches only for marriages, baptisms, and burials, others even after eleven hours' labor in the mill liked to spend their evenings improving their new church building. The more the structures, furnishings, and services resembled those of England, with bells in the steeples and surpliced choirs, the more fond of them the immigrants became.

In eighteenth- and nineteenth-century English industrial towns Methodism provided the emotional fervor and the chapels that the Church of England was slow to give the urban proletariat. Staffordshire miners, among whom were "a good many Methodees," had daily prayers underground. Thus many an English immigrant was an ardent Wesleyan. In a few places in the United States, such as isolated mining villages, Methodist congregations may have been mostly English. But since theirs was a major American sect, Methodists were likely to be swallowed up among their American fellow believers. And so were Baptists, Congregationalists, and other Non-conformists.

One group on the fringe of English Methodism, though originally inspired by an American evangelist, was unknown in the United States when immigrant members first arrived. The camp-meeting fervor of these primitive Methodists or Ranters had taken English miners and urban workingmen by storm. After the 1820's their little meetinghouses sprang up in coal and ore towns as soon as Englishmen—particularly Cornishmen—appeared. But the Primitive Methodists never numbered more than a few thousand in the United States.

Most newcomers from Scotland and Ulster, like their predecessors of colonial days, were Presbyterians of some stripe. Recurrent schisms had proliferated many rival shoots from the main stem alike in Scotland, Ireland, Canada, and the United States. Nevertheless, since families of Scottish or Scotch-Irish stock had planted their churches all through the frontier West, an immigrant Presbyterian could usually present his certificate to some American congregation. In New England, however, the Congregationalists had absorbed the few Scotch-Irishmen who had settled there in the eighteenth century. Rather than join them, the Scots, Ulstermen, and Scottish Canadians who came to Yankee towns to weave, dress granite, built houses, or sell dry goods at the same time replanted the Presbyterian polity. By 1904 they had nearly fifty New England churches, with more than ten thousand members. Furthermore, even in New York, Jersey City, Detroit, Chicago and other places where American Presbyterians abounded, the immigrants organized churches which were "Scotch" both in name and in membership.

Wherever they went, Scots were bound to maintain their kirk no matter whether the minister's clerical robes and the mode of worship surprised American Presbyterians. Although Taunton, Massachusetts, in 1887 already had fifteen Protestant churches, twenty Scots appealed for funds to put up a building of their own, saying that they, "still adhering to the faith of their fathers, 'do not feel at home' in any other church, and consequently have neglected attending any public place of worship." A Presbyterian minister of New York objected; one could remain true to the Westminster Confession within the existing Congregational churches. "If people who come to our country from Scotland, Ireland, Germany, or anywhere else do not like things as they find them when they get here," he admonished, "they had better either adjust themselves to the situation or go home." But the Scots persevered. Their countryman Robert Gilchrist, the Boston department-store owner, helped found several new chuches; without them, he feared, Scottish-Americans would think only of moneymaking.

Members of the smaller and more austere Presbyterian sects maintained to the last jot and tittle their mode of worship. In Cambridge, Massachusetts, a group of Prince Edward Islanders in 1895 organized the unique American congregation of MacDonaldites, a sect peculiar to their province, and modestly named it "the Church of Scotland." Adamant against singing hymns to an organ or other instrumental accompaniment in the lax fashion of most American Presbyterians, such minor sects as the

Covenanters, most of whom came from Ulster or the Maritimes, lined out metrical paraphrases of the psalms in tones that made even the minister think of untuned bagpipes. Covenanters refused to vote in a nation whose constitution did not explicitly acknowledge Christ as king. In so rigorous a congregation the way of the transgressor was hard indeed. Even though he had sinned—and escaped punishment—long before leaving the old country, the session of elders rebuked him and on the Sabbath held him up to public scorn. When called to account for Sunday tippling or football, immigrant Presbyterians were likely to grumble against "Holy Willies" and the "unco' guid" and to seek a more liberal church. But while America gradually softened the rigors of northern Calvinism, most Scottish immigrants were no rebels. They preserved old sectarian loyalties even after the parent groups in the homeland had reunited.

To the few Scottish Presbyterians who thought and spoke in Gaelic, distinct church services were vital. A Highland colony at Elmira, Illinois, in 1864 affiliated with the Canadian Presbyterian Church and, to choose a minister, heard fifteen sermons by applicants who claimed to have the Gaelic. In Boston, where many Highlanders from Cape Breton and Prince Edward Island settled, the Catholics among them apparently lost their separate identity in the Irish parishes. But in 1871 the United Presbyterian Church started Gaelic prayer meetings. Sixteen years later a Nova Scotian minister organized the Scotch Presbyterian Church, which held two Gaelic services each week. Several other Presbyterian churches in Boston, New York, and Chicago ministered to Highlanders whose English was poor.

Because of language, Welsh-Americans had to establish their own churches everywhere they settled. Those begun in the late seventeenth century by Welsh Quakers and Baptists near Philadelphia no longer worshiped *yn Gymraeg*. In the last century, moreover, Wales had been swept by a religious revolution. A new sect of Calvinistic Methodists—actually Presbyterians—had sprung up, and new fervor had entered the older Baptists and Independents (Congregationalists). Most Welshmen now belonged to these three sects. Anglicans were generally the gentry, who did not emigrate; Wesleyan Methodists and Unitarians were small groups. The large Welsh exodus of the early nineteenth century occurred at the height of the evangelical movement; in fact, discontent with the privileges of the established Church of England was at least a minor cause of emigration.

Thus religion pitched the tone of Welsh-American culture. In 1885 an immigrant remarked:

> The genuine *Cymro* can not talk two minutes with you about the pedigree of a horse, the points of a good cow, or the best method of tillage, but he can sit on his heels by the hour and with beaming countenance tell the points of a good sermon or argue a knotty theological dogma.

In new Welsh-American settlements of the early nineteenth century the immigrants' *hiraeth* (homesickness) was more for the chapels and preachers of the old country than for its scenery. "I wish to request someone who is coming over to this valley from the old country," a Gallia County farmer wrote in 1851, ". . . to bring a large Peter Williams Bible."

As soon as possible Welsh farmers, miners or ironworkers commenced prayer meetings, a Sunday school, and a Bible society and built a union meeting house. Usually within a few years the Calvinistic Methodists, the Congregationalists, and the Baptists each put up their own building. In Pennsylvania and the Middle West, which American Congregationalists had left to the Presbyterians, the Welsh Congregationalists—like Scottish Presbyterians in New England—in effect reintroduced their form of ecclesiastical polity. In the entire country in 1839, an immigrant minister estimated, there were 46 Welsh churches, of which 16 were Congregational, 13 Baptist, 12 Calvinistic Methodist, 3 Wesleyan Methodist, and 2 Episcopalian. Thirty-three years later, besides more than ten union congregations and two or three Episcopal churches, 384 chapels were counted: 154 Congregational, 152 Calvinistic Methodist, 71 Baptist, and 7 Wesleyan. Though many chapels disbanded, their number increased slightly through the rest of the century. Each sect organized state associations; in 1869 the Calvinistic Methodists united theirs in a general assembly.

Welsh chapels were distinct not merely because their congregations punctuated sermons with spontaneous cries of *"gogoniant"* when English-speaking evangelicals would shout "glory." Among what other people did a preacher have that "weird, peculiar intonation of his sermon . . . often strange and objectionable" to non-Welsh ears—the *hwyl*?

> The judicious use of it is confined to the more passionate or pathetic parts of a sermon. It differs entirely from that monotonous tone that is often heard in English churches or the chromatic chanting of the mass before papal altars; it is a *melody* of the purest nature . . . in which the minister pours forth his pathetic passages when under "full canvas" . . . It is the application of sentences in a chanting style to portions of the minor scale . . . The sentence is started, for instance, on E minor. The minister has his own peculiar melody. It ranges here and there from the first to the fifth, often reaching the octave, and then descending and ending in sweet cadence on the key-note . . . The introduction and the deliberative parts are in the major, and the voice continues thus until the emotional point is reached; then it glides triumphantly into a thrilling minor, which generally continues to the close.

Such eloquence made a *cymanfa bregethu* (preaching assembly), whether of a local chapel or one of the large associations, an annual red-letter event for a Welsh sect. Lasting two days or even a week if the *hwyl* started a revival, a *cymanfa* included a whole series of sermons, with prayers and hymns between, by a battery of ministers.

As austere as the Scots, Welsh chapel-goers long abjured organ music in their services, kept the Sabbath strictly, and condemned idle amusements. In the southern Ohio settlements, "parting the hair was looked upon . . . as a sign of too much pride. The men combed their hair straight down over their foreheads." Such extreme piety gradually relaxed as the American-born generations lost command of the Welsh language. In fact, their sects could continue only as long as the *hen iaith* survived. The dearth of books in Welsh handicapped their Sunday schools during the 1850's, but soon Welsh-American printers in Utica and New York brought out tracts, hymnals, volumes of sermons, and lives of preachers. As among other non-English-speaking foreigners in the country, the older immigrants who controlled church affairs long resisted the use of English. Having always heard the gospel in Welsh and suspecting in their children's secular interests a lapse from grace, they felt that *Cymraeg* was inherently more religious than *Saesneg*: "The English language is so used in business and earthly bargains of all kinds, high and low, that it is hardly fit to go to church and chapel on Sunday." An old Ohio Welshman complained, "When English came into the settlement, religion went out of it."

But when at last the choice lay between conducting Sunday schools and services in English and allowing the second and third generations to grow up ignorant of the scriptures and indifferent to the churches, bilingual and then only English services were held. In fact, it was difficult to find an American-born preacher fluent in Welsh, while a man from Wales might not suit the new generation. Thus as men and women who had grown up speaking Welsh passed off the scene, their congregations either melted away into American chuches or themselves became virtually indistinguishable from their American fellow believers. In 1919 the Calvinistic Methodists voted to merge their general assembly with the Northern Presbyterians; the state *cymanfaoedd* maintained their identity until the 1930's. Not that the Welsh were wholly submerged; in 1913 the choir of the largest Presbyterian church in Racine was solidly Welsh. But for immigrants who had known the valleys of Wales, their own chapels, whatever the language used, were always the strongest institutional link with the dearly remembered land of their fathers.

In the pages of their own newspapers and magazines British immigrants' old loyalties also shone. Like the churches, the Welsh-American press flourished while Welshmen still spoke their own language. From about 1840 through the rest of the century their three major sects each published monthly magazines of sermons and church news. Most notable were the Calvinistic Methodists' *Cyfaill o'r Hen Wlad* (Friend from the Old Country) and the Congregationalists' *Cenhadwr Americanaidd* (American Missionary). Commencing with the *Cymro America* (Welshman of America) of New York in 1832, more than a dozen secular weeklies, fortnightlies, monthlies and quarterlies—leaning heavily on the literary journals of the homeland—appeared at New York, Utica, Scranton, Pittsburgh, and other Welsh centers. There were a few musical papers and even two humorous magazines. Only the religious papers, however, survived more than five years.

At New York in 1851 the first number of *Y Drych* (Mirror) began an unbroken century of Welsh journalism. Moving to Utica in 1861, along its course it absorbed several rival weeklies: *Baner America* (Banner of America) of Scranton, 1866 to 1877; *Y Wasg* (Press) of Pittsburgh, 1871 to 1890; and the *Columbia* of Emporia, Kansas, and later Chicago, 1883 to 1894. At its peak at the end of the nineteenth century the *Drych* claimed twelve thousands subscribers.

Though the gradual decline of the Welsh language in the United States put an end by 1907 to all these periodicals except *Y Cyfaill* and *Y Drych,* several printed in English took their place. First and longest-lived was the *Cambrian,* a literary journal which began in 1880 at Cincinnati as a monthly and later appeared fortnightly at Utica. Besides providing for Welsh immigrants and their descendants who knew more English than Welsh, its founder aimed to record his people's history in America "in a language which shall not be an unknown tongue to future historians." The *Cambrian* suspended in 1919. After 1907 an English-language weekly, the *Druid* of Scranton and Pittsburgh, had nearly as many readers as *Y Drych.* Even the latter, which after 1939 was the only surviving Welsh-American periodical, in recent years likewise has printed most of its news in English.

Thus while language accounted for the profusion of periodicals in the small Welsh-American community, it was not the only reason for an immigrant press. Scots, Englishmen, and Canadians looked in vain in American papers for the news which interested them most—word from home. The first British-American newspapers, the *Albion* (1822 to 1876), the *Old Countryman* and the *Emigrant* (appearing separately or combined between 1829 and 1848), the *Scottish Patriot* (1840 to 1842), and the *Anglo-American* (1843 to 1847) reprinted news from the latest British papers to reach New York by packet ship.

After 1850, however, the rising immigrant community became as interested in news of its own doings as in the state of trade in Lancashire, some new sensation from the Old Bailey, or the Queen's latest excursion to Balmoral. Thus both *Y Drych* and the *Druid* were truly Welsh-American newspapers. The Scots stood next to the Welsh, in proportion to their numbers in the United States, as publishers and readers of their own papers.

From 1857 until 1919 the *Scottish-American Journal,* owned and edited for almost its entire span by Archibald M. Stewart, served as many as fifteen thousand subscribers throughout the country. A New York rival, the *Scotsman* (apparently combined with the *Caledonian Advertiser* in 1874), survived only from 1869 until 1886, and another weekly, John Adamson's *Boston Scotsman,* from 1906 until 1914. A literary monthly, the *Caledonian,* appeared between 1901 and 1923.

No newspapers designed solely for English immigrants lasted long. The New York *English-American* suspended in 1885 after only a year; two *Anglo-Americans,* one in Lawrence in the 1870's and the other in Boston between about 1899 and 1906, did little better. Several weeklies, however, catered to all British immigrants. A Chicago *British-American* appeared in 1864. The Queen's Jubilees first inspired the *British-American Citizen* of Boston (1887 to 1913), the *Western British-American* of Chicago (1888 to 1922), the *British-American* of New York and Philadelphia (1887 to 1919), and two monthlies, the *British Californian* of San Francisco (1897 to 1931) and the *British World* of Chicago (1898 to 1905). The first three each claimed as many as five to twenty thousand subscribers. . . .

Most of these newspapers, whether Welsh, Scottish, Canadian, or British, were eight-page weeklies. A typical issue culled a page or two of provincial news from the press of the United Kingdom and Canada and eked out a few more with British and American literary excerpts; but it concentrated—especially if a Welsh paper—on the immigrant community in the United States. For British immigrants no longer merely looked back to the old country. They had found their own identity, neither wholly British nor wholly American, but instead Welsh-American, Scottish-American, Canadian-American, or, at least among the English, simply British-American.

2.2

Urbanization, Migration, and Social Mobility in Late Nineteenth-Century America

STEPHAN THERNSTROM

Stephan Thernstrom here draws our attention to two significant facts about late nineteenth-century America: first, the crucial importance of the internal migration of native Americans from country to city, and second, the importance of geographical mobility among the lower classes. Thernstrom suggestively infers from the latter that the frequent moves of working people might help account for their failure to organize themselves more effectively. Thernstrom argues from structure (much mobility) to behavior (low level of militancy). Careful study of the intervening variables between structure and behavior might well modify the thesis. One such factor, for example, is culture, which, as we have seen, is often an extremely important factor in determining behavior.

From *Towards a New Past,* edited by Barton J. Bernstein. Copyright © 1967, 1968 by Random House, Inc. Reprinted by permission of the publisher.

The following book is suggested for further reading:

STEPHAN THERNSTROM, *Poverty and Progress,* New York: Atheneum Publishers, 1970.

The United States, it has been said, was born in the country and has moved to the city. It was during the half-century between the Civil War and World War I that the move was made. In 1860, less than a quarter of the American population lived in a city or town; by 1890, the figure had reached a third; by 1910, nearly half. By more sophisticated measures than the mere count of heads, the center of gravity of the society had obviously tilted cityward well before the last date.

If to speak of "the rise of the city" in those years is a textbook cliché, the impact of this great social transformation upon the common people of America has never been sufficiently explored. This essay is intended as a small contribution toward that task. It sketches the process by which ordinary men and women were drawn to the burgeoning cities of post-Civil War America, assesses what little we know about how they were integrated into the urban class structure, and suggests how these matters affected the viability of the political system.

I

The urbanization of late nineteenth-century America took place at a dizzying pace. Chicago, for instance, doubled its population every decade but one between 1850 and 1890, growing from 30,000 to over a million in little more than a generation. And it was not merely the conspicuous metropolitan giants but the Akrons, the Duluths, the Tacomas that were bursting at the seams; no less than 101 American communities grew by 100 percent or more in the 1880s.[1]

Why did Americans flock into these all too often unlovely places? There were some who were not pulled to the city but rather pushed out of their previous habitats and dropped there, more or less by accident. But the overriding fact is that the cities could draw on an enormous reservoir of people who were dissatisfied with their present lot and eager to seize the new opportunities offered by the metropolis.

[1] C. N. Glaab and A. T. Brown, *A History of Urban America* (New York, 1967), pp. 107–11.

Who were these people? It is conventional to distinguish two broad types of migrants to the American city: the immigrant from another culture, and the farm lad who moved from a rural to an urban setting within the culture. It is also conventional in historical accounts to overlook the latter type and to focus on the more exotic of the migrants, those who had to undergo the arduous process of becoming Americanized.

This is regrettable. To be sure, immigration from abroad was extremely important in the building of America's cities down to World War I. But the most important source of population for the burgeoning cities was not the fields of Ireland and Austria, but those of Vermont and Iowa. The prime cause of population growth in nineteenth-century America, and the main source of urban growth, was simply the high fertility of natives living outside the city.

We tend to neglect internal migration from country to city, partly because the immigrants from abroad seem exotic and thus conspicuous, partly because of the unfortunate legacy left by Frederick Jackson Turner's frontier theory, one element of which was the notion that the open frontier served as a safety valve for urban discontent. When there were hard times in the city, according to Turner, the American worker didn't join a union or vote Socialist; he moved West and grabbed some of that free land. This theory has been subjected to the rather devastating criticism that by 1860 it took something like $1,000 capital to purchase sufficient transportation, seed equipment, livestock, and food (to live on until the first crop) to make a go of it; that it took even more than $1,000 later in the century; and that it was precisely the unemployed workmen who were least likely to have that kind of money at their command. It is estimated that for every industrial worker who became a farmer, twenty farm boys became urban dwellers.[2] There was an urban safety valve for rural discontent, and an extremely important one. The dominant form of population movement was precisely the opposite of that described by Turner.

Since scholarly attention has been focused upon immigrants from abroad, upon Oscar Handlin's "Uprooted," it will be useful to review what is known about their movement to the American city and then to ask how much the same generalization might hold for native Americans uprooted from the countryside and plunged into the city.

Immigration is as old as America, but a seismic shift in the character of European immigration to these shores occurred in the nineteenth century, as a consequence of the commercial transformation of traditional European agriculture and the consequent displacement of millions of peas-

---

[2] Fred Shannon, "A Post Mortem on the Labor-Safety-Valve Theory," *Agricultural History*, XIX (1954), 31–37.

ants.[3] Compared to earlier newcomers, these were people who were closer to the land and more tradition-bound, and they generally had fewer resources to bring with them than their predecessors. One shouldn't overwork this; a substantial fraction of the German and Scandinavian immigrants had enough capital to get to the West to pick up land. But some of the Germans and Scandinavians, and most men of other nationalities, had just enough cash to make it to the New World and were stuck for a time at least where they landed—New York, Boston, or wherever. They swelled the population appreciably and the relief rolls dramatically, particularly in the pre-Civil War years, when they entered cities which were basically commercial and had little use for men whose only skill in many cases was that they knew how to dig. Eventually, however, the stimulus of this vast pool of cheap labor and the demands of the growing city itself opened up a good many unskilled jobs—in the construction of roads, houses, and commercial buildings, and in the manufacturing that began to spring up in the cities.

That they were driven off the land in the Old World, that they arrived without resources, immobilized by their poverty, and that they often suffered a great deal before they secured stable employment is true enough. But these harsh facts may lead us to overlook other aspects which were extremely significant.

One is that immigration was a *selective* process. However powerful the pressures to leave, in no case did everyone in a community pull up stakes. This observation may be uncomfortably reminiscent of the popular opinion on this point: that it was the best of the Old World stock that came to the New—the most intelligent, enterprising, courageous. But this should not lead us to neglect the point altogether. The traits that led some men to leave and allowed them to survive the harrowing journey to the port, the trip itself, and the perils of the New World, could be described in somewhat different terms: substitute cunning for intelligence, for example, or ruthlessness for courage. Still, whatever the emphasis, the fact remains: as weighed in the scales of the marketplace, those who came—however driven by cruel circumstance—were better adapted to American life than those who remained in the village or died on the way.

The other main point about the immigrants, and especially those who suffered the most extreme hardships—the Irish in the 1840s and 1850s, the French Canadians in the 1870s, the Italians and various East Europeans after 1880—is that they appraised their new situations with standards developed in peasant society. Lowell was terrible, with its

[3] For general accounts, see Marcus L. Hansen, *The Atlantic Migration, 1607–1860* (paperback ed.; New York, 1961); Oscar Handlin, *The Uprooted* (Boston, 1951).

cramped stinking tenements, and factory workers labored from dawn till dark for what seems a mere pittance. Children were forced to work at a brutally early age; the factories and dwellings were deathtraps. But Lowell was a damn sight better than County Cork, and men who knew from bitter experience what County Cork was like could not view their life in Lowell with quite the same simple revulsion as the middle-class reformers who judged Lowell by altogether different standards. It is not so much the objectively horrible character of a situation that goads men to action as it is a nagging discrepancy between what *is* and what is *expected*. And what one expects is determined by one's reference group—which can be a class, an ethnic or religious subculture, or some other entity which defines people's horizon of expectation.[4] Immigration provided an ever renewed stream of men who entered the American economy to fill its least attractive and least well rewarded positions, men who happen to have brought with them very low horizons of expectation fixed in peasant Europe.

That those Americans with greatest reason to feel outrageously exploited judged their situation against the dismally low standards of the decaying European village is an important clue to the stunted growth of the labor movement and the failure of American Socialism. Working in the same direction was what might be called the Tower of Babel factor. A firm sense of class solidarity was extremely difficult to develop in communities where people literally didn't speak each other's language. Even in cases where groups of immigrant workers had unusually high expectations and previous familiarity with advanced forms of collective action— such as the English artisans who led the Massachusetts textile strikes in the 1870s—they found it hard to keep the other troops in line; a clever Italian-speaking or Polish-speaking foreman could easily exploit national differences for his own ends, and if necessary there were always the most recent immigrants of all (and the Negroes) to serve as scabs to replace the dissenters en masse.

A somewhat similar analysis applies to the migrants who left the Kansas farms for Chicago. They were linguistically and culturally set apart from many of their fellow workers; they too had low horizons of expectation fixed in the countryside and brought to the city. The latter point is often missed because of the peculiar American reverence for an idealized

---

[4] For discussion of the sociological concepts of reference groups and the theory of relative deprivation, see Robert K. Merton, *Social Theory and Social Structure,* rev. ed. (Glencoe, Ill., 1957) and the literature cited there. The problem of assessing the level of expectations of any particular migratory group in the past is extremely complicated, and it is obvious that there have been important differences between and within groups. But the generalizations offered here seem to me the best starting point for thinking about this issue.

agrarian way of life. As we have become a nation of city dwellers, we have come more and more to believe that it is virtuous and beautiful to slave for fourteen hours a day with manure on your boots. Recently that sturdy small farmer from Johnson City, Texas, remarked that "it does not make sense on this great continent which God has blessed to have more than 70 percent of our people crammed into one percent of the land." A national "keep them down on the farm" campaign is therefore in the offing.[5] But it is damnably hard to keep them down on the farm after they've seen New York (or even Indianapolis), and it was just as hard a century ago, for the very good reason that the work is brutal, the profits are often miserably low, and the isolation is psychologically murderous. Virtuous this life may be, especially to people who don't have to live it, but enjoyable it is not—not, at least, to a very substantial fraction of our ever shrinking farm population.

This applies particularly to young men and women growing up on a farm. Their parents had a certain stake in staying where they were, even if it was a rut. And the eldest son, who would inherit the place eventually, was sometimes tempted by that. But the others left in droves, to tend machines, to dig and haul and hammer—or in the case of the girls, to sell underwear in Marshall Field's, to mind someone else's kitchen, or in some instances to follow in the footsteps of Sister Carrie.

There were some large differences between native-born migrants to the cities and immigrants from another land, to be sure. But the familiar argument that native workmen "stood on the shoulders" of the immigrant and was subjected to less severe exploitation is somewhat misleading. The advantages enjoyed by many America-born laborers stemmed more from their urban experience than their birth, and they did not generally accrue to freshly arrived native migrants to the city. The latter were little better off than their immigrant counterparts, but then they too were spiritually prepared to endure a great deal of privation and discomfort because even the bottom of the urban heap was a step up from the farms they had left behind. The two groups were one in this respect, and perceptive employers recognized the fact. In 1875, the Superintendent of one of Andrew Carnegie's steel mills summed up his experience this way: "We must steer clear as far as we can of Englishmen, who are great sticklers for high wages, small production and strikes. My experience has shown that Germans and Irish, Swedes and what I denominate 'Buckwheats'— young American country boys, judiciously mixed, make the most honest and tractable force you can find." [6]

[5] *Boston Globe,* February 5, 1967.
[6] Quoted in Oscar Handlin, *Immigration as a Factor in American History* (Englewood Cliffs, N.J., 1959), pp. 66–67.

II

The move to the city, therefore, was an advance of a kind for the typical migrant. Were there further opportunities for advancement there, or did he then find himself crushed by circumstance and reduced to the ranks of the permanent proletariat? Did his children, whose expectations were presumably higher, discover correspondingly greater opportunities open to them? Remarkably little serious research has been devoted to these issues. Historians who see American history as a success story have been content to assume, without benefit of data, that the American dream of mobility was true, apparently on the principle that popular ideology is a sure guide to social reality. Dissenting scholars have been more inclined to the view that class barriers were relatively impassable, an assumption based upon generalized skepticism about American mythology rather than upon careful empirical study. Some recent work, however, provides the basis for a tentative reappraisal of the problem.

We know most about mobility into the most rarefied reaches of the social order regarding such elite groups as millionaires, railroad presidents, directors of large corporations, or persons listed in the *Dictionary of American Biography*. What is most impressive about the literature on the American elite is that, in spite of many variations in the way in which the elite is defined, the results of these studies are much the same. It is clear that growing up in rags is not in the least conducive to the attainment of later riches, and that it was no more so a century ago than it is today.[7] There have been spectacular instances of mobility from low down on the social scale to the very top—Andrew Carnegie, for instance. But colorful examples cannot sustain broad generalizations about social phenomena, however often they are impressed into service toward that end. Systematic investigation reveals that even in the days of Andrew Carnegie, there was little room at the top, except for those who started very close to it.

Furthermore, this seems to have been the case throughout most of American history, despite many dramatic alterations in the character of the economy. It seems perfectly plausible to assume, as many historians have on the basis of impressionistic evidence, that the precipitous growth of heavy industry in the latter half of the nineteenth century opened the doors to men with very different talents from the educated merchants who constituted the elite of the preindustrial age, that unlettered, horny-handed types like Thomas Alva Edison and Henry Ford, crude inventors and

[7] For a convenient review of this literature, see Seymour M. Lipset and Reinhard Bendix, *Social Mobility in Industrial Society* (Berkeley, Cal., 1959), Ch. 4.

tinkerers, then came into their own; that the connection between parental wealth and status and the son's career was loosened, so that members of the business elite typically had lower social origins and less education, and were often of immigrant stock. Plausible, yes, but true, no. It helped to go to Harvard in Thomas Jefferson's America, and it seems to have helped just about as much in William McKinley's America. There were the Edisons and Fords, who rose spectacularly from low origins, but there were always a few such. Cases like these were about as exceptional in the late nineteenth century as they were earlier. The image of the great inventor springing from common soil, unspoiled by book-larnin', is a red herring. It is doubtful, to say the least, that the less you know, the more likely you are to build a better mousetrap. And in any event it was not the great inventor who raked in the money, in most cases—Henry Ford never invented anything—but rather the organizer and manipulator, whose talents seem to have been highly valued through all periods of American history.

These conclusions are interesting, but an important caution is in order. It by no means follows that if there was very little room at the top, there was little room anywhere else. It is absurd to judge the openness or lack of openness of an entire social system solely by the extent of recruitment from below into the highest positions of all. One can imagine a society in which all members of the tiny elite are democratically recruited from below, and yet where the social structure as a whole is extremely rigid with that small exception. Conversely, one can imagine a society with a hereditary ruling group at the very top, a group completely closed to aspiring men of talent but lowly birth, and yet with an enormous amount of movement back and forth below that pinnacle. Late nineteenth-century America could have approximated this latter model, with lineage, parental wealth, and education as decisive assets in the race for the very peak, as the business elite studies suggest, and yet with great fluidity at the lower and middle levels of the class structure.

Was this in fact the case? The evidence available today is regrettably scanty, but here are the broad outlines of an answer, insofar as we can generalize from a handful of studies.[8] At the lower and middle ranges

[8] The main sources for the generalizations which follow, unless otherwise indicated, are: Stephan Thernstrom, *Poverty and Progress: Social Mobility in a Nineteenth Century City* (Cambridge, Mass., 1964); Merle E. Curti, *The Making of an American Frontier Community* (Stanford, Cal., 1959); Donald B. Cole, *Immigrant City: Lawrence, Massachusetts, 1845–1921* (Chapel Hill, N.C., 1963)—for my reservations about this work, however, see my review in the *Journal of Economic History*, XXIV (1964), 259–61; Herbert G. Gutman, "Social Status and Social Mobility in 19th Century America: Paterson, N.J., A Case Study," unpublished paper for the 1964 meetings of the American Historical Association; Howard Gitelman, "The Labor Force at Waltham Watch During the Civil War Era," *Journal of Economic History*, XXV (1965), 214–43; David Brody, *Steelworkers in America: The Non-*

of the class structure there was impressive mobility, though often of an unexpected and rather ambiguous kind. I will distinguish three types of mobility: geographical, occupational, and property, and say a little about the extent and significance of each.

First is geographical mobility, physical movement from place to place, which is tied up in an interesting way with movement through the social scale. Americans have long been thought a restless, footloose people, and it has been assumed that the man on the move has been the man on the make; he knows that this little town doesn't provide a grand enough stage for him to display his talents, and so he goes off to the big city to win fame and fortune, or to the open frontier to do likewise. When you examine actual behavior instead of popular beliefs, however, you discover that things are more complicated than that.

It proves to be true that Americans are indeed a footloose people. In my work on Newburyport, a small industrial city, I attempted to find out what fraction of the families present in the community in the initial year of my study—1850—were still living there in the closing year, 1880, one short generation. Less than a fifth of them, it turned out—and this not in a community on the moving frontier, like Merle Curti's Trempealeau County, where you would expect a very high turnover. There the true pioneer types, who liked to clear the land, became nervous when there was another family within a half day's ride of them and sold out to the second wave of settlers (often immigrants who knew better than to try to tame the wilderness without previous experience at it). But to find roughly the same volatility in a city forty miles north of Boston suggests that the whole society was in motion.

The statistics bear out the legend that Americans are a restless people. What of the assertion that movement and success go hand in hand, that physical mobility and upward social mobility are positively correlated? Here the legend seems more questionable. It seems likely that some who pulled up stakes and went elsewhere for a new start did improve their positions; they found better land, or discovered that they possessed talents which were much more highly valued in the big city than in the place they came from. What ever would have happened to Theodore Dreiser in small-town Indiana had there been no Chicago for him to flee to?

But the point to underline, for it is less commonly understood, is that much of this remarkable population turnover was of quite a different kind. As you trace the flow of immigrants into and then out of the cities,

union Era (Cambridge, Mass., 1960); Pauline Gordon, "The Chance to Rise Within Industry" (unpublished M.A. thesis, Columbia University): Robert Wheeler, "The Fifth-Ward Irish: Mobility at Mid-Century" (unpublished seminar paper, Brown University, 1967): and the author's research in progress on social mobility in Boston over the past century, in which the career patterns of some 8,000 ordinary residents of the community are traced.

you begin to see that a great many of those who departed did so in circumstances which make it exceedingly hard to believe that they were moving on to bigger and better things elsewhere. There is no way to be certain about this, no feasible method of tracing individuals once they disappear from the universe of the community under consideration. These questions can be explored for contemporary America by administering questionnaires to people and collecting life histories which display migration patterns, but dead men tell no tales and fill out no questionnaires, so that part of the past is irrevocably lost. But some plausible inferences can be drawn about the nature of this turnover from the fact that so many ordinary working people on the move owned no property, had no savings accounts, had acquired no special skills, and were most likely to leave when they were unemployed. They were, in short, people who had made the least successful economic adjustment to the community and who were no longer able to hang on there. At the lower reaches of the social order, getting out of town did not ordinarily mean a step up the ladder somewhere else; there is no reason to assume that in their new destinations migrant laborers found anything but more of the same. When middle-class families, who already had a niche in the world, moved on, it was often in response to greater opportunities elsewhere; for ordinary working people physical movement meant something very different.

That is a less rosy picture than the one usually painted, but I think it is more accurate. And we should notice one very important implication of this argument: namely, that the people who were least successful and who had the greatest grievances are precisely those who never stayed put very long in any one place. Students of labor economics and trade union history have long been aware of the fact that there are certain occupations which are inordinately difficult to organize simply because they have incessant job turnover. When only 5 percent or 1 percent of the men working at a particular job in a given city at the start of the year are still employed twelve months later, as is the case with some occupations in the economic underworld today (short-order cooks or menial hospital workers, for instance), how do you build a stable organization and conduct a successful strike?

An analogous consideration applies not merely to certain selected occupations but to a large fraction of the late nineteenth-century urban working class as a whole. The Marxist model of the conditions which promote proletarian consciousness presumes not only permanency of membership in this class—the absence of upward mobility—but also, I suggest, some continuity of class membership *in one setting* so that workers come to know each other and to develop bonds of solidarity and common opposition to the ruling group above them. This would seem to entail a stable labor force in a single factory; at a minimum it assumes considerable stability in a community. One reason that a permanent proletariat along the lines envisaged by Marx did not develop in the course of American industrialization is perhaps that few Americans have *stayed* in one place, one workplace, or even one city long enough to discover a sense of common identity and common grievance. This may be a vital clue to the divergent political development of America and Western Europe in the industrial age, to the striking weakness of socialism here, as compared to Europe—though we can't be sure because we don't definitely know that the European working-class population was less volatile. I suspect that it was, to some degree, and that America was distinctive in this respect, but this is a question of glaring importance which no one has yet taken the trouble to investigate.

When I first stumbled upon this phenomenon in sifting through manuscript census schedules for nineteenth-century Newburyport, I was very doubtful that the findings could be generalized to apply to the big cities of the period. It seemed reasonable to assume that the laborers who drifted out of Newburyport so quickly after the arrival must have settled down somewhere else, and to think that a great metropolis would have offered a more inviting haven than a small city, where anonymity was impossible and where middle-class institutions of social control intruded into one's daily life with some frequency, as compared to a classic big-city lower-class ghetto, where the down-and-out could perhaps huddle together for protective warmth and be left to their own devices—for instance, those Irish wards of New York where the police made no attempt to enforce law and order until late in the century. Here if anywhere one should be able to find a continuous lower-class population, a permanent proletariat, and I began my Boston research with great curiosity about this point.

If Boston is any example, in no American city was there a sizable lower class with great continuity of membership. You can identify some more or less continuously lower-class areas, but the crucial point is that *the same people do not stay in them.* If you take a sample of unskilled and semiskilled laborers in Boston in 1880 and look for them in 1890, you are not much more likely to find them still in the city than was the case in Newburyport.[9]

---

[9] Recent work suggesting that even the most recent U.S. Census seriously undernumerated the Negro male population may make the critical reader wonder about the accuracy of the census and city directory canvases upon which I base my analysis. Some elaborate checking has persuaded me that these nineteenth-century sources erred primarily in their coverage—their lack of coverage, rather—of the floating working-class population. For a variety of reasons it seems clear that families which had been in the community long enough to be included in one of these canvases— and hence to be included in a sample drawn from them—were rarely left out of later canvases if they were indeed still resident in the same city. A perfect census of every soul in the community on a given day would therefore yield even higher, not a lower, estimate of population turnover for men at the bottom, which strengthens rather than weakens the argument advanced here.

The bottom layer of the social order in the nineteenth-century American city was thus a group of families who appear to have been permanent transients, buffeted about from place to place, never quite able to sink roots. We know very little about these people, and it is difficult to know how we can learn much about them. You get only occasional glimpses into the part of this iceberg that appears above the surface, in the person of the tramp, who first is perceived as a problem for America in the 1870s and reappears in hard times after that—in the 1890s and in the great depression most notably. But what has been said here at least suggests the significance of the phenomenon.

So much for geographical mobility. What can be said about the people who come to the city and remain there under our microscope so that we can discern what happened to them? I have already anticipated my general line of argument here in my discussion of migration out of the city —which amounted to the claim that the city was a kind of Darwinian jungle in which the fittest survived and the others drifted on to try another place. Those who did stay in the city and made their way there did, in general, succeed in advancing themselves economically and socially. There was very impressive mobility, though not always of the kind we might expect.

In approaching this matter, we must make a distinction which is obscured by applying labels like "open" or "fluid" to entire whole social structures. There are, after all, two sets of escalators in any community; one set goes down. To describe a society as enormously fluid implies that there are lots of people moving down while lots of others are moving up to take their place. This would obviously be a socially explosive situation, for all those men descending against their will would arrive at the bottom, not with low horizons of expectation set in some peasant village, but with expectations established when they were at one of the comfortable top floors of the structure.

Downward mobility is by no means an unknown phenomenon in American history. There have been socially displaced groups, especially if you take into account rather subtle shifts in the relative status of such groups as professionals.[10] But the chief generalization to make is that Americans who started their working life in a middle-class job strongly

---

[10] The assumption that discontent stemming from social displacement has been the motive force behind American reform movements has exerted great influence upon American historical writing in recent years. See for instance David Donald, "Toward a Reconsideration of Abolitionists," *Lincoln Reconsidered* (New York, 1956), pp. 19–36; Richard Hofstadter, *The Age of Reform: From Bryan to F.D.R.* (New York, 1955). Donald's essay is easily demolished by anyone wtih the slightest acquaintance with sociological method. Hofstadter's work, while open to a very serious objection, is at least sufficiently suggestive to indicate the potential utility of the idea.

tended to end up in the middle class; sons reared in middle-class families also attained middle-class occupations in the great majority of cases. Relatively few men born into the middle class fell from there; a good many born into the working class either escaped from it altogether or advanced themselves significantly within the class. There is a well-established tradition of writing about the skilled workman, associated with such names as the Hammonds, the Lynds, Lloyd Warner, and Norman Ware, which holds the contrary, to be sure.[11] This tradition still has its defenders, who argue that with industrialization "class lines assumed a new and forbidding rigidity" and that "machines made obsolete many of the skilled trades of the antebellum years, drawing the once self-respecting handicraftsmen into the drudgery and monotony of factory life, where they were called upon to perform only one step in the minutely divided and automatic processes of mass production."[12] Rapid technological change doubtless did displace some skilled artisans, doubtless produced some downward mobility into semiskilled positions. But defenders of this view have built their case upon little more than scattered complaints by labor leaders, and have not conducted systematic research to verify these complaints.

Careful statistical analysis provides a very different perspective on the matter. Two points stand out. One is that as certain traditional skilled callings became obsolete, there was an enormous expansion of *other* skilled trades, and, since many of the craftsmen under pressure from technological change had rather generalized skills, they moved rapidly into these new positions and thus retained their place in the labor aristocracy.[13] Second, it is quite mistaken to assume that the sons of the threatened artisan were commonly driven down into the ranks of the factory operatives; they typically found a place either in the expanding skilled trades or in the even more rapidly expanding white-collar occupations.[14]

As for workers on the lower rungs of the occupational ladder, the unskilled and semiskilled, they had rarely drifted down from a higher beginning point. Characteristically, they were newcomers to the urban

[11] J. L. and Barbara Hammond, *The Town Labourer (1760–1832)* (London, 1917); Robert S. and Helen M. Lynd, *Middletown* (New York, 1929), and *Middletown in Transition* (New York, 1937); W. Lloyd Warner and J. O. Low, *The Social System of the Modern Factory* (New Haven, Conn., 1947); Norman J. Ware, *The Industrial Worker, 1840–1860* (Boston, 1924).

[12] Leon Litwak, ed., *The American Labor Movement* (Englewood Cliffs, N.J., 1962), p. 3.

[13] This is evident from aggregated census data and from my Boston investigation, but we badly need an American counterpart to Eric Hobsbawm's splendid essay on "The Labour Aristocracy in Nineteenth Century Britain," in *Labouring Men: Studies in the History of Labour* (London, 1964), pp. 272–315.

[14] So, at least, the evidence from Boston and Indianapolis indicates; for the latter, see Natlic Rogoff, *Recent Trends in Occupational Mobility* (Glencoe, Ill., 1953).

world. A substantial minority of them appear to have been able to advance themselves a notch or two occupationally, especially among the second generation; a good many of their sons became clerks, salesmen, and other petty white-collar functionaries. And the first generation, which had less success occupationally, was commonly experiencing mobility of another kind—property mobility. Despite a pathetically low (but generally rising) wage level, despite heavy unemployment rates, many were able to accumulate significant property holdings and to establish themselves as members of the stable working class, as opposed to the drifting lower class.[15]

It may seem paradoxical to suggest that so many Americans were rising in the world and so few falling; where did the room at the top come from? The paradox is readily resolved. For one thing, our attention has been fastened upon individuals who remained physically situated in one place in which their careers could be traced; an indeterminate but substantial fraction of the population was floating and presumably unsuccessful. By no means everyone at the bottom was upwardly mobile; the point is rather that those who were not were largely invisible. Furthermore, the occupational structure itself was changing in a manner that created disproportionately more positions in the middle and upper ranges, despite the common nineteenth-century belief that industrialization was homogenizing the work force and reducing all manual employees to identical robots. The homogenizing and degrading tendencies that caught the eye of Marx and others were more than offset, it appears, by developments which made for both a more differentiated and a more top-heavy occupational structure. Third, there were important sources of social mobility that could be attained without changing one's occupation, most notably the property mobility that was stimulated by the increases in real wages that occurred in this period. Finally, there was the so-called "demographic vacuum" created by the differential fertility of the social classes, best illustrated in the gloomy late nineteenth-century estimate that in two hundred years 1,000 Harvard graduates would have only 50 living descendants while 1,000 Italians would have 100,000. The calculation is dubious, but the example nicely clarifies the point that high-status groups failed to repro-

[15] The clearest demonstration of this is in Thernstrom, *Poverty and Progress,* Ch. 5. It might be thought, however, that the remarkable property mobility disclosed there depended upon the existence of an abundant stock of cheap single-family housing available for purchase. It could be that where real estate was less readily obtainable, laborers would squander the funds that were accumulated with such sacrifice in places where home ownership was an immediate possibility. It appears from Wheeler's unpublished study of nineteenth-century Providence, however, that the working-class passion for property did not require an immediate, concrete source of satisfaction like a home and a plot of land. The Irish workmen of Providence were just as successful at accumulating property holdings as their Newburyport counterparts; the difference was only that they held personal rather than real property.

duce themselves, thus opening up vacancies which had necessarily to be filled by new men from below.

For all the brutality and rapacity which marked the American scene in the years in which the new urban industrial order came into being, what stands out most is the relative absence of collective working-class protest aimed at reshaping capitalist society. The foregoing, while hardly a full explanation, should help to make this more comprehensible. The American working class was drawn into the new society by a process that encouraged accommodation and rendered disciplined protest difficult. Within the urban industrial orbit, most of its members found modest but significant opportunities to feel that they and their children were edging their way upwards. Those who did not find such opportunities were tossed helplessly about from city to city, from state to state, alienated but invisible and impotent.

2.3

Class, Status, and the Gilded-Age Radical:
A Reconsideration.
The Case of a New Jersey Socialist

HERBERT G. GUTMAN

In this study of the political influence of the exiled Irish Fenian and socialist Joseph P. McDonnell, who became a prominent American trade unionist and social reformer, one of the co-editors suggests how ethnic self-awareness and working-class culture combined among the New Jersey Irish to sustain a coherent, but little understood, community structure. From such communities in Gilded Age cities came grass roots political movements that emphasized material betterment and social reform. A coherent community structure allowed these lower-class first- and second-generation immigrants enough leverage to begin to humanize the emerging industrial social system. Urban life for such persons involved more than the brutalized everyday existence frequently emphasized by that period's social historians. The evidence presented suggests that awareness of "poverty" did not await its discovery by sensitive members of the middle and upper classes in the early twentieth century.

Herbert G. Gutman, from a speech entitled "Class, Status, and the Gilded-Age Radical: A Reconsideration. The Case of a New Jersey Socialist," delivered on April 19, 1968 at the Thirteenth Yale Conference on the Training of Social Studies, "The Concept of the Radical in American History."

The following works are suggested for further reading:

HERBERT G. GUTMAN, "Class, Status and Community Power in Nineteenth Century American Industrial Cities—Paterson, New Jersey: A Case Study" in Frederic Cople Jaher (ed.) *The Age of Industrialism in America,* New York: 1968, pp. 263–87.

———, "Culture, Work, Conflict and Discontinuity in American Working Class History. The Recurrent Tension Between Pre-Industrial Cultures and Industrial Society, 1815–1920," *American Historical Review* (1973) (forthcoming).

———, "The Worker's Search for Power: Labor in the Gilded Age" in H. Wayne Morgan (ed.) *The Gilded Age,* Syracuse: Syracuse University Press, 1963, pp. 38–68.

This essay considers a single individual in order to assess his career but more important to reexamine certain general views of the Gilded Age American radical and of the Gilded Age itself. An Irish immigrant, Joseph Patrick McDonnell was a socialist, a trade union organizer, a lobbyist for protective and reform legislation, and a New Jersey newspaper editor. Orthodox labor history relates these facts and little more. Standard historical works of a broader sort entirely ignore men like McDonnell. Yet he was a figure of some importance between 1873 and 1893 and typified an entire generation of Gilded Age labor radicals. Men like McDonnell played dominant roles in the labor and radical movements of that time. They were harsh critics of the emerging industrial society. They pioneered in early legislative efforts to humanize a changing and an insensitive social order.

These are significant facts. Why, then, is so little known about radical and working-class leaders like J. P. McDonnell? Recreating the past is an ongoing and a selective process. But the principles that guide such selection are not objective and are often shaped by a particular overview (a general interpretation) of a past era. The dominant view of Gilded Age America allows little room for radicals like McDonnell and much else of importance. At best, such men are counted as nagging and ineffective reminders that conscience and moral purpose did not entirely wilt in that American Dark Age. At worst, such men exist beyond the fringe or simply are forgotten by a collective memory cramped by certain crude and misleading stereotypes that give conceptual shape to the Gilded Age. Men like McDonnell are misunderstood, minimized, or entirely neglected. Their role as critic escapes the historian. Their successes and failures confuse the historian. The Gilded Age radical lives outside the mainstream of his times. Even his own historians emphasize this fact and often study the radical and his movements as little more than exercises in exposure. Historians of the working-class accept this larger view, too, and their writing records mainly bitter industrial conflicts as well as the tiresome inner struggles between working-class leaders over principles of organization as well as strategy and tactics. Together with the more general historians, they concede that the age belonged to Andrew Carnegie. Disaffected workers, moralists like Henry George, Edward Bellamy, and Henry Demarest Lloyd, agrarians like the Populists, and scattered mugwump intellectuals were eloquent but powerless censors. Displaced craftsmen, rural folk, and utopian intellectuals, they were overwhelmed by a national ethos that thrived on an ugly materialism, deified the dollar, and worshipped in the marketplace. There is some truth in this perspective, and much has been learned from it. But it is defective in essential ways.

In examining McDonnell's role and influence, we do more than just study a single man. We reconsider the status of the Gilded Age radical and the character of the Gilded Age itself. The reason is important: careful assessment of his radical efforts challenges some of the comfortable clichés about the Gilded Age that saturate our historiography and obscure our past.

I

We first consider the dominant view of the Gilded Age more closely. Historians correctly emphasize indisputably significant themes such as industrialization, urbanization, and immigration and see the post-Civil War decades as a time (in Sigmund Diamond's words) when the "nation" was "transformed." Certain widely held assumptions affect their treatment of these themes and should be summarized (perhaps too simply, but this is a short paper). Industrialism was still new to most Gilded Age Americans —new as a way of work and new as a way of life. Its norms were not yet internalized, institutionalized, or legitimized. Yet the Gilded Age is described as a time when industrialization generated new kinds of economic power which, in turn, immediately altered the older social and political structure. Much follows from this flawed assumption. In another connection, I have summarized some of its implications. Studying Gilded Age social conflict as reported by most historians is to learn:

> that the worker was isolated from the rest of society; that the employer had an easy time and relatively free hand in imposing [new] disciplines; that the spirit of the times, the ethic of the Gilded Age, worked to the advantage of the owner of industrial property; that workers found little if any sympathy from nonworkers; that the quest for wealth obliterated nonpecuniary values; and that industrialists swept aside countless obsta-

cles with great ease. The usual picture of these years portrays the absolute power of the employer over his workers and emphasizes his ability to manipulate a sympathetic public opinion as well as various political, legal, and social institutions to his advantage.

No one has expressed this view more cogently than Louis Hacker. Writing in 1966, he insisted:

> The end of the Civil War . . . cleared the way for the triumph of American industrial capitalism . . . Far from being sharply critical of the capitalist processes of private accumulation, investment, and decision-making, Americans, *almost to a man,* veered to the opposite position; what before had been rejection now became assent. This new climate produced new institutions (values and attitudes) to support and strengthen industrial capitalism; in the law-text writers . . . ; in the writers of economy texts; . . . in the acceptance by the clergy of a market economy with its unequal distributive shares; in the programs and formulations of the labor organizations. *Americans, almost universally, during 1865–1900, when industrial capitalism made its swiftest progress in the United States, looked upon a market economy founded on the rules of laissez-faire . . . as the normal, more the right, way of life.* (italics added.)

So bold a statement exaggerates what others often accept in more quiet and subtle ways. J. P. McDonnell's career allows us to examine this view.

II

When Joseph McDonnell crossed the Atlantic in December 1872 to settle permanently in the Great Republic of the West (first in New York City and then in Paterson, New Jersey), he already was a radical. Then just twenty-five years old, he carried unusual baggage with him. Four arrests and three prison terms suggest that he was not typical of the immigrant millions pouring into post-Civil War America. Militant Irish nationalism and socialism had shaped his formative years. Never a worker, he was born to a middle-class Dublin family in 1847, attended Dublin's schools and its university, and prepared for the priesthood. Irish nationalism ended his formal education. He refused to take the Maynooth Oath, joined the National Brotherhood (the Fenians), helped edit Irish nationalist newspapers, and soon spent ten months in Dublin's Mount Joy Prison. Just twenty-one, he quit Ireland in 1868 to live in London for five years. Lectures and impressive public demonstrations that he organized urged amnesty for Irish political prisoners and independence for Ireland. In 1869, to cite one example, he led several thousand persons in a July 4 march from London to Gravesend. They carried Irish and American flags. London street demonstrations twice resulted in his arrest.

More than the cause of Ireland attracted McDonnell's concern and support during his London years. Working-class social movements won his allegiance. In 1869, the *Sheffield Journal* called McDonnell "a full-fledged Republican—disloyal but highly talented." He went to Geneva to an International Peace Congress, stayed in London for an International Prison Congress, and helped organize the Anglo-Irish Agricultural Union. The Franco-Prussian War caused yet another arrest after McDonnell formed an "Irish Brigade" that hoped to leave England illegally to support the French Republicans against their German enemies. McDonnell publicly endorsed the Paris Commune, won nomination to Parliament from London, and organized massive street parades and demonstrations to test the right of public assembly and free speech. He also joined the International Working Men's Association, associated with Karl Marx, became a socialist, and served as Irish secretary of the Internationals General Council. McDonnell brought these experiences and values with him to the United States in 1872. Few other immigrants carried to industrializing America so full and so complete a set of radical credentials.

His five years in New York City followed a predictable pattern. Socialist and labor agitation consumed his time. On his arrival, McDonnell's bitter letters filled long columns in the *New York Herald* as he exposed steerage conditions on immigrant vessels. "Better accommodation is provided for cattle . . . than . . . for human beings," fumed the new immigrant. Challenged in print by a less angry passenger, socialist McDonnell exploded:

> He evidently has more money than heart and belongs to that intelligent class of Englishmen who delight in discussing the qualities of dogs and horses over their punch and pipes. It is a well known fact that such men are very humane when horses or dogs are concerned, but their eyes are blind and their ears deaf to the miseries of the poor and toiling.

McDonnell told American readers he had "allied" himself "permanently with the great proletarian movement throughout Europe," and that steerage abuses of immigrants proved once more "that there is one law for the poor and another for the rich, even on the ocean."

Between 1873 and 1878, McDonnell involved himself deeply in the faction-ridden, tiny New York City socialist movement. These were busy but not fruitful years. Calling himself a "journalist and orator," McDonnell lectured widely and traveled the east coast to spread socialism and to strengthen existing craft unions and build collective strength among the unskilled factory workers. After 1876, he gave much time to editing the *New York Labor Standard,* a Marxist weekly. His public lectures revealed a large but not total debt to Marx: "The modern State has given them [the workers] perfect freedom to go whither they list and die when they please. It is that system which has turned earth into a Hell for the toiler and a Heaven for the idle monopolist." A second lecture told that the promise of America remained unfulfilled: "The despot Poverty seizes our noblest intellect by the throat and stifles out its genius. . . . Law which the founders of the Republic meant to be Justice is now only a farce when invoked for the protection of innocence or humanity," Even the *Labor Standard* survived a difficult birth, factionalism aborted the socialist movement that had given it life. McDonnell himself attracted little notice outside radical and labor circles. During the 1877 railroad strikes and riots (which McDonnell called a "a sort of guerilla warfare" by workers "for their rights"), he pleaded with New York City workers: "The laziest hog can grunt; if we are Men we shall not grunt any more, we shall act. . . . We must organize; unorganized we are a mob and a rabble; organized in one compact body we are a power to be respected. . . . Union is your shepherd." A similar speech in Baltimore (the scene of much bloodshed and industrial violence) finally caused the *New York Times* to notice McDonnell but only to warn that he preached "disorganizing doctrines" and "the unadulterated gospel of communism" to "loafers and ruffians." That was in August of 1877. A year later, McDonnell moved himself and his newspaper from New York City to Paterson and settled permanently in that New Jersey industrial city.

Failure and factionalism pushed the radical McDonnell from New York City. But the condition of the silk and other textile workers (the largest number of them women and children) together with his desire to organize them into the International Labor Union pulled McDonnell to Paterson. By then, he and a few other socialists had made common cause with New England labor radicals like Ira Steward and George McNeill hoping to organize unskilled factory workers and to spark a movement among them for shorter hours that would end by abolishing the "wages-system." Before that time, McDonnell had occasionally lectured to the Paterson workers. In 1876, he had helped some Paterson radicals celebrate bitterly the nation's centennial at an open air meeting at the Passaic Falls. A general strike by Paterson silk ribbon weavers in 1877 had commanded sympathetic attention in his New York newspaper. A year later, a nine-month strike by unorganized women and girls against the nation's largest cotton mosquito net manufacturer convinced McDonnell that Paterson was fertile ground to plant his radicalism. He moved there, helped organize the cotton strikers, and renamed his newspaper the *Paterson Labor Standard*. Across its masthead, he emblazoned the words of Karl Marx: "The Emancipation of the Working Classes Must be Achieved by the Working Classes Themselves." In its columns, he defended the Paterson workers and scorned their employers. McDonnell addressed the cotton strikers:

All hail! Your struggle is the struggle of humanity for humanity. Your warfare is the warfare of human hearts against a heart of stone. Your contest is that of human flesh against the Dagon of gold. . . . Those who serve a lordly autocrat to cut down the living of full grown human beings without a word do sell themselves for slaves. . . . Whoever holds his food at the will of another, he is the other man's slave.

McDonnell minced no words in demeaning the factory owner:

Sir, you are a man born to the image and likeness of your Creator. . . . You ought to remember that you have sprung from poverty, that you are nothing, and that in the natural order of events, death will close your eyes in a few more years. What will all your ill-gotten wealth then avail you? Your mills will stand as monuments of your cruelty. . . . The greatness that is won by shattering the health and happiness of thousands, driving young men to crime and young women to prostitution is the greatness of Lucifer. Be just and fear not. . . . Descend from the pedestal of your sinful pride, and wipe away some of the stains from your past life.

Paterson residents got a different message. In its first issue, the *Labor Standard* warned:

After a century of Political independence, we find that our social system is not better than that of Europe and that labor in this Republic is not better than that of Europe, and that labor in this Republic, as in the European monarchies, is the slave of capitalism, instead of being the master of its own products.

McDonnell argued that to save "the Republic . . . from monarchy and ruin"—even from "a dreadful revolution"—"steps" had "to be taken and at once to prevent the march of poverty and the growth of industrial despotism."

Such severe printed words were new to Paterson and shocked and worried otherwise uneasy manufacturers and their supporters. From his start, therefore, McDonnell faced critics who wanted to stamp out the growth that he and his newspaper nurtured. Soon after his arrival, in October 1878, loyal nonstrikers convinced a county grand jury to indict McDonnell because the *Labor Standard* had called them "scabs." A citizen's jury found McDonnell guilty of libel, and a judge fined him $500. A year later, McDonnell angered a local brick manufacturer. His newspaper published a letter from Michael Menton, a young, itinerant common laborer, which exposed working and living conditions in his Passaic River Brickyard. The manufacturer charged McDonnell and Menton with libel. A court found them guilty. They were fined, and in early 1880

McDonnell and Menton spent nearly three months in the Passaic County jail.

III

Nothing yet in McDonnell's career challenges the general view sketched earlier of Gilded Age America. Quite the contrary. His two trials and his imprisonment illustrate and strengthen that view. But these few facts are not the full story. McDonnell left prison in 1880. Despite much difficulty, his newspaper survived its early troubled years and remained a weekly labor paper until McDonnell's death in 1908. More important, less than four years after his release from prison a New Jersey governor appointed McDonnell as the state's first Deputy Inspector of Factories and Workshops. Although he held that position for less than a year, in 1892 he was chosen to head New Jersey's short-lived State Board of Arbitration.

Even these appointments lose significance beside other information about McDonnell's post-1880 career. McDonnell and a few other trade unionists, labor reformers, and radicals founded the New Jersey Labor Congress in 1879 and a few years later changed its name to the Federation of Organized Trades and Labor Unions of the State of New Jersey. Between 1883 and 1897, McDonnell headed the Federation's Legislative Committee. The Federation never was a powerful body. Its constituent organizations never represented more than 65,000 workers and less than a third of that number in the 1890s. For a few years, the dispute between the craft unions and the Knights of Labor severely weakened it. Its annual expenditures rarely exceeded $250 before 1900.

And yet, between 1883 and 1892, much of the spirit and pressure that resulted in remedial laws to check the freedom of the industrialist and to improve the condition of working people and other citizens came from this small group. Each year, McDonnell and other members of the Federation's Legislative Committee drew up laws and organized campaigns to prod Trenton legislators for their support. Not all of their efforts were successful. A factory inspector and several deputies were empowered to enforce these laws, but some laws were badly written. Few of these laws passed without bitter legislative battles, and some became statutes only after amendments had weakened them. But their range was impressive and their intent clear. McDonnell believed that the State's major duty was to satisfy "the wants of those who by their toil are the architects of the State's greatness," and the laws satisfied that objective. The list of laws passed after 1883 is too long to be catalogued fully but deserves brief summary. In 1883 and 1884, the state checked contract convict labor and child labor for the first time. A year later, the first of eight general factory laws passed between 1885 and 1893 took effect. These laws began civilizing primitive factory working conditions. Some provided for fire escapes and adequate factory ventilation; others required protective covering on dangerous machinery, belts, and gearing. Another limited the employment of children in dangerous occupations; factories were required to provide seats and suitable dressing rooms for women. Other laws incorporated trade unions, cooperatives, and working-class building and loan associations. Archaic conspiracy legislation was repealed. Non-residents, often Pinkerton police, were prohibited from serving as public officers. Labor Day became a legal holiday first in New Jersey. So did the fifty-five hour week for workers engaged in manufacturing. McDonnell and the Federation drew up and won even broader social reforms including ballot reform, the protection of tenants from landlords, the founding of public libraries, and, most important, the state's first comprehensive compulsory education law. "No better measure ever passed a legislative body," argued McDonnell, "and no state in the United States can boast of having a better system of compulsory education." Reviewing this law and others like it enacted between 1883 and 1892, McDonnell concluded: "The interests of the wage earners have been promoted through legislation. . . . No other state in the United States can show greater accomplishments by legislation for the welfare of the wage class during a like period."

After 1892, McDonnell's efforts were much less successful and he and others like him despaired greatly, but McDonnell deserved much credit for the earlier successes. "Every labor law on the state statute books of New Jersey owes its birth to the fostering care and indefatigable work of McDonnell," said the *Boston Post* in 1897. "Not a tithe can be told of all he has done for the betterment of mankind." But to say only this is to miss the larger significance of McDonnell's career. He could not have done this much alone. And it is here that we return to the larger view of Gilded Age America. McDonnell survived despite his Paterson critics; he won two state-appointed offices; he engineered significant legislative victories that industrialists bitterly opposed. Why was this possible? Why was this radical critic able to affect the political system in ways that promoted pioneering reform legislation? Answers to these questions require that we examine neglected but important aspects of the Gilded Age social, economic, and political structure.

IV

So brief a paper cannot entirely alter the larger view of Gilded Age America, but it can suggest new ways of looking at that world so that McDonnell's career and much else fall into place better. We must first put aside the view that the industrialist had authority as well as power because his ownership of "things" (machinery and a new technology) together with a widely shared set of beliefs that sanctified property, entrepreneurship, and social mobility gave him unexampled social prestige and exceedingly high status. British social historian Asa Briggs starts us looking in a more useful direction when he writes: "In order to understand how people respond to industrial change, it is necessary to examine fully what kind of people they were at the beginning of the process, to take account of continuities and traditions as well as new ways of thinking and feeling."

Industrialization caused the United States to change more rapidly and more radically after the Civil War than at any previous time, but these fundamental changes did not result in the hasty breakdown of an older social structure and in the disappearance of older patterns of thought among those most directly affected by such changes. Quite possibly, economic change occurred so swiftly that few had the "time," psychologically or historically, to be separated or alienated from a different but not distant past. Those who lived in Gilded Age America did not yearn to return to some mythic Golden Age but were a transitional generation that bridged two distinct social structures and ways of life. Many made the adjustment easily, but it does not follow that they shared values with the industrialist, sanctioned his new social role, and quickly granted him high status. For still others, the Gilded Age meant new and discomforting dependent relationships that violated deeply-held beliefs and norms and were alien to traditional American notions of independence and self-reliance. "Traditional social habits and customs seldom fitted into the new pattern of industrial life, and they had therefore to be discredited as hindrances to progress." So writes another British historian of his country. Similar "hindrances" existed in Gilded Age America. Industrial capitalism created new satisfactions and many opportunities, but to say only this is to neglect that it also threatened an older social structure and that the tension between the two was a major source of much of the violence and conflict so characteristic of Gilded Age America.

Many persons new to the urban-industrial world did not settle easily into a factory-centered civilization. McDonnell was one of them. More significant, however, is the fact that McDonnell's survival, much less his success, depended on such tension and conflict. Certain elements in the pre-industrial American social structure and in older patterns of popular ideology persisted strongly into the post-Civil War urban world, profoundly affected behavior, and served as a source of recurrent opposition to the power and status of the new industrialist. At times, they narrowed the industrialist's freedom of action and widened McDonnell's opportunities. Four such "factors" deserve brief note and then illustration:

First: Not all urban property owners and professionals shared common values with the industrialist. Older patterns of thought and social ties persisted among such persons and often alienated them from the new industrialist. Some became his severe critics. Others supported men like McDonnell.

Second: Vital subcultures among the immigrant and native-born poor as well as among the more substantial craftsmen and artisans thrived in Gilded Age America and were sustained by particular norms that shared little with the industrialist and his culture.

Third: Such subcultures were especially important in the Gilded Age industrial town and city and gave its social structure a particular shape and its quality of life a special tone.

Fourth: Politics in the industrial city was affected by these subcultures and an awareness of a potential (and, at times, active) working-class political presence. Many industrial city politicians had special ties to working-class and immigrant voters that usually filtered through a political machine but nevertheless affected the style of politics.

McDonnell's status and power rested on this world. Without support from it, his efforts would have failed, and he would have earned the anonymity that historians undeservedly have assigned to him.

V

It is unfortunate that so little is yet known about the Gilded Age industrial city because most of the significant changes that altered traditional American society focused on such places. Tensions between the old and the new social structure were sharpest there. Immigrant and working-class subculture was most vital there. To say this is not to minimize all else but to locate just where the factory, the worker, and the immigrant intersected. New Jersey was the nation's sixth largest industrial state in 1880. Ten years later, five major manufacturing cities (Camden, Jersey City, Newark, Paterson, and Trenton) counted one third of the state's population and more than half of its 150,000 factory workers. Immigrants (ninety percent of them in 1890 still from Ireland, Germany, and Great Britain) settled overwhelmingly in these and smaller industrial towns. Because its main industries were diverse (especially boots and shoes, jewelry, thread, shirts, scissors, felt hats, and leather goods), Newark, the state's largest city, was untypical. One or two industries characterized the usual New Jersey industrial city. The dock and railroad workers of Bayonne, Hoboken, and Jersey City gave those towns a special character, but large sugar refineries and the huge Lorillard tobacco factory centered in Jersey City and the mammouth Standard Oil refineries towered over Bayonne. Iron miners and iron mill workers lived in the Sussex and Morris county towns. Trenton had important iron and steel works, and its potteries made it the center of the American whiteware (common table dishes) industry. Camden was best known for its iron factories and shipyards. Orange specialized in the manufacture of hats. Southern New Jersey towns such as Bridgeton, Minatola, Millville, and Glassboro made that region a major producer of varied glass products. Paterson's silk and other textile factories caused it to be called the Lyons of America, but its workers also labored in locomotive, iron, and machine shops. Although the social history of such towns has not yet been written, sufficient scattered evidence indicates the presence of vital clusters of urban working-class subculture, a diversity of attitudes among nonworkers toward industrial power, and unique patterns of protest and politics essential to understand the larger developments of that time.

Let us turn first to McDonnell's trials and his imprisonment to see what it was that protected him from his early critics and allowed him to make Paterson his permanent home. Paterson was a model industrial city. Some of its nearly fifty thousand inhabitants (in 1878) were radicals like McDonnell but only a few. Campbell Wilson had been a Scot radical before working as a Paterson silk weaver and then running a working-class boardinghouse and saloon. A Lancashire Chartist, Samuel Sigley had fled England in 1848 after a threatened treason trial. He made out nicely as a Paterson house painter. Another Lancashire worker, Simon Morgan, had settled in Paterson after being blacklisted for leading a Fall River cotton strike. Irish and German radicals also befriended McDonnell, but by themselves they lacked the power to protect the socialist editor against his local critics.

Others in the city sustained McDonnell, and their behavior reveals much about the industrial city's inner structure. We consider first his supporters among nonworkers. Twenty "agents," including nearly every stationer and newsdealer on the city's main thoroughfares, sold the *Labor Standard,* and early issues earned advertising revenue from forty-five retail shopkeepers and other vendors of goods and services (among them eleven clothing and dry goods stores, ten saloons, eight boot and shoe makers, and eight grocers). Ethnicity varied among these petty retailers: the group included German, Irish, French, Dutch and ordinary "American" names as well as an Italian bootmaker and three Jewish clothing dealers. Such support may have been just good "business sense," but the sympathy McDonnell evoked during his first trial rested on other causes. His lawyer was a pioneer manufacturer who later grew wealthy as a real estate speculator, organized the city's waterworks, and fathered pre-Civil War banking and other reform in the state legislature. He had broken with the Whig Party over slavery and later quit the Republicans to protest the "money power." A jury of shopkeepers and successful independent artisans agreed that McDonnell was guilty but only after unusual pressure by a presiding judge. Even then, another judge, himself a poor Lancashire immigrant who then owned a small bobbin factory, convinced the presiding judge to fine McDonnell and not send him to prison. Some storekeepers and merchants helped McDonnell pay his fine. Aid also came from a prominent copper-smith and alderman as well as a third generation Yorkshire blacksmith who then headed a small bolt and screw factory. Orrin Vanderhoven also cheered McDonnell. Vanderhoven had traveled a long route from Jacksonian Democracy to Greenback reform and soon would return to the Democracy. "A scab," Vanderhoven wrote in his own newspaper, "is a man who deserts his fellows. . . . The name of 'scab' is not degrading enough for such a person. It ought to be a 'villainous, shameless, sneak-thief traitor'. . . . God bless the laboring classes. . . . May the God of fortune favor them through life. . . . May their beds be roses and their bolsters banknotes."

Others of local prominence joined editor Vanderhoven to side with McDonnell during his second trial. Two respected lawyers defended the troubled socialist. The son of a New Hampshire blacksmith, Socrates Tuttle was then sixty-one and Paterson's most revered Republican leader—a lawyer who had served as school commissioner, city clerk, state assembly-man, and mayor. Tuttle told the jury that silencing McDonnell meant to deny working people the essential right to "complain." William Prall, the son of a former Democratic mayor and cotton manufacturer, helped Tuttle defend McDonnell. A few years later, Prall went to the state assembly; after that, he gave up politics and became an Episcopal clergyman. Just before his trial, McDonnell had complained loudly that Paterson's clergy prayed to "that Trinity of Power, 'the Almighty Dollar, the Golden Eagle, and the Copper Cent'," but two prominent clergymen protested publicly in his behalf. A Baptist, one of them worked among the Paterson poor and later played a significant role as a midwestern anti-trust propagandist. The other, John Robinson, was an Irish Protestant, a Primitive Methodist, for a time Republican state senator, and Paterson's most esteemed clergy-man. Nor was this all. Two former silk factory foremen (one English and the other German) and soon to become prosperous business men orga-nized McDonnell's sympathizers. Thomas Flynn, then a saloonkeeper and ten years later speaker of the state assembly, posted bond for Menton, and a contractor financed the young man in a well-drilling business. Several aldermen, former aldermen, and county freeholders visited Mc-Donnell in prison. So did the nephew of the owner of the mosquito net mill that first brought McDonnell to Paterson. The young man gave McDonnell twenty dollars. Money also came from Garrett Hobart, then Paterson's State Senator, a rising corporation lawyer, the president of the

New Jersey State Senate, and the chairman of the New Jersey State Republican Party. (In 1896 Hobart won election with William McKinley and served as vice-president.) On McDonnell's release, a committee of seventy-five arranged a celebration. Not only workers organized the fete. The committee included a band leader, a contractor, a clothier, a doctor, five grocers, and twelve saloon and hotel keepers.

His first night in jail, McDonnell angrily confided in his diary: "Here in Jail for defending the poor in their Rights! Alas, for American Liberty'." Yet his prison stay was made less harsh than expected by a county jail warden, John Buckley, who was the son of Paterson's former Republican mayor and would himself soon head the county Republican organization. McDonnell's imprisonment apparently upset Buckley. He made his guest as comfortable as circumstances allowed. McDonnell spent some of his prison days writing letters for illiterate fellow-prisoners and himself appealing to the New Jersey Governor to enforce a moribund ten-hour law. Buckley also let him edit his newspaper and organize a national protest campaign from his cell. Visitors (twenty-one came on a single day, and children often called on McDonnell) met the editor in the warden's office. Meals came regularly from outside the prison. So did cigars, wines, and liquors supplied by friendly saloon and hotel keepers. Others brought fresh fruit, cakes, and puddings. Shamrocks came on St. Patrick's Day and two fancy dinners on McDonnell's birthday. On his release, Buckley commended McDonnell as a model prisoner.

Scores of ordinary working people supported McDonnell in their own way. They crowded the jail to console him and raised the money to pay his fines. But their support came in more significant ways. After his first trial, working-class sympathizers (and even some shopkeepers) jammed Democratic political rallies to humiliate the Democratic county prosecutor. They did not "riot," but at one meeting they created sufficient noise and disorder to prevent him from speaking. When he tried again, they packed the meeting hall, and as he rose to speak walked out in silent protest. On his release from prison eighteen months later, working people (organized mostly by skilled silk workers) arranged Paterson's greatest celebration to that time. Quite possibly more than half of the city's residents filled its streets and "almost mobbed" their hero. A band played; a carriage awaited him to carry McDonnell through the jammed streets; American flags decorated the parade route; a rally followed the street march; then came a festive banquet at which three young girls presented the socialist editor with a gold watch—a gift from "the ladies of Paterson." "No one ever purchased the title of martyr at so slight a cost," sneered a hostile Paterson newspaper. A sympathizer disagreed. "Paterson," he insisted, "is redeemed by the suffering of the innocent for the guilty." Such varied opinions did not matter as much as the fact that Paterson residents made it possible for McDonnell to survive in a social setting usually identified with little more than hopeless poverty, disorganized and ineffective protest, and God-like industrial power.

McDonnell's 1878–1880 Paterson experiences were never exactly re-peated in other New Jersey Gilded Age industrial cities, but events like them occurred with sufficient frequency to suggest that the Gilded Age worker was more than "a factor of production," that he was the sum of a total culture that has been scarcely recognized and little studied. That culture differed between groups of workers. Ethnicity and levels of skill counted for much in explaining these diversities. Despite them, however, Gilded Age workers had distinct ways of work and leisure, habits, aspira-tions, conceptions of America and Christianity, notions of right and wrong, and traditions of protest and acquiescence that were linked together in neighborhoods by extensive voluntary associations and other community institutions. Not all of this entirely separated the industrial city's workers from the larger community, but these strands wove together in ways that shaped a particular subculture.

The vitality of that subculture can be indicated by giving brief atten-tion to patterns of collective protest and local politics in the industrial city. Take the case of strikes, boycotts, and other forms of collective protest, including occasionally violent labor riots (such as those of the Trenton potters and railroad workers in 1877, the Hudson River coal heavers in 1887, the Newark threadmakers in 1891, and the Paterson silk dyers in 1894). Most labor historians agree that the Gilded Age was not conducive to building permanent unions, and there is much truth in that view. Union membership did not rise steadily in these years. It ebbed and flowed in an irregular fashion. But this fact does not mean that workers were powerless and that collective protest was ineffective. For the years 1881 through 1887, the New Jersey Bureau of Labor Statistics collected information on 890 strikes and lockouts. Many others occurred but were not recorded. These disputes involved mostly textile, glass, metal, trans-portation, and building trades workers. The Bureau's findings unsettle the traditional view concerning effective Gilded Age labor protest. Employers won only 40% of these disputes; 6% resulted in compromise settlements; strikers were victorious in the rest—54%. Workers won 80% of their walkouts for higher wages, and 78% of those for shorter hours. All of these happenings occurred in the absence of stable and permanent trade unions. We must therefore look elsewhere to understand them. Clues are found in the culture and social structure of the industrial town which sus-tained workers without formal protective associations, gave coherence to their behavior, often created sympathy for them, and shielded them against industrial power. How else can we explain that unorganized Paterson tex-tile workers managed to strike for nine months in 1878, and that lengthy disputes frequently occurred among other textile operatives, pottery, glass, and iron workers, threadmakers, and even ordinary dock hands? Although they misunderstood it, contemporaries noted the persistence of lower class "habits," "norms," and patterns of protest that strengthened disaffected Gilded Age workers in times of crisis. Three illustrations drawn from bitter strikes by Trenton potters and Paterson silk weavers and a boycott by Orange hatmakers indicate important aspects of that subculture as well as the ties between distressed workers and others in their communities that gave a special flavor to Gilded Age industrial conflict.

During a general strike of silk ribbon weavers (1877), Paterson manufacturers complained that many loyal workers refused to support employers because such behavior "entailed contempt, exile from the society of their fellow-workmen, and untold other annoyances." A silk manufacturer asked of his fellow entrepreneurs:

> Put yourself in their place. They cannot go anywhere without being molested or insulted, and no matter what they do they are met and blackguarded and taunted in a way that no one can stand, and which is a great deal worse than actual assaults, for it does not come within the reach of the law.

Another manufacturer agreed:

> All the police in the world could not reach the annoyances that the weavers have at home and on the street that are not offences—taunts and flings, insults and remarks. A weaver would rather have his head punched in than be called a "knobstick," and this is the class of injury they hate the worst, and that keeps them out more than direct insult.

These manufacturers confronted an ethic that confounded them. They appreciated it only as an obstacle to their objectives, not as the product of a way of life.

A traditional way of work bound together the Trenton potters. Old pre-industrial British craft habits dominated the Trenton industry. One historian writes: "The potters worked as they had always worked, bursts of great activity, spending long hours in the pottery eating and even sleeping there, and then laying off for several days at a time from sheer exhaustion." Their style of work was distinctly pre-industrial, and they fought bitterly to protect it, resisting efforts to mechanize and routinize their craft. Their tenacious efforts to control their habits of work caused a manufacturer's trade monthly, the *Crockery and Glass Journal,* to mock them and jokingly advise the Trenton manufacturers:

> Run your factories to please the crowd. . . . Don't expect work to begin before 9 A.M. or to continue after 3 P.M. Every employee should be

served hot coffee and a bouquet at 7 A.M. and allowed the two hours to take a free, perfumed bath. . . . During the summer, ice cream and fruit should be served at 12 P.M. to the accompaniment of witching music.

Such humor could not match the torchlight parades and effigy-burnings (traditional forms of craft protest) that characterized the potters' behavior during a bitter four-month strike (1877). Nor could it compensate for a cooperative store that sustained them along with "a generous local support" and the refusal of most Trenton storekeepers and landlords to follow the advice of manufacturers and "shut down" on the strikers.

Evidence of convincing support from nonworkers is drawn from an Orange hatters' boycott (1885). Nearly two thousand men and women worked in more than twenty Orange hat factories. The Knights of Labor won much sympathy from them, but a single manufacturer named Berg discharged women employees who wanted to join the Knights, refused to negotiate, and brought in new hands. A citywide boycott followed, and a labor journalist reported the attitude of the boycotters and their supporters toward Berg and the nonstrikers ("the foul"):

> They will not trade with any person who has any dealings with the boycotted foul or with any one who furnishes goods or supplies to Berg himself. Brewers refuse to furnish beer to foul saloonkeepers; bakers refuse to furnish bread to the fouls; and the knights of the razor turn them out of doors. One fair manufacturer discharged a man because he lived with his brother who is a foul, and two female trimmers were refused admission to the roller-skating rink because they were foul. . . . The foul cannot even find lodging places, and are compelled to resort to adjacent localities at night for bed and board. . . . One beer seller who has been threatened says he may be forced to sell beer to a foul, but he cannot be prevented from charging him a dollar a glass for it.

Although this reporter's enthusiasm caused some exaggeration, he insisted that the boycott had "the sympathy of nearly everybody in Orange."

What, finally, was politics like in the industrial city? The ballot gave the industrial city worker a presence, if not a power, that has been little studied. Political machines often disciplined the worker-voter and narrowed his choices. Votes were even purchased by "bosses" for cash and favors. That is an old story, but it is not the full story. Working-class voting behavior took many forms as a protest device. Camden and Phillipsburg had workers as mayors in 1877 and 1878. Some southern New Jersey counties sent glass blowers to the state legislature. Paterson elected two workers as state assemblymen in 1886 and two more in the early 1890s. A Paterson machinist and outspoken socialist twice served as city alderman. The direct election of workers on independent tickets, however, was not common. More typical was the elected official who was not a worker but nevertheless sympathized with the workers or feared alienating working-class electoral support. During the 1877 general silk strike, Paterson's Republican mayor (a Lancashire cotton worker who became a Paterson banker, manufacturer, and popular politician) and the Board of Aldermen publicly rebuked efforts by the Paterson Board of Trade to enlarge the police force and to deny strikers the use of the streets for their effective public demonstrations. Ten years later, Jersey City's Democratic mayor, a former congressman and also a manufacturer named Orestes Cleveland, declined to deputize Pinkerton police during a violent coal handlers' strike. After the *New York Times* condemned Cleveland as "a demagogue," the mayor fired back: "It is not the business of Jersey City to interfere between the great monopolies and their workmen. . . . If it were proper for Jersey City to interfere at all, we should interfere to assist and protect the men who are fighting for the right to live, instead of for the protection of the great monopolies . . ."

The Jersey City mayor may have been a "demagogue." It is also possible that he learned from the bitter experiences of other urban politicians who had sided with employers or broken promises to organized workers. Here a third pattern—punishment—emerged. During the 1877 potters' strike, Trenton's Republican mayor condemned the potters in the *New York World*. Their response was to vote him out of office that spring. Such flashes of independent political anger among urban workers recurred in the 1880s. A Camden Republican state assemblyman promised McDonnell's Federation his help but turned back on his pledge after the election. Aided by two Camden newspaper editors (one of them German), McDonnell organized Camden workers and prevented his reelection. The 1887 coal handlers' strike saw similar results. Bayonne aldermen and a Jersey City police official opposed the strikers and suffered defeat at the polls. These few examples suggest some of the ways in which working-class political presence affected industrial city politics. Such a presence also was felt on the state level and helped explain McDonnell's legislative victories.

VI

McDonnell won reform legislation between 1883 and 1892 by playing "pressure politics." Not enough is yet known to tell that story fully, but its outlines seem clear. For one thing, two state officials—one elected and the other appointed—supported McDonnell and eased his way in Trenton. One was Leon Abbett, twice elected Democratic governor (1883–1886 and 1889–1892), and the other was Lawrence Fell, the chief factory inspector from 1883 until 1895 when a hostile State Senate finally rejected his reappointment and began undoing his pioneering work. Fell's support was the more unusual, and Abbett's was the more important. The available evidence allows us to say no more than that Leon Abbett supported the efforts of McDonnell and the Federation. Just why remains obscure and is entangled in bitter controversy over his motives and his career. But it is sufficient in these pages to know only that Mc- Donnell had a powerful friend in Abbett, New Jersey's most significant nineteenth-century governor. During his two terms, Abbett gave much time battling the New Jersey railroads to tax them fairly, and in doing so he attacked the state's most well-organized private interest. Abbett won a public victory but twice lost a United States Senate seat as his reward. Abbett's methods aroused much public criticism. That he built "a machine" to fight "a machine" worried many as did his continued public appeal for electoral support from urban workers and immigrants. The son of a Phila- delphia Quaker journeyman hatter, Abbett was a wealthy Jersey City lawyer and state legislator. Even then (in the late 1860s and the 1870s), his actions showed a concern for the lower-class vote. As president of the State Senate (1877), he worked hard to abolish scrip money and com- pany stores then common in the southern and western New Jersey iron and glass towns. That same year, he represented workers in a successful suit for back wages against a bankrupt railroad and also defended strikers arrested in the aftermath of the 1877 railroad riots. Abbett accepted no fees in these cases. As candidate in 1883 (his Republican opponent was the judge who had sentenced McDonnell to prison in 1880), Abbett ap- pealed to immigrant and working-class voters. After his election, the Governor proclaimed: "Every citizen of this State, whether he be high or low, whether he be rich or poor, can always see me personally without the intervention of any man." Abbett was not a John Peter Altgeld, but McDonnell and the Federation found him sympathetic to their proposals. Historians, incidentally, have credited his administration's labor legislation solely to Abbett and not realized that it first came from men like McDon- nell. But Abbett's response should not be neglected.

Lawrence Fell is easier to explain than Abbett and is, in some ways, more interesting. His career suggests how new experiences remade even grown men. The 1883 legislature allowed the governor with the state senate's approval to pick a chief factory inspector to enforce the new laws. Fell was not the governor's first choice. Instead, a Newark hatter and outspoken trade unionist, Richard Dowdall, was nominated. But the senate turned him down because, according to the *New York Times,* it felt him "a labor extremist, a demagogue identified with the [Irish] Land League, and altogether an unfit person." An Orange hat manufacturer and real estate dealer, Fell was his replacement. If the conservative senate thought him a "safe" choice because of his background, Fell disappointed it. He became a vigorous proponent of enlarged and more effective labor legislation. He worked diligently under difficult circumstances to enforce the school and factory laws, and he cooperated openly with McDonnell and the Federation. When the opportunity existed, Fell urged the appointment of Mc-Donnell and a Newark trade unionist as his deputies. After their appointment and work angered industrialists and caused their removal, Fell praised them: "The manner in which they have acted is sufficient proof that the advocates of labor interests are fitted to fill the highest [public] labor offices."

What Fell learned as chief factory inspector made him a reformer and an advocate of extensive remedial and protective legislation. "Old faces and dwarfed forms are the offspring of the Child Labor System," his first report concluded. 'In a country where life is so intense as it is in this, where so much is expected in a little time, childhood and youth should be a time of free physical growth." Fell's second report detailed widespread illiteracy among "factory children." His description is a neglected classic of its kind. Fell told of his experiences with twelve- to fifteen-year-old boys and girls in the New Jersey factories:

> Nearly all the children examined were naturally bright and intelligent, but neglect, years of work and their general surroundings had left sad traces upon their youthful forms and minds. It is not possible in this report to enter into the details of every case, either of factory or child examination; to do so would be to fill the largest volume that the State has ever published. . . . There is no exaggeration in saying that three-fourths of the work-children know absolutely nothing. The greatest ignorance exists on the most commonplace questions. Most of these children have never been inside of a schoolhouse, and the majority have either been at school for too short a period to learn anything or have forgotten the little instruction they received.
>
> Not two per cent know anything about grammar or have ever been taught any. One of the few children who professed to know something about grammar said that the word "boy" was "a comma," when asked what part of speech it was. The vast majority could not spell words of more than one syllable, and very many could not spell at all. About ten per cent could answer questions in simple multiplication. Of the remaining ninety per cent, the majority know absolutely nothing about simple geographical and historical questions. The number able to read and write, in a distinguishable way, was shockingly small, and very many could neither read nor write even their own names.

Fell illustrated his experiences concretely:

> Very few of these children, the large majority of whom were born in the United States, ever heard of George Washington. Amongst the answers given about Washington, by those who heard of him, were the following: "He is a good man." "He chased the Indians away." "He died a few

years ago." "He is President." "I saw his picture." "He is a high man in war." "He never told a lie." "He discovered America." "The best man who ever lived," and so forth. Over ninety-five per cent never heard of the revolutionary war, Abraham Lincoln, the civil war, Governor Abbett or President Arthur.

At least sixty per cent never heard of the United States or of Europe. At least thirty per cent could not name the city in which they lived, and quite a number only knew the name of the street where they housed. Many who had heard of the United States could not say where they were. Some said they were in Europe and others said they were in New Jersey. Many big girls and boys were unable to say whether New Jersey was in North or South America. Girls were found in Jersey City and Newark who never heard of New York City. In Newark and Jersey City this was, of course, the exception, but in other parts of the State it was the rule. Some who had heard of New York said it was in New Jersey, and others answered that Pennsylvania was the capital of New Jersey. Not ten per cent could tell what an island was. Very few had heard of the city of Washington, and not three per cent could locate it. A girl aged fourteen years said Europe was in the moon. A few were found who never heard of the sun, or moon, or earth, and a large number who could not tell where or when they were born. . . . Children who had been brought to this country before their sixth year, in some cases, never heard the name of their native country, and others could not locate them.

One finding especially concerned Fell:

Boys and girls who had been brought to this country from Great Britain, Ireland and Germany, between the ages of twelve and fifteen years, were better educated and knew more about the geography and history of America than children born and reared in the State. . . . This sad tale of illiteracy is not overdrawn in the slightest degree. It is, alas, too true. . . .

Such evidence caused legislative critics in 1885 and again in 1886 to try to abolish Fell's office. But McDonnell and the Federation frustrated such efforts, and Fell continued his work for another decade.

VII

Although Fell and Abbett provided important help, McDonnell's legislative success depended on more than their support. It came only when McDonnell and the Federation could make a majority of the state's elected officeholders conscious, if not fearful, of the presence and potential power of the industrial city's workers and immigrant poor. This was not an easy task. The New Jersey legislature was a jungle of competing special interest groups, the railroads king among them. In addition, the State Senate increasingly under-represented the growing industrial cities and became a choice nesting ground for well-organized interest groups opposed to the Federation and its legislative programs. McDonnell scorned the typical state legislator, advising workers: "Leave him to himself and his surroundings, and he will forget all about you and his promises." So harsh a judgment was not unfair. Despite the Federation's important legislative gains, in 1897 New Jersey spent $222,400 for its National Guard ("our tin soldiers," McDonnell called the militia), a sum that nearly equalled the state's educational expenditures and was almost ten times the amount allotted to the Bureau of Labor Statistics and the Bureau of Factory Inspection.

In such a world, a single belief informed McDonnell's legislative efforts. His radicalism together with his experiences convinced McDonnell that neither rhetoric nor "right" won legislation. Only pressure worked, and the worker's weapon was the organized but "independent" vote. McDonnell preached and practiced this point for twenty-five years. As early as 1878, he advised *Labor Standard* readers: "Heaven help the laborers who rely upon their public officers to legislate for the good of labor. But honest legislation can be forced by labor unions." He regularly published the names of anti-labor legislators with the frequent admonition: "If there is courage, intelligence, and Manhood in the people, not one of these enemies will ever again be elected to a legislative position. Men of New Jersey, kick them out." McDonnell explained in 1882: "It is Power that men in office fear, and it is because the wage workers have not had organized Power that they have been treated with the grossest contempt." Legislative victories came because workers had "commenced to think and to act." "Politicians," he said in 1893, "are as a rule what we make them or what we permit them to be." Five years of decline in the Federation's influence (1893–1897) caused a similar outburst: "We should not forget that if we won't aid ourselves, no one else will, and that we shall get just as much as we fight for, *and no more.*" Nothing, McDonnell insisted, "of importance will be obtained from our Legislature unless they hear the workingman's and workingwoman's growl. We can get anything we want *by growling loud enough.*"

A "growl" unaccompanied by a "bite" was hardly enough, and that potential "bite" was the electoral power that rested in the industrial cities and their diverse but dense clusters of working-class subculture. McDonnell and men like him therefore cut the Federation loose from all formal political ties to enable it to apply non-partisan local pressure. The Federation supported Abbett when he favored its program, but it also gave its blessings to sympathetic Republican legislators. "The political policy of the Federation," a spokesman said in 1884, "has been and is to identify itself with no party but to support men of all parties favorable to their objects." In this way, McDonnell hoped to create effective working-class pressure and cement "natural" alliances with its legislative representatives. The regular procedure was simple. Each year the Federation convention established legislative priorities. Just before the fall election, it circulated a pledge among all candidates for public office:

> I pledge my word of honor that if elected to the Legislature, I will sup-
> port the bills introduced for the benefit of the wage class by the Legis-
> lative Committee of the New Jersey Federation of Trades and Labor
> Unions, whether said bills were approved or opposed by the political
> party to which I belong, provided that said bills are of a purely labor
> character; and I will support no measure, whether of a private or party
> nature, which may be introduced in opposition to labor measures and
> against the wishes of the organized wage-workers of New Jersey.

Approval of the pledge won Federation endorsement together with Federation scrutiny and pressure while the legislature met. For fifteen years, McDonnell spent the winter months largely in Trenton working this risky strategy. It depended for its success almost entirely on the Federation's ability to mount pressure from outside the party system. A Federation without close ties to the industrial city working-class was weak and lacked such strength. Between 1883 and 1892, such connections were sufficiently strong to win significant legislative achievements. And so in this neglected fashion, social reform came from "below." Such successes angered conservatives and those who found comfort in the ever-increasing gross national product. These victories so upset the *New York Herald* that it accused many New Jersey legislators of lacking in "courage." "Fear of the loss of the labor vote," moaned the *Herald,* "drives public men and parties into concessions against which their consciences and better judgments often rebel. . . . The law of supply and demand is offended at every tack and turn. The philosophy of trade is set at defiance." McDonnell did not share the *Herald's* rhetorical remorse.

Just what kind of industrial city legislators supported McDonnell and the Federation is difficult to tell. These men differed in social background and seemed to share only the fact that their constituents were mostly wage earners. Take the case of two quite different Paterson legislators: Thomas Flynn, a Democrat and for a time state assembly speaker, and Robert Williams, a Republican state senator.

Tom Flynn was a model Gilded Age ward politician. He started as a machinist, drove a horse car, fooled with firehouse politics, studied for the law, opened a saloon, built a personal political machine among the Paterson Irish, traded favors for votes, and went to the assembly several times starting in 1881. He became a Trenton power and critics identified him with corruption and the "racetrack lobby." The *New York Tribune* complained of his "unscrupulous conduct and aggressiveness." "A product of the slums, endowed by nature with more than an ordinary amount of acuteness, . . . and utterly without moral scruple or finer feeling," the *Tribune* saw in "Flynn's life from the first to the last . . . what any careful student of human nature might have predicted." But Flynn supported the Federation's legislative program from the very start. McDonnell often praised him and with good reason. He helped abolish an anti-labor conspiracy law and pushed the regulation of prison labor. He tried to get the legislature to lower utility rates and regulate insurance companies. Flynn worked so diligently for the fifty-five hour law that Paterson silk workers renamed him "Fifty-five Hour Flynn." A candidate for reelection, he emphasized his ties to the workers and his efforts in their behalf. Working-class voters learned that Flynn still "ranks among his friends the men who were then his comrades at the bench." A Democratic leader urged Paterson workers to reelect Flynn: "You have named him Fifty-five Hour Flynn, and he deserves the title. He fought your battle and kept the faith."

A graduate of the Columbia College Law School and a Republican newspaper publisher, Robert Williams was the antithesis of Tom Flynn. Democratic opponents mocked his upper-class style when Williams sought election to the state senate:

> Robby Williams. Nice boy, sweet little beard, dreamy way and langorous expression, long wavy hair. . . . Robby's a real nice fellow, but what does he know about labor? . . . He was born with a silver spoon in his mouth and never did anything but dandle it round his mouth. . . . Starvation has never stared him in the face. . . . and [he] cannot legislate for something of which he knows nothing.

Williams disappointed his political enemies: he knew his constituents well and regularly voted for Federation legislation. He even introduced bills drawn up by McDonnell. When Williams quit the senate, McDonnell had only words of praise: "This county has never had a Senator who more faithfully represented the interests of the common people." The real test for McDonnell was neither man nor party; only the issues counted. "Robby" Williams had also "kept the faith."

Just how McDonnell and other Federation leaders worked with men like Abbett, Fell, Flynn, and Williams can be illustrated briefly in 1884 and 1893. A fairly complete record relates McDonnell's Trenton experiences in 1884. He and the Federation's Legislative Committee met twice in December 1883 to discuss proposed labor legislation with a sympathetic Newark assemblyman and Abbett. After that, McDonnell drew up the several laws. Between mid-January and late March, he spent thirty-four days in Trenton and conferred with, cajoled, and pressured Democratic and Republican legislators from such industrial ciites as Paterson, Jersey

City, and Newark. He and other Federation spokesmen testified before legislative committees and brought pressure to bear in other ways. "We had hard work getting the child-labor bill through the Senate," reported McDonnell, "as they were trying to kill it by amendments, but several Senators were brought to terms by delegations of workingmen waiting upon them in their respective districts." When the Assembly Committee on Revision of Laws held back a strengthened factory inspection law for two weeks and then allowed only a brief public hearing, McDonald accused it of "discourtesy toward the labor organizations" to force it to hear him and Fell. The committee stalled again so Federation leaders conferred with Abbett. But the committee quickly won Assembly support for a badly amended bill. A labor journalist reported what followed:

> [McDonnell first] succeeded through Assemblyman Flynn. . . . in having the vote on the report reconsidered and the bill recommitted. The members of the Federation Legislative committee then went to work gallantly among the members, until they made things very unpleasant for the Committee on Revision of Laws. Mr. McDonnell at once telegraphed to the absent members in various parts of the State, urging them to come to Trenton at once, which they did early on Thursday morning. By this time, the aspect of things had changed. It was rumored among the Assemblymen that the labor men and their friends were swarming into Trenton like bees, and that their power was not to be made little of. The forenoon's work produced good results.

The factory inspection bill left the committee without its crippling amendments and soon became law. "What a change in twenty-four hours!," enthused McDonnell. "Would it have taken place if the labor men were not alive and doing?"

A different tactic prevented repeal of the fifty-five hour law in 1893. It had passed the year before, the first of its kind in the United States. Inadequately enforced, manufacturers nevertheless bitterly opposed it. Some went to the courts to test its constitutionality. Others mounted a campaign for its repeal, and in 1893 sent such circulars together with instructions to factory superintendents to get the signatures of workers. McDonnell quickly responded. A public appeal to the state's legislators defended the law, and a circular (entitled "Danger Ahead") urged every New Jersey trade union to elect delegates to attend a special Trenton convention on twenty-four hours' notice. The response was gratifying. Nearly all picked delegates and flooded Trenton with resolutions favoring the law. The manufacturers backed away from full repeal, but their supporters pushed two bills to emasculate the law. McDonnell worked for their defeat. The night before final adjournment, the Senate passed one of them. Then, Tom Flynn and others from the industrial cities stepped in. "Thanks

now and forever to Speaker Tom Flynn and other friends," McDonnell
explained, "neither . . . bill went through."

VIII

This journey has taken us from Dublin, to London, to New York, to
Paterson, and finally to Trenton. That was the route McDonnell traveled,
and we have followed it to fit the Gilded Age labor radical into the main-
stream of that era's history. To do so, several detours were necessary to
avoid the roadblocks set up by certain misconceptions concerning the
Gilded Age itself. Some of the larger implications of that trip through
America's Dark Age deserve summary. For one thing, McDonnell's New
Jersey career was not isolated and unique. Similar patterns of working-class
political pressure for reform were found in such states as New York,
Massachusetts, Pennsylvania, Ohio, Indiana, Michigan, Illinois, and even
Connecticut. Their success varied, but the men who led these movements
shared a common moral purpose with radicals like McDonnell. "The
foundation of the Republic," McDonnell insisted in 1882, "is men not
things, and to attend to the welfare of man, knowing that things will take
care of themselves is the true wisdom of statesmanship." McDonnell believed in the 1880s that strong trade unions and legislative reform would
open the way to more radical changes, but a litlte-studied conservative,
political backlash in New Jersey after 1892 that made it a one-party state
for more than a decade blocked such possibilities and began weakening
the ties that had given power and status to men like McDonnell. After
that McDonnell faded in significance, and his last fifteen years were filled
with much personal and political disappointment. It remains to be said,
however, that the modern "welfare state" was not just the child of con-
erned and sensitive early twentieth century upper and middle class critics
of industrial capitalism. A generation earlier, working-class leaders, including radicals like McDonnell, had helped give birth to a premature "welfare
state." They had arranged a marriage between the industrial city's workers
and immigrants and their political representatives. Such men, not the
Progressive reformers of a later time, were the founding fathers of modern
movements to humanize industrial society.

"What a comment upon our civilization it is that you who have given
so much of yourself have received so little for yourself," George McNeill
wrote of McDonnell in 1896. A worker who had matured in the world of
the New England abolitionists, McNeill was McDonnell's counterpart in
Massachusetts. His letter reassured his Irish friend by quoting a poem
McNeill had written some years before when another neglected American
radical, Ira Steward, had died:

Even now I see the coming day, the dawn appears,
The thoughtless brain will some day think
And at thy fountain pause and drink,
And praise thy name.

Although men like McDonnell deserved such recognition, it was not just because they gave so much and got so little. In 1873, McDonnell's first American letters had appeared in the *New York Herald*. The young social-ist denounced steerage abuse of poor, powerless European immigrants. He explained his concern for them by quoting John Milton, not Karl Marx:

Not to know at large of things remote
From use, obscure and subtle, but to know
That which before us lies in daily life
Is the prime wisdom. What is more is fume
Or emptiness or fond impertinence,
And renders us in things that most concern
Unpracticed, unprepared and still to seek.

Milton's words belong in this final paragraph. As more is learned of the world and the culture that bred men like McDonnell, more is revealed about the larger "forces" that have shaped modern American society. And that reason, not mere sentiment, is why we look with care at the life and times of radicals as obscure as Joseph P. McDonnell.

2.4

The American Railway Union

RAY GINGER

The Pullman boycott of 1894 possessed a significance far beyond its time and place. Fiercely contested, it pitted Eugene V. Debs, perhaps America's most famous unionist and socialist, against the powerful Pullman and railroad interests. It also saw the use of federal injunctions and federal troops to help the railroad leaders destroy the nascent American Railway Union and to jail its leader. The ARU, founded as an industrial union to combat the provincialism and conservatism of the railroad brotherhoods, was destroyed by the brotherhoods' cooperation with their employers.

The following works are suggested for further reading:

STANLEY BUDER, *Pullman*, New York: Oxford University Press, 1967.
WILLIAM CARWARDINE, *The Pullman Strike*, Chicago: Charles H. Kerr and Co., 1971.

Ray Ginger, *The Bending Cross: Eugene V. Debs; A Biography* (New Brunswick, N.J.: Rutgers University Press, 1949), pp. 123–29, 136–60, 161–62, 164–67. Reprinted by permission of the publisher and the author.

Henry David, "Upheaval at Homestead," in Daniel Aaron (ed.), *America in Crisis,* New York: Alfred A. Knopf, Inc., 1952, pp. 133–70.

The fierce, hard-fought Pullman boycott of 1894, named The Debs Rebellion by the commercial newspapers, began as a local dispute in the small Chicago suburb of Pullman, Illinois. During the previous year, more than sixteen thousand business firms had gone bankrupt, including fifty companies with a capital of more than a half million dollars each. Thousands of other firms were threatened with failure. The continued drop of wholesale prices made it increasingly difficult to produce goods at a profit. Companies, in a frantic attempt to cut their production costs and salvage their investments, repeatedly slashed the pay of their workers. These wage cuts and layoffs burst with a peculiar fury upon the residents of Pullman, where the Pullman Palace Car Company was the only employer and the only landlord. Since there was no competing demand for labor, and since most of the Pullman workers lacked the money to migrate elsewhere in search of better jobs, thy were forced to submit or starve.

Even in prosperous years, wages at Pullman were below the union scale for similar work in Chicago, and this difference was accentuated during the depression. A Federal commission later estimated that Pullman slashed wage rates 25 per cent between 1893 and May, 1894. The Rev. William H. Carwardine, a minister in Pullman who later wrote a book about the labor dispute there, believed that the reductions were even greater: "The average cut in wages was 33⅓ per cent; in some cases it was as much as 40 per cent, and in many was fifty per cent." Iron machinists in the streetcar department at Pullman charged that their wages were reduced 70 to 85 per cent. Vice-President T. H. Wickes of the Company, contradicting these claims, said that the average daily rate of earnings had declined only 19 per cent, but he failed to point out that few men worked every day. The size of the pay roll had declined drastically. In July, 1893, there were fifty-five hundred employees at Pullman, but the following May the total working force was only thirty-three hundred.

Just as wages were lower in Pullman, so rents were higher there. Jane Addams of Hull House, who investigated the town for the Civil Federation of Chicago, said that an eighteen-dollar-per-month cottage in Pullman could be rented for fifteen dollars in Chicago. In the words of the Federal commission: "If we exclude the aesthetic and sanitary features at Pullman, the rents there are from 20 to 25 per cent higher than rents in Chicago or surrounding towns for similar accommodations. The aesthetic features are admired by visitors, but have little money value to employees, especially when they lack bread." But the company refused to cut rents when it reduced wages, claiming that its rental of houses was a separate business from its manufacture of sleeping cars, and that there was no connection between the two enterprises.

Every foot of ground, every house, every church in the town was owned by the company, and they were run on a purely commercial basis. Even the sewage from the workers' homes was pumped to George M. Pullman's truck farm as fertilizer. Adults paid three dollars and children one dollar per year for the use of the town library, but the company said this charge was levied "not for profit, but to give the subscribers a sense of ownership."

The town was similar in many ways to a feudal manor, with George Pullman as absolute monarch. Since he believed that saloons and trade unions tended to inflame the workers, both were banned from the community. The eight-hour day was also banned, because Pullman thought that idleness would promote mischief. Professor Richard T. Ely and a Chicago judge both charged that the company hired spies to inform against the workers, and Mr. Carwardine wrote: "I am in a position to know that information of everything going on in the town of Pullman . . . is conveyed by letter every week to headquarters from the town proper." In order to maintain this absolute domination, the company freely interfered in local elections. Intimidation at the polls was common. The residents were advised how to vote, and the advice also held a poorly concealed threat. On one occasion a foreman was ordered to withdraw his name as a candidate for public office; when he refused he was fired.

Although most employees continued to live in Pullman because residents there were the last to be laid off and the first to be rehired, they deeply resented the destruction of their dignity. With grim humor one man declared: "We are born in a Pullman house, fed from the Pullman shop, taught in the Pullman school, catechized in the Pullman church, and when we die we shall be buried in the Pullman cemetery and go to the Pullman hell." Mr. Carwardine added that an awareness of George M. Pullman, not an awareness of God, ruled the community: "An unpleasant feature of the town is that you are made to feel at every turn the presence of the corporation. . . . This is a corporation-made and a corporation-governed town, and is utterly un-American in its tendencies." Four years later, the Supreme Court of Illinois agreed. Ordering the Palace Car Company to sell all property in the town of Pullman not needed for its manufacturing business, the Court declared that company towns were "opposed to good public policy and incompatible with the theory and spirit of our institutions."

The Pullman Company also exploited its monopoly position by charging exorbitant prices for its services, according to contemporary claims. Senator John Sherman, Republican of Ohio, who introduced a bill to bring the Pullman Company within the Sherman Antitrust Act of 1890, said to the Washington correspondent of the *Chicago Inter-Ocean:* "I regard the Pullman Company and the sugar trust as the most outrageous monopolies of the day. They make enormous profits, and give their patrons little or nothing in return." This attack aroused much comment, because George Pullman was a major source of campaign funds for Sherman's own party. Sherman exaggerated when he said that Pullman gave its customers "little or nothing in return," but he minimized when he said that it had made "enormous profits." Since its formation in 1867, the company had paid an annual dividend of 8 per cent, and during the depression dividends were increased while wages were being cut 25 per cent. For the year ending July 31, 1894, the corporation had an undivided surplus of $2,320,000, exceeding its total wage outlay for six months. Losses on the contracts received in 1894 were borne equally by the workers and the company, but, in the opinion of the Federal commission, "three-quarters of the loss for the company and the balance for labor would have more fairly equalized the division of loss on these contracts." Brushing aside the corporation's plea that, in addition to other losses, it had received no interest on its investment, the commission emphasized that much greater losses would have followed a complete shutdown.

As early as December, 1893, the Pullman Company was forced to issue a public statement denying the existence of extreme distress among its workers. The denial was easy to read, and easy to believe for men who had their own distress. Nobody cared much about poverty in Pullman except the residents of Pullman. During the harsh Illinois winter, want and suffering there became unbearable. Children lacked the money to buy school books, but that didn't matter—they also lacked the shoes and coats needed to go to school. In some homes they were kept in bed all day because there was no coal in the house; in others they were sent to bed early because there was no food for dinner. All joy passed from life. Sullen, tight-lipped women walked lead-footed through their worries. Men stood day after day by their windows and looked at the dirty black snow in the street—no work, no money, little hope. They erupted into violent rage, kicking the dog, swearing at the children, berating the wife for unmentionable evils. Nothing to do but stand at a window all day, looking at the dirty black snow and hearing a baby's whine from the next room.

Spring brought back hope, not much but a little. Men began to talk about striking one good blow against Pullman. During March and April, a majority of the employees joined the American Railway Union—they were eligible because the company operated a few miles of track near the factory. Finally on May 7, 1894, a committee of forty employees visited vice-president Wickes to present their complaints about wages and working conditions. Wickes told the committee to return two days later with their grievances down in writing; but on May 9 Wickes again delayed, promising to personally investigate the shop abuses. The men were not satisfied. Words were cheap, they thought; you couldn't trust Wickes. The next night the grievance committee held an all-night session at the Turner Hall in Kensington, an adjoining town, to discuss the advisability of a strike. George Howard and Sylvester Keliher were both at the meeting to urge delay until Wickes had completed his investigation. Howard had previously wired to Debs, who was in Terre Haute, that a walkout might occur. Debs, knowing nothing of conditions in Pullman, had advised caution until the union could learn the facts. But Howard's oratory, Keliher's ebullient charm, and Debs' influence all went for nothing. The workers were mad. God Himself could not have stopped them. On the third ballot they voted unanimously to strike.

At noon on May 11, three thousand workers left their jobs in the Pullman shops, and the remaining three hundred men were quickly laid off by the company. The walkout was calm, with no hint of violence. The strikers posted guards around the plant to make certain that vandals would have no chance to damage corporation property. Driven to the end of the tether, these men had snapped the chains and struck, but they struck without much hope. Resigned desperation was the major key in a May 13 statement by Thomas Heathcote, the strike committee's chairman: "We do not expect the company to concede our demands. We do not know what the outcome will be, and in fact we do not care much. We do know that we are working for less wages than will maintain ourselves and families in the necessaries of life, and on that proposition we absolutely refuse to work any longer."

Notified that the strike had begun, Debs at once hurried to Pullman to investigate its causes. The ARU had neither called nor authorized the walkout but these men were members of the union and Debs' clear responsibility was to ascertain the justice of their action. Seven years earlier he had protested against George Pullman's labor policies, but he was ill prepared for what he found in 1894. The Pullman employees told incredible but truthful stories of hardship. One skilled mechanic worked ten hours a day for twelve days, and then received a pay check for seven cents; his wages had been $9.07, but nine dollars rent for his company-owned house had been deducted in advance. A fireman worked "428 hours per month or about sixteen hours per day, and receives therefrom $40.00 per month pay," according to Mr. Carwardine. A blacksmith, paid forty-five cents for working six hours, declared that he was not willing to starve and wear out his clothes on Pullman's anvil at the same time. "I have a wife and four children," another employee said, "and it was for them that I struck, as I think that when a man is sober and steady, and has a saving wife, one who is willing to help along, and after working two and a half years for a company he finds himself in debt for a common living, something must be wrong."

Working conditions, almost as much as wages, had stimulated the revolt. There was a rigid hierarchy in the shops, no official daring to contradict his superiors. Foremen were free to curse and abuse their men, confident their authority would be always upheld. One worker explained how the company systematically used the speed-up system: "cabinetmakers were rated at seventeen to nineteen cents [per hour], and prices for piece work were supposed to be made to enable men to make that rate; wherever a man made over one or two cents per hour above day rate, that particular job was again pruned in price." There was no recognition of merit in the company's policies, and thirty years of loyal service were no guarantee against discharge without cause. One man was blacklisted for a trivial offense; forty employees were blacklisted in another case. There was no pension for laid-off or retired workers, many of them spending their last days in a poorhouse. Mr. Carwardine charged that the company did not pay disability damages "unless absolutely compelled to, to those who are injured or die in its service." All inventions by employees were simply appropriated by the corporation, the inventor receiving neither payment nor recognition.

On May 14, Eugene Debs spent the entire day wandering through the town of Pullman, inspecting the houses, talking with the women and children, noticing the size of pay checks, hearing complaints by the score, by the hundred. That night Debs left for St. Paul, but four days later he was back in Pullman and spent most of the day and evening there. As one link clutched the next to form an ugly chain of greed and injustice, his hesitation disappeared. Finally he told a meeting of Pullman employees:

> If it is a fact that after working for George M. Pullman for years you appear two weeks after your work stops, ragged and hungry, it only emphasizes the charge I made before this community, and Pullman stands before you a self-confessed robber . . . The paternalism of Pullman is the same as the self-interest of a slave-holder in his human chattels. You are striking to avert slavery and degradation. . . .

The Pullman Company did not retreat, nor did the workers. At noon on June 26, the deadline set by the convention, Debs ordered all sleeping cars cut from the trains and sidetracked. The railroads at once took an active rôle in the conflict; they refused to move any trains without Palace Cars on the grounds that their contracts with Pullman were inviolable. The General Managers Association,* which was the employers' general staff

---

* Hereafter called The Managers.

throughout the boycott, welcomed a showdown fight with the ARU. The railroads had consistently discriminated against ARU members, and they had refused to give Debs and his colleagues the free passes which they handed out to officials in the Brotherhoods. Thus the ARU came into immediate conflict with one of the strongest groups of employers in America; The Managers represented the twenty-four railroads terminating or centering in Chicago, which had a combined capital of eight hundred and eighteen million dollars, operated forty-one thousand miles of track, and had two hundred twenty-one thousand employees.

Foreseeing opposition from the railroads, Debs had already asked for assistance from the AFL and the Brotherhoods. A return wire from Samuel Gompers showed the reluctance in that sector: "Just received telegram signed your name. Verify same by letter giving full particulars." Only president John McBride of the Mine Workers promised full cooperation; the others replied evasively or negatively, and most of the Brotherhoods worked against the boycott. When four hundred engineers struck on the Wabash, P. M. Arthur denounced the act as a violation of the Engineers' rules. Under the circumstances, he said, unemployed engineers would be permitted to fill the vacancies left by the strikers. The chief of the Conductors took the same stand, replying that he had "neither authority nor inclination" to help the ARU. He later said that the craft jurisdiction of his organization made it hostile to the industrial union led by Debs, and that the boycott was wrong, "no matter what the conditions at Pullman were." The Brotherhood of Trainmen instructed its members to "perform their regular duties and no others, that is to say, they were not expected to leave their trains as conductors or brakemen and go into the yard where the switchmen had struck out of sympathy or otherwise." Since the Trainmen had itself organized switchmen, this provision had little practical meaning. The BLF was more cautious in its hostility; Frank Sargent later said:

> The B. of L.F. could not take part in the strike because our Constitution prohibits it. The B. of L.F. must observe their agreements. B. of L.F. committees should immediately call upon railway officials and make arrangements so that they would not be called upon to fire engines vacated by strikers.

But Debs had no time to send Gompers "full particulars" or to negotiate with the Brotherhood leaders. The nerve center of the boycott was set up in Uhlich's Hall, the ARU offices, at 421 Ashland Block, being much too small. Coordination of five hundred local unions and thousands of men rested in the hands of Debs, Howard, Keliher, Rogers, a few organizers, and Theodore Debs, who was again working side by side with his brother. The boycott began slowly. In spite of the convention orders, each ARU lodge was constitutionally forced to hold its own vote to determine whether it would support the boycott. Every lodge voted to enforce the convention's decision. The boycott was not called solely from sympathy with the Pullman workers; the railroad employees were also suffering from blacklists, short hours, wage cuts, discrimination. Also the feeling was widespread that, if the corporations succeeded in conquering the unorganized workers, they would next move against the organized men. Even among skilled workers there was agreement with Debs' statement: "Every concession the railway companies have ever made, has been wrung from them by the power of organized effort." As lodge after lodge voted to quit work, Debs sent them all the same instructions: Use no violence. Stop no trains. Elect a strike committee and send me the name of the chairman. In this way he hoped to keep control over the entire boycott.

By June 27 only five thousand men had left their jobs, but fifteen railroads were tied up. The Managers opened offices in Pittsburgh, Cleveland, Philadelphia, New York, and Buffalo, to recruit strikebreakers; they also opened a central publicity office in Chicago to furnish information to the newspapers. Soon the commercial press raised the cry of "Anarchy"; this charge was doubly effective because President Sadi Carnot of France had been assassinated by an anarchist just two days before the boycott began. The third day, more than forty thousand men had quit work. Traffic was stopped dead on all lines west of Chicago. In spite of Debs' orders to move mail trains, the Postal authorities reported that mails were obstructed at Chicago, St. Paul, and on the Southern Pacific in the Far West. United States Attorneys were instructed by the Justice Department to ask for warrants against all offenders.

One day later, nearly a hundred twenty-five thousand men had joined the boycott. Twenty roads were tied up. A crowd of a thousand strikers and sympathizers stopped a train on the Chicago & Erie at Hammond, Indiana, and forced the crew to detach two Pullmans. The head of the Switchmen warned that any member of his union supporting the strike would be subject to expulsion, and the Conductor's chief attacked the boycott in the public press.

But several unions rallied to the ARU. J. R. Sovereign pledged aid from the Knights of Labor. The Chicago Federation of Labor, with one hundred fifty thousand members, offered to call a city-wide general strike to enforce the boycott. In view of the probable effects on public opinion, Debs refused to sanction such an extreme measure at that stage. During the entire boycott he divided his attention between the need to maintain the strikers' morale and the equal need to win support among other trade unions and the general community. On one occasion he even relaxed the boycott in order to implement its ultimate chances. The Illinois Federation of Labor had called a conference to meet in Springfield on July 1, to consider the political program of the AFL and to organize "independent political action" by the labor movement. In order to reach Springfield, the Chicago delegates would be forced to travel over a struck railroad. Finding himself "at sea," president W. H. Madden of the state federation went to see Debs. The strike leader quickly grasped the publicity value of the conference, which planned to use July Fourth to "dedicate anew the common people to the principles of the Declaration of Independence." So he willingly gave the delegates permission to employ any service available to reach Springfield.

Throughout the East, The Managers continued to hire strikebreakers, and the depression provided hordes of recruits. Intimate grudges also motivated many railroaders to become scabs. One group in New York City told a reporter: "We are going to settle an old account. We were strikers on the Gould roads under Martin Irons [1886], and we haven't handled a switch since then. The men who are striking now are the men who helped to fill our places then. Now we are going west to take their jobs." The Managers easily hired from one hundred to two hundred fifty men daily; by the strike's end nearly twenty-five hundred strikebreakers had been sent to Chicago.

On June 30, in spite of Debs' orders to the contrary, minor violence again occurred. Crowds in Chicago temporarily halted two express trains on the Illinois Central and Panhandle lines. Union leaders were arrested in Indiana and Missouri. The first demand for militia in Illinois came from the Illinois Central, which claimed that its property in Cairo was endangered. Under the laws of Illinois, the governor could call out state troops when the legislature was not in session, but only at the request of the mayor or sheriff. As soon as he had secured permission from these local authorities, Governor Altgeld sent three companies of militia to Cairo. Thomas Milchrist, the Federal district attorney in Chicago, telegraphed to Washington that strikers had stopped mail trains in the suburbs the previous night. He also reported that conditions in Chicago were so bad that special deputies were needed, and recommended that the United States marshal in Chicago be empowered to hire such deputies. This wire by Milchrist exaggerated the actual situation. Five days after he sent the telegram, total strike damages were still less than six thousand dollars. There had been no major riots. The trains halted on the Chicago & Erie, Illinois Central, and Panhandle had soon been allowed to proceed. The telegram from Milchrist was contradicted by a simultaneous telegram from the Superintendent of Railway Mail Service in Chicago, telling the Postmaster General that no mail had accumulated in the city.

Most important of all, the local authorities were confident of their ability to handle the situation. Mayor Hopkins had not even applied to the governor for help, although Altgeld had shown both his willingness and efficiency in controlling labor violence. As recently as June 16, striking coal miners at Mount Olive, Illinois, had interfered with the movement of trains to prevent the shipment of nonunion coal. Mail trains were among those detained. The Federal court had issued an injunction against the rioters; and the United States marshal, believing that his forces were inadequate, had applied to the Attorney-General for advice. Attorney-General Richard Olney had immediately wired an answer:

Washington, June 16, 1894.

Allen, U.S. Judge, Springfield, Ill.:

Understand State of Illinois is willing to protect property against lawless violence with military force if necessary. Please advise receivers to take proper steps to procure protection by civil authorities of the State. If such protection proves inadequate, the governor should be applied to for military assistance.

Olney, Attorney General

Within one day after application was made to Altgeld, the state militia had arrived in Mount Olive and succeeded in moving all trains. Thus Richard Olney had established a procedure for such situations in which deputy marshals were not required; but Milchrist now asked for Federal marshals without first going to the Federal courts, the local authorities, or the governor of Illinois.

The newspaper campaign against the boycott was in full swing, with the Chicago *Tribune* leading the onslaught. On June 30 the *Tribune* let fly with both barrels. One headline read, "Mob Is In Control"; another charged, "Law Is Trampled On"; a third story began: "Through the lawless acts of Dictator Debs' strikers the lives of thousands of Chicago citizens were endangered yesterday." The Chicago *Herald* editorialized: "The necessity is on the railroads to defeat the strike. If they yield one point it will show fatal weakness. If the strike should be successful the owners of the railroad property . . . would have to surrender its future control to the class of labor agitators and strike conspirators who have formed the Debs Railway Union." There were recurrent charges in the press that Debs was a dictator, that he was personally profiting from the strike, that he had called the strike without consulting the union membership. It was widely, and falsely, reported that Debs had ridden in a Pullman car from Chicago to Terre Haute during the boycott.

Immediately after Milchrist sent his telegram to Washington, the General Managers Association met in closed session at the Rookery Building in Chicago. All newspaper reporters were excluded. At this meeting the railroads agreed that they would not rehire any of the strikers. They also sent a wire to Richard Olney, suggesting that he appoint Edwin Walker as special Federal attorney to handle the strike situation. Walker was, at that time, attorney in Illinois for the Chicago, Milwaukee & St. Paul Railroad, a job he had held since 1870. This railroad was involved in the strike, and was a member of the Managers Association. A few days earlier, Walker had been asked to handle all strike cases for the railroads. But within two hours, without even pausing to consult Milchrist, Olney had appointed Walker to represent the Federal government.

Eugene Debs, who had just tried to resign his job because of ill health, was being subjected to tremendous strain. He was working at top speed clear around the clock. Detailed instructions had to be sent to hundreds of railroad towns in order to bolster the weak spots. Constant warnings against violence and the obstruction of mail trains were necessary. Howard, Keliher, Rogers—they were burning up their lives with harried but jubilant abandon. Uhlich's Hall had become a delivery room for chaos. The executive board was in practically uninterrupted session, discussing this development, considering that possibility. The large hall was packed with excited men, screaming, yelling, shouting questions, singing. Exhausted men staggered out of executive board meetings in the small room, spoke briefly to the excited throng in the hall, went back to the board room. They hammered out press releases, sent appeals for help to labor unions from New York to San Diego. Couriers were constantly running back and forth to the Western Union—in three weeks the executive board sent more than nine thousand telegrams. And Debs moved from one room to another, talking, making decisions, always smiling, seeming strangely misplaced in an immaculate tweed suit and hard white collar. Even the reporters noticed that the calm assurance and control of the strike leader seemed indestructible. They always looked to him, watched him, wrote reams of copy about him, little realizing the expert organization that was working with him. Theodore was always at hand, the other ARU officers were indispensable.

Opposition to the boycott was gathering intensity. The railroads began deliberately to disrupt their schedules, hoping that the resultant inconvenience to the public would force government intervention. Pullmans were attached to trains that did not customarily carry them—freights, suburbans, and, most important of all, mail trains, trying to force the strikers to halt the mails. The Brotherhoods accelerated their campaign against the ARU. Conductors in Fort Wayne, Indiana, denounced the strike, declaring that they would not aid in any way. P. M. Arthur announced that he did not care whether the railroads employed union or nonunion engineers and firemen; any engineers who refused to work with strikebreakers could be fired without protest from the Brotherhood. Frank Sargent declared that any fireman who joined the strike would have to look to the ARU for help— he would get none from the BLF.

Never before had there been such a strike in the United States. More than a hundred thousand men had voluntarily quit work. Between Chicago and the Golden Gate, only the Great Northern was maintaining a semblance of its regular schedule. Everybody in the country had taken sides in the dispute. Debs clearly stated the situation in a speech to the railroaders:

> The struggle with the Pullman Company has developed into a contest between the producing classes and the money power of the country. . . . The fight was between the American Railway Union and the Pullman Company. . . . Then the railway corporations, through the General Managers' Association, came to the rescue, and in a series of whereases declared to the world that they would go into partnership with Pullman, so to speak, and stand by him in his devilish work of starving his employees to death.

On July 1, the union was firm at every point, and there was "no sign of violence or disorder," as Debs said. He later claimed that the railroads were losing a fortune daily: "Their immediate resources were exhausted, their properties paralyzed, and they were unable to operate their trains." Although the ARU had few members in the East and South, it seemed that the boycott might spread to northern New York and perhaps to Pennsylvania. The Central Labor Union of New York City endorsed the boycott, and urged people not to ride in Pullmans until the company accepted arbitration. The Central Labor Union of Chicago took similar action. In spite of the massed billions of Pullman and the railroads, in spite of the newspaper barrage, in spite of strikebreaking by the Brotherhoods and inaction by the AFL, Eugene Debs saw the road to victory stretching bright and certain into the future.

Deb's confidence reckoned without one possibility—Federal intervention. Throughout the critical period of the boycott, President Cleveland was occupied in a bitter fight with Congress over the Wilson Tariff Bill, and his only information about the strike came from Attorney-General Olney.

Richard Olney, from 1859 until his elevation to the cabinet in 1893, had been a corporation lawyer in Boston, representing mainly railroad interests and trust estates. He had also been a director of several railroads: the Eastern, the Boston & Maine, lesser New England lines, the Kansas City & Fort Scott, the Atchison. Since 1889 he had served on the board of the Burlington, which was involved in the Pullman dispute. His very appearance indicated his dominant characteristics—a narrow honesty, truculence, and stubbornness. He was tall, with open and quivering nostrils, a drooping mustache, dark brown hair just turning gray. His body tilted aggressively forward, he stalked swiftly in pursuit of Duty. Olney's violent and unpredictable temper had been illustrated by an incident several years earlier, when he forbade his daughter to enter his house following her marriage, even though he himself had approved the daughter's choice. The edict was still in effect.

Olney proposed to deal with the strikers much as he had dealt with his daughter. As soon as the Debs Rebellion started, the Attorney-General launched a series of maneuvers to defeat it. He thought that a nation-wide boycott was so essentially violent that Debs' order for peaceful conduct was a mere sham. In a memorandum about the Pullman affair, Olney later wrote: "The President might have used the United States Army to prevent interference with the mails and with interstate commerce on his own initiative—without waiting for action by the courts . . . But . . . it is doubtful . . . whether the President could be induced to move except in support of the judicial tribunals." So the Attorney-General decided to prod Cleveland by securing an injunction against the strike, and then use the Army to enforce the court order. This plan, as well as Olney's intention of smashing the boycott, was revealed in his telegram to Edwin Walker on June 30: "It has seemed to me that if the rights of the United States were vigorously asserted in Chicago, the origin and centre of the demonstration, the result would be to make it a failure everywhere else and to prevent its spread over the entire country. . . . I feel that the true way of dealing with the matter is by a force which is overwhelming and prevents any attempt at resistance."

Olney's attitude rested on three premises: (1) Any national railroad strike is automatically illegal; (2) The causes of the strike in Pullman were not relevant to the legality of the boycott; (3) The state and local officials could not be trusted to enforce the law. Altgeld, after all, had pardoned the Haymarket survivors, and Mayor Hopkins of Chicago had openly contributed to the relief fund at Pullman. Olney later claimed that Hopkins "even went so far as to openly wear the distinctive badge of the rioters"— a white ribbon was the emblem of the strikers, and Olney thought all strikers were "rioters" in this instance.

In accord with this interpretation, the Attorney-General was trying to persuade the President that the Army should be used at Chicago, and the troops at Fort Sheridan, Illinois, were ordered to hold themselves in readiness. Meanwhile a constant demand for the maintenance of law and order was emanating from the pulpits and the commercial newspapers. On July 2 a headline on the Chicago *Tribune* screeched:

STRIKE IS NOW WAR

And the lead editorial had a shrewd caption:

Six Days Shalt Thou Labor—BIBLE
Not Unless I Say So   —DEBS

In New York the Reverend Robert S. MacArthur said that there were "more Anarchists today in Chicago than in St. Petersburg . . . Anarchists should be excluded from the United States." He added that all boycotts are "unmanly and un-American." The Reverend A. C. Dixon of Brooklyn also contributed to calm consideration of the matter: "the Anarchist is a savage in a civilized country who is trying to turn civilization into barbarism."

That same day, in a crushing blow, Judges Peter Grosscup and William A. Woods of the Federal Court in Chicago issued an omnibus injunction against the ARU leaders. The previous Decoration Day, Judge Grosscup had said in a speech: "The growth of labor organizations must be checked by law." It was later shown that Judge Woods had accepted such important favors from the railroads that his impartiality was doubtful. Their irregular procedure in this case is therefore not surprising: Milchrist and Walker had prepared the application for the injunction, and the two judges had helped them to revise it before court opened. The breadth of their order was astonishing. Using the Sherman Antitrust Act of 1890 as authority, the injunction prohibited the strike leaders from any action to aid the boycott. They were forbidden to answer questions, to send telegrams. They were denied the right to urge men, by word of mouth, to join the boycott. Their constitutional rights to speak, write, and assemble freely, were ignored. They were, in short, completely shackled. Even Grover Cleveland was forced to admit that "a sweeping injunction had been granted against Eugene V. Debs."

Richard Olney, in a letter to Edwin Walker, September 24, 1894, justified the injunction under both the Sherman Antitrust Law and the powers of a court of equity "to enjoin a public nuisance when it threatens a public injury." Under his second thesis Olney made six points: (1) the obstruction of a public highway is a public nuisance; (2) railroads are public highways; (3) interstate railroads are Federal highways; (4) any obstruction of a Federal highway is enjoinable; (5) "the concerted, sudden, and simultaneous withdrawal from service of the trained corps of expert employees necessary to the operation" of railroads is an obstruction; (6) any act to promote a railroad strike can be enjoined. Olney's basic argument was used by scores of professors who defended the writ in law journals. Congressmen, without understanding the doctrine, spoke for days in its defense. Ministers solemnly identified the injunction with the voice of God.

The attack on the injunction was equally savage. The New York *Times,* while opposing the strikers, referred to the court order as "one of those peculiar instruments that punishes an individual for doing a certain thing, and is equally merciless if he does not do it, so it is difficult to understand how the strikers can maintain their present policy and at the same time evade its operation or escape its influence." The trade unions claimed that this injunction had taken from the railroaders the only weapon with which they could fight against corporate injustice, and that it gave the railroads unqualified power over all employees. Railroad workers still had the right to quit work individually, but where could they find other jobs during a depression? The unions objected to the absolute power of Judges Grosscup and Woods to punish violations of an order they themselves issued. They protested against issuance of the injunction without giving the ARU a chance to present its objections. They vehemently exclaimed that the government had shown scant knowledge and no respect for the rights and problems of the workingmen.

As soon as the injunction was served, Debs called the ARU executive board into session to decide their response. Violation of the writ might result in jail sentences for the union officials, and also have the effect of placing all strikers outside the law, in active opposition to the Federal government. On the other hand, obedience to the order would crush the strike, and would end all hope of forcing compromise by the Pullman company. Obedience would destroy the ARU and cause thousands of men to lose their jobs, since the railroads had pledged themselves not to rehire any striker. The job, already begun at Homestead, Buffalo, and Coeur d'Alene, of crushing the morale of labor would be completed; moreover, it would be a signal for the employers to move immediately against every trade union in America. The executive board came to a decision—they would ignore the injunction. Eugene Debs bitterly declared: "the crime of the American Railway Union was the practical exhibition of sympathy for the Pullman employees."

The ARU officials realized that they would surely be called into court to answer for this decision. Legal advice had been supplied, up to this point in the boycott, by the regular ARU attorneys and by William Irwin, a well-known Minneapolis lawyer; but Debs now resolved to hire an expert in equity and constitutional law. His choice seemed rather strange on the surface—he went to Clarence Darrow, attorney for the Chicago & North-western Railroad, which was involved in the dispute. Darrow had come to Chicago in 1887 from Ashtabula, Ohio, a young, poorly trained, country lawyer. Having few clients, Darrow was able to take an active part in Grover Cleveland's campaign in 1888. He gave several speeches without attracting any notice, but then he was invited to speak with Henry George at a Free Trade Conference in the Central Music Hall. His address that evening was splashed all over the front pages; he became a celebrity. In the audience had been DeWitt C. Cregier, who was elected Democratic mayor of Chicago a few weeks later. Judge John Peter Altgeld urged Cregier to give his friend Darrow a job. Cregier agreed. Darrow was named special assessment attorney of Chicago. Three months later a po-litical shift forced the resignation of the Assistant Corporation Counsel, and Darrow was promoted. Soon after that, ill health caused the retirement of the Corporation Counsel, and Darrow, a resident of Chicago less than two years, became head of the city's legal department. In 1892 he left public office to become general attorney of the Chicago & Northwestern. The Northwestern Railroad thought that their new employee was rather eccentric—he sympathized with labor, was always speaking at meetings of radicals and free-thinkers, played a leading rôle in the amnesty campaign for the Haymarket survivors—but they knew that he was a brilliant lawyer. Debs' choice was not so strange after all.

This request by the ARU put Darrow in a ticklish position. He had previously been named by the Chicago & Northwestern as their representative on the committee that was conducting the strike for the railroads, and had refused the appointment on the grounds that his sympathies were with the union. But he was now being asked, in effect, to resign completely his job in order to take a series of cases that would involve little pay and gruelling work. The courts' preference for property rights over civil liberties would make it almost impossible to successfully defend his clients. It was a hard choice to make. Darrow's conviction, Debs' persuasiveness, and the arguments of several mutual friends, finally turned the trick. Darrow became special counsel for the ARU.

The situation was indeed becoming desperate. An increasing number of strikebreakers were being brought into Chicago. The ARU charged that the railroads were even trying to inflame religious divisions among the strikers. The governor of Michigan ordered out the militia, although the United Press stated from Battle Creek: "The company has no men here that it can use to pull the trains if there were 1,000,000 soldiers here, and it is esteemed unwarranted. Then again the men have done nothing to prevent the company from moving its trains. The strikers say they will furnish all the men wanted for mail trains."

Throughout the country the injunction was being used against the strikers. As sweeping as the court order had been, the interpretations of it were even more sweeping. George Howard later testified to the Federal investigating commission:

> Men have been arrested in Chicago because they refused to turn switches when told to; they were arrested when they refused to get on an engine and fire an engine; . . . in Albuquerque, New Mexico, they arrested a man and he was sentenced to fifteen days in jail because he refused to get on an engine and fire it when told; the fact that he did not get on the engine was considered contempt of court.

And then, on July 4, Grover Cleveland played the leading rôle in the last great act of the drama. The issuance of the injunction had severely increased the problems and anxieties of the strike leaders. Debs had slept only a few hours a night since the beginning of the boycott; with this added strain it was long after midnight when he and Theodore arrived at their room in the Leland Hotel for some brief and troubled rest. Early on the morning of Independence Day, they were awakened by the sound of bugles and voices right under their window. Thinking that it might be a parade, Debs sleepily walked to the window and gazed down at Jackson Street and Lake Michigan. The sight he saw caused instant consternation. Hundreds of Federal soldiers were encamped along the lake front.

Richard Olney, who furnished the guiding hand for Cleveland's act, could cite a precedent for the use of the Army in such cases. During the railroad strikes of 1877, United States troops had been sent into Maryland, Illinois, Pennsylvania, and West Virginia, at the request of the governors. Moreover, and this was of critical significance to Olney's plan, on that occasion the Army was used in Indiana and Missouri on application of Federal marshals, not of any state officials. Already during the Pullman boycott, the Army had been sent to Los Angeles, to Raton, New Mexico, and to Trinidad, Colorado. Although violence had occurred in these places, Governor Davis Waite of Colorado had violently objected to the Administration's action on the ground that the militia was competent to handle the small disturbance in his state.

When Olney first proposed sending troops to Chicago, Secretary of War Daniel S. Lamont and General Nelson A. Miles had both opposed the suggestion. But only July 3, Olney received from Judge Grosscup, Marshal J. W. Arnold, Walker, and Milchrist, a telegram that was misleading in five respects. This telegram stated that violence had occurred in Chicago, when it actually occurred in a suburb. The telegram failed to mention that the violence, which flared up briefly on July 2, had subsided by July 3. The wire also alleged, without proof, that no authority less than the Army could protect the mails, that the workers of Chicago would join a general strike "today, and in my opinion will be joining the mob tonight, and especially tomorrow . . ." Secretary Lamont and General Miles now approved Olney's plan.

President Cleveland promptly ordered the entire command at Fort Sheridan to Chicago for the following purposes:

1. To protect Federal property
2. To prevent obstruction of the U.S. mails.
3. To prevent interference with interstate commerce.
4. To enforce the decrees of the Federal courts.

The facts were that no Federal property had been destroyed in Chicago, and there seemed to be no imminent danger. The Superintendent of Railway Mail Service had stated that no mail had accumulated there. Mail trains were still moving. Trains, including mail trains, had been detained in the suburbs, but this had not happened since July 2. The chief obstruction to interstate commerce lay in the workers' refusal to haul Pullman cars. If the ARU was right in its contention that the injunction was illegal, there was no court decree to be enforced.

Cleveland's action involved him in a heated dispute with Governor Altgeld. The President had relied for authority on two Civil War statutes, which had never been used in time of peace. The President has power, according to the United States Constitution, to send the Army into a state "on Application of the Legislature, or of the Executive (when the Legislature cannot be convened)" in order to protect the state "against domestic Violence." In a lengthy telegram to Cleveland, Altgeld protested that neither he nor the Legislature had applied for assistance. There were three regiments of militiamen in Chicago that could have been mustered into service, but "nobody in Cook county, whether official or private citizen," had asked for their help. It was true that violence had occurred, but it was easily handled by the local and state authorities. "At present some of our railroads are paralyzed," wrote Altgeld, "not by reason of obstruction, but because they cannot get men to operate their trains. For some reason they are anxious to keep this fact from the public, and for this purpose they are making an outcry about the obstruction in order to divert public attention. . . . The newspaper accounts have in many cases been pure fabrications, and in others wild exaggerations." The Governor protested lastly, "that local self-government is a fundamental principle of our Constitution. Each community shall govern itself so long as it can and is ready and able to enforce the law . . ."

President Cleveland briefly replied that the postal authorities had asked for the removal of obstructions to the mails, that Judge Grosscup had asked for help in enforcing the injunction, and that there was "competent proof that conspiracies existed against commerce between the states." On any of these grounds, wrote Cleveland, he could have ordered Federal troops into Illinois.

Altgeld, however, was not to be put off so easily. In a second long telegram he protested that Cleveland's action violated state's rights, established military rule in Illinois, and indicated a swollen and unconstitutional judgment of the powers of the President. The conclusion of Altgeld's wire was plain enough: ". . . believing that the ordering out of the Federal troops was unwarranted, I again ask their withdrawal." But Cleveland was even more brusque: "While I am still persuaded that I have neither transcended my authority nor duty in the emergency that confronts us, it seems to me that in this hour of danger and public distress, discussion may well give way to active efforts on the part of all in authority to restore obedience to law and to protect life and property."

Altgeld was forced to yield to the power of the Army, but similar protests were made by the governors of Kansas, Colorado, Texas, and Oregon. Neither Cleveland nor Olney had any doubts about the correctness of their action. When reporters called at Olney's office on July 4, they found him sending a wire to Milchrist instructing the immediate indictment of the strike leaders. He seemed pleased with developments, and told the reporters: "We have been brought to the ragged edge of anarchy, and it is time to see whether the law is sufficiently strong to prevent this condition of affairs. If not, the sooner we know it the better, that it may be changed." Cleveland had succinctly expressed his views to a friend: "If it takes every dollar in the Treasury and every soldier in the United States Army to deliver a postal card in Chicago, that postal card shall be delivered." A political colleague later said the President thought his action in the Pullman boycott was one of the best moves he made in either of his administrations.

Debs, like Altgeld, was unable to find any justification for the use of the Army. The militia were under arms in twenty states. In a few western states, the railroads were so unpopular that the state troops had refused to act against the strikers, but this was not true in Illinois. It seemed to the ARU officials that Cleveland and Olney had joined the railroads in a campaign to destroy their union, and this belief was heightened when The Managers announced that they would not confer with the municipal authorities or any other party to arbitrate or compromise the dispute. The Administration had exerted tremendous pressure on the strikers, but it had not said a single harsh word about George M. Pullman or the railroads. Debs had not objected to the use of state troops and local police, but he deeply resented the implication that the strikers were in rebellion against their government, and that the United States Army was needed to quell the riots. His protest to the President, made jointly with J. R. Sovereign, warned Grover Cleveland that his course would lead to rebellion. The two unionists contended that "a deep-seated conviction is fast becoming prevalent that this Government is soon to be declared a military despotism." The railroad themselves, who were accused of refusal to carry mail on trains to which Pullmans were not attached, were charged with full responsibility for the interruption of the United States mails.

Debs feared that the presence of Federal troops in Chicago would serve, not to keep the peace, but to inflame the populace, and he heatedly told a United Press reporter:

> The first shots fired by the regular soldiers at the mobs here will be the signal for a civil war. I believe this as firmly as I believe in the ultimate success of our course. Bloodshed will follow, and ninety per cent of the people of the United States will be arrayed against the other ten per cent. And I would not care to be arrayed against the laboring people in the contest, or find myself out of the ranks of labor when the struggle ended.

This prediction proved all too true. Although there had been brief but serious outbreaks in the suburbs on June 30 and July 2, no violence had occurred in Chicago before July 5. On that day railroad tracks were blocked, a freight train was stalled, a signal house was burned. The regular soldiers made a bayonet charge against a crowd, and several people were injured. Strike damage in the city still totaled less than six thousand dollars, but Mayor Hopkins was sufficiently alarmed to issue a proclamation which forbade riotous assemblies.

At the suggestion of Governor Altgeld, Hopkins formally requested state troops on July 6. Railroad property valued at three hundred forty thousand dollars was destroyed in Chicago on that day alone, although on no other day did damage exceed four thousand dollars. The presence of the Army had indeed proved to be a "signal for civil war," as Debs said; but the hundreds of special Federal deputy marshals had an even worse effect. Since men with regular employment were unwilling to accept these temporary jobs, Marshal Arnold had deputized labor spies, professional strikebreakers, racketeers, petty gangsters, the flotsam and jetsam of the city. Several public officials fiercely attacked these special deputies. Governor Waite of Colorado called them "desperadoes" who had been hired "without any regard for their qualifications but simply for military purposes." On July 6 near Pullman, where a mob of hoodlums was overturning freight cars, one of these deputies deliberately killed an innocent spectator. Accidentally shot while standing nearly a hundred yards from the scene of the riot, the victim tried to rise, but the deputy advanced upon him and shot him again. The killer was never arrested, although his identity was well known. Police Chief John Brennan of Chicago later testified that, on one occasion, these deputies fired into a group of people when there was no disturbance and no reason for firing. "Innocent men and women were killed by these shots," he added. "Several of these officials were arrested during the strike for stealing property from railroad cars. In one instance, two of them were found under suspicious circumstances near a freight car which had just been set on fire. They were dangerous to the lives of the citizens on account of their careless use of pistols."

The union also claimed that the railroads had burned their own cars in order to discredit the strike and collect damages and insurance on obsolete equipment. According to Debs, the assistant fire chief of Chicago once caught several deputy marshals cutting fire hoses when some cars were burning. Some newspapers supported the union's claim. "The railroads had everything to gain by a little well advertised rioting which could be attributed to the strikers," said the New York *Morning Journal.* "The strikers had everything to lose by violence and they knew it." Although the maximum pay of Federal deputies was $2.50 per day plus $1.50 expense money, the government paid out three hundred seventy-five thousand dollars to deputies during the boycott. In Chicago alone, the cost to the Treasury was a hundred twenty-five thousand dollars, and many deputies were paid their salaries by the railroads.

It was charged that soldiers also deliberately tried to provoke violence. Brand Whitlock, Governor Altgeld's secretary, told about one colonel, drunk in a Chicago club, who wished that he might have an entire regiment to shoot the strikers, "each man to take aim at a dirty white ribbon." But several Army officers in Chicago, according to Mayor Hazen S. Pingree of Detroit, soon realized that the newspaper stories about the strike were biased. These officers, at a small meeting in a hotel, decided that the strikers had a just cause and that the Army had been called out solely to break the strike. Resolving to publicize their views, they scheduled a second meeting to draft a statement. Before this second meeting could be held, news of the first gathering leaked out. All of the participating officers were held for courts-martial. This action was squelched by direct order of the President, said Pingree, "but the colonel was retired from active service and the other officers cowed by pressure from Washington authorities." Pingree was convinced that the troops had been used, "not so much to quell a riot as to crush labor unions."

Debs, continuing his efforts to stop violence, repeated his instructions to the strikers.

> I appeal to you to be men, orderly and law-abiding. Our cause is just, the great public is with us, and we have nothing to fear.
>
> Let it be borne in mind that if the railroad companies can secure men to handle their trains, they have that right. Our men have the right to quit, but their right ends there. Other men have the right to take their places, whatever the opinion of the propriety of so doing may be.
>
> Keep away from railroad yards, or right of way, or other places where large crowds congregate. A safe plan is to remain away entirely from places where there is any likelihood of an outbreak.
>
> The railroad managers have sought to make it appear that their trains do not move because of the interference of the strikers. The statement is an unqualified falsehood, and no one knows this better than the managers themselves. They make this falsehood serve their purpose of calling out the troops.
>
> Respect the law, conduct yourselves as becomes men and our cause shall be crowned with success.

The riots, the arson, the bloodshed, the deliberate provocations to violence by soldiers and special deputies, had created new worries for Debs. He was nearly always at ARU headquarters, where the men had daily grown more serious, more intense, wondering how the mad holocaust would end, whether it would ever end. Only two days had passed since the Army entered Chicago, but those forty-eight hours had bred a lifetime of torture and anxiety. The ARU leaders were still united in their determination to see the boycott through to the end. The future of the entire labor movement rested with them; if they failed, the workers would suffer for years to come. Clinging to this conviction, Debs sent a wire to all ARU lodges urging them to stand fast:

> Every true man must quit now and remain out until the fight is won. There can be no half way ground. Men must be for us or against us. Our cause is gaining ground daily and our success is only a question of a few days. Do not falter in this hour. Stand erect. Proclaim your manhood. Labor must win now or never. Our victory will be positive and complete. Whatever happens, do not give credence to rumors or newspaper reports.

The opposition was equally confident. Edwin Walker wired to Olney that he had gathered sufficient evidence on an ARU conspiracy to warrant presenting it to the grand jury, which was scheduled to meet July 10. This wire was a strange statement from a neutral official. Before anybody had been indicted, Walker wrote about the probable results of their trial: "I firmly believe that the result of these trials and the punishment of the leaders will be so serious that a general strike upon any railroad will not again occur for a series of years." The same day, the chief of the Brotherhood of Trainmen defended the actions of The Managers on the grounds that they had merely fulfilled their contracts with Pullman, while P. M. Arthur said of the boycott: "Inevitably it must fail. It is a question of but a short time. . . . The Engineers Brotherhood cannot take part in such an unwise movement. It informed Mr. Debs at the outset that we could give him no assistance. Engineers are employed to draw trains, not to build cars." In return, The Managers made it clear that they bore no ill feeling against the Brotherhoods, and Attorney-General Olney later intervened in behalf of the Trainmen in a legal case.

By July 7, the events in Chicago had captured the headlines of every metropolitan newspaper from coast to coast. Some of the headlines were truly terrifying. Destruction of railroad property had been widespread the previous day, with damages amounting to three hundred forty thousand dollars, but the press made it seem that the entire city had been despoiled. A headline in the Washington *Post* told its readers:

Fired By the Mob
Chicago at the Mercy of the Incendiary Torch

and the New York *Sun* was on the same general track:

Wild Riot in Chicago
Hundreds of Freight Cars Burned by Strikers

The most extreme headlines came from the center of the dispute—Chicago —where the *Inter-Ocean* might have been describing the razing of Carthage:

Flames Make Havoc—Unparalleled Scenes of Riot,
Terror and Pillage

Anarchy is Rampant—Mobs at Pullman and Burnside
Apply the Torch

Two Chicago newspapers—the *Daily News* and the *Record*—remained neutral during the boycott, while the *Dispatch,* the *Mail,* and the *Times* defended the strikers. Also individual writers on other papers disagreed with the policy of their employers. The Chicago *Tribune* was forced to fire one reporter who refused to authenticate before the grand jury the printed version of his interview with Debs. Finley Peter Dunne, through the words of that shrewd Irish saloonkeeper Mr. Dooley, contradicted the headlines of the Chicago *Evening Post,* which carried the Mr. Dooley columns. The *Evening Post* on July 7 let its vocabulary run wild:

THIRSTY FOR BLOOD
Frenzied Mob Still Bent on Death and Destruction
Violence on Every Hand

But, in the same issue, Mr. Dooley delivered some pointed gibes at George M. Pullman, who had taken his family to their mansion at Elberon, New Jersey, early in the strike:

This here Pullman makes th' sleepin' ca-ars an' th' constitootion looks after Pullman. He have a good time iv it. He don't need to look afther himself. . . . He owns towns an' min. . . . Whin he has trouble ivry wan on earth excipt thim that rides in smokin' ca-ars whin they rides at all r-runs to fight f'r him. He calls out George Wash'nton an' Abraham Lincoln an' Gin'ral Miles an' Mike Brinnan an' ivry human bein' that rayquires limons an' ice an' thin he puts on his hat an' lams away. 'Gintlemin,' says he, 'I must be off,' he says. 'Go an' kill each other,' he says. 'Fight it out,' he says. 'Defind the constitootion,' he says. 'Me own is not of the best,' he says, 'an' I think I'll help it be spindin' th' summer,' he says, 'piously,' he says, 'on th' shores iv th' Atlantic ocean.'

The most novel touch in this press war was provided by the Chicago newsboys. Most of them wore the strikers' white ribbon, and they dropped those journals which opposed the boycott into sewers.

Violence in Chicago, although abated somewhat from the previous day, was still serious on July 7, when two separate troops of militia were provoked into firing upon crowds of rioters who had taunted and stoned them. Four rioters were killed and forty wounded, some women among them. But at no time during the disorders in Chicago was an ARU member wounded by the police or troops. Debs had constantly argued that the rioting was being done by thugs and riffraff, not by the strikers, and he was determined to keep his men away from the riots. On July 7 he again said in a speech to the ARU men:

> We have repeatedly declared that we will respect law and order, and our conduct must conform to our profession. A man who commits violence in any form, whether a member of our order or not, should be promptly arrested and punished and we should be the first to apprehend the miscreant and bring him to justice. We must triumph as law-abiding citizens or not at all. Those who engage in force and violence are our real enemies.

Debs was guided both by his dislike for violence and by the example of the Great Northern strike, in which peaceful tactics had won a great victory. Seeking to control the strikers, he and the other ARU leaders now moved rapidly from one open-air meeting to another. Each of them addressed from two to six meetings a day, everywhere urging the workers to stand fast and remain away from the railroad lines. During the entire disturbance, the union did not hold a single secret meeting. The leaders spoke on the public highways, near railroad yards or in districts where the railroad workers lived. They moved hastily to any scene of reported rioting and begged the crowds to return peacefully to their homes.

Support for the strike continued to mount among the trade unions. The Central Labor Union of New York City condemned the interference of the Federal government and referred contemptuously to the Brotherhoods as "the Benedict Arnolds of the labor movement." Grand Master Sovereign of the Knights of Labor wired an urgent appeal for fair play to the President. Sam Gompers sent a telegram to Debs: "Have protested Tuesday to President against base action judiciary and improper use of military." But the acts of military tyranny continued to multiply. Debs charged that one soldier had forced a switchman to work at the point of a bayonet. Governor Altgeld later described the arrest of George Lovejoy, a striking trainmaster at LaSalle, Illinois. Lovejoy was taken one hundred miles to Chicago, held for two days by the police, and then was told that they did not care to prosecute.

Debs, still trying to broaden his support, again wired on July 7 to several local labor bodies: "We ask your cooperation . . . we are making a great fight for labor, and deserve the support of all railroad employees. Capital has combined to enslave labor. We must all stand together or go down in hopeless defeat."

Events were moving swiftly. The deadlock could not last much longer. In Hammond, Indiana, one man was killed and several injured when the Army fired into a crowd of rioters. The man killed was a respected carpenter who had no connection with the boycott or the riots; he had gone to the railroad tracks in search of his young son who had wandered away from home. President Cleveland issued a proclamation which in effect declared martial law for the entire area. At that time, there were already six thousand state and Federal troops, five thousand extra deputy marshals, and thirty-one hundred policemen, in Chicago and vicinity.

The Chicago labor movement was infuriated by the events in Hammond and by Cleveland's proclamation. All locals in the city and the heads of seven national unions met at Uhlich's Hall, and demanded that Samuel Gompers call an immediate session of the AFL executive council in Chicago. This meeting also appointed a committee to request Pullman to arbitrate. If he refused, a city-wide general strike would be called. The three representatives from this meeting joined three aldermen in their visit to Pullman, but Vice-President Wickes told the delegation that "the Company was not able to consider the question of arbitration." Therefore the Trades and Labor Council called a general strike as planned, but not more than twenty-five thousand men left their jobs. Thousands of others had already quit work voluntarily in support of the strike, but the majority preferred to await the results of the AFL executive council session scheduled for July 12 in Chicago. . . .

The end was in sight by July 10. Two more men were killed by soldiers at Spring Valley, Illinois. Another contingent of troops was sent to Chicago, locating there a total of 1,936 Federal soldiers. The House of Representatives approved a joint resolution "endorsing prompt and vigorous action of the military forces in suppressing interference with the mails and with interstate commerce." A Federal grand jury also met in Chicago to consider an indictment for conspiracy against the strike leaders. E. M. Mulford of the Western Union Company, the sole witness examined, produced copies of of all telegrams sent from ARU headquarters during the strike. Only the most incriminating telegrams were submitted to the grand jury; not one counselled violence and many advised against it. But Debs, Howard, Keliher, and Rogers were indicted for conspiracy to interfere with interstate commerce. They were arrested at once.

When Debs was picked up, his books, personal papers, and private unopened correspondence were seized by the Federal marshal. This act was clearly unconstitutional, and Judge Grosscup ordered the items returned the following day. Richard Olney later pointed to the prompt restoration of Debs' property as an indication that the Administration had "done its best to hold an entirely even hand as between the striker on the one hand and capital on the other." The four accused men were released on bail of ten thousand dollars each, after they had been held only a few hours.

Only a miracle could now save the boycott. John M. Egan, Chairman of The Managers, had wired to the metropolitan newspapers: "The strike was broken Monday. All roads moved trains to-day, and to-morrow a general resumption of business will take place." Debs was very worried when he got back to his room in the Revere Hotel on North Clark Street —he had left the Leland soon after the Army camped under his window. The hotel clerk handed him a note in small, precise handwriting, "like fine steel print," Debs thought. Eugene Field, the famous poet who was then working for a Chicago newspaper, had sent a prediction and an offer: "You will soon need a friend; let me be that friend. . . ."

By July 11, trains were moving even in California, where the boycott had been most effective. When Mayors Pingree and Hopkins and Erskine Phelps called in Vice-President Wickes to again request arbitration, they met an emphatic refusal. "The issue at question, which was simply that of reopening the shops at Pullman, and carrying them on at a ruinous loss, was not a proper subject for arbitration," said Mr. Wickes. Meanwhile a committee from the Knights of Labor was conferring with the President. They left Cleveland with the clear understanding that a commission to investigate the dispute would be appointed within a few days.

The AFL executive council met in the Briggs House in Chicago on July 12, with the leaders of several other national unions present. Gompers had ignored the boycott for more than two weeks, and had called the conference only at the request of the Chicago unions. Thomas J. Morgan, a Chicago socialist, even charged that Gompers had said, "I'm going to the funeral of the ARU," when he boarded the train in Indianapolis, but Gompers flatly denied the charge. The first act of the executive council was to send a wire to Cleveland asking him to attend its meetings, and urging him to "lend your influence and give us your aid so that the present industrial crisis may be brought to an end," but not discussing the causes of the boycott. Cleveland did not bother to answer the telegram.

Then Debs appeared, with a request that Gompers carry to The Managers an offer to call off the boycott if all ARU members would be rehired. Gompers refused, believing that such action would prejudice the interests of the AFL, but he offered to accompany Debs on such a mission. The railroads would not meet with Debs, and the ARU chief declined the offer. Becoming angry, Debs asked the AFL to declare a sympathetic strike. This request was very unreasonable, since the Army and the courts would obviously crush any move to spread the strike. The ARU was certain to be destroyed—nothing would be gained by the added destruction of all other unions. Gompers, by his rigid neutrality early in the boycott, had lost his chance to aid the strikers. If, from June 26, the AFL had sought to keep the courts and Federal government from entering the dispute, if it had sought to counteract the misleading newspaper stories, if it had tried to restrain the strikebreaking actions of the Brotherhoods, it would have rendered great service to the strikers. By July 12, the ship was already sinking. But Gompers' comment in his autobiography revealed the motives for his inaction: "The course pursued by the Federation was the biggest service that could have been performed to maintain the integrity of the Railroad Brotherhoods. Large numbers of their members had left their organizations and joined the A.R.U. It meant, if not disruption, weakening to a very serious extent."

After discussing the situation for a full day, the executive council issued a statement on July 13:

> The public press, ever alive to the interests of corporate wealth, have, with few exceptions, so maliciously misrepresented matters that in the public mind the working classes are now arrayed in open hostility to Federal authority. This is a position we do not wish to be placed in, nor will we occupy it without a protest . . .
>
> We declare it to be the sense of this conference that a general strike at this time is inexpedient, unwise, and contrary to the best interests of the working people. We further recommend that all connected with the American Federation of Labor now out on sympathetic strike should return to work, and those who contemplate going out on sympathetic strike are advised to remain at their usual vocations.

The statement concluded with an appeal for continued labor organization, and for the settlement of the issue at the ballot box so that the workers could wrench the government "from the hands of the plutocratic wreckers and place it in the hands of the common people."

The Chicago Building Trades Council at once called off its city-wide strike, and other unions followed suit. On July 14 the Chicago *Tribune* was pleased with these developments:

DEBS' STRIKE DEAD
It is Dealt Two Mortal Blows by Labor
Federation Hits First
Trades Council Follows with a Crusher

Mayor Hopkins carried to The Managers Debs' offer to call off the boycott if all ARU members were rehired; the offer was of course rejected. The merchants on Chicago's State Street were so hostile to the ARU that they began a boycott of the advertising columns of the Chicago *Times,* which had supported the strikers. In Chicago the disorders were at an end. The streets were clear, and flames no longer seared the evening skies. Train schedules were returning to normal. George M. Pullman, who had spent the strike in seclusion but had maintained direct contact with his general offices throughout the dispute, again showed his face to the country by issuing a statement to the press:

> The public should not permit the real question which has been before it to be obscured. That question was as to the possibility of the creation and duration of a dictatorship which could make all the industries of the United States and the daily comfort of millions dependent upon them, hostages for the granting of the fantastic whim of such a dictator. Any submission to him [Debs] would have been a long step in that direction, and in the interest of every law-abiding citizen of the United States was not to be considered for a moment.

For ten years Pullman had protected his employees from liquor dealers and union organizers—he was now offering to extend the same courtesies to everybody in the country.

But the workers at Pullman were feeling distress which exceeded their want during the previous winter. Although Mayor John Hopkins of Chicago, owner of a large grocery, had donated twenty-five thousand pounds of flour and the same amount of meat to the relief fund in May, this food had been used in a few days. Most contributions came in small drops from other workers and local unions. Thomas Heathcote, on July 15, announced that the original strikers were being starved into submission, but the ARU refused to quit.

Fifteen meetings were held that day in Chicago, and Eugene Debs spoke to most of them. He bitterly jibed at his old enemy: "Grand Chief Arthur, of the engineers, is a jobber and he will go down in history as a traitor to organized labor. He instructs his men to work with non-unionists and tells them it is honorable. He is a tool in the hands of the general managers." The ARU was sending out organizers to encourage the strikers on several roads, and Debs still thought they would win in the Far West, where they were better organized: "Men there are loyal, fraternal and true. When they believe they are right, they all go out and stay out until the fight is over."

Eugene Debs, a lifelong Democrat who three times campaigned for Grover Cleveland, was deprived of faith in the major political parties by the actions of Cleveland and Olney. He could no longer advocate labor's adherence to parties which were firmly controlled by the large corporations. At the last strike meeting, Debs made a personal appeal to the workingmen: "I am a Populist, and I favor wiping out both old parties so they will never come into power again. I have been a Democrat all my life and I am ashamed to admit it. I want every one of you to go to the polls and vote the People's ticket."

On July 17, Debs and the other strike leaders were again arrested on a contempt of court charge for violating the July 2 injunction. This time they refused bail and were imprisoned. The railroads, quickly seizing this opportunity to deal the strike a last blow, sent agents to each town to tell the workers that the men in neighboring towns had returned to work. Doubtful of the truth of these reports, the locals wired to Debs for information; but he was in jail and unable to answer them. In this way the strikers were tricked into returning to their jobs.

Twenty-four hours after the ARU leaders were sent to jail, a large notice was posted on the gates at Pullman: "These gates will be opened as soon as the number of operatives is sufficient to make a working force in all departments." Two days later, the United States Army left Chicago. The Debs Rebellion was over.

section

3

A Mature Industrial Society
1894-1919

The half century between 1843 and 1894 witnessed the transformation of preindustrial America. The accumulation of real wealth did not end in the 1890s, but by that time the nation had become a modern, industrial society. The United States had become the world's most powerful industrial nation, and the changes that occurred in this half century were reflected in the internal class and social structure, too. Power and decision making had different definitions in the world of Theodore Roosevelt than in the world of Andrew Jackson and in that of Benjamin Franklin. Newly integrated large-scale organizations altered traditional patterns of decision making. The factory and the city replaced the farm and the plantation as the major foci of work and life. A city like Chicago, for example, increased in population from 503,185 in 1880 to 1,698,575 in 1900. Old America had become New America.

An ethos that had stressed the accumulation of real wealth took on a new shape, and the years between 1890 and 1914 saw important adaptations to modern industrial society. Historian Robert Wiebe intelligently has called these decades the time of a "search for order." The "politics of accumulation" shifted in emphasis to the "politics of adaptation." What historians call the Progressive Movement was, in its many phases, a politics less concerned with the accumulation of real wealth than with the uses of real wealth in a developed industrial society. These processes of social integration and adaptation were not, of course, unique to the United States. All advanced industrial societies knew them.

In America, however, these years witnessed more than a preliminary accounting of the costs and benefits of "modernization." Large numbers of immigrants and native rural Americans continued to be drawn into the new society. Here, however, a major shift occurred. At the very time that American society entered into a new phase of development, its population changed radically. In 1890, only 3 percent of the foreign-born (290,000 of 9,200,000 immigrants) had come from eastern and southern Europe. In 1910, that figure stood at 30 percent. Between 1894 and the First World War, new patterns of migration and immigration began to alter the nation's social character. Consisting overwhelmingly of Roman and Greek Catholics and Jews from eastern and southern Europe, the "new" immigrants came to a developed and organized industrial society, not a country itself undergoing profound economic and social transformation. In addition, southern blacks were drawn into this process for the first time and migrated in increasing numbers to northern and southern towns and cities. By 1910, two-thirds of the workers in twenty-one major manufacturing and mining industries were eastern and southern European immigrants or native American blacks. Culture and society interacted again, but the cultures were new and so was the society. In that interaction, we see the beginnings of contemporary America.

3.1

Contadini *in Chicago:*
A Critique of The Uprooted

RUDOLPH J. VECOLI

Eastern and southern Europeans, nearly all Catholics and Jews, had migrated to the United States in small numbers before 1890, but their number increased spectacularly after the depression in that decade and remained high through the start of the First World War and the few post-war years before the passage of national immigration restrictive legislation. The following two articles focus on southern Italian immigration to the United States and the process of cultural adaptation to a new country, new work patterns, and urban-industrial life.

Rudolph Vecoli's detailed study of the Chicago Italian immigrant community before the First World War demonstrates convincingly that the second great wave of immigration to the United States (1890–1925) deserves the same type of study as the earlier migration from Great Britain, Ireland, Germany, the Scandinavian countries, China, and Canada has received.

Rudolph J. Vecoli, "*Contadini* in Chicago: A Critique of *The Uprooted*," *Journal of American History,* 51 (December, 1964), 404–17. Copyright The Organization of American Historians, 1964. Reprinted and footnotes omitted by permission of the copyright owner and the author.

Southern and eastern European immigrants entered a different country from their foreign-born predecessors, but their responses to it also were shaped by the interaction between the cultures they carried with them and the culture and society they encountered. The distinctive adaptations made by the Italians and described by Vecoli were unique to that group, but the process of adaptation was shared by all immigrant groups, including migrant blacks who quit the rural South for northern cities in larger and larger numbers starting in the first two decades of this century.

In *The Uprooted* Oscar Handlin attempted an overarching interpretation of European peasant society and of the adjustment of emigrants from that society to the American environment. This interpretation is open to criticism on the grounds that it fails to respect the unique cultural attributes of the many and varied ethnic groups which sent immigrants to the United States. Through an examination of the south Italians, both in their Old World setting and in Chicago, this article will indicate how Handlin's portrayal of the peasant as immigrant does violence to the character of the *contadini* (peasants) of the Mezzogiorno.

The idealized peasant village which Handlin depicts in *The Uprooted* did not exist in the southern Italy of the late nineteenth century. Handlin's village was an harmonious social entity in which the individual derived his identity and being from the community as a whole; the ethos of his village was one of solidarity, communality, and neighborliness. The typical south Italian peasant, however, did not live in a small village, but in a "rural city" with a population of thousands or even tens of thousands. Seeking refuge from brigands and malaria, the *contadini* huddled together in these hill towns, living in stone dwellings under the most primitive conditions and each day descending the slopes to work in the fields below.

Nor were these towns simple communities of agriculturists, for their social structure included the gentry and middle class as well as the peasants. Feudalism died slowly in southern Italy, and vestiges of this archaic social order were still visible in the attitudes and customs of the various classes. While the great landowners had taken up residence in the capital cities, the lesser gentry constituted the social elite of the towns. Beneath it in the social hierarchy were the professional men, officials, merchants, and artisans; at the base were the *contadini* who comprised almost a distinct caste. The upper classes lorded over and exploited the peasants whom they regarded as less than human. Toward the upper classes, the *contadini* nourished a hatred which was veiled by the traditional forms of deference.

This is not to say that the south Italian peasants enjoyed a sense of solidarity either as a community or as a social class. Rather it was the family which provided the basis of peasant solidarity. Indeed, so exclusive was the demand of the family for the loyalty of its members that it precluded allegiance to other social institutions. This explains the paucity of voluntary associations among the peasantry. Each member of the family was expected to advance its welfare and to defend its honor, regardless of the consequences for outsiders. This singleminded attention to the interests of the family led one student of south Italian society to describe its ethos as one of "amoral familism."

While the strongest ties were within the nuclear unit, there existed among the members of the extended family a degree of trust, intimacy, and interdependence denied to all others. Only through the ritual kinship of *comparaggio* (godparenthood) could non-relatives gain admittance to the family circle. The south Italian family was "father-dominated but mother-centered." The father as the head of the family enjoyed unquestioned authority over the household, but the mother provided the emotional focus for family life.

Among the various families of the *paese* (town), there were usually jealousies and feuds which frequently resulted in bloodshed. This atmosphere of hostility was revealed in the game of *passatella,* which Carlo Levi has described as "a peasant tournament of oratory, where interminable speeches reveal in veiled terms a vast amount of repressed rancor, hate, and rivalry." The sexual code of the Mezzogiorno was also expressive of the family pride of the south Italians. When violations occurred, family honor required that the seducer be punished. The south Italian was also bound by the tradition of personal vengeance, as in the Sicilian code of *omertà.* These cultural traits secured for southern Italy the distinction of having the highest rate of homicides in all of Europe at the turn of the century. Such antisocial behavior, however, has no place in Handlin's scheme of the peasant community.

If the south Italian peasant regarded his fellow townsman with less than brotherly feeling, he viewed with even greater suspicion the stranger —which included anyone not native to the town. The peasants knew nothing of patriotism for the Kingdom of Italy, or of class solidarity with other tillers of the soil; their sense of affinity did not extend beyond town boundaries. This attachment to their native village was termed *campanilismo,* a figure of speech suggesting that the world of the *contadini* was confined within the shadow cast by his town campanile. While this parochial attitude did not manifest itself in community spirit or activities, the sentiment of *campanilismo* did exert a powerful influence on the emigrants from southern Italy.

During the late nineteenth century, increasing population, agricultural depression, and oppressive taxes, combined with poor land to make life ever more difficult for the peasantry. Still, misery does not provide an adequate explanation of the great emigration which followed. For, while the peasants were equally impoverished, the rate of emigration varied widely from province to province. J. S. McDonald has suggested that the key to these differential rates lies in the differing systems of land tenure and in the contrasting sentiments of "individualism" and "solidarity" which they produced among the peasants. From Apulia and the interior of Sicily where large-scale agriculture prevailed and cultivators' associations were formed, there was little emigration. Elsewhere in the South, where the peasants as small proprietors and tenants competed with one another, emigration soared. Rather than practicing communal agriculture as did Handlin's peasants, these *contadini,* both as cultivators and emigrants, acted on the principle of economic individualism, pursuing family and self-interest.

Handlin's peasants have other characteristics which do not hold true for those of southern Italy. In the Mezzogiorno, manual labor—and especially tilling the soil—was considered degrading. There the peasants did not share the reverence of Handlin's peasants for the land; rather they were "accustomed to look with distrust and hate at the soil." No sentimental ties to the land deterred the south Italian peasants from becoming artisans, shopkeepers, or priests, if the opportunities presented themselves. Contrary to Handlin's peasants who meekly accepted their lowly status, the *contadini* were ambitious to advance the material and social position of their families. Emigration was one way of doing so. For the peasants in *The Uprooted* emigration was a desperate flight from disaster, but the south Italians viewed a sojourn in America as a means to acquire capital with which to purchase land, provide dowries for their daughters, and assist their sons to enter business or the professions.

If the design of peasant society described in *The Uprooted* is not adequate for southern Italy, neither is Handlin's description of the process of immigrant adjustment an accurate rendering of the experience of the *contadini.* For Handlin, "the history of immigration is a history of alienation and its consequences." In line with this theme, he emphasizes the isolation and loneliness of the immigrant, "the broken homes, interruptions of a familiar life, separation from known surroundings, the becoming a foreigner and ceasing to belong." While there is no desire here to belittle the hardships, fears, and anxieties to which the immigrant was subject, there are good reasons for contending that Handlin overstates the disorganizing effects of emigration and underestimates the tenacity with which the south Italian peasants at least clung to their traditional social forms and values.

Handlin, for example, dramatically pictures the immigrant ceasing to be a member of a solidary community and being cast upon his own resources as an individual. But this description does not apply to the *contadini* who customarily emigrated as a group from a particular town, and, once in America, stuck together "like a swarm of bees from the same hive." After working a while, and having decided to remain in America, they would send for their wives, children, and other relatives. In this fashion, chains of emigration were established between certain towns of southern Italy and Chicago.

From 1880 on, the tide of emigration ran strongly from Italy to this midwestern metropolis where by 1920 the Italian population reached approximately 60,000. Of these, the *contadini* of the Mezzogiorno formed the preponderant element. Because of the sentiment of *campanilismo,* there emerged not one "Little Italy" but some seventeen larger and smaller colonies scattered about the city. Each group of townsmen clustered by itself, seeking, as Jane Addams observed, to fill "an entire tenement house with the people from one village." Within these settlements, the town groups maintained their distinct identities, practiced endogamy, and preserved their traditional folkways. Contrary to Handlin's dictum that the common experience of the immigrants was their inability to transplant the European village, one is struck by the degree to which the *contadini* succeeded in reconstructing their native towns in the heart of industrial Chicago. As an Italian journalist commented:

> Emigrating, the Italian working class brings away with it from the mother country all the little world in which they were accustomed to live; a world of traditions, of beliefs, of customs, of ideals of their own. There is no reason to marvel then that in this great center of manufacturing and commercial activity of North America our colonies, though acclimating themselves in certain ways, conserve the customs of their *paesi* of origin.

If the south Italian immigrant retained a sense of belongingness with his fellow townsmen, the family continued to be the focus of his most intense loyalties. Among the male emigrants there were some who abandoned their families in Italy, but the many underwent harsh privations so that they might send money to their parents or wives. Reunited in Chicago the peasant family functioned much as it had at home; there appears to have been little of that confusion of roles depicted in *The Uprooted.* The husband's authority was not diminished, while the wife's subordinate position was not questioned. If dissension arose, it was when the children became somewhat "Americanized"; yet there are good reasons for believing that Handlin exaggerates the estrangement of the second generation from its immigrant parentage. Nor did the extended family disintegrate upon emigration as is contended. An observation made with respect to the Sicilians in Chicago was generally true for the south Italians: "Intense family pride . . . is the outstanding characteristic, and as the family unit not only includes those related by blood, but those related by ritual bonds as well (the *commare* and *compare*), and as intermarriage in the village groups is a common practice, this family pride becomes really a clan pride." The alliance of families of the town through intermarriage and godparenthood perpetuated a social organization based upon large kinship groups.

The south Italian peasants also brought with them to Chicago some of their less attractive customs. Many a new chapter of an ancient vendetta of Calabria or Sicily was written on the streets of this American city. The zealous protection of the family honor was often a cause of bloodshed. Emigration had not abrogated the duty of the south Italian to guard the chastity of his women. Without the mitigating quality of these "crimes of passion" were the depredations of the "Black Hand." After 1900 the practice of extorting money under threat of death became so common as to constitute a reign of terror in the Sicilian settlements. Both the Black Handers and their victims were, with few exceptions, from the province of Palermo where the criminal element known collectively as the *mafia* had thrived for decades. The propensity for violence of the south Italians was not a symptom of social disorganization caused by emigration but a characteristic of their Old World culture. Here too the generalizations that the immigrant feared to have recourse to the peasant crimes of revenge, and that the immigrant was rarely involved in crime for profit, do not apply to the south Italians.

To speak of alienation as the essence of the immigrant experience is to ignore the persistence of traditional forms of group life. For the *contadino,* his family and his townsmen continued to provide a sense of belonging and to sanction his customary world-view and life-ways. Living "in," but not "of," the sprawling, dynamic city of Chicago, the south Italian was sheltered within his ethnic colony from the confusing complexity of American society.

While the acquisition of land was a significant motive for emigration, the south Italian peasants were not ones to dream, as did Handlin's, of possessing "endless acres" in America. Their goal was a small plot of ground in their native towns. If they failed to reach the American soil, it was not because, as Handlin puts it, "the town had somehow trapped them," but because they sought work which would pay ready wages. These peasants had no romantic illusions about farming; and despite urgings by railroad and land companies, reformers, and philanthropists to form agricultural colonies, the south Italians preferred to remain in the city.

Although Chicago experienced an extraordinary growth of manufacturing during the period of their emigration, few south Italians found employment in the city's industries. Great numbers of other recent immigrants worked in meatpacking and steelmaking, but it was uncommon to find an Italian name on the payroll of these enterprises. The absence of the *contadini* from these basic industries was due both to their aversion to this type of factory work and to discrimination against them by employers. For the great majority of the south Italian peasants "the stifling, brazen factories and the dark, stony pits" did not supplant "the warm living earth as the source of their daily bread." Diggers in the earth they had been and diggers in the earth they remained; only in America they dug with the pick and shovel rather than the mattock. In Chicago the Italian laborers quickly displaced the Irish in excavation and street work, as they did on railroad construction jobs throughout the West.

The lot of the railroad workers was hard. Arriving at an unknown destination, they were sometimes attacked as "scabs," they found the wages and conditions of labor quite different from those promised, or it happened that they were put to work under armed guard and kept in a state of peonage. For twelve hours a day in all kinds of weather, the laborers dug and picked, lifted ties and rails, swung sledge hammers, under the constant goading of tyrannical foremen. Housed in filthy boxcars, eating wretched food, they endured this miserable existence for a wage which seldom exceeded $1.50 a day. Usually they suffered in silence, and by the most stern abstinence were able to save the greater part of their meager earnings. Yet it happened that conditions became intolerable, and the *paesani* (gangs were commonly composed of men from the same town) would resist the exactions of the "boss." These uprisings were more in the nature of peasants' revolts than of industrial strikes, and they generally ended badly for the *contadini*.

With the approach of winter the men returned to Chicago. While some continued on to Italy, the majority wintered in the city. Those with families in Chicago had households to return to; the others formed cooperative living groups. Thus they passed the winter months in idleness, much as they had in Italy. Railroad work was cyclical as well as seasonal. In times of depression emigration from Italy declined sharply; many of the Italian workers returned to their native towns to await the return of American prosperity. Those who remained were faced with long periods of unemployment; it was at these times, such as the decade of the 1890s, that the spectre of starvation stalked through the Italian quarters of Chicago.

Because the *contadini* were engaged in gang labor of a seasonal nature there developed an institution which was thought most typical of the Italian immigration: the padrone system. Bewildered by the tumult of the city, the newcomers sought out a townsman who could guide them in the ways of this strange land. Thus was created the padrone who made a business out of the ignorance and necessities of his countrymen. To the laborers, the padrone was banker, saloonkeeper, grocer, steamship agent, lodging-house keeper, and politician. But his most important function was that of employment agent.

While there were honest padrones, most appeared unable to resist the opportunities for graft. Although Handlin states that "the padrone had the virtue of shielding the laborer against the excesses of employers," the Italian padrones usually operated in collusion with the contractors. Often the padrones were shrewd, enterprising men who had risen from the ranks of the unskilled; many of them, however, were members of the gentry who sought to make an easy living by exploiting their peasant compatriots in America as they had in Italy. The padrone system should not be interpreted as evidence "that a leader in America was not bound by patterns of obligation that were sacred in the Old World"; rather, it was a logical outcome of the economic individualism and "amoral familism" of south Italian society.

In their associational life the *contadini* also contradicted Handlin's assertion that the social patterns of the Old Country could not survive the ocean voyage. The marked incapacity of the south Italians for organizational activity was itself a result of the divisive attitudes which they had brought with them to America. Almost the only form of association among these immigrants was the mutual aid society. Since such societies were common in Italy by the 1870s, they can hardly be regarded as "spontaneously generated" by American conditions. Instead, the mutual aid society was a transplanted institution which was found to have especial utility for the immigrants. An Italian journalist observed: "If associations have been found useful in the *patria,* how much more they are in a strange land, where it is so much more necessary for the Italians to gather together, to fraternize, to help one another." Nowhere, however, was the spirit of *campanilismo* more in evidence than in these societies. An exasperated Italian patriot wrote: "Here the majority of the Italian societies are formed of individuals from the same town and more often from the same parish, others are not admitted. But are you or are you not Italians? And if you are, why do you exclude your brother who is born a few miles from your town?" As the number of these small societies multiplied (by 1912 there were some 400 of them in Chicago), various attempts were made to form them into a federation. Only the Sicilians, however, were able to achieve a degree of unity through two federations which enrolled several thousand members.

The sentiment of regionalism was also a major obstacle to the organizational unity of the Italians in Chicago. Rather than being allayed by emigration, this regional pride and jealousy was accentuated by the proximity of Abruzzese, Calabrians, Genoese, Sicilians, and other groups in the city. Each regional group regarded those from other regions with their strange dialects and customs not as fellow Italians, but as distinct and inferior ethnic types. Any proposal for cooperation among the Italians was sure to arouse these regional antipathies and to end in bitter recriminations. The experience of emigration did not create a sense of nationality among the Italians strong enough to submerge their parochialism. Unlike Handlin's immigrants who acquired "new modes of fellowship to replace the old ones destroyed by emigration," the south Italians confined themselves largely to the traditional ones of family and townsmen.

The quality of leadership of the mutual aid societies also prevented them from becoming agencies for the betterment of the *contadini*. These organizations, it was said, were often controlled by the "very worse [sic] element in the Italian colony," arrogant, selfish men, who founded societies not out of a sense of fraternity but to satisfy their ambition and vanity. The scope of their leadership was restricted to presiding despotically over the meetings, marching in full regalia at the head of the society, and gaining economic and political advantage through their influence over the members. If such a one were frustrated in his attempt to control a society, he would secede with his followers and found a new one. Thus even the townsmen were divided into opposing factions.

The function of the typical mutual aid society was as limited as was its sphere of membership. The member received relief in case of illness, an indemnity for his family in case of death, and a funeral celebrated with pomp and pageantry. The societies also sponsored an annual ball and picnic, and, most important of all, the feast of the local patron saint. This was the extent of society activities; any attempt to enlist support for philanthropic or civic projects was doomed to failure.

Since there was a surplus of doctors, lawyers, teachers, musicians, and classical scholars in southern Italy, an "intellectual proletariat" accompanied the peasants to America in search of fortune. Often, however, these educated immigrants found that America had no use for their talents, and to their chagrin they were reduced to performing manual labor. Their only hope of success was to gain the patronage of their lowly countrymen, but the sphere of colonial enterprise was very restricted. The sharp competition among the Italian bankers, doctors, journalists, and others engendered jealousies and rivalries. Thus this intelligentsia which might have been expected to provide tutelage and leadership to the humbler elements was itself rent by internecine conflict and expended its energies in polemics.

For the most part the upper-class immigrants generally regarded the peasants here, as in Italy, as boors and either exploited them or remained indifferent to their plight. These "respectable" Italians, however, were concerned with the growing prejudice against their nationality and wished to elevate its prestige among the Americans and other ethnic groups. As one means of doing this, they formed an association to suppress scavenging, organ-grinding, and begging as disgraceful to the Italian reputation.

They simultaneously urged the workers to adopt American ways and to become patriotic Italians; but to these exhortations, the *contadino* replied: "It does not give me any bread whether the Italians have a good name in America or not. I am going back soon."

Well-to-do Italians were more liberal with advice than with good works. Compared with other nationalities in Chicago, the Italians were distinguished by their lack of philanthropic institutions. There was a substantial number of men of wealth among them, but as an Italian reformer commented: "It is strange that when a work depends exclusively on the wealthy of the colony, one can not hope for success. Evidently philanthropy is not the favored attribute of our rich." Indeed, there was no tradition of philanthropy among the gentry of southern Italy, and the "self-made" men did not recognize any responsibility outside the family. Projects were launched for an Italian hospital, an Italian school, an Italian charity society, an Italian institute to curb the padrone evil, and a White Hand Society to combat the Black Hand, but they all floundered in this morass of discord and disinterest. Clearly Handlin does not have the Italians in mind when he describes a growing spirit of benevolence as a product of immigrant life.

If there is one particular in which the *contadini* most strikingly refute Handlin's conception of the peasant it is in the place of religion in their lives. Handlin emphasizes the influence of Christian doctrine on the psychology of the peasantry, but throughout the Mezzogiorno, Christianity was only a thin veneer. Magic, not religion, pervaded their everyday existence; through the use of rituals, symbols, and charms, they sought to ward off evil spirits and to gain the favor of powerful deities. To the peasants, God was a distant, unapproachable being, like the King, but the local saints and Madonnas were real personages whose power had been attested to by innumerable miracles. But in the devotions to their patron saints, the attitude of the peasants was less one of piety than of bargaining, making vows if certain requests were granted. For the Church, which they had known as an oppressive landlord, they had little reverence; and for the clergy, whom they knew to be immoral and greedy, they had little respect. They knew little of and cared less for the doctrines of the Church.

Nor was the influence of established religion on the south Italian peasants strengthened by emigration as Handlin asserts. American priests were scandalized by the indifference of the Italians to the Church. Even when Italian churches were provided by the Catholic hierarchy, the *contadini* seldom displayed any religious enthusiasm. As one missionary was told upon his arrival in an Italian colony: "We have no need of priests here, it would be better if you returned from whence you came." As in their native towns, the south Italian peasants for the most part went to church "to be christened, married or buried and that is about all."

Because they were said to be drifting into infidelity, the south Italians were also the object of much of the home mission work of the Protestant churches of Chicago. Drawing their ministry from Italian converts and Waldensians, these missions carried the Gospel to the *contadini,* who, however, revealed little inclination to become "true Christians." After several decades of missionary effort, the half dozen Italian Protestant churches counted their membership in the few hundreds. The suggestion that Italians were especially vulnerable to Protestant proselyting was not borne out in Chicago. For the *contadini,* neither Catholicism nor Protestantism became "paramount as a way of life."

According to Handlin, the immigrants found it "hard to believe that the whole world of spirits and demons had abandoned their familiar homes and come also across the Atlantic," but the *contadino* in America who carried a *corno* (a goat's horn of coral) to protect him from the evil eye harbored no such doubts. The grip of the supernatural on the minds of the peasants was not diminished by their ocean crossing. In the Italian settlements, sorcerers plied their magical trades on behalf of the ill, the lovelorn, the bewitched. As Alice Hamilton noted: "Without the help of these mysterious and powerful magicians they [the *contadini*] believe that they would be defenseless before terrors that the police and the doctor and even the priest cannot cope with." For this peasant folk, in Chicago as in Campania, the logic of medicine, law, or theology had no meaning; only magic provided an explanation of, and power over, the vagaries of life.

The persistence of Old World customs among the south Italians was perhaps best exemplified by the *feste* which were held in great number in Chicago. The cults of the saints and Madonnas had also survived the crossing, and the fellow townsmen had no doubt that their local divinities could perform miracles in Chicago as well as in the Old Country. Feast day celebrations were inspired not only by devotion to the saints and Madonnas; they were also an expression of nostalgia for the life left behind. The procession, the street fair, the crowds of townsmen, created the illusion of being once more back home; as one writer commented of a *festa:* "There in the midst of these Italians, with almost no Americans, it seemed to be truly a village of southern Italy." Despite efforts by "respectable" Italians and the Catholic clergy to discourage these colorful but unruly celebrations, the *contadini* would have their *feste.* After the prohibition of a *festa* by the Church was defied, a priest explained: "The feast is a custom of Sicily and survives despite denunciations from the altar. Wherever there is a colony of these people they have the festival, remaining deaf to the requests of the clergy." The south Italian peasants remained deaf to the entreaties of reformers and radicals as well as priests, for above all they wished to continue in the ways of their *paesi.*

The *contadini* of the Mezzogiorno thus came to terms with life in Chicago within the framework of their traditional pattern of thought and behavior. The social character of the south Italian peasant did not undergo a sea change, and the very nature of their adjustments to American society was dictated by their "Old World traits," which were not so much ballast to be jettisoned once they set foot on American soil. These traits and customs were the very bone and sinew of the south Italian character which proved very resistant to change even under the stress of emigration. Because it overemphasizes the power of environment and underestimates the toughness of cultural heritage, Handlin's thesis does not comprehend the experience of the immigrants from southern Italy. The basic error of this thesis is that it subordinates historical complexity to the symmetrical pattern of a sociological theory. Rather than constructing ideal types of "the peasant" or "the immigrant," the historian of immigration must study the distinctive cultural character of each ethnic group and the manner in which this influenced its adjustments in the New World.

3.2

Patterns of Work and Family Organization: Buffalo's Italians

VIRGINIA YANS McLAUGHLIN

Like Rudolph Vecoli, Virginia Yans McLaughlin studies the process of Italian immigration and lower-class adaptation to new world work and life. Her study of the Buffalo, New York, Italian immigrant family focuses on the interior structure of a particular ethnic sub-culture. In quite original ways, she shows how traditional family patterns adapted to a new and difficult challenge. Her findings suggest again the need for caution in generalizing about "the immigrant experience." The striking difference between Italian and Polish immigrant family adaptation in Buffalo demonstrates these distinctive patterns, and raises serious questions about an historical perspective that views the process of migration merely as a disruptive process of social disintegration.

Virginia Yans McLaughlin, "Patterns of Work and Family Organization: Buffalo's Italians," *Journal of Interdisciplinary History*, 2 (Autumn, 1971), 299–314. Reprinted and footnotes omitted by permission of *The Journal of Interdisciplinary History* and the M.I.T. Press, Cambridge, Mass.

In their discussions of industrialization and urbanization, some social scientists have described the family as a dependent variable. Implicitly or explicitly, they view technical and economic organization as the prime determinant of family organization. Not surprisingly, power relationships within the family are also frequently considered to be dependent upon economic roles within the larger society. A common assumption, for example, is that because the industrial city offers work opportunities to women, they can become less reliant upon their husbands and fathers, especially if the latter are unemployed. And so, the argument continues, female employment outside the home encourages the decline of "traditional" family relationships in which the chief power and control reside with the male. In extreme cases, the unemployed male deserts his family altogether and female-headed households result.

Not all social scientists, of course, agree with this interpretation. Historians have a specific task in this dispute—to seek empirical evidence which will sustain or weaken generalizations concerning the dependent and causal relationships between the family, urbanization, and industrialization. As Goode put it, one of our difficulties is a "simple lack of information about the past history of family systems under varying conditions of urbanization and industrialization."

In line with Goode's suggestion, this paper attempts to add to our knowledge of family history by examining the relationship between female occupational patterns and family organization among south Italians in Buffalo from about 1900 to 1930. It questions the idea that the family should be viewed simply as a dependent variable by demonstrating that female assumption of new economic functions did not necessarily alter family power arrangements or disrupt the "traditional" family.

Any historian attempting to deal with working-class families immediately confronts the problem of documentation. Until recently, scholars have relied upon the reports of reformers and social workers for evidence concerning "the inarticulate." Thus, we have viewed working-class history through a filter of middle-class values. In order to overcome this problem, as well as the scarcity of literary sources concerning the family, historians have increasingly relied upon manuscript censuses and other statistical data. Much, but not all, of the argument presented in this paper is based upon such evidence, and I should caution the reader concerning its limitations. With the help of census materials, we can inform ourselves about the percentage of husbandless families, of unemployed males, and of employed wives. On the basis of these formal indices, inferences can be drawn regarding possible power relationships within the family. Statistics concerning household organization, however, cannot tell us to what degree traditional arrangements were being strained without actually being eliminated, nor can they describe the quality and "normal" tensions of family life. The picture that emerges tends to be static: If the family were broken, we can assume conflicts occurred. But if a family remained together, we cannot conversely assume that it did so free of tension. This is a problem, especially with relatively stable groups such as Buffalo's south Italians, who did not exhibit extreme family pathology in the process of becoming assimilated into American society. Statistics simply do not permit absolute conclusions concerning conflict and change among Italian families remaining together. But female occupational arrangements can tell something about family power alignments. Buffalo's south Italians favored conservative female employment patterns, patterns which usually kept women working at home or under relatives' supervision despite possibilities of better pay and opportunities elsewhere. These occupational styles, it will be argued, are a strong indication that patriarchal control continued.

An examination of south Italian families within the context of one city, Buffalo, makes one thing abundantly clear. The usual question— "What is the impact of 'urban-industrial life' upon the family?"—is much too general, too imprecise. The class and ethnic identity of the families in question, as well as the type of city and range of industrial development existing in the communities under consideration, must be specified because each can play a critical part in determining the family's relationship to the social order. First, in some cases, ethnic background and associated cultural ideals had an important impact upon the way immigrant families responded to their new environment. Buffalo's south Italian women, for example, expressed, and acted upon, a decided preference for occupations which permitted minimal strain upon their traditional familial arrangements. In this way, Old World family values could continue to operate effectively even within an advanced industrial city such as Buffalo. Other options were available, and other ethnic groups took them. This clearly suggests that south Italian values played an important part in determining family work patterns; in other words, the family acted as an independent variable. Some may wish to argue that immigrant family values, not the family itself, were the prime determinant here. Such an argument makes a strict distinction between the family as a formal structure and the system of values, norms, rights, and obligations associated with it. Although such a distinction is useful in some cases, in this paper values and organization are considered together as parts of the family as a social institution.

In discussing the relationships between economic and familial organization, it should also be noted that actually available work opportunities define the perimeters of behavior. In a small city dominated by one industry, the relationships between family and economy should be relatively clear. In the early twentieth century, for example, Homestead, Pennsylvania was a typical steel mill town, offering work to men on a fairly regular basis. Women could find employment only occasionally. Therefore, the possibilities for varying family occupational patterns were obviously limited: In Homestead, the overwhelming majority of working-class families adopted the attitude that men should be the breadwinners and that women should contribute to the family economy through their housekeeping skills, and not by leaving the home to work. In a cotton mill town, another type of one-industry city, we would expect to find women from needy families working; ethnic or cultural biases against female employment would probably be modified to meet the family's economic needs. In short, in one-industry towns, family occupational patterns would ultimately be determined by that industry regardless of cultural preferences. In larger, highly diversified manufacturing centers such as Buffalo, a variety of economic opportunities for both men and women existed; despite the city's emphasis on heavy industry women could, and did, find work. In such cities, the relationship between occupational patterns and family organization was, as we shall see, correspondingly much more complex. The nature of work opportunities permitted freer expression of cultural preferences concerning women's work role, and Old World family values could operate easily despite the urban-industrial context.

Finally, it should be emphasized that the subjects being considered, south Italian immigrants, were "working-class." I use that term here to refer not only to their occupational status as an unskilled, frequently unemployed group, but also to their relatively stable life style and culture, much of which represented a survival from traditional European peasant life. In such families, the occupational positions of husband and wife are frequently related to family structure. Hence, our original question regarding the family's status as a dependent or an independent variable is raised once again. Most social scientists argue that working-class and lower-class family structures are dependent upon occupational arrangements. They frequently cite unusual work patterns, for example, as a cause for family disorganization. The Moynihan report is a case in point. It stressed male employment difficulties in conjunction with more stable female employment as a key cause for male desertion and consequent female control of the family. Some historians similarly suggest that disrupted preindustrial work patterns upset family stability among first-generation immigrants. The move to industrial America supposedly caused radical changes in the traditional male-dominated family economy and hence forced a restructuring in family roles and relationships.

Although this model appears logical enough, it is not in agreement with historical fact. Buffalo's south Italians provide a fine example. Because tradition bestowed upon the mother great prestige, authority, and power (frequently including control of the household budget), south Italian peasant family organization was not purely patriarchal. Male superiority and paternal control, however, were the norm. To this degree at least, the south Italian family resembled the traditional peasant form described by Handlin in *The Uprooted*. The New World's industrial work patterns, however, did not destroy it. Specifically, women leaving the home to work did not necessarily cause an erosion of male control. This was true throughout the decades under consideration, despite the existence of certain female prerogatives in south Italian familial culture which could have emerged during times of family crisis, such as periods of male unemployment.

In southern Italy economic functions and family functions were closely integrated. Tradition required Italian men, the majority of them poor peasants without farms of their own, to support their families; children contributed their work in the fields or at home; wives ran their households, and, from this area, most of their rights derived. But the basis for each person's status within the family was *not* purely economic. Thus, strong cultural traditions sustained male authority despite seasonal or year-round unemployment. Although wife and children worked outside the home at harvest time in Sicily and more often elsewhere, the father's domination over family affairs remained unchallenged. Apparently this "family constellation" was strong enough to endure periods of male unemployment in America when women worked. Consequently, family disorganization among Italians (measured by male desertion and non-support, at least) remained relatively rare, and female-controlled families were unusual. This appears more remarkable given the existence of certain female privileges in south Italian culture. The point is that male authority did not depend entirely upon fulfillment of economic obligations; therefore, when a woman co-opted the male's economic function in whole or in part by becoming a wage-earner, she did not necessarily obtain greater bargaining power and so tip the balance of family authority in her favor.

Despite a potentially disruptive work situation, Buffalo's Italian men performed exceedingly well as husbands and fathers. Until the 1920s brought slightly improved conditions, the majority worked in low-paying construction, railroad, and other seasonal outdoor occupations; most were unemployed six or more months a year. This condition was not peculiar only to Buffalo Italians. Outdoor laborers all over the nation faced similar difficulties. Frequently, construction work drew Italians away from the city and their families. In addition, the immigration process itself had caused temporary separations for many. Buffalo Italians, then, endured two conditions commonly associated with family breakdown and female domination—irregular male employment and temporary absence of the father from the household—but the proportion of husbandless or female-headed families among them remained surprisingly low. Calculations based upon the 1905 New York State manuscript census reveal that only 4 per cent of more than 2,000 first-generation families were headed by women with no spouse present. And some of these were widows, not deserted wives. In 1908–09 Italians were the least likely Buffalo ethnic group to obtain welfare because of neglect or desertion by a family head. And, although the proportion applying for welfare had increased by the 1920s, the percentage giving desertion or non-support as their justification actually declined from 6 per cent in 1908 to 4 per cent in 1926.

These figures dispute the notion that male unemployment or contact with industrial city life disrupted immigrant working-class families; they also invite comparison with other urban groups who did not fare as well. How can the south Italian family's relative stability be explained? Undoubtedly inherited ethnic traditions supporting male authority helped, but let us look elsewhere before coming to definite conclusions. The answer resides, at least partially, in long-term female employment patterns, for they, and not male unemployment, distinguished Italians from less stable working-class families.

The south Italian family's traditional work patterns and economic roles were not seriously disturbed after immigration to a modern industrial city. Most important of all, women's work roles were adapted to the new industrial situation. This resulted to some extent from Buffalo's peculiar occupational structure. Unlike other upstate cities, heavy industry and transportation dominated its economy. The city offered comparatively little in the way of light industrial production for unskilled women. But it should be emphasized that even though alternatives were available, Italians *preferred* specific types of labor—occupations on the fringes of Buffalo's industrial structure—where customary family relationships could be and were effectively maintained. This preference helps to explain why Italian immigrant families remained stable. There was for them a period of transition, a time of adjustment, rather than rapid family disorganization or reorganization. Thus there was a lot of room in some late nineteenth- and early twentieth-century cities for immigrant families who wished to avoid a head-on collision with the new way of life. It was not simply a case of occupational arrangements determining family organization; cultural preferences also played a part in determining patterns of work. In short, traditional family values acted as an independent variable, and the occupational opportunities of industrial cities provided enough variation for individual families to find work arrangements appropriate for their cultural needs.

Let us first turn to the occupational patterns of Buffalo's first-generation Italian women in the period preceding World War I. In 1905, for example, less than 2 per cent of more than 2,000 wives reported to census-takers full-time employment which could have taken them from domestic concerns; some involved themselves in family enterprises which did not draw them permanently from the home or give them the status of independent wage earners. Only three women worked because their husbands were unemployed; only 1 per cent of the working women had children. Clearly, in 1905 Italian women did not sacrifice child-rearing responsibilities for work and no trend toward female assumption of the role of chief provider existed. Most women who contributed to the family budget in this year did so by providing housekeeping services to roomers and boarders residing with their families. Twelve per cent of all first-generation wives belonged to this category. The remaining 86 per cent reported no occupation at all, but we know that several hundred women engaged in part-time work as part of family groups. They did so most commonly as migrant laborers in northwestern New York's canneries and vineyards during the summer. A smaller number worked in Buffalo's domestic industries.

Italian women and girls rarely left their homes unsupervised by relatives or friends to work either as housekeepers or as factory laborers. Buffalo's Irish, Polish, Swedish, and German women commonly sought employment as domestics in middle-class homes, but jealous Italian men would not permit their wives to work under another man's roof, no matter how serious the family's economic circumstances. For example, efforts of various organizations in Buffalo and elsewhere to interest Italian women in such positions failed to erode this Mediterranean attitude toward female honor. The women themselves preferred employment which would not separate them from their families; even second-generation Italians failed to find service occupations as agreeable as did those of other ethnic groups. Italian husbands and fathers apparently appreciated the dangers of female employment outside the home. A National Federation of Settlements survey, noting that Italian parents tended to be more careful than most regarding their daughters' place of employment, cited parental concern for their children's morality as a reason.

Buffalo Italians responded to economic need by removing male children from school and sending them to work so that the women could remain in a sheltered environment. The 1905 manuscript census reveals that sons and daughters under fifteen, for example, had an equal chance to remain in school. From the ages of fifteen to nineteen, they dropped out of school at the same rate—79 per cent of the sons and 82 per cent of the daughters left school or were not attending. But the sons generally entered the labor force, while the daughters remained at home. Boys withdrawn from school had to pay the price of restricted occupational mobility, which helps to explain the Italians' slow rise up the social ladder. Considerations of female honor restricted the girls' freedom and achievement. As a result, Italian women almost always worked within the confines of their homes or as part of a family group, especially before World War I. Most who labored did so only part-time or by the season. This continued to be true throughout the 1920s. If these occupational patterns are examined in detail, it becomes clear that they minimized strain upon the traditional family system.

An examination of the homework industry indicates that Italians were especially noted for their preference for this type of occupation, which also acted as a kind of shock absorber for other ethnic groups including, for example, Russians and Germans. There are a number of ways in which homework did not challenge Old World family organization. The mother's roles as arbiter of household organization and tasks and as disciplinarian and child-rearer were reinforced by her economic position as manager of the domestic undertaking, be it artificial flower-making, basting, or sewing. Because she still had not become, in the strict sense of the term, a wage-earner, she presented no clear threat to her husband's authority and power. The basic unit of homework industries continued to be just as it had been in the Old World—the family, not the individual. The seasonal nature of most homework industry meant that the wife and child were only sporadically occupied. Finally, and critically, the wife did not leave the home, and therefore did not abandon her important roles of childbearing and child-rearing. These two responsibilities clearly exceeded in importance any economic obligation, for homework wages were lower than those a women could earn working full- or even part-time away from home. The similarity between the family as a working productive unit in preindustrial southern Italy and in America under the homework system is striking.

Although some domestic manufacture existed in Buffalo and Italians worked in it, the women and their children earned better pay as migrant laborers on farms and processing sheds near Buffalo. The canneries, which also utilized the family as the basic work unit, permitted the same sort of easing of family members into a potentially disruptive work situation. Due to the immigrants' handling of the situation and the industry's special character, the Italian family was able to maintain its Old World complexion. Once again, although Italians preferred this kind of work, other ethnic groups in different parts of the nation engaged in it, probably for similar reasons.

At first glance it seems surprising that conservative south Italian men would sometimes permit women and children to leave their Buffalo homes without husbands and fathers. The men sought and often obtained city construction jobs during the summer. South Italian mores, after all, required a husband to guard his wife with a jealous eye. In Italy, moreover, the wife who left home to work was viewed disapprovingly. But was going to the cannery really such a radical departure? In the first place, seasonal migration had not been an unusual experience for south Italian families. Laborers frequently followed harvests throughout the *Mezzogiorno*. Second, though many fathers remained in Buffalo, some found employment with their families as harvesters or as canning factory mechanics. Third, the women and children did not drift as separate family members into the labor market. They were recruited, lived, and worked as a family under the close scrutiny of the Italian-American community of migrant workers, many of whom were close associates, *paesani,* and kin. Fourth, as was the case in Italy, the seasonal income earned by wives and children who ventured into migrant labor camps was never understood as a replacement of the father's wages, as earlier figures on low desertion and non-support rates indicated, but as a supplement. The Italian father did not relinquish his obligation to support his family; likewise, he did not forfeit his control and authority over it. Finally, like the domestic industries, the migrant labor camp permitted close integration of living and working quarters and therefore did not separate the family's productive from its child-rearing capacities. Here a close integration of economic and family functions, similar to those which existed in Italy, prevailed. In short, the initiation of women into the factory system did not necessarily cause disruption of the traditional south Italian family.

The seasonal and part-time character of female employment patterns also prevented disruption. In the pre-World War I era, when Italian males were most likely to be chronically unemployed, their wives were also likely to be unemployed for at least as long. If women contributed to the family budget the year round, they generally did so by keeping boarders, an activity which did not contribute to their social or financial independence. Rarely did the Italian wife provide greater financial stability than her husband. Cultural tradition prevented her from taking the one suitable readily available job for unskilled women which would have guaranteed more steady employment than her husband—work as a maid or domestic. The contrast with black women who continue to depend upon this important source of income is striking. Equally striking are the contrasting attitudes between Italian and Polish families toward women entering the work world. Unfortunately, none of the evidence presented in the following pages allows for class distinctions between ethnic groups. (Because the overwhelming majority of both Italians and Poles were unskilled laborers, the difficulty is not a serious one.)

Buffalo's Polish women eagerly sought work in factories and as domestics. According to a 1910 survey of 146 Buffalo firms employing almost 11,000 individuals of Polish background, two Polish women found employment in the city's manufacturing and industrial establishments for every eight Polish men. If *all* Italian women who worked in all occupations —excluding those in cannery work and those with boarders in their households—are considered, the ratio for 1905 was only one to twenty. Even granting a higher proportion of Polish women to men, these differences are significant. They were not peculiar to Buffalo alone. Butler, noting the relative unimportance of Italian women in Pittsburgh's industrial life, also emphasized cultural differences between Italian and Polish women. "The Polish women," she wrote in 1910, "have not the conservatism which keeps the Italian girl at home. They have not the same standard of close-knit family relations. There is a flexibility in their attitude toward life and toward their part in it." In 1909 Tobenkin compared Chicago's Italian, Polish, Jewish, and Lithuanian girls and came to similar conclusions regarding the Italians' conservatism. In New York City, Italian girls left domestic and personal service work to other ethnic groups and entered the factory. Still, they viewed factory work chiefly as an opportunity to learn a skill such as sewing, which they might keep up at home after marriage.

During the war and pre-depression years when more Italian women began to leave their homes to work, Italian men were also more likely to be employed, or at least more likely to be earning higher incomes. Hence female employment did not represent a serious challenge to male authority at this time. Even after World War I female employment patterns had not changed radically, at least insofar as first-generation wives were concerned. An analysis of fifteen densely populated blocks in the Buffalo ward most heavily settled by Italians in 1925 indicated that although daughters had gone to work in silk factories, clothing trades, or offices, not one mother or wife in this district had left her home to work. Very few households in these blocks, moreover, contained boarders or lodgers, so the number of women contributing to family income in this way had actually declined. Italian women continued to work in the canneries during the summer after the war, but, as I have argued, this work tended to sustain, not challenge, traditional family relationships.

Italians retained a cultural bias against female employment even among the second generation. A survey of all second-generation families in sixteen wards, once again including those most heavily populated by Italians, revealed that in 1925 only 12 per cent had working wives (120 of 1,022). Moreover, these women were not forced to work because their spouses were unemployed or had deserted their families. Only one had no husband, and she may have been a widow. The remaining wives had employed husbands. The evidence produced by the 1905 data and suggested by the 1925 samples is amply substantiated by other local and national sources. In some cities, especially those with significant light industry, Italian women worked more often than they did in Buffalo, but even in these cases they tended to enter occupations which, like the canneries, assured the security and protection of working closely with fellow Italians or at least within Little Italy's confines.

Even if women entered factories in greater numbers, they could not have been the family's chief support. Italian female factory laborers, like most women in industry, tended to be irregularly employed. For example, in 1909 Odencrantz, known for her studies of women wage earners, found that one-half of a group of 1,000 New York City working girls held their jobs for less than six months, chiefly because most had seasonal occupations and their employers frequently discharged them. Most of the light industries to which women flocked for employment, such as clothing, textiles, food, candy, and paper box manufacturing, responded to irregular seasonal demand. Employers in these trades could not afford to maintain a year-round labor force if they wished to maximize profits. The situation was worst in cities like Buffalo where heavy industry predominated. Thus, even if other working-class ethnics took a more open-minded approach toward female labor than did Buffalo's south Italians, the nature of work opportunities for unskilled females in early twentieth-century America made it possible, albeit difficult, for them to supplant their husbands as chief bread-winners.

Why was family disorganization minimal and why were female-headed families rare among Italian-Americans? First, Italians had strong cultural and historical traditions regarding their women's role which survived long after emigration. The male continued to dominate in spite of his own unemployment and despite the existence of certain matriarchal privileges within the south Italian family. The conservatism of female employment patterns is clear evidence for continuing male domination. Male unemployment, furthermore, was not an entirely new experience for this group of former peasants any more than it was for other agricultural laborers, and the Italians withstood it as well in America as they did in Italy. Once in the United States, the peculiar occupational patterns of Italian women permitted the traditional family system to survive. Rather than permit their wives to leave the home, men who needed money resigned themselves "rather painfully" to daughters working in factories. The general disposition toward women's work, however, remained one of disapproval. This attitude persisted well into the 1920s, and it had a considerable influence upon second-generation families, which looked unfavorably upon female employment.

More Italian women entered the labor force after World War I, but generally these were daughters, not mothers. By contributing to the family income, they merely fulfilled the proper function of children, and hence represented no challenge to their father's prestige and control. In any case, because daughters and sons—not wives and mothers—left the home to work, the latter had little opportunity to enhance their bargaining power within the family by way of significant economic contributions.

Although Buffalo's Italians differed in some ways from other working-class groups, on the basis of their experience it is possible to offer a few speculations regarding the white working-class of late nineteenth- and early twentieth-century America. Single and unmarried sons and daughters, not wives and mothers, were the most likely candidates in these families to supplement the male head's earnings. Most were not occupied full-time or year-round. The white working-class male family head, though poor and unemployed, therefore probably found himself in a stronger familial position than does today's urban unemployed male, who is forced to depend upon his wife's wages. In the case of blacks, of course, wives and mothers supposedly assumed year-round employment or at least significantly more stable positions than their husbands and so challenged male control and authority within the family. Further studies of white working-class families, especially those in which wives worked year-round and husbands remained unemployed, and of ethnic groups with strong matriarchal tendencies, are required to determine the relative importance of ethnicity, the slavery heritage, and employment patterns. The findings of this paper, however, caution against assuming, as Moynihan and others have, that partial or total female control of the economic function necessarily predicts family power arrangements. Furthermore, before applying Moynihan's matriarchal model to the past, we should examine historical evidence to see if matriarchal families existed. As TenHouten suggests, conceptual muddling has caused many scholars to confuse matriarchies with female-headed families, a structure in which no male is present.

In conclusion, contrary to general descriptions of European immigrant adjustment, Buffalo's Italians suffered no immediate or radical disruption in family life. Although the Italian family had its share of poverty and unemployment, it did not develop a characteristic frequently associated today with lower-class life—a female-headed family system. In fact, there is little evidence of family disorganization among Buffalo's Italians. This is not to suggest that these Italians and their contemporaries were superior or more adaptable than today's urban minorities. First-generation European immigrants entered an industrializing economy and responded to it with the equipment of a traditional peasant background. Their historical experience as a class was strikingly different from today's urban workers.

We have moved throughout this discussion from the narrow focus of women's history to the broader realm of women, the family, and working-class culture. The seasonal, part-time, sporadic work patterns of wage-earning women stemmed partly from their sexual peculiarities, for most women dropped out of the labor market during the childbearing and child-rearing years. But the demands of a developing capitalist industrial economy for a cheap labor force which could be discharged periodically with a minimum of difficulty also explains their position. In this case the demands of employers and working-class cultural priorities coincided. The traditional, conservative character of this era's working-class culture advocated keeping women at home in order to avoid familial tensions, and in this manner worked toward providing the part-time labor force which employers sought.

We are now in a position to question clichés concerning the impact of industrialization and employment upon the family and woman's role. Probably no one generalization will hold for all women in all families everywhere. One can only plead for careful examination of women within the context of family life by class, ethnic group, region, city, and perhaps by religious background.

3.3A

Swislocz:
Portrait of a Shtetl

ABRAHAM AIN

The following articles by Abraham Ain (Chapter 3.3A), which was translated from the Yiddish, and by Abraham Menes (Chapter 3.3B), when read together suggest some of the important cultural and social determinants that shaped the behavior of immigrant Jews who made it from the towns and villages of eastern Europe to the industrial and commercial cities of the United States between 1890 and 1924. Ain does not idealize the pre-American communal life of the Swislocz Jews and even suggests the ways in which "modernization" there already had begun to alter their settled ways. In describing the emergence of the New York City Jewish labor movement, Menes suggestively indicates that its secular objectives had deep roots in traditional religious and larger cultural beliefs. His emphasis on the communal aspects of adaptation deserve particular attention.

Abraham Ain, "Swislocz: Portrait of a Shtetl," trans. by Shlomo Noble, YIVO Annual of Jewish Social Science, 4 (1949). Reprinted by permission of the YIVO Institute for Jewish Research.

I. GENERAL ASPECTS

Population and Appearance

Swislocz (Yiddish name: *Sislevich*) was considered one of the larger towns (*shtetl*) in the district of Grodno. According to the census of 1847, there were 997 Jews in Swislocz. Fifty years later, the town numbered 3,099 persons, of whom 2,086 were Jews. In the beginning of the present century the population again increased substantially. A leather industry of considerable size sprang up and a railway was built, linking the town with the industrial centers of Western Russia. Jews and non-Jews from surrounding villages flocked to the town. In 1906 it had some 600 families, of whom 400 were Jewish.

The town consisted of a market, five large and a dozen small streets and alleys, and a synagogue yard. The market covered an area of about two city blocks in the center of the town. It housed all the town's business places. All larger streets, which extended on the average to three or four city blocks, began in the market and terminated in the suburbs. These streets were known after the towns to which they led. Thus the Grodno Street led to the Grodno highway. Two of the larger streets, the market, and the synagogue yard were inhabited by Jews. The other large and most of the small streets were inhabited by both Jews and non-Jews. The non-Jews consisted of White Russians, Poles, a score of Russian civil servants and a dozen or so Moslem Tartars. . . .

The Vicinity

The immediate surroundings of the town were dotted with villages. Their inhabitants, chiefly White Russians, were, in the main, poor peasants who had to supplement their meager incomes by doing chores in town or laboring in the forests. Some of them worked in the leather factories in town; others were engaged in hauling timber from the forests to the railway depot. In the villages close to the forest skillful peasants carved all sorts of articles out of wood: pails, kneading troughs, felloes, yokes, and shingles. These articles they brought to town for sale, and with the money thus realized they purchased not only farm implements, but occasionally also flour and barley, for some peasants had so little land that they could not raise enough food for their families. There were also in the vicinity several large and small estates that belonged to Polish landlords.

Nearly every village and estate had a Jewish family, engaged as millers or lessees. On the eve of the first World War there were practically no more Jewish millers in the villages, for two Jews, former millers in a village, by installing two motor mills in town rendered the village miller superfluous.

Administrative Authorities

Administratively and juridically the town was linked with Wolkowysk, the county seat, which was at a distance of some twenty-eight versts. Economically, however, the town was closely bound up with Bialystok, some seventy versts away. In 1906, the railway through our town was completed, and a closer contact was established with Wolkowysk and other nearby towns.

To maintain order the town had a chief of police and a constable (*uryadnik*). In 1905 this force was augmented by eight policemen. The chief of police (*stanovoy pristav*) was the ruler of the town; his word was law. Frequently, this official would tyrannize over the town, but a way was always found to placate him. As a rule, he was not averse to a little gift. . . . In 1903, a new chief of police came to our town. Forthwith he launched a vigorous campaign against "subversive" elements, particularly among the young people. His zeal knew no bounds. Once, encountering on the outskirts of the town two young men reading a book, he had them arrested and questioned for two weeks. Subsequently, they were released. Another time, he raided a meeting of the clandestine Jewish Labor Organization "Bund" in the forest and arrested ten young men and three girls. The arrested maintained that their gathering was in the nature of a harmless outing and as no forbidden literature was found on them, they were released. The young bloods of the town decided to teach the chief of police a lesson. On a dark night they set fire to the woodshed of a school on the outskirts of the town. The regulations called for the chief of police to be present at a fire. A group of young people lay in wait for him and gave him a thrashing. This experience considerably diminished his zeal for discovering conspiracies. The constable, too, who began to peer into closed shutters, was given a beating, while in a somewhat intoxicated state.

The town had, moreover, a justice of the peace (*zemski nachalnik*), who adjudicated minor litigations of the rural population, and three excise-men, who supervised the manufacture and sale of alcoholic beverages.

Controversies in Town

The town, consisting exclusively of *misnagdim* (opponents of Hasidism), had a Synagogue and three Houses of Study, in which services were conducted three times a day. The Houses of Study possessed rich collections of books, and at dusk, between the *minkhe* (late afternoon) and the *mayriv* (evening) services, numerous groups could be seen busily pursuing their studies of the Scriptures, the Talmud, or some ethical text. The untutored had a teacher who instructed them in the weekly portion of the Bible on Friday evenings and Saturdays. The older folks were pious but tolerant toward the young generation, which was largely heterodox in its religious views. The young people, in turn, refrained from publicly offending the religious sensibilities of the orthodox.

On one occasion, however, a sharp conflict broke out between the young and the old generations. An itinerant preacher came to town. He was a man of eloquence and power and opposed to the "progressives," whom he attacked in his sermons. These sermons led to strained relations between some of the parents and their children. Once several young people entered the House of Study and interrupted one of the preacher's customary diatribes against them with catcalls. Some of the older people rose to the defense of the preacher and a fight ensued. During the altercation a butcher called out that the young people were justified in deriding the preacher because he was sowing discord in the community. The older folks avenged the slight to the preacher by prohibiting the butcher from selling kosher meat. The prohibition would have ruined the butcher, had not the Jewish Labor Organization or "Bund" sent an ultimatum to the trustees of the Houses of Study to repeal the prohibition, or it would adopt strong measures. The trustees were frightened and complied with the request.

There were also deep-seated and prolonged dissensions within the camp of the orthodox. They began toward the end of the past century, when the old rabbi of the town, Rabbi Meyer Yoyne, died, leaving a son, Rabbi Motye, who aspired to the position. Although he had been duly ordained and was qualified for the rabbinate, the old and prominent members of the community opposed his candidacy. The reasons for their opposition were that the deceased had not left a will designating his son as successor and that the aspirant because of his youth and familiarity would not command the respect due that office. They, therefore, selected one Rabbi Shneyer Zalman as rabbi. The artisans and small tradesmen, however, sided with Rabbi Motye and argued that since he was qualified for the position, the fact that he was a local man or that he was not well advanced in years should not be to his detriment. And so he, too, remained rabbi in our town. Rabbi Shneyer Zalman was a quiet and tactful person, and the tension between the two factions was kept at a minimum.

In 1903, Rabbi Shneyer Zalman died and Rabbi Joseph Rosen was chosen as his successor. The conflict flared up anew with increased bitterness. The young people remained largely outside of the struggle, although their passive sympathy was on the side of Rabbi Motye. Shortly before the first World War, Rabbi Motye died and his adherents chose no successor. After the war, Rabbi Joseph Rosen left for America, and the two factions were reconciled and agreed on one rabbi.

The Community Council

The Community Council administered all religious and community affairs. It gave financial aid to the various religious and charitable associations, paid the salaries of the rabbi and other functionaries, and maintained the ritual bathhouse (*mikve*) and the poorhouse (*hekdesh*). The budget for these activities came from the tax on kosher meat known in our parts as *korobke*. The *korobke* was usually leased by one person, or by several partners, called the tax lessees. The *shokhtim* (ritual slaughterers) could not slaughter an animal or a fowl without a permit from the tax lessee. The permit for a chicken cost three kopeks; it was somewhat higher for a duck, goose, and turkey. The permit for a calf was sixty kopeks. For slaughtering a cow or an ox there was a certain tax, and an additional tax was levied on the meat, exclusive of the lungs, liver, head, and legs. To guard against the importation of meat from nearby towns, the rabbis prohibited the sale and consumption of such meat. In cases where this prohibition proved ineffective, recourse was had to the police.

Some twenty or twenty-five prominent members in the community, who were the trustees of the Houses of Study and the various associations, constituted the Community Council and ruled the community. They were the choosers and the chosen. The elections took place in the following way. By order of the rabbi a meeting was called, to which the Houses of Study sent delegates. The delegates were chosen in this manner. The trustee of the House of Study told the sexton to call out the name of the delegate. The sexton called out: "Rabbi Shmuel, son of Rabbi Mendel, first delegate! Will anybody second the motion?" The prominent members chorused, "Second." The sexton then called out: "Rabbi Mendel, son of Shmuel, second delegate! Will anybody second the motion?" The same members responded again, "Second." And so on, till the required number of delegates were "elected." The delegates met and elected the Community Council or passed upon matters of policy under discussion. Popular dissatisfaction with their decisions did not affect them.

Thus the Community Council ruled the town up to the first World War. During the German occupation of the town, the tax on meat was abolished. After the war, the Community Council was elected in a more democratic manner.

Associations

The Holy Burial Association (*Khevre Kadishe*) played a leading role among communal institutions in town. Its membership consisted of old and pious Jews. Membership in the Holy Burial Association was restricted. Admission took place in one of the following ways: first, members could enroll their children or grandchildren as minors and upon attaining maturity they became full-fledged members; or, second, an adult wishing to be admitted to the association had to serve for a year as a sexton, whose duties were the calling of the membership to meetings and attendance at funerals. The association purchased the site for the cemetery and took care of the surrounding moat (the cemetery had no fence). It obtained the necessary funds from the families of the deceased, in accordance with their financial abilities. To the credit of the association be it said that it never wronged these families. It was fair and reasonable in its demand and always conciliatory in its dealings.

The most popular of the organizations in town was the Nursing Association (*Khevra Line*). The function of this association was to provide nursing service for cases of prolonged illness. Constant attendance on the patient, in these instances, would leave the other members of the family exhausted, and this service would give them an opportunity for a brief rest. The association sent two members—to a male, two men, and to a female, one man and one woman—to attend the patient from ten o'clock in the evening to seven o'clock in the morning. The association had its medical supply department that lent thermometers, icebags, heating pads, and similar sick-room needs to poor patients. The very poor were also supplied with medicine and nourishing food. The association obtained its funds from weekly dues paid by practically every adult in town, from special pledges in the synagogue, from the collection on the eve of the Day of Atonement, and from grants of the Community Council.

Two types of visitors came to town frequently: poor Jews who went begging from door to door and itinerant preachers. The former were lodged in the poorhouse and the latter in a specially provided guest house (*hakhnoses orkhim*), consisting of a large room with several beds in it. The sexton would arrange for their meals in some household. The more distinguished preachers and the collectors for charitable organizations (*meshulokhim*) usually stayed at the inn.

The small merchants were always short of money and in need of a loan. Most of them had to resort to a private lender who charged usurious rates. For a loan of twenty-five rubles for a period of a half-year he charged four rubles interest, which he deducted initially. Repayments had to be made from the first week, at the rate of one ruble a week. There was in a town a traditional loan association, *Gmiles Khasodim*, granting loans up to twenty-five rubles without interest. But many people refused to apply to the *Gmiles Khasodim*, for they regarded such a loan as a form of charity.

In 1908–1909, a cooperative savings and loan association was established with the aid of the Jewish Colonization Association in St. Petersburg. The members of the association could borrow money at the rate of

8%. The state bank gave the association a loan of several thousand rubles. People had confidence in the association and instead of depositing their savings in the savings bank, they deposited them in the association, which paid 6% interest. Even the non-Jewish population did business with the association. In time the private lender with his usurious rates was banished from the scene.

Sanitary and Hygienic Conditions

Sanitary conditions in town were far from satisfactory. Some inhabitants had to attend to their needs in the open. The wells were not covered, and dust and dirt would find their way into them. Before the war some wells were covered, and water was obtained by means of a pump.

The Jewish community had a bathhouse, too small for the needs of the population. On Fridays it was badly overcrowded, particularly in the winter. In the summer conditions in the bathhouse were better, since a number of people bathed in the river. All types of disease were prevalent in town, though they rarely attained epidemic proportions. Only during the German occupation in the first World War and immediately thereafter, epidemics of dysentery and typhus raged in town. . . .

Education

At the age of five, a boy was sent to a school (*kheyder*) where he was taught the alphabet and reading. In the *kheyder* the boy usually spent a year or a year and a half, and was then promoted to a higher grade, where he took up the study of the Pentateuch and the rest of the Bible. The next step in his education was the study of the Talmud. Some teachers (*melamdim*) also instructed their pupils in writing and in the elements of arithmetic. Thus, at the age of ten, a Jewish boy knew a little of the Bible, could write Yiddish, had a smattering of elementary arithmetic, and was studying the Talmud.

For the study of Russian there was a special teacher. Some boys studied in *kheyder* only part of the time and devoted several hours daily to the study of Russian, arithmetic, and writing.

Ordinarily the *kheyder* was in the home of the teacher. Study hours, except for beginners, were from nine in the morning to nine in the evening, with an hour for lunch.

For children whose parents could not afford the fee, there was a Talmud Torah, in which the fee was very low or tuition was altogether free. The Talmud Torah had three classes. In the first class instruction was given in reading, the Pentateuch, and the rest of the Bible; in the second class, in Bible, Talmud, and in writing Yiddish and Russian; in the third class, in Talmud, writing Yiddish and Russian, and in arithmetic. Instruction in the secular studies was given by two teachers who came for that purpose to the Talmud Torah for two hours daily, except Friday and Saturday. One teacher taught Yiddish writing and arithmetic and the other, Russian.

The years between twelve and fourteen were years of decision for the boys. Most of them entered at that age the leather factories, or were apprenticed to artisans. A small number of ambitious and promising boys left for the Yeshivas. Boys from the wealthier homes helped their parents in their factories or stores and simultaneously continued their education with a private tutor.

As for girls, their education was delayed to the age of seven or eight. It began with instruction in reading Hebrew and Yiddish, after which came instruction in writing Yiddish and Russian, and in the elements of arithmetic. At the age of thirteen or fourteen girls were usually apprenticed to seamstresses. The poorest became domestics. Some girls worked as saleswomen in their parents' stores part of the time and continued their education.

At the turn of the century a general public school, of four grades, and a modern Hebrew school were opened in town. These schools gave the foundation of a systematic education to a number of Jewish children. Moreover, some of the well-to-do parents began sending their children to secondary schools in the larger cities. At the time of the first World War, under German occupation, a secular Yiddish school was opened. After the war the old-fashioned type of *kheyder* became practically extinct. It was replaced by a net of Yiddish and Hebrew schools, which existed till the second World War.

Educational facilities for the non-Jewish population were provided by the Russian government. It maintained two elementary schools, one for boys and one for girls, and a seminary for the training of teachers for the elementary schools in the villages. The seminary had some 300 students. These students came from the entire district of Grodno and were provided with board and lodging by the school. Together with the faculty and staff the seminary population comprised some 350 people, who were a considerable economic factor in town.

Political Parties

The first political party in our town was the Zionist organization. On a winter eve, some time in 1898 or 1899, the Jews were summoned to the House of Study, where an out-of-town preacher and some local men addressed them and Hebrew songs were sung. As far as I recall, the speakers appealed to the audience to become members in the Zionist organization, and the response was good. The work of the organization consisted mainly in collecting money for the Jewish National Fund. Before every Zionist congress there was some activity in town in connection with the election of delegates. The Zionist organization also opened and maintained the Hebrew school in town.

From 1905 to 1907 the town had an organization of Zionist Socialists, known by the abbreviated Russianized name of S.S. The leadership of the group consisted of some temporary residents: a teacher and several workmen. Upon their departure, the group dissolved. The town also had an anarchist club, with a leader who also came from out of town. Upon his departure, the club closed its doors.

The Jewish Labor Organization or "Bund" had its beginnings in our town about 1900. By 1905 it had grown into a powerful organization. Its membership was drawn from all classes of the Jewish population. The organization conducted strikes in the leather factories and in the shops. It helped elect to the first Duma a "Bund" representative, who received some 80% of the Jewish votes cast in our town. But the years 1907 and 1908, the period of political reaction in Russia, saw a decline of the organization in our town. Some active members left town; others became disillusioned and gave up political activity. In 1909, the group was reorganized, concentrating mainly on cultural activities: symposia, lectures, discussions.

The heroic period in the history of the "Bund" in Swislocz was the year 1905. In the fall of that year a peculiar tension was felt in town. People awaited eagerly the arrival of the mail to obtain the latest news. Rumors of pogroms spread and there was talk of organizing a Jewish self-defense. Money was needed for the procurement of arms; and the following way of obtaining the required sum was decided upon, although the organization was in principle opposed to confiscation.

The town had two government stores for the sale of liquor. It was decided to stage an attack on one of these and to take its money. Once a month there was a fair in town, to which peasants and merchants from the neighboring villages and towns would come. During the fair the government stores took in considerable sums of money. The day of the fair was, therefore, deemed ideal for such an enterprise. Some time in October, 1905, in the evening following the day of the fair, as soon as the front door was closed, several of the most active members of the organization entered the store and, intimidating the salesgirls, departed with the money. Although the street was full of people and police (the chief of police summoned for the fair the police forces of the neighboring towns), no one noticed what had happened. When the salesgirls raised an alarm that they had been held up, no one believed them. Rumor had it that they embezzled the money and that the story of the burglary was an invention. It was only after the "Bund" published a proclamation taking responsibility for the act that suspicion of the salesgirls was allayed.

The attack was well organized, save for one serious slip. The participants entered the store undisguised, and the salesgirls identified two of them. One fled abroad; the other was arrested, and faced a long term at hard labor. After several months' imprisonment, he was freed on bail of five hundred rubles and likewise fled abroad. With the aid of the chief of police a false death certificate of the arrested was secured. The certificate was submitted to the district attorney and he released the bail. In the final analysis, the affair cost considerably more than it brought in.

Theatre

Formerly, Joseph and Esther plays were given in Yiddish during the Purim season. The actors, who were young men, took the parts of both men and women. Some time in 1905 or 1906 the first Yiddish play was given in which women, too, acted. This play was sponsored by the "Bund"; it was followed by several Yiddish plays given by the Zionist Socialist group.

Great difficulties were involved in these dramatic presentations, mainly in securing the requisite permission, which the chief of police was very reluctant to grant. Another difficulty was finding a suitable place. For a time a large barn was used, later on, a vacant factory loft. Under the German occupation and thereafter, dramatic presentations in Yiddish were given more frequently, with the dramas of Jacob Gordin enjoying great popularity.

Folkways

. . .

At the birth of a child, for the first seven days of confinement, the beginners in *kheyder* would come at sunset to the house of the lying-in woman and recite in unison several passages from the Bible, for which they were rewarded with sweets. If the newborn infant was a boy, a celebration called the *sholem zokher* was held on the Friday night following his birth, at which the guests were served boiled peas and broad beans. Some considered it particularly beneficial to have the child circumcised in the House of Study.

In case of death, the *Khevre Kadishe* was notified, and its representatives came and "lifted" the deceased, that is, strewed a little straw on the floor and placed him with his feet at the door. The grave digger was ordered to bring the coffin and dig the grave. Female members of the *Khevre Kadishe* sewed the shrouds. The sexton was sent to call out through the town, *"mes mitsve!"* implying that attendance at the funeral was requested. While these preparations were going on, a group of men would recite psalms in the house of the deceased. The *Khevre Kadishe* then washed the body, dressed it in a shroud, placed it in the coffin, covered it with a black cover, and carried it to the cemetery. One of the members of the *Khevre Kadishe* descended into the grave and put away the body, placed potsherds over the eyelids, two forked twigs in the hands, and boards over the body. . . .

The women believed in the evil eye, which they greatly feared. If a child was ill, particularly if it yawned, the mother immediately concluded that it had been given the evil eye. The only remedy was exorcism. For that purpose the women had several Yiddish incantations. One of them was in translation:

> There are three cracks
> In the ceiling wide.
> There the child's evil eye
> Will depart and hide.

Another incantation was:

> Three women sit on a stone.
> One says: "The child has the evil eye."
> The other says: "No!"
> The third says: "Whence it came
> Thither it shall go."

The incantation was followed by spitting three times.

· · ·

II. ECONOMIC ASPECTS

Occupationally, the Jews of the town were divided, in the main, into three categories: leather manufacturers and workers, merchants, and artisans.

The Leather Industry

Some 70% of the Jewish population were directly or indirectly connected with the leather industry. Its beginnings date from the 1870's, when Pinkhes Bereznitski opened a factory, in charge of a German master craftsman. Thereafter a number of other Jewish employers established factories. From 1900 to the German occupation (1915), the leather industry was the decisive factor in the general economic life of the town. At the beginning of this century the town numbered eight leather factories employing between forty and fifty workers each, and a dozen or so smaller shops employing from six to twelve workers.

The factories were divided into wet tanneries and dry shops. They produced leather from horse hides, which was used in the making of leggings and uppers for shoes and boots. The process of converting a raw hide into leather took about three months. The hide was taken into the wet tannery, soaked, scoured, and set out ready for the dry factory. These several steps took some ten weeks. In the wet tanneries the work was mainly unskilled, and most of the workingmen were non-Jews. In the dry factories it took another three weeks or so to curry, grain, wash, and otherwise make the leather ready for the use of the cobbler. Here the work was entirely skilled, and most of the workers were Jews. In both the wet tannery and the dry shop the work was done without machinery. It was hard work, the lighter tasks being performed by boys fourteen or fifteen years old. The big employers owned both wet tanneries and dry shops, with capital invested from twenty to forty thousand rubles. The business was conducted in a modern way. The raw hides were purchased in Bialystok with payments by drafts made out to a Bialystok bank. The leather was sent by freight to the leather merchants and the receipts for it were discounted in the Bialystok banks.

Practically all the manufacturers had to resort in part to borrowed capital. Some they obtained in the banks and some from private individuals on promissory notes. The interest private people charged on such loans ranged from eight to ten per cent. Every big employer went once a week to Bialystok to purchase raw hides and to settle his accounts with his banker. The smaller operators had no wet tanneries, but purchased half-finished hides in town or in nearby towns and finished them. The capital involved in such a business was between two and three thousand rubles.

Earnings of factory workers were good. From 1904 to 1908 earnings were the highest. An apprentice earned from two to four rubles a week; a semi-skilled worker, from eight to twelve rubles; skilled workers, from sixteen to twenty-five rubles. In 1908 and 1909 earnings declined about one-third. This lower level of earnings obtained up to the first World War. From 1904 to the first World War the working-day was eight hours: from eight o'clock to twelve o'clock and from one o'clock to five o'clock, with the exception of Friday, when the workers quit at three. Jewish workingmen did not work on Saturdays. Since the workers in the leather industry earned good wages, their standard of living was comparatively high. They were well-fed, well-clothed, and contributed freely to many a charitable cause. Frequently they extended loans of small amounts to hard-pressed merchants.

Merchants

There were some sixty stores in town, mostly small establishments, whose stock was worth fifty to a hundred rubles. A dozen or so were operated by women, with the husbands engaged in another occupation, such as tailoring or bricklaying. However, most of the merchants drew their entire sustenance from their stores. A few stores whose stock was valued at ten thousand rubles enjoyed the patronage of the landowners, officials, and leather manufacturers.

The big merchants took several business trips in the course of the year to Bialystok or Warsaw, where they purchased some of their stock. Otherwise, they purchased what they needed through a kind of commission merchant who did a two-way business. These commission merchants brought to town such farm products as butter, eggs, and mushrooms and shipped them to Bialystok on hired peasants' carts, usually on a Monday. Simultaneously, they took from the merchants in town orders for their immediate needs. On Tuesday mornings they would leave by train for Bialystok, attend to the orders given them, and sell the farm products that had in the meantime arrived in the city. On Thursday they would dispatch the carts back to town laden with merchandise and then go home the same evening by train. There, usually with the aid of wife and children, they delivered the merchandise to those who ordered it. Several of the more enterprising purchased some wares on their own account and sold them later on to the local business people.

Up to 1898 there were in town a dozen or so tavern keepers. After 1898, when the sale of liquor became a state monopoly, there were no more Jewish taverns. Several Jews obtained a license for a beer-hall (*raspivochno*), where bottled beer, tea, and a light bite were sold. Several Jews were grain dealers, buying from the landowners and the rich peasants. Part of the grain they ground to flour and sold to the bakers, and part they sold to wholesale merchants.

The district around the town abounded in forests; some were state owned and others the property of Polish landowners. (The Bialowiez forest, the property of the Czar, was a distance of fourteen versts from town.) A number of Jews were engaged in the timber business, some on a very large scale. The big timber merchants employed managers to supervise the work; the small merchants, who bought strips of forests (*otdelianka*), usually did all the work themselves. Occasionally, two or three small merchants formed a partnership. The better types of logs were floated down the Narew to the saw mills or to Germany. The others were used for railway ties. Defective logs were cut into fire-wood.

Artisans

There were two types of men's tailors in town: those that catered to the town's trade and those that worked for the peasants in the vicinity. The former were generally proficient in their trade and comparatively well-paid. Frequently, they employed two or three apprentices. The latter were less fortunate. In the summer time, when the peasants were busy in the fields, the tailors depending on them had a slack season. They had to resort to supplementary occupations, such as orchard-keeping and selling fruit. (The latter was usually the task of the wife.) Even in the winter time, when these tailors were fully employed, their earnings were meager. The materials they received from the peasants were home-made rough cloth, or sheepskins for coats. These materials could not be sewn by machine, but for the most part had to be stitched by hand.

The town had several women's tailors. Some employed one or two apprentice seamstresses. These tailors sewed bridal wardrobes, ladies' coats, or worked on orders for the wives of the landowners. They were proficient and well-paid. There were, furthermore, a few seamstresses who sewed blouses and skirts for the town women. Other women sewed blouses or jackets (*kurtka*) for the peasant women. The remuneration for this work was very low: twenty or twenty-five kopeks per blouse. In addition, a few women were engaged in sewing underwear, pillowcases, and the like.

The shoemakers catered almost exclusively to the town population. Because the peasant went barefoot in the summer, a pair of boots lasted many years. The shoemakers made their wares to order. The uppers were cut according to measurement by the cutter (*zagotovshchik*). The soles, shanks, and heels were purchased in a store. The well-to-do shoemakers would purchase these supplies in larger quantities, and the poor, for each pair of shoes individually. A few wealthy shoemakers purchased leather for both uppers and soles in large quantities. These shoemakers employed several apprentices. During slack times, when orders were few, they kept on working, preparing a stock of shoes, and selling them later on, in the pre-holiday season. Before the first World War, when two merchants began to import shoes from Warsaw, the local shoemakers saw in this step a threat to their existence. They banded together and declared a boycott on the imported shoes: they refused to repair them. Some of the shoemakers were truly masters of their trade. They made a pair of shoes that vied in attractiveness with any displayed in the stores of the large cities.

The few blacksmiths in town catered, in the main, to the village population. They put rims on wheels, hammered out plows, and sharpened scythes. In the winter time, work fell off. It was practically limited to putting iron runners on sleds or shoeing horses. Some blacksmiths would purchase wheels in the winter time, put rims on them and sell the finished wheels in the summer, when there was great demand for them.

The town had eleven bakers. Two baked black bread, four baked both black and white bread, rolls, and *khale* for the Sabbath. Five baked cake, cracknels, and pastries.

The town also had a number of Jews without a definite occupation, shifting from one calling to another, or engaging simultaneously in two or more. Such a man would own one or two cows and sell milk, bake bread for sale, fatten geese, and bake matza for Passover. These tasks were carried out by the women. The men would go to the market, buy a measure or two of grain, and resell it to an export merchant. In the winter time, some of them would buy a calf or a lamb, have it slaughtered and sell the skin and the meat, retaining the head and the legs and other minor parts. Others would buy from the peasants skins of foxes and martens, wool, bristles, mushrooms, and berries, and resell them to export merchants.

These Jews without a definite calling were indirectly engaged in agriculture. The Jews who kept cows or horses had manure. The peasants in the vicinity were always short of manure. Those who owned fields near the town would sublet a strip of land for two years to a Jew who had manure. The Jew would hire laborers to strew the manure on the field and plant potatoes. The following year, he would plant barley, oats, or buckwheat. On the third year the field was returned to the peasant in a fertile state, ready for planting rye. The Jew, in turn, would have enough potatoes and barley, or any other cereal planted, for his use, and even a small quantity for sale. The straw, chaff, and very small potatoes served as food for the cattle.

Strikes and Lockouts

Until the turn of the century, working conditions in the leather industry were very bad. The working-day was fourteen or fifteen hours and even more; wages were very low. Gradually, conditions improved. The number of factories increased and some of the smaller establishments expanded. More workers were needed, and wages rose. The higher wages attracted a number of young people from well-to-do homes, who deemed it below their dignity to become artisans. (These usually entered the more specialized branches of the trade, such as trimming and cutting, which were better paid.) Also young people from the vicinity came to work in the leather factories.

In 1900–1901 the "Bund" called the first strike in the leather factories. Members of the organization assembled a large number of workers and together formulated their demands: a raise of wages, and a twelve-hour working-day, from seven to seven, with one and a half hours for breakfast and one hour for lunch. Thereafter, a general assembly of the workers was called, at which these demands were discussed. A strike committee was appointed and a resolution adopted that no one should resume work until all demands were granted by the factory owners. This resolution was confirmed by an oath taken on a pair of phylacteries by each worker.

When the strike committee presented the demands to the factory owners, the latter remained unimpressed. They were inclined to regard the entire affair as a boyish prank. On the following day, however, when not a single worker reported for work, the factory owners began to take a serious view of the strike. They attempted to break the solidarity of the workers by promising higher wages to the older workers. Some of these workers remained unmoved by the tempting offers and in the case of others, the oath on the phylacteries acted as a powerful deterrent. The strike lasted only a short time and ended in complete victory of the workers.

A second strike in the leather factories took place in the summer of 1904. This was during the Russo-Japanese war, when the profits of the factory owners were high and the cost of living had gone up. By then the "Bund" was firmly entrenched in town, conducting systematic organizational and educational activities among the workers. The "Bund" called a general assembly of leather workers in a forest one verst and a half from town. To impress the assembly, a speaker from the neighboring town of Wolkowysk was invited. The speaker presented the demands formulated by the "Bund": 1) a raise of about 35% in wages; 2) a working-day of nine hours, from eight to five; 3) job tenure, no worker to be discharged without sufficient cause; 4) medical aid, the employer to pay the medical bills of the ill employee.

That evening the demands were presented to the factory owners. They were ready to negotiate a reduction in working hours and a raise of wages, but would not consider the other two demands. They were particularly incensed by the demand for job tenure, which to them appeared highly arbitrary. The strike committee refused to negotiate their demands piecemeal, and a strike was called. It lasted three weeks and again ended in a victory for the workers. The newly acquired working conditions were in effect till the end of 1907.

The political reaction, which set in after 1905, began to show its effects in the economic sphere. In November, 1907, the factory owners called a general assembly of their workers and put before them the following conditions: 1) a reduction of 35–40% in wages; 2) discontinuance of medical aid; 3) abolition of tenure. Refusal to accept these conditions, they threatened, would be answered with the closure of all factories. The workers rejected these conditions and countered with a strike. Although the "Bund" was then considerably weakened, it took over the direction of the strike.

In the first weeks of the strike it became evident that the developments had more than a local character. The leather factory owners of the entire district were anxious for a victory of their fellows, in which instance they would follow suit and put before their workers similar conditions. On the other hand, the workers of the entire region were hoping for the success of the strikers in Swislocz. The Tanners Union of the district sent a professional organizer to advise and guide the strikers. He was an energetic young man and an eloquent orator, who inspired confidence. He also traveled throughout the district to collect funds for the strikers. The Tanners Union also enlisted the interests of the union in the district of Vilna and there, too, collections were made for the benefit of the Swislocz strikers.

Most of the strikers did not require aid. Before the strike, they had earned decent wages and had managed to accumulate some savings. The few less skilled workers whose earnings were in need of aid, were given one and a half rubles per week, if single, and three, if married. To keep up the spirit of the strikers, daily meetings were called. Since it was the winter and assemblies in the open were impossible, the strikers met daily, with the exception of Saturday, in the House of Study. The trustees of the House of Study raised no objection, for the majority of the Jewish population was in sympathy with the strikers.

At first there were no difficulties with the police. At the time of the strike the chief of police was a quiet and liberal man who gave assurances that as long as the strike was conducted peacefully, he would not interfere. It was difficult, however, to conduct the strike peacefully, and a clash between the strikers and the police occurred. The strikers had pinned their hope on the factory owners' need for money to cover their outstanding notes. When these notes became due, the factory owners decided to raise cash through the sale of half-finished leather. This transaction led to the clash. In the seventh or eighth week of the strike, the strikers were told that a factory was shipping half-finished leather to other towns. A group of strikers left for the factory to prevent the loading of the leather. At the entrance to the factory yard several policemen denied entry to the strikers. When they attempted to force their way into the yard, the police fired a salvo in the air. The strikers retired and marched to the homes of the factory owners, demanding that the police be withdrawn from the factories. In the altercation that ensued, a factory owner was beaten up. The chief of police took a grave view of the situation and called for soldiers to patrol the streets. Tension mounted steadily.

Fortunately, the strike committee kept cool heads. An ultimatum was presented to the factory owners to withdraw the police and the military from the factories and the streets, or they would bear responsibility for the consequences. The police and military were soon recalled, and the strike again assumed a peaceful character.

The strike continued into the ninth and tenth week. Some strikers began to feel discouraged. At the meetings of the strikers in the House of Study demands were made for opening negotiations with the owners. The strike committee decided to call a conference of the Tanners Union of the Bialystok and Vilna districts. The conference met in Swislocz in the twelfth week of the strike. (The chief of police might have known of the conference, for it met in the neighborhood of his office.) It lasted two or three days and was attended by delegates from a number of towns. After prolonged discussions, it was decided to continue the strike. Following the conference, a general meeting of the strikers was called at the House of Study. Several delegates addressed the strikers, moving the audience to tears.

When the strike entered its fifteenth week, the spirits of the workers flagged. Aid from the neighboring towns came irregularly. The Passover festival was approaching, and the needs of the strikers were great. The demands for a settlement became more urgent, and the factory owners, too, were in a conciliatory mood. A week later the strike was settled with a compromise on wages. The workers won on the other points.

The Leather Industry from 1908 to 1919

A few weeks after the strike, the factory owners renewed their demands for the abolition of tenure of job under the threat of a new lockout. When the workers refused their demands, they carried out their threat. The "Bund" was then weak and the workers were exhausted by the previous strike. After three weeks of lockout, the workers capitulated and accepted all the demands of the owners.

The workers were quite demoralized. Since several factories had closed, a number of them were unemployed. Furthermore, the large factories began selling their product in half-finished form, which meant that the workers in the dry factories were left without work. Dry factories that had previously employed forty and fifty workers reduced the number to fifteen or ten. In these factories the percentage of Jewish employees was very high, and the growing unemployment affected chiefly the Jewish workers.

Some of the unemployed workers opened their own shops. Two workers would usually go into business in partnership. For about two thousand rubles they could rent a shop, hire a couple of workers, buy a quantity of half-finished leather and finish it. The small shops paid lower wages than the factories. Thus, a worker who had received before the strike some sixteen rubles a week in the factory, was paid for the same work in the small shop ten or nine rubles. Even at their best these small shops could give employment to only a small fraction of those who were out of work. A large number of workers then decided on emigration to the United States and Canada.

Emigration

Up to the turn of the century few Jews emigrated from our town. In 1896, several families left for Argentina to settle in the colonies of Baron de Hirsch. In the beginning of the present century there was a slight rise in emigration. After the depression resulting from the strike in 1908, the tempo of emigration quickened, with England, the United States, and Canada as destinations. In 1916, under the German occupation, several groups of women went to America. Emigration assumed mass proportions after the first World War, chiefly to the United States. There was also considerable emigration to Canada, Palestine, and Argentina.

3.3B

The East Side
and the Jewish Labor Movement

ABRAHAM MENES

When the Jewish immigrants from Eastern Europe began settling in great
numbers in New York's East Side in the early eighteen eighties, they little
dreamt that they were opening a new chapter in the history of Jewish life
in America, let alone in the history of the Jewish people throughout the
world. The East Side ghetto came into being without plan. Indeed, the
seething and frenetic life that filled the narrow streets and crowded tenements of the East Side more nearly resembled a symbol of chaos and
planlessness. . . .

The importance of this immigrant Jewish community on the East Side
becomes apparent when we recall some figures. A bit more than a century
ago there were about five million Jews in the entire world. Eighty-five
percent of this number lived in Europe. Only slightly more than one percent lived in America, and the remaining thirteen percent were scattered

Abraham Menes, "The East Side and the Jewish Labor Movement," in *Voices from the
Yiddish: Essays, Memoirs, Diaries,* eds. Irving Howe and Eliezer Greenberg (Ann Arbor,
Mich.: University of Michigan Press, 1972). Copyright © by The University of Michigan
1972.

throughout Asia and Africa. The number of Jews in Palestine was insignificant. Ninety years later, at the time of the outbreak of World War II, the number of Jews in the world exceeded sixteen million. In the course of not more than four generations the Jewish population in the world more than tripled its numbers. The distribution of the Jewish population shifted radically. America and Palestine became important centers. But the bulk of the Jewish people remained in Europe, primarily in the eastern part of the continent.

It is generally assumed that the mass Jewish emigration from Europe was caused by external factors, and that the emigrants themselves performed only a passive role. It is undeniable that economic pressure within the Jewish communities in Eastern Europe, and the wave of anti-Semitism and pogroms that swept Southern Russia in the early eighties, were potent factors. Nevertheless it would be a grievous error to overlook the fact that the Jewish emigrants themselves were the chief factor in the exodus from Eastern Europe. It was not the weak elements, ready to resign themselves to fate, who began to trek. Even under the conditions of disenfranchisement which prevailed in Russia it required courage to resolve to leave home and family and native town. Effort, determination, and pioneering initiative were required to embark on the long, and then unfamiliar, journey. Though many rumors were current regarding opportunities in America, it remained a remote and strange country. It was the poorest elements, who in most cases even lacked the fare to a port city, who were the ones to go. So far as paying the ocean passage was concerned, the majority did not even dream of possessing the requisite one hundred rubles ($50)—a sum that was considered a veritable fortune in the impoverished Jewish towns of Poland and Russia.

How, then, did they reach America? Some of the emigrant pioneers made the trip in stages. The first stage of the journey brought them across the Russian border. At the time of the pogroms in Russia in 1881–82, the commercial city of Brody on the Austrian side of the Russian border was the main first stopover. In 1881 alone, about four thousand emigrants received assistance in Brody from the large Jewish philanthropic organizations which gradually provided them with the means to continue their journey to America. Others settled temporarily in Germany, France, or England. If luck was with them, they obtained employment here and saved enough to resume their trip. The number of emigrants who left home with sufficient means to pay for the entire trip was infinitesimal.

But this trickle did not by itself account for the mass emigration of hundreds of thousands. The path of these pioneers was not an easy one even after they reached America, yet despite their hardships it was they who made possible the subsequent flood from Eastern Europe in the later eighties. The decisive factor stimulating the mass Jewish emigration to

America from 1885 to 1890 was the assistance from relatives already in America who were themselves still strangers in the country. "Everyone who came here," writes B. Weinstein, one of the pioneers of the Jewish labor movement in America, "constantly cherished one hope—to save enough money to bring other members of the family."

The growth of the East Side becomes comprehensible from Jewish writing in America five and six decades ago. Here we find a host of touching descriptions of how poor immigrant laborers, burdened with a sense of guilt, work far beyond their strength, denied themselves necessities, and went into debt in order to provide passage for some member of the family still in the Old Country.

They were obsessed by one idea: to work as hard as possible and spend as little as possible in order to save passage for the family. *The accusation leveled against the Jewish immigrants of that time that they were themselves to blame for the intolerable working conditions in the sweatshops was not entirely unfounded.* A theory was then propounded that it was in the "nature" of Jews to work endless hours and to drive themselves at their tasks, in disregard of the fact that Jews were the historical pioneers of the idea of definite periods of rest (Sabbath and holidays) and just as firmly defined hours for prayer and study during week days. Also overlooked was the fact that the sweatshop system already had a long tradition in America. It is undeniable, nevertheless, that the sweatshop system became especially acute in the needle trades at the time when Jews became prominent in this industry as workers and contractors. It is equally an established fact that the manufacturers and contractors met with but little resistance from their workers when they tried to extend the work day. *The workers themselves wished to work longer hours and thus to earn a little more, so as to hasten the day when they could bring their families to America.* It was this intense devotion to family and friends in the old home that made possible the mass influx of Jewish immigrants in the late eighties.

The aid extended by the new immigrants to their relatives still overseas merits our attention as *an example of the decisive role that can be played by purely moral factors in the life of a people.* Had the concern of the Jewish arrivals in America at that time not been directed so intensely to their native towns, they would have sent less material assistance and the number of immigrants would have been much smaller.

The distinctive nature of the Jewish immigrant is readily confirmed by statistical analysis of the immigration trends, as a whole, to America at that time. Our attention is at once drawn to the fact that the Jewish immigrants came to America to stay. As a general rule about one third of all immigrants left the United States; Jewish re-emigration, however, amounted to somewhat less than five percent. The figures also show that the percentage of women and children was considerably higher among Jewish immigrants than among others. This fact imposed a greater burden of duties on the family heads and compelled them to work harder and longer hours.

The pressers and operators of the East Side provided their kin with more than mere passage money: they also secured for them opportunities to earn their livelihood. As long as Jewish immigration was limited in scope, the problem of employment was virtually nonexistent. As late as the seventies of the last century, the majority of Jewish immigrants found their livelihood in peddling and trade. These callings were especially characteristic of the Jewish immigrants from Austria and Germany. It should be noted in passing that peddling was a grueling occupation, and that the immigrant peddler of the frontier performed a difficult and responsible task.

But such middlemen's occupations could absorb only a small number of immigrants, and many opportunities in commercial life were not available to the newcomers because of language difficulties. . . .

Industry did not everywhere welcome the immigrants. A number of trades excluded them altogether. The skilled and organized workers looked at the newcomers as competitors who served as instruments in the hands of capital to depress the wage scale. Nor were these suspicions entirely unfounded. Religious factors added to the difficulty of economic integration. Most of the Jewish immigrants of that time tried to observe the Sabbath and *kashrut* as far as possible, and many avoided employment in factories and businesses where the majority of workers were non-Jewish. Not knowing the language, they felt themselves strangers in such shops and factories, and even when need compelled them to take such employment they did not give up their search for work in traditional Jewish vocations.

Since the characteristic Jewish trades were not yet in existence in America, these had to be created. The garment industry was still in its infancy in the eighteen nineties, as is demonstrated by the following table:

Production of Women's Clothing

Year	Number of Enterprises	Number of Workers
1879	562	25,192
1899	2,701	83,739
1914	5,564	168,907

Thus the opportunities in this field, for workers as well as for manufacturers, were considerable, and it was not necessary to storm an already-occupied economic position. The opportunities were still further enhanced by the fact that as far back as the seventies Jews, largely from Germany and Hungary, were already prominent in the garment industry both as workers and as employers. The dominant role of the Jews in the garment industries of Eastern Europe, from which most of the immigrants now came, was still another factor contributing to the ease with which they entered this field.

Concentration in specific trades was a distinctive feature of the Jewish communities in Eastern Europe. In America this concentration assumed extreme forms. More than half of all Jewish workers (wage workers and self-employed) were engaged in garment manufacturing. Of the wage workers, two-thirds were employed in the needle trades. Since the eighties the needle trades increasingly passed into Jewish hands.

The sweatshop system may have contributed to the predominance of Jews in the needle trades, but it was not the sole or even most important factor. There is no doubt that Jewish skill in these trades, as well as Jewish initiative, played the chief role in the development of the garment industry. Thus it came about that the pioneering labors of the Jewish tailors and cloakmakers during the eighteen eighties and nineties paved the way for "the great migration" early in the twentieth century, when nearly one and one-half million Jews entered the United States in the course of fifteen years.

As might have been expected, the growth of the East Side was also marked by negative aspects which at one time were quite prominent. The sweatshops may have performed a necessary function in the development of the garment industry, then in the period of primitive exploitation characteristic of pioneering capitalism. But the methods it employed could not but retard the emergence of a sound and normal community. . . .

The Jewish immigrant coming to America from his small native town was . . . profoundly shaken by this transition. For though there had been no social equality in the East European town, the Jewish community nonetheless felt united by family bonds:

> In my town everything was done in common. The town was like one large family . . . Jews clung together, like children abandoned in a desert. . . . The Jew felt more secure when he was with others. . . . Should anything happen to a small town Jew, the entire community would share his joy or his sorrow.

Upon coming to America the immigrants clustered together and tried to recreate the *shtetl* in the guise of the *landsmanshaft*. The Jewish immigrants from Russia felt little sympathy for the czarist empire whose victims they were, but they cherished a powerful nostalgia for their families and native towns.

The cultural and historical role of the *landsmanshaft* has been beautifully described by Professor Morris Raphael Cohen in his autobiographical work, *A Dreamer's Journey*. Though Cohen became integrated in American culture, he displayed a profound understanding for the generation of pioneers. He did not break completely with the old home, though spiritually he had become an integral part of the culture of the new home. His *landslayt* from the town of Nieswiez remained close to him. On November 5, 1936, two days after his mother's death, he wrote:

> My last two years with her made me appreciate her qualities more than I did in the years when I saw little of her. If I had to make a speech, I would have spoken of the spiritual importance of the Neshvieser Verein —how it enabled the hardy pioneers to adjust themselves to the new land, to keep people in self-respect and to make a home for the new generation; how the tradition of learning was a light—not like the modern electric but like the ancient candle or torch—which enabled people to interpret the new life.

Yet, the *landsmanshaft* could not take the place of the *shtetl,* because the immigrant now lived in the turmoil of New York where he frequently felt isolated, with that peculiar sense of alienation of one who has been uprooted from his old home but has not yet struck new roots. Economic adaptation was the easiest aspect of the problem, and here the process of Americanization proceeded rapidly; but cultural and social integration went on at a much more laborious pace. And during his first years in America the immigrant had no time for anything except material survival.

It is therefore not surprising that economic success became the center of the immigrant's ambitions, and that its attainment also paved the way to social recognition. Material success became the yardstick with which values were to be measured, and this, in turn, engendered an attitude of contempt for spiritual values and the cultural traditions of the old home in particular. The successful "allrightnick" was not content with his place in economic life, he also felt the need to assert his claim to position of spiritual leader. This accounts for the defeatist moods that seized some of the Jewish intellectuals. America was lampooned in the pun *Ama reka* (hollow people) which recurs in a large number of articles and critical essays both in the Yiddish and Hebrew press of the past century. The situation of the intellectuals was indeed difficult, and especially so in the case of the older ones. They could no longer hope to adapt themselves to a regimen of manual labor, and their intellectual attainments were not in demand. The great upheaval which the migration caused created many weird situations. Former *melamdim* who were sufficiently aggressive assumed posts as rabbis, whereas modest and gentle scholars, unable even to attain positions as teachers, turned in desperation to hard physical labor. The following is a touching description of this phenomenon:

There are few more pathetic sights than an old man with a long beard, a little black cap on his head and a venerable face—a man who had been perhaps a Hebraic or Talmudic scholar in the old country, carrying or pressing piles of coats in the melancholy sweatshop; or standing for sixteen hours a day by his push-cart in one of the dozen crowded streets of the ghetto.

Since material success seemed to make up for all shortcomings, there appeared to be no need to ascribe importance to moral principles. The danger of moral degeneration became still greater, because the success of the self-made man brought out in greater relief the want and loneliness of the immigrant mass. Concentration in the most neglected sections of the big cities, overcrowding, dirty streets and equally dirty tenements, combined to undermine the moral discipline of the older generation, and were a poor backdrop for the moral education of the young. The insecurity of the immigrant went hand in hand with uncertainty regarding moral values. He lived in two cultural realms and was estranged from both. Hillel Rogoff, an authority on the East Side, gives the following description of the spiritual instability prevailing at the turn of the century:

Physical exhaustion was aggravated by moral and spiritual anguish. The old-fashioned religious Jew saw his traditions discarded and even ridiculed. He saw his children drift away from him to pick up strange new ways. The safe old moorings of Jewish family life loosened, the privacy of the home was invaded and its sanctity frequently profaned by boarders, the minds of the children were often poisoned against their parents by the ridicule of the gutter and by the ill-digested enlightenment of the school.

Many immigrants held financial success to be synonymous with the ideal of Americanization—a fallacious conception yet also a partial truth. The American philosophy of rugged individualism, in part a heritage of Puritan theology, was vulgarized. Furthermore, the dominant strata in American society had little understanding and still less respect for the culture of the later arrivals, even though they were themselves children or grandchildren of immigrants. . . .

The Jewish immigrants from Eastern Europe brought an entirely different approach to the questions of happiness and misery in life. Jews found it hard to become reconciled to the idea that material success is an outstanding indication of God's favor. The Puritan theology was well suited for the courageous pioneers who achieved their goals by means of stubborn diligence. But the Jewish historical experience was of a different kind, and scholarly thought was preoccupied with those who failed despite all efforts. Jewish thinking propounded the election of the injured and the suffering. Job's tragedy consisted not so much in his physical suffering as in his painful recognition that not even his friends believed in his innocence. "You have sinned," they repeatedly said to him, "and God has punished you for it." Job protested with all his strength against being abandoned by God and deprived of consolation and encouragement even from his closest friends.

The Job problem and the Jewish problem were basically alike, and to the question posed by the existence of suffering in the world, the Jews counterposed the old answer of faith in the coming of a new world at the end of time. This old, yet ever-new, Jewish solution to the problem of suffering was now propounded by the tailors and cloakmakers of the East Side.

It is impossible to account for the unique response of the East Side to socialist propaganda without taking into consideration the Messianic tradition. To the Jewish masses, socialism was incomparably more than the program of a political party. It was more than a dream of a beautiful future. For the workers of the East Side socialism was a new faith which helped them endure the hardships and disappointments of everyday life. Socialism bolstered their faith in themselves: it saved them from despair and from the loss of respect for both themselves and their fellows in need.

The problem of human dignity was no less important than that of material want. In the *shtetl* even the poorest Jew was a personality in his own right. "In my *shtetl* every Jew was a secret prince; every pauper concealed within himself the spark of secret aristocracy," wrote M. Olgin. The individual was not easily lost in a small town, and everyone had his recognized status, even if on the lower rungs of the social ladder. In the capitalist metropolis, on the other hand, it was much easier to lose one's individuality. Of what account is an individual among millions of his fellows? True, there were some among the immigrants who had left the old home with the express desire to "disappear," to shed their past and become "new" people. But only seldom was it possible genuinely to become a new person with a distinct individuality.

Work in the sweatshops could not provide moral satisfaction. The attitude of the bosses and subcontractors, themselves mostly former workers, was galling. It was an everyday occurrence for workers to be abused and fired without cause, and there were even instances of bosses beating their workers. Some of the early strikes were called because of such mistreatment. The workers also lacked permanent homes. The bachelors lived as boarders, three or four to a room, which was merely a place to spend the night. Even married workers with families seldom had homes to themselves. The sense of forlornness was great even when there was employment; if a worker lost his job, his situation became intolerable.

There has been a tendency to overlook the moral factors influencing the social and political conflicts of our time. It is very easy to see the material needs of the masses. Yet the unrest which agitates so many is often the product of the mounting depersonalization characteristic of modern society. This unrest is the protest of the *mass man* who refuses to become reconciled to his fate. He resents having to remain a *mass man* all his life. He wants recognition as an individual. The class conflict between rich and poor is becoming overshadowed by another social conflict—the struggle between those who have status in social life, the class of *somebodies,* and the great and nameless mass lost in the turmoil of modern life, the class of the *nobodies*. The East Side fought with especial vigor against this trend toward depersonalization. The entire labor movement in the country fought the same battle, but there was one distinction between the general and the Jewish labor movement. Until the time of the New Deal, the American labor movement, as represented by the American Federation of Labor, had been strongly influenced by the Puritan philosophy. This was apparent in the structure of the union movement. The principle of industrial unionism would without a doubt have been more practical in many instances, yet the unions stubbornly clung to the principle of craft unionism. The Puritan philosophy of "calling" was effective here. The skilled and better-paid workers proudly guarded their superior status and their privileged position as skilled labor. They did not care to mingle with the unskilled and thus lose their separateness.

The Jewish workers lacked this attitude toward a "calling" that was so characteristic of the Anglo-American tradition. For one thing, the conditions of work were very different here from what they were in the old home. The skilled Jewish workman, in particular, was frequently depressed because his craftsmanship was superfluous here. Most of the workers were what was then known as "Columbus' tailors," people who had learned the work after coming to America. As a result of an increasing division of labor, few truly skilled workers were needed. This was one reason the needle trades largely escaped the conflict between craft and industrial unionism. The ideology of "unionism pure and simple" as classically formulated by Samuel Gompers likewise found little response here. Even trade unionism as such appealed but little to the workers of the East Side.

For what the East Side yearned for was a reevaluation of values. It needed a philosophy that would give the worker comfort and status. In the course of generations of trials, the Jew had found consolation in his faith in his chosenness. This faith was now shattered, and the spiritual crisis of modern times further undermined the authority of religion. Moreover, the old-fashioned religious leaders were themselves at a loss in America; they did not comprehend the new reality and had no answers to the problems it posed. As for the philosophy of Reform Judaism, it was altogether alien to the workers of the East Side.

The socialists introduced a new scale of values. Today we can scarcely grasp what the teachings of the socialist propagandists, who stressed the unimportance of individual success and the insignificance of money as a yardstick for social values, meant for the Jewish workers of the East Side. If the poor were indeed the righteous and if the workers were the true creators of wealth, then they need not be ashamed of their social status. Socialism restored to them their human worth and aroused their sense of individual pride.

Socialism lent added prestige to spiritual values. While a segment of the Jewish intellectual class found it especially hard to adapt to the new conditions, this was not the case for those within the socialist camp. Socialist intellectuals enjoyed a sense of historic mission, as well as the balm of enthusiastic audiences, and since they were in the forefront of the struggle against the cult of success, they found it easy to stress the importance of spiritual values. Enlightenment and social justice were the two main themes of socialist propaganda. Young workers, boys and girls, enthusiastically undertook their self-education. They read, studied, discussed problems after their hard labor in the shops. The ancient Jewish tradition of individual and group study was revived in a new form. How important these intellectual pursuits were, can be judged from the fact that the majority of Jewish immigrants came to this country with but scanty education—many were, in fact, almost illiterate. Intensive educational work was therefore required in order to prepare a reading public for the socialist newspapers, books, and Yiddish literature in general.

Socialist educational work on the East Side was integrated into the broad framework of the social and political problems of the world. These were extensively reflected in the Yiddish socialist press as far as the nineties. Morris R. Cohen remembers:

> As I look back on the Yiddish and English press in the last decade of the nineteenth century I cannot help feeling that the former did more for the education of its readers than the latter. Having no army of reporters to dig up sensational news, the Yiddish press necessarily paid more attention to things of permanent interest. It tried to give its readers something of enduring and substantial value. . . . The Yiddish press has prepared millions of Jewish people to take a worthy part in American civilization while also promoting the natural self-respect to which Jews are entitled because of their character and history.

The pioneers of the Jewish labor movement gave the Jewish worker a sense of his own dignity. First they won for the Jewish worker the respect of the American labor movement. Working conditions in the sweatshops of the East Side were not of a kind to win the sympathy of organized labor. But this attitude changed almost overnight when a series of bitter strikes in the garment industry aroused public opinion, and the world became aware that the Jewish workers knew how to defend their rights.

The Jewish labor leaders were keenly aware of the importance of winning public opinion, perhaps because Jewish labor was still weak and urgently needed the moral support of the native American workers. The Jewish workers gained a reputation as good strikers but poor union people. This reputation was not unfounded, though their shortcomings as union people were not the result of a lack of understanding of the importance of organization.

How account for the fact that Jewish workers so frequently resorted to strikes when their unions were so weak? For there were even instances when they struck before formulating their demands.

The workers of the East Side often went on strike for reasons other than formulated economic demands. For them the strike was frequently a way of expressing their protest against a form of society that tried to transform the laborer into a robot. In an article published in the *Forward* (July 27, 1910) concerning the historic cloakmakers' strike, the poet A. Liessin characterized the mood of the workers as follows: *"The seventy thousand zeros now became seventy thousand fighters."* The worker refused to maintain his passive role in the shop or in social life, and struck for his rights as citizen and man. . . .

3.4

The Sources of Stability:
The Immigrants

DAVID BRODY

In part, the behavior of immigrants was shaped by their aspirations and expectations. In the nation's most important manufacturing industry (the iron and steel industry), David Brody suggests that their willingness to work long hours for wages that were low by American standards related closely to what they expected from their short-run American experience. Leaving their families behind, "single" men migrated to America and saw their wages as a way of supporting families in eastern and southern Europe, not in the United States. Large numbers, in fact, fulfilled that dream and returned to Europe. Over a generation, however, and especially after the First World War closed off that option, those who remained developed different expectations and as a result behaved in quite different ways.

The following books are suggested for further reading:

DAVID BRODY, *The Butcher Workman,* Cambridge, Mass.: The Harvard University Press, 1964.

————, *Labor in Crisis: The Steel Strike of 1919,* Philadelphia: J. B. Lippincott Co., 1965.

Before 1880, "English-speaking" workmen had manned America's iron and steel plants. Then immigrants from South and East Europe began to arrive in increasing numbers. More than 30,000 were steelworkers by 1900. The newcomers soon filled the unskilled jobs in the Northern mills, forcing the natives and earlier immigrants upward or out of the industry. In the Carnegie plants of Allegheny County in March 1907, 11,694 of the 14,359 common laborers were Eastern Europeans. The recent arrivals dominated the bottom ranks of the steel industry.

The Slavic influx shaped the labor stability at the unskilled level. A lowly job in the mills, however ill-paid and unpleasant, was endurable if it enabled the immigrant to leave in a few years with funds enough to resume his accustomed place in his native village. That was his original purpose. The majority, who in time decided to stay in America, usually had by then risen into higher paid jobs. In either event, the acceptance of the hard terms of common labor was the necessary prelude to a better life. Immigrant mobility was at the center of the peaceable adjustment of the unskilled steelworkers.

Fixed for centuries, by 1900 the peasant society of Eastern Europe had begun to disintegrate. The abolition of serfdom gave the peasant the right to mortgage and sell his land, and, later, to subdivide it. The falling death rate upset the ancient balance between population and acreage, leaving sons unprovided for or with insufficient land. Manufactured goods destroyed the peasant's self-sufficiency, raised his living standards and costs, and emphasized the inefficiency of his farming methods. When misfortune struck—a destructive storm, a drought, an outbreak of phylloxyra in the vineyards or disease in the livestock—he fell into debt, or, already mortgaged, lost his farm.

The peasant was linked to a chain of family inheritance and tradition. He had a name, a reputation, and a posterity. His self-esteem went with property, independence, and an assured social position. All this rested on his land, located in a certain village and held by his family from the immemorial past. The peasant with mortgage payments he could not meet faced an intolerable decline into the dependent, propertyless servant class. Rooted to the land, he saw his salvation only in emigration to a country from which men returned with money.

Inhabitants of the Western provinces of Austria-Hungary had long been accustomed to migrate seasonally to Germany for the harvests. To supplement meager farm incomes, Slovaks had peddled goods or followed wandering trades as wiremakers, potmenders, and glaziers. From the peasant viewpoint the longer move to America differed from seasonal migration only in degree. Men went to Germany to add to a slender livelihood. In America they would save enough to pay off the mortgage or to buy the land that would restore their social position. A Polish immigrant expected to "remain for some years and return with something to our country, so that later we might not be obliged to earn [as hired laborers]." The Atlantic crossing meant a heavy investment, a long absence, unaccustomed work in mill or mine; but the essential purpose did not differ from seasonal migration. The immigrant hoped to earn a stake and return to his village. With this end Slovaks, Poles, Croats, Serbs, Magyars, and Italians made the passage to America, and many found their way into the steel mills.

They entered the mills under the lure of wages. Earnings of $1.50 or $2.00 a day, it was true, would not support a wife and children. In the Pittsburgh district, where a family required $15 a week, two-thirds of the recent immigrants in the steel plants made less than $12.50, and one-third less than $10. The Pittsburgh Associated Charities in 1910 found that, if a steel laborer worked twelve hours every day in the year, he could not provide a family of five with the barest necessities. Every steel center had large numbers who earned much below the minimum for family existence.

But the immigrant steelworkers had not expected to support families in America. The vast majority came alone. One-third of those surveyed by the Immigration Commission were single, and roughly three-quarters of the married men who had been in the country under five years reported their wives abroad. The minority with families supplemented its income by lodging the others.

A "boarding-boss system" developed, benefiting all except perhaps the overburdened women. The workmen paid the "boss" $2.50 or $3.00 a month for lodging, including cooking and washing. The wife, or occasionally a hired housekeeper, bought the food for the household, and at the end of each month the total bill was divided among the adult males. There were variations. The boss might charge a flat monthly rate, or provide only a specified amount of food. In Granite City, Illinois, the Bulgarians economized by doing their own housework. But the system was essentially the same. A boarder could live for about $15 a month, and even after spending another $10 on clothing and trifles, could put aside $15. The boarding boss increased his income usually by more than half his mill earnings, and, in addition, was likely to be made a foreman.

The immigrants, moreover, counted the value of their hoards in terms of the increased buying power in their native villages. Mentally converting dollars into roubles, they estimated carefully that a few years of steady work would bring enough to buy a piece of land. "If I don't earn $1.50 a day," figured a prospective immigrant, "it would not be worth thinking about America." He could surely get that much in a steel mill. The large sums deposited in banks or sent home during prosperous years like 1907 verified the calculations. America, a Polish workman wrote home, "is a golden land as long as there is work." The wages in steel mills appeared to enable the peasant to achieve his purpose.

The newcomers harbored no illusions about America. "There in Pittsburgh, people say, the dear sun never shines brightly, the air is satu- rated with stench and gas," parents in Galicia wrote their children. A workman in the South Works warned a prospective immigrant: "if he wants to come, he is not to complain about [reproach] me for in America there are neither Sundays nor holidays; he must go and work." Letters emphasized that "here in America one must work for three horses." "There are different kinds of work, heavy and light," explained another, "but a man from our country cannot get the light." An Hungarian churchman inspecting Pittsburgh steel mills exclaimed bitterly: "Wherever the heat is most insupportable, the flames most scorching, the smoke and soot most choking, there we are certain to find compatriots bent and wasted with toil." Returned men, it was said, were worn out by their years in America.

Knowing about the taxing labor awaiting them, only the hardier men immigrated. Letters cautioned, "let him not risk coming, for he is still too young," or "too weak for America." The need to borrow for the trip tended to limit the opportunity to those who expected to make "big money." This selectivity gave the steel mills the best of Europe's peasant population.

Accustomed to village life, the adjustment to the new world of the steel mills was often painful. An Austrian Jew recalled his first day in a plant.

> The man put me in a section where there was [sic] terrible noises, shoot- ing, thundering and lightning. I wanted to run away but there was a big train in front of me. I looked up and a big train carrying a big vessel with fire was making towards me. I stood numb, afraid to move, until a man came to me and led me out of the mill.

Most weathered the first terror, the bewildering surroundings, the shouts in an unknown tongue. Appearing passive and unflinching, they grew used to the tumult and became skillful in their simple tasks.

A fat pay envelope overshadowed heavy labor and long hours; a few years' hardship was a cheap enough price for the precious savings. "I should like to have piecework, for work is never too hard," wrote a Polish peasant. "The work is very heavy, but I don't mind it," a brick factory worker informed his wife, "let it be heavy, but may it last without interruption." Russian steel laborers in Pittsburgh told an investigator they were glad to work extra days. A majority voluntarily reported on Sundays in 1907 to clear the yards and repair equipment. An immigrant characterized his twelve-hour position: "A good job, save money, work all time, go home, sleep, no spend." Thus did the immigrant's purpose match the policies of the employers.

The hazards of the mill alone troubled the workmen. Dangerous to experienced men, steelmaking was doubly so to untutored peasants. The accident rate for non-English-speaking employees at the South Works from 1906 to 1910 was twice the average of the rest of the labor force. Almost one-quarter of the recent immigrants in the works each year—3,273 in the five years—were injured or killed. In one year 127 Eastern Europeans died in the steel mills of Allegheny County. Letters told, sometimes in gory detail, the sudden end of friend or relative. The debilitating effects of industrial life took their quieter toll on the health of the immigrants.

In misfortune, the peasant had depended on his kin and parish, whose obligations to assist were defined and certain. He left this secure web of mutual help when he came to America. A Pole explained to his wife the hard lot of an immigrant.

> As long as he is well then he always works like a mule, and therefore he has something, but if he becomes sick then it is a trouble, because everybody is looking only for money in order to get some of it, and during the sickness the most will be spent.

Illness meant expenditure without income; a lengthy convalescence drained his savings and completely frustrated his ends.

Accidents were equally catastrophic. Illiterate, ignorant of the law, unable to speak the language, the immigrant had small likelihood of successfully presenting his compensation claim. If he was killed, the chances of his dependents were even more dubious. The Pennsylvania courts had ruled that the liability statute did not extend to nonresident aliens. Whatever the company's negligence, the victim's family in Europe was helpless. More than one-fourth of the men killed in Allegheny County in the year ending July 1907 had left their dependents in Europe, and the families of a score more departed soon after the funeral. Destitution awaited them. Friends learned from letters that "the widow begs, and the children are in rags," that the woman "works in the fields" or has "gone out to service," or that the family returned to the grandparents "who are old and have nothing."

Very early, the immigrants sought to ease the heavy individual risks. As soon as a number gathered in a mill town, they set up an informal mutual help society obligating each member to assist at sickness or death.

These became local insurance associations, in time affiliating with national benefit societies which were able to provide better and cheaper coverage. For example, the National Slovanic Society for monthly dues of 60 cents paid a death benefit of $1,000 and a sick benefit of $5.00 for the first thirteen weeks and $2.50 for another thirteen weeks. Immigrant steel-workers joined in large numbers. The Polish National Alliance had thirty locals in Pittsburgh in 1908. In Homestead 421 men belonged to the Greek Catholic Union, 363 to the National Slavonic Society, 460 to the First Catholic Slovak Union, 130 to the National Croatian Society. In much the same way as the native steelworkers, the immigrants partially coped with the hazards of the new world.

Bleak prospects faced the newcomers outside the mill. They settled on the low ground never far from the smoke and clamor of the plant, but also within easy walking distance to work. At Lackawanna they oc-cupied the marshy land surrounding the works, living in houses on "made ground" surrounded by stagnant, filthy pools. In the older mill towns they pushed the inhabitants of the dreariest streets into better neighborhoods. They huddled apart in enclaves often called Hunkeyvilles—in Gary, the Patch; in Granite City, Hungary Hollow; in Vandergrift, Rising Sun.

Flimsy, dilapidated structures lacking the most elementary sanitary facilities sheltered the immigrants. The Pittsburgh Bureau of Health re-ported after its 1907 inspection of tenement houses:

> The privy vaults were often found to be foul and full to the surface, sinks without trap or vent, the rain conductor serving to carry off waste water; damp, dark, and ill-smelling cellars used for sleeping purposes; cellars filthy; leaky roofs causing the walls and ceilings to become watersoaked, rendering the rooms damp and unhealthy; broken and worn floors; broken stair railings . . . plaster broken and paper torn and dirty.

Conditions were little better outside urban centers. Croatian workmen in Johnstown occupied frame houses edging a courtyard. A low four-room closet serving over fifty groups stood in the center directly over an exposed cesspool. The houses were dark, poorly ventilated, and in bad repair. Sim-ilarly, families depended on outside hydrants in the dismal immigrant courts of Homestead's Second Ward.

The inadequate dwellings were greatly overcrowded. The boarding boss and his family slept in one downstairs room in the standard four-room frame house. The kitchen was set aside for eating and living pur-poses, although it, too, often served as a bedroom. Upstairs the boss crammed double beds which were in use night and day when the mill was running full. Investigators came upon many cases of extreme crowding. Thirty-three Serbians and their boarding boss lived in a five-room house in Steelton. In Sharpsburg, Pennsylvania, an Italian family and nine boarders existed without running water or toilet in four rooms on the third floor of a ramshackle tenement. According to the Immigration Commission report, the number per sleeping room in immigrant households averaged around three; a sizable portion had four; and a small number six or more.

Ignorance compounded the living problems. Country people, the immigrants could not fathom the ways of urban life. Before the Pittsburgh filtration plant went into operation in 1908, many contracted typhoid fever. Doctors complained of the refusal to boil water. Despite warnings, men persisted in going to the river to quench their thirst as they had at home. Nor did they easily adjust to crowded, indoor life. Investigators found their rooms filthy, windows shut tight, sanitary facilities neglected and clogged. The occasional indoor bathrooms were left unused or served as storerooms.

The landlords, for their part, considered the immigrants fair game. When the newcomers invaded neighborhoods, property depreciated and frequently passed into new hands. The speculators ignored housing regulations, made no repairs or improvements, and in the continuing housing shortage and animus against immigrants, charged exorbitant rents. In some instances they received an extra dollar a month for each boarder. For much inferior accommodations, immigrant steelworkers paid an average 20 per cent more per room than did English-speaking tenants.

The local courts also fleeced the immigrants. The "squires" of the aldermanic courts in Pennsylvania received no salary, but were entitled to the fees incident to minor criminal and civil cases. Untutored in the law, they were usually brokers or real estate agents who regarded their office as a source of easy profit. And their prey were the foreigners, ignorant, inarticulate, and frightened. On pay nights the aldermen reaped handsomely from the workmen corralled into their dingy "shops" on dubious charges. An investigation of two aldermen revealed that only a small part of their criminal cases justified indictment. A Ruthenian boarding boss who had been fined $50 for disorderly conduct commented scornfully:

> Huh! The police are busy enough all right stopping disorder when the men have got money. But when there's hard times, like there is now, a man can make all the noise he pleases. . . . It ain't law they think about. It's money.

Indiana, Ohio, and Illinois justice was equally corrupt.

Harsh as life in the mill towns was, room still remained for a happier side. The newcomers went usually to friends and relatives, and worked with men from their own villages. The benefit societies were convivial, and from them sprang other social organizations. Priests arrived as soon as there were people enough to support a church. The parish emerged to unite the activities of the ethnic, religious group into a coherent community. The later arrival in steel towns found his social needs relatively well satisfied.

There were other means of consolation. Intemperance, particularly during pay nights and marriage and birth celebrations, dismayed social workers. The immigrants had ready money, beer and whiskey cost little, and saloons served as social centers. Investigators counted 30 saloons in Duquesne, 65 in Braddock, 69 in McKeesport. Gary had one saloon for less than every hundred inhabitants; barrooms lined solidly the immigrant end of the main thoroughfare, known locally as Whiskey Row.

But the main consolation was the knowledge that the hard life was temporary, a few years' sacrifice in exchange for a competence at home.

The one essential was not wages, working conditions, or living standards, but employment itself. "When there is none," wrote one Polish laborer, America "is worth nothing." Prospective immigrants wanted to know only "whether work is good and whether it is worth while to go to America." Favorable reports emptied the villages. "An awful multitude of people are going from here to America," a Polish peasant informed his brother during the high prosperity of early 1907. The peak years of American industry—1892, 1903, 1907, 1910—matched the heights of immigration.

The newcomer's stay depended directly on his employment. "I have had no work for four months now," a workman wrote his brother in February 1904. "If conditions don't improve by Easter, we will go back to our country, and if they improve and I get work, I will immediately send a ship ticket and you will come." In depressed years immigration dropped sharply; one Polish woman reported in 1908 "whole throngs of people coming back from America." More Austro-Hungarians and Italians departed than arrived that year.

The effects of trade fluctuations were, if anything, exaggerated in the unstable steel industry. And the immigrants were the first to be let go. Non-English-speaking men constituted 48 per cent of the South Works labor force in 1907, 37 per cent in 1908. Thirty per cent of the immigrant steelworkers surveyed by the Immigration Commission in 1908 worked less than six months, almost two-thirds under nine months. Approximately 2,425 recent immigrants left Steelton, where only half the normal work force had employment. By the end of the depression, nine-tenths of the Bulgarians, the chief unskilled labor of Granite City, had departed.

Unemployment frustrated the immigrant's aims in much the same way as illness or injury. If the depression was prolonged, he might be reduced to real want. Granite City's Hungary Hollow came with reason to be called Hungry Hollow during 1908. But the boarding boss system mitigated the worst of extreme hardship; the fortunate boarders shared with the others, and the boss rarely forced a penniless workman to leave. In every case, nevertheless, the lost job meant the collapse of the immigrant's plan. Not only did his savings stop, but his accumulation quickly drained out. Unemployment, impossible to accommodate within the immigrant's purpose, alone disturbed the unskilled labor pattern. Otherwise, the Slavic steelworker found entirely acceptable the terms of work imposed by the system of economy.

The immigrants intended to return to their villages, and many did. From 1908 to 1910 (including a bad, middling, and prosperous year) forty-four South and East Europeans departed for every hundred that arrived; altogether, 590,000 left in the three years. But more remained.

Many forces turned the immigrant away from his homeland. He saw little enough of the new country, but he was nevertheless influenced by it. He at once discarded his peasant garb, and he sensed, despite the hard life and the hostility of Americans, the disappearance of clear lines of class and status. Nothing revealed more of the American influence than the complaints of the gentry that immigrants, when they returned, were disrespectful.

Migration weakened the familial solidarity of peasant society, clouded the purposes and inherited values of the immigrant, and, particularly after the wife arrived, dimmed the image of the home village. Moreover, the presence of friends and relatives and the developing social institutions began to meet the needs of the immigrants. They in time regarded their jobs, not as temporary chances, but as their careers, and their goal became promotion rather than property at home.

The crucial fact was that in the steel mills immigrants did rise. Thomas Huras, for example, came to America in October 1910 and the following February found a job in the open-hearth department of the Gary Works. He transferred to the merchant mill, where there was more opportunity, gradually rose, and in 1918 was a catcher in the ten-inch mill. Walter Stalmaszck, at fifteen going to work on a blast furnace in the South Works, eventually became a straightener on No. 1 rail mill. When in 1914 the Joliet Works picked out men to serve as safety supervisors for their sections, many immigrant workmen received their first chance to advance.

Statistics showed the process. At one large Pittsburgh mill in 1910 none of the recent immigrants with under two years' service had skilled jobs, 56 were semiskilled, 314 unskilled; between two and five years, 17 were skilled, 243 semiskilled, 544 unskilled; between five and ten years, 79 were skilled, 441 semiskilled, 475 unskilled; and over ten years, 184 were skilled, 398 semiskilled, 439 unskilled. The income of immigrant steelworkers increased steadily. Less than one-tenth of any ethnic group resident less than five years earned over fifteen dollars a week; between 13 and 25 per cent resident from five to ten years; and 20 to 33 per cent resident over ten years. Altogether, 13 per cent of the recent immigrants in the industry held skilled jobs, another 42 per cent semiskilled.

The pattern of life changed with lengthening residence and rising earnings. The immigrant steelworker sent for his family; two-thirds in America under five years reported wives abroad, one-third from five to nine years, and one-seventh after nine years. His living standards rose; more money went for food, clothing, and luxuries. He was willing to pay higher rent for better lodging, frequently moved his family out of the densest immigrant sections, and abandoned the boarding boss system. Habitually saving, he often bought his house. One-sixth of 1,675 immigrant steelworkers in the Immigration Commission survey owned their homes. In time he learned to speak English with fair fluency. Steve Augustinovitch, a Croat who immigrated at the age of eighteen, was typical. Foreman of a repair crew at the Gary Works at twenty-eight, he owned his house, had savings, a large family, and his first citizenship papers.

In short, he merged with other skilled steelworkers. Distinguishable ethnically and perhaps socially, within the plant he moved in the same orbit of dependence and repression. If anything, the immigrants were more susceptible to the employers' strategy, for the peasant mentality sharply distinguished between independent farming and hired labor. The immigrant felt less secure in his job than the native steelworkers, whose experience encompassed only hired employment, and he therefore became a more docile, loyal employee.

The stability in the unskilled ranks thus rested on mobility. The newcomers either moved up into the skilled force; or they moved out at the first depression or with a satisfactory accumulation. Despite the harsh terms of work, therefore, steel companies enjoyed peaceful relations with their common laborers.

The employer's part in maintaining the pattern was essentially passive. He was generally ignorant of the reasons why the immigrants came to America. But he recognized them as a "floating supply of labor." That simple, crucial fact governed his decisions.

Hiring and firing policies assumed the mobility of common labor. Employment officials did not investigate the immigrants, kept no detailed records, and observed individual capacity only for physical strength. When labor was plentiful, foremen usually picked likely men out of the jobless crowds that gathered before the mill gates at the changing of the shift.

To insure a steady supply, companies reached understandings with immigrant leaders. The employment manager, said the labor supervisor of the South Works,

> . . . must not only be aware of the location of all the groups of foreign settlement in the community, but he must become personally acquainted

with the individual boarding bosses, steamship agents, clergymen, and other influential agents. . . . These are his supply depots, and only by perpetual, personal reconnoitering can he remain familiar with the quality and quantity of available applicants.

The steel plants in Granite City, for instance, had an agreement to employ all the applicants of a Bulgarian leader. Boarding bosses, when they were gang foremen, could hire as well as lodge workmen. Before the immigrant channels to mill towns developed, steel companies had sent agents to New York City docks or employed labor agencies. That was rarely necessary in later years except during serious shortages.

Welfare efforts, designed to attach workmen to the company, did not extend to common labor. "The problem of maintaining a force of skilled workmen is realized by every employer" and "much attention has been given to" their welfare, observed the *Iron Age,* "but the unskilled employee of shop or foundry gets little attention." The difference could be seen most clearly in housing programs. One company in the Eastern district provided excellent facilities at low cost for its higher paid men. For unskilled labor, the firm offered "shanties," an appropriate designation. Ten by fourteen feet, these were constructed of ordinary rough pine boards weatherstripped on the outside. Four men ate, washed, and slept in each shanty. Four "barracks," built like the shanties, housed twenty men each. All the structures were primitively furnished, and damp and cold in winter. According to the federal Bureau of Labor estimate, the rent amounted each year to more than 200 per cent of the company's original investment. In less isolated areas employers generally ignored the housing problems of the immigrants.

The few efforts at improvement proved dismal failures. Lackawanna erected a village of monotonous but substantial houses around its new plant for low-paid employees. And the Steel Corporation put up fifty dwellings—"double dry goods boxes"—for its laborers at Gary. But the men did not understand the need for sanitation and objected to the lack of amusements in the vicinity. The Gary houses were filthy, used as boarding houses, and greatly overcrowded. Within a few years the Corporation evicted the inhabitants of the notorious Hunkeyville and razed the houses. The experiment was admittedly unsuccessful.

> The housing provided by the Corporation is perhaps better suited to the needs of the skilled workmen than to the wages of the unskilled laborers [who are] largely foreigners without families. . . . These men earn low wages, out of which they seek to save the utmost amount possible.

The Steel Corporation thereupon left the immigrant steelworkers to their own devices, erecting housing designed only for the higher ranks. Other measures to reduce labor turnover—pensions, profit sharing, stock purchase—likewise bypassed the unskilled.

The steel manufacturers had ready answers for the criticisms of re- formers. The immigrants, they said, were eager to work the long hours for the greater earnings. They received wages higher than for similar work in Europe. Their living conditions were worse than the skilled workers' not because of smaller income, but because their wages were dissipated in "debauch." However bad their life appeared, said a Pittsburgh employer, it "is probably somewhat better than that to which such foreign workmen were accustomed in their own countries."

It was not that steel manufacturers undervalued the immigrants. Al- though claiming natives to be superior workmen, employers understood very well their good fortune. They dealt with the immigrant steelworkers as they did because nothing else was necessary. Developing without any effort on their part, the unskilled labor pattern of mobility fitted perfectly into the scheme of economical steel manufacture. The steelmakers were content.

3.5

Labor Conflict and Racial Violence: The Black Worker in Chicago, 1894-1919

WILLIAM M. TUTTLE, JR.

Starting in the early decades of this century and increasing rapidly during the First World War when European immigration dried up, southern blacks, mostly from rural communities, migrated to northern industrial cities. That process has continued through the subsequent decades. Blacks shared the challenge of cultural adaptation with white immigrants, but in quite particular ways. Prevailing racial ideology and caste beliefs put up unique blocks to their entry and gave it a special character. The opportunities, however limited, available to immigrant laborers and their children were not accessible to blacks. Employers often saw blacks as little more than an available cheap labor force that could be used to dampen efforts by white workers, both native and immigrant in birth, seeking self-protection. Weaker but still powerful craft unions also usually denied access to black workers.

In this analysis of the background to the 1919 Chicago race riots,

William M. Tuttle, Jr., "Labor Conflict and Racial Violence: The Black Worker in Chicago, 1894–1919," *Labor History*, 10 (1969), 86–111. Copyright Greenwood Press, Inc. Reprinted and footnotes omitted by permission of the publisher, the copyright holder, and the author.

William Tuttle uses unusually striking evidence to reveal the tensions between black and white workers that exploded into violence in Chicago and other northern cities after the First World War. Just how and why prevailing native racial ideology had penetrated into the value system of recent immigrants to the United States remains unstudied. Tuttle's evidence makes it clear, however, that it needs careful attention.

The following books are suggested for further reading:

ELLIOTT M. RUDWICK, *Race Riot at East St. Louis,* Carbondale: Southern Illinois University Press, 1964.

WILLIAM TUTTLE, *Race Riot: Chicago and the Red Summer of 1919,* New York: Atheneum Publishers, 1970.

On a crowded South Side Chicago beach on the afternoon of Sunday, July 27, 1919, white and black swimmers clashed in savage combat. Sparked by this clash during which a Negro youth drowned, the inter-racial resentment that had been smoldering in Chicago for the past few years exploded in furious rioting. The violence raged uncontrolled for five days, as whites mauled Negroes and Negroes in turn assaulted white peddlers and merchants in the "black belt." Members of both races craved vengeance as stories of atrocities, both real and rumored, rapidly spread throughout the city. White gunmen in automobiles sped through the ghetto shooting indiscriminately as they passed, and black snipers fired back. Roaming mobs shot, beat, and stabbed their victims to death. The under-manned Chicago police force was an ineffectual deterrent to the waves of violence that soon overflowed the environs of the black belt and flooded the North and West Sides as well as the Loop, the city's downtown business district. Only six regiments of state militiamen and a cooling rain finally quenched the passions of the rioters, but by then thirty-eight lay dead, twenty-three Negroes and fifteen whites, and well over 500 others had sustained injuries.

There were several factors precipitating this riot. From July 1917 to the eruption of the disorders two years later, for example, no less than twenty-six bombs were hurled at isolated Negro residences in once all-white neighborhoods and at the offices of certain realtors who had sold to blacks. Well over half these bombings occurred during the six tense months leading up to the riot. Politics, too, were important. Chicago's notoriously corrupt Republican mayor, William H. ("Big Bill") Thompson, was anathema to reformers and Democrats alike. Many of these Democrats, moreover, were blue-collar workers who lived in neighborhoods contiguous to the black belt and who felt threatened, politically and economically, by the "invading" Negroes. Yet Thompson was a favorite of the predominantly Republican black electorate, some of whose leaders had been rewarded with posts in his administration. The mayor was reelected in April 1919, after a bitter campaign which had racial overtones, and the Democratic organ, the *Chicago Daily Journal,* boomed out at dusk on election day in bold front-page headlines: "NEGROES ELECT BIG BILL." As racial friction mounted with the heat in the spring and summer of 1919, whites and blacks battled on the city's streetcars and in parks and schools. Several Negroes were murdered in mob assaults, and both blacks and whites armed themselves for the riot that numerous Chicagoans feared would erupt at any moment.

This riot was also the result of longstanding discord between white and black job competitors in the Chicago labor market. Several contemporaries claimed that job competition was not only a cause but perhaps the most significant one. Later students of the riot, however, while admitting that interracial labor friction might have precipitated some bloodshed, have listed it as merely a minor cause. The most exhaustive study, *The Negro in Chicago,* by the Chicago Commission on Race Relations, for example, concluded that it was relatively unimportant since "race friction" was "not pronounced in Chicago industries." Recently Allan H. Spear in *Black Chicago* has similarly asserted that the riot "had little to do with labor conditions. . . ."

Both the Chicago Commission and Spear support this contention by pointing out that during the riot there was an almost total absence of violence in the stockyards, which was by far the largest single area of employment for black Chicagoans. And, indeed, there was far less bloodshed there than knowledgeable observers had feared. But does this negative evidence prove anything other than that black workers did not dare return to the stockyards until after the militia had been ordered out of the armories to protect them? The absence of violence in the stockyards in the early days of the riot was, as Negro Alderman Louis B. Anderson explained, simply the result of fear of attack. "Colored men," Anderson said, "have refused to go to the stockyards to get paid even though their families were starving. . . ." And what happened when Negroes returned to work? Even under military and police protection, on the first day back, one worker was savagely struck with a hammer wielded by a white man. A mob then chased the dazed Negro through the sheep pens and finally killed him with shovels and brooms. When police rescued a second black man after a severe beating, white workers retaliated, and a vicious battle against police and soldiers ensued. Several days later the packers notified non-union black workers that order had been restored to the yards, and that additional police and soldiers armed with rifles and machine guns would be there to insure their safe return to work. Organized labor disagreed, arguing that the situation was still volatile. The packers "thought that if they would be able to jamb [*sic*] the colored laborers," charged President John Fitzpatrick of the Chicago Federation of Labor, "that is, the great body of colored laborers, and the white union men in the stock yards . . . that there would be murder there, and that they would destroy our organization. There was no other purpose in it, absolutely no other purpose in it. . . ."

Herbert Gutman has recently made a plea to labor historians "to explore in detail the confrontation of the black worker and industrial America in particular settings." The history of the black worker in Chicago from the Pullman strike of 1894 to the race riot of 1919 provides such an opportunity—in large part because the race riot was in many ways the tragic culmination of this twenty-five years of conflict between blacks and whites in the labor market.

The seeds of discord between white and Negro job competitors in the Chicago labor market had been planted in the stockyards in 1894, when masses of packing and slaughterhouse workers had conducted a sympathetic strike with Eugene V. Debs' American Railway Union. Violence marked this strike; and, in the midst of it, Negro strikebreakers were hired for the first time in the history of the meat packing industry. Although the packers initially disclaimed any intention of adopting this practice, less than a week later Negro strikebreakers were working, eating, and sleeping in the stockyards, and their presence fired racial animosities. "Cases of attacks on colored men were numerous yesterday," the *Chicago Record* reported on July 19. "Swinging from the cross tree of a telegraph pole . . . near the entrance to the yards, the effigy of a negro roustabout was suspended. A black false face of hideous expression had been fixed upon the head of straw, and a placard pinned upon the breast of the figure bore the skull and crossbones with the word 'nigger-scab' above and below in bold letters. . . ."

The strike ended in August, and the Negro strikebreakers were intimately associated with the defeat. The workers had been thoroughly vanquished. They seemed "unmanly and without self-respect," recalled Mary McDowell of the settlement house "back-of-the-yards." "A community cowed is a sad sight to one who has been used to freemen."

Gradually, the workers built a new union—the Amalgamated Meat Cutters and Butcher Workmen (A.M.C.B.W.). Chicago was its target, for "if a start could be made in Chicago," the center of the industry, the A.M.C.B.W.'s president Michael Donnelly wrote Samuel Gompers, "our success nationally would be virtually established." Success was slow in coming, but by 1902 Donnelly could proudly announce that twenty-one locals had been chartered in Chicago and that the union rolls had burgeoned to 4,000. Accompanying organizing successes were concrete gains in wages and hours.

Yet these benefits went only to skilled workers, and at the turn of the century less and less skill was required in the meat packing industry because of the minute subdivision of labor. The "facts are these," Homer D. Call, the A.M.C.B.W.'s secretary treasurer, explained to Frank Morrison of the A.F.L., "twenty years ago the trade of the butchers was one of the best in the country." Then, after the consolidation of smaller packing houses into a handful of "large packing houses . . . they began a system to crowd out the expert butchers and replace them by cheaper men in every way. . . ." The owners "divided the business up into gangs consisting of enough to dress the bullock, one man doing only one thing . . . , which makes it possible for the proprietor to take a man in off from the street . . . and to day [*sic*] the expert workers are, in many cases, crowded out and cheap Polackers and Hungarians put in their places. . . ." The skilled worker realized that this specialization enabled unskilled workers with "muscle" to replace him; it appeared inevitable that unless a minimum wage were obtained for the unskilled, cut-throat job competition would drive all wages down. The unskilled were "the club held above our heads at all times," a skilled butcher complained. "If the packers refuse to agree to any minimum wage for the unskilled," asked Call, "how long will it be before they attempt to reduce the wages of the skilled men?" The skilled workers thus championed the demand for a minimum wage of 20 cents an hour.

This minimum was the union's objective, but it still faced an obstacle that had perpetually plagued unionization of the stockyards—the vast heterogeneity of races and nationalities that competed for jobs. No other divisive force more ominously threatened the union's goal of solidarity. Racial jealousies and antagonisms crumbled, however, as the unskilled enthusiastically joined the union because of dissatisfaction with the prevailing wage of 15 to 18½ cents an hour, and Negroes joined as well as whites. Many of the 500 black workers in the Chicago yards had become members, U. S. Labor Commissioner Carroll D. Wright reported to President Theodore Roosevelt. The women's local reportedly greeted its black applicants with "a hearty welcome," and Mary McDowell noted that "black men sat with their white comrades" at union meetings. This fellowship extended beyond the confines of the meeting room. The A.M.C.B.W., for example, held a funeral for "Bro. Wm. Sims (colored) tail sawyer at Swift's east house," with sixty-eight whites and seven Negroes attending these last rites.

Negotiations with the packers over the minimum wage were fruitless, breaking down in late June 1904, and when the packers announced a wage reduction, 23,000 packing house workers struck. Seven thousand mechanical tradesmen later joined the strike, which dragged on for ten weeks before the workers sporadically drifted back to work. The A.M.C.B.W. had launched its strike in the face of a depression. Outside the stockyards each morning as many· as 5,000 men stood lined up to replace the strikers. The strike was further doomed because the strikers' resources were so paltry compared to the combined assets of the packers. Moreover, the heterogeneous nationalities, races, and foreign languages, which had united confidently in 1903 and 1904, were in the final analysis divided and weak.

Despite the hopelessness of the strike, the arch villains to emerge from the defeat were the packers and their black strikebreakers. One observer estimated that upwards of 10,000 Negroes served as strikebreakers, with almost 1,400 arriving in one trainload. To white workers their disturbing presence seemed to be ubiquitous. Five white women strikebreakers described the prevalence of Negroes in the yards. These women, who had been hired by a black man representing Armour, worked in the canning room, ate their meals in a massive improvised dining hall one floor below, and at night slept in the canning room which "had 40 cots arranged as close together as possible." They reported seeing many Negro strikebreakers, including thirteen- and fourteen-year-old boys.

Since the violence of the 1894 strike had alienated public opinion, in 1904 the union posted notices on trees and fences which admonished the strikers "to molest no person or property, and abide strictly by the laws of this country." Non-violence was also the theme of union meetings. These exhortations notwithstanding, the strikers' animosities frequently boiled over. A mob of 500 mauled a black laborer and his 10-year-old son, and in another skirmish white strikers stabbed both eyes of a Negro strikebreaker. Other black people were hauled off streetcars. A full-scale riot threatened to erupt when 2,000 angry strikers hurled brickbats and other missiles at 200 Negro strikebreakers and their police escorts. Harry Rosenberg, a worker at Mary McDowell's settlement house, reported witnessing a mob of women and children chasing a Negro down the street, crying "kill the fink," and in late August union pickets fatally stabbed a Negro suspected of strikebreaking.

Their fortunes waning in late August, union leaders desperately wired Booker T. Washington. "Hundreds of Negroes are acting as strikebreakers," they informed Washington, as they begged him to come to Chicago to lecture on the subject, "Should Negroes Become Strike Breakers?" Washington, however, declined the offer.

The words "Negro" and "scab" were now synonymous in the minds of numerous white stockyards workers; and, lest they forget, anti-Negro labor officials and politicians were present to remind them. The strike, one union official wrote, was broken "by such horrid means that a revelation of them makes the soul sicken and the heart faint with an awful fear." It was broken by Negroes, most of them "huge strapping fellows, ignorant and vicious, whose predominating trait was animalism." South Carolina's Senator Ben Tillman traveled to Chicago a month after the end of the strike. "It was the niggers that whipped you in line," he told a group from the stockyards district. "They were the club with which your brains were beaten out."

It was not mere words, however, but another strike, the bloody teamsters' strike of 1905, that made the image of Negroes as a "scab race" even more indelible. Just days after the teamsters struck in April, trainloads of Negroes began streaming into Chicago. Shootings, knifings, and stonings soon paralyzed the city's commerce. Showers of bricks and stones greeted the black drivers as they attempted to deliver milk, coal, and other merchandise; and the injuries inflicted were recorded in the box scores of "strike victims" that Chicago's newspapers printed as front-page news. Pummeled with brass knuckles, "right ear almost torn off"; "injured by bricks, severely bruised and cut, struck on head and left leg with clubs during riot at Rush and Michigan"; struck on the head by a brick "said to have been thrown from the tenth floor"; beaten into unconsciousness, "three shovels broken over his head"—these were but a few of the injuries.

Fearing that such acts of violence would erupt into full-scale rioting, the city council enacted an order requesting the corporation counsel to file an opinion "as to whether the importation of hundreds of Negro workers is not a menace to the community and should not be restricted." The employers' association responded by consenting not to import any more Negroes, though it refused to discharge any of its black drivers.

Not only was the employers' gesture futile, but its very futility indicated that new elements had entered into the relationship between labor conflict and racial violence in Chicago. In this dispute, unlike the stockyards strike of eight months before, the hostility of striking whites toward strikebreaking Negroes had been generalized into hatred for the black race as a whole; any Negro was a potential target. Now, no longer were mob assaults limited to just one district; presaging the 1919 riot, racial violence had spread throughout the city but it was especially prevalent in the blue-collar neighborhood to the west of the black belt. "You have the Negroes in here to fight us," the teamsters' president told the employers' association, "and we answer that we have the right to attack them wherever found." Moreover, as Graham Taylor of the Chicago Commons settlement house observed, the "great intensity of class consciousness" in the teamsters' strike forged a firm bond between strikers and their families, neighbors, other wage-earners, and even the little children who supported them by hurling rocks at the strikebreakers. The focus of their violence was

facilitated by the distinguishing physical characteristic of the Negroes—
the black skin that represented so many varieties of evil and danger to
them. Finally, the besieged Negroes were determined to defend themselves,
unlike 1904 when, unarmed, they had generally fled.

Some of the non-strikebreaking black victims were mistaken for non-
union drivers. One of these was a dishwasher, who was kicked and beaten
and his head smashed through a car window; when policemen came to his
aid, the crowd began to yell: "That's what they will all get." Another was
a porter who was attacked by a crowd that ran after him screaming that
he was a scab; beaten into unconsciousness, the porter died several days
later of a fractured skull. The only offense committed by other Negroes,
however, was that their color was "black and displeasing." A Negro medical student, for example, was pummeled to the ground. Even a black
union member was pelted with rocks; when he called out to his attackers
that his employer was not involved in the strike, one of them replied that
being a "nigger" he deserved a beating anyhow.

Perhaps there was no better example of white solidarity during these
turbulent weeks than the sympathy strike conducted by hundreds of grade-
school students. Protesting the delivery of coal at school buildings by
black strikebreakers employed by the Peabody Coal Company, the students
not only hurled missiles at the drivers but organized a "skilled pupils' "
union with a kindergarten local affiliated. "We are on strike. Hurrah for
the unions," read the paper badges of the students who threw bricks,
stones, and pieces of wood at those classmates refusing to join the picket
line. Many parents supported the strike, some asserting that they would
never permit their children to return so long as scabs continued to deliver
coal. They also sanctioned violence. One father, for example, told a judge
that his son was "amply justified" in flinging coal at Negro drivers because
these men were "black" and "nonunion." Even teachers encouraged the
strikers. "I will invite the pupils to strike," one principal allegedly said,
"if the dirty 'niggers' deliver coal at this school."

Negroes appeared resolved to defend themselves. When a white man
made a crude remark about a black strikebreaker who was standing at
the rear of a custom house, the Negro leaped down from the platform
and leveled a revolver at the white. "Why, I was only joking," the white
man quickly said. "You're just white trash and I ought to shoot you anyhow," replied the Negro.

It was this resolve that helped to precipitate unrestrained violence in
mid-May. An 11-year-old boy died on May 16, after two Negro strikebreakers, leaving work at the Peabody Coal Company, had fired into a
group of jeering children. Hysteria swept the neighborhood as enraged
mobs hunted for Negroes. White anger swelled menacingly, so that black
people feared to appear in the streets. Then, on the evening of May 20,

rioting surged out of control. Parading down the streets and proclaiming their intention of "driving the blacks off the face of the earth," whites met armed resistance. Surrounded by attackers, another strikebreaker from Peabody fired and fatally wounded a white man. The next day, as the rioting spread to other districts, police were unable to prevent the outbreaks and disturbances that grew bloodier as night approached. That evening a Negro was murdered by a white bartender in a saloon brawl, and other black men were dragged off streetcars. In the black belt, where Negroes marched the streets crying for "justice" and "down with the white trash," white men were chased and beaten. When the violence subsided on May 22, two people were dead and a dozen severely injured. It had been, as Allan Spear has written, "the bloodiest racial conflict in the city before the riot of 1919." Labor conflict, it was readily apparent, could easily escalate into racial violence.

The image of black people as a scab race no doubt continued to fester in the minds of white workers, even though Negroes did not reinforce it again until 1916. Pullman car porters and other black men and women replaced striking railroad car cleaners in the spring of that year. Fed in dining cars and sleeping in the Pullmans, the Negroes, according to the employer, were hired "not as strikebreakers, but with the understanding that their positions would be permanent," and they were "proving themselves much more efficient in every way than the cleaners who left. . . ." Most of these workers stayed on the job after breaking the strike.

In 1916, too, as a result of increased meat production to feed Europe's armies and a sharp decline in immigration, the lines of men waiting outside the stockyards each morning evaporated. "In the past years," Mary McDowell wrote a friend, "we have seen three to five thousand men and women waiting every morning for work and have been told that while there was such a surplus of labor a raise in wages could not be given to the unskilled workers." Surely, this must change.

Union leaders realized not only that the moment was propitious to organize all the stockyards workers, but that in this mass-production and minutely specialized industry some sort of industrial unionism would be required to do it. Under the leadership of John Fitzpatrick, president of the Chicago Federation of Labor (C.F.L.), and William Z. Foster, an organizer for the railway carmen's union, all the trade unions in the yards, with the exception of the A.M.C.B.W., united in July 1917 to form the Stockyards Labor Council (S.L.C.).

Next to persuading the nationals to lay aside jurisdictional jealousies for the benefit of central organization, the S.L.C.'s most formidable problem was that of unionizing Negro workers, of whom there were between 10,000 and 12,000 in the yards, or about one-quarter of the total laboring force. The C.F.L. asked Samuel Gompers to provide a method by which the S.L.C. could grant membership to Negroes without violating the constitutions, rituals, and other color bars of the nationals. Gompers' solution was that the A.F.L. would award federal charters to all-Negro locals, if no serious objections were raised by the nationals. Despite the established unworkability of federal locals, and the cries of "Jim Crow" that they would arouse, the S.L.C. confidently embarked on its campaign to organize Negroes. To assist in the drive, the Illinois coal miners donated two black organizers, and others later joined the team.

The yards, rather than the steel mills or other mass-production industries, were the focus of the unions' efforts to solicit Negro membership. Not only were the packers by far the major employers of Negro labor but, nearly as significant, success in organizing Negroes in the yards was generally considered a gauge of the unions' ability to organize them in any of Chicago's industries. Moreover, the slaughtering and meat-packing industry was the city's largest, employing over one-eighth of Chicago's wage-earners and ranking first in value added by manufacture and told value of its products.

A mass organization drive began in September 1917, with parades, smokers, hall and street meetings, and the distribution of 50,000 pieces of literature in various languages. "Brother's [sic] in all the Packing Houses. . . . BE MEN—JOIN THE UNION" read the handbills summoning black workers to a union meeting. The strike failures of 1894 and 1904 haunted union members, and it was rumored that the packers wanted a strike and had imported an enormous labor reserve of Negroes to break it and crush unionization. And, indeed, it seemed to be a fact, though a much disputed one, that employers were importing black laborers from the rural South.

On March 30, 1918, however, through the intervention of the federal government, Judge Samuel Alschuler, who had been appointed U. S. Administrator for Adjustment of Labor Differences in Certain Packing House Industries, awarded the eight-hour day and other benefits to workers in the yards. Such gains, the workers felt, were a tremendous union victory. Fitzpatrick jubilantly proclaimed to an excited crowd of thousands assembled in a Chicago public park: "It's a new day, and out in God's sunshine, you men and you women, black and white, have not only an eight-hour day but you are on an equality." Union membership soared in the weeks following these awards.

"I suppose you have heard from official sources that the Stockyards will soon be a hundred percent organized," Ida Glatt, an officer of the Women's Trade Union League, happily recounted to Agnes Nestor, former president of the League. "From intimate connection with the white and colored English-speaking women workers I can tell you firsthand that the women are just rolling into the organization." The unions' secretaries "do nothing but take in applications from morning to midnight." Negro men and women were also participating in the meetings of the S.L.C.

Not everybody shared Miss Glatt's optimism. Irene Goins, a Negro who was actively organizing in the yards, expressed her disappointment: "My people . . . know so little about organized labor that they have had a great fear of it, and for that reason the work of organizing has proceeded more slowly than I anticipated." Another black organizer, John Riley, echoed her disappointment.

The urgent need to organize black workers increased in the fall of 1918. The war was drawing to a close, and accompanying demobilization would be the termination not only of government contracts but of the federal wartime agencies which had supported union recognition, collective bargaining, and non-discrimination against union members. It was imperative for labor to meet with greater solidarity the employers' efforts to re-establish the pre-war pattern of industrial relations. Unorganized Negroes, union leaders feared, would be pawns of the employers in the future struggle. Southern Negroes continued to pour into the city; in recent years the Negro population in Chicago had more than doubled, increasing from 50,000 to over 100,000, while the Negro industrial force had risen from 27,000 to almost 70,000. In 1910, black men comprised just 6 percent of the laboring force in the yards; ten years later, they comprised 32 percent. The black laboring force of every packing house, reported Dr. George E. Haynes of the Labor Department's Division of Negro Economics, had increased rapidly from three to five times over the level of January 1916.

In addition, the image of Negro strikebreakers had not dimmed during the war. Hotel keepers, for example, locked out waiters in April 1918, hiring Negroes in their place. "This is a deliberate attempt to start a race war," Fitzpatrick wrote Secretary of Labor William B. Wilson. Wilson's conciliator in Chicago agreed that the dispute was "full of danger because of the Race problem." Negroes also broke strikes of egg candlers and garment workers.

With the Armistice, as the forces of demobilization touched all levels of the economy, the battle lines between employers and workers hardened. But the peace was also portentous to black Chicagoans whose employment security was in large measure attributable to the government's demands for war products. That spring, the prospect of a peacetime labor market disturbed people who were usually the first to feel the effects of the immediate postwar unemployment. Negro women were the first to be discharged; Negro men and white women soon followed. At the stockyards' National Box Company, where half of the workers and almost all the unskilled workers were black, Negro women were discharged after a pay raise for women workers. "After they gave that," a black woman complained, "there came a whole lot of white ladies." This woman, who wanted to remain at National Box, was told she could stay if she were willing to do the gruelling work of loading trucks formerly done by men. "If you don't want to do that," her foremen told her, "you will have to go home, because they are going to have all whites."

Upwards of 10,000 Negroes were unemployed in early May 1919. Employment in the stockyards had fallen from over 65,000 in January to 50,000. Returning soldiers aggravated this situation, and thousands of black troops were mustered out in or near Chicago, many of them southerners who had little desire to return home. A. L. Jackson of the Wabash Avenue YMCA pleaded with the Chicago industrialists to hire these veterans; and in boosting their qualifications he even invoked the nativism so prevalent in 1919: "These boys are all good Americans. There are no slackers, no hyphens among them." To alleviate this distress, the Chicago Urban League distributed portions of the labor surplus to Battle Creek, Flint, and Detroit, and to areas of Wisconsin and Illinois, but it could place only a few hundred compared to the many thousands of placements it had made during the war. Even during the prosperous summer months of 1919, black Chicagoans doubtless realized that during a labor depression they were the most expendable, and many did not want to jeopardize their tenuous positions by unionizing.

In early June the stockyards unions kicked off their most spirited organization drive since 1917. Following a parade and the distribution of campaign buttons on June 8, John Kikulski, an organizer of butchers and meat cutters, outlined the goals of "this great campaign," in which "Polish, Irish, Lithuanian, and in fact every race, color, creed, and nationality is to be included. . . ." "While there will be varied differences in our physical makeup and thoughts," he continued, "there is one thing which we all hold in common, and that is our right to a living wage, and our rights in the pursuit of happiness as American citizens. . . ." In other attempts to organize black workers, and to convince them that labor's cause was also theirs, the C.F.L. devoted portions of its newspaper, *The New Majority*, to the Negro. The organ of the A.M.C.B.W., the *Butcher Workman*, likewise published pointed appeals to black workers. An article authored by a Negro woman appeared in the May issue. Entitled "The Negro's Greatest Opportunity as I See It," it was both a slashing attack on race prejudice and an announcement that the A.M.C.B.W. had "broken down the bars and . . . invited us in." "Therefore, the black man should take advantage of this great opportunity [membership in the A.M.C.B.W.], so that he may be the instrument through which discrimination may be driven out of this country—the home of the free and the home of the brave."

White and Negro workers paraded through the black belt on Sunday, July 6, and congregated in a playground near the yards. Brass bands led the way, and the marchers waved miniature American flags and carried placards, on one of which was printed: "The bosses think because we are of different colors and different nationalities that we should fight each other. We're going to fool them and fight for a common cause—a square deal for all." Union leaders delivered speeches at the playground. The seven speakers, of whom three were Negroes, did not betray the advertised purpose of the meeting—to organize Negro workers. "It does me good . . . to see such a checkerboard crowd," said J. W. Johnstone of the S.L.C. in welcoming the workers. "You are standing shoulder to shoulder as men, regardless of whether your face is black or white." John Kikulski then addressed the Polish in their native language to explain the need for "cooperation between blacks and whites."

Yet events just two days later belied the union leaders' rhetorical optimism. For on July 8, as a hot spell settled on the city, the most violent strike of the summer occurred. Two thousand employees of the Corn Products Refinery at Argo struck that morning, after the company's president had reneged on an agreement to hold a referendum on the closed shop. Anticipating trouble, the company had requisitioned a shipment of rifles and reinforced its special police force. The next day, during a fracas at the plant's entrance, armed guards shot and killed two strikers and seriously wounded eighteen others, one of whom soon died. A howling, stone-throwing mob of strikers' wives and daughters added to the turbulence by chasing the mayor of Argo, who was also superintendent of the company's machine shops, two miles to Chicago's city limits for threatening local grocers and druggists with discontinuance of the refinery's accounts if they extended credit to the strikers. The day after the shootings, the strikers and several thousand other Russian, Lithuanian, and Polish workers, mainly from the stockyards district, marched in a guard of honor at the funeral of the murdered men. During the funeral the rumor was rife that the company had asked numerous Negroes to "come back Monday and bring all of your friends." Argo's citizens feared that the introduction of Negroes would ignite another round of bloodshed; and on Monday refinery officials deputized a number of black men whom they strung out in a line in front of the plant. Their presence particularly incensed the strikers, and disorder erupted during which three strikers were wounded. A mother of four was shot in the leg and then beaten down from a trolley wire, but not before she had disengaged it in order to allow strikers to hurl bottles and bricks at a stalled streetcar filled with strikebreakers. Altogether 600 Negroes were brought in as strikebreakers in this bloody dispute; doubtless, the immigrant strikers in Argo and around the stockyards did not forget the Negroes' role.

A confrontation between labor and management in the yards was not long in coming. The first week of July witnessed the introduction of 300 mounted policemen to patrol the stockyards district, apparently to reverse the union's organizing successes. As workers gathered around a union speaker, the police would ride into the crowd and disperse it. After protesting to the packers, 10,000 workers walked out on Friday, July 18. Although they returned to the stockyards Monday, it was evident that one of the most serious strikes in Chicago's history was imminent. That evening, union members voted to demand wage increases and other benefits, to submit these demands Saturday, July 26—just the day before the outbreak of the race riot—and to allow the packers forty-eight hours either to accept them or prepare for a strike. Ninety percent of the whites were unionized by that fateful weekend, while three-fourths of the Negroes, or 9,000 workers, were still outside the labor movement. What had retarded unionization among black workers?

Negroes in labor histories too often appear as faceless figures either to be praised, pitied, or damned. It is evident that black workers had very real reasons for resisting unionization. Many unions, of course, barred black craftsmen in order to control their portions of the labor market. These Negroes thus had to seek out unskilled positions, and it would be unreasonable for them then to unionize with common laborers, especially if they accrued employment benefits as non-union men. Unfortunately for the stockyards organization drive, neither all the A.F.L. national unions nor their members followed the lead of the C.F.L. Negroes were induced to join the federal locals recommended by Gompers, although some overzealous organizers enlisted black workers with the false promise that they would be transferred later to the locals of their respective crafts. A steamfitter expressed the dilemma of many of the Negro tradesmen in the yards: "I have worked as a steamfitter at the stockyards for fifteen years and tried to get into [all-white] Local 563 as have others of my race, but we have always been put off with some excuse until we gave up the attempt to get in." Other Negroes had become union members during labor disputes, only to be discharged after the strike was over. They felt betrayed, certain that unions were motivated not by a spirit of brotherhood but solely by self-interest. The exclusionist policies of southern unions had likewise alienated Negroes from the labor movement, and some of the migrants to Chicago during the war had traveled there to escape the job control exercised by the unions. Other migrants had peculiarly individual motives for not unionizing; some Negroes' life insurance policies were even voided if they did. Still others hesitated to join with whites who, during earlier labor depressions, had replaced them in domestic services, in the operation of barbershops, bootblack parlors, and contractual janitorial services, and in cooking, waiting tables, and dishwashing.

Negroes who traveled from the South to work in Chicago's industries brought with them not only a rural psychology but, in many cases, a total ignorance of strikes and unions. Fully 90 percent of the northern-born black workers in the yards, for example, wore the union button, but few of the migrants did. Other Negroes, however, were fully aware of how Negroes broke strikes, undermined wages, and reduced the white workers' bargaining power. Strikebreaking presented an opportunity to enter industries which formerly had been closed. Even if a Negro strikebreaker were employed at less than the union scale, he was generally paid more than he was accustomed to earning; and by refusing to go out on strike with whites, Negroes received promotions into more highly skilled fields which had not been previously open to them.

The readjustment from life on the farm to that of industrial wage-earner was so immense that Negro migrants often followed the advice of black leaders. Their advice was understandably more influential than that of white union members. A frequent source of counsel was the Urban League, the main employment agency in the black belt. The Urban League took a pragmatic view of unions, although the officers of the local branch were clearly cognizant of the danger of post-war labor conflict along racial lines. Robert E. Park, a white sociologist and president of the Chicago Urban League, feared that all the Negroes' perplexities after the Armistice would be "intimately bound up with the labor scene"; and, as early as November 1917, the League announced that it "would welcome any effort tending to an amicable settlement of this vital problem." It met with officers of the Chicago and Illinois Federations of Labor, and it advised the Women's Trade Union League during its campaign to organize Negro women in the yards, but these efforts accomplished little toward persuading unions to lower their color bars. The dilemma of the League, as of many Negro leaders, was that though it recognized the exigency of unionizing Negroes, it left little doubt that the first move had to be the unions' obliteration of all discriminatory membership policies. The League sought to plot a course between management and organized labor. For two reasons, however, it was more often on management's side: the unions did not lower their color bars, and Chicago's large industries could provide immediate opportunities for the migrants.

The attitude of Chicago's most widely circulated Negro newspaper, the *Defender,* paralleled that of the Urban League. "We have arrayed ourselves on the side of capital to a great extent," the *Defender* proclaimed in an editorial in late April 1919, "yet capital has not played square with us; it has used us as strikebreakers, then when the calm came turned us adrift." If it were to the race's "economic, social and political interest to join with organized labor now, it should not make the least bit of difference what was their attitude toward us in the past, even if that past was as recent as yesterday. If they extend the olive branch in good faith accept it today." In July, however, after the A.F.L. convention had done nothing to remove the exclusion clauses of some A.F.L. unions or the segregation clauses of others, the *Defender* complained: "Unwillingly we assume the role of strikebreakers. The unions drive us to it."

To most leaders in the black belt, exclusion and segregation were the roots of the problem. There was also a widespread attitude that employers were the Negroes' natural allies and that they, rather than unions, provided security and industrial opportunity. Negroes have found, Booker T. Washington wrote in 1913, that "the friendship and confidence of a good white man, who stands well in the community, are a valuable asset in time of trouble." For this reason, the Negro worker "does not always understand, and does not like, an organization [that is, a union] which seems to be founded on a sort of impersonal enmity to the man by whom he is employed. . . ." Mary McDowell recalled an example of the personal relationship which Negroes often believed existed between employer and employee. During the campaign to organize the stockyards, an organizer approached a newly-arrived Negro and explained to him the advantages of union membership. "It all sounds pretty good to me," the Negro replied, "but what does Mr. Armour think about it?"

Union leaders accused the packers of subsidizing black clergymen and other professional people, YMCAs, and welfare clubs to spread anti-union propaganda. Certain clergymen, among them unprincipled labor recruiters, did urge their parishioners to spurn union advances. Others, however, endorsed the endeavors of unions that were organizing without regard to race, arguing that union membership would help to minimize racial conflict; and among these were two of the city's most eminent ministers, L. K. Williams of the Olivet Baptist Church and John F. Thomas of Ebeneezer Baptist. In addition, black clerical associations, such as the Colored Baptist Ministers' Alliance and the AME Sunday School Convention, invited union organizers to use their groups as forums for outlining labor's views.

The YMCA, where at least two packers, Wilson and Armour, financed "efficiency clubs," was anti-union. Armour also gave an annual membership to the YMCA to each black worker after his first year of employment. Negroes at the club meetings, J. W. Johnstone charged, were "lectured and taught that the thing they have to do is to keep out of organized labor."

But were ministers and the YMCA witting instruments of the packers? Dr. George E. Haynes thought not. It was obvious, he reported after investigating the origins of the race riot, that certain black leaders were adamantly opposed to workers unionizing, "but there was no evidence that could be obtained that they were influenced to these opinions or used as tools of the employers."

It is not so difficult to determine the motives of Richard E. Parker, a notorious anti-union propagandist. Parker admitted that in 1916 he had distributed 20,000 handbills to "All Colored Working Men in the Stock-yards," warning them not to "Join Any White Man's Union." He claimed that he had paid for these himself because of his "personal interest" in his race; but he also acknowledged that he had gone to the South in 1916 while working for several packing and steel companies, and had "imported more Negroes than any man in Chicago." Parker edited a newspaper in which he advised black workers not to join the established unions but to join the American. Unity Labor Union, which he had founded and of which he was business agent. A card from his union, he boasted, would secure employment for Negroes in the building trades, steel mills, and stockyards. Parker was a demagogue and he was doubtless on the payroll of employers, but he might also have been working in the race's interest, as he perceived it. Because "the Negro happened to be born black," he wrote, "the Unions have labelled him inferior." As a result, they barred him not only from membership but also from apprenticeships and the chance to secure work in skilled jobs. "For this reason we formed the American Unity Labor Union," for we could expect "fairness from no local."

Above all, it was conflict between the white rank and file and their black counterparts that retarded unionization. Labor historians have wasted much energy debating the A.F.L.'s attitudes toward black workers, when the truly bitter, and functional, racial animosities were not at the national but at the shop level. Unions have too often directed their recriminations at anti-union Negroes, rather than conceding their own inability to control the racial hatreds of white members. Evidence of racial conflict at the shop level is scarce and difficult to find, but it is extant; and in few places was such conflict more pervasive than in the stockyards in 1919, where just a month before the race riot there was a series of spontaneous walk-outs, all racially inspired.

"Well, are you going to join or not," the smokehouse floor steward impatiently asked the black worker. "No, I would rather quit than join the union." "If you don't join tomorrow, these men won't work with you." "Fuck you." "God Damn you." Then the black man drew a knife from the pocket of his overalls. "He was big enough to eat me . . . ," the floor steward recalled, so "I called for help." The union men, "practically all of them are in the union except . . . these three colored fellows," came to his assistance. It was after this encounter that the white men in the smoke-house walked out, declaring that they could no longer work with non-union blacks. Similar confrontations were occurring simultaneously in various shops at the yards. Leaving dead hogs hanging on the conveyor belt or after only partially dressing the beef, hundreds of workers informed their foremen that black men on the floor were non-union, and that they would not return until these men were discharged or made to join the union.

"We are paying the union and wearing the buttons," one member complained, "and they are getting just as much." Other members echoed this resentment. "Fuck the Union," a black worker had reportedly told one of them. "I am making as much money as you are. What is the use of joining the Union?" Another grievance was that Negroes allegedly received preferential treatment, such as not being docked for reporting late or punished for stealing meat.

Negro as well as white members accused certain black men who used abusive language and incited violence of being anti-union agitators. The only task of "Heavy" Williams, they said, was to bring new workers from the company employment office to the cattle-killing floor, and "he brings up all non-union men and keeps the non-union men from joining the union." " 'Let me tell you,' " he would instruct the new men, " 'when they get after you about this union, don't you join it. . . . You stay out. If you don't you won't be here long.' " Williams also fought with whites, among them "Tubs," whom he threatened to "split open" with a meat cleaver. Williams had been a union member; so had Joseph Hodge, until a black friend of his had been hit over the head with a blunt instrument. Hodge continually cast such vicious and obscene slurs at the union that whites warned that he would "agitate a race riot or perhaps . . . get killed." Another anti-union Negro stabbed a white man on the killing floor after damning the union and branding black union men "a lot of bastards," "a lot of white folks' niggers."

Negroes frequently replaced striking whites in the stockyards that summer. In the hair house, for example, the all-white union of spinners struck, and Negroes from various other departments were recruited to fill their jobs. Few whites in the yards could have been unaware of the strike; for, as one man reported, "at the noon hour these colored men are looking out of windows and doors, and these [white] men come out for lunch, and . . . it creates a dis-harmony and hard feelings among the races. . . ." It was also a fact, however, that sometimes Negroes who joined unions were also discharged.

Organizers and black workers had difficulty communicating with each other, and this was a major cause not only of friction but also of the unwillingness of Negroes to unionize. Numerous floor stewards and union committeemen spoke English poorly, if at all. How, a non-English-speaking Polish steward was asked by an interpreter, did he expect to explain the benefits of unions to black workers? He did not even try, he said, but there was a Negro committeeman who "talks the best way he can." Well, then, did he instruct the Negro committeeman? "I don't tell him nothing," he replied. "They have got to get it for themselves."

A Negro who did not "get it," however, would have "it made hot for him," with his "face pushed in" or bricks hurled at him. Frustration as well as racial bitterness provoked these acts of violence. "When I was coming in [to work]," recounted a Negro, "6 or 7 or 8 Polocks grabbed a colored fellow out there, and carried him on the [union] wagon, and said 'you son-of-a-bitch, you will join the union,' and made him go up, and one had him by this arm, and the other by this arm, and one fellow had him by the neck. . . ."

Black resistance—and, with it, interracial abuse and violence—only mounted in the weeks before the riot. "Fuck the union, fuck you in the [union] button," raged a black worker. Knives and revolvers proliferated on both sides. "If I catch you outside I will shoot you," a Negro warned an insulting committeeman. Yet the unions became even more aggressive. "Where is your button?" demanded an organizer. "I ain't got none on," was the angry reply, "but [if I did] I would put it on the end of my prick."

Union leaders claimed that there was no racism involved in this bitterness—that it was simply a labor matter. But it was obviously much more than that by late July 1919; the two were inseparably fused. The Irish, Polish, Lithuanian, and other workers who clashed with Negroes in other spheres of human relations had their racial antagonisms reinforced if not initiated at the stockyards and in other industries. Labor in Chicago, moreover, was possessed of an intense class consciousness; anyone who was not with it was against it—and the black workers were notoriously not with it. The hostility was so intense that, as in 1905, hatred of Negro "scabs" could be generalized into hatred of an entire race. The factors retarding unionization—Negro distrust of unions and white workers, the economic advantages to be accrued as non-union workers, the manipulation of black workers by management, and, above all, the hatred of black workers by whites arising from racial antipathy and conditioned by strikebreaking and by other anti-union acts—left a legacy of twenty-five years of violence and helped produce a bloody race riot in 1919.

3.6

San Francisco Labor
and the Populist
and Progressive Insurgencies

ALEXANDER SAXTON

It remains true that most Progressive reformers between 1900 and the First World War were products of middle- and upper-class families. But it does not follow that the "Progressive Movement" was entirely a "middle-class movement." That such reformers drew significant support from the settled working-class urban population is carefully shown in Alexander Saxton's study of San Francisco voting patterns in the early twentieth century. Populist, Progressive, and Socialist candidates depended in part on their support, and the rhetoric and programs reflected the presence of such a constituency. "Coalition" politics, drawing together critics of the established industrial order from diverse social classes, also shaped national elections, such as that of 1916 and, of course, the elections of 1932 and 1936.

Alexander Saxton, "San Francisco Labor and the Populist and Progressive Insurgencies," *Pacific Historical Review*, 34, No. 4 (1965), 421–37. © 1965 by the Pacific Coast Branch, American Historical Association. Reprinted and footnotes omitted by permission of the Branch and the author.

The following book is suggested for further reading:

MICHAEL ROGIN and JOHN SHOVER, *Political Change in California,* Westport, Conn.: Greenwood Press, Inc., 1970.

Historians of the Populist and Progressive insurgencies have frequently assumed that the Populists failed to win support of urban labor, and that the Progressives, led as they were by middle-class professionals, remained hostile to labor's interests. The course of events in San Francisco, in the light of an examination of assembly district voting records, appears not to have conformed to this generalization. San Francisco in 1890 contained 25 per cent of the population of California, including a substantial proportion of the non-agricultural labor force. Throughout both the Populist and Progressive periods, the city completely dominated the organized labor movement of the state. It would seem difficult to argue, therefore, that a generalization with respect to labor's political relationships which did not fit the city could have applied to the state. But if the state of California represents an exception to the generalization, it is rather a large one. That question, however, is beyond the scope of this paper. What follows here will be an analysis of voting behavior of San Francisco labor electorates in several decisive Populist and Progressive contests.

Working-class politics had been traditional in San Francisco at least since the late seventies. By the time of the first Populist campaigns, labor identification was thoroughly institutionalized into urban party structure. Of 180 San Francisco assemblymen elected between 1892 and 1910, biographical information available for 120 shows that 49 were laborers or skilled or semi-skilled workers, as opposed to 23 lawyers and 31 business and professional men. By way of contrast, in Los Angeles County, 48 assemblymen elected in six elections during the same period included 19 lawyers and one workingman—a solitary carpenter. It would be a mistake, however, to assume that because of its labor component, the San Francisco delegation exerted a radical influence at the state capitol. Franklin Hichborn, a progressive journalist, by no means totally hostile to labor, described the situation as follows:

> With rare exceptions the San Francisco delegation has been made up of ignorant and for the most part vicious men, thoroughly in accord with the tenderloin and groggery interests. . . . Such a delegation lent itself for easy manipulation . . . a dependable trading quantity . . . readily adjustable under all conditions to corporation plans and purposes.

And Abraham Ruef, who, as last of the great bosses before the Progressive purification, was certainly in a position to know, observed that upon the San Francisco delegation "the railroad always depended for a strong voting support for its program."

Since the main thrust of both Populist and Progressive campaigns was against railroad domination of the state, their message to labor necessarily involved a plea to break out of the *system,* to repudiate those labor politicians who did the bidding of the "interests." Such an appeal would almost certainly have failed—as pleas from outside a constituency against its own leaders generally do—had it not been for the fact that labor leadership was divided. Or to put it more accurately, there were two leaderships: a trade union leadership devoting itself to economic activities and eschewing politics like the plague; and a political leadership which exploited its working class, ethnic, and religious connections to win votes. The Populist and Progressive approaches to labor therefore implied not simply an attack on leaders, but an appeal to one leadership group against another. At this level, the conflict proceeded through public pronouncements, and the dialogue can easily be followed in the labor press. But beneath the approach to leadership lay the more important approach to the constituency. In this regard, public pronouncements are inconclusive and only the voting records themselves will serve.

Reference to voting records at once raises the problem of identifying the labor constituency. And here history, merging into folklore, suggests that such an identification might not be too difficult in San Francisco; where the nabobs, according to legend, dwelt on Nob Hill, while the workingmen lived "south of the slot" and out among the sand dunes and little sheltered valleys of the Mission district. A map of the city as apportioned in 1892 shows the "south-of-the-slot" and Mission areas as a contiguous group of assembly districts—eight in the city's eighteen—lying along the bayshore south and east of Market Street. If we may begin by taking this tradition for hypothesis, it remains to apply whatever checks can be found. The biographical data on San Francisco assemblymen referred to earlier, when arranged according to groups of assembly districts, show that 41 per cent of the assemblymen elected in the eight "south of the slot" districts (Group I) were laborers or skilled or semi-skilled craftsmen. The corresponding percentage for the ten assembly districts in the remainder of the city (Group II) was 16 per cent. Thus the incidence of workingmen among assemblymen elected from Group I was two and a half times that for Group II. On the other hand, the incidence of lawyers was four times greater in Group II than in Group I.

This is suggestive, although far from conclusive. But fortunately San Francisco history provides what is probably the most decisive test that could be found for any American city at any time—the series of Union

Labor party elections which occurred between 1901 and 1909. The politics of these elections will be discussed in greater detail below; here it is sufficient to note that in five elections analyzed the eight districts of Group I gave 37 Union Labor party victories out of a possible 40. The ten districts composing the remainder of the city (Group II) gave 18 labor victories in a possible 50.

To sum up then: a voting area of preponderant labor identification has been indicated on the basis of: (1) local tradition; (2) occupational status of assemblymen elected over a twenty-year period; and (3) outcomes of a series of elections spanning a nine-year period. The results are an approximation, yet the long-sustained preponderance of attitude seems sufficiently evident to justify examination of the response of this area as a labor response to the Populist and Progressive appeals.

Populism in California was built from the top down. Its leaders included veterans of earlier third-party campaigns and a good many old radicals—single-taxers, Nationalists, Socialists—who were also active in the Knights of Labor and in the beginnings of trade union organization. In 1890, following the pattern already apparent in the Midwest and South, they organized a California farmers' alliance, which grew rapidly and was soon converted into a vehicle for third-party action. The Populist party was founded in 1891 and a year later polled approximately 9 per cent of the statewide vote for its presidential nominee, General James Weaver. In 1894, the high water mark of Populist success in California, this percentage was doubled. Then followed merger with the Democrats to support Bryan in 1896, and a series of splits and fusions, leading to gradual disintegration by the turn of the century.

From the beginning, the efforts of Populist leaders to appeal to urban labor seem to have been hampered by the religious-ethnic cleavage between city and country. The American Protective Association, a Protestant nativist organization, national in scope, was active in California throughout the nineties and exerted strong influence among rural Populists. Urban Catholics rallied in self-defense around the San Francisco diocesan newspaper, the *Monitor,* and Populist candidates were occasionally caught in the crossfire. Nonetheless, the Populists achieved substantial success in establishing communications and forms of joint action with the city workingmen. Here the Populist manifesto of 1892—the Omaha Platform with its declaration that all workers, "rural and civic," shared common interests and identical enemies—laid the basis. Early in 1894, upon call of the Federated Trades Council of San Francisco, a joint farmer-labor conference drew up a program of demands which was adopted in full by the Populists. The new party consequently went into the campaign of 1894 with several significant additions to the Omaha platform. These included a ban on all Oriental immigration, factory and workshop inspection by the state, public works for the jobless, a general eight-hour law, and universal suffrage. To make their message unmistakably clear, the Populists nominated a carpenter, A. J. Gregg, for lieutenant-governor, and a printing tradesman, M. M. McGlynn, for secretary of state. McGlynn was an organizer for the Knights of Labor and later served as secretary of the San Francisco federated trades.

The depression of 1893 favored Populist strategy. Through the winter and into the spring of election year, contingents of unemployed "industrials" gathered in San Francisco, preparing to join Coxey's Army for the march to Washington. The Populists rallied support, collected food from farmers to sustain the workmen on their journey, all the while pointing to events as verification of their warnings. In May came the Pullman strike. Since farmers and laborers could easily agree that the railroad was chief villain, this served for demonstration of the *identical enemies* text from the Omaha platform. The Populists organized mass meetings, raised money, and denounced the governor for calling out militia at the demand of the Southern Pacific. A Populist newspaper in San Francisco, the *Voice of Labor,* was designated official west coast organ by the striking railroad workers.

All these developments furthered an appearance of harmony with labor. So too did the decision of Adolph Sutro to run for mayor of San Francisco on the Populist ticket. Sutro was not exactly a Populist, but he was enormously popular, and especially with workingmen, since he was thought to have defended the honest miner of the Comstock against the "interests." More recently he had served San Francisco as philanthropist on the grand scale and especially had endeared himself by fighting the Southern Pacific's grip on the city streetcar system. Sutro would have won on any ticket, and he was in fact elected by a landslide. It is clear however that his victory represented a non-partisan tribute to a very highly esteemed old man rather than a mass conversion to Populist principle: for while Sutro polled 50 per cent of the city's vote, the Populist gubernatorial candidate, J. V. Webster, received only 11 per cent, considerably less than his statewide showing of 18 per cent. Examination of the results for the two groupings of assembly districts (Table I) indicates that San Francisco

TABLE I. *Votes cast for assemblymen in San Francisco, 1894*

	For All Candidates	For Populist Candidates	Percentage to Populists
Group I (8 A.D.s)	20,767	4,783	23%
Group II (10 A.D.s)	29,821	3,265	11%
City Total	50,588	8,048	16%

—if we leave aside the Sutro candidacy—was by no means uniform in its response to Populism.

Voters of Group I, the area of preponderant labor identification, were more than twice as sympathetic to Populist assembly candidates as voters in the remainder of the city; and the degree of their sympathy equalled or slightly exceeded that for the state as a whole. In 1894 only two Populist assemblymen were elected in California; one came from Santa Barbara, the founding county of the farmers' alliance, the other from the 35th assembly district of San Francisco, one of the eight included in Group I.

It seems evident from the foregoing that in their best year, 1894, the Populists received a favorable, though not spectacular, response from San Francisco labor voters. The response may be assumed to have reflected: (1) the basic labor appeal of the issues raised by the Populists; (2) skilful use by Populist leaders of special circumstances which they turned to their party's advantage; and (3) efforts of a number of trade union leaders sympathetic to Populism.

From the disintegration of Populism at the turn of the century to the first election of Hiram Johnson in 1910, the San Francisco labor movement experienced a period of growth, industrial conflict, and intense political activity. Trade union membership increased from some 20,000 in 1900 to probably well over 50,000 in 1910. Local unions clustered around two distinct and frequently rival power centers, the Building Trades Council and the San Francisco Labor Council. So complete was the division between, that the building trades forbade their locals to participate in the other council, and the two customarily held separate Labor Day parades. In 1901, the labor council initiated the formation of the California State Federation of Labor, while the building trades, as counterweight, established their own statewide organization under the wing of their San Francisco council. Between these centers—both nominally fraternal bodies within the American Federation of Labor—appeared significant differences of strength, membership, and policy.

The building trades were long-established, clearly definable craft skills, difficult to acquire and therefore irreplaceable. Once organized, as they were by 1900, they achieved a leverage of bargaining power which enabled them to maintain closed shop conditions, high wages, and a general eight-hour day. Council structure centralized power in the executive committee and especially in the hands of its president, Patrick Henry McCarthy. An Irish immigrant, a carpenter—and master craftsman of organization as well—McCarthy enjoyed for many years the position of a Lorenzo the Magnificent among west coast labor leaders. Under his generalship, building trades' power penetrated deeply into local politics. This resulted partly from the ties between construction and such city hall functions as street grading and paving, fire and sanitary inspection, and issuance of building permits; and partly from the fact that building tradesmen themselves formed a stable group of resident—and consequently *voting*—citizens. The relationship was formalized in 1900 by the appointment of President McCarthy as city commissioner of civil service.

The labor council, on the other hand, although larger in numbers, was weaker economically and politically. Its membership, based at first on the sailors, dockworkers, and teamsters, was less protected by skills than were the building tradesmen and formed a more transient and fluctuating group—especially the sailors, virtually disfranchised as they were by their occupation. The labor council exerted little influence at city hall. Outstanding among its leaders were Andrew Furuseth and Walter Macarthur of the sailors' union, and Michael Casey of the teamsters. Two of these at least surpassed McCarthy in national reputation, but none wielded centralized authority comparable to his.

Driven by its own economic weakness and its impotence in local politics, the labor council tended to seek remedial legislation at the state level. Thus it pressed for factory inspection, an eight-hour law, child labor restrictions, regulation of employment agencies, and expansion of the bureau of labor statistics. One of its primary purposes in calling for statewide federation had been to strengthen labor's voice at Sacramento; by 1907 the labor council and the state federation which it fathered were able to maintain a regular labor lobby during the sessions of the legislature. The building trades council on the other hand, secure in its craft skills and strongly entrenched in city politics, remained locally oriented. Toward advocates of statewide labor unity, as well as toward political reformers, it displayed an eloquent lack of enthusiasm, if not outright hostility. It was for these reasons that the Progressive insurgents in 1909 and 1910 would find their first working-class allies in the San Francisco labor council rather than in the building trades.

The relationships that subsequently developed between labor and the Progressives were deeply affected—in some respects poisoned—by the rise and decline of the Union Labor party. Despite its name, this party was not the official creation of any trade union body. Organized in 1901 in the aftermath of the bitterly contested teamster strike, it was fuelled by labor resentment at the use which the Democratic city administration of Mayor Phelan had made of police and special deputies in protecting, and apparently in some cases actually aiding, strikebreakers. The sponsors of the new party, however, were all second-stringers. McCarthy and the building trades—at most lukewarm in their support of the teamster strike, and tied to the city administration—remained dead set against any independent ticket. Furuseth, Walter Macarthur, and Casey of the labor council, although sympathetic, were inhibited from taking a hand by their traditional

AFL dread of overt political action. Into this partial vacuum moved the aspiring young Republican politician, Abraham Ruef, and the Union Labor party was launched upon its baroque career.

The new party triumphed in 1901, 1903, and 1905; while Ruef, like many bosses before him, organized municipal government to maximize payoffs and bargained statewide with the *system* for the best available price in money and patronage. All this, of course, was nothing new. Ruef's real innovation was his direct appeal to labor voters. In the past, city bosses had been content to handle labor politicians as they came along at the ward level; Ruef, to undercut them, roused and deployed the labor constituency. McCarthy, after watching with grim hostility through two elections, brought the building trades over to the new party, and in fact claimed credit for its victory in 1905. Then in 1906 came the famous graft prosecution: Ruef went to San Quentin, Mayor Schmitz was convicted and removed from office, while almost the entire union labor board of supervisors confessed to receiving bribes. McCarthy, who was not implicated, denounced the graft prosecution as an anti-labor conspiracy. He then took over the leaderless party and had himself nominated its candidate for mayor. In 1907 he was defeated, but ran again and captured the city in 1909.

The leaders of the labor council, in contrast to the building trades officials, accepted the revelations of the graft trials at face value. They repudiated the Union Labor party, including its new chief, Patrick Henry McCarthy. Furuseth and Walter Macarthur of the sailors' union never receded from this position. Casey, however, wavered. His friend and spiritual advisor, the Catholic priest, Father Yorke, editor of the Irish weekly *Leader,* was backing the Union Labor party. Father Yorke arranged a reconciliation between Casey and McCarthy, and Casey was later able to mollify the labor council, which supported McCarthy in the election of 1909, although with partially weaned affections.

There remains one note to be added to complete this outline of the labor power structure which confronted the Progressive approach to San Francisco: the Progressives themselves made their entrance as sponsors and initiators of the graft prosecution. Fremont Older, Rudolph Spreckels, Francis Heney, and Hiram Johnson—all key northern California leaders of the Progressive insurgency—were the men who organized, financed, and generalled the prosecution of Union Labor party city officials. Consequently, San Franciscans who identified with labor were inclined to see Progressivism as an enemy, and it was upon this inclination that McCarthy and his supporters based their appeals to labor voters. The result of the election of 1909 showed that they had been remarkably successful. Despite all the vicissitudes his party had suffered, McCarthy carried every assembly district in Group I and polled 58 per cent of the total Group I vote, as compared with 54 per cent in 1901 and 56 per cent in 1903.

The insurgent Progressives captured the Republican party, then the state of California, in the summer and fall of 1910. This upheaval precipitated a four-year struggle between the two councils for control of the San Francisco labor vote. Eearly in 1910, the *Clarion,* organ of the labor council, and the *Seamen's Journal,* which Walter Macarthur edited, made clear their progressive sympathies. Labor council secretary Andrew Gallagher and a number of other union officers including the teamster Michael Casey issued public endorsements of Hiram Johnson, the Progressive candidate for governor. For Casey this represented a break with his old friend, Father Yorke, whose weekly remained conspicuously silent throughout the gubernatorial campaign. Thus, after the separation of 1909, Casey rejoined his labor council colleagues, Furuseth and Walter Macarthur, who were now committed to an alliance with Fremont Older and his radically progressive San Francisco *Bulletin.* Macarthur, in fact, casting aside earlier Gomperish scruples with respect to politics, was now running for Congress as a progressive Democrat against an incumbent Republican "standpatter" —and with full backing of the *Bulletin.* Statements of support for Macarthur carried the names of almost all prominent labor men in the city, with one notable exception—that of the president of the building trades council and mayor of San Francisco, Patrick Henry McCarthy. His silence echoed that of Father Yorke's *Leader.*

The November returns gave Hiram Johnson 46 per cent of the statewide vote as against 40 per cent for his Democratic opponent, most of the remainder being accounted for by an unusually large Socialist showing. Table II shows the vote in San Francisco by groupings of assembly districts.

While Johnson had carried the city for the (Progressive) Republicans, he carried it by a smaller edge than his statewide margin, and his showing was 8 per cent lower in the labor districts of Group I than in the remainder of the city. Lack of enthusiasm for both major candidates (most noticeable in Group I) was evidenced by the high Socialist vote, as well as by the decline in total vote cast. For Group I this was down by 2,400, and for

TABLE II.   *Election of November, 1910, by assembly districts in San Francisco*

	(Rep.) Johnson	(Dem.) Bell	(Soc.) Stitt-Wilson
Group I (8 A.D.s)	8,201 (38%)	7,993 (37%)	5,278 (25%)
Group II (10 A.D.s)	16,676 (46%)	15,397 (43%)	4,113 (11%)
City Total	24,877 (43%)	23,390 (40%)	9,391 (17%)

the city as a whole by almost 7,000 from the municipal election of the preceding year. To this extent, the efforts of the labor council leaders for Johnson had proven ineffective. They had failed also in their campaign for Walter Macarthur who was defeated for Congress. But the fact remains that Johnson did carry the Group I districts. Since Johnson appeared on the Republican ticket and Macarthur on the Democratic, as long as the voters failed to distinguish some non-partisan quality of progressivism, the efforts of the union leaders for Johnson could only have worked against Macarthur.

In the election of 1912, California voters had the choice between Woodrow Wilson and Theodore Roosevelt for the presidency. Taft's role in the contest was minimal since the Progressives had pre-empted the Republican ballot designation for Roosevelt and for Johnson, now governor of the state, who was running with Roosevelt for the vice-presidency. Labor at the national level inclined strongly to the Democrats. In San Francisco, the three major labor papers had been hostile to Roosevelt for years, and this hostility outweighed any sympathies for Hiram Johnson. During the final weeks before election, Father Yorke's *Leader,* in a series of bitter editorials, revived all the old charges against Roosevelt, especially that of being soft on the Japanese; then coupled its criticism of the national Progressive leader with an attack on *local* Progressives—and upon certain unnamed labor leaders who had permitted themselves to be "copper-riveted to Hungry Hiram's pie counter." Despite these flurries of infighting, however, all factions of the San Francisco labor movement found themselves united in 1912 in support of the Democratic presidential ticket. While the two major parties ran neck and neck in the statewide race, the Democrats rolled up a comfortable 10 per cent lead in San Francisco. Yet in sharp contrast to this apparent Democratic sweep, urban voters, most of them in the Group I districts, elected a Republican-Progressive, John I. Nolan, to Congress. An officer of the labor council and head of the state federation's labor lobby at Sacramento, Nolan embodied the political outlook of the labor council and state federation leadership. He won 53 per cent of the vote cast in his congressional district.

So far, however—with the single exception of Nolan's victory—the Progressives and their allies in the labor movement had made rather a poor showing in San Francisco. 1914 brought a dramatic change. (See Table III.) The California insurgents, banking on the growth of their new national party, had by this time shuffled off the old Republican label: Hiram Johnson made his bid for re-election to the governorship as a third party candidate. In the three-way split that followed, he took 50 per cent of the statewide vote, while his Republican opponent held 29 per cent, and the Democratic contender only 12. San Francisco displayed an even more massive swing to the Progressive column. Thus the city was running 5 per

TABLE III.   Election of November, 1914, by assembly districts in San Francisco

	(Prog.) Johnson	(Rep.) Fredericks	(Dem.) Curtin	(Soc.) Richardson
Group I	26,438	7,283	5,392	2,826
(5 A.D.s)	(63%)	(17%)	(13%)	(7%)
Group II	45,819	29,323	10,775	3,520
(8 A.D.s)	(51%)	(33%)	(12%)	(4%)
City Total	72,257	36,606	16,167	6,346
	(55%)	(28%)	(12%)	(5%)

cent ahead of the state for Johnson. But most striking here is that this divergence to the advantage of the Progressives was due to a Johnson land-slide in the labor assembly districts of Group I. These ran 12 per cent ahead of the rest of the city.

San Francisco labor's response to Progressivism then, although de-layed, and although contained within a national commitment to Democratic candidates, was favorable and strong. The policy eventually accepted by the labor constituency was that advocated by the San Francisco labor council and state federation leadership—and generally opposed by the Union Labor party, the building trades, and the Catholic *Leader*. A read-ing of the labor press for the period suggests that three events in 1911 were decisive in determining the later swing of San Francisco working class voters to the Progressives.

Most important of these was the enactment of an unprecedented batch of labor laws by the first Progressive-controlled legislature. Even those unionists who had endorsed Hiram Johnson in 1910 were apparently unprepared for such a bonanza. Measures which organized labor had been pushing unsuccessfully for twenty years were suddenly passed without opposition. Statutes previously dormant were made operative. New under-takings were written into law, including the eight-hour day for women and the establishment of workmen's compensation and employer liability. In addition, labor was able to block a "compulsory" arbitration measure which it distrusted; and in fact suffered only one major setback—the lost of a bill to limit issuance of injunctions in labor disputes.

Report of the achievements of the 1911 legislature occupied seventeen pages in the *Proceedings* of the State Federation and hailed the lawmakers as "progressive builders" to whose actions "future generations" would "point with gratitude." The *Seamen's Journal* declared that the session "marked an epoch in the labor movement of California"; and that Governor Johnson had "proved himself not only different from but better than any of his predecessors." On the basis of these results, the labor council–state federation leaders moved to cement their alliance with Progressivism. Clearly such an entente held attractions for the Progressives as well, since they could hardly expect to maintain control of the state without San Francisco. Thus the alliance, which involved favorable legislation on one hand, hinged upon delivery of the San Francisco labor vote on the other. But in 1911, the San Francisco labor vote seemed still firmly under the control of Mayor Patrick Henry McCarthy and the Union Labor party.

McCarthy was up for re-election in 1911, and his summer primary campaign provided the second decisive event of the year. Despite the mayor's appeals for labor unity, those leaders most closely identified with the Progressive alliance—especially Furuseth and Walter Macarthur of the sailor's union, whose prestige was now at high tide due to the benefits just won in the legislature—led the attack against him. McCarthy was beaten without even getting into the finals. Afterwards he retired from public politics and the Union Labor party declined rather rapidly, leaving the road open for the labor council and state federation leadership.

The third decisive event, although it deeply affected labor politics in San Francisco, actually occurred in Los Angeles. It was the confession of the McNamara brothers to the bombing of the Los Angeles *Times*. For labor as a whole, the deed and the confessions were disastrous. They set back organization in the south by many years, and torpedoed the nearly victorious campaign of Job Harriman, Socialist and labor-backed candidate for the Los Angeles mayoralty. But the *indirect* effect was to strengthen the alliance of labor and the Progressives in the north. The leaders of the labor council and state federation were now more, rather than less, dependent upon those Progressives who were willing to be sympathetic to them; and more than ever obliged to deliver the San Francisco vote. At the same time, they had acquired an extremely strong argument in the labor legislation of the Johnson administration. And beyond this, they had moved closer to being masters in their own house. For the events of 1911 had, on the one hand, weakened the Socialist appeal to labor voters; and on the other had forced McCarthy and the Union Labor party to the back of the stage.

The Populist and Progressive insurgencies then both had needed urban support and wooed labor. Their methods of approach, even the content of their appeals, were in large part similar. Both included labor issues in their platforms and placed labor men on their slates; both sought out trade union leaders, trying to persuade them to take the field against the established labor politicians. Both movements also appealed directly to labor voters, conceiving them as being of all urban groups, the most inclined to democratic reform.

Here the similarities end.

The Populists first presented themselves as a third party. They were unable to enlarge the initially favorable response of urban labor because they never succeeded in staking out a solid rural base for their movement. Consequently they had little to offer in the way of legislative backing for labor's demands, and could not compete with the already established labor politicians. Populism failed in the city essentially because it had first failed in the country.

The Progressives on the other hand presented themselves as a reform movement within the Republican party. Labor had not been deeply involved in the 1910 primary contest, and many workingmen probably viewed the Johnson slate in November as simply another bevy of Republican office seekers, possibly more anti-union than their predecessors. In 1912, Progressive candidates appeared under even less favorable auspices. In 1914, however, Progressivism finally broke through to labor voters. The major factor here seems to have been the legislature of 1911, and the enthusiasm of part, at least, of the labor leadership. But the fact that Johnson ran in 1914 as a third party nominee doubtless made the crossing of party lines easier for traditionally Democratic voters. The pattern, once established, continued strongly into 1916.

The role of radicals in the two periods is more difficult to assess. In 1892 and 1894, it seems clear that various single-taxers, Nationalists, and Socialists were pushing the new party. The influence of such men in labor organizations may have contributed substantially to the Populist showing in Group I of San Francisco in 1894. During the period 1910 to 1916, however, the Socialists were strongly organized and committed to their own tickets. Their twenty-five per cent of the vote cast in Group I in 1910 was obviously detrimental to both major candidates. Indirectly, the Socialists may have aided the Progressives, since they were agitating many of the same issues and probably drew, or pushed, a middle group of urban voters to Progressivism. At all events, the coincidence of the decline of Socialist strength with the rise of the Progressive vote is striking in 1914 and 1916.

Just as the Progressive insurgency, despite certain similarities, was different in kind from the Populist movement, so labor in 1910 differed *in kind* from what it had been in 1894. It had, among other things, grown larger; but the change was not principally one of size. What was new was that the expanded base made possible a professional leadership. Whereas, in 1894, labor leaders were for the most part either full-time politicians or else workingmen who pursued their union duties after hours, by 1910 a corps of salaried organizers, business agents, secretaries, and legislative representatives had taken the field. Here was a group with time and energy for politics, yet not dependent on politics—if we leave aside *intra*-union politics—for their livings. The Progressive alliance was, in one respect, a relation between two leadership groups. The triumph of the Progressives in 1910 helped the labor council–state federation leadership to win dominance in the labor movement; and this dominance in turn helped the Progressives to maintain control of the state. Both groups of leaders, Labor and Progressive, grew rapidly less insurgent, and the narrowing of their horizons tended further to unite them.

After 1911, a major goal of the labor council–state federation leadership appears to have been to secure a permanent place for itself in the California establishment; and by rallying San Francisco labor voters to Progressivism, it accomplished precisely this. But the accomplishment was unstable in two respects. In the first place, the basic labor voting area— Group I—was suffering a rapid erosion. Population was moving south and west into newer portions of the city. This shift may have been due in part to the earthquake and fire, but basically resulted from the steady encroachment of industry and warehousing into the old working-class residential areas. There would still be voters of labor identification, and perhaps as many as before, but they would be more difficult to identify and to control. In the second place, the labor leadership, bargaining from weakness after the McNamara disaster, had given away rather more in exchange for the Progressive alliance than it had received—at least in terms of values for the movement as a whole. The situation in Los Angeles, unresolved since 1911, would be certain to undermine labor's position in San Francisco. But the war years intervened, and this particular reckoning was to be postponed until the twenties.

3.7

Socialist Electoral Strength, 1912-1918

Progressive reformers disagreed among themselves about the specific changes
needed to improve American society, but most did not quarrel with the
essential structure of the social system. Some favored reform through the
centralization of elite decision making, hoping that a detached and
well-educated elite would substitute "national" interests for "class" interests.
Others believed that democratizing the political process and making it more
accessible to popular pressures would bring needed reforms and correct
injustices. Socialists offered yet a third alternative, and unlike the
Progressives, quarrelled with the central economic structure itself.

Between 1900 and 1918, the Socialist Party of America grew in
importance. Its electoral successes in municipal politics and in the 1912
national election made those two decades quite distinctive in the history of
American radicalism. James Weinstein details that presence for us. Important
questions, however, remain unanswered. Its evident electoral successes did

James Weinstein, *The Decline of Socialism in America* (New York: Monthly Review Press,
1967), pp. 93, 103–18. Copyright © 1967 by Monthly Review Press, Inc. Reprinted and
footnotes omitted by permission of the publisher.

not sustain the Socialist Party beyond the First World War, and the reasons for the collapse following its unusual growth need further study. What did socialist-dominated municipal governments accomplish? How did Woodrow Wilson's successful legislative program undercut their early strength among native American critics of capitalism? What effect did the First World War and the Bolshevik Revolution have on the socialists' electoral and organizational strength?

If 1912 represented the high point of the Socialist movement in any area, it was in electoral strength; in that year Debs polled 6 percent of the total Presidential vote, a figure never again equalled by a Socialist candidate. At the same time, Party members held their greatest number of public offices—some 1,200 in 340 municipalities from coast to coast, among them 79 mayors in 24 states. In 1916, the Socialist Presidential vote declined from 897,000 to 590,000, and the percentage dropped even more sharply. Similarly, after 1912, the number of Socialists elected to local office decreased progressively. The number of Socialist mayors, for example, dropped from 74 elected in 1911 to 32 in 1913, 22 in 1915, and 18 in 1917. The Presidential figure is most often cited as proof that the history of the party after 1912 is that of a "trailing penumbra."

Social reforms and a more sophisticated approach to conservative trade union leadership did operate to circumscribe Socialist influence during Wilson's first administration. Many Party leaders anticipated a continued rise in Party strength; at the 1912 convention, Hillquit spoke of a Party of 200,000 members in the near future. Others viewed the 1912 vote as a rock-bottom Socialist core from which the Progressive Party had already scraped the decayed organic matter. Yet some also understood that more reforms were coming, and that these would include government regulation of industry. The *International Socialist Review* commented that "the clearest thinkers among the capitalists and their politicians" realized that if American manufacturers were "to compete with Germany in the world market," they must have "the same sort of help from the government in conserving the labor supply which the German employers get." In this the editors found "no ground for anxiety on the part of Socialists," explaining that the " 'Progressive' reforms that are coming will be, so far as they go, a good thing for 'all the people.' " Child labor laws and other progressive reforms, they concluded, were good for both capitalist and labor.

The left wingers on the *International Socialist Review* understood this better than Hillquit. In an exchange of letters with Ralph Easley of the National Civic Federation over the Federation's sponsorship of workmen's compensation acts, Hillquit had charged that the game played by the businessmen's organization was "the shrewdest yet devised by the employers of any country." As Hillquit observed, the Federation understood that to ignore the movement would be to "face the danger that this agitation may give rise to a powerful labor movement along Socialist lines." But he would not admit that the Federation's activity in behalf of compensation had improved matters. Instead he accused it of seeking "to divert the movement of the workers into the shallow channels" of reform. In reply, Easley insisted that the workers had a right to better conditions in the present, and read Hillquit (who was open to the charge) to mean that improvement could only come after the Socialists had captured power. Hillquit did not see, or would not admit, that the Federation could distinguish "between proposals and direct undertakings" which were "socialistic and anarchistic in principle," and those which Socialists "would naturally favor, although not necessarily in conflict with the underlying principles of the existing industrial order."

The *International Socialist Review* not only admitted this but went further to observe that the "next step" would be for the businessman "to act on the discovery that he can carry on certain portions of the productive process more efficiently through *his* government than through private corporations." "Some muddleheads," the *Review* continued, "think that will be Socialism, but the Capitalist knows better." The right of "wageworkers to organize and to control the conditions under which they work—that is the issue that must be fought out between the two great opposing classes."

The reforms that came during Wilson's first term were impressive. In 1913, the Sixteenth and Eighteenth amendments, authorizing the income tax and providing for the direct election of senators, were finally adopted, and labor gained representation in the Cabinet with the appointment of William B. Wilson as the first Secretary of Labor. In 1914, Congress adopted the Federal Trade Commission Act, for which the National Civic Federation had agitated since 1907, and the Clayton Act, hailed by Gompers as "labor's Magna Carta." Then in 1915, the La Follette Seaman's Act, sponsored by the International Seaman's Union, became law. Finally, in 1916, the Federal Farm Loan Act and the Child Labor Law were passed. These reforms entailed no substantial change in the lives of most workers, but their cumulative impact was sufficient to halt the steady growth which the Socialist Party had enjoyed during the previous four years.

In 1916, even such leading Socialists as A. M. Simons and Gustavus Myers voted for Wilson. Casting his first Presidential ballot in 1916, John Reed expressed the classical dilemma of minority party supporters: whether to support the party in whose principles they believe or to use their ballots to achieve immediate practical results. Reed decided he would vote for Wilson "as considerably the lesser of two evils," revealing at the same time his superficial understanding of the President by commenting that "the only real principles he has (few enough) are on our side."

However, Debs' refusal to run for re-election in 1916 was also instrumental in the decline of the Socialist vote. Ill, and desiring to give a younger man the opportunity, Debs stepped aside, and for the first time since the organization of the Socialist Party of America, was not the Party standard bearer. In his place the Socialists nominated Allan L. Benson, a journalist, in a Party referendum. Compared to Debs, Benson was not only unknown, even within Party ranks, but he campaigned poorly and ran badly. Debs had generally run well ahead of the ticket; Benson trailed his running mates in almost every state.

Early in the campaign the Socialists had optimistically looked forward to receiving two million votes for their Presidential candidate and to electing ten congressmen and a United States senator. Before election day, however, there were many indications that Benson would fall well short of this mark, although, at the same time, the Party's popularity did not appear to have diminished substantially, if at all, since 1912. The *Literary Digest,* for example, in a pre-election forecast considerably more accurate than its attempt two decades later, predicted that the labor vote would go heavily for Wilson. At the same time, the *Digest* found "a widening undercurrent of strength" for the Socialists, and suggested that "on some occasions Wilson was preferred "only because in the way of actual accomplishments he can do more for the Socialists than Mr. Hughes." In a later report on three thousand local communities, the *Digest* predicted that while Benson would carry only forty-seven, their informants "not infrequently noted" that the local Socialist vote would be stronger than it had been in 1912.

In fact, although they failed to achieve their goals, Socialists did fare better in legislative and local elections in 1916 than they had in 1912. The Party elected Meyer London to Congress in 1916, whereas no congressman had been elected in 1912. They also came closer to electing a United States senator in 1916 than ever before, when Grant A. Miller polled 30 percent of the vote for that office in Nevada. In elections to the various state legislatures, the Party also surpassed its record of 1912, electing twenty-nine legislators compared to twenty, four years before. Fusion against them, not a decline in their voting strength, led to some Socialist defeats in 1916. In California, both Socialist legislators lost to fusion candidates, despite an increase in their vote.

In municipal elections the Socialist vote increased in 1916 in several major cities. Most prominent were Minneapolis and Milwaukee, both of which elected Socialist mayors by majority votes. The victory in Milwaukee was most significant because Emil Seidel, elected mayor in a three-way race in 1910, had been unable to overcome fusion in 1912 and 1914. In 1916, Daniel Hoan finally succeeded in winning a majority and began his long tenure as mayor of the city.

The decline in the number of Socialist municipal office holders after 1911 had several causes. In part, it was a result of the Party's earlier emphasis on the pressing need for reform in American cities and towns. Even Woodrow Wilson had commented on this aspect of Socialist popularity. In *The New Freedom,* Wilson inquired of his readers if they had "noticed the growth of socialistic sentiment in the smaller towns." Not many months before, Wilson explained, he had stopped in a small town in Nebraska and met the mayor, who was a Socialist. "What does this mean?" Wilson asked. "Does this mean that this town is socialistic?" "No Sir," replied the mayor; "I have not deceived myself; the vote by which I was elected was about 20 percent socialistic and 80 percent protest."

After 1911 the old parties showed an increasing willingness to adopt many of the reforms advocated by the Socialists, who were severely limited in what they could do when in control of a municipality. They could not bring socialism to one city while the rest of the country remained capitalist. Furthermore, even if charter restrictions permitted (which they rarely did), Socialists could not put through reforms which would seriously impinge upon business interests, lest industry be driven from their city. In practice, a Socialist administration could press for public ownership of utilities and transportation facilities; increase social, recreational, and cultural services; and adopt a friendly attitude toward unions, especially in time of strikes. But some or all of these things could be done, and at times were done, by non-Socialist reformers such as Tom Johnson and Newton D. Baker in Cleveland, Samuel Jones in Toledo, and John Peuroy Mitchel in New York, and by business groups under city manager charters.

On a municipal level, Socialist administrations often met with the approval, implicit if not explicit, of the larger and more sophisticated business interests. This was brought home in dramatic fashion to David I. Nelke, editor of the anti-Socialist Catholic magazine, *The Common Cause,* when he went to see Charles A. Coffin, president of the General Electric Company, in February 1912. Nelke had gone to Coffin to ask for support for his anti-Socialist venture at the suggestion of Ralph Easley. After Nelke had waited for "some little time," Coffin rushed into the room, "evidently very much excited," and without even asking Nelke to be seated, "he began roaring about [the] magazine." Coffin attacked the statements against socialism it had made, and said that as far as he was concerned "Dr. Lunn was the best man that had ever been Mayor of Schenectady," and that he (Coffin) was "going to work hand in glove with him." Nelke "was unable to get in a word in any way whatsoever," and Coffin "kept edging toward the door, evidently with the desire of leaving." At the door, Coffin turned to Nelke and stated that he was "simply tearing down socialism and offered nothing in the way of reforms."

The ability of some progressive administrations to match Socialist demands, or the failure of municipal Socialist platforms to go beyond reform, gave rise to many criticisms of the leadership from within the Party. The Left took the lead in these attacks, but it was not alone. Some complained that the old parties were "only too anxious to copy this weak stuff." Walter Lippmann, on his first job as secretary to Mayor Lunn, wrote Carl D. Thompson suggesting that the Socialists include in their platforms only those planks which the progressives could not steal. He was highly critical of the administrations both in Milwaukee and in Schenectady for failing to follow this path, and was perturbed by the reluctance of the Socialists in Schenectady to raise the tax rate and thereby "expropriate private capital for social use."

Unfortunately, neither Lippmann nor any of the other critics offered real alternatives. Nor were their critiques well directed, for, as Berger had pointed out, with each reform won it was the responsibility of the Socialists to go on to the next demand. Only thus could the Party retain its popular following while it moved on toward socialism. In fact, in local elections, left wingers gave implicit support to this approach and espoused programs indistinguishable from those of the Right. In 1912, for example, the Cleveland left winger Charles E. Ruthenberg admitted that "it was on municipal reform issues that most of the Ohio victories were won." When appealing for votes on a local level, both Left and Right pointed to the miserable conditions created by capitalist government, and both promised, if elected, to solve their city's most pressing problems.

Debs also looked with mixed feelings on the early municipal victories, fearing that the Party would attract reform elements it could not assimilate. He believed that Socialists should seek only to register the "actual vote of Socialism," and criticized members who regarded "vote-getting as of supreme importance." To Debs, socialist propaganda was not "bait for votes" but a means of education, and the only meaningful election victories were those which would occur when the workers developed a solid socialist consciousness.

In this view of political action, Debs was further from Haywood and the IWW than were Berger and Hillquit. Debs tended to believe only in the educational value of the ballot, while Haywood believed it had only practical value. Berger, on the other hand, saw both aspects, believing that election campaigns provided the dual opportunity to conduct mass socialist education, and to win the chance to demonstrate in practical terms the civilizing values for which the Socialists stood.

Eventually, even the right wingers came to share Debs' fears. In 1915, four years after Debs had warned of false victories, Oscar Ameringer issued a similar injunction. Observing that in many cities Socialists had disguised themselves as reformers, "sneaked into the camp of the enemy and yelled 'victoria,'" Ameringer went on to relate that when the foe "woke up," he "kicked us out of camp." The lesson to learn, Ameringer stated, was that the "revolution in the economic world must be reflected in the brains of the workers." Agreeing with Debs, he concluded that "every campaign must be a campaign of education first," since power without mass consciousness "is weakness."

This attitude on the part of Socialists of all tendencies led Party members to value the number of votes received above the election of officials, and even to look upon fusion against them as a positive blessing which allegedly placed the issue of capitalism versus socialism squarely before the voters. Thus, when the Socialists were defeated for re-election in Milwaukee in 1912, they claimed a victory because in a "straight vote" against a combined capitalist enemy they had increased their percentage. Nor, if one can project oneself back into the spirit of those years, does the explanation appear to have been concocted entirely of sour grapes.

But if Debs' position had no ideological foundation at variance with that of his comrades to the right, there was a difference of mood, a greater degree of alienation, which Debs shared with many left wingers in the Party. This hostility to their society reflected itself in an attitude which made the idea of Socialists holding public office under capitalism almost unbearable, and which caused many to view any practical activity of elected Socialists with extreme suspicion. In many places Socialists were expelled or hounded to the point of resigning from the Party simply because they had performed their normal duties. In Ashtabula, Ohio, for example, W. E. Boynton, Socialist president of the city council, resigned from the Party after he had been attacked by the "reds" in his local for voting in favor of a commission charter which included proportional representation, and was, therefore, fully in accord with Party policy. Similarly, in Duluth, Minnesota, Socialist State Senator Richard Jones was expelled from his local, dominated by an IWW-oriented Finnish branch, apparently only because he managed to get himself elected. In Pittsburg, Kansas, two Socialists were brought up on charges of diluting Socialist principles in the "quest for mere election" because they accepted Trades and Labor Council support as well as Socialist endorsement. Finally, in Los Angeles, the Socialist councilman was forced to resign from the Party for voting for a Democrat for council president, there being no Socialist member other than himself.

Many Socialist officials were expelled once they reached office, and it appears that most of them were vicitms of the alienation of their comrades, rather than of their own misdeeds. This, of course, was not always the case. Some were expelled for violating Socialist principles—e.g., H. K. Davis, a Socialist state assemblyman in Nevada, who voted against women's suffrage. Others were expelled for more practical reasons, as in Ashtabula, where a councilman voted "dry" when the local was "wet"; or as in the case of school board members in Edmonds, Washington, who refused to appoint a Socialist as principal of the local high school. On the whole, however, left wing Party members were quick to expel their elected comrades for reasons that now appear quite flimsy.

While the Party debated the correct approach toward municipal elections, municipal reformers came to life after 1911. Of national scope and highly successful, the commission and manager movements swept the country after the adoption of commission government by Des Moines, Iowa, in 1907, and the victory of a manager charter in Dayton, Ohio in 1912. Designed to rationalize city government and to enable municipalities to meet some of their more pressing commercial and social needs, these plans were the adaptation, under the guiding hands of local chambers of commerce, of corporate methods to city government. For the first time, in hundreds of cities throughout the United States, organized business threw its support behind civic reformers, adopted programs that often differed little from those of the Socialists on municipal issues, and carried the day for reform.

Under these new charters, the likelihood of Socialists gaining office was lessened both by the strength of the new coalition of business and traditional reform groups, and by the mechanics of commission and manager government. The number of elected city officials was sharply reduced, and ward representation was replaced by a commission, usually of five, elected on a city-wide vote. This often meant the elimination of minority representation, since minorities, racial, national, and political, were usually concentrated in specific wards. In Dayton, for example, the Socialists had polled 25 percent of the vote in 1911 and elected two councilmen and three assessors, but after the adoption of the manager charter, they elected no one, although their vote rose to 35 percent in 1913 and to 44 percent in 1917. The "nonpartisan" ballot, a standard feature of commission and manager charters, acted against the Socialists in the same manner as fusion. Under this feature of the plans only two sets of candidates competed in the final election; where the Socialists had formerly been able to win with slightly more than one-third of the vote, they now needed an absolute majority.

In cities without commission or manager charters, direct fusion was commonly used to prevent reelection of Socialists. Here, also, the Socialist vote often increased while the number of elected officials declined. In 1915, for example, in the face of an increase in their vote in each case, Socialist

TABLE I.   *Cities and towns electing Socialist mayors or other major municipal officers, 1911–1920*

State	City	State	City
1911 (74)			Fostoria
Arkansas	Winslow		Lima
California	Berkeley		Linden Heights
	Watts		Lorain
Colorado	Nederland		Martin's Ferry
	Victor		Mineral City
Idaho	Coeur d'Alene		Mineral Ridge
Illinois	Davis		Mount Vernon
	Dorrisville		Osnaburg
	Grafton		St. Marys
	Granite City		Salem
	O'Fallon		Sugar Grove
	Thayer		Toronto
Iowa	Madrid	Oklahoma	Antlers
Kansas	Arma	Oregon	Coquille
	Curransville	Pennsylvania	Broad Top
	Girard		Township
Michigan	Flint		Hazeldell
	Greenville		New Castle
	Kalamazoo		North Versailles
	South Frankfort		Roulette
	Wilson		Wheaton
Minnesota	Crookstown	Utah	Cedar City
	LaPorte		Eureka
	Pillager		Mammoth
	St. Hillaire		Murray
	Ten Strike		Stockton
	Two Harbors	Washington	Edmonds
Missouri	Buffalo		Tukwila
	Cardwell	West Virginia	Star City
	Gibson	Wisconsin	Manitowoc
	Minden Mines		Milwaukee (1910)
Montana	Butte		West Salem
Nebraska	Beatrice		
	Red Cloud	**1912 (8)**	
	Wymore	California	Daly City
New Jersey	Rockaway	Florida	Gulfport
New York	Schenectady	Louisiana	Winnfield
North Dakota	Deslacs	New Jersey	Haledon
Ohio	Amsterdam	West Virginia	Adamston
	Ashtabula		Miami
	Barnhill		Star City
	Conneaut	Wisconsin	Manitowoc

State	City	State	City
1913 (32)			Jerseyville
Arkansas	Chant		Lincoln
	Hartford		Phelps
Colorado	Buena Vista		Riverton
	Edgewater		Torrino
	Grand Junction	Indiana	Hymeria
	Lafayette		Clinton
	Longmont	Michigan	Gustin
Connecticut	Naugatuck	Minnesota	Cloquet
Illinois	Canton	New York	Schenectady
	Granite City	Ohio	Conneaut
Michigan	Harbor Springs		Krebs
Missouri	Liberal		Cleveland
Minnesota	Brainerd	Pennsylvania	Pitcairn
	Crookstown		Williamsport
	Eagle Bend		(Commissioner)
Montana	Butte	Virginia	Brookneal
New Jersey	Haledon	West Virginia	Star City
North Dakota	Minot (1	Wisconsin	Manitowoc
	Commissioner)	**1916 (6)**	
	Rugby	Michigan	Traverse City
Ohio	Canal Dover	Minnesota	Minneapolis
	Conneaut	New Jersey	Haledon
	Coshocton	Vermont	Barre
	Hamilton	Wisconsin	Milwaukee
	Martins Ferry		West Allis
	Shelby	**1917 (17)**	
	Talent	Illinois	Buckner
South Dakota	Sisseton		Granite City
Washington	Burlington		Sylvis
	Hilyard	Indiana	Elwood
West Virginia	Hendricks		Gas City
	Star City	Kansas	Frontenac
Wisconsin	Manitowoc		Hillsboro
1914 (5)		Minnesota	Duluth
Florida	Lakeworth		(Commissioner)
Montana	Missoula (2		Dawson
	Commissioners)	Ohio	Byesville
New Jersey	Haledon		Jenera
West Virginia	Star City		Piqua
Wisconsin	Manitowoc	Pennsylvania	Garrett
1915 (22)			McKeesport
Alabama	Birmingham		(Controller)
	(Commissioner)		Pitcairn
California	Eureka		Union City
Illinois	Canton	Utah	Eureka
	Eagle River	Washington	Camas

State	City	State	City
	1918 (2)	Ohio	Byesville
Illinois	Mascoutah		Massillon
Wisconsin	Milwaukee	Wisconsin	Sheboygan
			(assessor,
	1919 (5)		municipal judge)
New York	Buffalo (High vote		
	for Councilman-		1920 (2)
	at-Large)	Iowa	Davenport
	Lackawanna	Wisconsin	Milwaukee

administrations lost to fusion of Republicans and Democrats in Coshocton, Hamilton, and Martin's Ferry, Ohio.

Over-all, Socialist electoral strength varied unevenly from 1911 to 1917. The Presidential vote dropped sharply in 1916 (although it made a comeback in 1920 when Debs polled 923,000 votes from his cell in Atlanta penitentiary). In legislative elections the Party reached its high point in 1914, yet the decline through 1918 was slight. In 1918, for example, thirty-two Socialist state legislators were elected, compared to twenty in 1912, thirty-three in 1914, and twenty-nine in 1916. There was, however, a reduction after 1914 in the number of states electing Socialist legislators, from fourteen in 1914, to nine in 1916, to four in 1918. Finally, in municipal elections, 1911 and 1917 were high points, although there was a change in the pattern of the vote in these years. In 1911, Socialist strength was greatest in many semirural towns and small cities (see Table I), whereas, as we shall see, the Socialist vote in 1917 increased principally in the larger cities of the industrialized East and Midwest (see Table II).

What emerges is a patchwork pattern which does not lend itself to generalizations. The period of more or less steady growth that characterized the Party in its first dozen years obviously came to an end at least by 1914. Yet the years after 1912 did not constitute a period of break-up and decline as most historians have asserted.

After the low Socialist vote in 1916, the *Nation,* recognizing the specific circumstances, commented that "the future of the Socialist Party should not be predicated from its showing at the last election." Only a few months later the United States entered the war, and soon after, the world entered a new era of revolution. Caught up in this stormy course, the Socialist Party was to emerge battered and torn. But during the war, the Party made a rapid comeback at the polls, as the *Nation* had prophesied.

TABLE II.   *Socialist state legislators, 1910–1920*

State	1910/11	1912/13	1914/15	1916/17	1918/19	1920/21
California	1	1	2			
Idaho			1			
Illinois		3	2			
Kansas		3	1	2		
Massachusetts		1	1	1	1	
Minnesota	1	1	3	2	4	2
Montana		1	2			
Nevada		2	2			
New Mexico			1			
New York	0/1		0/1	2/10	3/5	5
North Dakota	1					
Oklahoma			6	1		
Pennsylvania	1		1	1		
Rhode Island	0/1					
Utah			1	1		
Vermont				1		
Washington		1				
Wisconsin	13	7	9	10	22	10
TOTALS	19	20	33	29	32	17

Crisis in the New Order
1919-1945

More than half a century has passed since the start of the First World War. Over that time, preindustrial and even industrializing American society have faded from the memories of many Americans. Instead, they have experienced in different ways the social processes characteristic of a mature, industrial, capitalist society. Overall, the half-century was one of powerful but irregular economic growth. That growth resulted in new ways of life for most Americans and altered in essential ways the patterns of decision making rooted in the earlier industrializing process itself.

In the years between 1914 and 1945, military and diplomatic crises, together with economic crisis, encouraged state intervention in ways unknown to nineteenth-century Americans. This powerful thrust, however, was shaped by problems and difficulties rooted in *modern* industrial society. War and depression encouraged the political "integration" of society. But so did the desire for social justice and equality. These "pressures" toward state intervention had a different weight, came from different groups in the society, often had contradictory objectives, and had different consequences. Despite the many changes that occurred in the 1920s, for example, (national income increased from $60.7 billion in 1922 to $87.2 billion in 1929) 26 million of 27.5 million American families earned less than $2500 at the end of the 1920s. The Great Depression that started in 1929 exposed in new ways the profound political, economic, and social consequences of this fact. "We find our population suffering from old inequalities, little changed by past sporadic remedies," admitted the American President in the midst of the Great Depression. What occurred then meant to integrate and balance the social system in new ways. The "New Deal" involved massive but often inconsistent patterns of government intervention. "Its policies," the political theorist Walton Hamilton wrote years later, "were expediencies improvised to meet the instant emergencies. . . . All were fitted out with techniques which were the inventions of the political arts. The great separation of state and economy was gone." It was as if earlier and long-forgotten mercantile patterns had emerged to deal with the multiple crises of modern industrial society.

"The story of the New Deal is a sad story," one of its historians had recently concluded, "the ever recurring story of what might have been." That "story," however, had many chapters. Some belong to the decades before 1930 and others to the decades after 1940. Others belong to the 1920s and 1930s themselves and are descriptions and analyses of the ways in which rural southern and western whites and blacks, blacks who had migrated to the North, and first- and second-generation immigrant workers in the North responded to "prosperity" and then to depression.

4.1

The Rights of the Mine Workers

CARTER GOODRICH

Patterns of work-discipline have complex origins and change over time. Some are imposed from without—the product of external pressures. Others are the byproduct of the work process itself. In addition, "tradition" often affects the attitudes of men and women toward work and toward technology. The economic historian Carter Goodrich examined the subtle interplay between such "pressures" among early twentieth-century coal miners. Coal miners, of course, have a particular history. So do all groups of workers identified with special industries. Goodrich here dealt with a specific group of workers, but the process he described occurred in all industries and everywhere had its historical dimension. It is important to note, moreover, that the workers Goodrich described lived at a time when "scientific management" was yet in its infancy.

Carter Goodrich, *The Miner's Freedom* (Francestown, N.H.: Marshall Jones Company, 1925), pp. 56–100.

The technique of coal mining leads very naturally, as has been shown, to conditions of indiscipline, but it does not completely explain them. For room-and-pillar mining may in fact be carried on with thoroughly submissive workmen—with serf labor as in the early days of British mining or with negroes still under the spell of slavery as in isolated Southern mines to-day; and the prevailing freedom of the miners is in part a matter of vigorous human tradition.

The teaching of this tradition goes on largely in the working place itself. A certain anthracite miner, for example, was telling how he had given a lesson in the ways of the mines to the newly-landed "hunky" who was working as his laborer. "Come here, Frank, says I. Here's the boss. Don't work. Always sit down when the boss is around." The story comes from an allied industry, and the particular custom in question seems within the last generation to have dropped out of the bituminous mines, but there is no doubt that the process of teaching is typical of both industries. Just as the younger worker picks up from the older one the greater part of his craft knowledge, so also he learns from him most of his attitude toward the boss and toward the industry. The vivid phrase of a union leader, moreover, throws light on another part of the process. "It's the *gob pile oration*," he said, "that makes the miners less submissive than other workers. A miner hears the boss bawling out the man in the next place. Pretty soon there's a delay or something and the men get together on the piles of slate out in the heading and talk it over." "The bolder ones," he added, "teach the others;" and out of it comes a common attitude toward the boss. "It's the delays," said another union man, "that makes the miners debaters." It is certainly the delays that bring them together in the small groups on the gob piles, and very likely it is true that the "orations" that are delivered there are of more importance in setting the manner of life in the mines than all the speeches of the official union leaders outside. There are many other things also in the daily life of the miners that make for their solidarity. There is a suggestion of this in the group of men gathered at the end of the day at a crossroads inside the mine waiting to be jostled out together in the "man-trip," but it is in the villages to which the men go home at night that the background of common feeling is most evident. "We haven't got a farmer or anybody else in the town," said a miner, "except one hotel-keeper." That is the extreme, but the mining of bituminous coal is for the most part carried on far from cities and far from other industries; and the miners, more often than almost any other workers, live in isolated camps and villages of their own. The communities, to be sure, are usually made up of a great mixture of nationalities; but they are communities in which the talk in the pool room or on the log across from the company store is largely the talk of the one industry—communities, most of them, to which all the men come home black.

The talk of the working place, the orations of the gob pile, the public opinion of the mining village—there are thus many ways, even aside from the formal organization of the union, in which the traditions of the miners are passed on and strengthened; and, as a matter of fact, some of them are older than the union itself and many of them are forces to be reckoned with even beyond the boundaries of the union fields. John Mitchell and other leaders of the United Mine Workers have referred to the importance of the "conditions that have grown up with the industry" and "the practice of the trade" that is older than the union organization; and the tradition of the "square turn," for example, "that no man should have more cars than another man," which is often thought of as merely a union restriction, is clearly of much longer standing. "Even without contracts," said a prominent operator in the early years of the union agreement in Central Pennsylvania, "the question of unequal distribution has always arisen. That is an old question that has been up for twenty-five or thirty years." And there is even reason for believing that this and other "customs and conditions" of the industry may have had a still longer history in the British mines where so many of the early American miners learned their trade.

Coal mining is an old industry with old traditions as well as in part a union industry with union traditions, and many of the characteristic elements of this old indiscipline may be found in the attitudes of unorganized as well as organized workers throughout the greater part of the industry. "Even the non-union miner," declares an active member of the U.M.W., "is freer than a factory worker." There *are* mines, to be sure, in which it can be said of the workers that they "only know what the coal company teaches them" because they are fresh from the farms of Virginia or Poland or because "the majority of the men is just the men the company made them out of the timber that lived here when a mine was an unheard-of thing"; but the ordinary non-union mine has among its employees a number of old miners and often a group of former union miners, and from these men the rest of the workers acquire much of the traditional attitude of personal independence. The miner's right to go home when he pleases does not end at the union border; in fact, one miner told me that he "had to come from West Virginia to solidly organized Illinois to find a mine where they'd discharge a man for coming out early." Absenteeism is no less frequent in the non-union fields, and it was a non-union foreman who declared that "if a man has been in here loading three or four days, he's done something, and if he lays off the next day, that's his own business." Even in some of the fields most securely beyond the reach of organizers, the customary rights of the mine workers are felt as a serious obstacle to the stiffening of discipline, and I have heard non-union miners stating as eloquently as any union ones the advantages of mining as a job in which you were "more your own boss" than in a factory.

The democracies of the gob piles assert much of the traditional freedom of the miners even beyond the union frontier, but there is no doubt that on the whole they speak much more boldly in the union mines. "Non-Union Towns are Towns of Fear," declared a card circulated during the 1922 strike:

> "Non-Union Miners Have Lived in Fear!
>   Fear of the Boss
>   Fear of Spies and Spotters
>   Fear of Gunmen and Coal and Iron Police
>   Fear of anti-union Civil Authorities
>   Fear of Blacklist
>   Fear of Evictions."

To be sure, the communities in question, even those in which all the weapons named are used quite ruthlessly against organizers and strikers in time of struggle, do not usually seem like "Towns of Fear" to their loyal inhabitants. Sometimes, even, they may seem like Kingdoms of Love, at least according to the ingenuous language of a poster issued by a certain church of colored miners:

> "8 P.M. The Hon. Mr. ———, the owner of this beautiful plant and the greatest Negro friend in West Virginia, will address the audience. 8:30 P.M. Mr. ———, *the second man in the Kingdom,* the honored and highly respected *superintendent of this town,* the man we hope whom when the mantle falls from Elijah it will fall upon him as it did upon Elisha, will also address us." (italics mine.)

But in either case, whether the motive be fear or a sort of plantation loyalty, it would be surprising if the miners in these villages were very vigorous in asserting the traditions of the workers at the points at which they ran counter to the wishes of the management. And surely there must be some reflection underground of the difference between the community in which the coal company which owns the land is all the local government there is, as is frequently the case in the non-union fields, and the community in which, as sometimes happens on the other side of the line, the president of the local union is elected mayor or burgess. To the question, "What do the men think of a certain change?" two non-union superintendents gave the significant answers:—"What does that matter?" and "We have no organization here." No union boss could have answered so nonchalantly. The organization would have furnished a channel through which the men's opinion would have made itself felt, and in case after case the union appears as the great bulwark of the traditional independence of the miners.

The relationship of the union to these individualistic rights, however, is not always one of direct defense. In fact there are certain elements in the old indiscipline that the organization expressly disavows. It makes no claim for the right of miners to go home early or to stay away from work at will. "And if they do lay off," declared one leader, "as some of them do by getting too much booze . . . they will have to settle their own grievances with the employer. . . . He is at liberty to discharge them if he sees fit." This position, moreover, is now taken in the majority of agreements. "Should any employee absent himself from work for two days," reads a typical provision, "or persist in working irregularly, unless through sickness, or by first having notified his Foreman and obtained his consent, it shall be construed as a dischargeable defense;" and there are a number of districts also in which the contracts either "jointly recommend and request" or else require that the man remain in the working places "the full eight hours, or such part of the eight as they have work to perform." But for the most part these rules are "treated with impunity by the employees," and no doubt a sweeping campaign of enforcement would meet with more opposition, in spite of the agreements, in the union than in the non-union mines. A passage from the diary of Mr. Edward A. Wieck, a mine committeeman in Southern Illinois, throws a much clearer light on the actual relation between the union and the old custom of irregularity. The mine manager had just posted notices requiring the miners to stay in their places until 3:45 in the afternoon. "Such orders are strictly according to the contract," comments the diary, "and have been in effect in various parts of the district for twelve or fifteen years, but . . . no doubt some of the men will buck this, which will mean work for the committee to do trying to get their jobs back." The boss asked the committeemen to take an active part in getting the miners to obey the rule; they were not quite willing to put themselves in the position of seeming to "help the management impose onerous conditions on the men" but decided instead to "ignore the matter and let the boss enforce it as he saw fit." "I called his attention, however," continues the committeeman's account of the interview, "to the fact that it was a new departure in this field to insist that piece workers work up to the last minute. 'Customs and habits of a lifetime are not easily changed,' I reminded him. 'You can't expect to put up a notice and get immediate results, especially when you are dealing with men.' " And the final comment in the diary is:—"I think there are no discharges imminent." The picture is doubtless thoroughly typical. When a movement toward the new discipline starts, "the men don't like it," and the leaders of the union are more interested in protecting the jobs of their members than in campaigning for efficiency; but it is clear that the basis of the resistance lies in the old customs of the mine workers and not in anything the union has added to the tradition.

The union fights neither for nor against the position that a man "ought to know when he is tired" and when he feels like working, but it does assert and defend many of the other customary privileges of the miners. A number of these rights are written into the joint agreements, not merely under the head of the significant clause—"customs and conditions to remain the same"—but in specific provisions as well. The principle of the square turn, or equal distribution of mine cars, for example, that expresses the traditional feeling of the miners that "they ought to get a fair share of the work that is going," has become institutionalized in the contracts in an elaborate body of rules and exceptions and safeguards; and the right of miners to separate and special working places is either stated or implied in all the agreements. In most of the districts there are clauses making the arrangement definite—providing, for example, that each man shall have a separate place, or that a pair of loaders shall have two rooms unless the machine runners can keep them in steady work with one, or that two men shall have three rooms, and so on. Even in the longwall mines of Texas and Northern Illinois, the contracts expressly provide that the miners shall work by ones and twos and "assume the responsibility of the place" very much as in the more usual type of mining. There are occasional rules also, probably reinforcing a more widespread custom, that declare the right of the miner under certain conditions to choose his own "buddy" to share the place with him. Moreover, the union is almost everywhere successful in its contention that the foreman "cannot force a miner to leave his place and go and drive mules (or do other company work), unless he is willing to do so, and that he cannot stop the cars on such a person" if he declines to make the change. Under certain circumstances, to be sure, one man's place may be given temporarily to another worker, but the rule expressly provides that "such loader must leave rooms in as good condition as found." One agreement provides that a man's place must be held for him during his absence on union business or during an annual vacation of two weeks, if he notifies the company in advance; and the actual practice of the industry, as indicated in the decisions interpreting the agreements, goes much farther than this in confirming a miner in his property right to a particular place in the coal. A number of such decisions hold that a man has a claim to his old place even after a period in which the mine has been shut down, and another case throws an even more interesting light both on the customs of the industry and on the position taken by the union. A certain miner in Central Pennsylvania was slightly injured in the mine and stayed away from work for some time without sending word to the boss. "The mine foreman held the place for him for three weeks, and then upon learning that he was working about his store, driving a team in delivering goods, etc., gave his place to another miner." At the end of *six* weeks the man returned to the mine and demanded not only re-employment but re-employment in his own old place. The union backed his claim; and the case was referred, according to the usual procedure, to the commissioners, or representatives, of the union and of the operators' association. "In view of . . . the fact that Gravich followed the advice of the physician, but did not keep the foreman advised," reads their decision, "and his place having been given away to another miner, we decide that Gravich be reinstated, either in his own place or in an average place in the mine."

In defending claims like this and in enforcing these provisions in the contracts, the union appears as the supporter of certain elements in the old indiscipline; but its most important contribution to the individualistic freedom of the mine workers comes in the protection it gives them from arbitrary discharge. The contract provisions on the subject, to be sure, always start with the statement that the union has nothing whatever to do with it. "The right to hire and discharge," the contracts declare, "is vested exclusively in the operator, and the United Mine Workers shall not abridge that right;" but this ringing declaration is contradicted, and this right is certainly shared and abridged, both in the provisions of the contracts and in the practice of the industry. In the first place, the general power of discipline is limited in all the agreements by clauses that prescribe specific penalties for particular offenses. "A miner who sends out 'dirty coal' shall be suspended one day for the first offense," reads a typical contract, "three days for the second offense, five days or discharge for the third offense within any thirty days." Moreover, the very section of the contract that states the principle of the employer's right to hire and fire almost always follows it with a "but" and an important qualifying clause. "It is not the intention of this provision," explains one such statement, "to encourage the discharge of employees . . . on account of personal prejudice or activity in the United Mine Workers of America." The more usual type of contract goes even farther and specifically recognizes the right of the union to "take up" all cases of discharge. If "in the opinion of the mine committee, . . . any employee . . . has been unjustly suspended or discharged, the mine committee shall endeavor to have him reinstated;" and if necessary the case shall be carried up through the various "courts" provided for the adjustment of disputes. The employer's right to discharge is absolute, says the contract, but if he uses it "unjustly" the man must be put back to work and, in many cases, be given back pay for the time lost!

The curious logic of this position reflects the modification of the contract with the growing power and activity of the union, and even now its actual power outruns the contract provisions. "You must have a just cause"—and, as the Coal Commission points out, good evidence—"before you discharge a man" if you want the penalty to "stick;" and there are many operators who would amend the statement to read that you can't get rid of a man even if you *do* have a just cause, or at least that "you have to bring it around to the point where it would be absurd *not* to discharge a man." Certainly it is often felt to be the duty of the mine committee to contest every case of discipline that arises. An Illinois committeeman, for example, was looking ruefully at the enormous pile of "clod" that a certain miner had tried to load out as coal. Another miner came up and grinned sympathetically, "You'll have a hell of a time getting that fellow's job back!" Evidently where there is an active committee, no man need lose his job, no matter how flagrant the case, without a hearing and without benefit of economic counsel. The benefit of the doubt, moreover, is usually given to the miner, and very often the decisions of the commissioners or arbitrators take the form of sustaining the contention of the company but recommending that the man be put back to work! In certain districts, also, the general statement of the right to hire and fire has been so overshadowed by other provisions that it is officially held that discharge cannot take place except for offenses that are definitely stated in the agreement. It is said that in Northern West Virginia, for example, men who have been discharged for running disorderly houses in the mining camps have been put back to work on the ground that "the agreement prescribes no special kind of conduct outside working hours;" that men who have been fired for loafing have been reinstated on the ground that "the scale agreement does not say just how hard a man has to work;" and that men who have been discharged for swearing at their foremen and for "threatening them with bodily harm" have been given their jobs back because these things were not "dischargeable offenses under the agreement." But these cases are exceptional, and the careful discussion of the matter in the Labor Relations Report concludes that "over most of the areas where relations under union conditions have obtained for a longer period, . . . discharge, when merited, can be made and the maintenance of effective standards insured at the same time that unfairness in discharge is avoided. . . . The outstanding fact (however) is that discharges and other disciplinary acts are very much more difficult than formerly" and very much more difficult than in the non-union mines. It is not true that the union's power makes discharges impossible. It is not even proven that it is what makes them infrequent. Discharges are rare enough, to be sure, in the union fields to-day—one company with a payroll of six thousand fired only twelve men in a year in which it was taking advantage of a depression to rid itself of "reds;" but it is not clear that they were any more numerous in the past—an operator of fifteen years ago declared that in his experience "suspensions (were) simply and solely for loading dirty coal;" and it is not even clear that they are much more frequent in the non-union fields, except where the weapon of wholesale discharge is used as a campaign measure to get rid of union men and "agitators" or to force the men to sign the "yellow-dog" anti-union contracts. Both union and non-union bosses know how to "freeze men out" or "ease them off" by giving them poor working places, but in ordinary operation outright discharge is comparatively rare in either part of the industry.

It is not the number of discharges, however, that is the important point for the study of freedom and indiscipline, and the essential and significant difference is that under union conditions discharge cannot take place as a simple act of the employer's will or the foreman's temper. It is the effect of this on the attitudes of men and bosses underground that gives meaning to the organizing slogan, "Join the Union and Quit Being Afraid of the Boss!" and the assurance of a hearing and the sense of power given by the organization go far in making the miners readier and bolder in asserting their individualistic privileges.

Sometimes, also, the very discharge cases themselves are fought by the union officials on the ground, not of the contract rights of the employees, but of their traditional—or "natural"—rights as mine workers. An arbitration board in Central Pennsylvania, for example, was hearing the case of a pair of machine runners who had been fired for refusing to obey the foreman's orders. "The men considered the place wasn't safe to cut, the foreman ordered the men to cut the place, and they refused to do it." "The posts were cracking all around," testified the cutter, "and in the morning a fall was down pretty close to where he wanted me to go in and the post was broke in two. . . . I refused to go in there while the roof was working." "You see," explained the mine committeeman, "when they put up a jack to get in, the machine might loosen the roof up and maybe it is easy to come down." To an outsider this seems like a vivid picture of danger, but the more prosaic testimony of the company showed that the place was in fact cut that same night without accident by the foreman and another worker. "The question involved," summed up Mr. Mark for the union, "is whether a man is supposed or required by the contract or this Board or the law of the States to work in any place that he considers as dangerous to life and limb." "The whole matter is determined by law," argued the operators' commissioner. "The mine is exclusively in the hands of the mine foreman. If this Arbitration Board is going to lay down the principle that every man for himself shall determine for himself whether he will work in a given place or not, you are laying down a dangerous principle." "By Heavens," declared the union leader, "I would not let any mine superintendent or mine foreman determine for me whether my life was safe to work in a place or not;" and it was on this appeal to the logic of individual rights that the union won the decision for the men.

It is in ways of this sort that the union intensifies the customary independence—or indiscipline—of the miners, and in the process it adds an important new element to the tradition. For in defending the miner's freedom in regard to his own work, the organization secures for the miners as a group something of a collective freedom in regard to the running of the mines. This new power, to be sure, has grown up without definite intention on either side. The United Mine Workers of America drives forward towards its major goals of wages and hours under strong conservative leadership and with little attention to modern doctrines of "workers' control." And surely the operators have not intended any such sharing of authority. "The management of the mine and the direction of the working force . . . are vested exclusively in the operator" according to the emphatic language of the contracts; and this provision is often reinforced by a clause that attempts to limit the activity of the mine committees to "the investigation and adjustment of disputes" and declares that they "shall have no other authority or exercise any control nor in any way interfere with the operation of the mine." But the frequent disputes over these clauses and the frequent charges of "interference with management" are good evidence that the "dividing line" is very much blurred in the actual practice of the industry. This fact was well brought out in the course of an early scale conference in Central Pennsylvania. "We are coming to the point," said Mr. J. L. Spangler, "where we will have to determine just how far we have any authority as operators in the management of our own works and how far we concede that our men take part in management." The remark led to an honest attempt to clarify the issues in which Mr. W. B. Wilson, later Secretary of Labor, was the chief spokesman for the miners:

> "I still don't see," persisted the operator, "how far you go in the management, the joint management of our mines."
>
> "So far as our interests go, Colonel."
>
> "Well, your interest, it seems to me, goes to the extent that if you get your wages and the proper conditions . . . under an annual scale that is made and we keep that contract with you, that is the limit. You ought to be satisfied. But when you ask us to submit to you any changes in the hiring and discharging of men, or in doing anything outside of that, you are interfering with our business."
>
> Mr. Wilson met this with a partial disclaimer. "Our position . . . is this, that (in case of) any change in the methods of operating the mine that does not affect the conditions of the employee or his earning capacity . . . we would not have the right to interfere."
>
> "Well," said one of the operators, " 'conditions of the employee' is awful wide."
>
> "I know," replied the miners' leader. "That is the reason I used the word!"

"Conditions of the employee" is still a very "wide" term, and the everyday work of maintaining and enforcing them keeps the mine committees and the higher union officials continually "dipping into management that is none of their business," as many operators would still put it, and gives them, in fact if not in name, an active and a significant share in the running of the mines.

Oftentimes, indeed, this comes about as the result of the simplest issues of wage rates and earning capacity. In order to ensure honest weight, for example, the men place one of their number on the tipple to check and verify the weights as taken and recorded by the company's weighman, and this checkweighman often becomes the spokesman of the men on other issues as well. Many grievances, however, require more than this informal handling. The enforcement of the scale of payment for dead work, for example, calls for representatives of the men who know the complicated set of customs and contract clauses that govern the matter, and who can go to the working places where the disputes arise and check over the foreman's measurements and interpret the agreement on the spot. It is for this and for similar purposes that a mine committee is elected in each mine—typically three working miners who are paid by the local union for the time spent in investigating grievances; and the committee's primary duties of defending the wages of the miners frequently carry it into active contact with the operation of the mine. Sometimes, even, they put it in the position of passing judgment on the efficiency of the management. "All necessary props, rails, and other supplies," say the contracts, "shall be delivered at the working places;" and this and other clauses are intended to make sure that the company will provide the piece workers with the proper facilities upon which their earnings depend. Often these provisions are badly enforced, and the miners have to scurry around in abandoned rooms hunting for rails and timbers that have been left behind; but at least in Illinois and in the Southwestern fields it has become the accepted principle that the men must be paid for the time that is lost on account of these and similar failures on the part of the management. Compensation is sometimes paid not only for time that is wasted in waiting for supplies but also for time lost in waiting for the boss to give proper instructions or for the company men to lay the necessary track, switches and the like, and it has been claimed in cases where machine runners and loaders have lost time because the machines were out of order. The principle has not been pushed to the point of compensating the men for all the time spent in waiting for cars—a claim that might revolutionize the industry; but, even as it is, it means that in case after case the committees must investigate the actual operation of the mine and decide whether or not the company has "done all that could reasonably be done" to give the men work. It has been pointed out that "the genuine interest of the (British) miners in the problems of mine management (is) partly traceable to their piece-work system;" and here in a similar way the claims of the American miners for the facilities with which to earn their wages frequently place their representatives in the position of prosecuting their employers for inefficiency in the courts of the industry.

The enforcing of the square turn also leads to similar controversies. Here again there is no such far-reaching intention. The chief purposes of the rule are the simple ones of preventing favoritism in the supply of cars on which the men's earnings depend, and of preventing men who might be favored in cars from returning special favors to the company by working for less than the scale rates. Nevertheless its day-to-day application sometimes puts the committeeman in the position of an unofficial motor boss. "They couldn't keep a square turn in one part of the mine with the other," reported one motorman at a union convention. "They went to the mine foreman about it and he told them they couldn't do anything about it, it is up to the mine committee. So whenever one side of the mine got behind, the next day they (the committee) sent that motor over in the other side and give them a trip or two to help them out and we hain't no trouble getting a square turn." The question of permitting exceptions to the rule, moreover, involves the committee in much more complicated questions. The union recognizes that there are certain conditions—the need of opening up new territory to provide working places or the danger of losing coal in a "squeeze" of the roof—that justify favoring one part of the work at the expense of the others; and in these cases a "free turn" is allowed under certain safeguards. It is in judging when such exceptions are really necessary, and when they are simply cloaks for favoritism, that the committees come into most direct conflict over the actual planning and lay-out of the mines. How this happens may be illustrated by a story from a district in which the union's privileges in the matter are not very firmly established. Te local union at Nanty Glo, Pennsylvania, had passed a rule that no man should load coal on the days that the mine itself was not working, with the proviso that "the mine committee had the full rights and privileges to order the men to go to work on idle days" if there was danger of a squeeze ("since no man wants to see anyone losing anything"), "or if the mine committee saw that it was necessary to advance this or that place." One of the companies attempted to work certain headings on idle days, the committee ordered the men not to go in, and the members of the committee were discharged for interfering with the operation of the mine. In the arbitration case that followed, the committeemen pointed out that they had not been consulted and claimed that the advancement of the headings in question was not in fact necessary for the development of the mine. When they started to present evidence on the latter point, however, the operators' commissioner cut one of them off with the remark that he "didn't need to qualify as superintendent of the mine" and asked one of the others if he presumed to "set up (his) opinion as to the necessity of certain development" against that of the superintendent. "I would," declared the committeeman. "He has the maps under his hand, but I can find my way and notice the development . . . from my own knowledge. I have a practical idea of . . . the progress and what effort has been made to develop in previous times." The question of the committee's right to concern itself with such matters was vigorously debated. The foreman hotly declared that he "didn't know it was the rule for the mine foreman to go to the committee and ask what to do." The union's representative argued that without such consultation the principle of the square turn could not be enforced. The umpire to whom the case was finally referred declared that the committeemen were not "modest" (though he gave them back their jobs) and affirmed the company's absolute right, both under the contract and under what he called "the common sense relations between man and man," to advance its headings on idle days if it believed it to be necessary. "Whether such belief is right or wrong," continued the decision, "is not an official concern of the mine committee. The management of the mine is in no way in their hands." But the rights that are denied by this particular decision are recognized by the agreements in several other districts —one expressly provides that miners shall work on idle days only "on the order of the mine committee . . . except in urgent cases"—and over a very large portion of the industry the "condition" of the square turn does in fact lead to a recognized right and practice of consultation over questions of development.

This same feeling that lies at the basis of the square turn clause— that every man "ought to get a fair share of the work that is going"—runs also through other elements of union policy. The industry as a whole characteristically meets a depression not by drastic reduction of the working force—sometimes the total force actually increases—but by spreading what work there is over a great number of men; and in this situation also the union presses vigorous claims for its equal division. If one section of a mine is to be shut down, the union frequently demands that the men who work in it shall share equally in the work of the other sections; if the mine closes altogether, the union is likely to claim work for the men in other mines of the same company; and there is even a clause in one contract that provides that the miners of nearby mines of *other* companies "may at their option"—not the companies'—"share work with those thrown idle, either by doubling up in the working places or some other manner mutually agreeable." Here again the principle brings the union into contact with vital questions of management, and in working out its application the representatives of the men often come very near to exercising "the right to control and distribute the jobs."

A similar right is sometimes exercised by the union even on other grounds. In certain regions, particularly in the Southwest, the union is quite literally the distributor of jobs, under local rules and customs that provide that the operator shall hire men in the order in which they appear on the "applicant lists" of the local union: "With tonnage men the burden of proof rests with the operator to show why the man is not to be hired, and with day men the burden of proof rests with the union to show that they are capable of performing a day's work." This practice extends over only a relatively small part of the industry, but over a much wider area the union exerts a considerable influence over transfers from one job to another and over the customary promotions from extra fireman to fireman, from trip-rider to motorman, and the like. "It was put in the hands of the bank (mine) committee," reads a familiar sort of record, "and they talked to the superintendent . . . and put the man in that belonged in." Usually this action is based on the principle of seniority—it is the youngest man in point of service that "belongs" off if the force is to be reduced; but occasionally a contract clause carries the significant provision that disputes over competency are to be settled jointly by the mine manager and the pit committee; and there are even cases in which the foreman leaves the question of the possession of a particular job entirely to the mine committee to settle according to its own judgment.

Very often, also, the especial dangers of coal-mining lead to the exercise of independent judgment by the representatives of the men. Under the agreement in the state of Washington, a safety committee at each mine, composed of the president of the local union, the mine superintendent and a third member chosen by them, is expressly commissioned to make regular bimonthly examinations of the mine and "to investigate all serious and fatal accidents." In most districts, however, activity of this sort is without official sanction, and sometimes an arbitration board takes occasion to remind the union that "the safety of the mine rests with the mine management and not (with) the committee." But whatever the contract position, story after story from the mines leaves no doubt of the frequency and vigor of committee action on questions of ventilation and safety. If a group of men have quit work on account of bad air, it is often a matter of course that the mine foreman and the mine committee should go together to inspect the places in question; and such a tour is quite likely to begin with the boss down on his knees in the coal dust sketching the ventilating system—at the committee's request—as the beginning of a long discussion of remedies. If the men are afraid that a certain creek will break in and flood the mine, if the airshaft that serves as an emergency outlet from the mine is slippery with ice, and in countless similar cases, it is the mine committee that fights out the issue with the management, and often it is the committee or the local union that sends for the state mine inspector to settle the dispute. If there is danger from men crowding into the cages in the morning, it is likely to be the mine committeemen who take upon themselves the job of seeing to it that the men line up instead. If the hoisting engineer raises cages of men as recklessly as he would hoist cars of coal, it may be the mine committee and not the management that successfully disciplines him. And occasionally a committee takes positive and dramatic charge of a dangerous situation. One story that comes from Herrin, Illinois, illustrates the point—a different sort of story from most of those that have made the town's name known. At one of the mines there had been a small gas explosion. "The following morning it was decided by the Pit Committee that men should not risk their lives in the mine unless the operator would place three good men on watch at the old workings." The company did this under protest. A week later there was a sudden alarm, the men were ordered to put out their lights, and the bosses led them to the shaft bottom by the light of their safety lamps. The manager directed that one mule should be sent up along with every cage full of men. The order "almost started a riot as the men felt men's lives were of more value than mules," and the men were finally sent up first. A few days later it was proposed that the mine should be opened again. The committee insisted upon making its own inspection before the men were allowed to go in. "They went into the old workings and were compelled to wade in water up to their necks to get to the lower part of the mine. . . . (They) spent two days down the mine making this examination, and most of the time they were over their hips in the water. A proper cut was finally opened through which the air current was forced and the gas and black damp cleared out of the mine." It cost the local union $64 for doing work that the operator should have paid for," complained some of the men, but the committeemen "felt sure that their caution"—and their independent activity—"had saved the lives of many men." Here again, as in the issues arising from wages and the distribution of jobs, the defense of the "conditions of the employees" had led the representatives of the men into vigorous "dipping into management."

In these and in other ways, the local representatives of the union exert a considerable degree of control over the day-to-day running of the mines, and many of the issues raised in these cases are carried farther in the activities of the higher branches of the union. The question of safety has led the organization into many legislative campaigns for the adoption and the strengthening of mining codes. The principle of the fair division of work is often carried further in claims for "equal running time" as between mines of the same company and in protests against practices that prevent the equal distribution of railroad cars between different mines; and the famous demand for the thirty-hour week was in large part based on the feeling that an industry that on the average provided little more than thirty hours' work a week ought to share that work equally among all the men engaged in it. The right of consultation over methods of work, moreover, becomes of great importance when it is applied to the question of the introduction of machinery or of completely new methods. For many purposes these wider policies are of much more significance than those of the mine committees, and the attitude of the organization toward new techniques will require separate treatment in the last chapter; but the present interest lies less in these issues than in the effect of the typical local forms of control upon the quality of the everyday life inside the mines.

It is clear that this power of the mine committee has a twofold effect on the freedom of the individual miner. In the first place, it cuts across the indiscipline of the mines, perhaps paradoxically, with a new group discipline. For the enforcing of these conditions involves control by the representatives of the group not only over the company but over the individual worker as well. Sometimes this takes the form merely of persuasion, and the committeeman passes on the traditions of the union in much the same way that the other traditions of the miners are passed on in the talk of the gob pile. This is illustrated by another revealing story from the Wieck Diary. The boss was trying to get a certain miner to do a bit of company work for nothing on the ground that he had just been treated too liberally in a dispute over dead work.

> "The digger, being a little soft," so the committeeman's account runs, "took it seriously and did not answer. The boss continued, 'Well, what do you think about it?' The digger stammered, 'I—I don't know.' 'You don't!' I exploded, and then on second thought continued, 'Well, damn it, I won't interfere,' vexed as I was at the man's denseness and ignorance of the contract. Then thinking again, the poor devil needs a little help, I said, 'Huck, listen to me. If the boss tells you to do anything, you do it. He's the boss. If he comes in here to tell you to throw your shovel in the gob and load coal with your hands, you do as he tells you, and if at the end of the day you think you haven't made enough money because of your instructions, and if you can't settle it with him, bring your complaint to us.'" "The man looked at me a little queerly after this lecture," ends the narrative, "and I think he got the point."

Sometimes, however, the men do not "get the point" so easily, and the union adopts other forms of pressure. When the eight-hour day had just been won, the new condition was continually violated by certain piece workers who insisted on coming to work long before daylight "with a lantern in their hand." "There seems to be no way," reported a union delegate, "to stop the men from going to work anywheres from twelve o'clock (midnight) to seven;" but another answered that in his local they had "caught four brothers working thirteen hours" and had tried to settle the question by fining them fifteen dollars apiece. The enforcing of the square turn, also, has frequently meant pressure exerted upon the union's own members as well as upon the company. Sometimes this is turned upon the men who receive special favors; "any man accepting a free turn," reads an occasional resolution, shall be considered as having violated his sworn "obligations" to his fellow-members; and occasionally more drastic action is proposed. More often the pressure is directed against the motormen and drivers who distribute the cars unfairly. Get them into the union, said one delegate in the days when the organization was weak, and there'll be no trouble about the turn. And when the transportation men are in the union, it is sometimes proposed that they should be fined if they fail to give a square turn. "A man who will give mine cars for beer is not much of a man," argued a rank-and-file delegate; why shouldn't the union discipline him? Higher officials of the union, to be sure, sometimes point out that the drivers are company men and therefore "under the bosses" and can hardly refuse to take the cars where they are told; but it has been shown that in actual practice they have great latitude in the matter, and there is no doubt at all that the union influence exerted directly upon them has a powerful effect in enforcing the rule. And occasionally this power is even used not in keeping the turn square but in enforcing some other matter of group discipline; a man's turn may be stopped, for example, to force him to join the organization or to obey its orders. "Back in our locality," said one miner, "the day man is the best man we have got to keep the diggers in line." The effectiveness of the discipline that the union can exert in this and other ways is recognized in the frequent pleas of the operators that the union should help, as it sometimes does, in enforcing this or that rule of the company's; and occasionally the union itself gets rid of a man whom it will not permit the company to discipline but whose poor work is a drag on the other members. In all this there is clearly compulsion, and a typical picture of it is that of the mine committeeman standing at the drift mouth ordering men not to work on an idle day. In his testimony in the case already discussed, Committeeman Varish told of a dramatic encounter one morning with a group of men who wanted to go to work in spite of the union rule:

> "One of them came in there special and he commenced to kick to the assistant mine foreman. . . . He says, 'What is the matter, a fellow no can go in on idle day?'
>
> I say to him, 'Listen here, didn't you insist on these rules to be drawed up?'
>
> He says, 'Yes.'
>
> I say, 'What in the name of God do you want to go in and tell that mine foreman you can't go in? Go ahead in, then . . .' I says. 'If you fellows wants them rules reversed,' I says, 'call a meeting . . . I am not objecting against having them rules wiped off;' and I says, 'Let every man go into the mines if they have any work.'
>
> 'Nothing doing, we don't want the old conditions we had before we had those rules.' That is the statement they made."

The encounter illustrates two aspects of the effect of workers' control on the working life. In defending the "conditions of the employee" and in protecting its members from the rigors of the companies' discipline, the union imposes a new and occasionally rigorous discipline of its own; but in the same process it gives to its members an important sense of group control. Here in this story the rules enforced by the committee are clearly felt as limitations on the freedom of the individual worker. But they are rules of which it can be said more literally than of those of most democracies that the men themselves have had them "drawed up" and that the men themselves can "call a meeting" to "wipe them off;" and at the end of the argument the group of miners come to the point of admitting that the committee is doing their business and really enforcing their will. In the great range of union activities, moreover, this second aspect— that of control *by* the group—is much more conspicuous than the aspect of control *over* its individual members. The range and vigor of this activity, to be sure, vary greatly from district to district and from mine to mine. "When you haven't got a live mine committee," said one union delegate, "you know how we suffer, you know how the grievances creeps in." And just as there are some union mines without "live" committees, so also there are a number of non-union mines that permit mine committees of varying degrees of independence. But on the whole vigorous committee activity is a characteristic of the union mines, and in most cases it is to the union and its officers and committees that the men turn for the carrying out of their wishes. "They go to the committees" for everything, the operators sometimes complain; certainly they do go to them on a surprising range of subjects—from matters of a stolen pair of shoes or a broken shower in the wash-house, or the troubles of a pair of buddies who are temperamentally unsuited for sharing a place, to questions of bonding the payroll of a company in danger of bankruptcy or matters of life and death as in the story from Herrin; and it is in providing these agencies for group activity that the union exerts its most direct and most distinctive influence on the quality of the working life. It is the union that gives to the democracies of the gob piles something of the feeling and practice of a collective freedom.

[This chapter has] attempted to describe the working life in the soft coal industry in terms of the technique of the mines and also of the traditions of the miners, for by the standards of other industries both mining and the miner are more than "a little peculiar." It may be that in lumbering the methods of work sometimes leave the individual as much to his own devices as in coal mining. It may be that in the printers' chapels and elsewhere there are groups of workers that cling to traditions even older than those of the gob piles. And in the clothing trades at least there are union shop chairmen who exercise a group control over the working arrangements that is no less vigorous and even more conscious than that of the mine committees. But there are not many industries that are like soft coal mining even in one of these respects, and there is surely no industry, unless it be anthracite, in which all these things are combined. The type of working life that results is unique in American industry.

On the side of technique the key to the peculiar nature of this life lies in the way in which the workers are scattered by ones and twos in the many miles of dark tunnels that make up the underground workings of a mine. Almost of necessity, therefore, the working arrangements place a quite old-fashioned reliance—for better or worse—on "the skill, dexterity and judgment of the individual workman." To the independence that comes from this source, the traditions of the miners add other elements. It is the organization of the mine that determines how rarely a miner shall see his boss, but how he shall act when he does see him is also a matter of the custom of the trade and the orations of the gob pile. These traditions are of the more importance because many times they are crystallized in the policies of the union, and the activity of the organizaiton not only defends the miner's independence in regard to his own work but adds to it also something of a new collective control over the running of the mine.

Out of these two sets of influences, then, comes the freedom of the miners or the indiscipline of the mines. It *is* indiscipline, certainly, as well as freedom; if "the mine is a friendly place," as some of the reforming engineers admit, it is partly because bosses are likely to be easy-going where the piece-workers themselves stand so many of the costs of inefficiency and loose discipline; and some of the miners' privileges are hardly more than signs of the general slackness that goes with chronic underemployment. To one idealistic leader of the union, in fact, who sees in the idea of workers' control the promise of a larger freedom for the miners as a group, the mere freedom from being bossed that arises out of this looseness of mine organization seems little better than that of the sweated home-worker. The work of mining must not be idealized; it is rough and dirty and arduous, and it is carried on under conditions of semi-darkness and stale air and constant danger; but even among rough jobs there are significant differences in the quality of life and discipline; and if the occupations of modern wage-earners were to be "graded," as John A. Hobson suggests, "according to the measure of the scope of skill, judgment and self-determination" that they afford to the individual, surely there are very many that would be placed below those of the mine workers. "The miners of Luzerne," said the delegate from a Pennsylvania local, "do feel for more liberty than money." Their friends among the engineers and economists may well point out that what they have now is precisely "more liberty than money," more freedom on the job, that is, than opportunity for a good life away from the job; but independence is a rare thing in industry and a thing that draws many men back from the factories to the mines. "If there's anything that gives me the willies," explained one of them, "it's a boss standing and looking down my shirt collar;" and the relative freedom of the miner in this respect is enough to justify the claim that there are human values in the present type of working life underground that are worth careful consideration in comparison with those of the *new discipline* that prevails in modern factories and that threatens or promises to replace the *old indiscipline* of the mines.

4.2

Mexican Labor in the United States: Dimmit County, Winter Garden District, South Texas

PAUL S. TAYLOR

Before 1900, Mexican and Mexican-American labor was important to the economy of the Southwest. Its place in that economy, however, increased greatly in the first three decades of the·twentieth century. More than this, such workers grew in number in the Far West and even in and around places like the city of Chicago. The decline of European migration during and after the first World War intensified the need for unskilled and semi-skilled labor from rural areas within the United States and from countries nearby. Mexican workers figured importantly in this calculus.

Few immigrant and native-born working-class groups have been studied in such careful detail as the Mexicans and Mexican-Americans. That was largely so because of the work of Paul S. Taylor, a distinguished agricultural economist and student of American society. Taylor paralleled his study of

Paul S. Taylor, "Mexican Labor in the United States: Dimmit County, Winter Garden District, South Texas," University of California Press Publications in Economics, 6:5 (1930). Originally published by the University of California Press; reprinted and edited, omitting footnotes and Tables 1, 3, and 4, by permission of The Regents of the University of California.

Texas farm workers with equally penetrating studies of Mexican and Mexican-American workers in California, Colorado, and Chicago. Although the following study focused on a particular ethnic group, it also probed deeply into the general condition of farm workers.

Dimmit County lies in the Rio Grande Plain, in the southern portion of the Great Plains. Most of its surface is gently rolling, with some hilly portions in the southwest; it is covered with a native vegetation consisting chiefly of mesquite, chaparral, prickly pear, guajillo, and catclaw. The principal drainage is furnished by the Nueces, a river of intermittent flow. In the west a number of creeks flow into the Rio Grande. Soils are productive when sufficient water is available, either from rainfall or irrigation. The climate is semi-arid. True normal rainfall is perhaps close to 21 inches . . . but there are important fluctuations which affect crop growth.

The inquiring visitor in Dimmit County is soon told that "only fools and new-comers prophesy the weather." The reply is not facetious, as observations of the Weather Bureau show. Through the greater part of southwest Texas, annual precipitation varies greatly from year to year; rainfall is local in character, and subject to great fluctuations from place to place within the area. The average rainfall diminishes slightly from east to west. There is also a great range in the amount of precipitation during the same months of different years. . . .

The uncertain rainfall makes irrigation necessary to assure uniform crops. While a small amount of dry farming is practiced in Dimmit County, crop failures frequently result with this method. . . .

In the early days even gardens were rare. By the late nineties a little dry farming, subject to the vicissitudes of the seasons, had sprung up and a small surplus of vegetables was shipped to market. People also began to irrigate small garden patches from flowing wells, or from wells equipped with windmills. One rancher dammed a creek to irrigate a garden. These projects, however, were still so unimportant in 1900 that Hill, who reported some twenty-five flowing wells at Carrizo Springs, stated, "The quality of the water is good, but it is allowed to waste, practically no irrigation being done." But the potential importance of the underground waters had already been glimpsed. At the close of the century a number of artesian wells were developed, and earthen tanks or reservoirs were constructed to irrigate a few acres of garden truck.

About the same time the waters of the Nueces were utilized. Commencing construction in 1896, J. S. Taylor built a dam at Bermuda, cleared land, and by 1899 was ready to begin irrigation. In 1904 this water system, which is still in operation, was irrigating 100 acres by gravity, and 75 acres by pumping. Irrigable land in the vicinity, which originally sold for $1.50 per acre, had advanced to $10 and $15 per acre.

From this time on new wells were bored steadily, settlers began to move in, land sales were made, and land values rose rapidly. With the optimism of the day the editor of the Carrizo Springs *Javelin* exclaimed:

> The man with the hoe is crowding in. His approach to this artesian belt where the water supply is inexhaustible and the soil productive, is inevitable. There is no keeping him out. He is like Johnson grass when it gets started in a rich field.

In 1904, thirty wells were reported to be supplying water for the irrigation of 1026 acres in the vicinity of Carrizo Springs. Average flows varied from 40 to 300 gallons per minute; a few flowed very strongly. One of the Richardson wells flowed 1200 gallons per minute, and an Eardley well attained 1400. By 1906, there were over sixty artesian wells in the county, ranging in depth from 300 to 700 feet. In 1909 there were said to be over two hundred flowing wells. By 1911 so many wells had been bored that pressure was greatly reduced. Flow ceased or became so weak that pumping was resorted to generally, although some excellent artesians continued to afford irrigation. . . .

The evidences of the southern cultural heritage of Dimmit County, of its past frontier isolation and conflicts, profound present economic changes, and hopes for future development are visible not only in its material environment, but in the mental attitudes of its people as well. From a sparsely settled cattle and sheep range of the southwestern frontier, it has been passing to an irrigated district which watches intently the daily fluctuations in the market price of Bermuda onions in New York. Although agriculture has spread over but a fraction of its surface, the county today is dominated by farmers.

Settlement by white men dates from the middle sixties. Practically simultaneously, three races closed in together on this frontier—white, Mexican, and colored. From the first, the whites have been economically, socially, and politically the dominant group. The whites came principally from Frio, Atascosa, and Goliad counties, east and northeast, crossing the prairies in Chihuahua wagons and "prairie floats," behind oxen or horses, and driving their cattle. Most of them were Texans. Some of them had made previous westward migrations, stopped a while, then again moved west. With the whites came a few slaves. The western fringe of the black belt has remained more than a hundred miles to the northeast; the number of Negroes in Dimmit County has never reached fifty.

Mexicans came in principally from the adjacent state of Coahuila, just south of the Rio Grande, but as far southeast as Matamoras, and Cerralvo, Nuevo León; and some of them settled. Among these was Ramón Sánchez, and later his nephew Diego. Ramón came first at the head of a band of mustang hunters, and liking the country and the security furnished by the presence of newly arrived American settlers, he remained. In 1874 he was joined by Diego, who had left Mexico because of dislike of military operations in the war against the French, and had gone to the vicinity of Corpus Christi as a *pastor*. Diego and his descendants, with their wives, now number approximately sixty; they either live on the original 160 acres on Pendencia Creek, raising a little corn, *calabazas,* and truck, irrigating their garden from the windmill, grazing a herd of goats, and working on neighboring ranches as vaqueros, or have moved to neighboring towns. Raphael Condé, of Coahuila, like others, came to work as a vaquero for American ranchmen; Indelasio and Guero Gonzales, and Pedro Treviño, of Presidio, close by, came to graze herds of cattle on the open range. Santana Rodríguez, of Matamoras, was a cattleman and land-owner. Simón García, a veteran of the Texas revolution on the Texan side, Trinidad Sánchez, a guide to the soldiers of Captain Benavides, of Laredo, and descendants of the Sánchez family, founders of Laredo, be-came landowners; some of these probably were Texas-born. Some were escaped *peones,* who, like the Negroes before the Civil War, found liberty by crossing the Rio Grande. In their flight they were sometimes aided by Americans as well as by other Mexicans.

By 1870 the population of the county was 109. Its origins, already given in some detail, are shown in their numerical proportions by the census. Eighty-four were born in the United States, and twenty-five abroad. Of the latter all were born in Mexico except one from the British Americas; of the former, sixty-four were Texas-born, fourteen were born in five specified states of the Old South, data on six were not published. Settlement was by a converging movement from areas lying northeast, east, southeast, south, and southwest. The subsequent growth of population is shown in the United States census data in table I. . . .

Characteristic of pioneer cattle ranges, there was cattle stealing, and the buying of stolen cattle. While the emotions engendered by these prac-tices in the Americans of Dimmit County are prone to line up Mexicans against Americans, the fact is that some Americans as well as some Mexi-cans were participants. A tinge of the feelings between early Mexicans and Americans appears even in the conflicts between Americans and In-dians. The Indians sometimes took refuge in Mexico, and perhaps partly because of that, it is reported by a descendant of first settlers that, "My father always thought that the Mexicans were mixed upon with the Indians in the raids."

TABLE I.   *Population of Dimmit County, Texas, according to race and nativity, 1870 to 1920* *

	1870	1880	1890	1900	1910	1920
Total	109	665	1,049	1,106	3,460	5,296
White	103	649	1,012	1,065	3,431	5,265
Native born	84 †	510 †	900	899	2,806	3,384
Foreign born	25 †	155 †	112	166	625	1,881
Born in Mexico	24 †	149 †	93 †	141 †	566	1,806
Other	1	6	19	25	59	75
Negro	6	16	37	41	29	31

* Compiled from United States Census. The 1930 census population is 8467.
† Irrespective of race, but almost entirely "white" within the census definition which classes "Mexicans" as "whites."

In the early eighties, wire fencing was introduced and rapidly extended. This put out of business those who owned herds and flocks, but no land. By the latter half of the eighties the open range was gone.

The first heavy invasion of the cattle country by farmers was barely twenty years ago. The men and women who entered the prairie, settled it, lived through the Indian raids and cattle stealing, drove the trail to Kansas, bored the first artesian wells and began to farm, were in comparative isolation. Many of them are still living there, together with their children, and their grandchildren. Interrelationship is extensive, the product of large families and isolation. This isolation is breaking down. In 1908 came telephone connections with the outside world; the first automobile ride to San Antonio was reported in 1909. Within another year or so, two railroads entered the country, and homeseekers poured in to clear brush and begin farming. The process is continuing: in 1926 a paved highway was run the length of the county; electric light and power lines and real estate development projects are preparing the way for additional homeseekers.

On April 1, 1929, Mexican children comprised 73 per cent of all children reported in the scholastic census. The federal census of April, 1930, reported a total county population of 8467. Assuming that the ratio of Mexican children to all children may be applied as the ratio of all Mexicans to total population, that the 1929 ratio applied in 1930, and that the Federal census was correct, there were approximately 6100 Mexicans in the county in 1930. But applying the method previously employed in these studies, . . . the 1929 Mexican population was nearly 8800, and the total population 12,000. The great discrepancy may be due to more than one cause. In part it is probably due to an actual decline in population during the intervening year; evidences pointing to such decline were observed among both Mexicans and Americans. In part it may be due to the greater assiduity of those who took the scholastic census, for the allotment of state aid placed a premium to the school district of about $15 for each name secured. Both censuses are taken at the time when Mexican population, much of which is of a floating character, is at its peak. Beyond these two estimates, and this explanation, it is not possible to go at the time this study goes to press, and at this distance from Texas. The estimates represent Mexicans, whether born in Mexico or the United States, and are not comparable with the figures of the federal census for foreign-born whites born in Mexico presented in table I.

The distribution of Mexican population is determined principally by the location of irrigated crops, because these create the major demand for labor. The areas within which irrigation is practiced are indicated by shading. The method employed to determine the area was consultations with persons in each part of the county who were best informed on the situation. The result is inevitably an approximation, with the degree of error varying somewhat from locality to locality. It represents an excess over the area actually irrigated probably of from 50 to 100 per cent; nevertheless it shows the manner and location of irrigation development. A more accurate map is in preparation by the United States Geological Survey. The largest concentration of Mexicans is at Asherton, because of its location within an important crop area, and its central position among the other crop areas of the county. Carrizo Springs is overshadowed as a labor center by Asherton and Crystal City. Catarina is both new and on the fringe of the irrigated zone, and still draws much of its labor from Asherton.

Probably well over half the Mexicans of Dimmit County live in towns. This urban concentration is stimulated by the character of the labor demand, which not only fluctuates seasonally but shifts every few days from field to field. The towns, therefore, serve as fluid reservoirs of agricultural laborers who ride out in the morning on trucks in whatever direction their work may lie on that day.

The growth of Mexican population since the development of irrigation has been very marked, both in absolute numbers, and relative to the total population of the county. This is clear from examination of the United States census figures presented in table I . . . Except for the decade of the nineties, which opened shortly after fencing of the open range had been completed, and closed before the irrigation boom was fully under way, the rate of population growth has been consistently rapid. The census tells equally clearly the numerical story of the Negroes who remain the inconsequentially small group they have always been.

The Mexicans, however, are not separately classified by the census. Its enumeration, therefore, has never given the full measure of this social group. The figures published by counties omit from separate classification even the children of Mexican immigrants, although the figures published by states include both Mexican immigrants and their children; beyond that, the Mexicans, although to a very great extent they remain a distinct social group, are lost among the undifferentiated "whites." Yet how far short of telling the whole story these figures of the federal census fell in 1920 is evident from a comparison of the federal and scholastic censuses. The former shows an increase of foreign-born whites from 141 or 12.7 per cent of the total population in 1900, to 566 or 16.4 per cent of the total population in 1910, and to 1806 or 34 per cent of the total population in 1920. The number of Mexican scholastics rose steadily from 376 or 39 per cent of total scholastics in 1911 to 51 per cent in 1915, 65 per cent in 1920, 72 per cent in 1925, and 2615 or 75 per cent in 1928. The recession in 1929 was slight.

This discrepancy between Mexicans by race and "foreign-born whites born in Mexico" is not uniform throughout the United States, but varies from place to place. It increases with the passage of time and is great wherever, as in New Mexico, there are many generations of this stock. In order to secure a count of the race group, the 1930 census created the separate classification "Mexican."

The effect of the development of intensive agriculture on composition of the population in a cattle range, then, was clearly to increase both numbers and proportion of Mexicans. This is similar to trends observed in both Imperial Valley, California, and the valley of the South Platte, Colorado, although the proportion of Mexicans to total population in Dimmit County is far greater than in either of the other areas. The percentage of Mexican school children in Imperial Valley in 1927 was 36.8, and in seven counties of northeastern Colorado it averaged but 5.7 per cent; in Dimmit County it was 73 per cent in 1929.

The origins of the Mexican vaqueros who joined the early white and colored settlers of Dimmit County have already been given. Another source of data on the origin of Mexicans in Dimmit County before its colonization by farmers is the record of marriages prior to 1910. Of 76 Mexican residents of Carrizo Springs married betwen 1884 and 1909, 36 had been baptized in Coahuila, 11 in Nuevo León, and 21 in Texas. Some of the Mexican towns appearing in the records for this period are the interior towns of Monclova, Saltillo, Nava, Zaragoza, and Torreón and the lower Rio Grande towns of Matamoras, Mier, Camargo, and Guerrero. Among the Texas towns are named Laredo and Palafox on the river to the south, Pearsall to the east, San Antonio to the northeast, and Carrizo Springs, the only town in the county at that time.

The slow infiltration of Mexicans during the days when sheep and cattle raising predominated was accelerated by the use of artesian water for irrigation during the first decade of the twentieth century, and became a flood when, with the coming of railroads at the end of the decade, American farmers began to colonize, clear brush, and sink wells. To attractions of the labor demands of expanding agriculture in the Winter Garden was added the expelling force of revolution in Mexico, entailing political and economic insecurity. The Mexicans came largely from the same areas as before. The majority are from Coahuila and Nuevo León lying just south across the Rio Grande, 48.7 per cent and 22.8 per cent, respectively, of those from Mexico having been baptized in these states. From the northeastern border states of Mexico came 87 per cent, and from the central plateau came 12 per cent. Practically all who came from the central plateau migrated to the Winter Garden district during or after the world war. In the fields I met a lone Mexican from Yucatán; the only other part of the United States where the presence of Yucatecans was reported to me was the vicinity of New York. Proximity is the most important explanation of the origins of this migration, as it was of the migration to Imperial Valley. This is not true of Chicago and the Calumet region, where the great majority of Mexicans are from the *mesa central* of Mexico. More detailed comparison of origins of Mexicans in Imperial Valley, the Winter Garden district, Chicago and the Calumet region, and perhaps other areas is reserved for a later study.

The great mobility of Mexican laborers and their families is observed in all parts of the United States where there are Mexicans. Some permanent movement of Mexicans from the Winter Garden to north Texas and even farther northward was reported. As a single but interesting instance of this, I met in the stockyards district of Chicago a Mexican musician who had worked on construction of the Uvalde-Carrizo Springs railroad twenty years before. And in Dimmit County I encountered or was told of Mexicans who had been to distant places. A majority of the Mexicans pick cotton in south, central, and west Texas. Most of them begin near Corpus Christi, some go as far north as Dallas and west to Amarillo. A very few pick cotton in Oklahoma. In 1925 some were transported to the Mississippi delta to pick cotton, but very few have gone there since. One family reported that it went east to work in potatoes at Eagle Lake, near Houston, before cotton picking started at Corpus. But these movements represent seasonal migrations only. One Mexican in an onion field, with whom I talked, had lived in Oklahoma, and another in Shreveport, Louisiana. One family had worked in sugar beets in Montana, Wyoming, and Colorado, and at a coal mine in New Mexico. Other Mexicans had worked in Michigan beet fields, in Detroit, Chicago, and Gary factories, and one on the railroad in Pennsylvania. Health or family reasons, or because some member of the family disliked northern climate, were the principal reasons given for return to south Texas. However, comments on the north were generally favorable. One old Mexican who had worked in the beet fields of Michigan and liked it, evidently did not realize why he did not return there, for he exhibited with pride a letter from the labor superintendent of the sugar company stating that he was "not adapted to beet work."

Most of the Mexicans who go from the Winter Garden to the sugar beet fields are shipped from Crystal City; the number from Dimmit County is small. Nor does Dimmit County send any considerable number to northern industry.

. . .

Written records of wage rates prevailing in Dimmit County in times past are inadequate. The historical data presented here are based largely upon recollections of old residents. Naturally, there were variations in the reports, owing perhaps as much to actual variations in wages paid as to the frailty of memory. The data presented are approximately general wage levels prevailing at intervals. At any given time there were departures from these rates, and between the dates named there were frequent intermediate variations exhibiting an upward trend.

From the sixties until the middle eighties Mexican and Negro cowboys received $10 a month and "grub." During the round-up they received $12. The boss cowboy received $15. From the middle eighties until the late nineties wages for these classes of labor were $15, $18, and $22, respectively. About 1900 they rose to $20, $25, and $30. Ten years later they had risen to $30 a month or $1 a day and grub, and $40 for the boss cowboy. From the time of the war to the present, wages have been $45 a month or $1.50 a day for cowboys, and from $75 to $100 a month for the boss cowboy. Cowboys have been both Mexicans and Americans from the first, and a very few Negroes. The Americans have generally received the higher pay and borne the greater responsibilities.

Shepherds were always Mexicans. They used to receive at first from $6 to $8 a month and grub, and later in the eighties, when sheep raising flourished in Dimmit County, from $9 to $10 a month and grub. One large rancher is reported to have started his Mexican *pastores* at $9 per month, Mexican money, raising them after six months to $9 American, or double the starting rate. Boss sheep herders received from $12 to $15 per month and grub.

Prior to the coming of the railroads, such farm labor as was required was generally performed at the rate prevailing among cowboys. This meant, from the latter eighties to the early years of 1900, 50 cents a day. When, in anticipation of the railroads, rapid colonization began in 1909, wages were still frequently 50 cents a day, for "all day," in the language of one resident. They quickly advanced, however. The Soil Survey, reporting conditions in 1910, stated, "The daily wage paid laborers ranges from 75 cents to $1, though help by the month can usually be obtained at the rate of 50 to 75 cents per day." These wages were without board, although sometimes housing was provided on the ranches to ensure the presence of labor when wanted. From this level wages rose to a war peak of $2 and even $2.50 per day. Since then, they have varied from $1.25 to $2, depending principally upon the season; occasionally wages as low as $1 are paid, but the usual amount is $1.50 for a ten-hour day.

Before the land can be farmed, it must be cleared of brush. This process of "grubbing" is performed generally by the use of grubbing hoes; occasionally a tractor is used to pull out small trees. This work is performed sometimes by day labor, but usually by the acre, on contract. The contract prices in 1910 were reported in the Soil Survey:

> The cost of clearing land ranges from about $7 to $20 an acre, depending on the size and density of the vegetation to be removed. The average cost is probably about $12.50 an acre, though in the vicinity of towns the sale of the wood for fuel is usually sufficient materially to reduce the cost.

Present contract prices for grubbing vary similarly with the difficulty of the task, and to some extent with the season, being less during periods of slack labor demand. An average price is about $14. Commencing with June, which is the slack season, and the date from which crop contracts customarily run, a timetable of the principal seasonal agricultural occupations in Dimmit County is as follows:

> *June:* Cultivation of corn and feed crops (milo maize and Kaffir corn) is in progress. Some feed crops are planted in May and some in June. Cow peas are planted to fertilize the ground; they are to be turned under twelve weeks later. Tomato seed beds are planted.
>
> *July:* Casaba melons are planted. Cotton is picked.
>
> *August:* "Fall crops" are planted: egg plants, peppers, squash, beans. Some of the planting is done in late July. If a grower made little money in onions, he probably plants "fall crops." These operations involve comparatively small amounts of labor since the acreage is small. Cotton picking continues.
>
> *September:* Spinach is planted: plantings continue to January 1. Onion seed beds are planted between September 10 and 25. Cultivation of July and August plantings of "fall crops" is in progress.
>
> *October:* Harvesting of July and August plantings of "fall crops" takes place. "Winter crops" are planted: lettuce, beets, carrots, turnips, broccoli; cabbage is transplanted. Little Romaine lettuce is raised now because of competition in recent years from the Salt River Valley of Arizona. In the last fifteen days of October a few onions are transplanted—about 10 per cent of the entire crop. Cotton picking (almost entirely outside Dimmit County) and onion transplanting overlap. In October those who have gone as cotton pickers to north and west Texas have not all returned to Dimmit

County. Citrus fruit is picked from the middle of October to the middle of January. Irrigation and mulching of citrus orchards take place in July and August; little attention is required from November to March. The citrus industry, because of its infancy, has not yet created an important labor demand.

Strawberry plants shipped from Arkansas are transplanted from mid-October to mid-November. Strawberries require the care and attention of the farmer himself. Forty thousand plants per acre are required. The plants carry through only two seasons satisfactorily, after which new plants must be set out.

November: Onion transplanting continues; about 60 per cent of the crop is transplanted during this month. Harvesting of "fall crops" is completed. The acreage of these crops fluctuates considerably from year to year.

December: Onion transplanting continues; about 30 per cent of the crop is transplanted in December. The spinach harvest begins with the harvest of the September plantings.

January: Spinach harvest continues; January is the most important month. "Spring crops," also called "mixed vegetable" crops, are planted: cucumbers, cantaloupes, tomatoes, beans, peppers, egg plant, roasting corn. The "spring crops" are practically the same as the "fall crops." Acreage fluctuates from year to year, depending upon what land is idle. Strawberries are picked in January, February, and on into March.

February: Planting of "spring crops" and spinach harvest continue. February is another important month of the spinach harvest.

March: Spinach harvest is completed. "Spring crops" are cultivated. Harvesting of "winter crops" is practically completed by the end of March or the early part of April.

April: The onion harvest begins, although a very little of the crop may have been harvested at the end of March. Cultivation of "spring crops" continues. Pulling of onion and tomato plants for shipment north extends from January through April.

May: The onion harvest is completed. "Spring crops" are harvested. The cantaloupe harvest comes during the latter part of May.

The peaks of the demand for labor in Dimmit County are onion transplanting from late October to January, and onion harvesting from the end of March to the first part of May. Onion sets raised from seed in the field are pulled up and transplanted by hand. The purposes of transplanting are an earlier crop, a more nearly perfect stand, and onions of better grade and quantity. In some districts where, because of market or other conditions, these advantages are insufficient to outweigh the higher costs of transplanting, the onions are seeded in the field and later thinned. In the Winter Garden, the desire to reach the market early has made the practice of transplanting almost universal. Working on hands and knees, with a short forked stick as a tool, a small hole is made in the soil, a plant inserted, the earth tamped, and the process repeated at three-inch intervals. Men, women, and children work, achieving great dexterity and speed.

Cultivation is usually by mule-drawn plows, or sometimes by hoeing. At harvest time the onions are first plowed up or lifted by a double curved blade, which passes under the roots of two rows. The onions are then pulled by hand and laid in piles or windrows. Sitting beside these piles with sheep shears in hand, the clipper with two clips cuts off the hair-like roots of the onion, then the stem, tossing the severed bulb into a waiting crate with a movement of the shears as he makes the second cut. Men, women, and children participate in this work. It is repetitious, and considerable speed is attained by experienced clippers. . . .

Almost all field labor in Dimmit County is performed by Mexicans, some living on farms, others in the towns. In seasons of peak labor demand, particularly onion transplanting and harvesting, many other Mexicans come temporarily to the Winter Garden. Advertisements distributed in the stream of cotton pickers that follows the opening bolls from the Lower Rio Grande Valley to the plains of west Texas invite them to the onion fields at the conclusion of picking and many come. At times, growers bring truck loads of Mexicans from San Antonio and from towns east of the Winter Garden, or from other points where they may be available. Sometimes they send transportation money to Mexican families to bring them to the onion fields from the cotton patch last picked. During and immediately after the war, when employers were permitted, under waiver of certain immigration restrictions, to secure Mexicans at the border for temporary purposes, Dimmit County farmers availed themselves of that source of labor. Some of the Mexicans were returned to the border by the farmers at the conclusion of employment; others were not returned. A few years ago growers in the vicinity of Asherton assessed themselves $1 per acre to secure labor through agencies at Eagle Pass and San Antonio. Further accretions to the labor supply are Mexicans who come to the Winter Garden at the conclusion of the earlier season of employment near Laredo, and immigrants fresh from Mexico.

Naturally, any disturbance of the labor supply is resented by the farmers. One such interference was the activity of the border patrolmen of the United States Immigration Service which was at its height during the spring of 1929. For a number of years enforcement of the immigration laws on this border had been very lax. Numbers of Mexicans had been crossing the international boundary illegally, and working on farms along the border or penetrating into the interior. Gradually since the war, but particularly during the past four or five years, a more effective patrol of the border has been developed. In the spring of 1929, along the entire Mexican border the Immigration Service was making a determined effort not only to stop the flow of surreptitious entrants, but to return to Mexico those who had previously crossed illegally and were subject to deportation.

The effectiveness of enforcement may be judged both from the protest of employers of Mexicans along the border, and from available statistics. During the month of March from 1925 to 1928 inclusive, the highest proportion of Mexicans legally admitted by the Immigration Service at El Paso, who had previously resided illegally in the United States, was only 3.2 per cent. For the six months' period July-December 1929, the United States Department of State reported that of the 8121 Mexicans who received visas, 1713 or 21.1 per cent were residents of the United States; they were either forced to go back or voluntarily went back in order to return and legalize an otherwise precarious residence. The southwestern border in 1929 was being held against illegal immigration far more tightly than most people had believed possible.

In order to determine the legality of their presence in the United States, Mexicans suspected of illegal entry are subjected to questioning by patrol inspectors. When this inspection was carried out with vigor in early 1929 numbers of Mexicans in Dimmit County and elsewhere were returned to Mexico by the officers. The inevitable result was to spread apprehension among the Mexican population. Some knew they were deportable; many had entered the country illegally, and though no longer subject to deportation, they were uncertain of their status. Others had no clear proof of an entry which was legal; others had been born in the United States, but lacked documentary proof. These, and even persons in possession of full proof of legal entry, were all subject to questioning at unexpected times and places. Furthermore, the whole process of interrogating newcomers and old residents alike is repeated when officers are changed, or new ones introduced.

In addition two new laws were passed, one increasing the penalty for attempted illegal entry, and another permitting persons of good character who had entered illegally prior to June 3, 1921, and had resided here continuously ever since, to legalize their residence in the United States. The second law was actually designed to help certain classes of aliens illegally in the United States, but neither American farmers nor Mexicans so understood it, the Mexican press in the United States gave out incorrect statements regarding it, so that its effect was to increase the general confusion of minds. At the same time the Mexican Consulate-General in San Antonio was advising Mexicans who were illegally in the United States to recross the Rio Grande and re-enter legally, while the United States consuls in Mexico were beginning to enforce more rigidly the laws having to do with immigration visas, and were thus greatly restricting the number of immigrants admitted.

The fears, real and fancied, which spread among an uneducated alien group in such a situation can perhaps be imagined. During the spring and summer of 1929, I was asked apprehensively by Mexicans, not only in south Texas, but also on the southern shores of Lake Michigan, whether it was true that the United States was about to send *all* Mexicans back to Mexico! The extent and character of the unfounded rumors is further indicated by the following which appeared in the Mexican press in the United States as recently as May 4, 1930 (translation):

> The 702 Mexicans were deported [at El Paso] by the authorities of the United States, accused of refusing to comply with the immigration laws, according to official communications.
>
> However, private dispatches indicate that our compatriots were deported from the neighboring country for having refused to naturalize themselves as Americans.

Incidents such as the two following, which occurred in Dimmit County, added to the grievances of the farmers:

> Farmer X paid the fines of two or three Mexicans from his ranch arrested for gambling. When they left court the patrol inspector apprehended the Mexicans in order to return them to Mexico for illegal entry into the United States. Farmer X objected that it was a "low trick" that the officer had not told him they were "wet" (i.e., illegally in the United States) before he paid the fine. The court thereupon remitted the fines.
>
> A patrol inspector was taking a Mexican from the ranch of Farmer Y. Prior to departure, when making financial settlement with the Mexican, the farmer asked the cost of a head tax and visa, and was informed by the officer that it was $18. After talking with the Mexican he then asked the officer if it was all right if he bought the Mexican's Ford, and received an affirmative reply. Obviously, the farmer wished to provide the Mexican with enough to pay the costs of legal immigration so that he might return, but he also wished to avoid violation of the law prohibiting payment of an alien's immigration fees. Unfortunately for the farmer, it turned out that the Mexican was in arrears in payments on the automobile, which was taken back by the owner; also that the Mexican was illiterate and consequently ineligible to return to the United States. Later when the permanent loss of his laborer and money was discovered, Y's wife complained to a colleague of the inspector that it was "mean" of the officer not to tell Y that the Mexican was inadmissible, and to permit him, after inquiring the amount of immigration fees, to "buy" the Ford of an alien known by the officer to be inadmissible. The colleague replied that the officer either had to believe that Y was making a bona fide purchase of the Mexican's Ford, or else arrest him for violation of the alien contract labor law.

Frequently local farmers supplied Mexicans whom they knew with letters stating the length of time they had known them, and other pertinent information. These were, of course, not acceptable to the officers as complete proof of legal residence in the United States. For example, as shown by his letter, a Mexican might have actually worked for the farmer over a period of say, seven years, and apparently be not deportable because of the statute of limitations; yet upon interrogation, he might admit recent departures to and re-entrances from Mexico, which render him subject to deportation.

Needless to say, such experiences annoyed the farmers, irrespective of the law, and they protested vigorously. As one aggrieved farmer said, "We couldn't farm this country without the Mexicans. They can take away about all the Mexicans they want; they can 'get something' on them [proving them technically deportable]."

Jeopardy of the supply of labor was undoubtedly the principal concern of the farmers. But they also protested in the name of the Mexicans, claiming violations of constitutional guaranties against search and seizure, and other abuses, and pointing out the danger of retaliation by Mexico, by annoyance of Americans in Mexico, or otherwise. Said a farmer:

> The immigration officers are pestering the labor we have got and scaring them to death. They take Mexicans who have been here 18 years or are native born and lock them up. Now Mexico is going to stop emigration. [The last referred to press reports similar to others both before and since that emigration would be checked by Mexico itself after May 1, 1929.]

And a county official protested vehemently:

> The immigration officers are violating the bill of rights against unlawful search and seizure, and are perjuring and throwing Mexicans in jail until they say they were born in Mexico. They tell them they will "help them out" if they admit this. Then they put them over into Mexico and say, yes, they are "helping them out" of the country. The officers took the petition against them which was at the store. They stop Mexicans who were born here and search them and throw them into jail and cuss them. This county went three to one Republican, but it never will again. These officers ought to be down by the river or in the brush and not on the highway.

If their work was confined to the river and the brush, the officers would of course miss the large number of illegal entrants who are able to reach a farm and secure employment. With their operations thus limited, effective patrol of the border would be impossible. Obviously, and sometimes admittedly, that is exactly what is desired by many persons in Dimmit County as well as elsewhere along the border.

In Dimmit County no charges of use of physical rough handling of Mexicans were made to me, as they were made in some other places. The officers operating in that county denied violation of civil liberties as well as other alleged abuses, and cited their authorization under federal statutes to search for and arrest without warrant any alien who in their presence or view is entering the United States in violation of law. So far as I could ascertain, none of the Dimmit County cases in which violation of rights was alleged, were presented and proved, although a local attorney offered his services gratis, and proof should not have been difficult had many such cases occurred. The officers made the countercharge that the zeal of the residents in defense of the rights of the Mexicans was not disinterested since *all* violations were not regarded as equally reprehensible; specifically, the officers cited the violation of the Mexicans' right to education, which takes place daily in Dimmit County without audible protest from local Americans; therefore, apparently, maintenance of the supply of Mexican laborers was considered more important than maintenance on principle of the latter's legal rights.

In order that the law might be enforced with a minimum of disturbance, it was informally understood that the patrol inspectors would not "disturb" labor at work on farms (although they would interrogate them on the roads or in towns), while the farmers would inform the patrolmen just prior to termination of employment to permit of a "check-up" before departure of the Mexicans. But this arrangement did not operate satisfactorily to the officers. It was discovered in one instance, for example, that the Mexicans knew of the approaching inspection in advance and that the "wets" had departed before the officers arrived. In another instance, when the end of employment was in sight, the Mexicans were gradually leaving, yet the farmer did not notify the inspectors. The officers, to prevent escape of "wets," appeared on the ranch early one morning and held an inspection. Neither party felt satisfied in this case—the officers charged the rancher with letting the Mexicans depart without notice to them, and the farmer maintained that, although Mexicans were leaving, the "end of work" when notice was to be given, had not arrived.

Not all the growers, however, are opposed to the activities of the patrolmen. One who cooperated with them said:

> Now I give orders to my contractor to ask the Mexicans if they have a passport. I don't want to give a Mexican $4 or $5 worth of grub and have him taken from me the next day. A lot of people say the immigration officers should not come on a farm and disturb labor. I think they should if the Mexicans have not paid their immigration fees.

Another disturbance of the labor market arose from competition between localities. The development of agriculture around Catarina, beginning in 1926, has drawn some labor away from other parts of the Winter Garden, particularly from Asherton. In 1929 this competition resulted in legal efforts by Asherton growers to hamper the movement of labor to Catarina. The complaint was partly against the payment of higher wages by the Catarina growers, and the fact that many of the Catarina farmers are from the North accentuated the tension. Said one Texan,

> Part of the trouble is due to the northern people with money and big acreages who don't know how to handle the Mexicans like the southerners. They offer them too high wages. . . .

Frequently contractors are paid by growers for securing and transporting labor, a practice followed by Asherton growers as well as others. Under stress of labor competition, Catarina growers not only paid wages a little higher than customary, but they also paid a little more per head for securing labor. Asherton growers thereupon secured an injunction against the Mexican contractors as operators of labor agencies without licenses. The injunction was subsequently overruled, but in the meantime it frightened the Mexican contractors and so accomplished its purpose. It also stirred the resentment of Catarina growers, one of whom pointed out, "The Asherton farmers helped the company to sell us this land, and then tried to keep us from getting labor."

This reliance on some device hampering to one's competitor and to the movement of labor is characteristic in south Texas. Another instance in point is the 1929 Texas emigrant labor agency law fathered by the representative from Carrizo Springs. Agitated by the activities of the patrol inspectors, south Texas interests as represented by the Winter Garden, South Texas, and West Texas Chambers of Commerce sought to check the drain on Texas labor principally through shipments of sugar beet fields of the North. First an occupational tax on "emigrant agents" was levied, to the amount of $7,500. Enforcement of this act was immediately enjoined by a Federal Court upon application of a Michigan beet-sugar company. Apprehending that the law might be declared unconstitutional on the ground of prohibitive fees, its sponsors had it repealed and new laws passed. These provide a state tax on emigrant agents of $1,000 plus a tax of from $100 to $300 depending on the population of the county in which they operate, and supervision by the State Commissioner of Labor Statistics. Emigrant agents are required to give bond that they will, upon written demand of the laborer, within thirty days after termination of the contract of employment, furnish return transportation. But an important proviso states that the laborer may waive his right to return transportation before the county judge at time of shipment.

The theory behind the laws was plainly stated by one of the sponsors:

> It is the same situation as where you have had a stream of water running through your ranch. If someone turns its source off you want to put up a dam to hold what you have. . . .

The same theory of holding labor away from more attractive opportunities was also used frequently in south Texas as an answer to the demands of organized labor for restrictive legislation:

> The labor unions are trying to stop Mexican immigration, but the Mexicans aren't competing with them at all; they aren't doing any work that the union men could be got to do. But in the North? Then they should stop them from going out of the four border states; they could stop them there as well as they can on the river here. . . .

The dominant view in the county is that "labor shortage" exists and that interference with fresh supplies of immigrant Mexican laborers bodes disaster. The concept, "labor shortage," is rarely defined, but its meaning to Dimmit County residents is revealed somewhat by their statements. A farmer said,

> We have two labor shortages every year—at transplanting and harvesting times. Three days of rain now would rot the onions. The scarcity of labor makes me pay what my crop is worth to get it harvested.
>
> We would be blowed up, without the Mexicans, or if they stopped immigration. If we had to pay Oklahoma prices for labor we could not exist. One dollar and a half [without board] is a high wage for us to pay.

One large landowner emphasized the need of more Mexicans for further land development, but thought the supply was adequate for present needs:

> We need plenty of Mexican labor if this [South Texas] country is to develop and make its proper contribution to the vegetable production of the nation. We have enough labor for the present area under cultivation but not for development.

Another stressed both further development and the flow of labor through this region and away from manual occupations:

> Yes, we must have a flow of labor. We need this for the development of new land for our intensive crops. There is a movement of our Mexicans north, and education of Mexicans takes them out of manual labor. We have got to have a class of people who will do this kind of labor. If we can't have the Mexicans it will stop all this development. . . .

It is clear, even from the statements of these men who wish more Mexicans, that there was no shortage of labor in Dimmit County in 1929. Despite the general loose but vehement assertions of the dire consequences of shutting off the influx of Mexicans, very few who were pressed for details of crop losses asserted so much as an occasional shortage, and the crop loss involved appeared then to have been an isolated rather than a general case. The prevailing wage level and assurances of plenitude in appeals to prospective settlers, furnish further evidence on this point, if it is needed.

The most emphatic claim of labor shortage which came to my attention was carefully checked and found to be an exaggeration. The details were as follows:

> This grower stated to me that on that very evening he had unexpectedly discovered that he needed a large number of Mexicans to go to work on the following morning. In great excitement he exclaimed:
> "If they stop Mexican immigration, we will be blowed up. I need 130 Mexicans tomorrow morning to pull plants. I am paying two Mexicans $5 each to get the other Mexicans. Yes, they will probably get them but look what it is costing me." The next morning there were by my count 70 men, women, and children engaged in pulling, packing, and loading plants. The last plants left the field about 2:30 P.M. The work, begun about 9:30 A.M., had been completed in approximately five hours by a little over half the number of laborers demanded.

Another farmer also preferred a flow of immigrants to paying transportation for Mexicans already in Texas:

> Yes, we need more Mexicans. I had to pay $50 to get my Mexicans out of Devine, Dilley, and Moore. If they came out of Mexico, I would not have to pay for them.

Frequently it was stated to the writer even by opponents of immigration restriction, that "We have had right plentiful labor." The manager of a large ranch, favorable to restriction, was emphatic in his statement, not only that no shortage existed, but that the labor market was glutted:

> I feel sorry for the Mexicans. The man who says there are not enough Mexicans has ten or fifteen acres of onions, and doesn't want to wait two days to harvest them. If they can't start the same day they want to, they say they can't get enough labor. We are overrun with hands. The Mexicans can't make a decent living. I could get 300 Mexicans in the morning just as easy as I could get fifty. Some of the town "farmers" say we need four times what we have, but they use them only a few days in the year. If they would handle it right, they now have more than they can feed. They may think they need more, but they don't feed them. We have to spread our work out now so they can have something to eat. . . . The Mexicans don't live they just exist. . . . They will come out nine miles from X for a job on which they will earn 80 cents. They starve themselves to save a few nickels to start hunting a new job. . . . They don't know when they are going to have a job. They come in absolutely hungry and you have to feed them up [with advances from the commissary]. . . . There is no need of dragging them into the country and starving them.

Figures of the Department of Agriculture corroborate the fact of a very large labor supply. The early loadings of onions to April 30 increased from 2,754 cars in 1928 to 4,151 cars in 1929 because of "larger supplies of Mexican labor. . . . In previous years it has been considered impossible to ship in excess of 125 cars of Texas onions daily, without demoralizing market conditions. However, during the last two weeks of April, daily forwardings generally ranged from 200 to 250 cars with a peak movement of 299 on April 18. Prices were low during this period and a few shipments were rolled unsold."

In some quarters "cheap labor" is a term of ill repute. When unskilled immigrant labor is desired, interested persons appearing before Congressional committees are usually careful—if necessary they are cautioned—not to ask for "cheap labor," but rather to deny that the desired labor is "cheap." In south Texas, such scruples are rare. Once, indeed, the adjective "cheap" was hastily withdrawn after its utterance. Now, on the contrary, the necessity of "cheap labor" is readily asserted without any of the sense of impropriety, economic, political, or moral, noted above. Said one grower,

> We have to have the Mexicans as cheap labor.

A land prospectus states:

> The cheapest farm labor in the United States is to be had in this section (close to the Mexican border).

There are two blunt statements, one by a real estate man,

> We would go broke on $2 a day labor. The land would go back to the cattle man.

and the other by a representative of a land development company:

> You have the Japs for cheap labor in California, I guess. We have to have the Mexicans for cheap labor. With the prices we get and tariff conditions and competition from other sections, we would be blowed up if we had to pay $2 a day for labor.

It is not without significance that during the hearings on the agricultural tariff in 1929, the customary argument for protection against foreign "cheap labor" was made on behalf of the onion growers by a representative from New York rather than from Texas. Yet one Dimmit County grower said to me,

> We have to go against onions grown by cheap labor in the Teneriffe Islands.

While the California anti-restrictionists have generally denied before Congress that Mexican labor is "cheap labor," the Congressman representing south Texas asserted what his constituents just quoted told me, viz., that they want and need cheap labor:

> Mr. Chairman, here is the whole situation in a nutshell. Farming is not a profitable industry in this country, and in order to make money out of this, you have to have cheap labor. You can not take it like any other industry and pay $5 or $6 or $7 a day and make a success of it. In order to allow landowners now to make a profit on their farms, they want to get the cheapest labor they can find, and if they get the Mexican labor it enables them to make a profit. If they have to pay a higher price for labor, there is a loss instead of a profit. That is the way it is along the border and I imagine that is the way it is anywhere else.

The advantage, and even necessity for cheap labor is the dominant economic philosophy in the Winter Garden district.

In the preceding pages, the term "cheap labor" has evidently referred to low-wage labor generally. Sometimes the term is used to mean "low-wage labor economical to its employer" or "low-wage labor paid less than others performing the same work." One grower recently from the northeast, with economy to the employer in mind, said:

> The company men and farmers here told us Mexican labor was cheap and plentiful. It's plentiful, but not cheap. A white man is better.

Another grower made a confused statement, asserting the superiority of white labor, admitting payment of less to a Mexican for the same work, and decrying the instability of white laborers even at wages somewhat above those paid to Mexicans.

> They're not cheap labor. I've had white men at $2.50 cheaper than Mexicans at $1.50. But one of my regular Mexicans is as good as any white man. I pay him $2. The white men you get at $2.50 don't usually stay very long.

An old settler cited the regret of the farmers at rising wages:

> Wages used to be 75 cents and $1 when we came out here [1911]. Now they are $1.50 and $2. Now the Mexicans drive tractors like a white man. We could not get along without the Mexicans. When we came down here, the southerners said to us, "There's no sense in you people coming down from the north and making dunces out of our labor by paying $2 a day." One said to me, "I don't want you paying over $1. I will send you some Mexicans you won't have to pay over $1." And he did. Now the farmers would like to kick the Mexicans' wages down, but they can't. . . .

Clearly, Mexican labor in Dimmit County is "cheap" both in the sense of "low-wage labor" and in that it frequently receives less than Americans receive for the same type and amount of work.

It is only natural that the growers observe apprehensively the "cheap labor" available to the Teneriffe Islands onion growers, and recall longingly the lower wages of the past, and of that part of the Old South from which the settler at Catarina next quoted came.

> Labor is high here. They tell me the Mexicans earn $2 a day. In the Mississippi delta we get twelve to fourteen hours out of the Negroes at this time of the year—from sun to sun, we pay $1.50.

But opinion of Dimmit County residents is by no means unanimously agreed that more immigrant Mexicans are needed. Indeed, from several viewpoints the belief is advanced that there are already too many Mexican laborers. The unsatisfactory market for onions in 1929 influenced some to express favor of the Box bill (which proposed a quota limitation of immigrants from Mexico to less than 1600 annually), who had not done so before. Said one grower:

> The abundance of labor is the farmer's ruin. He would be better off if he could hardly get any. There is no scarcity of labor here. The little grower is being crowded off the map. The big farmer beats the little fellow because he ships quicker. The market demands 100 cars of onions a day and we ship 300. There is no question that if labor was scarcer we could not ship such a volume of onions. The present situation will ruin us. The farmers would be better off here if we did not have so many Mexicans. . . .

Sometimes small growers expressed belief in a conflict of interest between them and the large growers. The following is illustrative:

> The bankers, and lawyers, and professional men who don't work want the Mexicans. If the Mexicans couldn't farm, the whites could and we would get better prices. X made $17,000 on onions last year and sat in town. Those men who don't do the work themselves want the Mexicans, but I wish they'd put every one of them back in Mexico. The big men want the Mexicans, but that's the way it always is; they run things against the small farmer.

Another small tenant farmer raising twenty acres of onions on halves, spoke in the same vein.

> Cheap labor is not a good thing for a small grower like me. If labor wasn't so cheap I could either get a job at good wages or work five acres of onions myself and make a profit. If there was no cheap labor, the bankers, merchants, and lawyers could not raise onions. If a man won't

work, it's better to have Mexicans, but for a man who works it is better to have no Mexicans.

Another put it briefly,

> It looks like people want more Mexicans so that they can raise more truck cheap. We are raising too much now.

And similarly,

> The big farmers want the Mexicans. They don't usually think they have anything in common with the small farmer. They don't feel on an equality with him.

The divided interest of a tenant farmer who also labors for others was plainly evident in the following quotation; his emotions were evidently mainly on the side of the laborer and small producer, though he could not quite overlook the fact that he paid wages as well as received them:

> The Mexicans are getting so they think a white man can't get a job picking cotton. They get a job and then 100 Mexicans come onto the field. A lot of white men would come down from the north and set onions, but they can't do it at Mexican prices, and we can't afford to pay more at the present prices of onions. At smaller acreages and better prices we could pay white men's wages. Nearly any working man would do any of this work if he got a white man's price. Millionaires are ruining the working man.

This group consciousness of the small farmers may not have been entirely derived locally, for some who expressed the view previously had been small farmers in north Texas or elsewhere. Large landowners, on the other hand, pointed out that even the small farmer uses Mexican labor, and that the larger growers bring it in for him:

> Even a small farmer needs the Mexicans to harvest his spinach, carrots, and onions, and to transplant onions.
>
> The small farmers are carried along on the skirts of the big farmers. We get the labor. We send trucks to San Antonio and elsewhere. We get it here a week or so before we need it, and advance the provisions, but charge them against them . . . when they go to work. Some leave us, and we are out that much; the small farmers will pay a cent or two more on their small acreage than we can, or want to, on our big acreage.

Several times, when sympathy with the Box bill was expressed, it was accompanied by the remark,

> I suppose I'm the only person in the country who has talked this way to you.

As a matter of fact, the view was expressed with surprising frequency, and more often on the farms than by farmers living in town.

In the battle of conflicting views on restriction of Mexican immigration, the question whether white men will or will not do the work performed by Mexicans is raised in Dimmit County, as elsewhere. A large grower presented in characteristic language, the view that he will not:

> The white men won't do the work on their hands and knees next to Mother Earth.

Others coupled with prevailing low wages the unwillingness to work of the whites (and Negroes). Said a large landowner,

> The white labor won't do this work. The Negro would not do it. He is getting $4 or $5 a day in towns. We are dependent on the Mexicans.

Another grower stated,

> We could not get whites to come in and clip at a price we could cover by selling.

And again,

> They work cheaper than white labor can afford to.

A land development agent also recognized the relationship between work and wages:

> The white people won't do the work and they won't live as the Mexicans do on beans and tortillas and in one or two-room shacks.

A Texas-Mexican said,

> Immigration officers have sent so many Mexicans back. What will the farmers do? The Spanish hands will work cheaper than the whites.

Of those interviewed in the Winter Garden district, only one person, a large grower near Eagle Pass, urged that whites *couldn't* do the work because they "can't stand the heat," but this assertion is not valid and was denied by those who do their own work.

The hand labor of Dimmit County is performed by Mexicans, and among the chief reasons for the absence of white labor are the character of the work and the low remuneration. White labor was not physically "displaced" here, for the farm labor supply was furnished by Mexicans from the beginning. Wages have been adjusted to standards of living of Mexicans, and rates attractive to Americans have never prevailed.

The result is the almost complete absence of Americans from this labor market. Their absence, in turn, gives rise to the opinion frequently expressed that "the Mexicans here are not competing with white labor." But this inversion of reasoning is recognized by the Chamber of Commerce of at least one town which actually advises American laborers to remain away because of the unequal competition in living standards:

> This is not a community for a man without money. That is due to the great supply of Mexican labor that we have. A man depending on common labor for the up-keep of his family cannot compete with them. Unless a man is a skilled workman or has a trade or profession, or is a good practical farmer with some capital as mentioned above, it is harder for him to get along here than in communities farther north or east. But to the man with $5,000 or more, Carrizo Springs offers a better opportunity than any other section in the country.

As noted before, when Mexicans rise above the lowest level, e.g., to become tractor drivers, they are frequently paid less for the same work than Americans receive. The exceptional occasion on which I found Americans doing the lowest grade of labor was also exceptional as to relative rates of pay. I met one white man who said he and his family had transplanted onions, and saw two white families, including girls, clipping onions. One of the latter was a tenant family, and the man of the other family was a trucker. The tenant said, "Of course, whites can do the work, and if more of them did they would make more money." Curiously, in this instance the whites were actually working for less than the Mexicans demanded. The latter had asked 8 cents a crate; the whites did the work for 6 cents and indicated that they were glad to get the employment. . . .

Significant of the attitude of the younger whites was the statement that a young brother chose a filling station job at $1 a day in preference to $1.50 on his father's farm. A young American in search of work replied to interrogations that he had never considered onion work; that the Mexicans were "best at that." And an old resident said, "the boys won't work. They loaf around town and burn up gasoline and spend their fathers' money, if any. They say that field work belongs to the Mexicans." Field labor has become stigmatized.

Some of the hand labor operations in truck crops are repetitive, and suggest the possibility of use of machines. This is true of both transplanting and clipping Bermuda onions. Indeed, a mechanical transplanter was used on about three acres in the fall of 1928, and on about thirty acres in 1929. Reports of its success are encouraging. A grower who has used them (and is interested in their sale) describes his method of operation:

> The machines plant flat (hand transplanting is on top of ridges), 3 rows at a time, require 3 hands to each machine, the regularity of the stand depends on the skill of the hands. I paid the hands by the hour, ran

two machines, and sometimes three, and had a foreman to look after regulating them, attend to oil and gasoline and direct the labor. I employed [at 15 cents an hour] boys and girls who were not earning 15 cents per hour by hand work. They averaged about 8 hours work daily. We never got in over 9 hours per day; more is too trying for them and they do poor work. They space plants 3½ inches in row, and rows can be spaced 14 inches to 18 inches. . . . After planting, I ran through with a three-row onion cultivator, threw dirt to the onions, and had my rows ready for irrigation. Just reversed the row-making practice in that rows were made after onions were in the ground. I did the same last year and liked the results. We had fewer weeds and better onions. . . . The machines averaged one-half acre per eight-hour run. . . . At 15 cents per hour per hand, my transplanting cost per acre by machine was $8 including pulling plants, labor, gas, and oil, but not including supervision, or overhead costs of the machine. Hand transplanting costs at 7 cents per row would have amounted to approximately $12 per acre. The cost of the transplanter is $295 f.o.b. Michigan.

The quality of work was reported to be satisfactory:

> We made better tonnage last year on the machine planted onions, but I think I have a better stand this year on hand work because there was so much labor we could force them to do good work.

Some growers were skeptical of the machine, following its 1928 demonstration. One declared he had investigated and believed it unsuitable, adding, "In agriculture it requires the human touch on the tool." But others were optimistic over its possibilities and even present advantage. The *ex parte* statement above, however, is given here not as the present writer's judgment of its practicability [a judgment he is not qualified to make], but because of the important bearing on the labor supply of even an approach to mechanization.

The abundance of labor and its low wage retard the introduction of machinery. Said one grower, "When labor goes to $2.50 a day, we will use the machine," and he wrote in December, 1929:

> While I have not seen the new one they have out this year, it is my understanding that it is very superior to the one they had last year; however, I do not believe that they have sold any, for the reason that we, again this year, have a big supply of labor.

As in northeastern Colorado where, because of peak labor demands for both thinning and topping of sugar beets, it was thought undesirable for the sake of the Mexicans to mechanize one operation alone, so in Dimmit County the same "make work" argument was advanced by a large grower,

An onion transplanter? My brother said it planted all right except it planted on the level instead of on the ridge, and we would have to irrigate by flooding instead of down the trough [but note that in 1929 ridges were made *after* transplanting]. Yes, we could do it. But we have to have the Mexicans around for harvesting anyway, so it's better to give them the work. Clipping machinery? Well, we'll wait until someone invents it. If they take the Mexicans away from us, then we'll have to use machinery or do something.

But another grower, previously quoted, who believes there is already a large surplus of Mexican labor said, "Onion transplanters will be cheaper than the Mexicans. But what will the Mexicans do?"

Generally, there was little consideration of aspects of Mexican immigration other than adequacy of labor supply, crop surpluses, or competition with American labor. A few persons, however, presented further analyses of problems involved, such as diversification of crops, stimulation of invention, competition with American tenant farmers. A merchant of northern origin, but twenty years resident in Dimmit County, said,

As an economic proposition there is nothing to cheap labor. It is just like the slaves before the war. There are no inventions where there is cheap labor. With fewer Mexicans there would be more dairies, etc. You could not convince the slave-holder that freedom was better than slavery. . . . The poor whites here can't ask for a better house, etc., because the landlords can get Mexicans who won't ask for more than $20 a month advances. If there were no Mexicans the landlords would fix their places up for the Americans a bit, buy paint, etc. When they can't get labor, they will get machines. Last year there were three or four home-made machines which worked fairly well transplanting onions, and they can also sow onions and thin them as well as transplant.

Different reasons were advanced for a similar attitude in a town not far from Dimmit County; it was atypical, and had drawn much fire from other business and agricultural interests in the region.

We have got about as far as we can with cheap labor. Our chamber of commerce can get only about 25 cents per capita, when the United States Chamber of Commerce estimates we should get a dollar, and we can't get any farther. Our merchants have no trading territory. Labor with $1.25 wages can't buy. Our lands of about 12,000 acres under cultivation are in the hands of about a dozen men. They live in hotels; they are not farmers; they are speculators in onions. The farms are practically uninhabited except for groups of Mexican laborers. I asked one of these men if we might show home-seekers his farm. He said he didn't want more people coming down here to raise onions in competition with him. What we need is more white farmers and more capital, and we can't go ahead until we get them. We don't need more cheap labor. We should not drive out our own labor in the North to provide ourselves with cheap labor here. It may make wages go to $2.50 a day, but in a year or two conditions will be adjusted. These Mexicans have large families, larger than the whites, and we will soon have plenty of labor from natural increase. We've got to educate the children. They are now holding back the progress of our children in the schools.

In a few instances, a non-economic reason—opposition to the immigration of foreigners—outweighed what the speaker believed to be their own economic interests. It is interesting to note that in the course of our conversations all three persons quoted below first expressed opposition to restriction of Mexican immigration, then opposition to immigration of foreigners, by which they meant Europeans or Asiatics, and finally, when the inconsistency of the two positions was suggested, said that their opposition to immigration was stronger than their desire for more labor. The farmer with whom the following dialogue took place began with an explanation of the need for Mexican labor and a protest against the Box bill.

> If they take away our labor it will knock the socks off us. The quota law against European immigration? Yes, there are too many foreigners coming in; they should be kept out. Then how about the Mexicans and the Box Bill? They ought to pass it. But it would knock the socks off you down here? Yes, it would hit us, but for the good of the country they ought to pass it.

A second farmer was perplexed by his dilemma, but preferred adherence to his "principles."

> Restrict immigration? I am opposed to European immigration; but I realize that if we get a good Mexican we like to keep him. I would vote to shut them out, although I realize we need them. My principles rule my selfishness, but I am kind of weak on that. We need them and they need us. We are sparsely settled here, and have not enough people.

At this point a neighboring farmer interjected, "I am for restriction of immigration of foreigners; there are more nationalities in San Antonio than I ever saw—dagoes, etc." It is curious, but common, to find in a community one-half or even two-thirds Mexican, as is Dimmit County, that the remote presence of foreigners in the country, particularly Italians, is resented, while the immediate presence of Mexicans, socially ostracized but economically desired, is accepted so unconsciously that the term "foreigners" does not seem to include them.

A real estate dealer, also a large grower of vegetables, in a Winter Garden town adjacent to Dimmit County, was evidently almost as perplexed as the second farmer quoted, but unlike him he conceded victory to his "interests" rather than to his "principles." In his office, in the presence of a number of people, he opposed restriction of immigration, yet advanced with disconcerting conviction several of the current arguments in favor of restriction. On another occasion, when we met alone on the street he concluded his statement frankly:

> It's selfish with us. We will fight restriction as long as we can; but it would be better for the United States.

Inquiry as to the attitude of Mexicans concerning restriction revealed diversity of opinion. A Texas-Mexican who knows his people thoroughly reported that "Most of the Texas-Mexicans think we have enough Old Mexico Mexicans; there isn't enough work." Another expressed a similar judgment, and indicated a hope that after restriction "wages would not be so low."

The attitude of Mexicans born in Old Mexico was influenced by knowledge of the plight of their countrymen who wished to immigrate. One of them said,

> Many are in positive misery in Mexico and seek only justice here and tranquility. They are not seeking high wages. Only it is a prejudice to us that they come and make wages lower. They say they go north where there are too many people, and become bandits. But here they are not bandits. The immigration officers send them back across the river, but they may kill three Mexicans, and two will still cross. They have no money, but they seek escape from misery in Mexico. If they take them back they will come again across the river. But it is harder to cross now than it used to be.

Another spoke in similar vein:

> Restrict immigration? No, we see the tears of the poor people who have no work in Mexico. The government doesn't want them to leave, but they have no work. If more come, we have a bigger town here, which is better. [Upon suggestion] Yes, if more come here, I won't get $2 a day; wages will go down. . . .

Dimmit County opinions of Mexicans as laborers exhibit the wide range observed both in Imperial Valley, California, and in the valley of the South Platte, Colorado. Some laud the Mexicans, as did an old cattleman and farmer:

> The Mexicans are fine laborers. You can tell them what to do and they will do it. Mexican cowboys are good. I would rather work Mexicans than Negroes.

One land agent said, "The Mexicans are good labor." Another praised them in similar strain, "Mexicans are obedient, and the best class of labor for this country." A farmer mingled praise of their honesty and loyalty with compassion for their low economic condition and their stoical acceptance of it:

> I have not lost one hundred dollars of the thousands I have advanced to the Mexicans. They will work. They are fine for what we use them. They are just barely keeping body and soul together. They are ragged, they are humble, they are loyal. The Mexicans take their meager share of this life and wait patiently and starve. I would rather see a Mexican get $3 a day if conditions warranted it. . . .

Others, however, spoke with less enthusiasm. The comments of a banker were particularly unfavorable:

> They will starve themselves before they will work. The consul comes out and tells them to get written contracts for everything, and to do this and that. They are Bolsheviks and want to run every deal they are in on. They will all sit down in the field, and not work if they hear somebody is paying a couple of cents more. You go out and either have to give it to them or fire them. Efficient? No, they are no good.

In similar vein a farmer said,

> Only the necessity for food makes them come down from their independence.

One of the few Americans in the county who uses Mexican share-tenants to raise cotton was unfavorably impressed with their financial integrity, complained of their chronic indebtedness, and cited the practice of assumption by the new landlord of the tenant's debt to the old:

> The Mexicans just walk off when they go too deeply in debt. They get sick and they quit every once in a while. . . . They are generally always in debt. Mine are always in debt. We pay them out when we take them over from somebody else to get them free. I paid $250 debt to get one Mexican, but this man has teams and is high class. I would not do it for a common *pelado*.

The preference common throughout the Southwest for contract work rather than day work was expressed by the next speaker:

> The Mexicans are just about like the Negroes as laborers. A few are good. Most of them aren't much good. They're good on contract work, but not on day work.

A dealer in building materials reported that unloading a car which at day rates had required a little over two days, was later accomplished at a contract price in a little less than a day by the same group of Mexicans. Another grower took a middle-ground position, saying,

> Some of the Mexicans are reliable, and others not. Some are pretty good farmers.

Those farmers who had been used to handling Negro labor frequently preferred the Negroes *as laborers,* although there was a general preference for Mexicans as members of the community. One such person from Missouri said,

> The Negroes are quicker and better workers than the Mexicans. The Mexicans are not good with teams.

The latter observation was heard frequently both in California and Colorado, and reflects the agricultural background of many of the Mexican immigrants. . . .

A Louisiana farmer indicated the natural preference of each person for the labor he best understood:

> I'd rather have niggers, but of course I've always worked them and am used to them. The Negroes demand and get more money [the Mississippi delta farmer quoted earlier reported the contrary] but they are worth it. They won't stay here because there are so few of them. The oldtimers here prefer the Mexicans.

Commenting on the method of handling the Mexicans he said,

> The worse you treat them, the more they do. You can't praise them like you can a nigger.

But another resident with considerable experience with both races expressed the opposite view.

> The Mexicans are social. They love a crowd. If there are only a few of them in a field you can just see the discontent grow and then they quit. The more in the field, the less likely they are to quit.
>
> The principal causes of discontent are the crop conditions and the owner's method of handling them. You can cuss a darky and he chuckles. If you cuss a Mexican it hurts his pride. The Mexicans pet fine.

This latter opinion was corroborated by a large landowner well liked by the Mexicans:

> You can't handle the Mexicans roughly and get them to work by cursing them. You get better results if you say to a man who is doing bad

work, "You will put me into bankruptcy and I won't be able to pay you Saturday," and then laugh; and they will do as you tell them.

And he added by way of praise,

The Mexicans are accustomed to subserviency.

An Oklahoma farmer with previous experience with Negroes expressed one of the most unfavorable opinions of Mexican labor:

I don't see how a horse could be so ignorant. They don't know anything when they arrive, and after a few years they get smart. If labor is scarce they will raise prices, and the more you pay the less they work. After they have made a couple of dollars they quit even in mid-afternoon.

The Negroes are better workers, although the Mexicans can do as well if they want to. They will lie to you. They will tell you they will come to work, and then will not come.

An old settler with the characteristic feelings of old Texans against Mexicans voiced a traditional view, similar to that of the Imperial Valley rancher who decried the uselessness of Mexicans who returned from Los Angeles wearing cloth-top shoes and carrying fountain pens:

There is a saying that if a Mexican wears *guarachas* [sandals] he is all right. If he wears shoes, he is tolerable, but if he wears boots and talks English, he is no good. . . .

The view that "the less you pay them the more work you get done" is common among south Texas farmers. The grower next quoted outlined the position in detail. Not knowing my identity, but suspecting my northern origin, he voiced doubt that I would understand the point of view:

I saw an article by a northern woman; she gave it to the farmers here pretty hard. Perhaps I'm talking to the wrong man; if you are from the North you won't understand. The Mexican is getting paid about four bits too much; he gets from $1.50 to $2 a day. He should get about $1. When he has a dollar in his pocket he won't work. You get more onions transplanted at 5 cents a row than you do at 10 cents. It's just the nature of the Mexican. He needs about $8 a week if he has a family, for clothes, shoes, and food. What a Mexican should be paid is just enough to live on, with maybe a dollar or two to spend. That's all he deserves. If he is paid any more he won't work so much or when we need him; he's able to wait around until we have to raise the price above what's legitimate.

Similar attitudes were exhibited by two farmers who said, "There's no use paying them more," and "We need them for their labor, for the same reason you need a mule."

In parts of south Texas talk of physical discipline of Mexican laborers by farmers is not uncommon. In Dimmit County, however, the statements of both Mexicans and Americans indicate that practically none of this method of handling labor is practiced there at the present time. One young farmer relating his experience with Mexican labor said,

> I kicked one down here who had been wasting water and fired him. The others laughed at him. He is the only one I have struck on this place. I should have just fired him, but I was mad. On another place [in another county] I had a fight with one bully and got him fired, and with one who was sleeping. I poured water and threw dirt to awaken him. I sent him in covered with mud, and the others laughed. They knew I was right. If any Mexican attacked me, the others would fight for me.

This was the only case of its kind in Dimmit County which came to my attention. But rumors and traditions of high-handed dealings between American farmers and Mexican tenants or laborers are in the air of south Texas. A Dimmit County landlord with an American tenant expressed it mildly when he said,

> Some people prefer the Mexican tenants because they can get out of paying them all they owe them. They just tell them they did not do the work right and tell them to go along.

In Dimmit County these dealings are mainly traditions of the past. A farmer of twenty years' residence there felt that the rising wages of Mexicans, which he regretted, were nevertheless just retribution for the past misdeeds of the farmers.

> In the early days of the cattle industry they used to shoot the Mexicans just like nothing. There is a man living in X now that has three Mexican graves around. The Texicans used to pay the Mexicans as little as possible and then try to cheat them out of that. But now the Mexicans have the upper hand, and as a community we have it coming to us.

The "shot-gun" settlement of which one hears, is a procedure by which the farmer drives his employee from the farm at the point of a gun, in lieu of financial settlement. I was informed of only one such recent case in Dimmit County. The official who was my informant pointed out also the moderating influence of the urgent seasonal demands for labor, and of the recent Raymondville peonage convictions.

> They have had their shot-gun settlements, but not in this county. They need the Mexicans too badly here—but we have had trouble with one man [in the county] over shot-gun settlements.

A Mexican working in Dimmit County when I talked with him, related a story of brazen chicane, which, had I not heard so much from both Americans and Mexicans in south Texas, would have seemed incredible. The man had been a cotton share-cropper in a neighboring county, and was waiting for the farmer to come to his Dimmit County ranch, in hopes that he might secure some legal aid against him there. This was his story:

> I rented on shares from a man at Hondo. I owed him $240 and my share of the crop was $380 [balance due $140]. He told me that the President—the big man in Washington—had sent a notice saying to send him any earnings of Mexican tenants, and told me to "vamos." I saw the sheriff here and he told me when the man comes to his ranch in this county to tell him. In this county the *dueños* [landlords] are good men.

The pressing need for Mexicans in certain seasons is indeed some protection to them. As was said by one grower who regretted that their wages are not higher,

> The Mexicans' only protection is that they are the only labor available, and you can't treat them too badly and hold them. The relations between Mexican laborers and American employers are fine, and are regulated under economic, not personal pressure.

Another grower cited a farmer who had refused to allow his Mexicans to remain on the farm in his labor house after the onion season. Word of this spread among the Mexicans, and the next season he was obliged to have another farmer secure and pay his labor, so they would not know they were working for him.

Sporadic, unorganized strikes are also efforts at protection. The record in the *Javelin* of a strike which took place some years ago shows not only how it was crushed, but also the temper of the farmers when inflamed by contemporary activities of the I. W. W. in agriculture:

> Onion clippers went on strike. Asherton Mexicans tried I. W. W. tactics —Got it in the neck.
>
> Some Asherton Mexicans got the idea that onion clipping was skilled labor, and that they ought to be fashionable and strike. Likewise they thought they had the onion growers where they couldn't kick. . . . The onion growers couldn't see the raise. They offered to come through with half the extra money, but the clippers said it was a whole loaf or no crust, and they were pretty crusty about it too. The onion men simply sent out for more Mexicans, and now the former clippers are in the soup, no money, no job, and no strike fund in the treasury.*

---

* April 27, 1912. There was some I. W. W. activity in the county in connection with its support of the Zapata revolution, led by Charles Cline, or Klein. See for example, *Javelin*, September 20, and November 28, 1913. Whether it had anything to do with local strikes I do not know.

Some years later again a potential strike was commented on by the editor of the *Javelin:*

> With the beginning of onion planting, there are a few Mexicans, mostly the ones who live in the county, begin urging a hold-up price. . . . *Javelin* would feel everlastingly disgraced were he to even countenance a scheme to defraud a peon of his wages, or to beat him down to less than it is worth, but the interest of the farmer should also be considered, and what the labor is actually worth to him. . . . Under such conditions, if a farmer is paying his transplanting force what the work is worth, and some copper fronted gentleman from the south tries to do a little I. W. W. propaganda among the working force, a pick handle would probably make a good lever to roll out the offender, or at any rate soften his views.

While opposing concerted action by the laborers and the wages which might result, three months earlier he had advocated concerted action by the farmers. Anticipating an ample supply of labor he proposed that

> . . . it would not be a bad idea for the onion and berry men to get to-gether and decide upon a fair and reasonable wage for the transplanting, and stick together on it. The *Javelin* would not for a moment stand sponsor to a plan for skinning the laborer out of his hire, but we would gladly as-sume responsibility for an agreement between the employers that would cut out the practice of bidding against each other, with the inevitable result that some of the fellows overpay. There will be labor enough to transplant all the crops, and at any rate, there would be just as many acres transplanted at a fair price as there would be at an exorbitant rate.
>
> What about it?

Similar attempts to adhere to an agreed price are still made, but the common complaint is that farmers themselves, especially the smaller men, do not hold to the agreement.

No general complaints of maltreatment by farmers of Dimmit County were reported by the Mexicans. Frequently they spoke warmly of their own employers, or of another in the vicinity, who was highly regarded among them. One contractor reported specific difficulties, but only one of them, the second, had occurred in Dimmit County.

> I know one farmer who chased a Mexican off his place with his pistol, and I know another who owed a Mexican now in this field $100, but did not pay, saying he was broke.

Another Mexican told of a difficulty which was remedied, and went on to express appreciation of the kindnesses shown by an American to his Mexican employee:

> One American did not want to pay his Mexicans. He said they did bad

work. The judge made him pay. The judge himself paid a doctor who came twelve times to the sick child of the Mexican who worked for him.

Another Mexican thought that the treatment received depended mainly on the Mexican himself, a view often expressed by Mexicans in south Texas:

> The farmers treat you all right. If a man is a *malo hombre* he gets *malo tratado*.

A temperate view was expressed by another who said,

> Most of the American employers are good men. There are some differences, and sometimes the farmers don't pay. Sometimes it is the fault of the Americans and sometimes of the Mexicans.

Most of the labor relations unsatisfactory from the point of view of the Mexicans, centered about wages, the importation of outside laborers, and the contractor system. Transplanting and harvesting onions, the major hand labor operations in the county, are usually performed on contract. Contractors are in almost all cases Mexicans.

Contractors work on different bases: (1) for a fixed piece price for the job, (2) a margin above the piece rate paid to the laborers, or (3) as supervisors by the day. This system was criticized by farmers, contractors, and Mexicans. Some of the farmers, as already stated in part, regard the contractors as representatives who organize their people and raise wages. In some cases this is probably true, but in many cases the contractor bids low in order to secure the contract. A resident who knows the farmers said,

> The Mexican laborers are fairly well organized. You can't go to individual families to secure labor as you do with the Negroes. You have to go to contractors. They get better pay than they would otherwise. Under the individual system everybody has some hands, but you may not be able to get any labor from the contractor if he has other work in progress.

An American contractor who, with a Mexican partner, handled from 100 to as many as 600 or 700 Mexicans explained the situation from his point of view, his chief difficulty arising from changes in rates after the contract was taken:

> Sometimes we take a contract at a fixed price. The trouble is that if someone else pays more, we may have to pay more; and if someone else offers more to our Mexicans, everyone in the field will stop until you pay it. Sometimes we make an agreement that the owner of the crop will meet current labor prices if they change. Sometimes we get paid by the day, and only oversee the work. I prefer the latter.

A Mexican contractor indicated the same difficulty, namely, the competition of contractors, particularly new ones, who cut prices, and the occasional non-payment of his men by the contractor. The latter was one of the grievances of the Mexicans who organized a union in Imperial Valley.

> Many contractors take contracts too low, so many Mexicans leave the contractor when others offer more. Then the contractor can't finish, and it takes two, three, or four gangs on one place sometimes. Here all the farmers pay. Some contractors do not pay their men, and go far away, to Mexico or other places. Many farmers pay their men directly; it is better. The contractors who are new take too low prices.

A group of Mexicans objected to bringing in outside Mexicans and to low wages; they answered some of the farmers' complaints against them, and some expressed complaint of the contractors who fail to pay their men, but, like the Mexican unionists in Imperial Valley, they showed no desire to abolish the contractor system.

> They say we live in a bad way. It is because we can't live better. The contractors come in here with other Mexicans from other places. The Americans pay them, and the Mexicans work, but no American would accept the situation [at the low wages]. It is all right for them to bring in other hands if there is danger of losing the crop, but the trouble is that it means less work for us.
>
> There is some trouble with the contractors. Sometimes they accept too little. Sometimes the contractor receives the money, but doesn't pay in full, especially if he is from other parts of Texas. They say it is because they don't have the money. The contractors accept too low prices in order to get the contract, and the farmer of course takes the low contract prices. Then the men can't make anything, and they strike. They say we won't work, but work is the only way we make our living. We recommend that the farmers pay a little more and give contracts to the Mexicans they know.

Another Mexican said,

> The Mexicans don't like the *contratistas* [contractors]. Last year three or four got their money and did not pay their men.

A large grower maintained what is undoubtedly true in the great majority of cases:

> The men get paid; if a farmer didn't pay, the Mexicans would all know about it very quickly. No farmer wants his check turned down by the bank when it is drawn to a Mexican, because the Mexican would think he was trying to cheat him, where a white man would understand a temporary shortage of funds.

This fails to recognize, however, the paramount importance of dissatisfaction over those relatively few cases in which the laborer is not paid.

At the beginning of the 1929 onion harvest, the farmers' side was stated by a large grower in these terms:

> Now we can go into the field and tell them what to do, and they will do good work; but in ten days when everyone is busy, they'll demand higher wages and tell us how it will be done. Of course the farmers themselves are partly to blame. They won't get together and all pay the same price, but they will offer a little more, especially the man with only a few acres, because it doesn't amount to much on a few acres, and he wants to get it over with.
>
> If the Mexicans would work ten hours a day when they were needed, we wouldn't need so many of them as we have now. But about one-third of them are not working. The Carrizo Springs Mexicans complained that we brought in Mexicans from Crystal City. At a meeting of farmers and contractors a farmer pointed out that the contractors couldn't guarantee completion of their contracts, and that sometimes local labor wouldn't work through the contract, so we have to bring in Mexicans.

The chief reason for failure to fulfil contracts, viz., higher wages paid elsewhere, has already been pointed out. There is also some truth to the statement that Mexicans do not always wish to work when work is to be done. As one Mexican acknowledged,

> Yes, the Mexicans don't always want to work. I have seen lots of Mexicans sit at home even when there was no complaint over the price paid in onions.

It is quite evident, however, from the statements of several growers that the labor supply is abundant, and that the necessity of bringing in additional numbers does not exist.

In the spring of 1929 the prevailing wages led to discussion among the Mexicans of the formation of a union, but the presence of outside laborers deterred them. As a local Mexican remarked,

> The Mexicans talked of a union this year, but didn't organize because many Mexicans come from other places, and they work cheaper.

Whether they actually do work for less than local Mexicans is open to doubt, but their presence undoubtedly did depress the wage level. The "home market" argument for employment of local Mexicans was also advanced by another Mexican who said, "But they take the work and spend the money away from here."

4.3

Unionism Among Southern Plantation
Sharecroppers, Tenants, and Laborers

STUART JAMIESON

All segments and social classes in American society felt the impact of the Great Depression of the 1930s, including southern black sharecroppers, tenants, and farm laborers. In earlier essays, William Ivy Hair and Lawrence Goodwyn examined the bitter conflicts in the 1880s between black Louisiana farm laborers and their employers and soon afterwards between black Texas Populists and their adversaries. In his study of labor unionism among twentieth-century American farm workers, Stuart Jamieson moved forward in time to study black Alabama farm workers in the 1930s. Jamieson related their behavior to larger economic and social processes, to the role of non-farm organizers among them, and to the violent responses to their efforts. His study, however, did not focus sufficiently upon the Alabama blacks themselves, and his quite traditional methods should be compared to those of Lawrence Goodwyn.

Stuart Jamieson, *Labor Unionism in American Agriculture*, U.S. Department of Labor Bulletin 836 (Washington, D.C.: Government Printing Office, 1945).

TENANCY AND DISPLACEMENT

The Plantation and Large-Scale Farming

The plantation based on sharecropping and share-tenancy as well as wage labor, has been the southern counterpart of the factory farm in California and other States. Fundamentally, both are large specialized and capitalistic agricultural enterprises which depend upon sizable numbers of seasonal workers for short periods each year to cultivate and harvest intensive cash crops. The lines between farm owners, tenants, sharecroppers, and wage laborers have long been fluid and uncertain in the Southern States. Where land ownership is highly concentrated, the distinctions between various categories of the propertyless become in many respects purely academic. The cotton plantation and the large commercialized farm differ primarily only in their methods of production, of financing necessary capital outlays, and of recruiting, maintaining, and paying their labor. The modern plantation scarcely differs even in these respects.

Cotton agriculture in the South during the last decade in particular has been adopting production techniques and labor relationships that give it more and more the character of California's large-scale farming. This trend, hastened by drastic cyclical and climatic changes, has generated landlord-tenant friction comparable to labor-employer conflict in other regions. The similarity in group relationships on the land in both instances would therefore justify a consideration of sharecroppers' organizations as part of labor unionism in American agriculture.

Sharecroppers and Laborers

Nominally the sharecropper is one kind of tenant whose income is, in part, remuneration for individual enterprise and assumption of risk. Extreme concentration of control and a high degree of supervision in the plantation system of the South in actuality give the sharecropper a status more like that of a farm laborer. Like the Mexican beet worker of Colorado, his work is closely directed by the owner, manager, or "riding boss," and his earnings, his hours of work, and the use to which he puts land, farm stock, and implements are all determined for him by his supervisor. The sharecropping system in the South was a means by which the plantation could make certain of an adequate labor supply at unusually low pay, after the Civil War had freed the slaves. In contrast to most other types of landlords in the United States, the southern planter had to assume almost all financial risk and control over farm operations in order to keep sharecroppers propertyless and dependent and therefore available at all times for work.

The South has been one region in America in which the concept of the "agricultural ladder" has never been widely accepted. The caste system, because of its clearly defined classes of well-to-do whites, poor whites, and Negroes, has precluded any frequent rising in the social scale. For the same reason, it has hindered the development of unions. Rigid social levels based on tradition and race have long prevented lower-income groups from acting collectively for their own material betterment. Landless farm laborers who organized for higher wages, or farm tenants who organized for written contracts and larger shares, met relentless suppression. This varied in degree from ridicule and social ostracism for promoting "racial equality," to extralegal violence by hooded and unhooded leaders of the community, among whom not infrequently were officers of the law. Laborers and sharecroppers, both white and colored, have been unable to protect themselves through political means. The poll tax in eight Southern States, in addition to school and property taxes and "Jim Crow" laws in many local communities, serve to disfranchise many lower-income groups.

Exploitation of sharecroppers and day laborers has been widespread on southern cotton plantations, because of the one-sided bargaining relations and the workers' lack of protection. Planters have been accused continually of charging croppers and laborers unnecessarily high prices at the plantation commissary, of charging exorbitant rates of interest for their credit, or "furnish," of paying them a lower price for their cotton than is received on the market, of misrepresenting the accounts, short-weighting the croppers on their share of the cotton, and overestimating their indebtedness. Not infrequently, through connivance between planters and law-enforcement authorities, sharecroppers appear to have been bound to plantations in a condition of peonage.

Planters and their advocates justified the prevailing modes of exploitation as their only means for survival, since the labor was inefficient and irresponsible, and farm income was on the average low. All these practices had been used so long and so commonly in the plantation system that they were for a long time accepted by both planters and croppers as an integral part of their relationship. Poverty and suppression, moreover, were not conducive to articulate protest or collective action. On the contrary, the enervating effects of long-continued exploitation fostered an apathy which precluded unionism. The older, more exhausted and depressed areas of Georgia, South Carolina, and Mississippi, where the economic and social status of Negro and white sharecroppers was lowest, did not produce the most militant movements. Such movements developed, instead, in the rich plantation areas of the Arkansas Delta and the Black Belt of Alabama, where sudden and drastic changes in the traditional planter-tenant relationship created hardship, unrest, and collective action. The changes were too rapid to allow for gradual adjustment or resignation to the new situation, and group dissatisfaction and discord developed. The attention of sharecroppers was turned to new and unfamiliar issues and injustices, and these in turn made them conscious of older deficiencies in the system which they had accepted as being almost in the nature of things.

Unrest, Mobility, and Conflict

Dissatisfaction and unrest among sharecroppers and day laborers on southern cotton plantations were usually expressed passively and individually. The most prevalent manifestation was a high rate of turn-over or individual mobility common to many unorganized groups. Arthur Raper and others estimated that, before the Federal Government initiated new agricultural policies during the thirties, typical southern tenant families, whether white or Negro, moved almost every 2 years. According to some authorities, personal discord between landlord and tenant, which often developed over the distribution of income from crop shares, was a major cause for mobility. Not infrequently such conflict culminated in lynching and other mob action. Sharecroppers had much less incentive to move during depression periods because of the greater difficulty of finding a "situation."

The increasing contact of the Negro sharecroppers with other social and occupational groups weakened the authority of the planter by lessening the dependency of his tenants. Rural Negroes who migrated in large numbers to industrial areas during the years of World War I made permanent contacts with people in localities having higher living standards and fewer restrictions for the colored race. Improved facilities of transportation and communication increased the mobility of croppers and laborers, and in periods of prosperity their opportunities for employment in other industries furnished an escape. A planter who was known for his violence or for mistreatment of his tenants sometimes found it difficult to recruit an adequate labor supply. The cropper, noting the prices advertised in newspapers or in stores of nearby towns and cities, became more aware of being short-paid for his cotton and overcharged at the commissary. Enterprising croppers on some occasions even hired attorneys for protection against usury or fraudulent division of crops and Government benefit payments.

Improved transportation and communication also made the plantation more subject to social and legal control from outside, and thus modified the more extreme forms of exploitation and intimidation. Lynching as an extralegal means of social control over Negroes attracted increasingly hostile public attention. By exerting strong pressure on the authorities, organized groups in the South, such as the Southern Women's League Against Lynching, during the past decade have reduced the frequency of mob action. Peonage also was more effectively prosecuted by Federal authorities in later years.

These changes had important effects on the Negroes' philosophies of race relations. Booker T. Washington's dictum of humble perseverance and avoidance of aggressive action that would cause racial antagonism has given way to the more militant doctrines of W. E. B. DuBois, as expressed in the policies of the National Association for the Advancement of Colored People. Many southern Negroes, seeing the weaknesses of both positions, turned during the 1930's to the broader programs of labor unionism, and, in a few instances, to revolutionary action. In the opinion of Prof. Guy B. Johnson of the University of North Carolina, these activities were the forerunner of a Negro movement to be characterized by new thought and leadership.

> The Scottsboro case, the Angelo Herndon case, the Alabama mine disorders, the sharecropper revolts in Arkansas and Alabama—these, although aided by "outside" white radical influences, are symptoms of the beginning of a new struggle for economic justice, a struggle which comes from the bottom and pushes upward. Eventually the various phases of the movement will strive toward integration, and a leader will be created.

The specific issues which led to organized conflict in the thirties arose suddenly and dramatically. They originated from the unprecedented displacement and migration of cotton tenants, who were uprooted from the land by severe depression conditions, by crop- and acreage-reduction programs sponsored by the Federal Government, and by the widespread adoption of power farming in place of hand labor.

Displacement

CONDITIONS DURING THE DEPRESSION.   Certain significant, though seemingly contradictory, changes in the status of southern farm operators took place during the years 1930–35; they indicated a further breaking down of the "agricultural ladder." The number of white and colored farm owners increased, many of whom were urban unemployed returning to the land, but they were concentrated in the poorer and already overpopulated hill farming areas where cheap land was obtainable. At the same time the number of farm laborers and unemployed in the Cotton States increased greatly. Of all operators, the percentage who were tenants declined for the first time since the Civil War.

Several steps may be seen in this major change. Displacement of Negro operators continued, as a long-time trend, but from 1930 through 1935 it was more than offset by an increase in the number of white farmers. The number of white and colored owners and "other tenants" together increased about 10 percent but the number of croppers altogether decreased about 8 percent. This decrease was concentrated in 4 States, roughly 28,600 croppers were displaced in Texas, 20,400 in Georgia, 9,400 in Arkansas, and 7,400 in Oklahoma. Changes in status for farm groups in other States were few and just about offset each other.

Although the total number of farms increased in every State in the country from 1930 through 1935, the number of 20- to 49-acre farms (which would include the typical cropper holdings) decreased in every Cotton State. The increase of "other tenants" was extremely small in Arkansas, Oklahoma, and Texas. Another indication of mass displacement or at least of a reduction in employment and income, was the decrease in cotton acreage, from 43 million acres in 1929 to 42 million in 1930, to 38 million in 1931, to 35 million in 1932, and to 29 million acres in 1933. According to Woofter—

> Disorganization of agriculture resulted in curtailment of operations by some planters and absolute cessation of planting by others between 1930 and 1932. . . . The result was a displacement of large numbers of croppers' families during these years. Rural youth, no longer able to get employment in urban centers and unable to gain entrance to the agricultural economy of the South, augmented the relief rolls.

Many of these relief cases were families who continued to live on the landowners' property. As Prof. Harold Hoffsommer pointed out—

> Although the conventional attitude of landlords and tenants was that the landlord was expected to "take care" of the tenant when the latter needed aid . . . there was evidence that many landlords were shifting responsibility to the relief agencies.

Relief, however, disturbed the relations between the planter and the croppers. Hoffsommer, in another study, found that where the croppers were dependent on the planters, about 40 percent of the landlords interviewed indicated that they opposed relief because of its "demoralizing effect." Specifically the planter feared that he would lose his control over the croppers, which was based on their personal dependence on him. The relief allowance would raise their standard of living so that they would refuse to bargain with landlords on the old basis.

The discord between the landlords and the sharecroppers was aggravated by the crop- and acreage-reduction program of the Federal Government's AAA. The hardships which this program imposed on southern tenants and sharecroppers provoked them to organize in self-defense. The secretary of the Sharecroppers Union of Alabama wrote on August 8, 1935:

> Wholesale evictions have taken place among sharecroppers and other tenants due to the acreage reduction under the AAA. The more than a million croppers, farm laborers, and other tenants that are landless, homeless, and starving as a result of the reduction program of the AAA are floating from place to place seeking farms to tend or be employed as wage laborers. (Letter from Albert Jackson, Birmingham, Ala., August 8, 1935.)

Literature of the Southern Tenant Farmers Union of Arkansas sounded the same keynote.

The various New Deal measures for agriculture—cotton plow-ups, rental for nonproduction, subsidies for soil conservation, loans of the Federal Land Bank and the Land Bank Commission—saved many plantation owners from bankruptcy. Federal emergency crop loans enabled many small owners and renters to produce crops. However, there was no commensurate service to the sharecroppers, except to those few who benefited from projects of Rural Rehabilitation and later the Farm Security Administration. Relief agencies, including the WPA and the CCC, were of real, though usually temporary, assistance to tenant families. On the whole, however, the AAA and other Federal farm policies merely accelerated the process of displacement which depression conditions had already made serious. For many sharecroppers, particularly the Negroes, the New Deal meant loss of work and income.

Benefit payments for acreage reduction at first were made directly to the planters, who often kept most or all of the money in payment for croppers' debts, real or imaginary. Many tenants and sharecroppers claimed that they never saw their benefit payments, because governmental agencies and private creditors were made joint payees. Provisions which were later written into the contracts, to assure justice to the sharecroppers, were in many cases shrewdly evaded or broken outright. New provisions were then made for paying the tenant directly. Many owners thereupon changed the position of their sharecroppers to that of wage hands (who were not entitled to the benefits) by the simple device of paying them a daily wage at the end of the week rather than advancing them food and clothes beforehand. Woofter points out that some displaced croppers were not actually driven off the plantation but were converted into casual laborers who were allowed to occupy their houses rent-free while they did odd jobs without the benefit of subsistence advances or crop agreements. The hardest hit were the Negroes. White families displaced 70,000 Negro tenants between 1930 and 1935, according to Raper. The dispossessed Negroes commonly became subtenant wage hands and casual laborers, the position they occupied in the years immediately following the Civil War.

MECHANIZATION OF AGRICULTURE.   The trend towards power farming in cotton was an even more dramatic and in the long run more important force than Government crop restriction in displacing tenants and sharecroppers. This development, in the opinion of Arthur Raper, is leading to "the emergence of large-scale mechanized farms in the most fertile areas of the Old South, and a type of peasantry in the hilly sections. Farm laborers working by hand and with one-horse plows on hilly fields cannot compete with power-driven machines on alluvial plains." (The South's Landless Farmers, p. 14.)

Tenant and labor displacement by power farming has been noted by Woofter, Power, and Cutler and others, and described by Paul S. Taylor. The use of tractors in cotton cultivation began on the outer fringe of the western Cotton Belt and penetrated into several important regions: the dry cotton area of Oklahoma and Texas, which is characterized by large farms, share tenants on thirds and fourths with managerial capacity, and a small proportion of Negroes and croppers; the Black Waxy Prairies of Texas (the outstanding producing section of the western Cotton Belt, with Negroes and white tenants and croppers in large numbers); the Delta region of Mississippi, Louisiana, and Arkansas; and the more fertile areas of the Black Belt of Alabama and Georgia, which are characterized by large plantations and a heavy concentration of Negro croppers on small family-acreage allotments.

The introduction of the tractor has had many results. The optimum size of farm units increased, and it became more profitable in many cases for owners to take over the acreage of their tenants and operate it themselves. Less labor was needed, except at the peaks of the chopping and picking seasons, because each worker could cultivate a much larger acreage. The difficulty of climbing the "agricultural ladder" was increased by the larger size of farms and heavier cost of capital equipment. Above all, the displacement of tenants and sharecroppers and their conversion into low-paid casual wage laborers were accelerated. Almost all the mechanized plantations in the Delta areas and the western region used day laborers to operate the tractors. Seasonal choppers and pickers employed for a few weeks each year were substituted for tenants and croppers supported the year round.

Displaced tenants migrated to cities to face unemployment and subsistence on relief and to furnish a pool of mobile seasonal labor. Mechanization disrupted the social structure of the plantation, particularly in making more casual and less personal the traditional relationships between landlord and tenant. Friction developed where the customary system of mutual dependence with its accompanying loyalties was destroyed and the urban employer-employee pattern of labor relations was established at a substandard level. The result, according to Taylor, has been—

an industrialized form of agriculture employing wage laborers, some of whom live on the farm, but many, if not most of whom live in the towns. Large-scale mechanized farming, with labor paid by the day or hour; labor swept off the land and into the towns from which it is drawn back only during seasonal peaks; labor which is increasingly mobile and without ties to the land—this pattern is incipient in the Cotton Belt. (U.S. Bureau of Labor Statistics, Serial No. R. 737, p. 20.)

FARMERS' AND SHARECROPPERS' UNIONS IN ALABAMA

Alabama has had perhaps the longest and most consistent history of militant agrarian unionism of any State in the southern Cotton Belt. Periodic group conflict was caused by several circumstances.

Alabama is sharply divided into topographically distinct sections, each carrying on different types of farming. About half way down the State lies a broad strip called the Black Belt, running in a general east-west direction just south of Montgomery. It is characterized by large plantations employing chiefly Negro sharecroppers. Several counties in the region have the highest ratios of Negroes to whites in the United States. The Gulf area lying south of the Black Belt is devoted to commercialized farming of special cash crops which are marketed and exported through such centers as Mobile. The third distinct area is the ridge or hill section in the northern half of the State. This is populated mainly by small-farm owners and tenants, many of whom are employed in coal and iron mines and steel plants in the Birmingham industrial area or in sawmills or lumber camps farther west.

Agrarian movements in Alabama represented incipient conflict between regions with contrasting patterns of land ownership, as well as between class or occupational groups within regions. Before the 1930's discord arose most frequently when small-farm owners and tenants of the ridge section protested against the encroachments of Black Belt plantations and urban business or commercial interests. Agrarian conflict in later years followed the attempts of plantation sharecroppers and day laborers to improve their position through organization and collective bargaining.

The militancy of its agrarianism has rested partly on the fact that Alabama has been the most highly industrialized of the southern Cotton States, with aggressive urban unions that have enrolled many rural Negroes and whites. The Birmingham area is a center of basic or heavy industries —mining, smelting, and fabrication of coal and iron and steel products. The requirements for jobs in these industries have tended to select a type of labor most partial to unionism. Perhaps more important, the jobs have been accessible to Negroes, many of whom migrated from surrounding farms areas. These workers have imparted to their rural kinsfolk the attitudes of urban labor, and this has conduced to unrest among the poorer farm population.

Farm Tenant and Labor Unionism in the Nineteenth Century

Agricultural labor agitation in Alabama and other Southern States began among freed Negroes immediately after the Civil War. They attempted to use their temporary voting privilege and their potential economic bargaining power to improve their material position. Negro labor unions were organized in many centers and sought to obtain agreements guaranteeing certain standard wages and working conditions, security of tenure, and opportunity for land ownership. These they proposed to win through legislation, if possible, and through strikes and demonstrations, if necessary.

This movement was defeated throughout the South by organized planters and dispossessed gentry who regained political power and destroyed the measures designed to protect labor. County associations were formed to protect planters' interests by setting maximum-wage scales and acting as courts of trial to enforce contracts drawn up by their members. Extralegal vigilante organizations, like the White Camelias and the Ku Klux Klan, functioned when economic and political pressure alone was insufficient to ensure absolute control.

The final victory of white supremacy was achieved in 1874, and the initiative in labor and agrarian movements had to come henceforth from whites in northern Alabama who were not under the immediate domination of the large plantation interests. Efforts were made to organize both urban and rural workers and small-farm operators in the Birmingham industrial area and adjacent agricultural sections. Branches of the Agricultural Wheel and the Farmers Alliance in the late eighties attempted to unite across occupational lines and to some degree across racial barriers. The more radical elements among organized farmers joined forces with urban unions affiliated to the Knights of Labor and formed a Union Labor Party. The Alliance in nearby Georgia, ignoring racial divisions, organized Negroes and attempted to protect them from violence and intimidation from white planters.

Collapse of these organizations in Alabama and other Southern States followed their decline throughout the country. The Alliance in Alabama suffered much internal strife because it included such diverse groups as Black Belt planters, small hill farmers, industrial union-labor elements, and Negroes.

FARMERS UNION OF ALABAMA IN THE 1930's. During the 1930's a branch of the Farmers Union was organized in Alabama. This organization of small-farm operators, devoted primarily to establishing cooperative enterprises, had risen rapidly and then declined during the early decades of the twentieth century. When it was revived in Alabama during the thirties its character was somewhat changed. Its locals in northern hill counties and in counties in or near the Black Belt organized both white and colored laborers and sharecroppers as well as independent farm operators. As a result, in some localities the organizations were more like farm-labor unions than associations of proprietors. Several locals, and to some extent the State organization itself, finally came under the control of left-wing labor organizers.

The Farmers Union developed strongly in counties adjacent to the Birmingham industrial area, among small part-time owners, tenants, and laborers. Urban industrial unionism was probably the chief influence in its growth. Since many farmers in this region had worked in the past in mines and steel mills, they had seen the tangible economic results of collective action. Olive Stone pointed out that—

> North Alabama members of the Farmers Union had the advantage over southern Alabama of cooperation from industrial workers. Whole counties were solidly organized into unions, from coal miners to washwomen, from preachers and teachers to hod carriers. Merchants who would not respect the "union label campaign" and buy according to union prices were boycotted, and farmers refusing to sell through union channels were isolated through the merchant boycott.

The Farmers Union, following the example of some industrial labor unions, organized Negro farm owners, tenants, and laborers (though there were few of these in the northern counties where the union was strongest). At its peak, according to one former official, it had some 75 colored locals with about 500 dues-paying members. Twenty of these were in Bibb County and the others were in Tuscaloosa, Marion, Walker, and Shelby Counties.

The Farmers Union of Alabama became more like a labor union in form and character during the mid-thirties. The State convention, in December 1936, drew up an ambitious program of cooperation with urban trade-unions, and planned to expand its organization and improve conditions among Negro and white tenants, sharecroppers, and day laborers in cotton. The resolutions that were adopted expressed the interests of wage workers as much as proprietors.

The divergent interests of the various geographic and occupational groups within the union caused administrative difficulties. During 1937 the union, as described in more detail below, agreed with certain farm-labor organizations to exchange some members in order to have greater homogeneity. These arrangements were made chiefly through the influence and organized pressure of left-wing members in the farm group, backed by urban industrial unions of the Birmingham area. They provoked opposition from some of the established leaders of the Farmers Union. The State secretary-treasurer in a communication to the Union News, organ of the Walker County Central Labor Council, in the spring of 1937 charged that—

> The Communists are breaking into our ranks, the leaders of the tenant farmer and other so-called farm union organizations. Clyde Johnson of Birmingham (ex-organizer of the Sharecroppers Union) and W. M. Martin (provisional president of the Farm Laborers and Cotton Field Workers Union, No. 20471, A. F. of L.) are the leaders, and they are getting good-meaning men to endorse their organization. Therefore the officials of the true Farmers Union have been placed in a position that we must take action against them at once. . . . The Walker County Union in session at Jasper has endorsed this labor organization, not knowing that Johnson and Martin are trying to put their organization ahead of the true union and are using this Farmers' Educational and Cooperative Union of Alabama as a cat's paw to put their RED stuff over with. (Union News, April 15, 1937, p. 6.)

Farmers Union locals in several counties—Bibb, Winston, Fayette, Franklin, Marion, Tuscaloosa, and Shelby—nevertheless, had all voted by July 1937 to affiliate to the C.I.O. through its newly established State Industrial Union Council. The two groups were drawn closer together by the increasing employment which small farmers were finding in the strongly unionized mining industry during the recovery period of the late thirties.

The Farmers Union of Alabama declined rapidly in membership during that period. In most counties it apparently depended upon a substantial labor membership, and upon the support of the urban labor movement. By 1940 it still survived only in industrial areas, including Walker, Andoga, Bibb, Shelby, Blunt, and Franklin Counties, and in farming areas having commercialized trade relationships with urban shipping centers, particularly Baldwin County in the Gulf area.

Origin of Sharecroppers' Union of Alabama

The most dramatic rural organization in Alabama during the thirties was the Negro farm workers' and tenants' Sharecroppers Union. This was one result of the Communist Party's organization campaign among southern Negroes, which also gave rise to such incidents as the celebrated Scottsboro case, the Angelo Herndon trial, and the numerous mine "disorders" in the

Birmingham area. Although initiated by "outside" white radical influences, these incidents were, nevertheless, symptomatic of underlying unrest and antipathy in the established relationships between the whites and Negroes.

The Communist Third International in the late twenties launched its program for mobilizing for revolutionary action the most exploited elements in capitalist countries. This was carried out in the United States through the Trade Union Unity League, which concentrated on organizing unskilled industrial mass-production workers and agricultural tenants and laborers who had been ignored hitherto by the American Federation of Labor. Special attention in the Southern States was paid to cotton-plantation sharecroppers (particularly Negroes), to textile workers, and to laborers in mines, smelters, and steel mills.

The most lasting successes in Alabama were in the Birmingham industrial area. A long and bitter history of race conflict arising from job competition, wage cutting, and strikebreaking was ended finally during the thirties when industrial unions under white domination began admitting Negroes to membership. The new labor movement met hostile legislative restrictions and violent suppression from employers and law-enforcement authorities. These tactics in the long run served to unify still further the labor interests of Negroes and whites and to strengthen the influence of Communist organizers. Much the same labor policy in regard to the Negro was continued after the Trade Union Unity League had been dissolved and its affiliates absorbed into the A.F. of L. and C.I.O. unions. An official of the United Mine Workers in Birmingham reported in 1937 that—

> We have completely unionized several of the mines here. We have both white and Negro members and they are learning to work hand in hand. The bosses tried to scare them with "social equality" stuff and with dynamite and machine guns, but they have stuck together. The Negroes are our best members. They were desperate. The union helped them, and now they are ready to fight and die before they see the union broken up. (Guy B. Johnson: Negro Racial Movements and Leadership in the United States, p. 69.)

Conservative whites in Birmingham admitted that the psychology of colored workers was changing, and complained that the Negroes were getting "uppity."

The doctrines of unionism found ready response among Negro tenants, sharecroppers, and laborers, who were undergoing severe hardships during the years of depression. It is difficult to judge whether the burdens of depression which fell so heavily on the cotton-growing areas of the South were especially severe in Alabama, and whether sharecroppers suffered more in this State than in others. Prof. Harold Hoffsommer in a study of 1,022 Alabama farm households receiving relief during 1933 estimated that in 89 percent of the years spent at sharecropping, the net economic outcome for this group was either to break even or to suffer a loss. He concluded that the so-called financial loss to the sharecropper was largely a decline of social or occupational status and an increased dependence upon landlords, since in most instances the sharecroppers had no finances to lose.

THE CAMP HILL AFFAIR, 1931.   The first local of the Sharecroppers Union (S.C.U.) was organized in Tallapoosa County in 1931, before Federal Government relief and crop-reduction programs had been introduced. Early in the year the Trade Union Unity League's official paper, the Southern Worker, reported receiving a letter asking that an organizer be sent to Tallapoosa County, Ala., to help the debt-ridden sharecroppers and renters of that area, who were burdened with mortgage foreclosures and ruinously low prices for their produce. Apparently the movement first took hold among tenants above the bottom rungs of the "agricultural ladder," in the section of the county which most resembled the plantation Black Belt area in farm values, tenancy, and racial composition of the population. Its proximity to Birmingham influenced the attitudes of the rural Negroes. Local men who had been to and from that city in search of jobs or who had worked in the coal mines of northern Alabama spread union doctrines among family members, friends, and acquaintances on the land.

The actual direction of the movement originated from Communist Party headquarters in Birmingham. Local authorities claimed that secret meetings were being held under the sponsorship of Negro and white agitators from Chattanooga. Literature of an "incendiary nature, designed to stir up race trouble between white landlords and Negro tenants," was reported distributed. The organizers, according to the Birmingham News of July 20, 1931, were urging Negro laborers to demand "social equality with the white race, $2 a day for work, and not ask but 'demand what you want, and if you don't get it, take it.'"

The reactions of the local community to these developments were duplicated many times in the South during the following years. A union of tenants, croppers, and laborers was by its very nature a threat to the plantation system. In seeking to release these groups from dependence upon the planter and to give them a voice in renting and sharecropping contracts, the movement was "revolutionary" and treated as such. Not only was the plantation system being menaced, but the biracial relationship of social classes was also being upset through the Negro's "getting out of his place." Hence the union soon faced violent suppression from growers and local authorities, aided by other resident whites.

Trouble first broke out openly on July 16, 1931, when the county sheriff and deputies broke up a meeting held to protest the Scottsboro convictions. At another meeting held the following night a Negro who was standing guard was reported to have shot and wounded the sheriff. A manhunt was started by the chief of police of Camp Hill (Tallapoosa County), and when authorities arrived at the Negro's house they found it barricaded and held by armed colored farmers. In the ensuing exchange of shots 1 Negro was killed, 5 were wounded, and 30 were later rounded up and imprisoned in the county jail.

Metropolitan newspapers emphasized the racial aspects of the sensational outbreak. The Birmingham News described it thus:

> This little community [Dadeville, the county seat] had the appearance Friday of an armed camp. . . . During the night the constant crackle of rifle and shotgun fire in the wooded slopes near Mary, Ala., recalled nights in No Man's Land. . . . All available men, armed with sawed-off shotguns, rifles, pistols, and other types of firearms, patrol the highways and search the fields. . . . Few Negroes are visible on the streets or in the fields. . . . It is estimated there are 600 white men under arms. (Quoted from Dadeville, Spot Cash, July 23, 1931, p. 4.)

The local newspaper, the Dadeville Spot Cash, vigorously denied these statements and charged Birmingham papers with misrepresenting the facts. It played down the incident, asserting that not more than 20 men were deputized and that very few more were armed. In an editorial it praised the coolness of the local population during the emergency:

> Both races did their part nobly and patriotically. . . . Both races displayed the spirit that characterizes a great people. . . . Particular praise is due to the colored citizenship of this part of the county for their conduct during the excitement which lasted for about 2 days. . . . [They] left it to the law to take its course. (Spot Cash, July 23, 1931, p. 2.)

THE REELTOWN AFFAIR, 1932. Suppression did not kill unionism among sharecroppers but drove it underground. Meetings were held secretly and local units were kept small in size. No further outbreaks occurred for more than a year, and the S.C.U. grew quietly. By the spring of 1932 it claimed 500 members, most of them in Tallapoosa and Chambers Counties. Organizing activities continued under the direction of the Communist Party headquarters in Birmingham, where city police were currently busy breaking up meetings of the Committee of the Unemployed and other such groups. Newspapers stressed particularly the "subversive" nature of the movement. A letter, reported to have been sent from the party headquarters to one Sharecroppers' Union local in Tallapoosa County, received wide publicity:

> The question should be the day-to-day agitation of all the comrades, not only in this local but in all the locals. Do not hold meetings in empty

houses. Do not face the lights of cars, and do not use flashlights. Never walk in too large crowds.

Never take action with arms before notifying us, unless it is impossible to get out of a trap without fire. If ever the meetings are run in on by the sheriff or other officers, don't attempt to hold the meeting next day or night, or that week.

Another outbreak accompanied by loss of life occurred in the county in December 1932, when the union came to the defense of a leading member, Cliff James, against whom a writ of attachment had been served by a deputy sheriff. James previously had been denied credit by merchants, and his landlord, to whom he had been making regular payments with interest until cotton dropped to 6 cents a pound, refused to allow him to defer a year's payment. James refused to give up his workstock when the writ of attachment was served. Union members claimed a deliberate effort was being made to ruin the leading organizers. When the sheriff and several deputies came to seize the property, they found armed Negroes barricading the house. In the ensuing combat, the sheriff and two deputies were wounded, while one Negro was killed and several others were wounded.

Mob action and violence far surpassing that of the previous year followed. Mobs invaded the houses of several union members and were reported to have shot, killed, and beaten several Negroes. Posses of more than 500 men went on a manhunt, tracking down Negro union members in the woods where they were hiding for safety. Sheriff Young, in an interview, stated that he did not know how many Negroes had been killed in the battle and the subsequent 4 days of rioting.

Popular metropolitan newspaper accounts again wrote sensationally of "race war" and "red violence," while the local Dadeville Herald played down the incident. That paper denied that the trouble was primarily an interracial clash, stating that "had the Negro James and his companions been whites, it couldn't have been handled differently. Sheriff Young and his deputies are to be commended." An editorial dated February 29, 1932, stated:

> Both our officials, including the sheriff and his deputies and all officers of the law, also our Negro citizens and the masses of our white people, are to be commended for the cool manner in which in two instances they have let uprisings pass.

Local and metropolitan papers both agreed that "agitators" were responsible for the incident. The attitude of the Birmingham News in an editorial dated December 22, 1932 (p. 8), was perhaps typical:

> The deplorable affair in Tallapoosa County is an example of what comes of the activities of Communist agitators in preying upon ignorant Negroes in these times of unrest and stirring up bitterness among some of them.

Only the Birmingham Post, according to John Beecher, in one editorial recognized the deeper causes of the conflict:

> It would be exceedingly superficial to regard the disturbance between Negro farmers and sheriff's deputies at Reeltown as a "race riot." . . .
>
> The causes of the trouble are essentially economic rather than racial. The resistance of the Negroes at Reeltown against the officers seeking to attach their livestock on a lien bears a close parallel to the battles fought in Iowa and Wisconsin between farmers and sheriffs' deputies seeking to serve eviction papers.
>
> A good many farmers, ground down by the same relentless economic pressure from which the Negroes were suffering, expressed sympathy with the Negroes' desperate plight, although thoroughly disapproving of their resistance to the law. (John Beecher: The Sharecroppers Union in Alabama, pp. 130–131.)

The rank and file were surprisingly persistent in spite of the forceful suppression of the union and the arrests of its most active leaders. Members and sympathizers poured into the county seat at Dadeville before dawn on the day set for the first trial of those arrested. When they filled the courtroom and overflowed into the square, the judge postponed the hearings. Care was taken on the second day to block the highways to town and to pack the courthouse with whites beforehand. The Negroes came, nevertheless, along bypaths and across streams and ditches. They demanded to be seated, and the judge requested the whites to clear one-half of the courtroom for them. The trial resulted in sentences of several years for those convicted.

Avoiding any outward signs of collective action, the S.C.U. continued to grow secretly despite the temporary crippling in Tallapoosa County. By the spring of 1933, according to its spokesmen, the union had some 3,000 members, including a few white sharecroppers, and had extended its influence to other counties. Expansion of rural and urban unionism in the South was encouraged at this time by financial support from the Garland fund. A philanthropist who had inherited a large fortune donated money to establish and maintain a southern organizing committee, designed to promote the work of "progressive organizations" in the South.

The Sharecroppers Union began to give more attention to collective-bargaining tactics, as new issues created friction and unrest. Federal Government programs for rural relief and for crop and acreage reduction were special sources of contention. In a survey of Alabama plantations in late 1933, Professor Hoffsommer found that sharecroppers had small financial profit from the AAA, because in 60 percent of the cases the money had passed on to the landlords. He concluded that planters were apprehensive of any Government program, whether for relief or rehabilitation, that promised to bring independence to sharecroppers and laborers and thus to threaten the whole plantation system. Landlords insisted that they have control over the granting of relief.

Some improvement in the position of Alabama sharecroppers and farm laborers was claimed during 1934. The State statistician reported that "the supply of farm labor is 97 percent of normal against 115 percent last year, while the demand this year is 74 percent of normal against 61 percent last year." Farm wages in Tallapoosa and nearby counties, however, remained at $15 per month without board. The local Director of Rural Rehabilitation complained that landlords were trying to have their crops subsidized indirectly by getting their tenants on relief.

The Sharecroppers Union in the fall of 1934 called its first strike. About 500 cotton pickers in Tallapoosa County struck for a wage rate of 75 cents per hundredweight. Organized sharecroppers and laborers refused to go into the fields unless they were paid the union rate they demanded. When they were threatened, they pleaded sickness. They won demands in a few local areas, spokesmen reported.

Organization in the Black Belt

In the mid-thirties the Sharecroppers Union of Alabama shifted the center of its activities to Lowndes, Montgomery, and Dallas Counties, in the Black Belt lying south of Montgomery, the State capital. The farm structure in this area was one of large plantations employing mainly day laborers, in contrast to most of Tallapoosa and Chambers Counties in the northeast Piedmont area, where smaller farms were operated by tenants and croppers. Sharecroppers and tenants in the Black Belt had been displaced in large numbers by mechanized farming methods and Government crop-restriction programs. A steadily growing proportion of plantation labor was being done by casual wage workers who found intermittent employment at seasonal jobs. The S.C.U. under these changed conditions became concerned primarily with the wage rates paid for the two chief seasonal jobs of cotton chopping and picking, rather than with the terms of leasing or crop-sharing over the year.

The union found that the task of organizing the Negro in the large plantations of the Black Belt was easier than in the smaller holdings in eastern Alabama because of homogeneity of the labor and the close contacts among workers on each plantation. They were more subject to attack and intimidation, however, since they lived in compact groups under the domination of individual planters. Strikes for higher wage scales were broken with violence and finality by a combination of landlords, managers, and overseers, and local law-enforcement officers.

The Sharecroppers Union of Alabama claimed 10,000 members by

1935. In the spring of that year it called a strike of cotton choppers in an attempt to raise wage rates throughout five counties. Approximately 1,500 workers were reported to have held out for almost a month for a basic wage of $1 per day. Compromise wage increases were won in several sections. According to union spokesmen a "great wave of terror broke out against the strike," particularly in Dallas County. Two white organizers, it was claimed, were arrested, and were beaten by a mob after being released.

Union organizers were intensely active during the summer of 1935 in cotton and other agricultural industries of Alabama. The employees of several dairies in the Birmingham milkshed area during July struck in protest against wages reported to be as low as $1 per working day of 15 hours. A federal labor union was organized by the strikers and affiliated to the A.F. of L., and plans were made to extend the union to the Montgomery area. Several thousand seasonally employed shrimp fishermen and part-time farmers along the Gulf Coast were reported organized in federal labor unions in such towns as Biloxi and Gulfport, Miss., Delacroix and Morgan City, La., and Bayou and La Batre, Ala. They claimed substantial gains in earnings after a prolonged strike of several months during the summer and fall of 1935.

The Sharecroppers Union, now having central headquarters in Montgomery to direct activities in the Black Belt region, prepared for a general strike in cotton picking over several States. Union spokesmen by this time claimed 12,000 members, 2,500 of these being scattered throughout Louisiana, Mississippi, Georgia, and North Carolina. Organized cotton pickers formulated demands for $1 minimum wage for 10 hours' work and $1 per hundredweight for cotton picking, as well as provisions for room, board, and transportation. The S.C.U. sought a "unity agreement" with the Southern Tenant Farmers Union, which at the same time was preparing for a similar strike in Arkansas and Oklahoma.

A strike was called in August 1935 to implement the union-wage demands throughout six counties in southern and eastern Alabama. It began on August 19 on one large plantation in Lowndes County, where the pickers were attempting to raise the wage rate to $1 per hundredweight in place of the prevailing 40 cents. The planter called for aid from County Sheriff Woodruff and his deputies. The strike spread to other plantations in spite of arrests of local union organizers and a formidable show of arms.

The struggle soon developed into a miniature civil war. The Montgomery Advertiser claimed that Communist organizers were employing force and intimidation, even to the point of using guns to "ambush" cotton pickers who refused to join the strike. Authorities claimed that white organizers from Montgomery were breaking Federal law by placing unmailed mimeographed literature in mailboxes, warning Negroes that they would be killed if they returned to work in the fields. Violent means were used to suppress the strike. Local newspapers reported at the end of August that "with the Federal, State, county, and city authorities cooperating in the hunt for Communist organizers, officers said they were confident that agitators would be apprehended if they continued long in this vicinity."

Union spokesmen on the other hand claimed that their members had to arm themselves in self-defense. Local authorities were charged with encouraging illegal mob action to break the strike. The union secretary stated that Sheriff Woodruff organized a gang of vigilantes for "night riding," breaking into strikers' homes, kidnapping and beating them in an effort to terrorize them into returning to work. A delegation of union officials traveled to Washington to protest these incidents to the Administrator of the AAA. They listed 20 strikers who were beaten or flogged and 6 who were killed (including 3 known local union members and 3 unidentified bullet-riddled bodies of Negroes reported found in swamps near Fort Deposit and Calhoun). A local postmaster was charged with illegally opening mail addressed to farm hands and sharecroppers as a means of identifying union members for the authorities. The Alabama State Relief Administration was charged with allowing relief workers to be transported in Government trucks from Montgomery to Black Belt plantations. There they were paid 50 cents per hundredweight for picking cotton, though they continued to receive relief from the Government. To counteract this move, union organizers attempted to extend the strike to relief workers in Lowndes, Montgomery, and nearby counties. This failed because of what the Montgomery Advertiser termed "drastic steps taken by delegated authorities to quell the spread of Communist doctrine and literature."

Forceful suppression limited the effectiveness of the strike to a few localities. The union reported in September that most strikers in Lowndes County had finally been forced to return to their plantations to pick cotton at 40 cents per hundredweight. The union secretary in a later report, however, claimed that the total income for cotton workers for the season was increased by approximately $40,000 as a result of the strike, and that wages had been raised in counties adjoining the strike area. Wages were reported increased from the prevailing 35 and 40 cents up to 65 cents per hundredweight in the vicinities of Burkeville and Lowndesboro in the southern part of Lowndes County.

The union had been established longer and had more members in Tallapoosa, Chambers, Lee, and Randolph Counties northeast of Montgomery. The strike began in scattered localities of this section during September, as the cotton crop became ready for picking. Though not so large and well organized as in the Black Belt, the strike met with less hostility and violence from the community. In Lafayette (Chambers County) 65 relief workers sent out to replace the strikers all quit work after 3 days. Union spokesmen claimed that in many places small farmers, both white and colored, supported the strikers with food and shelter.

Cotton sharecroppers throughout the South won temporary gains during 1935 and 1936, partly as a result of the strikes and the agitation against AAA on the part of the Sharecroppers Union of Alabama and the Southern Tenant Farmers Union of Arkansas. Late in 1935 the Federal Government announced that it would make cotton benefit payments for the following year directly to tenants instead of to landlords. The new contracts also provided that the sharecroppers' portion of total benefit payments to planters was to be raised to $25 out of every $100, instead of the previous year's $15.

Relations with A.F. of L. and C.I.O.

The chief interest of the S.C.U. during 1936 was to affiliate itself to larger farmer and labor organizations. It sought to organize Negro and white farm operators (sharecroppers, tenants, and small owners) and Negro and white farm laborers into separate but cooperating unions. The circumstances in which the S.C.U. operated made it difficult to conduct simultaneously activities benefiting both wage hands and farm tenants, since their needs were different. According to Clyde Johnson, former organizer, there was a growing tendency for tenants and small owners to dominate all locals; thus the wage workers were in a disadvantageous position.

The Sharecroppers Union was finally dissolved and its farm-operator membership was transferred to the Farmers Union of Alabama after much negotiation and numerous conferences between the two groups. The Farmers Union in turn released its labor membership to a newly organized Alabama Agricultural Workers Union, and an ambitious organization campaign was planned for both unions.

The Alabama Agricultural Workers Union early in 1937 received a charter from the A.F. of L. as the Farm Laborers and Cotton Field Workers Union No. 20471. By early spring it claimed a membership of more than 10,000 through the acquisition of wage laborers from the S.C.U. and the Farmers Union. It called a conference of agricultural workers in Birmingham during March to fix wage scales for farm labor in Alabama. The union planned to "popularize the scale throughout the State, utilizing every possible channel to make this scale known and to get public sentiment behind it." In line with farm-labor union policy in other States, the F.L.C.F.W.U. sought the cooperation of various farm organizations and urban trade-unions to establish a State-wide agricultural workers organizing committee.

More than 100 delegates from branches of the F.L.C.F.W.U. No. 20471 attended the conference together with fraternal delegates from the Alabama Farmers Union, the United Mine Workers, the National Association for the Advancement of Colored People, and kindred organizations. William Mitch, president of District 20, U.M.W., and former president of the Alabama Federation of Labor, promised the new union the "full support of the labor movement of this State." Standard wage scales far above the prevailing rates were endorsed for farm workers: $1.50 per day for cotton chopping, $1.25 per hundredweight for cotton picking, and $1.25 per day for general farm labor.

The F.L.C.F.W.U. No. 20471 was absorbed into the newly organized United Cannery, Agricultural, Packing and Allied Workers of America of the C.I.O. a few months later. Little was done toward meeting the announced farm-labor union objectives. The U.C.A.P.A.W.A.'s most important activities were carried on in other States, while in Alabama the C.I.O. was chiefly interested in organizing the steel industry in the Birmingham industrial area.

The U.C.A.P.A.W.A.'s most important gains in Alabama were won in northern and northeastern counties. As a result of a national agreement signed in Minneapolis in December 1937, between the Farmers Union and the U.C.A.P.A.W.A., branches of the two organizations in Alabama cooperated more closely. Together they directed a campaign to encourage tenants and sharecroppers to vote on the crop-control plan of the AAA, hitherto under the domination of larger planters.

The U.C.A.P.A.W.A. reported 4 locals in eastern Alabama by March 1938, and by late summer it claimed 17 locals with a total of 1,000 members. These organized sharecroppers late in 1938 successfully agitated for work relief divorced from the control of local plantation owners.

This was the last activity of the rural unions in Alabama. The national U.C.A.P.A.W.A. organization was forced to reduce the budget drastically because of business recession and loss of union revenue. Unionizing campaigns were restricted largely to metropolitan areas having important agricultural processing industries. U.C.A.P.A.W.A. organizations of farm laborers in Alabama and other States were abandoned.

4.4

Class War in Minneapolis, 1934

IRVING BERNSTEIN

In two scintillating syntheses (*The Lean Years* and *The Turbulent Years*), the labor historian Irving Bernstein detailed the history of organized and unorganized labor in the 1920s and the 1930s. Central to these decades was the Great Depression of 1929–1940, and the responses during this difficult decade by unorganized industrial workers (many of them first- and second-generation immigrants) to new labor organizations and, in particular, to the C.I.O. unions. Among the many strikes and lock-outs during the depression years, few were as dramatic or important as the Minneapolis truckers' strike in 1934. In this narrative account, as in other places in his two-volume study, Bernstein skillfully related the dispute between the workers and their employers to the changing contours of New Deal politics. The reader should give careful attention to the roles ascribed to leftist organizers and to the Minnesota governor and other local, state, and federal officials.

Irving Bernstein, *The Turbulent Years* (Boston: Houghton Mifflin Company, 1969), pp. 229–30, 231–52. Reprinted and footnote omitted by permission of the publisher Houghton Mifflin Company. Copyright © 1969 by Irving Bernstein.

Minneapolis in 1934 was ripe for class war. The town, like its twin, St. Paul, had run downhill. "The city of Minneapolis," Charles Rumford Walker wrote, "is a man in his late thirties who made a tremendous success at twenty-five." Its most prominent building was the high-rise Foshay Tower; but Wilbur B. Foshay's utility empire had gone bankrupt in November 1929 and Foshay himself had been sent to Leavenworth for fifteen years. The city's imperial role on the stage of the Northwest was now history. This had depended upon a quadrumvirate of industries—railroads, agriculture, timber, and iron ore, all now in serious trouble. The Panama Canal had undermined the Twin Cities as a transportation hub. Agriculture had staggered in the twenties and then collapsed in the early thirties; the Farm Holiday Association was now running sheriffs off foreclosed farms and the flour mills were moving out of town. The lumber industry had migrated to the Pacific Northwest; Minnesota's "cut-over" counties were bankrupt. With the severe reduction in steel output, there was little demand for the iron ore of the Mesabi Range. "Minneapolis," *Fortune* reported, "has outgrown the Northwest, from which it must live. . . ."

It had continued to grow by importing the displaced labor of the region—jobless railwaymen, farmers, lumberjacks, miners, and their families. In the spring of 1934 almost a third of the population of Hennepin County consisted of the unemployed and their dependents. Wages, low since the end of World War I, fell sharply during the depression. Textile workers earned $6 to $7 a week, upholsterers 25¢ an hour, warehousemen $9 a week. Truck drivers, who worked from 54 to 90 hours weekly, received between $12 and $18. Some were paid off in bruised vegetables.

Violence was a way of life in the Twin Cities. St. Paul had long rivaled Chicago as the crime center of the United States. The Citizens' Alliance, Minneapolis' belligerent employers' association, had not hesitated to use force in smashing union labor. A great kidnapping ring based in St. Paul stole off with the wealthy. John Dillinger was soon to shoot his way out of a St. Paul apartment. "If you want someone killed," *Fortune* advised, "inquire along St. Peter Street." . . .

Floyd Björnstjerne Olson, the Farmer-Labor governor of Minnesota since 1930, was the hero of the poor and the enemy of the rich. Measured by any yardstick, he was a phenomenon. In addition to possessing extraordinary skill with the English language on the hustings, Olson was fluent in Norwegian, Swedish, and Yiddish. His political genius had welded a winning political combination of those historically polar groups—the farmers and the workers. Olson was, doubtless, the farthest left of any man in high station in America. "I am not a liberal," the governor told the Farmer-Labor Association in 1934. ". . . I am a radical. . . . I want a definite change in the system. I am not satisfied with tinkering."

One change Olson certainly wanted was the unionization of labor in Minneapolis. He wanted to erase the city's reputation for the open shop and to undermine the Citizens' Alliance, which he detested.

The Alliance had been formed in 1908 allegedly to promote industrial peace. Its real purpose was to prevent the organization of labor, and its means included espionage, propaganda, planting stool pigeons in unions, hiring thugs to beat up labor leaders, and tampering with grand juries. A. W. Strong, a boiler stoker manufacturer, was the dynamo of the Alliance and he had 800 Minneapolis employers to back him up. "The businessmen are organizing and preparing for a showdown with Labor," Lorena Hickok wrote Harry Hopkins on December 12, 1933. "You find old friends ready to fly at each other's throats. . . . The Citizens' Alliance is getting into the show."

Because of the effectiveness of the Alliance, organized labor had not gotten far in Minneapolis. The case of the International Brotherhood of Teamsters was typical. This union had 800–900 members, mainly in separate locals of milk, ice wagon, local cartage, and other specialized drivers. In addition, it had General Drivers Local 574, a miscellaneous group with fewer than 200 members. This union had been chartered by the international in 1915 or 1916 and existed by virtue of a handful of closed-shop contracts with small firms anxious to obtain union labor business. Nothing whatever was remarkable about 574 except its charter, in which jurisdiction was so loosely drawn as to allow an industrial form of organization. This was odd for the unindustrial Teamsters, whose president, Dan Tobin, was presently a vociferous leader of the craft unionists in the deepening split within the AFL. And this charter was the magnet that drew the Dunne brothers and their followers to 574.

The Dunne brothers had made a family Odyssey through American labor and radical movements in the first part of the twentieth century. All six were active unionists and four were among the earliest Communists. Their father was an Irish immigrant laborer and their mother a French Canadian, both devout Catholics. The boys were raised in Little Falls, Minnesota, and attended parochial school. One day, as they were studying for first communion, the eldest, William F. ("Bill"), read to the others from a novel of Victor Hugo, borrowed from his grandmother's slender library. The priest seized the profane book, tore it to pieces, and preached a sermon to the class on the evils of worldliness. The Dunne brothers were expelled and the family disgraced. The boys became rebels.

Bill joined the Socialist Party in 1910 and entered the union movement as an electrician in British Columbia. During the first war he moved to Butte, Montana, where he led a violent metal trades strike and became the dominant figure in the local labor movement. He took the Butte Socialist Party into the Communist Labor Party in 1919. In the twenties he rose to very high position in the Communist Party of the United States. His expulsion as a Red from the American Federation of Labor was the high point of its 1923 Portland convention. He was an editor of the *Daily Worker* and American "ambassador" to the Comintern in Moscow. While never entirely comfortable as a disciplined Communist (the party expelled him in 1946), in the great split within the movement in the late twenties Bill Dunne chose orthodoxy with Stalin.

His younger brothers—Vincent Raymond ("Ray"), Grant, and Miles—elected heresy with Trotsky. Ray, everyone recognized, outshone the others because of his dedication and brilliance as a revolutionary. Born in 1891 in Little Falls, he was largely self-educated. About 1905 he migrated to Montana and became a lumberjack. He soon joined the IWW and was arrested in California for making a Wobbly speech. In 1908 Ray moved to Minneapolis, where he made his living principally in the trucking industry, at first driving a team and later a motor truck. He joined the Communist Party immediately following its creation. Between 1921 and 1933 Ray worked for the De Laittre Dixon Coal Company in Minneapolis, shoveling coal, driving a truck, as weighmaster, dispatcher, and even superintendent. The De Laittres found him an exemplary employee, offered him stock in the business, which he rejected, and indulged his vigorous activities in behalf of his political beliefs. Other Communists in Minneapolis were Carl Sköglund and Farrell Dobbs, both coal yard workers.

Following the world-wide split in the Communist movement, James P. Cannon and Max Schachtman called the first convention of the American Trotskyists in Chicago in May 1929, which formed the Communist League of America, Left Opposition of the Communist Party. Among its approximately 100 founding members were a dozen from Minneapolis, including Ray, Grant, and Miles Dunne, as well as Sköglund.

Ray was short, slender, and, excepting his keen eyes, unprepossessing in appearance. But his mind was quick and sharp and he was physically fearless, inspired the loyalty of his followers, and had a genius for organization in a military sense. In 1933 a subsidiary of the Ford Motor Company acquired the De Laittre coal yard and fired him for political activity. Dunne decided that the time had come to unionize the coal workers. If he had been a Stalinist, like his brother Bill, Ray would have put the union in the dual Trade Union Unity League. But this had been a central issue in the division within world Communism. As Cannon, the leader of the American Trotskyites wrote, "Despite the great conservatism, the craft-mindedness and the corruption of the AFL leadership, we insisted . . . that the militants must not separate themselves from this main current of American unionism. . . . The task of the revolutionary militants . . . was to plunge into the labor movement as it existed and try to influence it from within." Thus, Ray Dunne was led to the Teamsters and to the generous charter of Local 574. By one of those coincidences of history, the key man in the Minneapolis Teamsters, Bill Brown, international organizer and head of the joint council, welcomed Ray along with his brothers, Sköglund, and Dobbs. This was not because Brown was a Trotskyite; in fact, he was a Farmer-Laborite who supported Olson (Ray Dunne detested the governor). Rather, Brown was a militant trade unionist who felt the moment had struck to organize Minneapolis and that the existing union leadership was not up to the job. In Brown's judgment, it called for a Ray Dunne. But the latter was to lead 574 into the climax of its history while neither he nor his fellow-Trotskyites were officers of the local.

Ray Dunne began in the industry he knew best—the coal yards. The timing was right: the men were restive because of low wages and long hours, Section 7(a) had stirred interest in organization, and demand for coal was at its peak during the winter season. Since the employers categorically refused to deal with the union, Dunne expected and prepared for a strike. A map of the Minneapolis coal yards was drawn; picket captains were chosen and given mimeographed instructions; and cruising picket squads were set up. On February 4, 1934, 700 workers walked out at 65 of the town's 67 coal yards. The industry, it was said, was "shut as tight as a bull's eye in fly time." The employers, taken completely by surprise, capitulated within three days and granted recognition to Local 574.

Everyone realized that the coal strike was only a preliminary skirmish and that the major battle would be fought in the general trucking industry. Minneapolis, almost more than any other city, was strategically dependent upon the motor truck because it was the distribution center for the Northwest.

Dunne, capitalizing on 574's decisive victory in the coal yards, at once pushed for unionization of drivers and helpers. Again, bad conditions and expanded interest in unions made organization easy. The union conducted Sunday night forums climaxed by a huge rally at the Shubert Theater. By early spring of 1934, 2000 to 3000 men had signed up. On April 30 Local 574 served its demands: the closed shop, shorter hours, an average wage of $27.50 a week, and premium pay for overtime.

The Citizens' Alliance now stepped in to stiffen the backs of the trucking employers. In a strategy session at the West Hotel late in April a spokesman for the Alliance told representatives of the eleven major trucking firms that it had smashed the 1916 drivers' strike at a cost of $25,000 and that it could do the job again inexpensively. Shortly, the Alliance formed a much broader organization named the Minneapolis Employers of Drivers and Helpers. On May 7 this association categorically rejected 574's demands and its chairman, H. M. Harden, announced that the central issue was the closed shop; his members would never agree to an abridgement of the liberties of the individual workman. The union promptly withdrew its demand for the closed shop and offered to arbitrate wages. The employers refused to bargain. Brown announced that 574 would stop "every wheel in the city." Mediation efforts by the Regional Labor Board and the governor collapsed over the employers' unwillingness to deal with the union. On May 12 the membership of 574 voted overwhelmingly to strike the trucking industry and the walkout began on May 15, 1934.

Ray Dunne with the advice of Cannon, who flew to Minneapolis from the Trotskyite central office in New York, laid plans for war. The union rented an old garage at 1900 Chicago Avenue and converted it into a multipurpose strike headquarters. The office became the dispatching center. Four telephone lines brought messages on truck movements from picket captains stationed all over the city. They were written out and relayed to the dispatchers, Ray Dunne and Dobbs. They, in turn, ordered cars out over the loudspeaker by number and assigned men to them from a pool of hundreds of strikers who remained at headquarters. "Calling car 20. Wanted a driver and a helper. . . . Calling Danny. We might as well announce right now that we can't call husbands unless they have been away four nights running. Wives, remember that picketing is no grounds for divorce." The dispatcher gave the car picket captain secret written orders and he reported back at the end of his mission. When the strike was three days old, the police tapped the telephone wires. Thereafter messages were sent in code. A low-wave radio picked up police instructions. A union motorcycle squad of five cruised the streets 24 hours a day to report on trouble spots. The motorcyclists were under orders not to engage in direct action themselves. Pickets were posted on some 50 roads leading into the city with instructions to turn back trucks without union clearance papers. An internal guard was kept at headquarters to maintain order and watch for stool pigeons. Four sentries armed with tommy guns guarded the surrounding area from the roof.

The main section of the garage became an auditorium in which about 2000 people assembled nightly for speeches and entertainment. The overflow—said sometimes to reach over 20,000—was handled outdoors by a public address system. The car-wash section was whitewashed and converted into a kitchen with a dozen stoves. Here two chefs from the cooks' union directed 120 women in preparing and serving food around the clock. As many as 10,000 people—strikers and their families—ate here daily. Another wing of the garage became a hospital where two doctors and three nurses were in attendance. Finally, 15 mechanics in the shop kept about 100 trucks and squad cars in repair.

This operation was costly and was financed in large part by contributions—$2000 from the milk wagon drivers' local, lesser sums from other unions, and $500 from Governor Olson. The Farm Holiday Association contributed food to the commissary. But it was an extraordinarily effective strike machine. Excepting the unionized ice, milk, and coal wagons, hardly a truck moved in Minneapolis. The central market, the city's strategic transportation pivot, was shut down.

For the first few days a deceptive calm prevailed in the city. There was virtually no violence and the large fleet operators kept their vehicles off the streets. Local 574 enjoyed the backing both of other unions and of much of the public. It also won the support of a few students at the University of Minnesota, notably Dick Scammon, the towering son of the dean of the medical school, who was to do picket line duty, and Eric Sevareid, who left the university to cover the strikes for the *Minneapolis Star*. This support was encouraged by the local's moderateness in the aborted negotiations as well as by the obstinacy of the employers, now reaffirmed by their rebuffs to new mediation efforts of the Regional Labor Board and the governor.

On the fourth and fifth days the mood changed. The press carried ominous stories of a prospective food shortage and farmers protested the shutdown of the public market. A mounting chorus of statements by newspapers and employers denounced "Communists capturing our streets." A mass meeting of businessmen created a Committee of Twenty-five "to lay plans to move trucks through the picket lines if necessary" and to form a "citizens' army." Mayor A. G. Bainbridge and Police Chief Mike Johannes offered their support.

The employers' offensive opened on Saturday, May 19, in "the Battle of *Tribune* Alley." A stool pigeon and *agent provocateur,* James O'Hara, had been planted inside 574 headquarters and had won the confidence of the Dunnes. About 10 o'clock that night O'Hara took the microphone, called for several trucks, ordered them filled with both men and women, and dispatched them to the alley alongside the *Minneapolis Tribune* building. When the vehicles were inside the narrow area, police and special deputies sealed the exits and beat the people in the trucks with night sticks and saps. After treating the wounded, the union armed its pickets with lead pipe, bannister spokes, baseball bats, and the booty from a highjacked load of clubs manufactured by Clark Woodenware Company for the Citizens' Army.

The employers now established their own military headquarters at 1328 Hennepin Avenue, complete with barracks, commissary, and hospital. They recruited businessmen, doctors, lawyers, insurance agents, clerks, students from the University of Minnesota, and scions of socially prominent families. Many were under the impression that they had enlisted only to preserve order in the town; others knew they had been recruited to break the strike.

Whatever else divided them, both armies agreed that the public market would be the battleground. At dawn on Monday, May 21, the police and the Citizens' Army occupied this area, presumably in order to insure the movement of trucks. Alfred Lindley, a socialite sportsman, appeared in jodhpurs and polo hat. An advance party of pickets gradually worked its way between the police and the forces in mufti. When this was accomplished, strike headquarters ordered out the main body of pickets. They had gathered in two groups, one at the Central Labor Union and the other at 1900 Chicago Avenue. The former, 600 strong, marched into the market in military formation, four abreast, each armed with a club. The Citizens' Army seems to have lost its morale at this moment. Shortly, the second group arrived and the pickets surrounded the police. Over a period of several hours the pickets made occasional sallies to separate individual policemen. Then the police drew their guns. The strike leaders had anticipated this. A truck loaded with 25 pickets was ordered to drive into the police at high speed in order to break them into small groups in which use of firearms might be dangerous to their own forces. This is precisely what took place and the market became a melee of hand-to-hand fights in which the pickets had the advantage of numbers. The casualties consisted of three or four pickets and about thirty policemen, none dead on either side. No trucks had moved.

But this battle had been inconclusive and there surely must be another. Chief Johannes was determined to clear the streets; the employers adamantly refused to deal with the union; Local 574 would prevent truck movements at any cost. The newspapers on Tuesday morning, May 22, announced that produce houses would ship perishables. Would the trucks move? A crowd of over 20,000 gathered in the market to find out. Radio station KSTP broadcast the battle throughout the state as though it were the Minnesota-Iowa football game.

The immense crowd and the inherent tension in the situation made calculated strategy impossible for either side. For a time the two armies quietly faced each other. Then a minor incident broke the calm. A merchant moved several crates of tomatoes before his shop. A picket seized one of the boxes and heaved it through the plate glass window. This shattering of glass set off "the Battle of Deputies Run." Vicious hand-to-hand fighting broke out in the public market and the adjoining streets. The police did not use firearms. The pickets, more numerous and better armed with clubs, baseball bats, and pipe, won control of the market place within an hour. The fighting then spread over the city as the pickets pursued the disintegrating police and Citizens' Army remnants. Sporadic outbreaks took place until late evening. The battle had been a complete and decisive victory for the union. No trucks had dared to move. The union had taken control not only of the market but also of the streets of Minneapolis. That night, it was said, traffic was directed downtown by pickets rather than by policemen.

The casualties had been heavy, especially among the members of the Citizens' Army, two of whom were killed, notably C. Arthur Lyman, vice-president of the American Ball Company and attorney for the Citizens' Alliance. About 50 persons were wounded. That night, according to *Fortune*, "members of many of the first families of Minneapolis met in houses on Lowry Hill and hysterically talked of fleeing the city." There was no need because peace of a sort was soon to break out.

Governor Olson, by threatening to send in the National Guard, persuaded both sides to accept a truce, first for twenty-four hours and then for another twenty-four, during which the employers agreed to move no trucks and the union to halt picketing. Collective bargaining of a fashion proceeded at the Nicollet Hotel. Since neither negotiating committee could bear the sight of the other, each was closeted separately, mediators trotting back and forth with proposals and counterproposals. On May 25 an "agreement" was reached. In fact, it was issued as an "order" of the Regional Labor Board, but representatives of 574 and the employers' association had given their advance consent. It was notable for calculated ambiguity in which agreement on language disguised disagreement on substance.

This "order" provided for the termination of the strike and the re-employment of all persons on the payrolls as of May 1. Each employer was to "adhere to and be bound by" Section 7(a), which appeared in full text. This, presumably, was in lieu of union recognition and, given the uncertainty of the law and the history of the Citizens' Alliance, meant that 574 would be recognized only if it had the power to compel recognition. The employers agreed not to discriminate against union members, to respect seniority in hiring and laying off, to abide by NRA code hours, and, failing agreement on wages, to submit that question to arbitration by a seven-man tripartite board. Section 8 of the order, which was written by the governor himself and was to gain a certain notoriety in Minneapolis, defined the bargaining unit: "The term 'employees' as used herein shall include truck drivers and helpers, and such other persons as are ordinarily engaged in the trucking operations of the business of the individual employer." If 574 and the association were to disagree, as they soon did, over who these "other persons" were, that question would go to the Regional Board for determination.

On Saturday, May 26, trucking operations resumed in Minneapolis. The unknowing sighed with relief; those who were knowledgeable held their breath for they knew that peace could hardly last. The central issues had been postponed without being settled. The employers had no intention of either generally raising or arbitrating wages, and they obstinately refused to recognize 574 as agent for their "inside" workers or even for their drivers. The union, obviously, would not survive unless it forced these questions to a showdown. If its Trotskyite leaders had been inclined to show hesitancy here, the Stalinists would have been pleased to leap into the breach. The Communist Party denounced the Board's order as a "sell-out" by 574 to the Citizens' Alliance. Bill Brown replied, "The Stalinists have not only discredited Communism out here; they've discredited the mimeograph machine."

Thus, both sides prepared for the second war. The employers and the police profited from their humiliation in May. The Citizens' Alliance, it was said, raised $50,000. A propaganda barrage of paid ads and editorials filled the metropolitan newspapers and the radio waves. The charges were that 574 had broken the agreement, that the drivers were satisfied with their conditions, that Minneapolis was being ruined, and, above all, that the Dunne brothers and their followers were red Communists plotting revolution and the establishment of a Russian soviet in the city. Here an attack by Dan Tobin in the *International Teamster,* calling the leadership of 574 communistic, served as ammunition. Chief Johannes asked for a virtual doubling of the police budget to hire 400 added men, to maintain a training school, and to provide weapons—machine guns, rifles fitted with bayonets, steel helmets, riot clubs, and motorcycles. The union's newspaper advertised: "FOR SALE: One half bushel basket of special deputy badges—very slightly used."

Local 574 perfected the war machine that had performed so efficiently in May. A forty-day food supply was put in. To allay disaffection among farmers, the union arranged with the Farm Holiday and Market Gardeners' Associations to allow growers to drive their own trucks to a market in a vacant lot in town. The Communist League's top echelon migrated into Minneapolis: Cannon for grand strategy; Schachtman and Herbert Solow for journalism; Otto Oehler to organize the unemployed on the Toledo plan; and Albert Goldman as legal mouthpiece. The union had earlier launched its own newspaper. When the strike began, the *Organizer* became a daily, a new departure in labor journalism. It was said to have a circulation of 10,000 and actually to make money. The paper was written with vigor and wit, as in Mike's letter to "dere Emily":

> Here i am at strike head¼ an' its plenty hot. These here bosses we got in town keep yellin' in the papers that communism and payin' 54½ c an hr is one an' the same thing. Well, if thats what it is I guess I'm a communist an' I expect most evry one in the world except a small bunch of pot bellyd and titefisted bosses must be to.

On July 5 an immense parade and mass meeting were staged to show labor and farmer solidarity. Two airplanes zoomed overhead with "574" painted on their bodies. Members of many unions and farm organizations marched over the eighteen-block route from Bridge Square to the Municipal Auditorium. The end of the procession was just leaving the square as the grand marshal, Alderman Hudson, dismounted from his white horse at the auditorium. The meeting, addressed by AFL and farm leaders, was described as the biggest in the history of Minneapolis.

The decay of the May 25 agreement proceeded rapidly. Strikers who tried to return to work found that none was available. The union claimed 700 cases of discrimination. Paychecks were made payable only at the payroll windows, where they were cashed for discounted amounts. The employers refused to name their members of the wage arbitration board. When this refusal was referred to the eleven-man Regional Labor Board, it deadlocked five to five; Chairman Neil M. Cronin, in a galling display of dereliction of duty, refused to cast the deciding ballot. The employers also declined to negotiate over "other persons" in Section 8. When a committee, consisting of the governor, a union representative, and an employer representative, ruled two to one that it should be construed to include any employees whose work facilitated movement of merchandise by truck, the companies ignored the decision.

The employers, it seemed, invited another strike and the union, its patience worn down, had little choice. The arrival of a federal conciliator, E. H. Dunnigan, at the end of June proved fruitless. A 574 membership meeting on July 6 voted overwhelmingly for a showdown. The employers received these demands: recognition, negotiations over wages, hours, and conditions, and wage retroactivity to May 26. If these terms were not met, 574 said, there would be a strike. They were not met. Governor Olson interrupted a holiday at Gull Lake for last-minute mediation, which was profitless. The union membership voted to strike at midnight, Monday, July 16, 1934.

The first few days, as the walkout bit into the life of the city, were without incident. On Wednesday, Francis J. Haas, a noted priest and authority on labor relations, arrived as special mediator for the National Labor Relations Board. The next day Father Haas and Dunnigan proposed a settlement to the disputants: resumption of work, re-employment of strikers without discrimination, reinstitution of the RLB's May order, inside workers defined as all employees except drivers, office workers, and full-time salesmen, and wages and overtime unspecified. The union responded the same day, accepting the specific terms and asking in addition for a signed agreement, minimum wages of 55¢ for drivers and 45¢ for inside workers retroactive to May 26, and time and one half after eight hours daily and double time on Sundays and holidays. On July 20, in effect, the employers rejected the Haas-Dunnigan deal; the only provision they accepted was that 574 should call off its strike. The employers had other plans.

In close collaboration with the police they were plotting to stage a riot in order to force the governor to call out the National Guard to break the strike. The first incident had taken place on Thursday, July 19. From the onset of the strike 574 had cleared vehicles for deliveries to hospitals. With fanfare (the newspapers carried stories of the event before it took place), the employers dispatched a five-ton truck with banners reading "Hospital Supplies" on its sides to the Eitel Hospital guarded by 11 squad cars with 44 policemen armed with shotguns and under orders to shoot if attacked. The union was not trapped; the truck went through without interference.

On the next day, "Bloody Friday," July 20, the temperature in the streets downtown was 102°. At 2 P.M. a large yellow truck escorted by 50 heavily armed policemen drew up to the platform of the Slocum-Bergen Company in the market area. A few boxes were loaded. The truck then moved slowly off into Sixth Avenue and turned into Third Street closely followed by the police convoy. A vehicle carrying pickets cut across the truck's path. The police immediately opened fire on the occupants. Meridel Le Sueur described the scene:

> The movement stopped—severed, dismayed. Two boys fell back into their own truck. The swarm broke, cut into; it whirled up, eddied, fell down soundlessly. One's eyes closed as in sleep and when they opened, men were lying crying in the street with blood spurting from the myriad wounds that buckshot makes. Turning instinctively for cover, they were shot in the back. And into that continued fire flowed the next line of pickets to pick up their wounded. They flowed directly into the buckshot fire, inevitably, without hesitation, as one wave follows another. And the cops let them have it as they picked up their wounded. Lines of living, solid men fell, broke, wavering, flinging up, breaking over with the curious and awful abandon of despairing gestures; a man stepping on his own intestines, bright and bursting in the street, and another holding his severed arm in his other hand.
>
> Another line came in like a great wave and the police kept firing. As fast as they broke that strong cordon it gathered again. Wherever it was smashed the body filled again, the tide fell and filled. Impelled by that strong and terrific union they filled in every gap like cells in one body healing itself. And the cops shot into it again and again. Standing on the sidewalk people could not believe that they were seeing it.

The incident took only a few minutes. Sixty-seven persons were wounded, two fatally. Only one policeman was hurt. That night at the city hospital nurses showed the strikers' wounds to Eric Sevareid—almost all in the back of their heads, arms, legs, and shoulders. He wrote, "They had been shot while trying to run out of the ambush."

It is difficult to avoid the conclusion that the leaders on both sides deliberately sought bloodshed. In the case of the employers this is obvious; for the Trotskyite leaders of 574 the evidence is circumstantial. The fact that a trap was being laid must have been known to them. Thursday's incident had provided a lesson; that day the *Organizer* exposed the employers' decoy strategy; newspaper reporters and cameramen, obviously notified in advance, were stationed in the area of Friday's massacre. Most important, the governor's adjutant general, Ellard Walsh, phoned the strike leaders to notify them of the plot and to warn them not to interfere with the decoy truck. The Marxist doctrine of class war, with its inversion of ordinary means and ends, presumably justified in their minds the decision to send unsuspecting pickets into the rain of police gunfire.

The union now had slain martyrs. On Friday night an enormous protest meeting was whipped into a frenzy of revenge and began a march on city hall to lynch Mayor Bainbridge and Police Chief Johannes. A detachment of troops sent from Camp Ripley by General Walsh headed off the mob. Henry Ness, a picket who had served fifteen years in the regular army, two and one half in active service in World War I, the father of four children, received 37 slugs in his body. Despite repeated blood transfusions, Ness died on July 24. The union then staged a colossal funeral. The crowd is said to have ranged from 20,000 to 100,000 as the procession advanced from funeral parlor to strike headquarters to cemetery. The marchers included virtually the entire local labor movement and several posts of the Veterans of Foreign Wars, of which Ness was a member. At the headquarters, where a black flag flew overhead, Bill Brown broke down in mid-eulogy and Albert Goldman, looking at the Minneapolis Club, told the throng to hold its prominent members responsible for the killing. No policemen were in sight on the march to the cemetery; strikers directed traffic and instructed pedestrians to doff their hats. An army firing squad from Fort Snelling fired the last volley over Ness's grave.

By now Minneapolis was in chaos, and community pressure, as the employers had planned, was building up on Olson to send in the National Guard. Before giving in, he prodded the federal mediators into another effort. On July 25 Haas and Dunnigan gave both disputants and the press their recommendations for "a fair and impartial basis on which to work out an adjustment of the perplexing and even critical situation now confronting Minneapolis." They reaffirmed their earlier proposals and added these: The NLRB would conduct an employee election within three days of the end of the strike on this question—"Do you or do you not wish Local 574 to represent you for the purposes of collective bargaining?"

All employees of the 22 firms in the fruit and produce industry except salesmen and office workers would be eligible and would vote as a group; in nonmarket firms drivers, helpers, and platform men would be eligible but would not vote as a group unless both sides so agreed. Representatives chosen by the majority would bargain for all. Substantive issues would be resolved by arbitration. The five-man board would consist of two chosen by each side and a neutral chairman chosen by these four. If they failed to agree within 24 hours, the NLRB would name him. The board's award would be rendered within five days and would be retroactive to the date the strike ended. The minimum wages would be 52½¢ for drivers and 42½¢ for inside people, helpers, and platform men. These rates would form the floor from which arbitration would proceed.

The governor, threatening martial law at noon on Thursday, July 26, urged both sides to accept the Haas-Dunnigan plan. Local 574 voted 1866 to 147 to do so. In an involved letter on July 25 the employers in essence said, "We cannot deal with this Communistic leadership."

Olson, while dismayed by the prospect, now had no choice. His sympathies, of course, were wholly with the strikers ("Neither am I willing to join in the approval of the shooting of unarmed citizens of Minneapolis, strikers and bystanders alike, in their backs, in order to carry out the wishes of the Citizens' Alliance of Minneapolis"). Yet as governor of the state he had the duty to preserve order, a function in which the city officials had revealed their bankruptcy. Olson at 12:22 P.M. on July 26 proclaimed martial law.

The governor sought to frustrate the employers' hope that the militia would break the strike by guaranteeing free movement of vehicles. He both forbade picketing and imposed a military permit system. That is, no truck would move unless certified to do so, and permits were to be issued only for the delivery of milk, fruit, and other edibles. General Frank E. Reid, commander of the Guard, resigned: "If I were not permitted to let trucks operate, I could not conscientiously act as troop commander." Olson replaced him with Ellard Walsh.

The first phase of military control was both painless and funny. Parking was banned downtown; no drinks were served after 9 P.M.; night spots closed at midnight. The public debated whether community sings and walkathons were permissible; they were. The employers, claiming that Olson had abridged freedom of speech, publicly asked permission to send him a letter. His reply:

> Please be advised that you may write me in any terms you desire with complete immunity from any military regulation or the laws of the state with reference to libel. I solemnly warn you, however, to refrain from stating anything that will frighten the children of Minneapolis. . . . I

shall look forward with pleasure to receiving your communication and to read . . . the supporting editorials in the *Minneapolis Journal.*

But this mood soon evaporated when the union recognized that martial law in fact had restored truck movements in Minneapolis. The militia granted permits wholesale and many operators sent out unauthorized vehicles. By July 29, traffic was 65 per cent of normal. Olson, despite his intention, was breaking 574's strike.

That day the union called a protest meeting at the parade grounds, said to be attended by 25,000 persons. Bill Brown, himself an Olson supporter, denounced "the Farmer-Labor administration [as] the best strikebreaking force our union has ever gone up against." The meeting voted to stop trucks by force unless the permit system was abandoned within 48 hours. Miles Dunne phoned the provost marshal to order his "tin soldiers" off the streets before they were thrown off. "Submit to the governor," Ray Dunne said, "and the strike is lost. *The militia is moving trucks.*"

In the face of this defiance the governor had no choice but to assert the sovereignty of the state with the use of force. But his decision to do so wrung him emotionally; he retired to the Lowry Hotel in St. Paul, where he put in a sleepless night, leaving the execution of his plan to General Walsh.

At 4 A.M. on August 1, with Colonel McDevitt in command, several hundred guardsmen, a battery of light artillery, and a detachment of machine gunners surrounded the old garage that served as 574's headquarters. McDevitt ordered the evacuation of the building and arrested Ray and Miles Dunne along with Bill Brown. Grant Dunne and Dobbs escaped through a rear door. The strikers were disarmed, the three captured leaders were imprisoned in a stockade at the fair grounds, and warrants were issued for those at large.

Olson now called on the rank and file of 574 to choose new leaders to settle the strike. The members elected Ray Rainbolt and Kelly Postal. Rainbolt, a Sioux Indian, gave this account:

> We met with the governor, Kelly and I. He said to us, "Well, boys, we've got to settle this thing." We said to him, "First you let out our leaders; after that we'll talk." Kelly called him a copper-hearted son-of-a —— and I said to him, "Governor, you're right in the middle on a picket fence. Watch your step or you'll slip and hurt yourself bad."

As these "negotiations" proceeded, infuriated bands of pickets, now unrestrained by their leaders, carried out hit-and-run raids against commercial trucking. Instead of ending picketing, the governor's action had caused it to become violent.

Olson sent out word that he wanted to talk with Grant Dunne. Dunne, phoning from a service station in the suburbs, got the governor to call in the warrants for himself and Dobbs in return for a promise to come downtown. In the interview Dunne warned that the strike would continue without 574's leaders; the governor needed only to look in the streets to know that the threat was not idle. He turned his palms up and said, "Well, Grant, what do you want me to do?" Dunne replied, "Two things: first, release our leaders from the stockade; second, turn back the headquarters." "All right," Olson said, "I'll do it." He kept his promise.

He went further in order to mend his battered political fence with labor. On August 3 he ordered the National Guard to raid the Citizens' Alliance. The soldiers walked out with armfuls of documents. The governor had hoped that they would contain headline-rich damaging evidence. But the Alliance, tipped off in advance, had already shipped out its confidential files. Olson could merely announce that "the Citizens' Alliance dominates and controls the Employers' Advisory Committee," which was hardly news in Minneapolis. He received, however, a laudatory telegram from a supporter in Kentucky addressed to General ANDREW JACKSON OLSON: "I praise God, Confusius, Budda and the Farm Labor party because, You caused the Citizen's Alliance to be raided."

The governor, taking the suggestion of two United Press correspondents, now announced that effective 12:01 A.M., August 6, permits would be issued only to truckers who, on the one hand, handled either necessities or interstate shipments or, on the other, accepted the Haas-Dunnigan proposal or a mutually agreed-to modification thereof. While 47 firms signed up, the more important bitter-end employers resisted. On August 6 they petitioned the U.S. district court for an injunction restraining the declaration of martial law as an unconstitutional deprivation of property under the due process clause of the Fourteenth Amendment. Olson declared that he personally would argue the case for the state, but he first secured a two-day continuance.

The reason for this delay was that he needed to visit Rochester. President Roosevelt, en route back to the White House from his great-circle summer trip on the U.S.S. *Houston* through the Caribbean, the Panama Canal, and the Pacific to the Pacific Northwest, was, after avoiding Minneapolis, paying tribute to the noted Minnesota surgeons, Drs. William and Charles Mayo, at their clinic in Rochester. The governor and others involved in the strikes were eager to get the President's ear on matters having little to do with the progress of medicine.

On August 7 the employers sent Roosevelt, as they described it, a "purely informative and unbiased" chronology of the dispute. In essence, it branded the leadership of 574 as communistic, held it solely responsible for violence, blamed the union for rejecting the Regional Labor Board's ruling, denied that 574 represented their employees, denounced Olson for proclaiming martial law, etc. It is doubtful that Roosevelt saw this document; Louis Howe referred it to the NLB.

More important, on the morning of August 8 a delegation of Minnesota labor leaders visited the President's train in Rochester. They were received by Howe and, doubtless at his request, put their views in writing later that day. The group included no one from Local 574. Rather, they were old-line unionists—Gottfried Lindsten of the Railroad Trainmen, Roy Wier of the Minneapolis Central Labor Union, Emory C. Nelson and Patrick J. Corcoran of the Milk Drivers, A. H. Urtubees of the Building Trades Council, and R. D. Cramer, editor of the *Minneapolis Labor Review*. "The issue," they pointed out, "aside from wages and working conditions is the right of collective bargaining" as incorporated in the Haas-Dunnigan proposal. Here the Citizens' Alliance was the roadblock. And behind the Alliance, the labor men argued, stood "appointees of the federal government who through the control of credit are preventing a settlement of the strike." They named three local officials of the Reconstruction Finance Corporation: Joseph Chapman, manager; John W. Barton, in charge of industrial loans; and C. T. Jaffray, who, among his many interests, controlled the liquidation of assets of closed banks. "These people are all reactionary Republicans, held over from the . . . Hoover regime." Through these bankers, the union leaders charged, "employers must join [the Citizens' Alliance] and go along in the war on trade unions or they find their credit ruined."

Olson conferred with Roosevelt privately. While we do not know what the governor said, it may be inferred from what the President did that Olson must have taken a position approximating that of the labor men. That same day, August 8, Jesse Jones, chairman of RFC, telephoned Father Haas and, as the mediator's chronology put it, "suggested getting in touch at once" with Jaffray and Theodore Wold of the North West Bank Corporation. Haas and Dunnigan met the bankers at 2:30 that afternoon. Jaffray asked for a memorandum on the key obstacles to a settlement prior to conferring with the employers' committee. The next day Haas and Dunnigan wrote him that there were two critical issues: reinstatement of strikers, with dismissal of those hired after July 16, and arbitration of wages above the employer offer of 50¢ for drivers and 40¢ for others. The mediators felt that both sides would accept a representation election.

On the afternoon and evening of August 9 Haas, Dunnigan, Jaffray, Barton, and the employers' committee negotiated fruitlessly in Jaffray's office. Jones phoned from Washington and spoke separately with Jaffray and Haas, but to no effect. The trucking employers would not yield ground: they would arbitrate wages, but only without the specified floors, and they refused to fire some 800 strikebreakers. They almost certainly were stalling to learn the outcome of their injunction suit.

On August 10 judges Sanborn, Molyneaux, and Nordbye heard argument. Olson was at the top of his form. He majestically brushed aside the contention that he had abridged due process under the Fourteenth Amendment. In fact, the executive's decision to invoke martial law was not subject to court review. His duty to the people of Minnesota was to avert violence; if trucks must be locked in the barn to achieve this, he was empowered to issue such an order. In his reasonable judgment, the governor argued, martial law was necessary to protect life and property. If the court disagreed, it must assume the responsibility for the consequences. This last point was unassailable. While the judges in their decision on the morning of August 11 testily observed that they "personally disagree with Governor Olson as to the manner in which he has handled the entire situation," they helplessly sustained his power to invoke martial law. The legal ship on which the employers' hopes were riding was torpedoed.

That afternoon Haas and Dunnigan were back in conference with Jaffray and Barton. The employers now went halfway. Jaffray reported that they would either arbitrate and keep workers hired during the strike or dismiss these employees and not arbitrate. The next day 574 rejected both alternatives, standing by the Haas-Dunnigan proposal.

On August 14, with both sides reeling after almost a month of strike, the mediators submitted a new peace plan: a return to work; preferential re-employment of strikers; seniority in hiring and laying off; representation elections with only those on the payroll on July 16 voting; minimum wages of 52½¢ for drivers and 42½¢ for others; and misunderstandings to be arbitrated by the regional board. The union accepted and the employers turned down this proposal.

The latter now injected a new demand—representation elections in the 166 firms represented by the Employers' Advisory Committee prior to the conclusion of the strike. The union agreed. On August 15 Haas asked Lloyd K. Garrison, chairman of the National Labor Relations Board (which had just succeeded NLB), to order elections. The Board did so and, on August 17, P. A. Donoghue arrived in Minneapolis to conduct them. Meantime, the employers' committee had instructed its members on how to prepare for the voting: "A definite responsibility rests upon each employer to see that every one of his loyal employees goes to the polls. . . . It is recommended that employer provide transportation to and from polls." This document fell into union hands and was published in the *Organizer*. The union on August 17 notified Donoghue that it would not participate in elections. Mediation now collapsed in Minneapolis.

Once again, Jesse Jones, presumably at White House initiative, came to the rescue. On the evening of August 18 he phoned Haas to learn, in effect, what it would take to settle the strike. The mediator reported that two assurances to the union were needed: allowing strikers to vote even if they were charged with committing acts of violence and requiring arbitration of wages above the minima. Jones phoned Barton that evening and must have taken a hard line indeed. On August 19 resistance among the trucking employers collapsed; they conceded on both points.

On August 21, after ratification on both sides, the agreement settling the great 36-day Minneapolis trucking strike was promulgated: strikers would receive preference in re-employment. Within 10 days the labor board would hold elections both among the drivers, helpers, platform men, and inside workers of the 22 market firms and among the drivers, helpers, and platform workers of the 144 other companies. Only those on the payrolls on July 16 would be eligible to vote. Representatives chosen by the majority would bargain for all and "each employer shall deal with such person, persons, or organization . . . for purposes of collective bargaining." Minimum wages would be 50¢ for drivers and 40¢ for others; rates above these minima would be arbitrated by a tripartite board. Hours and overtime would conform to the NRA codes. This was the Appomattox of the Minneapolis civil war.

The agreement was a great victory for Local 574 and trade unionism in the Northwest. Minneapolis was no longer an open-shop city. "Inwardly," Walker wrote, "the civil war had raged over far deeper issues [than the terms of settlement], the first of which was the historic dictatorship over Minneapolis and the lives of its workers by the tightly organized camarilla of the Citizens' Alliance. The strike had challenged and broken that dictatorship." The strikers and their friends indulged in a well-deserved twelve-hour victory binge.

While the union did not do as well in the NLRB elections of August 29 as it had hoped, winning clear-cut victories in only 50 firms, this proved no more than a temporary setback. In fact, 574 bargained for the employees of all 166 members of the Employers' Advisory Committee and within two years was to win collective bargaining agreements with a total of 500 Minneapolis employers. The Trotskyite leaders—the Dunne brothers, Dobbs, and Sköglund—became officials of the local, taking it over in form as well as in fact. Thus, the Trotskyite faction of Communism gained a solitary bastion within the American labor movement. It is an irony that Jesse Jones should have been a principal architect of this achievement, for this banker was, in Francis Biddle's words, "Texas in the 'giant' sense, conscious of his power, proud of his wealth, a pioneer who found no limits to his spirit in the acquisition of material possessions; hard, shrewd, ruthless, strong, conservative." Among the minor results of the strikes was the education of the upper class of the Twin Cities in the more esoteric aspects of Marxism. Minneapolis was said to be the only town in the United States in which socialites at cocktail parties neatly distinguished Stalinists from Trotskyite Communists.

Soon the leaders of 574, with the imagination and drive they had evidenced during the strikes, expanded the organization of over-the-road drivers in the upper Mississippi Valley as the foundation for mass unionism on a semi-industrial basis. Dan Tobin, brooding at his rolltop desk in Indianapolis, observed this development with revulsion, waiting impatiently for the opportunity to destroy the leadership of 574.

4.5

The Negro in the Meat-Packing Industry

HORACE CAYTON
GEORGE S. MITCHELL

The shortage of unskilled, immigrant, white labor during and after the First
World War encouraged southern blacks to migrate to northern cities and to
seek work in new industrial occupations. In an earlier essay, William Tuttle
indicated some of the dimensions of conflict between black and white
Chicago workers before 1920. The Great Depression everywhere affected
black workers more severely than white workers, and the traditional hostility
of settled craft unions toward black workers made their condition even more
precarious. Interviews with black and white workers during the 1930s served
as the primary sources for George Mitchell and Horace Cayton in their
pioneering study of northern black workers and the changing trade-union
movement. Here, Catyon and Mitchell reported their findings in the meat
packing industry.

Horace Cayton and George S. Mitchell, *Black Workers and the New Unions* (Chapel
Hill, N.C.: University of North Carolina Press, 1939), pp. 228–31, 232–33, 235, 236, 238,
257–79. Reprinted, omitting footnotes, Tables 19, 23, and 24, and Figures 3 and 4, by
permission of the publisher.

Negroes were first employed in the Chicago Stockyards in 1881 when two colored men were hired, one as a butcher and one as a beef-boner. For the next nine years no mention is made in the literature of Negro employees in meat-packing, but in 1891 a Negro was reported to be a member of one of Armour's killing gangs. During the next few years there was some infiltration of Negro workers among unskilled and even skilled workmen in the Chicago plants. But this caused no conflict.

> Negro butchers were an oddity; even unskilled Negro laborers were few. To stand aside a black man was an unfamiliar experience which had first created an element of curiosity and interest rather than of conflict.

This situation was somewhat changed during the strike of 1894 when the workers in the stockyards struck in sympathy with the American Railway Union in its dispute with the Pullman Company. The Poles, who had been the first group to be used as strike-breakers, were joined by Negroes and both were brought into the yards to help the packers break the union. Colored workers, aware of the anti-Negro clause in the American Railway Union constitution, had first retaliated by forming the anti-Strikers' Railroad Union and later by breaking strikes in the stockyards. It was reported in a Chicago daily paper that "the colored men went to work out of revenge for treatment received at the hands of the American Railway Union." The resentment of the union men was especially directed against Negroes and the effigy of a Negro was publicly burned.

After the strike, a few Negroes retained their positions and, although they were numerically unimportant, their presence was a constant threat to labor organizations. Hiring Negroes was a strategic act on the part of the packers for:

> . . . by this move the packers profited on two accounts: first, they tapped an almost inexhaustible supply of cheap labor; second, they secured thereby a labor force offering even greater resistance to unionization, through racial antagonism, than that supplied by the immigrant through language handicap and nationality hatreds.

The next large influx of Negroes came during the stockyards strike of 1904. At the time of the strike Negroes constituted perhaps 5 per cent of the working force. Additional hundreds of Negro strike-breakers were recruited to defeat the union. Negro workers were smuggled into the yards on the same day that the regular employees laid down their tools and marched out. Such a large number of Negroes were employed that it was thought for a time that the packing industry was going to become overwhelmingly black. Estimates placed the number of Negroes employed in the Chicago plants during the strike as high as 10,000.

In this dispute the role of the Negro worker was different from that which he played in the strike of 1894. In the earlier dispute Poles had been numerically the more important and Negroes played, in spite of the publicity which was attached to their activities, a relatively incidental part in breaking the strike. But in 1904 Negroes were a much more important factor as strike-breakers. This change was recognized and an ever more intense resentment of union men against the black worker followed.

After the strike had been settled, a narrow majority of the colored men retained their positions. The rest were discharged or displaced by returning union men. The packers, having utilized the services of Negro workers in a time of need no longer cared to retain most of them as employees; so they were loaded into special trains and sent back to the South from whence they had been imported.

The nucleus of Negroes who stayed in the yards was augmented each year by a small but steady stream of new black employees. In the period from 1917 to 1921, due to the war and immigration barriers, there was a tremendous demand for unskilled labor. The packers again tapped the labor pool of the South and began importing Negroes. The influx was tremendous and by 1918 Negroes constituted 20 per cent of the workers in the industry, whereas in 1909 the 459 Negro employees constituted only 3 per cent of the workers. . . .

In these plants as early as 1920 the number had reached 5,110 or 27.8 per cent of the total employees. The highest point for Negro employment was reached in 1923 when 5,148 or 33.6 per cent of the workers in these plants were colored.

There were two factors which made possible the employment of large numbers of Negroes in the industry during the post-war period. In the first place, immigration had been sharply reduced and consequently the cheap foreign labor supply of the packers had been curtailed. In the second place, the war with its increase in production had accelerated the tendency for northern European workers to move into higher occupational levels. This is illustrated in Table I, which shows the changes in nationality among employees in Chicago plants between 1909 and 1928. The groups listed are those which had more than a thousand members employed in the industry in 1909.

*   *   *   *   *

Four cities have been investigated in this study: Chicago, Omaha, St. Paul, and St. Louis. Table II shows the number and percentage of Negro operators and laborers in these localities. Chicago is the nation's most important meat center and, as the table indicates, is also the most important center for Negro workers in the packing industry. In 1930 Chicago had 17.5 per cent of the total laborers in the industry for the

TABLE I.   Changes in nationality among employees in the slaughtering and meat-packing industry of Chicago between 1909 and 1928

	1909		1928	
	Number	Per cent	Number	Per cent
Native-born white	1,931	18.9	3,604	27.3
Negro	(a) 459	3.0	3,894	29.5
Czechoslovakian	1,490	9.6	274	2.1
German	1,605	10.5	382	2.9
Irish	1,164	7.5	390	3.0
Lithuanians	1,860	12.0	1,033	7.8
Polish	4,293	27.7	1,570	11.9
Mexicans	1	. . .	746	5.7

(a) Plus three foreign-born Negroes.

TABLE II.   Numbers and percentages of total and Negro laborers and operators in four cities in 1930 *

	Total for United States		Chicago		Omaha		St. Paul		St. Louis		Four Cities	
	Num-ber	Per cent	Num-ber	Per cent	Num-ber	Per cent	Num-ber	Per cent	Num-ber	Per cent	Num-ber	Per cent
(All Workers)												
Laborers	43,045	100	7,510	17.5	2,495	5.8	788	1.8	903	2.1	11,696	27.2
Operators	61,094	100	7,332	12.0	1,227	2.0	852	1.4	1,216	2.0	10,627	17.4
(Negro)												
Laborers	9,332	100	2,074	22.3	639	6.9	52	.6	425	4.6	3,190	34.2
Operators	7,167	100	2,373	33.1	247	3.5	106	1.5	350	4.9	3,076	42.9

* From the *Fifteenth Census of the United States,* Vol. V, Chap. VII.

country as a whole, but 22.3 per cent of all Negro laborers. The distribution of Negro operators also shows a disproportionate percentage in Chicago. Twelve per cent of all operators in the industry were located in Chicago and 33.1 per cent of all Negro operators. This same distribution tends to be true of all northern cities. In each of the cities investigated in this study, the percentage of Negro laborers and operators was greater than the percentage of total workers, showing the preponderance of Negroes in northern meat-packing plants. In the four cities combined there were 27.2 per cent of all laborers in the industry and 17.4 per cent of all operators, while in these same cities there were 36.7 per cent of all Negro laborers and 28.9 per cent of the Negro operators.

TABLE III.   *Percentage of laborers and operators who are Negroes in four cities ***

	Chicago	Omaha	St. Paul	St. Louis	Four Cities
Laborers	27.3	20.1	6.6	47.1	36.7
Operators	32.4	25.6	12.4	28.8	28.9

* From the *Fifteenth Census of the United States,* 1930, Vol. IV, Population.

The 1930 census enumerated 164,882 persons engaged in the meat-packing and slaughtering industry. The following distribution by race and nationality obtained:

	Number	Per Cent
Native-born white	107,238	65.0
Foreign-born white	35,384	21.5
Negro	18,426	11.2
Other races	3,834	2.3

Of the 18,426 Negroes in the industry, most were to be found in the semi-skilled and laboring divisions.

	Number	Per Cent
Officials, professional and highly technical	9	.05
Office employees	21	.1
Less skilled office help	191	1.0
Standard crafts	217	1.2
Skilled workers and foremen	59	.3
Semi-skilled workers	7,988	43.4
Maintenance employees	605	3.3
Laborers	9,332	50.7

The concentration of Negroes in the laboring and semi-skilled classi-fications was striking, as these two groups accounted for approximately 90 per cent of all Negroes in the industry. Less than 1 per cent of Negroes were in the divisions including officials, professionals, and technical workers; office employees and skilled workmen and foremen. Approximately 2 per cent were among the less skilled office help and standard crafts. The remaining three divisions, maintenance employees, semi-skilled workers, and laborers, had over 97 per cent of the entire Negro group. . . .

The actual operations in which Negroes were found indicated their position even more accurately. The ten operations in which the greatest number of Negroes were employed were as follows:

PERCENTAGE OF TOTAL NEGROES EMPLOYED IN SELECTED OPERATIONS

	Percentage		Percentage
Laborers	64.1	Firemen	.9
Semi-skilled	38.9	Clerks	.4
Chauffeurs and truck drivers	3.2	Shipping clerks	.4
Janitors	1.5	Coopers	.4
Porters	1.2	Elevator tenders	.4

When separate operations were considered, Negroes constituted more than their percentage in the industry in the following groups:

	Percentage		Percentage
Porters	82.0	Cranemen, derrickmen, hoistmen	18.2
Janitors	38.3	Housekeepers, stewards	14.7
Laborers	21.7	Elevator tenders	13.5
Firemen	18.3	Operatives	13.5

From these figures it can be seen that Negroes, after having been in the industry in some numbers for a period of over thirty years, had not risen much above the lowest occupational level. This material covers the United States as a whole and hence the distribution in a city favorable to the promotion of Negroes, such as Chicago, cannot be shown. It is likely that in such a locality the advance of Negroes into more skillful and lucrative positions has taken place to some extent.

THE UNION MOVEMENT
UNDER THE NEW DEAL

When the blanket code was passed, the meat-packing industry boasted three rival union organizations. The Amalgamated Meat Cutters and

Butcher Workmen of North America was the American Federation of Labor union. The company unions, organized in many plants in 1921, had been comparatively inactive but were brought to life by the packers in an attempt to retain control over their labor force. The Packing House Workers' Industrial Union, which reflected the revolutionary philosophy of the Communist Party, was the newcomer in the field.

Except for sporadic strikes in 1924, the Amalgamated Meat Cutters and Butcher Workmen had been phlegmatic since 1922. Its membership of 65,300 in 1920 had dropped to 10,400 in 1923 and had risen to only 11,800 in 1929. With the coming of the N.R.A. the union was spurred to action.

> Before the N.R.A. our national organization consisted of 26,000 members. Today a year later our membership numbers 60,000 men in 515 locals. As soon as Section 7-A of the N.R.A. was published we sent our organizers out to the packing plants to explain to the men that now there was nothing to fear in joining a union as the government was behind labor in this. Before the N.R.A. we couldn't say that the government favored the idea of the men joining a union. But after the N.R.A. was passed this helped, as their great belief in the government aided us in our organizational work. [Interview with Patrick E. Gorman, general president of the Amalgamated Meat Cutters and Butcher Workmen of North America (Chicago, Ill.).]

In St. Louis an organizer reported the growth of that local:

> In 1921 the number of members in good standing dwindled to 124, and stayed at that number for some time. In August of 1933 we had only 168 members in good standing. With the passage of the N.R.A. we began to reorganize and in six weeks got 1,500 members. In the next six weeks we had the industry 90 to 95 per cent organized. [Interview with Michael Roth, officer of the Amalgamated Meat Cutters and Packing House Workmen, local No. 545 (St. Louis, Mo.).]

The organization progressed rapidly and after a short time made demands for increased wages and better working conditions. Strikes were called in 1933 in Pittsburgh, South St. Paul, Austin (Minnesota), and Los Angeles. Perhaps the most extensive dispute arose in Chicago on November 26, 1933, when 1,000 members of the Livestock Handlers' Union, local No. 517, went out on strike. After three days the union formulated its demands and the men returned to work leaving the case in the hands of the Chicago Labor Board of the N.R.A. Several small strikes occurred in Chicago during December but met with little success.

Having in few cases received either recognition from the packers or satisfactory adjustments at the hands of the various regional labor boards, groups of workers throughout the country continued to precipitate strikes. On May 14, 1934, 2,500 packing house employees struck in St. Louis and demanded increased wages and a guaranteed minimum working week. On June 5, 5,600 butchers and other employees struck in thirty-five packing plants in Brooklyn. After a week these strikers were joined by a sympathetic walkout, increasing the number of participants to 6,000. The strike was for increased wages and recognition of the union. The packers agreed to meet with their own employees but refused to deal with the outside representatives.

On July 24 the livestock handlers of Chicago called a second strike. Nine hundred men walked out, 300 of whom were union men. Since the yards had received 45,000 cattle the day before—the largest single day's shipment since 1908—the strikers were in a strategic position to enforce their demands for increased pay. The handlers charged in their strike call that their employers had violated wage terms of a contract under which they had returned to work after a strike the previous winter. The dispute affected only members of the Livestock Handlers' Union, local No. 517.

By July 31 the strike had spread to the packing house workers. On that day, the members of the Amalgamated Meat Cutters employed by C. A. Burnette & Co. walked out in sympathy with the livestock handlers. The number of strikers in that company was estimated by the company foreman to be 150 and by the union to be 400. Workmen in the other packing houses in the city failed to respond to the strike call and the Burnette employees were the only ones to remain out. The sympathetic strike did not, however, receive the support of the international officers. General Hugh Johnson came to Chicago to take personal charge of the situation on August 3. One of the moot questions was that of a minimum wage guaranteed for the extra men hired as livestock handlers. On August 5 the twelve-day strike was settled by compromise and the strikers regained their old jobs in the yards.

A campaign for the organization of the industry was carried on in nearly all of the important meat-packing centers in the country, and its initial success caused the packers no little concern. Even company unions, which were hurriedly brought forward, did not stem the tide of workers anxious to join outside unions.

> Too, the fact that the packers immediately came out with company unions aided us in increasing our membership. We were in a position to point out that the companies were only offering this as a sop to the workers. That until then they had done nothing and that now they came wheedling for employee plant conferences. We could point out that the company union didn't do anything for the men in raising wages or meeting their grievances. Then too, the voting in the plants showed what a farce the company union is. [Interview with Patrick E. Gorman (Chicago, Ill.).]

Few of the unions, however, were recognized by the packers even when the employers were forced in a strike emergency to negotiate with them on specific issues. In most instances the unions were unable to obtain satisfactory settlements from the various regional boards. Such inefficacious results, combined with the well planned campaign of the employers to fire and intimidate union men, netted for the Amalgamated organization a decided loss of prestige. Company unions were continually played up and encouraged by the management, so that as the workers grew discouraged with the outside organization and were afraid to risk their jobs for intangible benefits, the employers' organization grew in strength.

The Packing House Workers' Industrial Union had also been active during this period. In some cities it appeared in the field before the Amalgamated organization. "The Communists started organizing in South St. Paul before the Amalgamated Meat Cutters and had some little success" [Interview with Roy Wentz, official of the Amalgamated Meat Cutters and Butcher Workmen of North America (St. Paul, Minn.).] They were at first interested in organizing their own unions and bitterly attacked the Amalgamated. As late as June 20, 1933, the *Daily Worker* encouraged the workers to avoid the A. F. of L. unions.

> The A. F. of L. stepped into the situation (a small strike in Chicago) and is working closely with the police to divide the ranks of the strikers. They are calling a meeting in the attempt to destroy the first struggle of the stockyard workers to organize and win better conditions since 1924. The workers are showing a fine fighting spirit and are determined to win the strike. Twenty-five have already joined the packing house union [Packing House Workers' Industrial Union].

The efforts of the Communists met with little success except in one or two of the small independent plants in smaller meat-packing centers. In November of 1933 a national conference of the Packing House Workers' Industrial Union was held in Chicago. Two weeks later Local No. 517 of the Livestock Handlers' Union went out on strike. This situation in itself indicated clearly the isolation of the Packing House Workers' Industrial Union from the great body of the workers and its inability to attract any large number of laborers. Despite the national conference in Chicago, just two weeks previously, its role in the strike was relatively unimportant. The *Daily Worker* stated editorially:

> We have no reports as yet regarding the role of our Party and the Trade Union Unity League in the strike of the Chicago stockyard workers.
>
> .   .   .   .
>
> First and foremost there stands out the isolation of our Party from the main body of the workers in Chicago. The strike took our Party by surprise.

The over-optimistic Communists had underestimated the strength of the A.F. of L.

> The third outstanding lesson is without doubt the underestimation of the role and influence of the American Federation of Labor. Even up to the end the leading comrades in the District Bureau were not aware of the extent of the A. F. of L. organization among certain sections of the workers in the stockyards and the role that they would play in any struggle.

The Packing House Workers' Industrial Union, however, continued its attack on the Amalgamated for some time. By May, however, the Communists had begun to work within the organization and to encourage a rank and file movement. At the time of the second Chicago strike, members of the P.H.W.I.U. were urged to establish real rank and file control of the strike through an elected strike committee which would include representatives of union groups other than the A. F. of L. In the latter part of 1934, the Packing House Workers' Industrial Union realized the futility of attempting to form an independent union and ceased to function. All subsequent work by the Communists was carried on within American Federation of Labor unions.

During the N.R.A. there was an increase in the membership of the Amalgamated Meat Cutters but indications that the union's hold on the great body of workers was diminishing had appeared before the Act was declared unconstitutional. The Amalgamated had failed to gain recognition and it had not forced out company unions. The Packing House Workers' Industrial Union had attempted an independent organization for a year and then abandoned it in favor of "boring from within" the Amalgamated. Company unions, with skillful employer management and intimidation of workers, crept to the front as the most powerful of the three organizations.

Before the N.R.A. there had been less than 200 Negro members in the entire international organization of the Amalgamated Meat Cutters and Butcher Workmen of North America. In the union campaign which followed the passage of the blanket code, Negroes came into the union with the rest of the packing house workers in large numbers. In January, 1935, there were "over 5,000 Negroes enrolled in [the] Chicago locals alone" [Interview with Patrick E. Gorman (Chicago, Ill.).] The St. Louis organizer reported similar success with Negro workers.

> When we began to organize in August of 1933 we attempted to include Negroes in our union on the same basis as the whites. At one time we had about 40 per cent of the colored in the industry in our union. There are 2,000 workers in the meat packing industries in St. Louis, of which about

750 are Negroes. When we were at the peak we had 180 Negroes in the organization and 1,600 to 1,700 whites. [Interview with M. R., union official, November 23, 1934.]

Most of the Negro members, however, were highly suspicious both of the advantages of contradicting the will of the packers and of the good intentions of white workers toward them. When the union showed the first sign of weakness, numbers of them dropped out. An incident which illustrates the deference of Negro workers toward employers was reported in Omaha.

They (the union) were doing fine for a while, but you know in everything the test must come, and so finally the test came at Armour's when they had planned to go nine hours. The Company said go nine hours, the Union said go eight. The floor men in the Kill were the key men, that is everybody looked to them to see what they were going to do. That would have been a test for the union to have showed their strength, but when 3:30 came the Timekeeper came up with a handful of time slips and went around to each man and asked, "What are you going to do?" Each man said, "I'm goin' to work," and from that time the colored men say that so long as the company has not reached any agreement with the union, what is the use of them paying their membership into the union. [Interview (Omaha, Neb.) January 19, 1933.]

With the strengthening of the employers' counter-offensive against the unions and the systematic firing of Amalgamated members, more Negroes dropped out of the organization. In St. Louis where the attempt to organize had met with some success there was a noticeable decline in Negro union membership as soon as the packers became active against the union. [Interview with M.R., a union official.] After that it was almost impossible to organize Negroes in that district.

. . . we had a great deal of trouble in organizing the Negroes at the Independent plant where there were 400 Negro workers and 900 white workers. During the strike which was at the plant only one Negro struck and showed up on the picket line. Most of the Negroes stayed at work. Before, during the strikes we had Negro members who were very active in some of the plants. At one of the yards we had nearly a 100 per cent organization of Negroes and whites. During the strike 100 per cent of the Negroes struck with us. At Kreys about 70 per cent of the Negroes struck and about 85 per cent of the whites struck. This membership had both white and Negroes. We held this membership until the plants began to victimize the union members. [Interview with M. R., a union official.]

In Omaha practically the same story was told by union officials.

I have been successful in getting their applications but cannot hold them. They understand the organization and will join, but there is just a small percentage that we can hold. They have doubts about the success of the organization and are afraid of their jobs. Negroes have been pushed around a lot and they have not much faith in their white brothers. [Interview with the president of the Amalgamated local at Omaha, Neb.]

A union official in St. Paul stated that their Negro membership had dwindled to 18 or 20 men from a former high figure of 100 or more. [Interview with a union official, January 17, 1935.]

There are several other factors besides the mistrust of white workers and fear of the management which undermined the loyalty of union Negroes. One important deterrent to continued union activity was the bitter memory of the strike of 1921, especially to those colored workers who had struck with the union.

> The reason the Negroes did not go back into the union for the second time was due to the happenings in the 1921 strike. During the strike the men would come around and say "Go ahead boys we're going to win, stick to it." All at once we heard statements that they had gone back to work in Kansas City, then Chicago, and then someone heard that the international president had been bought off for $10,000 and then most of our people [Negroes] got disgusted and felt that the big shots were getting all the money and we were letting our living go and exposing ourselves.
>
> Some of the men were out in the picket line there with patent leather shoes, that is leather on top and their bare feet patting the ground in weather which was fourteen degrees below zero. [Interview (Omaha, Neb.) January 19, 1935.]

Other employees and union officials made similar statements about the lack of morale among the workers as a result of the failure of the 1921 strike.

Discrimination against Negroes in the social activities of the union made them suspicious of the possibility of fair treatment from the white union brothers. The local at Omaha, Nebraska, although anxious to obtain Negro members, was unwilling to meet with them on terms of social equality.

> We had a picnic and we ruled that every other dance was for the colored. We have held no regular dances so that the colored would not think they were discriminated against. We have not asked Negro women to join, but there were four that did belong. [Interview (Omaha, Neb.) January 18, 1935.]

Negro members resented this treatment and believed it to be an indication of the insincerity to be expected from white workers.

> At the picnic which was held last year the same fellows that were there every day dipping snuff, cutting tobacco off the same piece and drinking

coffee out of the same cup with the men, at the picnic didn't want to drink lemonade with the Negroes and made the remark, "They didn't want to drink after niggers." It hurts the union and retards the progress of the whole organization for them to do that.

Then they were charging 5c a glass for beer, and for our folks they had a small glass and for the white people they had a larger glass and our folks went up in the air. At the dance they had a separate place for the colored and white to dance. [Interview with a Negro union member (Omaha, Neb.) January 18, 1935.]

This situation was further aggravated by the failure of the union officials to take a definite stand on these matters. When the behavior of the members in some locals was such that it might embarrass the colored workers union officials took a tolerant attitude toward the former.

When we had our largest colored membership we had around 100 to 200 coming to our meetings at the hall. They would pay their dues but when time for the meeting came only about 40 would stay and participate. I asked one of them why they left at the beginning of the meeting and he said because the Negroes did not feel that they were welcome. Probably the reason for this was that during and immediately after the strike some of the white members in talking about the colored strikebreakers would call them niggers rather than Negroes or colored people. Of course as soon as anyone called a Negro a nigger, he was called out of order and reprimanded but that might have caused ill feeling. [Interview with M. R., a union official (St. Louis, Mo.).]

Rather than face this issue and take a stand which would reassure the Negro workers, this union official suggested a compromise.

We have lately thought of a new idea. It might be possible to have a separate meeting night for Negroes but still maintain just one local. Two locals of course would lead to confusion. If we had a separate night for Negroes under the same local and under the same officers, this might get around the rather difficult situation existing now. Of course this would only be a temporary measure to show the Negroes they were welcome. We would also try to work on those white members among us who do not have the same liberal attitude. We have to deal with the prejudices of the white members against the Negroes. [Interview with M. R., a union official (St. Louis, Mo.).]

Although at one time approximately 11 per cent of the members of the union were Negroes, this local (St. Louis, Missouri) did not have a single Negro officer. The election of Negro officers in the union would have demonstrated fairness, but the white officers were not willing to sacrifice any of their power to gain racial solidarity, offering instead the compromise of a special appointive position—Negro representative.

We had a colored organizer at the Independent Plant to keep the colored in line. The colored fellows came to the meeting and said they wanted representation. As I did not know whom to appoint, I asked them to suggest a man and they chose their representative. I planted this man at the Independent Packing House to receive complaints, collect dues, etc. We paid this man $25.00 per week. Later we heard that he had been telling the colored workers not to pay dues, as the union did not mean them any good. After this I called a committee meeting of the colored members to ask them what was the best thing to be done. We cannot afford to pay out of this organization $25.00 per week when no new members were coming in. Ten persons were appointed to serve on this committee and only two showed up. They stated there was little use of trying to do anything with the colored workers as they were were afraid that they might be fired. [Interview with M. R., a union official (St. Louis, Mo.).]

The failure of local officials to take a definite stand on the question of equality for Negroes is condemnable in view of the fact that these officers realized that without the Negro an effective labor organization was impossible.

We are now at a standstill. We do not know how to get the colored in, and we cannot function without him. On the other hand we need him and he needs us. If we strike they gain the benefits without costs, and without helping in the fight. Whether we win or lose it reacts against him as against us. When we lose, he loses, when we win, he wins. We cannot progress without him and he cannot progress without us. [Interview with M. R., a union official (St. Louis, Mo.).]

In Omaha, although there were three Negroes elected to minor offices, the control of the union rested entirely in the hands of whites who were antagonistic to Negroes.

In different departments you have some prejudice. Some of our men will call a darkey a black son of a bitch. That happens in many cases. The darkey will resent this because they have been abused in the South. They feel that if this union man treats him like that he should not trust the organization. [Interview (Omaha, Neb.) January 19, 1935.]

In Chicago the attitude of the locals was more favorable to Negroes, but even there the number of Negroes holding elective positions was much smaller than would be expected from an organization whose effective existence depended upon the participation of Negro workers.

The international officers presented a no more encouraging picture. One of them expressed an open dislike for black workers.

Between you and me, I consider the Negroes poor union men. You know as well as I do that they are shiftless, easily intimidated and generally of poor calibre. They were brought up here by parties from the South in 1904 to keep the wages down. They came in here, settled in dirty tenements, with a high consumption rate and have been used by the packers to keep the wage scale down ever since. Of course it has been all the packers' doings that brought on the race riots which were partly due to the resentment on the part of the white workers, of their keeping the wage scale down.

Of course most of the trouble in labor here comes from the fact of having a large Negro population. Though many of them make good loyal union men, the others are for the most part not useful to the labor movement and would be much better off picking cotton in the South. What should have happened is what is being done in Calhoun County, Illinois, where Negroes are not allowed to stay over night. As a result there are no Negroes there and no Negro problem. [Interview with an international officer of the Amalgamated Meat Cutters and Butcher Workmen of North America (Chicago, Ill.).]

Another officer, although not so antagonistic to Negroes, did not care to have it known that he had associated with them.

I once traveled for nine straight weeks as president with our Negro organizer ——— on a speaking tour. He went wherever I went, it made no difference to me. But he often left me to stay in a small hotel in the Negro section. I never asked him why. I wish though you wouldn't mention this, for if it would be known where I ran on the Democratic ticket, that I had traveled together with a Negro, the Republicans would use it against me. That's their narrow mindedness. [Interview with another international officer of the Amalgamated Meat Cutters and Butcher Workmen of North America (Chicago, Ill.).]

In commenting upon the few Negro officers of local lodges, this officer stated:

I believe there are as many Negro officers in our various locals as there are in any other union with the same proportion of Negro members. For instance the Cattle Butchers local No. 87, the vice-president is I., a Negro; local No. 547 the Retail Meat Cutters Union is all Negro; the president of the Wichita, Kansas, local is a Negro named W——— and the vice-president of the Sioux City lodge is a Negro named S———, as is the vice-president of the St. Joseph lodge. [Interview with an international officer of the Amalgamated Meat Cutters and Butcher Workmen of North America (Chicago, Ill.).]

From time to time the international office has hired Negro organizers in an effort to draw Negro workers into the union. In the 1917 drive for membership, two Negro organizers were lent to the union by the Illinois Miners. Later, during the same campaign, two more colored organizers were added: George Reed, who was sent to Kansas City, and C. Ford, who was assigned to St. Louis. These men were hired in addition to I. H. Bratton, George Strather, and John Riley (the latter from the American Federation of Labor). From 1917 to 1921 the organization maintained a total of nine Negro organizers. [Interview with Patrick E. Gorman.] At present there are three colored organizers: William Tate, Isom Williams, and W. M. Woods. [Interview with Patrick E. Gorman (January 10, 1935).] Of these, William Tate, whose success in attracting men to the organization constitutes a brilliant record, is outstanding. Mr. Gorman stated: "Our Negro organizers are not entirely confined to working among Negroes. One of them, Tate, has been highly successful among both Negro and white." However, even the help of these Negro organizers, while successful during the first wave of enthusiasm, was not sufficient to keep Negro workers in the union. In Omaha it was reported:

> We haven't had much success organizing Negroes. The only one that helped us was Bill Tate. When he was here we had a mass meeting at the Dreamland Hall, and only 15 people attended. We were able to initiate only four new members. [Interview with union official (Omaha, Neb.) January 18, 1935.]

Nearly all of the Negroes interviewed were disillusioned with company unions. This was true even when there were colored representatives on the conference boards. A number of workers in Chicago complained.

> One thing which can't be remedied is there are three colored fellows there who will tell anything on the colored that they can find out. One is the representative. He thinks he owns the place. I don't think the colored representative means much because they don't take up anything. They just wait for the big bosses to call them in the office and give them a consultation and make them feel good. It don't mean anything. [Interview (Chicago, Ill.) January 14, 1935.]
>
> They already had the representative in 1925 when I started. I think it is more for the company than it is for the men or for the colored. [Interview (Chicago, Ill.) January 14, 1935.]
>
> There was a colored representative. His name was T———. I went to him and he said there was nothing he could do. Otherwise I don't think they do what they can. [Interview (Chicago, Ill.) January 11, 1935.]
>
> They have always had the representative plan. It doesn't mean anything because they would fire a representative as quick as anyone else. If representatives would object to anyone being laid off the superintendent would tell him that he is boss and he told the foreman what to do. [Interview (Chicago, Ill.) December 31, 1934.]

In Omaha a colored worker who had been a representative described the effectiveness of the plan in the following terms:

> There is nothing to the company union. I was on the division committee. It helps the worker about like you and me was fighting and you take the bullets out of a gun and hand it to me and say, "Now shoot me."

The secretary brings in the plans and reads them, then asks you what you think about them. Maybe a superintendent, your foreman, and time-keeper are all sitting there and unless you got a good backbone you are afraid to speak freely. Usually things pass without any dissenting vote.

Once in a meeting with the company union the assistant superintendent made a motion and they put it forth, and then they said "Question." I stated "Not ready." They blared their eyes in wonderment—what was wrong with me? I did this in order to get my other constituents awake. Then after I was through, others had statements of unreadiness to make. They don't pay any attention to parliamentary rules in their meetings. [Interview (Omaha, Neb.) January 19, 1935.]

About a third of the workers interviewed thought that the company unions could not adjust the larger questions between the employers and employees but were effective in settling minor difficulties. The following are typical statements from that group.

Like in the case of garnisheeing, the company wanted to lay men off who were garnisheed but the representative straightened it out. [Interview (Chicago, Ill.) January 7, 1935.]

The representative plan has been there for some time. In some cases he can do them [colored] good and some cases he can't. I say this, when I was laid off I know that I had no business being laid off. I was working days and that foreman told me in August to work nights. That is when the government contract came in for killing cattle. So when the contract was over, I was laid off. I went to the representative and he got me back on. But I worked only one month. I went back to the representative and he said he could do me no good unless I was there for one year. He represents only the colored. [Interview (Chicago, Ill.) January 11, 1935.]

In this group, as well as in the former group, fear of the company and of white workers effectively kept the Negro workers out of the union in spite of their attitude toward the employees' representative plan. The N.R.A., by setting up governmental support of unions, offered the union an opportunity to sweep the entire industry into organization. At a time such as that, the Amalgamated should have guarded against any behavior which would have alienated Negro workers and should have included Negroes in the union on terms of absolute equality. Instead, the union, in the hands of an intrenched group of leaders, resisted most attempts to allow Negroes to be more than dues-paying and almost non-participating members. That this behavior would necessarily defeat organization in the industry did not seem to disturb the officials.

The Amalgamated Meat Cutters and Butcher Workmen of North America was controlled during the N.R.A. period by a conservative group of American Federation of Labor bureaucrats who had neither the courage nor the ability to organize the industry. Many of the rank and file members seriously distrusted the international officers. It was openly rumored that one high official of the International Union had an interest in some of the larger packing houses and that was the reason no great effort had been made to organize the workers in the industry. Another, one of the vice-presidents, was reputed to have at one time misplaced money with which he had been entrusted. Other international officers were criticized for their high salaries and large expense accounts. Whether true or false, these stories did much to destroy the morale of the union. The only remedy, it seemed, was the election to office of an entire body of vigorous young men from among the workers themselves. At that time there was no rank and file movement of younger, more progressive men who were in a position to challenge the leadership of the old, conservative union officials.

It would have been possible, had Negroes joined the union in large numbers, to change the attitude of the local as well as international officers by the pressure of numbers. In some localities Negroes constituted from 30 per cent to 50 per cent of the workers under the jurisdiction of the lodge. If organized, these colored workers could have voted their own officers into office and made vigorous protests against any acts of discrimination within the union. They might also have combined with any growing rank and file movement of the progressive elements in the union and overthrown the chauvinistic international officers. Since Negroes constitute over 13 per cent of the semi-skilled workers in the industry, 20 per cent of the maintenance workers, and more than 21 per cent of the laborers, their alliance with a progressive group would have insured both the success and the recognition that each group sought.

The C.I.O. Drive to Organize
the Meat-Packing Industry

From its initial start during the N.R.A. period the Amalgamated by 1936 had been successful in a number of small independent shops but had been unsuccessful in its attempts to organize the large plants throughout the country and especially in Chicago. One of the organizers stated, "We don't have contracts with Wilson, Armour or Swift in Chicago. Chicago is a hard place to crack. For one thing, you can't really get in the plant or anywhere near." Company unions had become more intrenched and, even after the passage of the Wagner Act, had not been completely dislodged. The Amalgamated had originally organized along industrial lines, i.e., all workers in the plant had been taken into the union. After the initial period of the 1934 campaign, however, the membership had been divided into various craft organizations. This action, combined with the fact that the organization was making very little effort to push through aggressively a drive for the unskilled in the yards, made some of the more trade union conscious workers dissatisfied. In Chicago this incipient "rank and file movement" met the resistance of the Amalgamated leadership and there were some instances where individuals were expelled from the union. A worker who was active in the rank and file movement described the situation in his local:

> Finally they kicked M. out. He was branded as a "Red." I mean having no support for his stand, he was ousted in 1936. He was in the Park Department local. [Interview (Chicago, Ill.) October 19, 1937.]

> This worker, it was stated, was expelled from the union for insisting upon a new drive in the industry which the national office was not willing to undertake.

> A number of the "rank and file" from the various plants finally called upon the national officers to demand that a campaign be inaugurated, but this delegation met with no success. A Committee of Seventeen was organized which appointed a smaller group (upon which three Negroes served) to meet with officers of the C.I.O. The delegation met with Nicholas Fontecchio, Assistant Regional Director, who informed them that the C.I.O. was not prepared at that time to go into the stockyards. When the spokesmen for the group attempted to describe the "militant" sentiment of the workers in the stockyard Fontecchio was not convinced:

> He wouldn't talk to us on the basis of sentiment. He said that we would have to show him. [Interview (Chicago, Ill.) October 19, 1937.]

Following this conference the delegation reported back to the larger group and it was decided to call a mass meeting. Although the meeting was not well advertised, about three hundred and fifty persons attended and over two hundred signed pledge cards. Fontecchio, although informed of the results, still was not convinced that the C.I.O. should attempt to organize the industry. Members of the Committee of Seventeen then held another meeting and contributed from their own resources enough money to print two thousand pledge cards which they distributed throughout the plants in which they worked.

In May of 1936 the Committee of Seventeen opened a union office and actually succeeded in organizing one of the smaller plants before the C.I.O. decided to come into the industry. It was not until the latter part of the same month that the C.I.O. took over responsibility for the office and sent regular organizers into the plants. At that time the United Packing House Workers' Industrial Union was officially set up as a part of the C.I.O. This was not a permanent organization. One of the officers stated:

> A call for a national convention will be issued when the packing industry is completely organized. Then the constitution and bylaws will be drawn up and adopted and international officers will be elected. [Interview (Chicago, Ill.) October 27, 1937.]

Donald Harris was the National Director, Henry Johnson (formerly of the S.W.O.C.) became at a later date Assistant National Director, and Arthur Kompfert, Regional Director.

At the present time (1938) there are no reliable figures on the membership in the U.P.H.W.I.U. A few of the smaller independent plants have been organized. One of the national officers stated:

> P. T. Burham plant is 100% organized and has 100% dues paying members; sole bargaining rights are established. Miller and Hart has the same. Agar plant has 100% organization, as elections are being held this week to establish bargaining rights. Robert and Oak are 100% organized. Swift plant, with 5,000 workers in the plant, is 50% organized; Wilson (3,500 workers in the plant) is 50% organized; Armours, with 7,000 workers (and a maximum capacity of 10,000 workers) is 80% organized. [Interview (Chicago, Ill.) October 25, 1937.]

In the larger plants the unions have made some headway but have not been successful in organizing the majority of workers. Different union officials estimate rather uniformly that approximately 50 per cent of the workers are signed up in each of the large plants in Chicago. However, due to the confusion which exists in the industry caused by the competition between the company dominated independent unions, the Amalgamated of the A.F. of L., and the United Packing House of the C.I.O., no organization has been able to achieve a majority.

At the present the U.P.H.W.I.U. is following the policy of bringing the cases of union discrimination to the attention of the Labor Board and trying to build up membership before any real test of their strength is made. A typical case was described by a national officer:

> Last week a Negro shop steward was fired. We went to the company and gave them four hours to reconsider before we called the N.L.R.B. They took him back. In the meantime this man told us that he had been sick for thirteen weeks. The company told him that this broke his service record and that he would get no vacation. We brought these things up when we went back for their answer. They agreed to give him a clear record and two weeks' pay.
>
> We have an oral agreement at Wilson's but we don't intend to push for agreement [written contract] until later when work picks up. Then we will seek a national contract. [Interview (Chicago, Ill.) September 10, 1937.]

In a few instances, when the union believed that it had a majority of the workers organized, requests were made to the National Labor Relations Board for an election to see what organization would be the bargaining agency for workers in the plant. In Chicago the U.P.H.W.I.U. won an election in three of the smaller plants in the fall of 1937. However, the union was well aware of the fact that it did not control a majority of the workers in the larger plants and wished to avoid the possibility of a strike.

In 1937 the Amalgamated claimed a national membership of between 85,000 and 89,000 of whom between 5 per cent and 15 per cent were Negroes. [Interview with Patrick Gorman, president of A.M.C.O.B.W. and Isom Williams, organizer.] The officers stated that they had about 95 per cent of the independent companies throughout the country under contract. In Chicago it was claimed that about 50 per cent of the workers in the larger plants were members of the Amalgamated. As in the case of the U.P.H.W.I.U. these estimates are not very reliable and cannot be checked until there is a strike or a vote for recognition is taken. Until then, the relative strength of both unions is open to speculation.

The presence of three unions in the field has done much to hinder the organization of workers into either of the outside unions. One A. F. of L. official stated:

> It's a personal fight between big shots in the labor movement. But I'm a firm believer in the need for unity. There must be unity, or the entire labor movement will collapse; sooner or later this split will ruin the entire labor movement. [Interview (Chicago, Ill.) September 21, 1937.]

In spite of this division there is a surprisingly coöperative feeling between the two organizations. The president of the Amalgamated stated:

> In Minneapolis where Bill Green ordered the Central Labor Union to expel the C.I.O. unions this was done. But the packing unions [A. F. of L. and C.I.O.] continued to co-operate. In Chicago in the plant of the Oppenheimer Casing Co., our man, Novack, was called in by the bosses and told we could have a contract for sole bargaining rights. The C.I.O. was already organizing, so he called Van Bittner and told him of the situation. Van replied that if the A. F. of L. could get a contract, the C.I.O. would quit organizing there. He [Van Bittner] agreed to appear at a mass meeting of the workers with Novack and explain to the workers the situation in the shop. This was done and the contract was signed by the A. F. of L. [Interview, Patrick Gorman.]

Negroes are members in both unions in large numbers. They are, on occasion, encouraged to join the Amalgamated by employers who wish to defeat the C.I.O. Schuyler found that colored workers were often used in this method to keep out the more aggressive form of unionism. In competing for Negro membership the organizers of the U.P.H.W.I.U. claimed the Amalgamated had often shown prejudice and that there were no Negroes on the international executive board while the Assistant Director of the Industrial Union was colored. Officers of the Amalgamated stated, however, that at the last convention fifteen of the one hundred and forty delegates were Negroes and there were four national Negro organizers. One of the organizers was described in the following terms:

> Reverend G——— R——— is a Baptist minister. He has been organizing for us for twenty years. He's an itinerant preacher. Wherever he happens to be he goes in on Sunday and preaches. [Interview (Chicago, Ill.) October 26, 1937.]

Concerning the charge that there is no Negro on the executive board, Gorman said:

> We never have had any Negroes on the International Board. In the 1930 convention in Detroit there was a resolution introduced asking that a Negro be placed on the board, but this was overwhelmingly defeated because it was felt there was to be no representation just because of race or nationality. Why, in that case, we would have to have more Poles on the board because we have a great many Polish workers, and also Jews because we have three times as many Jews (butchers) as we have Negroes. In the 19th convention George Reade got a very big vote for the International Board but he was defeated by a white candidate. [Interview (Chicago, Ill.) October 26, 1937.]

Negroes are very prominent, however, in many of the locals of the Amalgamated. Schuyler reported in Philadelphia:

> The Amalgamated Meat Cutters and Butcher Workmen of North America, Local No. 195, A. F. of L., has been conducting an organization drive for over two months. Because of past discrimination against colored workers, organizers report a certain reticence of Negro workers in joining, but claim that it is being overcome.
>
> Of the 2,300 workers in the local industry, comprising 19 different nationalities, about 30 per cent are Negroes. A colored man, Dewey Bucannon, is vice president. William Banks is shop steward at Duffy Bros., Emmanuel Wyatt at Cross Bros., and Samuel Elliott at the Consolidated Dressed Beef Company. All are trustees of the union. The Negroes in the industry are both laborers and craftsmen.

Local No. 116 in Chicago has a colored organizer attached to it and the president, vice-president, recording secretary, and financial secretary are Negroes. Sixty per cent of the membership of the local is white and only 35 per cent Negro. The situation it was admitted was very unusual. [Interview (Chicago, Ill.), September 21, 1937.]

Of the two unions, however, there is little doubt that the U.P.H.W.I.U. is the more liberal. Not only has it made a very definite effort to guard against any form of race prejudice but it does not have to overcome the disadvantage of prejudice acts toward Negroes in the past or the racially conservative attitudes of its national leadership as is the case with the

Amalgamated. The entrance of the U.P.H.W.I.U. into the field has done much to liberalize racial attitudes in the industry. Material on the participation of Negroes in the Amalgamated in Omaha, St. Paul, and St. Louis (which were visited in 1934) is not available. However, correspondence with competent observers in these localities tends to confirm the facts found in Chicago. There, as in Chicago, the Amalgamated was not making much headway against the combined efforts of the C.I.O. and the independent company dominated unions. However, it also had liberalized its attitude toward Negroes in those localities in order to compete with the C.I.O. for their allegiance.

The meat-packing industry is an example of the harm to the organized labor movement which has resulted from the split between the A. F. of L. and the C.I.O. Negro workers can by their numbers and importance determine whether the A. F. of L. or the C.I.O. will be victorious and even whether the industry can be organized at all.

section **5**

Contemporary American Society
1945-the present

The years since 1945 have seen the acceleration of long-term economic trends that had begun earlier in the century and become especially important after 1929. If we focus just on the decade-and-a-half following the Second World War, some of these trends can be briefly sketched. Measured in 1957 dollars, the Gross National Product increased from $301 billion in 1946 to $440 billion in 1957. The output of goods doubled as compared to the 1920s. In three postwar years (1946–1948), business expenditure just for new plants and new equipment totalled $130 billion. New technology encouraged new investment, but so did the enlarged role of the government. Local, state, and federal spending as a percentage of the Gross National Product increased from 11 percent in 1929 to 20 percent in 1957. Military expenditures now consumed a staggering volume of dollars and shaped a mounting national debt. Forty billion dollars of public monies alone was invested in highway construction between 1946 and 1958.

Quantitative measures of economic growth masked significant social and economic changes following the Second World War. Short-term credit (mostly consumer installments) rose from $8.4 billion to nearly $45 billion between 1946 and 1958. Long-term credit (most mortgage debt) increased in the same years from $23 billion to $118 billion. Between 1946 and 1957, agricultural output rose 13 percent but agricultural employment dropped 25 percent. The relative importance of "self-employed" workers and production workers declined, too. Between 1947 and 1957, for example, the number of production workers remained constant but the number of non-production workers in manufacturing industries increased by 60 percent. The role of women in the economy also altered in important ways. In 1940, just over one in four eligible women worked; in 1956, it was one in three. For the same years, the percentage of married women working increased from one in three to three in five. Other changes of importance occurred in post-World War Two America. *Fortune Magazine* estimated that about nine million Americans had moved to the suburbs in the seven years before 1954, and that 30 million persons then lived in such places.

Much of this data suggested important changes in the shape of mature industrial American society. But these processes did not mean radical structural change. "Ours," Walton Hamilton worried in these years, "has become increasingly a corporate economy and yet the question of corporate responsibility is as insistent today as ever before." More than this, the social power that rested upon the distribution of income remained imbalanced. In 1957, more than 40 million Americans in families of two or more persons lived on cash income of less than $3000 or, if an individual, on cash income of less than $1500. A year later, the 7.6 million families at the bottom of the income pyramid received an aggregate income of $8.5 billion dollars while the 2.5 million at the pyramid's top received $65 billion dollars.

The importance of these changes and constants was often "masked" by differences in color, but these differences reflected long-term shifts in the status and behavior of depressed Americans. The editors faced numerous choices in choosing readings related to these and other broad social changes which have occurred in the United States since 1945. The readings selected, however, relate as much to the distant past as to the recent past and have been selected for comparative purposes. They focus on the common themes emphasized in other sections of these volumes: ethnic distinctiveness, violence and disorder, work and leisure, and the intersection of culture and society. The broad social changes of the past two-and-a-half decades have not pushed these common themes to the side. Instead, their importance was reasserted in the 1960s. The president of the United States is as good a witness to this fact as any ordinary American. He celebrated Labor Day in 1971 by proclaiming "the dignity of work, the value of achievement, the moraltiy of self-reliance." "None of these is going out of style," he insisted. But he worried a bit. "Let us also recognize," he added, "that the work ethic in America is undergoing some changes." These changes, however, were rooted in the problems and dissatisfactions of a mature industrial society, not a pre-modern social system. It was that fact, among others, that loomed larger and larger as the country prepared to celebrate the bicentennial of its national independence.

5.1

The Myth of the Happy Worker

HARVEY SWADOS

A novelist and a journalist, Harvey Swados was not a historian. In the 1950s, he worked for a time in an automobile factory and reflected on his experiences in a brief magazine article that attracted widespread attention. It should be realized that the article appeared at a time when large numbers of American social scientists and others celebrated the apparent social stability of post–World War Two America. In focusing on the work process and the satisfactions and dissatisfactions resulting from it, Swados pointed to a recurring concern of these two volumes. One need only remember Edmund Morgan's essay on labor in colonial Jamestown. But it should not be forgotten that the society itself has changed greatly over these three centuries.

Harvey Swados, A Radical's America (Boston: Little, Brown and Company, 1962), pp. 111–20. Reprinted by permission of Georges Borchardt, Inc., New York.

> "From where we sit in the company," says one of the best personnel men in the country, "we have to look at only the aspects of work that cut across all sorts of jobs—administration and human relations. Now these are aspects of work, abstractions, but it's easy for personnel people to get so hipped on their importance that they look on the specific tasks of making things and selling them as secondary . . ."
>
> —*William H. Whyte, Jr., The Organization Man*

The personnel man who made this remark to Mr. Whyte differed from his brothers only in that he had a moment of insight. Actually, "the specific tasks of making things" are now not only regarded by his white-collar fellows as "secondary," but as irrelevant to the vaguer but more "challenging" tasks of the man at the desk. This is true not just of the personnel man, who places workers, replaces them, displaces them—in brief, manipulates them. The union leader also, who represents workers and sometimes manipulates them, seems increasingly to regard what his workers do as merely subsidiary to the job he himself is doing in the larger community. This job may be building the Red Cross or the Community Chest, or it may sometimes be—as the Senate hearings suggest—participating in such communal endeavors as gambling, prostitution, and improving the breed. In any case, the impression is left that the problems of the workers in the background (or underground) have been stabilized, if not permanently solved.

With the personnel man and the union leader, both of whom presumably see the worker from day to day, growing so far away from him, it is hardly to be wondered at that the middle class in general, and articulate middle-class intellectuals in particular, see the worker vaguely, as through a cloud. One gets the impression that when they do consider him, they operate from one of two unspoken assumptions: (1) The worker has died out like the passenger pigeon, or is dying out, or becoming accultured, like the Navajo. (2) If he *is* still around, he is just like the rest of us—fat, satisfied, smug, a little restless, but hardly distinguishable from his fellow TV-viewers of the middle class.

Lest it be thought that (1) is somewhat exaggerated, I hasten to quote from a recently published article apparently dedicated to the laudable task of urging slothful middle-class intellectuals to wake up and live: "The old-style sweatshop crippled mainly the working people. Now there are no workers left in America; we are almost all middle-class as to income and expectations." I do not believe the writer meant to state—although he comes perilously close to it—that nobody works any more. If I understand him correctly, he is referring to the fact that the worker's rise in real income over the last decade, plus the diffusion of middle-class tastes and values throughout a large part of the underlying population, have made it increasingly difficult to tell blue-collar from white-collar worker without a program. In short, if the worker earns like the middle class, votes like the middle class, dresses like the middle class, dreams like the middle class, then he ceases to exist as a worker.

But there is one thing that the worker doesn't do like the middle class: he works like a worker. The steel-mill puddler does not yet sort memos, the coal miner does not yet sit in conferences, the cotton mill-hand does not yet sip martinis from his lunchbox. The worker's attitude toward his work is generally compounded of hatred, shame, and resignation.

Before I spell out what I think this means, I should like first to examine some of the implications of the widely held belief that "we are almost all middle-class as to income and expectations." I am neither economist, sociologist, nor politician, and I hold in my hand no doctored statistics to be haggled over. I have had occasion to work in factories at various times during the Thirties, Forties, and Fifties. The following observations are simply impressions based on my last period of factory servitude, in 1956.

The average automobile worker gets a little better than two dollars an hour. As such he is one of the best-paid factory workers in the country. After twenty years of militant struggle led by the union that I believe to be one of the finest and most democratic labor organizations in the United States, he is earning less than the starting salaries offered to inexperienced and often semiliterate college graduates without dependents. After compulsory deductions for taxes, social security, old-age insurance and union dues, and optional deductions for hospitalization and assorted charities, his pay check for forty hours of work is going to be closer to seventy than to eighty dollars a week. Does this make him middle-class as to income? Does it rate with the weekly take of a dentist, an accountant, a salesman, a draftsman, a journalist? Surely it would be more to the point to ask how a family man can get by in the Fifties on that kind of income. I know how he does it, and I should think the answers would be a little disconcerting to those who wax glib on the satisfactory status of the "formerly" underprivileged.

For one thing, he works a lot longer than forty hours a week—when he can. Since no automobile company is as yet in a position to guarantee its workers anything like fifty weeks of steady forty-hour pay checks, the auto worker knows he has to make it while he can. During peak production periods he therefore puts in nine, ten, eleven, and often twelve hours a day on the assembly line for weeks on end. And that's not all. If he has dependents, as like as not he also holds down a "spare-time" job. I have worked on the line with men who doubled as mechanics, repairmen, salesmen, contractors, builders, farmers, cabdrivers, lumberyard workers, countermen. I would guess that there are many more of these than show up in the official statistics: often a man will work for less if he can be paid under the counter with tax-free dollars.

Nor is that all. The factory worker with dependents cannot carry the debt load he now shoulders—the middle-class debt load, if you like, of nagging payments on car, washer, dryer, TV, clothing, house itself—without family help. Even if he puts in fifty, sixty, or seventy hours a week at one or two jobs, he has to count on his wife's pay check, or his son's, his daughter's, his brother-in-law's; or on his mother's social security, or his father's veteran's pension. The working-class family today is not typically held together by the male wage-earner, but by multiple wage-earners often of several generations who club together to get the things they want and need—or are pressured into believing they must have. It is at best a precarious arrangement; as for its toll on the physical organism and the psyche, that is a question perhaps worthy of further investigation by those who currently pronounce themselves bored with Utopia Unlimited in the Fat Fifties.

But what of the worker's middle-class expectations? I had been under the impression that this was the rock on which socialist agitation had foundered for generations: it proved useless to tell the proletarian that he had a world to win when he was reasonabiy certain that with a few breaks he could have his own gas station. If these expectations have changed at all in recent years, they would seem to have narrowed rather than expanded, leaving a psychological increment of resignation rather than of unbounded optimism (except among the very young—and even among them the optimism focuses more often on better-paying opportunities elsewhere in the labor market than on illusory hopes of swift status advancement). The worker's expectations are for better pay, more humane working conditions, more job security. As long as he feels that he is going to achieve them through an extension of existing conditions, for that long he is going to continue to be a middle-class conservative in temper. But only for that long.

I suspect that what middle-class writers mean by the worker's middle-class expectations are his cravings for commodities—his determination to have not only fin-tailed cars and single-unit washer-dryers, but butterfly chairs in the rumpus room, African masks on the wall, and power boats in the garage. Before the middle-class intellectuals condemn these expectations too harshly, let them consider, first, who has been utilizing every known technique of suasion and propaganda to convert luxuries into necessities, and second, at what cost these new necessities are acquired by the American working-class family.

Now I should like to return to the second image of the American worker: satisfied, doped by TV, essentially middle-class in outlook. This is an image bred not of communication with workers (except as mediated by hired interviewers sent "into the field" like anthropologists or entomologists), but of contempt for people, based perhaps on self-contempt and on a feeling among intellectuals that the worker has let them down. In order to see this clearly, we have to place it against the intellectual's changing attitudes toward the worker since the Thirties.

At the time of the organization of the CIO, the middle-class intellectual saw the proletarian as society's figure of virtue—heroic, magnanimous, bearing in his loins the seeds of a better future; he would have found ludicrous the suggestion that a sit-down striker might harbor anti-Semitic feelings. After Pearl Harbor, the glamorization of the worker was taken over as a function of government. Then, however, he was no longer the builder of the future good society; instead he was second only to the fighting man as the vital winner of the war. Many intellectuals, as government employees, found themselves helping to create this new portrait of the worker as patriot.

But in the decade following the war intellectuals have discovered that workers are no longer either building socialism or forging the tools of victory. All they are doing is making the things that other people buy. That, and participating in the great commodity scramble. The disillusionment, it would seem, is almost too terrible to bear. Word has gotten around among the highbrows that the worker is not heroic or idealistic; public-opinion polls prove that he wants barbecue pits more than foreign aid and air-conditioning more than desegregation, that he doesn't particularly want to go on strike, that he is reluctant to form a Labor Party, that he votes for Stevenson and often for Eisenhower and Nixon—that he is, in short, animated by the same aspirations as drive the middle-class onward and upward in suburbia.

There is of course a certain admixture of self-delusion in the middle-class attitude that workers are now the same as everybody else. For me it was expressed most precisely last year in the dismay and sympathy with which middle-class friends greeted the news that I had gone back to work in a factory. If workers are now full-fledged members of the middle class, why the dismay? What difference whether one sits in an office or stands in a shop? The answer is so obvious that one feels shame at laboring the point. But I have news for my friends among the intellectuals. The answer is obvious to workers, too.

They know that there is a difference between working with your back and working with your behind (I do not make the distinction between handwork and brainwork, since we are all learning that white-collar work is becoming less and less brainwork). They know that they work harder than the middle class for less money. Nor is it simply a question of status, that magic word so dear to the hearts of the sociologues, the new anatomizers of the American corpus. It is not simply status-hunger that makes a man hate work which pays *less* than other work he knows about, if *more* than any other work he has been trained for (the only reason my fellow workers stayed on the assembly line, they told me again and again). It is not simply status-hunger that makes a man hate work that is mindless, endless, stupefying, sweaty, filthy, noisy, exhausting, insecure in its prospects, and practically without hope of advancement.

The plain truth is that factory work is degrading. It is degrading to any man who ever dreams of doing something worthwhile with his life; and it is about time we faced the fact. The more a man is exposed to middle-class values, the more sophisticated he becomes and the more production-line work is degrading to him. The immigrant who slaved in the poorly lighted, foul, vermin-ridden sweatshop found his work less degrading than the native-born high school graduate who reads "Judge Parker," "Rex Morgan, M.D.," and "Judd Saxon, Business Executive," in the funnies, and works in a fluorescent factory with ticker-tape production-control machines. For the immigrant laborer, even the one who did not dream of socialism, his long hours were going to buy him freedom. For the factory worker of the Fifties, his long hours are going to buy him commodities . . . and maybe reduce a few of his debts.

Almost without exception, the men with whom I worked on the assembly line last year felt like trapped animals. Depending on their age and personal circumstances, they were either resigned to their fate, furiously angry at *themselves* for what they were doing, or desperately hunting other work that would pay as well and in addition offer some variety, some prospect of change and betterment. They were sick of being pushed around by harried foremen (themselves more pitied than hated), sick of working like blinkered donkeys, sick of being dependent for their livelihood on a maniacal production-merchandising setup, sick of working in a place where there was no spot to relax during the twelve-minute rest period. (Someday—let us hope—we will marvel that production was still so worshiped in the Fifties that new factories could be built with every splendid facility for the storage and movement of essential parts, but with no place for a resting worker to sit down for a moment but on a fireplug, the edge of a packing case, or the sputum- and oil-stained stairway of a toilet.)

The older men stay put and wait for their vacations. But since the assembly line demands young blood (you will have a hard time getting hired if you are over thirty-five), the factory in which I worked was aswarm with new faces every day; labor turnover was so fantastic and absenteeism so rampant, with the young men knocking off a day or two every week to hunt up other jobs, that the company was forced to overhire in order to have sufficient workers on hand at the starting siren.

To those who will object—fortified by their readings in C. Wright

Mills and A. C. Spectorsky—that the white-collar commuter, too, dislikes his work, accepts it only because it buys his family commodities, and is constantly on the prowl for other work, I can only reply that for me at any rate this is proof not of the disappearance of the working class but of the proletarianization of the middle class. Perhaps it is not taking place quite in the way that Marx envisaged it, but the alienation of the white-collar man (like that of the laborer) from both his tools and whatever he produces, the slavery that chains the exurbanite to the commuting time-table (as the worker is still chained to the time clock), the anxiety that sends the white-collar man home with his briefcase for an evening's work (as it degrades the workingman into pleading for long hours of overtime), the displacement of the white-collar slum from the wrong side of the tracks to the suburbs (just as the working-class slum is moved from old-law tenements to skyscraper barracks)—all these mean to me that the white-collar man is entering (though his arms may be loaded with commodities) the gray world of the working man.

Three quotations from men with whom I worked may help to bring my view into focus:

Before starting work: "Come on, suckers, they say the Foundation wants to give away *more* than half a billion this year. Let's do and die for the old Foundation."

During rest period: "Ever stop to think how we crawl here bumper to bumper, and crawl home bumper to bumper, and we've got to turn out more every minute to keep our jobs, when there isn't even any room for them on the highways?"

At quitting time (this from older foremen, whose job is not only to keep things moving, but by extension to serve as company spokesmen): "You're smart to get out of here. . . . I curse the day I ever started, now I'm stuck: any man with brains that stays here ought to have his head examined. This is no place for an intelligent human being."

Such is the attitude toward the work. And toward the product? On the one hand it is admired and desired as a symbol of freedom, almost a substitute for freedom, not because the worker participated in making it, but because our whole culture is dedicated to the proposition that the auto-mobile is both necessary and beautiful. On the other hand it is hated and despised—so much that if your new car smells bad it may be due to a banana peel crammed down its gullet and sealed up thereafter, so much so that if your dealer can't locate the rattle in your new car you might ask him to open the welds on one of those tail fins and vacuum out the nuts and bolts thrown in by workers sabotaging their own product.

Sooner or later, if we want a decent society—by which I do not mean a society glutted with commodities or one maintained in precarious equi-librium by overbuying and forced premature obsolescence—we are going to have to come face to face with the problem of work. Apparently the Russians have committed themselves to the replenishment of their labor force through automatic recruitment of those intellectually incapable of keeping up with severe scholastic requirements in the public educational system. Apparently we, too, are heading in the same direction: although our economy is not directed, and although college education is as yet far from free, we seem to be operating in this capitalist economy on the totalitarian assumption that we can funnel the underprivileged, underequipped, into the factory, where we can proceed to forget about them once we have posted the minimum fair labor standards on the factory wall.

If this is what we want, let's be honest enough to say so. If we conclude that there is nothing noble about repetitive work, but that it is nevertheless good enough for the lower orders, let's say that, too, so we will at least know where we stand. But if we cling to the belief that other men are our brothers, not just Egyptians, or Israelis, or Hungarians, but *all* men, including millions of Americans who grind their lives away on an insane treadmill, then we will have to start thinking about how their work and their lives can be made meaningful. That is what I assume the Hungarians, both workers and intellectuals, have been thinking about. Since no one has been ordering us what to think, since no one has been forbidding our intellectuals to fraternize with our workers, shouldn't it be a little easier for us to admit, first, that our problems exist, then to state them, and then to see if we can resolve them?

5.2

Liberal Intelligentsia and White Backlash

RICHARD F. HAMILTON

Changing attitudes toward work have constantly been a theme in American social history. So have the distinctive voting patterns of particular social classes and ethnic groups. In the 1920s and especially in the 1930s, "new" immigrants, and particularly industrial workers, identified strongly with social reform and with the Democratic Party. Changing material and cultural circumstances after the Second World War were bound to affect their political perception and behavior. One of these changes—perhaps the most important—was the challenge posed by Black Americans. Whites in all social classes reacted differently to the attack on institutional racism. The Alabama Governor George Wallace attracted widespread support on this and related issues, and political analysts and social scientists disputed the social origins of that electoral support. The sociologist Richard Hamilton

Richard F. Hamilton, "Liberal Intelligentsia and White Backlash," *Dissent Magazine*, Winter, 1972, pp. 225–32. Also published by Quadrangle/The New York Times Book Co. in *The World of the Blue Collar Worker* (New York, 1972). Copyright 1972 by *Dissent Magazine*. Reprinted, omitting bibliography, by permission of Quadrangle/The New York Times Book Co.

strongly quarreled with those who easily identified Wallace sentiment with just a working-class "backlash" vote.

In the world view of liberal intellectuals, those persons who share decent and humane values form a tiny minority standing on the edge of an abyss. In that world view they are always standing there, the problem being that there are so few people who share those values and so many potentially powerful and, if aroused, dangerous groups present in the society. The best one can hope for is that the threatening groups remain quiescent, that they not be aroused.

The American liberal finds himself in a difficult world; he is sincere, concerned about the pressing problems in the society, willing to see changes made, but he also is trapped by the inexorable dictates of the situation. If these hostile groups were to be aroused (at one time the dangerous lower-middle class was the problem, now there is also the dangerous white working class), the liberal minority would be unable to stem the reaction that would follow.

Are the liberals really as threatened as they imagine? Is it true, as John W. Gardner says, that:

> The collision between dissenters and lower middle class opponents is exceedingly dangerous . . . [that] as long as the dissenters are confronting the top layers of the power structure, they are dealing with people who are reasonably secure, often willing to compromise, able to yield ground without anxiety. [But that] when the dissenters collide with the lower middle class, they confront an unsure opponent, quick to anger, and not prepared to yield an inch.

Is it true, as Adam Walinsky puts it, that "There are now only two identifiable ethnic groups—blacks and those who hate them . . ."?

The white workers, so goes the sedulously repeated lesson, compete with blacks for jobs and hence are hostile to any moves that would tend to favor the latter. And a second major source of "strain" for the white workers appears when blacks move into "their" neighborhoods, the housing areas immediately adjacent to the ghettos. While working-class communities are broken up, property values suffer, hard-earned equities disappear or are seriously diminished, problems develop in the schools and intense racial hostilities result. Clear, tangible evidence of this reaction appeared in support for George Wallace provided by the white working class.

Again one may ask the question, is this true?

In 1963, the National Opinion Research Center (NORC) asked a representative sample of the American population a question touching directly on what is presumed to be the central area of the black-white struggle, the matter of jobs. In all that follows, the attitudes of the white working class and middle class will be contrasted (or, for the sake of stylistic variation, the white manuals and nonmanuals, the blue-collar and white-collar workers). Since the pattern differs in the South, we will consider first that three-quarters of the white population living outside the South and the border states, those who live in the North, Midwest, and the Western states.

The job question reads as follows: "Do you think Negroes should have as good a chance as white people to get any kind of job, or do you think white people should have the first chance at any kind of job?" Given the impressive agreement in liberal circles on the virtue of the educated and responsible middle class, it is not surprising to learn that 91 percent of the white-collar group favor equal treatment. It may well come as a surprise, however, to learn that approximately the same percentage, 87 to be exact, of the blue-collar group also say Negroes should have an equal chance.

One might conclude that this was 1963, before the black revolution took on such aggressive form, before there were any serious demands made on the available supply of jobs, that is, before the white working-class *reaction* had occurred. In April of 1968 the same organization asked a somewhat different job question, this one reading: "How do you feel about fair employment laws—that is, laws that make white people hire qualified Negroes, so that Negroes can get any job they are qualified for—do you favor or oppose such laws?" The non-Southern middle-class whites again indicate a commendable level of liberal virtue, 88 percent favoring such laws. Once again, despite the fervid assertions, the equivalent blue-collar group also shows that same high level of virtuous sentiment, in this case the figure being 89 percent.

What about housing? This is an area in which, once again, there is fierce antiblack and necessarily antiequalitarian sentiment present; or at least so it is said. In 1963 the NORC asked the following question: "If a Negro with the same income and education as you moved into your block, would it make any difference to you?" The percentages of blue-collar and white-collar respondents saying "no difference" were 72 and 71 respectively. Once again, the image of the liberals as a beleaguered minority is not supported; and once again, the assumptions that liberal virtue resides in the middle class and that intolerance is disproportionately found in the working class are not supported.

It might be, to repeat the previously mentioned objection, that the finding is "prebacklash." But when the same question was asked in April 1968, the result did not indicate a "backlash" or "reaction" at all; it showed rather an increase in tolerant sentiment in both groups, the respective figures then being 83 and 88 percent.

One might haggle over the wording of the question and object that the "same income and education" phrase might obscure the "real" distribution of opinion. A question asked by the University of Michigan Survey Research Center in its 1964 election study does not contain that kind of clause; it asks: "Which of these statements would you agree with? White people have a right to keep Negroes out of their neighborhoods if they want to. Or, Negroes have a right to live wherever they can afford to, just like white people." The percentages favoring open housing were 72 among the blue-collar workers and 80 in the white-collar ranks. The same question, when asked four years later during the 1968 election campaign, found 85 percent of the manuals and 84 percent of the nonmanuals favoring the open housing option. There was, it will be noted, no reaction in the course of the intervening four years, with the long-term trend of recent years toward ever higher levels of tolerance continuing unabated.

When asked about school integration a similar result appeared. The 1963 NORC question read as follows: "Do you think white students and Negro students should go to the same schools, or to separate schools?" Of non-Southern manual workers 79 percent and of the nonmanuals 81 percent said they should go to the same schools. The same question was asked in April 1968, the percentages being 80 and 89 for manuals and nonmanuals respectively. Again, the evidence provides no indication of a reaction.*

Not all the evidence is as positive as these results. A 1968 statement read: "White people have a right to keep Negroes out of their neighborhoods if they want to, and Negroes should respect that right." In this case somewhat lower percentages disagreed, that is, took the tolerant position, the figures being 45 and 63 percent for manuals and nonmanuals respectively. This result comes from the same study that asked about the Negro with the same education and income moving in. The discrepancy between the two results may mean that some whites, particularly those in the manual ranks, subscribe to an equality position and to a "neighborhood auton-

---

* People who find such responses difficult to believe, perhaps because they are somehow attached to the idea that manual workers must be a repository of bias, will sometimes ask the question: how do you know that they are *really* expressing their genuine feelings when they respond in the polls? Aren't they perhaps giving what they think are the proper or expected answers, while in their actual conduct they go by different, less attractive values? There is of course no way of discounting this possibility entirely—with regard to blue-collar workers who are polled, or with regard to *anyone else.* But my own assumption would be that such a response bias is more likely to occur among middle-class respondents, who are much more involved with current views preaching or assuming tolerance, than among blue-collar workers, whose milieu might be more supportive to a frank expression of intolerant attitudes.

omy" position at the same time. Even in this case, were the nervous liberal once again to feel beleaguered, it should be noted that there are still some 45 percent of the blue-collar workers who are with him on this matter. There is no warrant for seeing the wall of opposition suggested by Walinsky's remark.

When questions were asked about closer contacts, the amount of approval fell off sharply from the high levels indicated in the questions about job equality, housing, and equal schooling. Asked about objections to one's teen-age child dating a black boy or girl, the percentages with "no objections" fell to 6 and 13.

To summarize the evidence briefly: among the non-Southern whites there is immense support for equality with respect to jobs, housing, and educational opportunities. In both these areas, contrary to widespread alarm, there is very little difference between manuals and nonmanuals in their stated positions. When it is a question of closer contacts, much less equalitarian sentiment is indicated and in these cases there are some larger differences between manuals and nonmanuals.

The responses among Southern whites are quite different, as may well be expected. The overall levels of tolerance are considerably lower and there are also rather consistent and fair-sized differences between manuals and nonmanuals. It is in the South that one finds a relatively intolerant working class. The respective percentages approving of a Negro moving into their neighborhood were 55 and 63. The percentages favoring integrated schools were 35 and 64. But, even in the South, there are some striking exceptions. Taking the April 1968 question on equal job opportunities, the percentages of manuals and nonmanuals taking the tolerant position were 79 and 77.

The focus on the "competition for jobs" appears, therefore, to be misleading. This study indicates that four-fifths of the Southern white workers hold an equalitarian position on that question. A majority of the white workers also take an equalitarian position on the housing question. The situation is less favorable with respect to school integration but even here one-third of the white workers take the tolerant position.

These attitudes also vary considerably within the South, the lowest tolerance appearing in the Goldwater or Wallace states and the highest in the border states. Even these attitudes are not constant, for in recent years they have shown the same tolerant trend found elsewhere in the nation. The percentages favoring integrated schools in 1963, for example, (as compared to the 1968 figures cited in the previous paragraph) were only 21 and 49.

If one did not make the regional separation but simply presented the overall figures for manuals and nonmanuals in the entire nation, the result would obscure the fact that the class differences do *not* appear in the non-Southern states. The conventional presentation, in other words, lends credence to the notion of working-class intolerance by averaging diverse regional patterns.

Against this survey evidence, to be sure, one has the evidence of the elections, both the 1964 and the 1968 presidential elections having involved attempts to stimulate a backlash. Such evidence, involving as it does a kind of behavior (as opposed to the mere expression of opinions to pollsters), is of a much "harder" character. And, as is well known, in both elections the white working class is supposed to have indicated its preference for those proffering backlash appeals. Theodore White, for example, tells us that the "disturbance of spirit" felt by white workingmen in 1964 was "absorbed in the Goldwater vote."

Once again we may ask, is that true? The University of Michigan's Survey Research Center's 1964 election study shows only 20 percent of the non-Southern white workers supporting Goldwater in that election, a level of Republican sentiment well *below* normal levels. Rather than absorbing the "disturbed spirits," the Goldwater candidacy repelled hundreds of thousands of them. Among relatively low-income middle-class groups approximately a third favored Goldwater. Among the high-income middle-class group, which for short we may call the upper-middle class, approximately half favored his candidacy. In the case of the upper-middle-class white Protestants, the level of Goldwater support ran to 70 percent. And it would be a mistake to write these voters off as untutored *arrivistes,* since 22 percent of that group had at least some college education and another 42 percent had finished college or gone on for a higher degree.

Speaking of that other remarkable event of the 1964 campaign, the appearance of George Wallace on the national scene, Theodore White observes:

> . . . Wallace astounded political observers not so much by the percentage of votes he could draw for simple bigotry . . . as by the groups from whom he drew his votes. For he demonstrated pragmatically and for the first time the fear that white working-class Americans have of Negroes. In Wisconsin he scored heavily in the predominantly Italian, Polish and Serb working-class neighborhoods of Milwaukee's south side. . . .

That is all true enough, Wallace did score heavily to take approximately one-third of the votes there. The only point omitted in White's account is that Wallace drew almost twice as high a percentage in the elegant north-side suburbs. Outside of the ghetto, his vote in that primary was *lowest* in white working-class neighborhoods. In general, the richer the suburb the higher the Wallace percentage. In Dane County, which contains the state capital, the most elegant suburb, Maple Bluff, also had the more elegant level of Wallace support. It seems likely that much of this Wallace vote came from those out to punish the Democratic "favorite son," a governor who had brought in a sales tax. Such misrepresentation of the sources of Wallace's 1964 strength is quite wide-spread. The political sociologist Seymour Martin Lipset, for example, writing in *Encounter* later that year, claimed that Wallace "received his highest vote in the predominantly Catholic working-class areas of Milwaukee. . . ." One fact that has been completely overlooked amidst the talk of a *growing* reaction is that Wallace's vote in the south side of Milwaukee was considerably lower both in percentage and in absolute numbers in the 1968 presidential election than in the 1964 presidential primary.

All this, however, is mere play as against the most telling demonstration of the "working-class racism" thesis: the vote for Wallace in 1968 election. Again, taking the words of the eminent commentator Theodore White, we learn that

> No less than 4.1 million [of Wallace's 9.9 million votes] came from the Northern and Western states; and these were, overwhelmingly, white workingman votes. . . . Despite all the influences of the media, all the pressure of their labor leaders, all the blunders and incompetence of the Wallace campaign, they had voted racist.

Again, it is true? Did *they* vote racist?

According to most political surveyors, the best available studies of the American electorate are those undertaken by the Survey Research Center of the University of Michigan. Taking their study of the 1968 election and examining the non-Southern white respondents and their political preferences, one finds that Theodore White's claim is not supported. Of the non-Southern blue-collar workers, 9 percent voted for Wallace as against 8 percent of the equivalent white-collar workers. The manual–nonmanual difference in Wallace support is a matter of *one* percentage point.

In assessing this "difference" it is worth remembering that as a result of migration the non-Southern manual ranks contain a somewhat larger percentage of white ex-Southerners than do the nonmanuals. And one should also bear in mind that the non-Southern middle-class ranks gain a special edge in "liberalism" as a result of the disproportionate number of Jews present there. Without these two special contributions, it seems likely that even this one-percent difference would disappear.

In the South, by comparison, the traditional hypothesis is supported. A sizable minority of the white workers, some 39 percent, favored Wallace as did approximately one-third of the lower-income middle-class. Only one-eighth of the Southern white upper-middle class favored Wallace, most of them preferring Nixon.

A discussion of the 1968 election by Seymour Martin Lipset and Earl Raab, which is based on Gallup data, shows results that are very similar to those of the Survey Research Center study. Here the difference between the manual and nonmanual vote for Wallace was a matter of four percentage points within the non-South population. In the South the difference was again considerably greater. These authors also added the percentage of those who "considered Wallace" in the course of the campaign and, looking at the "Total Wallace Sympathizers," came up with a larger difference, one of 12 percentage points. Whether "considering Wallace" derived from *sympathy* for him or from the absence of a more attractive alternative is not indicated in Lipset's presentation. The frustration of the voters in that election is indicated by one poll result which showed that 43 percent of the electorate were not satisfied with any of the three candidates who had presented themselves. In any event, a majority of the manual workers who "considered" Wallace eventually rejected him so as to yield the 4 percent difference.

There is a striking congruence between these voting results and the attitudinal evidence discussed above. Outside the South, there were no class differences on those issues which were presumably of key concern, manuals and nonmanuals alike showing very high tolerant–equalitarian percentages. The voting evidence shows much the same pattern, a very limited attraction to the Wallace appeals and essentially the same level of such interest indicated by both groups. The Wallace appeal, incidentally, was exactly the same in both the lower-middle and upper-middle-class segments.

One might add further details to this picture of the Southern Wallace vote. It was a vote centered in smaller communities and middle-sized cities. In those locations he took approximately two-fifths of the total as against less than one-fifth in the larger cities. Intolerance in the responses to the attitude questions is also concentrated in the same communities. Why do the smaller Southern communities have the outlook they do? It might be owing to the influence of fundamentalist Protestant sects preaching the inferiority of the sons of Ham. It might be owing to competition for jobs, although rural blacks are in general located in different areas from the majority of rural and small-town whites, the former being found disproportionately in lowland plantation areas and the latter in the uplands and hill country.

Another question deserving some attention is stimulated by this discrepancy between the evidence presented here and the productions of liberal intellectuals. One might sum it up with a modification of a current slogan: they are "telling it like it isn't." How come?

There are a number of reasons. Most of the Gallup presentations during the 1968 presidential campaign made no separation by region, thereby averaging in two divergent patterns. The Southern pattern would come through in the nationwide figure and suggest general, across-the-board confirmation for the "working-class authoritarianism" thesis.

Another tendency involves the magnification of small percentage differences. The Gallup results throughout the campaign showed the manual workers to be only a few percentage points ahead of the nonmanual categories in their level of Wallace support. The relationships indicated in the monthly polls were somewhat erratic, and in some cases the manual percentage even fell below that of some of the nonmanual groups. Despite this, the formulations tended to be categorical; it was the "racist workers" and the virtuous (or "moderate") middle class. Where some conception of *relative* magnitudes was indicated the tendency still was to magnify the differences—as, for example, in Theodore White's use of the adjective "overwhelming."

Some data presentations make use of attitude scales. In such cases, a range of questions would be used, some having high, some middling, and some low tolerance response levels. They would then be combined so that the result would, typically, be single-scale scores rather than a number of percentages for each of the separate questions. This allows some methodological gains and a considerable degree of economy in the presentation of findings. In the case of the NORC studies reported here, it would mean combining the questions on jobs, housing, and schooling (which showed either small or no class differences) with the questions on more intimate contacts (which did show such differences). The overall result, mixing as it does two diverse orientations, would hide the lack of difference in those areas of greatest public concern. In this case the conventional wisdom would gain some support even if there were a separate presentation by region.

Some presentations have shown tolerance and intolerance by educational level (presumably a surrogate for or close equivalent to occupation). These presentations characteristically show a very strong relationship and one is invited to translate the result back to the "obvious" implications for the poorly educated and the well-educated occupational groups. But education is a poor surrogate for occupation, for the simple reason that education is very strongly related to age. And what is showing up in this education–tolerance relationship seems to be that older people are less tolerant than younger people. Put somewhat differently, this means that older, small-town or rural, (and poorly educated) Southern women are less tolerant than young urban non-Southern (and college-educated) men.

Put still another way, this means that there are a lot of other factors operating besides education to yield those handsome distributions.

The evidence presented here is not entirely new. Similar results have appeared from time to time, but not fitting in with dominant preconceptions, they have generally been ignored. Some ten years ago Charles Herbert Stember reviewed a large number of national studies in his book *Education and Attitude Change* (published by the Institute of Human Relations Press, New York, 1961). He found that many of the conventional judgments were unfounded or at least not as clearly and unambiguously supported as some have thought. His summary conclusion reads: "Socioeconomic status has no uniform effects of its own on attitudes toward the rights of Negroes." Regrettably, his work has not gained the attention it deserves, and one result is that the conventional wisdom persists. One study that presented evidence challenging the conventional wisdom was treated as follows by two sociologists: "There is just too much independent evidence that prejudice toward Negroes is inversely associated with current occupational status for us to contemplate seriously the possibility that the zero order associations revealed by this data are substantively correct." The "independent evidence" they then cite consists of three community studies and one very erratic sample of veterans. All of those studies, incidentally, involve very small percentage differences.

Intellectuals of a literary persuasion are compulsively hostile to systematic data presentations, preferring instead their own "free" and uninhibited associations stimulated by the *New York Times* accounts of the day's events. A few thousand construction workers, following a scenario very similar to that of the motion picture *Z,* attack peace demonstrators on Wall Street, and for these intellectuals those few thousand become the "typical" blue-collar workers. The available evidence does not support that interpretation. Yet demonstrations against open-housing marchers (once again in the notorious south side of Milwaukee) are presented as further proof of the sentiments of the entire population in that area. Lost from view was a small survey of the area's population, which indicated that 70 percent of it favored open housing.

It is correct that most incidents of black-white conflict occur in white working-class neighborhoods on the edge of the ghettos. But then, one might ask, where else could they occur? In order to have conflict one must have contact. For there to be conflict between upper-middle-class whites and blacks, one or the other of them would have to go on a long march or take a long bus ride. Where that has happened—as for example when open-housing marchers went to two upper-middle-class suburbs in Milwaukee—the receptions were similar to the marches to the south-side working-class areas. The location of the conflict, in most cases, is determined by urban social geography. It is a serious question, however, as to whether the actions of small minorities of counterdemonstrators (many of whom are not from the immediate area) speak for or express the feelings of the majority of white workers. The evidence reviewed here would indicate that they do not.

The point, in short, is that literary–political intellectuals read their special preconceptions into the day's news. In this respect they exhibit all the perceptual biases and distortions that have been so amply documented in experiments in social psychology. A review of "the nation's malaise" by any of these writers will dwell on an assortment of awesome backlash campaigns. Such an account would have mayors Stenvig and Yorty of Minneapolis and Los Angeles figuring very prominently. When one asks, however, about Peter Flaherty and Sam Massell, the mayors of Pittsburgh and Atlanta—both of whom beat back the established powers in their respective cities, fighting all the standard weapons in the backlash arsenal —the characteristic response is, who are they? In such a case, the literary intellectual has either submerged the evidence or, worse, failed even to see it. In the antiseptic language of the social sciences, this would be called "selective perception."

If one compulsively rejects systematic evidence and has a trained, aesthetic disgust when faced with "data," with numbers, percentages, or correlation coefficients, then clearly that kind of contact with reality is never going to affect one's understanding. In great measure, the understanding that then comes to dominate has roughly the same basis as that of neighborhood or backyard gossip. Interpretations are passed around within a narrow circle of acquaintances. Those people within that circle support and mutually reinforce each other so that in time their special understandings appear to be indisputable.

Such selective perception and continuous misreading of the evidence gives rise to the alarm felt by liberal policy-makers and, in turn, provides the basis for "go slow" policies and "benign neglect." The evidence reviewed here indicates that the policy-maker genuinely concerned with equality and human decency has considerably more support for his initiative than he ever dreamed.

The evidence reviewed here covers events through November 1968. One of the difficulties of survey research is that the day after one can always say—"That was yesterday." In some ways "backlash" is an indestructible hypothesis. Throughout the 1964 election campaign commentators of all varieties were predicting it, regardless of the evidence of the pollsters, and only when the result was in did they, for a moment at least, desist. There was a period of quiescence and then again, slowly, the hypothesis reappeared in all its glory for its George Wallace flowering. Once again, the result did not match the grim prognostications of the professional alarmists and, in the face of some more positive results in the 1969 elections, the concern again faded. But then, prior to the 1970 congressional elections, there it was once again. It was difficult to add up the results of that year's elections as evidence of the efficacy of hard-line, backlash campaigns and therefore the sounds of alarm again faded away.

There is little point in making a priori stipulations as to what the evidence on that "day affair" will or will not hold. It is always possible that the long-term trend toward greater tolerance might be, or might already, since 1968, have been reversed. It is also possible that in some localities there could be tensions that would reverse the national trend. But the evidence above suggests the need for some restraint before jumping to a conclusion based on impressions or on a few spectacular or dramatic events. The mistaken conclusion can, in some circumstances, give rise to the very eventuality one would ardently wish to avoid.

5.3

Who Are the Chicanos?

JOHN WOMACK, JR.

John Womack, Jr., a Professor of History at Harvard University and the author of a distinguished social history of Mexican peasant movements in the early twentieth century, here reviews an outpouring of books and anthologies about Mexican Americans published in the early 1970s. His is, however, much more than a mere review essay. A penetrating summary of recent Mexican-American historical experiences, the essay puts into perspective emergent and changing ethnic self-consciousness among Mexican Americans. Womack's sharp evaluation of the strengths and weaknesses of many of these recent "studies" applies to much of the literature published about other ethnic groups in the 1960s and early 1970s. The larger questions he poses about historical perspective as a clue to understanding ethnic self-awareness also apply to these other groups.

John Womack, Jr., "Who Are the Chicanos?" Reprinted with permission from *The New York Review of Books*, 19 (August 31, 1972), 12–18. Copyright © 1972 NYREV Inc.

Seventy years ago there were no "Mexican Americans." There were people in the Southwest who were somehow both from Mexico and natives of the United States. But in the view of the regular Americans who knew them best, the transplanted Easterners, Midwesterners, Southerners, Irish, Italians, Jews, and Chinese busy Americanizing the Southwest, and the Negroes serving them, these people did not belong there as Americans. They were "Spaniards" if they were prosperous and pale, and "greasers" or "spics" or "Mexicans" if they were poor and brown.

In their own view these people did not belong in America either. The "Spaniards" deliberately performed as noble exotics in the most pretentious California cities. The "greasers" only reversed the terms of exoticism. The regular Americans were all *anglos* or *gringos* or *gabachos* to them, except for the *negritos*. As for themselves, they were *tejanos, hispanos, pochos, mexicanos, cholos, la raza*. Bunched in little communities scattered throughout the Southwest, Catholics whom regular American Catholics despised, speaking dialects of Spanish no longer if ever heard in Spain, Mexican provincials in their courtesies and food, they were born aliens—a conquered people who could not give in.

Until 1836 the Southwest from Texas to the Pacific had been Mexican territory. By 1848, after American subversion and invasion, it had become US territory, and the 75,000 Mexican citizens there had become US charges. The treaty ending the war had assigned them full title to their property and made all who stayed American citizens. But as regular Americans settled in the newly acquired territory, the ruthless among them freely cheated and killed the newly adopted citizens. After railroads linked the Southwest into national markets in the 1880s, regular Americans flooded into the territory, seized the land they wanted, and drove all the conquered families they needed onto the new cotton plantations and into the new copper mines. Only in New Mexico had the conquering Americans compromised, dealing with a few formidably entrenched native families to exploit the others.

The conquered protested their degradation. Some resorted to the courts, in vain. Others went against the law, like the bandits who had terrorized California in the 1850s and the Lower Rio Grande during the 1860s and 1870s. Others went beyond the law, like the cowboys who had joined the Knights of Labor in Texas in the 1880s or the sheepmen who had organized the *Gorras Blancas* in New Mexico to fight for the range in the 1890s.

But these protests failed. By the turn of the century, of the 100,000 souls the conquered then numbered, probably only a tenth were in families in town, surviving on little businesses and handiwork and a few years of schooling—enough people to support forty-odd Southwestern newspapers in Spanish, but all confined in every town to the wards the regular Americans called "Mextown." The rest were not only humiliated, dispossessed, and impoverished, without skills they could sell dear, but isolated out in the sticks—on ranches lost in the South Texas chaparral, on plantations marooned on the central Texas Black Waxy, in villages hidden in the wooded hollows of northern New Mexico's Sangre de Cristo Mountains, in mining camps, tiered up Arizona's bare and baking Gila Hills, on the big farms and orchards and vineyards fenced into California's San Joaquin and Sacramento valleys, in boxcars barracks stationed along the railroad tracks, always on the wrong side, from Chicago through Kansas City to Houston and Santa Fe, from New Orleans through El Paso to Los Angeles and San Francisco. Kept apart, the conquered kept to themselves, cherishing their religion, language, manners, and tastes, the estrangements that were their consolations.

Consolidating the conquest was the Reclamation Act of 1902, which provided federal funds for irrigation in the Southwest. Bankers now began financing regular American farmers to produce fruit and vegetables for back East and up North. In Texas the lucky farmers promptly drafted local conquered families for migrant labor in their "winter gardens"; when they needed labor dirt-cheap, they had *enganchistas* (contractors) recruit it from across the Big River. In Golden California they became "growers" in the "agribusiness," but reduced local conquered families to migrants and resorted to *enganchistas* too.

In 1910 a revolt broke out in Mexico. At first only an overthrow of seven-term President Porfirio Diaz, it soon exploded into a revolution that lasted a decade. In its course it destroyed the bonds of hundreds of thousands of peons and uprooted villagers even in remote mountains. Most joined revolutionary or counter-revolutionary armies roaming through their country. But in the northern provinces thousands every month escaped farther north, across the open frontier or past the guards at Eagle Pass, Laredo, El Paso, Nogales, and so into this amazingly foreign country, where big pinkish men laughed out loud, spat in public, and wore their hats indoors, where ladies as creamy as the Virgin were wives to such men, rode bicycles for fun, and did their own shopping, where black men and women boldly half-rendered services to them, where one never inquired after another's family, deferred to elders, or begged permission to leave a room, and where the national saint was a furious San Afabichi.

The refugees immediately took shelter in local communities of the conquered. There they learned the ropes of the new country and how much their work would be worth here—not much, but more than at home. There they also picked up a nickname, given in sympathy and exasperation, *Chicano*.

From 1910 to 1920 probably 800,000 Mexicans entered the United States. During the 1920s, while Congress restricted immigration from Europe and Asia, probably 1.5 million entered the country. Many came only to hurry back to Mexico. But many stayed to work in the booms of World War I and Normalcy. Dreaming year after year of the return home, refusing to naturalize as US citizens, they forged lives out of expatriation.

By 1930 the natives of this country whom census officials then called "of Mexican race," greatly reinforced by the Chicanos, numbered probably two million. Maybe 100,000 were off in cities like Detroit or Chicago, working in plants and mills with immigrants from other countries, becoming regular immigrants themselves, and so regular Americans. But almost all the rest were still in the Southwest, probably a tenth of them hanging on in Mextowns, but the huge majority still out in the fields and mines and on the roads, still working in gangs almost exclusively with their own kind at the lowest wages in dead-end labor, housed in camps segregated from regular Americans, "white" and "Negro," their children begrudged a few weeks of school a year, forever on the move and forever hungry. There was then a regular joke about "the Mexican breakfast: a cigarette and a piss."

The struggle against contempt and exploitation never died. In South Texas border towns the local notables of "Mexican race" rallied in a euphemistic League of United Latin-American Citizens (LULAC) "to develop within the members of our race the best, purest, and most perfect type of a true and loyal citizen of the United States of America." In Southern California migrant workers organized a Confederación de Uniones Obreras Mexicanas and staged strikes in the Imperial Valley in 1928 and 1930. But the tougher the fights, the uglier the defeats—though LULAC citizened along, the Confederación was busted with tear gas and clubs.

The Great Depression was a special trial for the "Mexican race" in America. It devastated the small businesses in the Mextowns. And jobless families that went on relief infuriated their regular American neighbors, who often had officials deport them to Mexico. Officially the program was "repatriation." It really was that, when the deportees were Chicanos. It was exile, however, for those "Mexican" by "race" but American by birth. Beginning in Los Angeles, the deportations eventually reached as far as Detroit and altogether involved probably 500,000 people, probably half of them American citizens.

Families lucky enough to hold jobs during the Depression joined unions in droves, especially in California, and contributed mightily to the strikes in the cities and on the big farms and mines throughout the West in the mid-1930s. But they lost out too—the unions retreated or were busted, the strikes were broken, and the leaders of "Mexican race," whether or not they were US citizens, were deported. As an officer of the law in the San Joaquin Valley said, "We protect our farmers. . . . They are our best people. They are always with us. They keep the country going. . . . But the Mexicans are trash. They have no standard of living. We herd them like pigs."

By 1940 there were 2.5 million people in the Southwest whom the census officials now defined as "Spanish-speaking." Though they were twenty-five times as many as the conquered people at the turn of the century, they had gained nothing on regular Americans. The 150,000 congregated in Los Angeles were still in a ramshackle Mextown on the east side. The millions who remained out in the sticks were still almost all without property or valuable skills and dismally poor. Still Catholics, still speaking Spanish at home, still Mexican in their manners and tastes, they still kept intensely to themselves. Only in New Mexico, where Republican and Democratic bosses had long manipulated them, did they vote and hold office. Elsewhere they usually could not even register, or would not, for voting or for New Deal welfare, because they feared the registries might go to the Immigration Service for more deportations. The strongest political surge among them was *Sinarquismo,* Mexican fascism, whose apostles reminded them of "the sorrowful and magnificent . . . land of their ancestors," which might be the Southwest or Mexico but was not the United States.

The first good chances for these people to get in on America opened only during World War II, which made masses of them valuable for more than common labor. And the chances had many takers, starting on December 8, 1941, when "Spanish-speaking" New Mexico National Guardsmen began defending Bataan. Some 400,000 eventually served in the army, navy, marines, and air force, in all theaters of the war. Hundreds of thousands of others streamed into California's cities, to work in the new defense plants or in the construction, services, and vices then booming there. They too had to live in Mextowns. But they made them into barrios, neighborhoods, and sent the kids regularly to school.

Their breaks infuriated regular Californians. And after "relocating" the "Japanese," the Sons of the Golden West took aim at the "Spanish-speaking." Around Los Angeles they concentrated on the kids they called "zoot-suiters," the boys in the barrios who boogied in the drapes (from Harlem), ambled like *pachucos* (El Paso hoods), and sported duck-tail haircuts (which they invented). And when the "zoot-suiters" began jiving downtown, tangling with the servicemen there, the reaction was what regular Angelenos called "a lesson." For a week in June, 1943, "zoot-suiters"

—and hundreds of other men and women who dutifully worked for a living, paid their bills, and prayed for the Allies, and children who dutifully attended school and pledged their allegiance, all normally dressed and most fluent in English, but all obviously "Spanish-speaking" (as well as scores of "Negroes")—went down bloody in the streets under rampaging regular soldiers, sailors, marines, policemen, and civilians. The arrests were of the victims, the publicity by the criminals, whose incantation of "Zoot-Suit Riots" passed for the truth for years.

But inexorably chances multiplied for "Spanish-speaking" Southwesterners to break into America. The maintenance of twenty-odd military bases in the region after the war, the vigorous military recruitment there for the Korean war, the boom of the California defense plants into full-fledged cold war industries, the burgeoning of cold war industriettes in Arizona, New Mexico, and Texas, and the proliferation of freeways, motels, shopping centers, and housing "developments"—all this was the biggest bonanza ever in the land of bonanza.

The cushiest new tricks went to the pinkish tycoons already on the scene or swarming in from back East. And the sweatiest and filthiest drags went to the "Negroes" and the "Spanish-speaking," the locals and the hopeful multitudes whom the *enganchistas* were bringing in from Mexico's poorest provinces, legally on permanent visas or as *braceros* under the new Public Law 78, illegally as *mojados* (wetbacks in American). But so open now were the Southwestern markets that barrio lawyers were developing into real estate brokers, and keepers of corner stores into proprietors of department stores. Such was the need for workers that pickers and packers in the agribusiness were graduating to changing tires at a Sears garage or sheets at a Holiday Inn, maybe to a shift at a Ford plant or the sales staff at a J. C. Penney's. And such was the corruption that hoods were swelling into racketeers. Anyway the "Spanish-speaking" were fast getting into regular Southwestern occupations and company. Already by 1950 the census officials had tellingly redefined them as only "Spanish-surnamed."

The humiliations went on—police invasions of family parties, municipal swimming pools open to them only once a week (the same day as for "Negroes," the day before the pool was cleaned), their children smacked for speaking Spanish at school and given new Christian names by the teachers (Jesús mutated into Jesse, Magdalena into Maggie). Dispossession went on as garnishments, foreclosures, attachments, and eminent-domain expropriations. Poverty remained the classic beginning, and not far from the classic end. Exclusion to Mextown continued, to the west side in San Antonio, East El Paso, South Barelas in Albuquerque, Maravilla, the Heights, Chavez Ravine, and the dozen other barrios in the now enormous colonial city of East Los Angeles. And politics still offered more frustration than relief. New Mexico kept an assortment of "Spanish surnames" in its legislature and congressional delegation. But Texas allowed only one in its legislature, and Arizona and California allowed none anywhere. And harassment from the federal government resumed in "Operation Wetback," in effect to deport any "Spanish-surnamed" nuisance who could not immediately show US citizenship or the resources for a bribe.

Most disappointed were the veterans, who learned on their return from war that even "Spanish-surnamed" buddies killed in action could not be respectably buried in the hometown cemetery, and that their own medals, honorable discharges, and GI benefits were often not enough to get them into a regular American bar, much less into a subdivision of "prestige ranchettes on low FHA."

But by 1960, because of the bonanza, most of the four million "Spanish-surnamed" then in the Southwest had worked their way deep into America. Through the Community Services Organization (CSO), founded in California in 1947 "to promote the general welfare in the Spanish-speaking neighborhoods," and the GI Forum, founded in Texas in 1948 "to foster and perpetuate the principles of American democracy based on religious and political freedom for the individual and equal opportunity for all," the vets in particular were asserting new claims on their regular compatriots. By 1960 over half the "Spanish-surnamed" families from Texas through California owned their own homes, mostly a crowded dilapidated little place, but the family's castle; and most of them also owned a TV and a car, which in the barrios the dudes lowered, channeled, chopped, and primed into rolling sculpture. Between 1950 and 1960 the median income of "Spanish-surnamed" families in the region had risen by more than 70 percent, much faster than that of regular American families there. (Even so it was only 65 percent of the median income of the white families.)

So fast had the "Spanish-surnamed" in the region streamed into cities, or the cities expanded around them, that by 1960 almost 80 percent of them lived around "urban" centers. As Catholics, they were attracting fervent attention from newly conscientious hierarchs, priests, and nuns. The souls lost to the Church were being saved in increasing numbers in Pentecostal sects. By 1960 probably half the "Spanish-surnamed" in the region were bilingual; in California the proportion was probably three-quarters. "Mexican" no longer explained how they behaved and what they liked to eat, for probably 80 percent of the "Spanish-surnamed" in the region were native Americans. And many who could afford it were indulging in quite regular neglect of their sorrier kin, disregard of elders, and scorn for grace and care in public and private, as well as in caesar salad and roast beef instead of *pozole* and *gorditas*.

Despite frustrations, the politically inclined were mobilizing potent blocs. The Mexican American Political Association (MAPA), organized in California in 1958, yielded Viva Kennedy clubs that brought out 95 percent of the "Spanish-surnamed" vote in the state for JFK in 1960, and two years later helped elect Democrat Edward R. Roybal to Congress. The Political Association of Spanish-speaking Organizations (PASO), organized in Texas in 1960, helped Democrat Henry B. Gonzalez win a special congressional election in 1961, and three years later helped elect Democrat Eligio de la Garza to Congress too. Within a generation an alien minority had turned into what sociologists were calling an "ethnic minority," Americans on parole.

Now, after all the recent revivals of the American conscience, the civil rights movement, and antidiscriminatory legislation and rulings, the insults and outrages still go on. A California Superior Court judge tells a "Spanish-surnamed" juvenile who has confessed to incest, "You are lower than an animal. Even animals don't do that [sic]. . . . Mexican people, after thirteen years of age, it's perfectly all right to go out and act like an animal. . . . You are no particular good to anybody. . . . We ought to send you out of the country—send you back to Mexico. . . . You ought to commit suicide. . . . You . . . haven't the right to live in organized society—just miserable, lousy, rotten people. . . . Maybe Hitler was right. The animals in our society probably ought to be destroyed because they have no right to live among human beings." He speaks for enough Americans to make life extraordinarily dangerous for "Mexican people" in this country.

Still stuck in the crummy jobs, an average "Spanish-surnamed" worker in the Southwest now makes only 60 cents for every dollar an average white American worker there makes. With wives and kids working, the median income of "Spanish-surnamed" families in the region remain two-thirds that of white families there, around $6,000 a year, not enough even for the family on the median to afford more than a four-room house or a rattletrap car, or both a dentist and a daily paper, both school supplies and six-packs. Of the probably seven million "Spanish-surnamed" now in the Southwest, probably three million are still miserably poor, keeping alive on beans and greens.

Yet in the last ten awful and affluent years "Spanish-surnamed" Southwesterners have been integrating into America even faster than before. So many young men have borne so well the uses made of them in the armed services, for "action" in Indochina or "intelligence" in Latin America, that by now the roster of junior commissioned officers is studded with names like Ernest L. Medina (now retired). The fortunates with cunning, connections, and capital or degrees have extended their businesses, careers, and rackets out of the barrios into the insatiable surrounding markets. And by now some thirty of the most successful have received honors from President Nixon—Sandoval (an El Paso newspaper distributor), head of the Small Business Administration; Villarreal (a Los Angeles R&D executive), head of the Urban Mass Transportation Administration; Sanchez (a Fresno County administrator), director of the Office of Economic Opportunities; Ramirez (a Whittier, California, New-Horizons superintendent), chairman of the Cabinet Committee on Opportunities for Spanish-speaking People; Banuelos (a Los Angeles Mexican-food manufacturess), Treasurer of the United States—to surname only a few.

Workers in the proper industries have passed into America too, into the UAW, the United Steelworkers, the Rubberworkers, the Teamsters. Thanks to the end of the *bracero* program, the courage of Cesar Chavez, and the determination of thousands of migrant families to show how valuable they were, even the farmworkers have a union. And the "Spanish-surnamed" poor in the Southwest are slowly merging into the worn ranks of the regular American poor there, the Southwestern branch of the fifth of this nation that serves as its inland pariahs, all racked in the same stupefying and crippling torment.

Most significantly, politics has been ever more popular. Though the congressmen have turned into regular savings-and-loan flag-flappers, a rising proportion of "Spanish-surnamed" Southwesterners has participated in local and national elections, most of them so far as Democrats, the largest contingent of them happy McGovernites.

This integration would be even faster except for the continuing immigration from Mexico, which has kept heavy the number of "Spanish-surnamed" who are not only poor but also really Mexican. Through the 1950s and 1960s some 750,000 Mexicans entered the United States on permanent visas. Until 1964, when Public Law 78 expired, some 200,000 to 450,000 *braceros* came into the United States every year on temporary contracts, and many stayed. Since then, under provisions of the McCarran-Walter Act, they have come as "greencarders" (on permanent work permits) or "bluecarders" (seventy-two-hour permits); by 1970 there were some 150,000 in the country. Depending on the season, and the weather in Mexico, there have been between one and two million *mojados* here illegally. Listed or not, the immigration from Mexico since World War II has probably been twice that from any other country. (Hyperbolically, it has been as if the recent "black" experience has included a large immigration of destitute Africans.)

But the trends now seem clear—that this "ethnic minority" is dissolving like the others into an "ethnic category," which within another generation will no more than statistically and nostalgically bring together

people living in different classes. "Spanish-surnamed" Southwestern notables were right on time in pressing census officials in 1970 to let respondents define themselves as "Mexican Americans."

The most dramatic result of the integration is the new Chicano movement, to boost la raza, "the people, our kind of people." What sparked it
was the resentment of "Mexican American" politicos in the early 1960s
—for their help in electing Democrats their people were getting nothing,
while "Negroes" were attracting federal attention and liberal money and
admiration. The movement itself began inadvertently in 1964–65, when
LBJ's warriors on poverty began dribbling federal money into the Southwestern barrios and publicizing the misery in them. As new sources of local
patronage appeared, so did conflicts between local Democratic bosses and
their "Spanish-surnamed" counselors and barrio captains, who now saw a
chance to build their own machines.

For a while, in spite of the example of Watts, the conflicts were on the
inside. Then the Delano grape strike revealed a "Spanish-surnamed" organizer who was openly defying all the lords of California's agribusiness. And
from the ancient New Mexico land grant suits, Reies Lopez Tijerina
emerged loudly challenging the very powers of state. Thus inspired, fifty
"Spanish-surnamed" notables staged a walkout at an Equal Employment
Opportunities Commission Conference in Albuquerque in March, 1966. By
1967, while Chavez's grape boycott and Tijerina's courthouse raid were
catching most "Spanish-surnamed" notice nationally, gangs in East LA
barrios were outfitting as Brown Berets, and students in universities
throughout the Southwest were forming aggressive associations. At Berkeley
young "Spanish-surnamed" professors were preparing to publish *El Grito,*
the first "journal of contemporary Mexican-American thought." After the
Black Power Conference on the East Coast that July, the thought in many
"Mexican American" circles was, why not a Brown Power Conference on
the West Coast?

That October the new federal Inter-Agency Committee on Mexican-
American Affairs held hearings in El Passo to control the agitation.
(Chavez refused his invitation; Tijerina never received one.) But the show
was stolen by the "Mexican American" guests who lambasted the federal
government and staged a rival Raza Unida Conference in El Paso's slum-
miest barrio, where the banners read, "Mañana is here!" They shied away
from Brown Power, but they did "affirm the magnificence of La Raza, the
greatest of our heritage, our history, our language, our traditions, our contributions to humanity, and our culture."

The response from back East was conciliatory—the Bilingual Education Act and healthy Ford Foundation grants to a Mexican American Legal
Defense and Education Fund and a Southwest Council of La Raza ("for

the development of the barrio through the organization and encouragement of local cooperative community groups"). But by spring, 1968, the spirit of protest was even upon the kids. In March, 15,000 in East LA staged "blowouts" from their high schools, demanding transfers of racist teachers, revised curricula ("to show Mexican contributions to our country"), no punishments for speaking Spanish, unlocked toilets, unfenced campuses, and so on. While riots and rebellions exploded around the world that spring and summer, "blowouts" hit the San Antonio and Denver barrio schools too.

Five years after it began, vibrant now with the nation's terrific tensions, the movement produced its professionals at a Youth Liberation Conference in Denver. The host for the 1,500 delegates assembled there on Palm Sunday, 1969, was Rodolfo Gonzales, already locally famous as "Corky." A native of the city's barrio, ex-slaughterhouse-worker, ex-NBA-listed featherweight, ex-bailbondsman, ex-coordinator of Viva Kennedy clubs, ex-general agent for Summit Fidelity and Surety in Colorado, and ex-chairman of the board of Denver's War on Poverty, now at forty the father of eight, a poet, a playwright, director of the Crusade for Justice (a lively barrio service center), and probably the most blatantly *macho* public figure in America, redolent of mod Elvis Presleyism and raving about emasculation, Corky managed the conference like a fiesta.

During its proceedings he pulled three strokes of genius. The first was to establish a name for the new militants, Chicanos. Its original meaning forgotten, the name cut the clumsiness of "Spanish-speaking," "Spanish-surnamed," and "Mexican Americans" (hyphenated or not) to announce a distinct people, once suppressed but now reclaiming their integrity. Corky's second stroke was to establish a militant lingo, barrio slang, *pochismos*. A swinging syntax of Southwestern American English and Northern Mexican Spanish, pocho talk suddenly became the Chicano language.

Third was Corky's divulging that the Southwest was Aztlán, the mythical fatherland of the mythical Aztecs, who, he said, had erected the great civilization of ancient Mexico, of which, he said, Chicanos were descendants. Lifted from the sappiest pages of romantic historiography (Mexican and American), garbling recent scholarship, this exegesis allowed an image of the Southwest as la raza's by right of lineage. With a people, a language, and a homeland, the delegates proclaimed their Plan Espiritual de Aztlán—"the call of our blood is our power, our responsibility, and our inevitable destiny. . . . We are a nation. . . . *Por La Raza todo, Fuera de La Raza nada.*"

Implied then and elaborated later were all the old contradictions of nationalism. Devotion to la raza is not racism, for la raza is only one kind of mankind, except that it has good traits galore and the other kinds have none. (In one Chicano's translation the Plan de Aztlán concludes, "To hell with the nothing race. All power for our people.") And within la raza the rule is one for all and all for one, except that the *carnales* (brothers) who want to liberate la raza cannot control the *Malinches* and *vendidos* (sellouts) and *Tios Tacos* (Uncle Toms); and *macho* as the *carnales* are, they can no longer intimidate the Chicanas blowing out of the bedroom and the kitchen.

At the call of the blood, the goal of liberation itself has shifted between "cultural and economic independence" and an independent state. And strategy has wavered between "defense of the community" and "armed revolutionary struggle."

Chicanismo has left many in the movement cold, like those on the Southwest Council, who gladly call themselves Chicanos but reckon that a new alienation would ruin la raza. And it has scandalized the LULACs, GI Forumites, MAPAs, and PASOs, who now have their investments in "Mexican Americanism." Since their first encounter with him the nationalists have repelled Chavez, who is committed far beyond Aztlán to buildling solidarity among farmworkers of every complexion. Lately they have even lost Tijerina, who is committed after all to the sad *hispanos* of the Sangre de Cristos, and is now evangelizing against nations and states everywhere.

Most galling to the professionals, who expected to take off like the blacks, has been their manifest failure to touch many white consciences. As ignorant of the East as the East has been of them, they did not understand in 1969 that the special reservoirs of white guilt the blacks could tap would never open to them—and that outside the South precious little guilt was open even to blacks. Only slowly some have learned that they can make gains only by their muscle.

Within these limits Chicano nationalism has been flourishing. Brown Berets who "hate Amerika" are now active in barrios throughout the Southwest. Chicano "cultural groups" have hatched in the penitentiaries. Several major student associations have allied into the Movimiento Estudiantil Chicano de Aztlán, or MECHA (which means "fuse," and in rural slang "down home stuffing"). Young academics have proclaimed their Plan de Santa Barbara, the blueprint for Chicano Studies departments and programs now available in scores of Southwestern universities. Two quarterlies have appeared, *Aztlán* ("Chicano Journal of the Social Sciences and the Arts") and *Con Safos* ("Reflections of Life in the Barrio"), as well as at least a dozen Chicano newspapers, varying from *El Grito del Norte,* published in Española, New Mexico, to *¡Basta Ya!* in San Francisco. Repeated "blowouts" have put the fear of a Brown God in Southwestern high-school principals. There have been Chicano conferences in Albuquerque, Houston, Kansas City, and South Bend, annual rejuvenations in

Denver, and last spring the first joint Chicano-Boricua (Puerto Rican) Conference, in Cambridge, Massachusetts.

Even politically the nationalists have been thriving. In 1970 they organized a Raza Unida Party in South Texas "as a unifying force in our struggle for self-determination," and won control of the school board in the Zavala County seat, Crystal City, which brought on a local social revolution. They also organized a Raza Unida Party in Denver, where Corky ran for mayor, and in Oakland and Los Angeles. In 1971 the Texas party won city council elections in Crystal City and in the neighboring county seats of Carrizo Springs and Cotulla, in the heart of the Winter Gardens. Last April the National Chicano Political Conference in San Jose spurned McGovern, endorsed the California party's drive to get on the ballot this fall, and voted to build a Raza Unida Party throughout the country. By now the Texas party is operating seriously in more than twenty of the state's southern and central counties, where most of the population is "Spanish-surnamed," and it has its own candidate for governor on the ballot.

Meanwhile the amateurs of the movement have been carrying on their own campaigns to boost la raza within America, to seat Chicano delegates at the Democratic Convention, elect candidates indebted to them, stop defamatory advertising, prevent job discrimination, halt freeway construction through barrios, sue state legislatures for fair reapportionments, recruit more kids into college, correct the history books, etc. Their version of the movement has off and on attracted many "Mexican Americans," young and old, integrated and still alien, loaded, hustling, and strapped. It is where their sympathies go when they too are sure that their kind has suffered more than any other kind of people in America, when they yearn to know that they are as good as the other kinds (maybe better than the blacks), that only prejudice keeps them from getting more out of the country, and that they should not have to sacrifice their most consoling sense of themselves to get it.

It attracts them especially when the offenses against their kind are most flagrant—20,000 from throughout the Southwest were Chicanos at least for a day in August, 1970, when they marched in the East LA Moratorium against the Vietnam war, and probably fifty times 20,000 throughout the country were Chicanos for weeks after the Los Angeles sheriff's deputies willfully destroyed the demonstration and three "Mexican American" lives.

So altogether the Chicano movement is only another ethnic movement, at its bitterest a threat not to integrate which cannot stop the integration but which can wrest some reparations for the loss of old certainties. Eventually it will win for its surviving professional and amateur chiefs their quota of revenge and power in America, and for its winter and summer members a little better deal than they would otherwise have had for the stakes in their class.

II

From the beginning this has been a curious history. Never a melting into an American pot, or an assimilation to an American archetype, or an acculturation to an American civilization, or a preservation within America of a separate culture, it has become an ethnic history—like the histories of the Old Stocks, the Early Immigrants, the New Immigrants, the Blacks, the Indians, the Orientals, the French Canadians, the Puerto Ricans, and the Cubans here, like all American histories. But it remains as different from them as they have been from each other. And after fifty years of study, its peculiar character is still obscure. The reason is fear, of Mexico and America.

In quiet dread of discovering too much pain in Mexico and too much promise in America, regular Americans have treated the "Mexicans," the "Spanish-speaking," the "Spanish-surnamed," and now the "Mexican Americans" as intruders in this country, whom they could always "send back to Mexico." And students of the treatment, almost all of the regular kind themselves, almost all anthropologists or sociologists (or behaving like them), have taken it as a reflection not on the stingy but on the denied.

On this prejudice they have been fairly productive. As advanced-degree candidates, journalists, professors, and researchers for state and federal commissions, they have delivered titles that now amount to a 200 page bibliography. But precisely because they have treated their subjects as intrusions, their work has made almost no dent on American historians, either the monographists who transmit only within the AHA, or the popularly talented from whom the reading public recollects its ideas of who Americans are. Between 1928 and 1934 Paul S. Taylor published five signal volumes of *Mexican Labor in the United States,* Manuel Gamio his perceptive *Mexican Immigration to the United States,* and Emory S. Bogardus his useful synopsis, *The Mexican in the United States.* Yet "Mexicans" did not figure even as hyphenated Americans in any of the US histories that came out before or during World War II. They were all, as a "Spanish-surnamed" author described New Mexico's *hispanos* in 1940, "forgotten people" in American history and society.

After more sociology published just after the war, and the culmination of Carey McWilliams's brave, solid, and brilliant reportage in *North from*

Mexico (now published in a new edition), they did receive their first historical consideration, brief but wise, in Oscar Handlin's *The American People in the Twentieth Century* (1954). But despite still more sociology and Octavio Paz's fascinating essay on *pachucos* in *The Labyrinth of Solitude,* they soon faded back almost into oblivion. They received notice again only from Handlin, three tiny references in his grand synthesis, *The Americans* (1963). Even in 1966 la raza remained, as another "Spanish-surnamed" author subtitled yet another attempt to bring it fully into the public view, "forgotten Americans."

Because of the United Farmworkers, the Tijerina rebellion, and the Chicano movement, books on "Mexican Americans" are now coming out in a rush. For a while the hottest topic was the farmworkers, who are not all "Mexican Americans," and in particular Cesar Chavez, who is. Chavez himself has approved Mark Day's *Forty Acres,* which is the name the Delano strikers gave their headquarters. Mostly an insider's account of the union's tribulations from 1967 to 1970, the book is best at conveying the innocence of the freshly indignant, who, blind to the odds against them, fight until they win.

Much more composed is Joan London's and Henry Anderson's *So Shall Ye Reap.* A sober and lucid report on "the long effort of agricultural workers in California to organize themselves," it traces the endeavors of the early unions in the 1920s and 1930s and the complicated intra- and extramural battles of the National Farm Labor Union (NFLU), the National Agricultural Workers Union (NAWU), and the AFL-CIO's Agricultural Workers Organizing Committee (AWOC) in 1940s, 1950s, and 1960s. Most of the book is on four men especially memorable from the campaigns of the last twenty years: Thomas McCullough, the priest who first seriously engaged the Church in defending farmworker unions; Fred Van Dyke, a "grower" who supported the unionizing (and lost his farm); Ernesto Galarza, an intellectual free agent, who fought like the hedgehog and the fox for the NFLU, the NAWU, and the AWOC; and finally Cesar Chavez, "The Organizer."

Of all the recent books on farmworkers, the truest is Peter Matthiessen's *Sal Si Puedes.* It was born in a deathly time, in the wretched summer of 1968, after the assassinations, the riots, and the mournful mud of Resurrection City, when Matthiessen journeyed to Delano to interview "one of the few public figures that I would go ten steps out of my way to meet." Courting disaster, he expected Chavez to "impress" him. If Chavez had, and Matthiessen had taken it, the book would have been only another exposé of one more fraud by one more exhibitionist. But on the quiet Sunday morning when he received Matthiessen at his house, walked with him to early Mass, and drove out to Forty Acres to sit and visit with him,

Chavez was just himself—which "startled" Matthiessen. The result is this splendid and inspiring book.

It is not a biography, in style or purpose. Only at random Matthiessen concedes Chavez's past—one of six kids on a family farm in the Gila Valley, at ten thrown into the Great Depression's western migrations, at fourteen done with school, at eighteen a navy enlisted man (two years on a destroyer escort out of Saipan), after the war following the crops again, at twenty-one married and settling to sharecrop outside San Jose, moving again to cut timber on the Smith River, settling again to a lumberyard job in San Jose, living in its Mextown, Sal Si Puedes (Get Out If You Can), actually getting out in the 1950s as a paid organizer for the CSO, then its statewide coordinator, then its national director. He does not even suggest why Chavez, hobnobbing with congressmen, hustling mayors and legislators, meeting in "the best motel in town," quit it all in 1962 to settle his wife and eight kids in Delano and start building from scratch without violence a movement that had always before failed, a farmworkers' union.

But Matthiessen does have the man Chavez has become as alive as he can be in print, "an Indian's bow nose and lank black hair, . . . sad eyes and an open smile that is shy and friendly, . . . centered in himself so that no energy is wasted, . . . as unobtrusive as a rabbit, . . . 'so stubborn, so irrational—oh, he can be a sonofabitch!' . . . praising, teasing, needling, cajoling, comforting, and gently chastising," full of tales, organizing even in his sleep, and constantly in danger of assassination. Because Chavez gave him the nerve to write in praise without idolatry or shame, Matthiessen gives others the nerve to believe that "warmth and intelligence and courage, even in combination, did not account for what I felt at the end of the four-hour walk on that first Sunday morning. . . . What welled out of him was a phenomenon much spoken of in a society afraid of its own hate, but one that I had never seen before—or not, at least, in anyone unswayed by drugs or aching youth; the simple love of man that accompanies some ultimate acceptance of self."

Chavez bores many professional Chicanos, who think that his rural concerns bore the barrios and that nonviolence is crazy for Brown Berets under a hysterical policeman's gun; Corky has insinuated that Chavez is an idiot. But Matthiessen shows Chavez already containing more power than his nationalist *carnales* have yet dreamed of releasing, through the "impossible gaiety" he spread in the desperate struggle against American selfishness, the invincible faith he has fortified in a "New American Revolution."

Last spring Chavez finally returned to his beginnings, to organize the Arizona valleys where thirty-five years ago the county seized his father's farm for taxes. The "growers" think the union is "bad for the country."

And the Arizona legislature has passed a law that prohibits farmworkers from striking, picketing, and boycotting. When the workers protested, Governor Jack Williams observed, "As far as I'm concerned, these people do not exist." Chavez has called for massive civil disobedience in Arizona on August 15, the day the law is to go into effect. The "simple love" Matthiessen felt is now defying the state itself, to test its interest in injustice.

For a while Tijerina also excited crowds of writers. Of all the reports on him, the most thorough and engaging is Richard Gardner's *¡Grito!* It is a deft weaving of straight agrarian history of northern New Mexico, sensitive accounts of contemporary life in its towns and out in its woods, and a canny biography of Tijerina himself in triumph and in court, thick throughout with nice quotes from locals pro and con. The book is dense, for Gardner respects the *hispanos* and Tijerina's weird vision too much to gut the subject of its intricacy; but the writing is crisp and clean.

Now the publishers are pushing sets of "readings." At least six have come out in the last couple of years, most of them so inanely edited that they do not merit mention as collections. Just passable is Edward Simmen's *Pain and Promise,* thirty-odd articles (twenty from "Spanish-surnamed" authors) that fit into a plausible guide to "the Chicano today."

The only collection commendable for more than meeting an emergency in the market, for being a book in its own right, is Luis Valdez's and Stan Steiner's *Aztlán.* Valdez's introduction is the most assured, eloquent, and intriguing statement so far of the professional Chicano ideology, complete with rancid cracks about "eternal foreigners" from Europe. The notes introducing each selection, which smack of Steiner, are concise and apt. The order of the selections (130-odd of them!) is constructive. The selections themselves are 85 percent of them from "Spanish-surnamed" authors; they include the best lot of Chicano short stories and poems now at hand in the East. Especially welcome are the pieces on the barrios and the bits on Chicanas, the Albuquerque walkout, the blowouts, the El Paso and Denver conferences, the Brown Berets, the Comancheros del Norte, the Church, and Chicano theater.

The editors commit only a few gaffes—like ordaining Bernal Diaz and supposing Don Porfirio to have said, *"Pobres de México. . . ."* The value of the collection is less than it could have been, because, as Valdez observes, "When the writer is a victim of racism and colonization, . . . the poet in him flounders in a morass of lies and distortions about his conquered people." Because neither Valdez nor Steiner knows enough about Mexico to have avoided swallowing the theosophical sinkers in Mexican Indianism, they waste pages on Mayans and Aztecs that would have been better spent, for instance, on the *hispano* diaspora, long the leaven in "Spanish-speaking" business and politics throughout the Southwest; El Paso, for two generations now the main source of sartorial, linguistic, and social styles in the barrios; the Sinarquista movement, the first serious touting of la raza in the United States; GI ordeals, during and after the war; work in the plants; programs and practices of CSO, MAPA, PASO, etc.; recent experiences in the "service," above all in Indochina; and the Raza Unida parties—all of which they omit. But at least the editors have shaped an argument.

Dwarfing these collections is the immense report by Leo Grebler, Joan W. Moore, and Ralph C. Guzman, *The Mexican-American People*. Ten years ago this was a gleam in the eye of a slew of professors, each beseeching the foundations for funds to go after the "Spanish-surnames" in the 1960 census. It became Grebler's baby in 1963 when he won a "generous" grant (reportedly $400,000) from Ford for his Mexican-American Study Project at UCLA. With Moore, a sociologist, as associate and Guzman, a political scientist, as assistant, and a supplementary grant from the College Entrance Examination Board, Grebler, himself an economist, directed a team of some twenty "collaborating scholars" through probably 2,000 interviews and five years of research and reporting. The product is easily the most comprehensive and rigorous study now available of "the nation's second largest minority."

The book combines abundant statistics, observations, and accruals from previous literature on the Southwest itself, immigration from Mexico, demography, education, incomes, occupations, jobs, earnings, housing, segregation, classes, mobility, the family, ethnic relations, intermarriage, tradition, the Church, Protestant sects, and politics. It presents a diverse people strenuously and alertly contending for their parts in America. It is bound to have a strong influence on federal policy toward "Mexican Americans." It already enjoys a reputation, which its authors invite, as the equivalent of Myrdal's *An American Dilemma*.

For all the money and the work, however, the book has several serious faults. At the start the authors waffle on whether to stress the voluntary or the compulsory features of Mexican immigrant life. (Here the question is much harder than for Myrdal, who could take it for granted that "Negroes" had come as slaves, but the authors never decide even on a point of view.) The inconsistency haunts the book to the end—did Mexicans stay in the Southwest (a bad territory for them) because they did not want anything better or because they could not get anything better?

The authors also never resolve whether "Mexican Americans" are "a distinctive people," so exceptional from regular Americans that a special study of them is legitimate, or are typical Americans, at least so close to typical that money and patience will soon render them ideally typical. (Here too the authors have it harder than Myrdal did, who could take "Negroes" as obviously distinctive; but the question becomes incomprehensible when they take it in isolation instead of knitting it into the patterns of modern American exploitation, which is how Myrdal solved its dilemma.)

Their own dilemmas arise from a confusion central to the book, inherent in its assumptions about assimilation. The authors take assimilation only abstractly as a process. They do not take on the question of who makes the process happen, whether it is a process of assimilating or being assimilated, whether "Mexican Americans" are becoming similar (actively, intransitively, reflexively, because they will it) or are being made similar (passively, because they cannot help it). They nowhere, for instance, query "Mexican American" military experience. Nor do they ask to whom the "Mexican Americans" are becoming or being made similar. If they had, they would have seen through their assumption, because there are no "typical Americans" to be similar to, and the Americans who consider themselves the regular kind are themselves changing as they have to admit that others, whatever their apparent irregularities, are thoroughly American too. The authors reveal their trouble in their concluding sentence, where they take poverty among "Mexican Americans" as a "challenge . . . to create the conditions in which the Mexican-American people can become ever more active participants in *our* society [my emphasis]. . . ."

Because of their central confusion, they flub the most pressing question in the book. "The schooling gap," they write, "is a fundamental cause of the depressed economic condition of the minority." But they cannot explain the gap. Leaning on the Coleman Report, they indicate that it might derive from "family background" (as if families were immune to a "depressed economic condition"). But then they note Bowles's and Levin's criticism of the report, granting that it applies especially in the "Mexican American" case. Finally they sigh that "much more research is needed. . . ."

Most sorely missing in the book is an understanding of what the changes of the last generation have meant historically. Though the authors proudly measure many of them, they nowhere convey how fatefully the meanings of their measures have themselves changed. It was one fate to be getting in on America in the 1940s, and another in the 1950s. It was quite another in the 1960s. It will be yet another in the 1970s. This change is incalculable, but it is the heart of what Mexican and other Americans have been living through.

The UCLA work reappears handily condensed in Joan Moore's own *Mexican Americans*. In her version, because she decided by herself what to write, the argument is clearer and subtler. And because she makes more of the politics of being "Mexican American," she gives keener insights into "Mexican American" suspicions and into Chicanismo.

The grounding for all this work should have come from Southwestern histories but it could not. Because of the vast and ominous space, the manic fantasy of dominating Nature, and the silent knowledge of the rattlesnake in the dark on the road, because so many strangers come and stay or go, because they themselves have come so recently and still yearn for benedictions from back East (North or South), the regular Americans in the Southwest have not made the absolute commitments to the region that would allow them to behold it honestly—and have therefore produced no profound history of it. For Perry Miller on New England, W. J. Cash or S. Vann Woodward on the South, Henry Nash Smith or Ray Allen Billington on the Midwest, they have only J. Frank Dobie or Paul Horgan or Robert Glass Cleland, whose best efforts have been merely entertaining.

And because of the prevailing contempt for the conquered people, and for those afterward who looked and talked and worked like them, there has been almost no history at all of the "Mexican Americans." For years Carey McWilliams's *North from Mexico* was the only general report on their past. Not until 1966 did a professional historian publish a monograph on them. Even now, though publishers and foundations are bidding high, there is only one new history, Matt S. Meier's and Feliciano Rivera's *The Chicanos*.

Without question their book is welcome—at last a professionally informed summary of the alienation and integration, coherent and readable. Its principal virtue is momentous, to focus historical controversies on the Southwest as a borderland unique in America, a region where societies have always been precarious, fluid, and intermingling; on different "Mexican American" heritages in Texas, New Mexico, and California; on the constraints that regular American rule imposed; on the continuing immigration; and on the recent involvement in America, most significantly through the armed services.

But major defects in the book indicate what misconceptions sociologists and the reading public must still expect from historians. Meier and Rivera imagine that "Mexican American history begins with the early story of man in the western hemisphere," which is a stunning anachronism. They refloat the myth of the "Aztecs," which is eighteenth-century Mexican creole propaganda. They see "life style" as the reason why Mexicans disgusted the regular American conquerors, which is nineteenth-century regular American propaganda. They fancy that Mexican immigration into the Southwest is "the return of the Indian Mexican to the land of his origins," which is the daffiest current Chicano propaganda. And they put Chavez into the same league with Tijerina and Corky, which is a misrepresentation of the United Farmworkers and the Chicano movement.

Missed by sociologists and historians, the quality of "Mexican American" experiences is clearest in "Mexican American" narrations of them. The judgment required in this art has so far eluded the novelists; the most competent is John Rechy. It is also absent from the various confessions now coming out. (One nevertheless worth mentioning is Armando B. Rendon's *Chicano Manifesto,* a Sacramento reporter's rap and rant, dull on Mexico, America, and Chicanos, but laced with enticing data on la raza's politics.) But the right timing and tone do distinguish the creations of several short-story writers. Particularly remarkable are Tomas Rivera, who has a fine story about migrants, "On the Road to Texas," in Valdez's and Steiner's *Aztlán;* and Mario Suarez, who has produced several good vignettes of Tucson's barrio, three of them being "Señor Garza," in Edward Simmen's *The Chicano,* and *"El Hoyo"* and *"Las Comadres"* in *Aztlán.*

The funniest, brightest, most moving, accomplished, and prolific "Mexican American" writer used to be Amado Muro, a veritable Isaac Babel of the Southwest; three of his many stories are in the recent anthologies, *"Mala Torres"* and "Maria Tepache" in Ed Ludwig's and James Santibanez's *The Chicanos,* and "Cecilia Rosas" in Simmen's *Chicano.* But Muro was really an anglo, Charles Seltzer, and is now dead.*

So far the masterful "Mexican American" narrations have been memoirs, most of them tales for the family. Among the few written down are the short reminiscences that Manuel Gamio published in 1931, now out in a new edition, *The Life Story of the Mexican Immigrant.* Here Isidro Osorio from Guanajuato tells how he came to the United States ten years before so that "boys of my town who had been here . . . could not tell me stories." Señora Ponce from Puebla laments that her husband brought her to the United States fourteen years before in a tantrum, because a priest had told him her confession that she (aged nineteen) did not love him (aged sixty-six)—in the years since she has had three children by him and been let out on the street twice. Then there is Guillermo Salorio, a Los Angeles construction worker who chummed around with Wobblies, longed for a business of his own, and was "studying many books and I now lack very little of being well convinced that God doesn't exist." Seventy-odd more original Chicanos recount their adventures.

With a humor just as arch, Ernesto Galarza has written a long and vivid memoir of his childhood, *Barrio Boy.* This original Chicano is one of the unheralded wonders of modern America. Born in 1905 in the mountains of western Mexico, uprooted with his family by the revolution, fleeing north with his mama and uncles, growing up in the Sacramento barrio, he came into his forte debating in high school. By a series of miracles he went on to a scholarship at Occidental, to Stanford for an MA in economics, to Columbia for a PhD, and to the Foreign Policy Association. First director of the Pan American Union's Division of Labor and Social Information in 1940, a hell-raising inspector of conditions for

* This is the word from Philip D. Ortego, short-story writer and professor of English and Chicano Studies at the University of Texas at El Paso.

Mexicans working in the United States during the war, he resigned in 1946 because of the government's postwar Latin American policy.

For the next fifteen years he was the western dynamo of the NFLU and the NAWU. Though the AFL-CIO scrapped him for its own AWOC in the early 1960s, it was Galarza who was most responsible for the end of the *bracero* program in 1964, the key to the rise of the United Farmworkers. The author of three solid books—*La Industria Eléctrica en México* (his dissertation), *Merchants of Labor* (a study of the *bracero* business), and *Spiders in the House and Workers in the Field* (a study of congressional harassment of the NFLU and NAWU)—and of the most thoughtful essay on la raza today ("Mexicans in the Southwest," in Edward H. Spicer and Raymond H. Thompson, eds., *Plural Society in the Southwest*), crusty, meticulous, passionate, he has been the brains of the Southwest Council of La Raza.

His new book is only partly personal history, to represent "the experiences of a multitude of boys like myself." It is also to refute psychologists, psychiatrists, social anthropologists, and other manner of "shrinks" [who] have spread the rumor that these Mexican immigrants and their offspring have lost their "self-image." By this, of course, they mean that a Mexican doesn't know what he is; and if by chance he is something, it isn't any good. I, for one Mexican, never had any doubts on this score. I can't remember a time I didn't know who I was; and I have heard much testimony from my friends and other more detached persons to the effect that I thought too highly of what I thought I was. It seemed to me unlikely that out of six or seven million Mexicans in the United States I was the only one who felt this way.

The opening pages on Jalcocotán, his native village in the Sierra de Nayarit, are a soft and excellent evocation of how a child takes root in tradition. The section on his family's "peregrinations" down to Tepic, the state capital, and then to Mazatlán, in the next state north, in search of peace and work, is an illuminating record of the forebodings of ordinary rural Mexicans at the beginning of the revolution. The passage on the flight north from Mexico to Nogales, Tucson, and finally Sacramento, where Uncles Gustavo and José had found work "on the track," belongs among the choicest accounts of debarkation into America. The depiction of "life on the lower part of town, . . . between Fifth Street and the river from the railway yards to the Y-street levee," jammed with Mexicans, Japanese, Chinese, Filipinos, Hindus, Portuguese, Italians, Poles, Slavs, Koreans, and gringos, richly portrays Northern Californians who Joan Didion cannot sketch into her romances.

The closing pages, where the family moves out "on the far side of town where the open country began," then Uncle Gustavo and Mama die, and the boy spends his first summer as a migrant worker, are the most personal in the book, particularly because they end with the boy daydreaming of the high school he knows he will attend in the fall, a rare chance for a Chicano then. This is the only disappointment in the book, that it does not go on for another couple of volumes to recount its author's rare career in redefining America.

Almost twenty-five years ago Carey McWilliams predicted that when "Mexican Americans" produced "a significant autobiography, . . . a new chapter will be written in the history of the Southwest." Now they have one. And through Medina, Gonzales, Tijerina, Banuelos, Chavez, Galarza, and all the other names they are making recognized as American, they are writing their chapter into the history of the entire country—its horrors, swindles, and hopes.

5.4

Migration and
the Rise of Disorder in the Cities

FRANCES FOX PIVEN
RICHARD A. CLOWARD

In the two and one-half decades following the Second World War, no pattern of social behavior so tested the stability and structure of American society as the internal migration of southern blacks to northern and western cities. More was involved than the traditional resettlement of the rural poor in a new urban environment. Institutional racial constraints together with changing patterns of economic growth shaped the adaptation of rural blacks to the northern city. Therefore, it was not merely a "repetition" of the experiences known to earlier immigrant groups. Black behavior and white responses to such behavior assumed a variety of forms. Frances Fox Piven, a political scientist and an urban planner, and Richard A. Cloward, a sociologist and a social worker, assessed the relationship between black protest (particularly black voting blocs and ghetto disorders and violence) and white responses (particularly the loosening of "welfare" regulations to absorb and contain black discontent).

From *Regulating the Poor*, by Frances Fox Piven and Richard A. Cloward. Copyright ©
1971 by Frances Fox Piven and Richard A. Cloward. Reprinted by permission of Pan-
theon Books/A Division of Random House, Inc.

. . . [T]he main facts are indisputable. A large mass of economically obsolete rural poor were redistributed to the cities, particularly to Northern cities. Very large numbers of these newcomers (especially blacks) were not absorbed into the urban economy but were left to subsist on incomes well below established welfare payment levels. Only a small percentage were admitted to the welfare rolls during the 1950's.

Why did the AFDC caseloads rise so rapidly in the 1960's, especially after 1964? As outlined earlier, we believe the explanation to be the increasing political trouble caused by blacks—trouble in the streets, and trouble at the polls. Although we shall discuss each of these political disturbances in a separate chapter, they are, of course, intertwined. They occurred more or less simultaneously, for as mass disorder among urban blacks mounted, so did the number of black voters. Moreover, each of these forms of political influence was heightened by the existence of the others. Disorder among some blacks (such as civil rights protests) alerted and activated many others, leading them to shift their voting allegiances. White voting blocs also became aroused by black turbulence, leading some to defect from their traditional parties and leaders. . . .

THE WEAKENING OF SOCIAL CONTROL

If the blacks remaining in the rural South were still subject to a near-feudal pattern of control, those who migrated were freed from it. They were also cut loose from their own traditional institutions—especially from their churches and from the established patterns of community relations that shape and direct people's lives.

The potential for disorder unleashed by these breakdowns might have been moderated if the institutional structures of the city had absorbed and integrated the newcomers. What the institutions of the city offered instead was resistance, which worsened the strains toward disorder.

There were several reasons for this resistance. For one, the host institutions were confronted by very large numbers: some 4 million blacks came to the cities in less than three decades, and they tended to concentrate in the largest cities. (White rural migrants, by contrast, tended to disperse among smaller cities, towns, and villages.)[1] By 1960, half of the blacks in each of the six cities with the largest black populations (New York, Chicago, Philadelphia, Detroit, Los Angeles, and Washington, D.C.) had been born elsewhere, chiefly in the South.[2] Sheer numbers made the task of absorption formidable.

[1] In 1965, about 33 per cent of all blacks lived in America's twenty largest cities, compared with only 13 per cent of whites (Center for Research in Marketing, 1).

[2] Bureau of Labor Statistics, 1968, 15.

Further, the institutions of the city—not least the economic institutions—were dominated by whites who resisted the newcomers. The grossest forms of racial discrimination persisted, indeed hardened, in many occupations which unskilled and semi-skilled blacks might otherwise have entered (as a prime example, the construction industry). Meanwhile, automation wiped out thousands of other low-skill jobs. To make matters much worse, the years after the Korean War were marked by periodic recessions and rising unemployment. High labor demand would have eased the transition to the cities and thus modified the strain toward disorder, for the occupational role has been the main agency of social control throughout history. But blacks came to the cities during a period when jobs were scarce.[3] Even those who did get work often remained in financial straits. Many found their wages too small to support a family in the expensive urban environment. Others were employed only sporadically, never sure from week to week when there would be another paycheck. In prosperous 1963, for example, "29.2 per cent of all Negro men in the labor force were unemployed at some time during the year. Almost half of these men were out of work 15 weeks or more." [4]

The consequences of migratory upheaval followed by persistent unemployment and subemployment were predictable enough. Especially important, the structure of the family system eroded, further weakening the already shaky structure of social control in the ghettoes. Men who are chronically unemployed will mate like other men, but they are not so likely either to marry or to sustain a stable relationship with women and children. Year by year, the proportion of black female-headed families grew, rising from about 19 per cent in 1949 to almost 27 per cent in 1968.[5]

The erosion of the family was far greater in the cities than in rural areas. In 1960, 23.1 per cent of urban black families were headed by females, compared with 11.1 per cent in rural farm areas. In the Northeast and West, the differences were especially striking: 24.2 per cent and 4.3 per cent respectively in Northeastern cities and rural farm areas; and 20.7 per cent and 5.5 per cent respectively in Western cities and rural farm areas.[6] These proportions increase considerably if one looks at only the poorest stratum of blacks within the cities. Although precise data are

[3] Comparing the circumstances of European immigrants to those of blacks, one observer had this to say: "For one thing, the United States has far less need for unskilled labor today than it had when European immigrants were flooding our shores. . . . The gap is widening between Negro education and training, on the one hand, and the requirements of the labor market, on the other. . . . The Negroes' economic position has actually deteriorated over the last ten years, relative to that of whites" (Silberman, 40–41).

[4] Moynihan, 21.

[5] A slightly greater part of this increase occurred in the 1960's: between 1960 and 1968, the proportion of non-white households headed by females increased from 22.4 to 26.4 per cent (Bureau of Labor Statistics, 1969, 22).

[6] Moynihan, 17.

not available, it is likely that the proportion of female-centered families among the ghetto poor of the larger cities ranges well above half.[7]

The weakening of the family as an agency of social control was crucial for the young.[8] And it was the young who were especially prone to disorder in the cities. In any circumstance, teenagers and young adults are the most volatile age group because they are partly loosed from the family system but not fully absorbed into the occupational system; compared with older groups, moreover, they are much more sensitive and vulnerable to social change. Two simple measures suggest the seriousness of family breakdown and unemployment for the urban black young. In a study of Harlem conducted in the early 1960's, it turned out that "only about half of the children under eighteen . . . [were] living with both parents compared with 83 per cent in New York City as a whole." [9] At the same time, black young people also found themselves confronted by shrinking occupational opportunities. In 1948, 7.6 per cent of non-white male teenagers were unemployed; by 1963, the figure had risen to 25.4 per cent.[10] In some ghettoes, it ranged upward to 50 per cent.

The litany of urban disorders in the wake of declining occupational and family controls is by now familiar: rising rates of gang delinquency and other forms of juvenile delinquency, such as school vandalism; spreading drug addiction; an alarming increase in serious crimes, such as armed robbery and burglary. Eventually, of course, disorder took the form of widespread rioting, and the rioters, too, were predominantly young, single, and marginally related to the occupational structure.[11] They were unmistakably unintegrated.

[7] For the nation as a whole, including rural areas, where there are proportionately fewer female-headed black families, 42 per cent of black families with incomes under $3,000 were headed by females in 1966 (Bureau of Labor Statistics, 1967, 71).

[8] We make no judgment about the relative merits of different family systems, female-headed or otherwise. Our point is a different one—that *any* type of family system undergoing rapid change is likely to be at least temporarily less effective as an agency of social control.

[9] Clark, 47.

[10] U.S. Bureau of Labor Statistics, 1968, 83–84.

[11] Although rioters were not more likely to be unemployed than nonrioters, they were more likely to have been periodically unemployed, according to the *Report of the National Advisory Commission on Civil Disorders* (132). This report contains a detailed description of the characteristics and attitudes of rioters and non-rioters.

The reader should be aware that our interpretation of the ghetto disturbances in the 1960's varies sharply from prevalent views, mainly in the great weight we give to the breakdown of regulatory institutions (especially to the breakdown of work patterns) in accounting for disorder. Others have tended to ascribe the disturbances either to the injustices suffered by blacks or to the thwarting of their expectations, which had presumably risen with the trek north. Neither condition seems to us a sufficient explanation. Throughout history, most people have suffered at the hands of a few; if this is what is meant by injustice, it surely does not account for what have been rare moments of rebellious behavior; in effect, such an explanation attributes occasional events to ever-present conditions. Nor does it seem to us that thwarted expectations among the poor account for recent disorders. The evidence suggests that it was

THE WEAKENING OF LEGITIMACY

In the 1960's, disorder worsened substantially. Moreover, it came to be directed outward, at the white world. Street crime spread beyond the ghettoes and make many areas of the cities unsafe. The roving gangs of black youth who in the 1940's and 1950's fought one another for control of sections of the ghetto now attacked whites on the streets. Teachers in ghetto schools were assaulted with much greater frequency; so were public welfare caseworkers making "home visits" in the ghettoes. The police found it dangerous to make arrests on ghetto streets, for they risked the anger of crowds that gathered to protest. When the riots broke out, mobs of young black did not simply loot and burn indiscriminately; they often selected white establishments, and they engaged policemen, firemen, and National Guardsmen in pitched battles, sometimes even in gun battles.

The main conclusion to be drawn from an appraisal of the disorder of the 1960's is that old patterns of servile conformity were shattered; the trauma and anger of an oppressed people not only had been released, but had been turned against the social structure. Disorder, in short, had become at least partly politicized. Both the rising magnitude of the disturbances in the 1960's and the fact that the disturbances came to be directed against whites probably owe much to this process of politicization.

There is nothing in the process of social disintegration as such that would account for the politicization of poor blacks in the nation's ghettoes during the 1960's. The weakening of occupational and familial roles may engender many forms of disorderly behavior, but that behavior is ordinarily apolitical. When men violate social norms, it does not follow that they have changed their views about what is right and what is wrong, nor does it follow that they will strike out against the larger social structure. Rules may be broken simply because men find it impossible to do otherwise (as when fathers abandon families because they cannot support them), or because conformity is so poorly rewarded (as when men quit work because the pay is so low), or because nonconformity evokes so few sanctions (as when crimes by blacks against blacks are more or less ignored by the police). The acceptance of social rules as just and proper is itself a constraint on deviant behavior, to be sure; but if these sentiments find no

---

among segments of the black middle class, rather than among the black poor, that expectations rose sharply after World War II. However, rising expectations, as we shall subsequently note, probably did have something to do with the emergence of civil rights activism in the black middle class, and that in turn redounded on the black poor, politicizing the disorder created by the weakening of community and occupational controls.

support in the conduct of daily life—if conformity yields no rewards and nonconformity no sanctions—then they alone may be an insufficient force to regulate behavior. Social rules lose saliency; to acknowledge their legitimacy is to impute moral validity to abstractions.

Under these conditions, disorder may occur just because of its intrinsic values: it may yield profit, as in much crime; or provide escape from the boredom and frustration of daily life, as in much drug addiction; or drain off rage, as in much violence. A society can retain its legitimacy, in other words, and still lose control over large masses of people simply because the structures that ordinarily regulate behavior have weakened or collapsed.

Sometimes, however, the events that create disorder are accompanied by repudiation of the rules; disorder is then likely to spread and worsen, for the disorderly act comes to be defined as morally proper, as the appropriate response of a victimized group toward the victimizers. The difference is an important one: men may stop working because for one reason or another they are unable to work, or they may repudiate the obligation to work, as the young black does who remains idle on the ground that blacks are denied any but the most menial jobs. Thievery is one way of surviving; but it may sometimes come to be justified on the ground that whites have always stolen from and exploited blacks, so reparations are due. To the extent that such a transvaluation took place in the 1960's, worsening disorder, the question is why?

The main cause, we suspect, was the denunciatory climate created by the civil rights movement. Between 1955 and 1965, various groups coalesced to repudiate American racism in the most unambiguous terms. As civil rights activists arose to attack caste arrangements in the South, similar groups mobilized in the North to attack discrimination in employment, in housing, and in education. The main legislative result was the enactment of the Civil Rights Act of 1964 and the Voting Rights Act of 1965, neither of which had much direct impact on poor blacks in the Northern cities. But the dramatic and prolonged struggle that led to the legislation probably *did* have the consequence of politicizing and alienating people, especially the young, in the black ghettoes.

The emergence of civil rights as a major national issue very likely owes much to the changing posture of various white elites.[12] During the

12 The role of elites in precipitating the breakdown of legitimacy has often been noted. Edward C. Banfield, for example, has this to say about the origins of the violent draft riots of 1863: "How did the mass of rioters come to have this feeling of moral immunity? Partly from the presence among them of a few leaders who did have political ideas or were at any rate motivated mainly by righteous (as they thought) indignation. (A longshoremen's association had been organized the month before and its 300 or so members seem to have been in the vanguard of the rioters.) Partly from the failure of the authorities to take stern action against them, a failure

1940's and 1950's, men in the highest places in business, philanthropy, and government began to speak out against racial discrimination. The new posture can probably be traced to changes in the economic role of blacks, changes that undermined the traditional economic uses of racism and also meant that discriminatory attitudes and practices were beginning to create economic and related problems of their own.

The stakes of large-scale corporate enterprise in domestic racism have been declining since the Depression. Before that, racism ensured a surplus of cheap black labor which was used against white workers, chiefly to undermine wage levels. It was also used against whites more directly, for blacks were hired as scabs and goons to impede unionization; the history of labor violence in this country has also been a history of racial violence.

Since World War II, however, the accelerated development of machine technology and the growing ability of corporations to manage markets have made low wages a relatively less important factor in profits, at least for large-scale enterprises. Accordingly, racism is also less important, for many corporate enterprises have less incentive to depress wages. As for inhibiting unionization, it has become clear that by helping to discipline the labor force, large-scale unions dominated by "bread and butter" concerns perform a useful function for mammoth industrial organizations.

But even as corporate stakes in domestic racism declined, corporate stakes in blacks as workers also declined. In recent decades, industry has come to require an increasingly skilled labor force. This change occurred just as unskilled blacks reached the cities in large numbers from the fields of the South, with the result that Northern industrial elites were becoming as indifferent to black labor as Southern agricultural elites already were.

But corporate elites could not long remain indifferent to unemployed and underemployed blacks as a source of disturbances in the cities. The disturbances had partly to do with outright disorder in the ghettoes, such as rising crime rates. Far more disruptive, however, at least at first, were the reactions of urban whites who panicked at the black "invasion." To be sure, the streets became less safe and the public schools seemed to deteriorate. But these changes were greatly exaggerated by the fear that the

---

that seemed to imply some degree of assent. (The Archbishop's refusal to address the rioters in the first days of the riot seemed particularly significant.) Partly—and this I believe to have been the main part—from having for months been told by leading politicians that they were victims of outrageous injustices and were therefore likely (was this prediction or invitation?) to rise in righteous wrath. (Consider, for example, the words of Governor Seymour: 'One out of about two-and-a-half of our citizens is destined to be brought over into Messrs. Lincoln and Company's charnel house' and his warning—or was it a suggestion?—a few days before the riot that 'the bloody and treasonable and revolutionary doctrine of public necessity can be proclaimed by a mob as well as by a government.') As Orestes Brownson wrote, the draft rioters 'only acted out the opinions they had received from men of higher religious and social position than themselves' " (Banfield, 57).

mere presence of growing numbers of blacks on the streets and in the schools evoked. Whether the dangers were real or imagined, however, more and more middle-class whites joined the exodus to the suburbs as the ghettoes enlarged, forcing economic enterprises to follow or risk being stranded in a central city without affluent customers. Taken together, black disorder and white panic were costly, and they threatened to become more costly, not least because they endangered the great property investments in the urban core.

Religious and philanthropic elites were also disturbed by the changing population of the cities. Many churches and social welfare agencies followed the white middle class to the suburbs, but many remained in the cities, and for them the black poor posed a new reality. In some "inner-city" neighborhoods, blacks became the only constituency available to these institutions. Protestant leaders especially were impelled toward racial liberalism because blacks were predominantly Protestant and the strength of blacks within church councils had been growing steadily.

Finally, it was inevitable that some Northern political leaders would also be affected by these events, especially those who were susceptible to a mass of new black voters or who depended on corporate, religious, and philanthropic elites whose opposition to racism was hardening. Accordingly, some Northern political leaders began tentatively to advocate racial reforms (which mainly threatened the interests of Southern whites rather than those of Northern whites).

The effects of this growing climate of racial liberalism can be seen in events dating back to the 1930's: the congressional struggle (albeit an unsuccessful one) for an antilynching law in 1934 and 1935; efforts by federal administrators to see that Southern blacks got at least something from New Deal programs; a 1941 Executive Order prohibiting discrimination in employment; the appointment of a presidential Commission on Civil Rights in 1947, followed by strenuous efforts by some congressmen and senators to enact a civil rights law; the Supreme Court decision in 1954 declaring *de jure* school segregation unconstitutional; the passage of the first Civil Rights Act of the twentieth century in 1957, together with the ordering of federal troops into Little Rock in the same year.

There were also attempts to deal more directly with trouble in the cities by measures intended to facilitate the "assimilation" of blacks. Some of the larger foundations, especially those with national interests and perspectives, were the first to act on this view of the problem. In the late 1950's, for example, the Ford Foundation inaugurated a "Great Cities" program through which money was funneled to urban school systems for experimental programs designed to reverse the high rates of academic failure among black youth. Later, Ford funded "Grey Areas" projects in several cities to encourage local leaders to get together on plans for new approaches to "urban problems." Foundation money, in other words, was used in an attempt to activate local professional and political elites, and to induce them to be more responsive to the urban black populace.

Few of these events led to a direct and immediate improvement, if any at all, in the lives of poor blacks. But they did reveal that sentiments supporting traditional racial controls were weakening, at least among some elites. This was to have consequences far beyond the symbolic actions of the elites themselves.

As the legitimacy of many racist attitudes and practices came to be questioned by prominent Northern groups, organized protests began to spread in the black community, mainly among the new black middle class. It was they who launched the "direct action" phase of the civil rights struggle, attracting thousands of followers, black and white. This group was itself being shaken by economic changes, although in a very different way than the black lower class. Even while high rates of official unemployment and subemployment afflicted those at the bottom of the black community, better-educated blacks had come to be in greater demand than ever before as a result of the growing need for skilled manpower during and after World War II. Thus, "in 1966, 28 per cent of all Negro families received incomes of $7,000 or more, compared with 55 per cent of white families. This was 1.6 times the proportion of Negroes receiving comparable incomes in 1960, and 4 times greater than the proportion receiving such incomes in 1947." [13] However, "about two thirds of the lowest income group—or 20 per cent of all Negroes—are making no significant economic gains. . . . Half of these hard-core disadvantaged—more than two million persons—live in central-city neighborhoods." [14] In other words, two opposing income trends were at work in the black community: rising affluence in an expanding middle class, and persisting poverty in a shrinking lower class.

These opposing income trends suggest why protest developed first among blacks at higher income levels. As is often the case, ascending economic fortunes stimulated ambitions in this rising group which outpaced their actual rate of advance.[15] They were, after all, as well-educated as the traditional black middle class, but they were younger, they tended to have slightly less prestigious occupations, and they had lower incomes.

[13] U.S. National Advisory Commission on Civil Disorders, 251.

[14] *Ibid.,* 252.

[15] As Alexis de Tocqueville was to say regarding economic improvement and the origins of the French Revolution: "It is a singular fact that this steadily increasing prosperity, far from tranquilizing the population, everywhere promoted a spirit of unrest. The general public became more and more hostile to every ancient institution, more and more discontented; indeed, it was increasingly obvious that the nation was heading for a revolution.

"Moreover, those parts of France in which improvement in the standard of living was most pronounced were the chief centers of revolutionary movement" (175).

Various studies of the Southern protest leader who emerged in the 1950's show that he

> is the young, somewhat underpaid Negro professional. He is of the Negro middle class but his occupational position does not yet provide him with either economic security or a comfortable income. . . . Protest leaders, like leaders in general, are a group of a much higher class position than the subcommunity as a whole. But among their fellow race leaders their class position is relatively low. The "typical" protest leader is not the well-established M.D., but the struggling young optometrist.[16]

The civil rights activism of the past decade can thus be understood in part as a struggle by a rising group to consolidate its position in the middle class.[17]

Direct action, in turn, accelerated the process of racial liberalization. The new black protest leaders found ready support in the Northern white community, especially among the sons and daughters of the affluent, who went south in large numbers to join the freedom rides, the "Mississippi summers," the protests and the marches, there to be beaten, jailed, and sometimes killed. With many groups in the North aroused and sympathetic, various elites were even more inclined to repudiate publicly the nation's racist practices, and the movement won victories, first in the courts, and then in the Congress. Each victory—even each symbolic victory—demonstrated that America's caste system was not only illegitimate but vulnerable.

The resulting climate could not help but affect the mass of poor blacks, for even as they were freed from institutional controls, they were led to think of themselves as exploited and oppressed by white institutional arrangements. Under the impact of these combined influences, it is hardly surprising that unrest mounted among poor blacks. This unrest, in turn, redounded on some of the new activists, producing a rising tide of militancy among black leaders. Integrationist goals gave way to the raised black fist and the call for "black power," to an ideology that celebrated race pride and race anger and proclaimed the need for violent struggle against oppressive white institutions. All this heightened restlessness in the ghettoes.

[16] Ladd, 255. See also Killian and Smith; and Burgess.

[17] Within this rising group, tendencies toward activism were strongly influenced by occupation and source of income. As economic conditions improved for some in the black community, it was possible for a growing number of entrepreneurs and professionals (e.g., physicians, dentists, ministers) to derive their incomes from the black community itself, thus reducing their vulnerability to white retaliation. Others, such as social workers, teachers, and civil servants, were much more dependent on the good will of whites. It was from those enjoying more "independent" sources of income that the protest leadership was mainly drawn, for in the South, if not elsewhere, it has been "a basic fact of life for Negroes . . . that one does not actively engage in the work of protest organization unless he is secure from economic sanctions" (Ladd, 254).

With social controls weakening and delegitimizing forces at work, disorder in the cities continued to increase. School vandalism provides one example. Pitching rocks through school windows is a not unfamiliar form of juvenile delinquency, but in recent years it has become so widespread as to represent something more than the aimless sport of uncontrolled youth. In New York City, for example, 161,000 panes of glass were broken during 1959; ten years later, the figure had risen to 275,000 panes, an increase of 71 per cent. Other types of school vandalism showed similarly sharp increases. Fewer than 800 unlawful entries to schools were reported in 1959; 3,000 were reported in 1969. The number of fires set in schools also rose—from 109 in 1959 to 330 in 1969. Data on the color of those who committed these acts of vandalism are not available, but the acts themselves occurred disproportionately in ghetto schools.[18] The sharp increase in vandalism suggests not only that social controls over youth were weakening, but that youth were turning against the schools, deliberately making them a target of their anger and frustration.

In the same vein, comparisons of rioters and non-rioters reveal marked differences in attitudes toward economic and political arrangements. First, the rioters were much more likely than non-rioters to possess accurate information about the economic and political condition of blacks. They were also more resentful than non-rioters: "69 per cent, as compared with 50 per cent of the noninvolved, felt that racial discrimination was the major obstacle to their finding better employment."[19] Rioters were more likely to have participated in protest actions (such as civil rights meetings and demonstrations); their hostility to whites and their "pride in race" were significantly greater; they were more likely to be contemptuous of efforts by local government in their behalf; and they were less likely to feel that "the country was worth fighting for in the event of a major war." They were more knowledgeable about the political system even while they were much less likely to feel that traditional electoral arrangements afforded an efficacious channel to promote justice and equality for blacks. The rioters were, in short, far more politicized, alienated, and rebellious than their non-rioting contemporaries.[20]

The political transformation of a part of the black poor should not be exaggerated. There have been periods in our history when blacks erupted in activities that were more clearly insurrectionary—for example, the slave conspiracies during the first third of the nineteenth century: Gabriel Prosser's plan to capture Richmond, Virginia; the plantation uprising around New Orleans led by Deslandes; Denmark Vesey's conspiracy to capture Charleston, South Carolina; or the Nat Turner rebellion in

[18] These figures were provided by the New York City Board of Education.
[19] U.S. National Advisory Commission on Civil Disorders, 133.
[20] *Ibid.*, 133–135.

Southampton County, Virginia. The number of blacks who participated ran into the thousands, and although these efforts were usually betrayed and always crushed, they represented political action of a clearly insurrectionary kind.[21]

If the riots of the 1960's were not insurrectionary conspiracies, they still reflect a marked change from the relative passivity that characterized black reaction to white oppression in the years between 1880 and World War I. Throughout this period, blacks were kept terrorized by lynchings in the South and by mobs of whites (many of them unemployed) who periodically invaded ghetto neighborhoods in the cities of both North and South. An early example of these mob actions occurred in Cincinnati in 1829, when half of the black population was burned out and driven from the city.[22] Ghetto invasions became more frequent as black migration increased after the Civil War, and especially after the turn of the century. At least a dozen major incidents occurred between 1900 and World War I, a period of greatly accelerated black migration. For example, white mobs killed, looted, and burned the ghetto of Springfield, Illinois, with the result that several thousand blacks fled the city and had to be cared for in camps established by the state.

Blacks offered little resistance to these events. But that was to change, and the turning point was probably the Chicago riot of 1919. Racial controls had already been weakened greatly—by enlarging black numbers, by unprecedented job opportunities in war industries, and by the return of many black men who had served in the armed forces during World War I. In any event, the Chicago riot saw armed bands of blacks defending their neighborhoods against white mobs and sometimes retaliating by invading white neighborhoods.

Beginning with the Harlem riot in 1935, self-defense against white incursions escalated into black aggression against the symbols and agents of white domination—notably the white police, merchants, and landlords. Although aggression has rarely extended beyond ghetto boundaries, policemen and firemen within the ghetto have been frequent objects of direct attack—in just two years between 1965 and 1967, for example, twelve law officers were killed and twelve hundred injured in the course of ghetto riots.[23] Looters and arsonists also tended to single out white establishments, although fires, even when set on white property, often raged out of control and enveloped black stores and homes as well.

Many of the riots during the 1960's were triggered by civil rights demonstrations, again suggesting that these riots had a distinctly political

---

[21] For a discussion of these revolts, see especially Franklin, and Aptheker.

[22] U.S. National Advisory Commission on Civil Disorders, 209.

[23] However, white riots against blacks in earlier periods of our history resulted in a much greater loss of life.

character. In 1961 and 1962, "freedom riders" and other activists were the targets of violence by whites in one place after another throughout the South, with, at first, little overt reaction by blacks. By 1963, however, white aggression began to precipitate a black response, usually taking the form of mass rioting, as in Birmingham, Savannah, and Charleston (S.C.). A predominant feature of these Southern riots was attacks on the police. On May 24, 1964, for example, blacks in Jacksonville attacked the police, assaulted other whites, looted and damaged property, and introduced the use of Molotov cocktails—all this in the wake of court convictions of black sit-in participants. The rioting which was to follow in the big cities between 1964 and 1968—such as New York, Newark, Los Angeles, Philadelphia, and Detroit—was far more widespread and destructive, and its political character was evident; it was often precipitated by some real or imagined act of official brutality, the police were frequent targets, and the violence was not just aimless.

Finally, it should be said that the urban riots appear to have been most severe where social controls were weakest. One of the differences between cities that experienced serious riots and those that did not was the rate of increase of the black population. A precipitous population increase, especially if migration accounts for a significant part of the increase, probably provides a crude index of weakening social control, for the larger and more rapid the increase, the greater the social disorganization. Among the nation's fifty largest cities, nineteen experienced less than a doubling of their black populations between 1940 and 1960, and only three of these cities (13 per cent) had serious disorders; but of the thirty-one cities where the proportion of blacks at least doubled, twenty (60 per cent) had serious disorders.[24] What, then, was government's response to the rising disorder in American cities.

[24] In classifying the seriousness of disorder, we followed the criteria used by the "Riot Commission" (see the *Report of the National Advisory Commission on Civil Disorders,* 112–113). Our use of the term "serious" disorder includes both what the Commsision calls "major" and what it calls "serious"—that is, violence lasting more than one day, with at least some fires and rioting, at least one sizable crowd or many small groups, and the use at least of the state police (in addition to the local police) to quell the disturbance. To obtain descriptive information on the disorders themselves, we relied mainly on the Civil Disorder Chronology in the 1967 *Congressional Quarterly,* the "Riot Commission" report, and newspaper accounts. No incidents occurring after the summer of 1968 were included. Our grouping of cities by "serious" and "minor or no" disorders follows:

Serious Disorders

Atlanta	Dayton	Oakland
Baltimore	Detroit	Philadelphia
Birmingham	Jersey City	Phoenix
Boston	Los Angeles	Rochester
Buffalo	Miami	San Francisco
Cincinnati	Milwaukee	Tampa
Chicago	Newark	Washington
Cleveland	New York	

(*Footnote continued on page 479.*)

LOCAL RESPONSES TO DISORDER

Considering that migration brought blacks into urban electoral politics in large numbers, the initial unresponsiveness of local government is remarkable (low rates of registration among blacks notwithstanding). In the areas from which they migrated, blacks were generally disenfranchised; in the cities, they became at least nominal participants in electoral politics. By 1960 at least one in five residents in our 50 largest cities was a black.[25] Some of these cities had few blacks (El Paso, for example, had fewer than 10,000), but others (such as Newark, Cleveland, Detroit, and Philadelphia) were well on their way toward black majorities. But despite their growing votes, urban blacks got little from the urban political apparatus—not jobs nor housing nor health care nor even much by way of relief payments.

Indeed, it can be said that in some respects the circumstances of urban blacks worsened precisely because their numbers increased. As the central-city ghettoes, swollen by thousands of newcomers (as well as by a high birth rate), began to spill over into white neighborhoods, schools, parks, and hospitals, bitter resistance was generated among the older inhabitants of the city. The trouble was often publicly attributed to blighted housing or inferior schools; but its main source was white resentment of black incursions. Even the fiscal troubles of the city, while real enough, aroused intense political ire because rising costs were associated with the influx of the black poor.

That these feelings were so bitter was partly a result of changes in the style and method of urban politics. In the era of the political machine, a degree of consensus could be maintained by converting public goods into private favors to be divided among competing groups. What one group got ordinarily did not directly (or at least, not obviously) infringe on the interests of other groups. But with the growth of bureaucratically organized municipal services, whether in education, housing, law enforcement, or urban renewal, the policies controlling the allocation of these

---

Minor or No Disorders

Akron	Long Beach	St. Louis
Columbus	Louisville	St. Paul
Dallas	Memphis	San Antonio
Denver	Minneapolis	San Diego
El Paso	New Orleans	Seattle
Fort Worth	Norfolk	Pittsburgh
Houston	Oklahoma City	Toledo
Indianapolis	Omaha	Tulsa
Kansas City	Portland	Wichita

[25] Center for Research in Marketing, 9.

services became the grist of urban politics. Unlike private favors, public-service concessions cannot easily be divvied up; if schools or housing are provided for one group, it is usually at the expense of another, and it is usually obvious that this is the case. And so the allocation of municipal services among competing groups emerged as the chief focus of political conflict.

Confronted by seemingly irreconcilable group demands regarding the allocation and control of municipal services, mayors generally favored the various white blocs with which they were aligned, ignoring their new black constituents. New public housing, for example, was reduced to a trickle despite the availability of federal funds because the projects generated fierce opposition from whites who feared the invasion of the black poor. Other federal programs, such as urban renewal, were turned against blacks; renewal projects were undertaken in most big cities to deal with the black invasion through "slum clearance," by reclaiming land taken by the expanding ghettoes and restoring it to "higher economic uses" (i.e., to uses that would keep better-off whites and businesses in the central city). Seventy per cent of the families thus uprooted were black.

But with blacks becoming more disorderly and more demanding in the early 1960's, local government began to make some concessions. Urban renewal provides one example. By the early 1960's, black protests were mounting against "Negro removal" in the guise of slum clearance, and political leaders in some cities with large black populations became apprehensive. They did not halt the demolition of black neighborhoods, however, for that would have displeased the commercial and civic interests that benefited from urban renewal.

Instead, to conciliate blacks while still pushing forward with renewal projects, local officials began to implement new federal guidelines which required that relocation services and subsidies be provided to those who would have to be removed from the neighborhoods designated for clearance. In other words, although black votes and protests did not yet have sufficient force to prevent the destruction of their homes and the usurpation of their neighborhoods, they at least produced modest services and financial aid for some of those who were driven out.

During the early 1960's, as black voting numbers in the cities continued to build up and mounting unrest among blacks gave these votes some power, city governments responded a bit more. To have acceded to some of the demands of blacks—a halt to urban renewal, integrated schools, access to white neighborhoods, apprenticeships in white unions, and the like—would doubtless have spelled the demise of many political leaders tied to traditional white constituencies, so blacks got few concessions in these areas.

What they *did* begin to get was more relief benefits: more people began to apply for relief, and more of those who applied were admitted to the rolls. In all likelihood this happened because it was easier to give relief than to grant other concessions. The rising rolls were objectionable to whites, to be sure, but considerably less so than locating public housing projects in white neighborhoods or integrating schools or enforcing fair-employment statutes. Urban politicians, in other words, permitted modest concessions in relief-giving as a means of placating the discontented.[26]

And so the urban welfare rolls began to rise during the early 1960's, especially in the North. The seventy-eight Northern urban counties where the welfare rolls had risen by only 41 per cent in the earlier decade experienced increases of 53 per cent in the next four years alone.[27] In many places, the rises were quite substantial. The rolls in Baltimore, for example, rose 128 per cent; in Hartford, 120 per cent; in Newark, 98 per cent; in Cleveland, 96 per cent; and in Kansas City (Kan.), 80 per cent.

Some Southern cities also began to respond. Civil rights agitation in the South reached a crescendo during this period: local whites repaid sit-ins, demonstrations, and boycotts with killings, jailings, burnings, and bombings. At the same time, and partly as a result of voter-registration campaigns by civil rights activists, blacks were beginning to emerge as a modest electoral force in the South. Even before the congressional enactment of voting-rights legislation in 1964 and 1965, black voter registration had risen sharply—by 800,000 between 1962 and 1964[28]—and this electorate was being alerted and activated by civil rights turmoil. Therefore, even as they publicly condoned repression of civil rights demonstrators, some Southern officials permitted a modest liberalization of relief policies. During 1960–1964, while the rolls in the South as a whole rose

[26] Welfare programs are usually administered by the county, not by the municipality. But in larger cities, county programs are usually subject to the vicissitudes of city politics. Where the municipality includes a very large proportion of the county population, city politicians frequently run the county political organization as well, or at least have substantial influence in it.

[27] However, these increases are exaggerated because of the addition of AFDC-UP cases beginning in 1961. We estimate that about 29 per cent of the total national increase between 1960 and 1964 can be attributed to this new category (see Appendix, Source Table 3). Since most of the AFDC-UP programs were enacted in Northern states, the proportion of the increase attributable to AFDC-UP in that area may be as much as one third, and it may be even larger in the Northern urban centers. (This general statistical problem is discussed in Chapter 6.) Even without AFDC-UP, however, the rate of welfare increase in the early 1960's was greater than in the 1950's.

[28] Between 1952 and 1962, black registration increased only from 1 million to 1.4 million: in just the next two years, 800,000 additional registrants were added. (These figures apply to the eleven states that are normally defined as Southern for purposes of political analysis, rather than to the seventeen-state census region that is used elsewhere in this book. The states omitted are Delaware, Maryland, Oklahoma, West Virginia, Tennessee, and the District of Columbia.) See the press release dated November 15, 1964, Southern Regional Council.

by only 7 per cent, the rolls in the forty-three urban counties showed an increase of 24 per cent.[29] In some cities, the rises were large enough to more or less offset the steep declines that had occurred during the 1950's. In New Orleans the rolls had fallen by 48 per cent in the 1950's, but they rose by 35 per cent between 1960 and 1964; in Atlanta, the rolls declined by 30 per cent in the 1950's but rose by 19 per cent in the early 1960's; in Savannah, the rolls dropped by 40 per cent in the 1950's and then rose by 50 per cent in just four years. In the light of the deepening distress of the black poor in the South, however, these rises were modest.

None of this should be taken to mean that welfare restrictions gave way in the early 1960's. As before, many families that applied for aid were turned down. Indeed, the rising tide of black migrants, and of white hostility toward them, led some jurisdictions to begin enacting new restrictions. In 1962, for example, New York State passed a "welfare abuses" act, a special type of residency law under which a person can be denied benefits if it can be shown that he came into the state for the express purpose of obtaining them. Although the New York law placed the burden of proof regarding motive on the local welfare department, the mere fact that an applicant came from out of state was often used as prima facie evidence that he had migrated for the purpose of collecting welfare; consequently, many thousands of families were disqualified and given bus tickets back to their states of origin.[30] Despite a number of such efforts to impose new restrictions, however, a general pattern of liberalization did begin across the country. In the nation's 121 urban countries, the rolls rose 47 per cent in four years, compared to a rise of only 35 per cent during the entire preceding decade.

If the relief rise in the early 1960's coincided with the rise in disorder, this relationship was even more striking after 1964. As protests, demonstrations, riots, and other forms of disorder reached unprecedented heights between 1965 and 1968, the relief rolls climbed 58 per cent, having already risen 31 per cent in the preceding four years. The 121 urban counties showed an increase of 80 per cent after 1964; in the "big five" urban counties, the rolls more than doubled (up 105 per cent). And in the South the first significant rise in fifteen years, an increase of 43 per cent, took place after 1964.

At first glance, these data might suggest a simple and direct relation-

[29] Since only a handful of these states enacted AFDC-UP, these percentage increases are more substantial than they seem in comparison to the Northern urban increases, where AFDC-UP cases constituted a significant proportion fo the increase in the early 1960's.

[30] Such practices were especially prevalent in New York City, where the city administration succeeded in turning away large numbers of "non-resident" families until a lawsuit initiated by antipoverty attorneys in 1964 compelled them to desist.

ship between growing black turbulence, on the one hand, and greater responsiveness by local government, on the other. However, local government was also under pressure to conciliate blacks from quite another source during the 1960's; namely, the federal government. Even as many urban political leaders continued to fight a rearguard action against blacks on behalf of their white constituents, national political leaders were developing programs that represented concessions to blacks. The main significance of these new programs—especially the anti-poverty program, which was initiated in 1964—is that they led to "reform" in the practices of local government. In other words, under prodding from the federal government, local government was made to revise some of its service policies so as to give more to blacks. Thus, as we shall presently see, it was the federal programs that washed away one local relief restriction after another, especially after 1964. To understand why the national government intervened in local service arrangements, it is necessary to examine the impact of both growing blocs of black voters and rising black disorder on national political alignments.

REFERENCES

APTHEKER, HERBERT, *American Slave Revolts.* New York, Columbia University Press, 1943.

BANFIELD, EDWARD, "Roots of the Draft Riots," *New York Magazine,* July 29, 1968, 55–57.

BURGESS, MARGARET ELAINE, *Negro Leadership in a Southern City.* Chapel Hill University of North Carolina Press, 1962.

CENTER FOR RESEARCH IN MARKETING, INC., *The Negro Population: 1965 Estimates and 1970 Projections.* Peekskill, N.Y., The Center, 1966.

CLARK, KENNETH B., *Dark Ghetto: Dilemmas of Social Power.* New York, Harper & Row, 1965.

DE TOCQUEVILLE, ALEXIS, *The Old Régime and the French Revolution,* trans. Stuart Gilbert. Garden City, N.Y., Doubleday & Company, 1955.

ELKINS, STANLEY M., *Slavery: A Problem in American Institutional and Intellectual Life.* Chicago, University of Chicago Press, 1959.

FRANKLIN, JOHN HOPE, *From Slavery to Freedom: A History of American Negroes.* Chicago, University of Chicago Press, 1956.

KILLIAN, LEWIS A., and SMITH, CHARLES V., "Negro Protest Leaders in a Southern Community," *Social Forces,* 1960, 38, 253–257.

LADD, EVERETT CARYLL, *Negro Political Leadership in the South.* Ithaca, N.Y., Cornell University Press, 1966.

MOYNIHAN, DANIEL P., *The Negro Family: The Case for National Action.* Washington, U.S. Department of Labor (Office of Policy Planning and Research), 1965.

SILBERMAN, CHARLES E., *Crisis In Black and White*. New York, Random House, 1964.

U.S. DEPARTMENT OF LABOR, BUREAU OF LABOR STATISTICS, *The Negroes in the United States: Their Economic and Social Situation, June 1966*. Washington, U.S. Government Printing Office, 1968. (BLS Bulletin No. 1511.)

U.S. DEPARTMENT OF LABOR, BUREAU OF LABOR STATISTICS, *Recent Trends in Social and Economic Conditions of Negroes in the United States, July 1968*. Washington, U.S. Government Printing Office, 1969. (BLS Report No. 347.)

U.S. DEPARTMENT OF LABOR, BUREAU OF LABOR STATISTICS, *Social and Economic Conditions of Negroes in the United States, October 1967*. Washington, U.S. Government Printing Office, 1967. (BLS Report No. 332.)

U.S. NATIONAL ADVISORY COMMISSION ON CIVIL DISORDERS, *Report of the National Advisory Commission on Civil Disorders*. New York, Bantam Books, 1968.

5.5

The Way It Is in the Alleys, The Way It Is on the Porches

A child psychiatrist at Harvard University, Robert Coles has authored a
multi-volume study entitled *Children of Crisis* (the fourth volume, now in
progress, examines southwestern Mexican-Americans and Indians).
In-depth studies of families, together with a particular sensitivity to children
and to the larger historical and cultural patterns that affect behavior and
belief, make for an analytic awareness and sensibility that is without parallel
among social scientists and "contemporary historians" of the poor. Coles
understands the tension between "past" and "present" and is able to convey
that tension in strikingly effective ways.

Robert Coles, "Like It Is in the Alley." Reprinted and footnotes omitted by permission of
Daedalus, Journal of the American Academy of Arts and Sciences (Boston: Fall, 1968,
The Conscience of the City). Also appeared in *The South Goes North,* by Robert Coles
(Boston: Atlantic-Little, Brown, 1972).

A thousand miles and only the Lord knows how many "social" and "cultural" differences and how much psychological distance separates the two Peters from one another—even though they share certain kinds of experiences. Yet, they both occasionally talk about how things are going in their lives, and I have heard from both of them those words "like it is." One Peter is black; one Peter is white. One Peter's family came to the Northeast by way of Alabama; one Peter came to the north central region of this country by way of some mountains that straddle the East and Midwest. (Even now those Appalachian Mountains are a sort of frontier, defining two sections of a great nation.) One Peter's family was, long ago, slaves; more recently they have lived under the constant domination of sheriffs and plantation owners. The other Peter's parents boast of their family's long-standing independence; no one, absolutely no one, could ever tell them to do or believe anything they didn't want to do or believe. Today the Peters live in buildings that are quite similar, and both Peters hear their mothers make mention of another kind of life, a kind that is gone and yet seems curiously attractive, even as it was "awful, awful, awful." Both boys know poverty, have felt the state of exile and the consequences of upheaval.

The boys were both nine years old when I sat down to write about them. They were both in elementary school, in the fourth grade. Neither Peter was (or is) a particularly good student, which is an understatement; in fact, each boy has never liked school, which is another understatement. I leave it to them, a little later on, to put their feelings into words. Yet, for all their troubles at school, and for all the critical things I have heard about the boys from their teachers, the fact is that each boy, each *young man,* has his own kind of intelligence, guile, sharpness of vision, breadth of understanding. And each Peter has a rhythm to his mind and body that is partially his and his alone, but also partially of a kind he shares with other children like him.

I cannot, I have no wish to, define words like *rhythm* or *grace* or *style* as they apply to something called "the personality" of a child, any more than I quite know how I would define what runs through me when I come to feel that a child's *spirit* is hurting, is faltering, is in jeopardy. At times I have found myself wishing that the two Peters were patients, or research subjects or, yes, characters in a short story or a novel I was trying to construct. Then maybe I could capture the spirit of the boys and feel satisfied that I know just what to say and just how to say it.

All one like me need do to lose his smug sense of professional competence is keep on going back on those home visits. Both Peters have told me in dozens of ways, direct and indirect, to watch myself and not be so sure about what I decide to conclude and assert and insist upon as "right" or "the answer." Their message is, I suppose, every individual's eventual message to the observer, be he professionally sanctioned or driven by those "inner" and "private" rages or compulsions or desires that prompt writers and artists to seize from the world events they find significant and give them all the coherence or illumination they as particular human beings can summon. I refer to the message implicit in this remark the black boy named Peter made to me, perhaps because he sensed that I had been thinking days before *how much* I knew about him and others like him, now that I had spent four or five years in their neighborhood and knew my way around: "You're learning, man. You're learning. But I haven't started telling you about a lot of things, a whole lot of things. Then, when I do, there'll still be something else that I've got to bend your ear about."

I suppose as a psychiatrist I have always known that the mind's preoccupations are as endless as time itself; furthermore, given half a will on the part of a given speaker and a corresponding degree of responsiveness on the part of a genuine listener, what Peter called "a whole lot of things" can come to light, only to be followed by a whole lot more, and then yet more, until either or both parties say *enough*—with reluctance or relief or out of weariness or boredom. It is necessary at times to mull over "things" at very great length and to make statements and formulations and "diagnoses" which have about them a flat, unequivocal, authoritative spell that no one dares dispute, not the patient, let alone a somewhat doubtful colleague. It is necessary, I mean, the way death and taxes seem necessary; it happens and happens and happens—so one cannot envision a profession, never mind *a kind of existence,* in which each person is seen and responded to as *himself* or *herself* and, further, discussed in words that he or she evokes, as a very particular and special and individual human being. The other Peter, the white boy, has said it in his own special way: "I heard the teacher talking about all of us from Appalachia. I never heard us called 'from Appalachia' until I came up here from Letcher County. First they told me I was from Kentucky, and I tried to tell them no, I was from Letcher County. Then they told me I was 'from Appalachia' and I tried to tell them no, I was from Hot Spot, that's where we lived in Letcher County. But they never do listen to you."

When he spoke he didn't emphasize that last word, that *you;* he had obviously almost given up trying to emphasize such a word. He had learned that the more he will pull himself away from Appalachia and Kentucky and Letcher County and Hot Spot and realms more familiar to *him,* the more his teacher (and all of us) will start tugging him away toward the ever larger generalizations those geographical names symbolize. Peter's mother, when she heard what he had told me, turned to him: "Well, even if they don't listen to you, don't you stop listening to yourself. No matter what anyone says about you, there's more to tell than they'll ever know. My daddy would say that to me when I was a girl. If I got a compliment or if someone said something bad, he'd always tell me I had the last laugh on them, because I could always think to myself and come up with something that would contradict them plenty."

And with that warning, I will try to say something relatively brief, but not so general, about alleys and porches and two boys and two mothers—testifying to what I have witnessed of how it goes, how it is for them.

"In the alley it's mostly dark, even if the sun is out. But if you look around, you can find things. I know how to get into every building, except that it's like night once you're inside them, because they don't have lights. So, I stay here. You're better off. It's no good on the street. You can get hurt all the time, one way or the other. And in buildings, like I told you, it's bad in them, too. But here it's OK. You can find your own corner, and if someone tries to move in you fight him off. We meet here all the time and figure out what we'll do next. It might be a game, or some pool, or a Coke or something. You need to have a place to start out from, and that's the way it is, like it is, in the alley; you can always know your buddy will be there, provided it's the right time. So you go there, and you're on your way, man."

Like all children of nine, Peter is always on his way—to a person, a place, a "thing" he wants to do. "There's this here thing we thought we'd try tomorrow," he'll say, and eventually I'll find out that he means there's to be a race. He and his friends will compete with another gang to see who can wash a car faster and better. The cars belong to four youths who make their money taking bets and selling liquor that I don't believe was ever purchased and pushing a few of those pills that "go classy with beer." I am not completely sure, but I think they also have something to do with other drugs, and again, I can't quite be sure what their connection is with a "residence" I've seen not too far from the alley Peter describes so possessively. The women come and go—from that residence and along the street Peter's alley leaves.

Peter lives in the heart of what we in contemporary America have chosen to call an "urban ghetto." The area was a slum before it became a ghetto, and there still are some very poor white people on its edges and increasing numbers of Puerto Ricans in several of its blocks. Peter was not born in the ghetto. His family are Americans and have been here "since way back before anyone can remember." That is the way Peter's mother talks about Alabama, about the length of time she and her ancestors have lived there. She and Peter's father came North "for freedom." Americans, they moved on when the going got "real bad," and Americans, they expected something better in the new place. They left Alabama on impulse and found Peter's alley by accident.

Peter's mother believes that "something will work out one of these days." She believes that "you have to keep on going, and things can get better, but don't ask me how." She believes that "God wants us to have a bad spell here, and so maybe it'll get better the next time—you know, in Heaven, and I hope that's where we'll be going." Peter's mother, in other words, is a pragmatist, an optimist, and a Christian. Above all she is American: "Yes, I hear them talk about Africa, but it doesn't mean anything to us. All I know is Alabama and now it's in Massachusetts that we are. It was a long trip coming up here, and sometimes I wish we were back there, and sometimes I'd just as soon be here, for all that's no good about it. But I'm not going to take any more trips, no sir. And like Peter said, this is the only country we've got. If you come from a country, you come from it, and we're from it, I'd say, and there isn't much we can do but try to live as best we can. I mean, live here."

What is "life" like for her over there, where she lives, in the neighborhood she refers to as "here"? Her answer provides only the beginning of a reply: "Well, we do OK, I guess. Peter here, he has it better than I did, or his daddy. I can say that. I tell myself that a lot. He can turn on the faucet over there, and a lot of the time, he just gets the water, right away. And when I tell him what it was like for us to go fetch that water—we'd walk three miles, yes sir, and we'd be lucky it wasn't ten—well, Peter, it doesn't register on him. He thinks I'm trying to fool him, and the more serious I get, the more he laughs, so I've stopped.

"Of course, it's not all so good, I have to admit. We're still where we were, so far as knowing where your next meal is coming from. When I go to bed at night I tell myself I've done good, to stay alive and keep the kids alive, and if they'll just wake up in the morning, and me too, well then, we can worry about all the rest come tomorrow. So there you go. We do our best, and that's all you can do."

She may sound fatalistic, but she appears to be a nervous, hardworking, even hard-driven woman—thin, short, constantly on the move. I may not know what she "really" thinks and believes. Like the rest of us she has her contradictions and her mixed feelings; and there are some things that she can't say to me—or to herself. Sometimes she doesn't tell me something she really wants me to know. She has forgotten, pure and simple. More is on her mind than information I might want: "Remember you asked the other day about Peter, if he was ever real sick. And I told you he was a weak child, and I feared for his life, and I've lost five children, three that was born and two that wasn't. Well, I forgot to tell you that he got real sick up here, just after we came. He was three, and I didn't know what to do. You see, I didn't have my mother to help out. She always knew what to do. She could hold a child and get him to stop crying, no matter how sick he was, and no matter how much he wanted food, and we didn't have it. But she was gone—and that's when we left to come up here, and I never would have left her, not for anything in the world. But suddenly she took a seizure of something and went in a half hour, I'd say. And Peter, he was so hot and sick, I thought he had the same thing his grandmother did and he was going to die. I thought maybe she's calling him."

Actually, Peter's mother remembers quite a lot of things. She remembers the "old days" back South, sometimes with a shudder, but sometimes with the same nostalgia that the region is famous for generating in its white exiles. Now, she has moved from the country to the city. Her father was a sharecropper, and her son wants to be a pilot (sometimes), a policeman (sometimes), a racing-car driver (sometimes), and a baseball player (most of the time). Her husband is not alive. He died one year after they all came to Boston. He woke up, in the middle of the night, vomiting blood. He bled and bled and vomited and vomited and then he died. A doctor does not have to press very hard for "the facts": "I didn't know what to do. I was beside myself. I prayed and I prayed, and in-between I held his head and wiped his forehead. It was the middle of the night. I woke up my oldest girl and told her to go knocking on the doors. But no one would answer. They must have been scared, or have suspected something bad. I thought if only he'd be able to last into the morning, then we could get some help. I was caught between things. I couldn't leave him to go get a policeman. And my girl, she was afraid to go out. And besides, there was no one outside, and I thought we'd just stay at his side, and somehow he'd be OK, because he was a strong man, you know. His muscles, they were big all his life. Even with the blood coming up, he lookd too big and strong to die, I thought. But I knew he was sick. He was real bad sick. There wasn't anything else, no sir, to do. We didn't have no phone, and even if there was a car, I never could have used it. Nor my daughter. And then he took a big breath and that was his last one."

When I first met Peter and his mother, I wanted to know how they lived, what they did with their time, what they liked to do or disliked doing, what they believed. When particular but not unrepresentative or unusual human beings are called in witness, their concrete medical history becomes extremely revealing. I cannot think of a better way to begin knowing what life is like for Peter and his mother than to hear the following and hear it again and think about its implications: "No sir, Peter has never been to a doctor, not unless you count the one at school, and she's a nurse, I believe. He was his sickest back home before we came here and, you know there was no doctor for us in the county. In Alabama you have to pay a white doctor first, before he'll go near you. And we don't have but a few colored ones. I've never seen a one. There was this woman we'd go to, and she had gotten some nursing education in Mobile. No, I don't know if she was a nurse or not, or a helper to the nurses, maybe. Well, she would come to help us. With the convulsions, she'd show you how to hold the child and make sure he doesn't hurt himself. They can bite their tongues real, real bad.

"Here, I don't know what to do. There's the city hospital, but it's no good for us. I went there with my husband, no sooner than a month or so after we came up here. We waited and waited, and finally the day was almost over. We left the kids with a neighbor, and we barely knew her. I said it would take the morning, but I never thought we'd get home near suppertime. And they wanted us to come back and come back, because it was something they couldn't do all at once—though for most of the time we just sat there and did nothing. And my husband, he said his stomach was the worse for going there, and he'd take care of himself from now on, rather than go there.

"Maybe they could have saved him. But they're far away, and I didn't have money to get a cab, even if there was one around here, and I thought to myself it'll make him worse to take him there.

"My kids, they get sick. The welfare worker, she sends a nurse here, and she tells me we should be on vitamins, and the kids need all kinds of checkups. Once she took my daughter and told her she had to have her teeth looked at, and the same with Peter. So, I went with my daughter, and they didn't see me that day, but said they could in a couple of weeks. And I had to pay the woman next door to mind the little ones, and there was the carfare, and we sat and sat, like before. So, I figured it would take more than we've got to see that dentist. And when the nurse told us we'd have to come back a few times—that's how many, a few—I thought that no one ever looked at my teeth, and they're not good, I'll admit, but you can't have everything, that's what I say, and that's what my kids have to know, I guess."

What *does* she have? And what belongs to Peter? For one thing, there is the apartment, three rooms for six people: a mother and five children. Peter is a middle child with two older girls on one side and a younger sister and still younger brother on the other side. The smallest child was born in Boston: "It's the only time I ever spent time in a hospital. He's the only one to be born there. My neighbor got the police. I was in the hall, crying I guess. We almost didn't make it. They told me I had bad blood pressure, and I should have been on pills, and I should come back, but I didn't. It was the worst time I've ever had, because I was alone. My husband had to stay with the kids, and no one was there to visit me."

Peter sleeps with his brother in one bedroom. The three girls sleep in the living room, which is a bedroom. And, of course, there is a small kitchen. There is not very much furniture about. The kitchen has a table with four chairs, only two of which are sturdy. The girls sleep in one big bed. Peter shares his bed with his brother. The mother sleeps on a couch. There is one more chair and a table in the living room. Jesus looks down from the living room wall, and an undertaker's calendar hangs on the kitchen wall. The apartment has no books, no records. There is a television set in the living room, and I have never seen it turned off.

Peter in many respects is his father's successor. His mother talks things over with him. She even defers to him at times. She will say something; he will disagree; she will nod and let him have the last word. He knows the city. She still feels a stranger to the city. "If you want to know about anything around here, just ask Peter," she once said to me. That was three years earlier, when Peter was six. Peter continues to do very poorly at school, but I find him a very good teacher. He notices a lot, makes a lot of sense when he talks, and has a shrewd eye for the ironic detail. He is very intelligent, for all the trouble he gives his teachers. He recently summed up a lot of American history for me: "I wasn't made for that school, and that school wasn't made for me." It is an old school, filled with memories. The name of the school evokes Boston's Puritan past. Pictures and statues adorn the corridors—reminders of the soldiers and statesmen and writers who made New England so influential in the nineteenth century. And naturally one finds slogans on the walls about freedom and democracy and the rights of the people. Peter can be surly and cynical when he points all that out to the visitor. If he is asked what kind of school he would *like,* he laughs incredulously: "Are you kidding? No school would be my first choice. They should leave us alone and let us help out at home, and maybe let some of our own people teach us. The other day the teacher admitted she was no good. She said maybe a Negro should come in and give us the discipline, because she was scared. She said all she wanted from us was that we keep quiet and stop wearing her nerves down, and she'd be grateful, because she would retire soon. She said we were becoming too much for her, and she didn't understand why. But when one kid wanted to say something, tell her why, she told us to keep still and write something. You know what? She whipped out a book and told us to copy a whole page from it, so we'd learn it. A stupid waste of time. I didn't even try, and she didn't care. She just wanted an excuse not to talk with us. They're all alike."

Actually, they're all not alike, and Peter knows it. He has met up with two fine teachers, and in mellow moments he can say so: "They're trying hard, but me and my friends, I don't think we're cut out for school. To tell the truth, that's what I think. My mother says we should try anyway, but it doesn't seem to help, trying. The teacher can't understand a lot of us, but he does all these new things, and you can see he's excited. Some kids are really with him, and I am, too. But I can't take all his stuff very seriously. He's a nice man, and he says he wants to come and visit every one of our homes; but my mother says no, she wouldn't know what to do with him when he came here. We'd just stand and have nothing to talk about. So she said tell him not to come, and I don't think he will, anyway. I think he's getting to know."

What is that teacher getting to know? What *is* there to know about Peter and all the others like him in our American cities? Of course, Peter and his friends who play in the alley need better schools, schools they can feel to be theirs, and better teachers, like the ones they *have* in fact met on occasion. But I do not feel that a reasonably good teacher in the finest school building in America would reach and affect Peter in quite the way, I suppose, people like me would expect and desire. At nine Peter is both young and quite old. At nine he is much wiser about many things than my sons will be at nine, and maybe nineteen. Peter has in fact taught me a lot about his neighborhood, about life on the streets, about survival: "I get up when I get up, no special time. My mother has Alabama in her. She gets up with the sun, and she wants to go to bed when it gets dark. I try to tell her that up here things just get started in the night. But she gets mad. She wakes me up. If it weren't for her shaking me, I might sleep until noon. Sometimes we have a good breakfast, when the check comes. Later on, though, *before* it comes, it might just be some coffee and a slice of bread. She worries about food. She says we should eat what she gives us, but sometimes I'd rather go hungry. I was sick a long time ago, my stomach or something—maybe like my father, she says. So I don't like all the potatoes she pushes on us and cereal, all the time cereal. We're supposed to be lucky, because we get some food every day. Down South they can't be sure. That's what she says, and I guess she's right.

"Then I go to school. I eat what I can, and leave. I have two changes of clothes, one for everyday and one for Sunday. I wait on my friend Billy, and we're off by eight-fifteen. He's from around here, and he's a year older. He knows everything. He can tell you if a woman is high on some stuff, or if she's been drinking, or she's off her mind about something. He knows. His brother has a convertible, a Buick. He pays off the police, but Billy won't say any more than that.

"In school we waste time until it's over. I do what I have to. I don't like the place. I feel like falling off all day, just putting my head down and saying good-bye to everyone until three. We're out then, and we sure wake up. I don't have to stop home first, not now. I go with Billy. We'll be in the alley, or we'll go to see them play pool. Then you know when it's time to go home. You hear someone say six o'clock, and you go in. I eat and watch television. It must be around ten or eleven I'm in bed."

Peter sees rats all the time. He has been bitten by them. He has a big stick by his bed to use against them. They also claim the alley, even during daylight. They are large, confident, well-fed, unafraid rats. The garbage is theirs; the land is theirs; the tenement is theirs; human flesh is theirs. When I first started visiting Peter's family, I wondered why they didn't do something to rid themselves of those rats, and the cockroaches and the mosquitoes and the flies and the maggots and the ants and especially the garbage in the alley which attracts so much of all that "lower life." Eventually I began to see some of the reasons why. A large apartment building with many families has exactly two barrels in its basement. The halls of the building go unlighted. Many windows have no screens, and some windows are broken and boarded up. The stairs are dangerous; some of them have missing timber. ("We just jump over them," says Peter cheerfully.) And the landowner is no one in particular. Rent is collected by an agent, in the name of a "realty trust." One day I went with three of the tenants, including Peter's mother, to see if someone in the city administration couldn't put some pressure on the trust. I drove us to City Hall, which is of course all the way across town. After waiting and waiting, we were finally admitted to see a man, a not very encouraging or inspiring or generous or friendly man. He told us we would have to try yet another department and swear out a complaint, and that the "case" would have to be "studied," and that we would then be "notified of a decision." We went to the department down the hall and waited another hour and ten minutes. By then it was three o'clock, and the mothers wanted to go home. They weren't thinking of rats any more, or poorly heated apartments, or garbage that had gone uncollected for two weeks. They were thinking of their children, who would be home from school and, in the case of two women, their husbands, who would also soon be home. "Maybe we should come back some other day," Peter's mother said. I noted she didn't say *tomorrow,* and I realized that I had read someplace that people like her aren't precisely "future-oriented."

Actually, both Peter and his mother have a very clear idea of what is ahead. For the mother it is "more of the same." One evening she was tired but unusually talkative, perhaps because a daughter of hers was sick: "I'm glad to be speaking about all these things tonight. My little girl has a bad fever. I've been trying to cool her off all day. Maybe if there was a place near here, that we could go to, maybe I would have gone. But like it is, I have to do the best I can and pray she'll be OK."

I asked whether she thought her children would find things different, and that's when she said it would be "more of the same" for them. Then she added a long afterthought: "Maybe it'll be a little better for them. A mother has to have hope for her children, I guess. But I'm not too sure, I'll admit. Up here, you know, there's a lot more jobs around than in Alabama. We don't get them, but you know they're someplace near, and they tell you that if you go train for them, then you'll be eligible. So, maybe Peter might someday have some real good steady work, and that would be something, yes sir, it would. I keep telling him he should pay more attention to school and put more of himself into the lessons they give there. But he says no, it's no good; it's a waste of time; they don't care what happens there, only if the kids don't keep quiet and mind themselves. Well, Peter has got to learn to mind himself and not be fresh. He speaks back to me these days. There'll be a time he won't even speak to me at all, I suppose. I used to blame it all on the city up here, city living. Back home we were always together, and there wasn't any place you could go, unless to Birmingham, and you couldn't do much for yourself there, we all knew. Of course, my momma, she knew how to make us behave. But I was thinking the other night, it wasn't so good back there either. Colored people, they'd beat on one another, and we had a lot of people that liquor was eating away at them; they'd use wine by the gallon. All they'd do was work on the land, and then go back and kill themselves with wine. And then there'd be the next day—until they'd one evening go to sleep and never wake up. And we'd get the bossman, and he'd see to it they got buried.

"Up here I think it's better, but don't ask me to tell you why. There's the welfare, that's for sure. And we get our water, and if there isn't good heat, at least there's *some* heat. Yes, it's cold up here, but we had cold down there, too, only then we didn't have any heat, and we'd just die, some of us would, every winter with one of those freezing spells.

"And I do believe things are changing. On the television they talk to you, the colored man and all the others who aren't doing so good. My boy Peter, he says they're putting you on. That's all he sees, people 'putting on' other people. But I think they all mean it, the white people. I never see them, except on television, when they say the white man wants good for the colored people. I think Peter could go and do better for himself later on, when he gets older, except for the fact that he just doesn't *believe*. He doesn't believe what they say, the teacher, or the man who says it's getting better for us—on television. I guess it's my fault. I never taught my children, any of them, to believe that kind of thing, because I never thought we'd ever have it any different, not in this life. So maybe I've failed Peter. I told him the other day he should work hard, because of all the 'opportunity' they say is coming for us, and he said I was talking good, but where was my proof. So I went next door with him, to my neighbor's, and we asked her husband, and you know, he sided with Peter. He said they were taking in a few here and a few there and putting them in the front windows of all the big companies, but that all you have to do is look around at our block and you'd see all the young men, and they just haven't got a thing to do. Nothing."

Her son also looks to the future. Sometimes he talks—in his own words—"big." He'll one day be a bombardier or "something like that." At other times he is less sure of things: "I don't know what I'll be. Maybe nothing. I see the men sitting around, hiding from the welfare lady. They fool her. Maybe I'll fool her, too. I don't know what you can do. The teacher the other day said that if just one of us turned out OK she'd congratulate herself and call herself lucky."

A while back a riot excited Peter and his mother, excited them and frightened them. The spectacle of the police being fought, of white-owned property being assaulted, stirred the boy a great deal: "I figured the whole world might get changed around. I figured people would treat us better from now on. Only I don't think they will." As for his mother, she was less hopeful but even more apocalyptic: "I told Peter we were going to pay for this good. I told him they wouldn't let us get away with it, not later on." And in the midst of the trouble she was frightened as she had never before been: "I saw them running around on the streets, the men and women, and they were talking about burning things down, and how there'd be nothing left when they got through. I sat there with my children, and I thought we might die the way things are going, die right here. I didn't know what to do: if I should leave, in case they burn down the building, or if I should stay, so that the police don't arrest us, or we get mixed up with the crowd of people. I've never seen so many people going in so many different directions. They were running and shouting and they didn't know what to do. They were so excited. My neighbor, she said they'd burn us all up, and then the white man would have himself one less of a headache. The colored man is a worse enemy to himself than the white. I mean, it's hard to know which is the worse."

I find it as hard as she does to sort things out. When I think of her and the mothers like her I have worked with for years, when I think of Peter and his friends, I find myself caught between the contradictory observations I have made. Peter already seems a grim and unhappy child. He trusts no one white, not his white teacher, not the white policeman he sees, not the white welfare worker, not the white storekeeper, and not, I might add, me. There we are, the five of us from the one hundred eighty million white Americans who surround him and the other twenty million blacks. Yet, Peter doesn't really trust his friends and neighbors, either. At nine he has learned to be carfeul, wary, guarded, doubtful, and calculating. His teacher may not know it, but Peter is a good sociologist and a good political scientist, a good student of urban affairs. With devastating accuracy he can reveal how much of the "score" he knows; yes, and how fearful and sad and angry he is: "This here city isn't for us. It's for the people downtown. We're here because, like my mother said, we had to come. If they could lock us up or sweep us away, they would. That's why I figure the only way you can stay ahead is get some kind of deal for yourself. If I had a choice I'd live someplace else, but I don't know where. It would be a place where they treated you right, and they didn't think you were some nuisance. But the only thing you can do is be careful of yourself; if not, you'll get killed somehow, like it happened to my father."

His father died prematurely, and most probably, unnecessarily. Among the poor of our cities the grim medical statistics we all know about are encountered as terrible daily experiences. Among the black and white families I work with—in nearby but separate slums—disease and the pain that goes with it are taken for granted. When my children complain of an earache or demonstrate a skin rash I rush them to the doctor. When I have a headache, I take an aspirin, and if the headache is persistent, I can always get a medical checkup. Not so with Peter's mother and Peter; they have learned to live with sores and infections and poorly mended fractures and bad teeth and eyes that need but don't have the help of glasses. Yes, they *can* go to a city hospital and get free care, but again and again they don't. They come to the city without any previous experience as patients. They have never had the money to purchase a doctor's time. They have never had free medical care available. (I am speaking now of Appalachian whites as well as southern blacks.) It may comfort me to know that every American city provides some free medical services for its "indigent," but Peter's mother and thousands like her have quite a different view of things: "I said to you the other time, I've tried there. It's like at City Hall, you wait and wait, and they push you and shove you and call your name, only to tell you to wait some more, and if you tell them you can't stay there all day, they'll say, 'Lady, go home, then.' You get sick just trying to get there. You have to give your children over to people or take them all with you, and the carfare is expensive. Why, if we had a doctor around here, I could almost pay him with the carfare it takes to get there and back for all of us. And you know, they keep on having you come back and back, and they don't know what each other says. Each time they start from scratch."

I took Peter to a children's hospital and arranged for a series of evaluations which led to the following: a pair of glasses; a prolonged bout of dental work; antibiotic treatment for skin lesions; a thorough cardiac work-up, with the subsequent diagnosis of rheumatic heart disease; a conference between Peter's mother and a nutritionist, because the boy has been on a high-starch, low-protein, and low-vitamin diet all his life. He suffered from one attack of sinus trouble after another and from a succession of sore throats and earaches, from cold upon cold, even in the summer. A running nose was unsurprising to him—and so was chest pain and shortness of breath, due to the heart ailment.

At the same time, Peter is tough. I have to emphasize again *how* tough and, yes, how "politic, cautious and meticulous," not in Prufrock's way, but in another way and for other reasons. Peter has learned to be wary as well as angry, tentative as well as extravagant, at times controlled and only under certain circumstances defiant: "Most of the time, I think you have to watch your step. That's what I think. That's the difference between up here and down in the South. That's what my mother says, and she's right. I don't remember it down there, but I know she must be right. Here, you measure the next guy first and then make your move when you think it's a good time to."

He was talking about "how you get along" when you leave school and go "mix with the guys" and start "getting your deal." He was telling me what an outrageous and unsafe world he has inherited and how very carefully he has made his appraisal of the future. Were I afflicted with some of his physical complaints, I would be fretful, annoyed, petulant, angry—and moved to do something, see someone, get a remedy, a pill, a promise of help. He has made his "adjustment" to the body's pain, and he has also learned to contend with the alley and the neighborhood and *us,* the world beyond. "The cops come by here all the time. They drive up and down the street. They want to make sure everything is OK to look at. They don't bother you, so long as you don't get in their way."

So, it is live and let live—except that families like Peter's have a tough time living, and of late have been troubling those cops, among others. Our cities have become not only battlegrounds, but places where all sorts of American problems and historical ironies have converged. Over the past ten years I have been asking myself how people like Peter and his mother survive in mind and body and spirit. And I have wanted to know what a twentieth-century American city "means" to them or "does" to them. People cannot be handed questionnaires and asked to answer such questions. They cannot be "interviewed" a few times and told to come across with a statement, a reply. But inside Peter and his brother and his sisters and his mother, and inside a number of Appalachian mothers and fathers and children I know are feelings and thoughts and ideas—which, in my experience, come out casually or suddenly, by accident almost. After a year or two of talking, after experiences such as I have briefly described in a city hall, in a children's hospital, a lifetime of pent-up tensions and observation comes to blunt expression: "Down in Alabama we had to be careful about ourselves with the white man, but we had plenty of things we could do by ourselves. There was our side of town, and you could walk and run all over, and we had a garden, you know. Up here they have you in a cage. There's no place to go, and all I do is stay in the building all day long and the night, too. I don't use my legs no more, hardly at all. I never see those trees, and my oldest girl, she misses planting time. It was bad down there. We had to leave. But it's no good here, too, I'll tell you. Once I woke up and I thought all the buildings on the block were falling down on me. And I was trying to climb out, but I couldn't. And then the next thing I knew, we were all back South, and I was standing near some sunflowers—you know, the tall ones that can shade you if you sit down.

"No, I don't dream much. I fall into a heavy sleep as soon as I touch the bed. The next thing I know I'm stirring myself to start in all over in the morning. It used to be the sun would wake me up, but now it's up in my head, I guess. I know I've got to get the house going and off to school."

Her wistful, conscientious, law-abiding, devoutly Christian spirit hasn't completely escaped the notice of Peter, for all his hardheaded, cynical protestations: "If I had a chance, I'd like to get enough money to bring us all back to Alabama for a visit. Then I could prove it that it may be good down there, a little bit, even if it's no good, either. Like she says, we had to get out of there or we'd be dead by now. I hear say we all may get killed soon, it's so bad here, but I think we did right to get up here, and if we make him listen to us, the white man, maybe he will."

To which Peter's mother adds: "We've carried a lot of trouble in us, from way back in the beginning. I have these pains, and so does everyone around here. But you can't just die until you're ready to. And I do believe something is happening. I do believe I see that."

To which Peter adds: "Maybe it won't be that we'll win, but if we get killed, everyone will hear about it. Like the minister said, before we used to die real quiet, and no one stopped to pay notice."

Two years before Peter spoke those words he drew a picture for me, one of many he has done. When he was younger, and when I didn't know him so well as I think I do now, it was easier for us to have something tangible to do and then talk about. I used to visit the alley with him, as I still do, and one day I asked him to draw the alley. That was a good idea, he thought (though not all of my suggestions were). He started in, then stopped, and finally worked rather longer and harder than usual at the job. I busied myself with my own sketches, which from the start he insisted I do. Suddenly from across the table I heard him say he was through. Ordinarily he would slowly turn the drawing around for me to see, and I would get up and walk over to his side of the table, to see even better. But this time he didn't move his paper, and I didn't move myself. I saw what he had drawn, and he saw me looking. I was surprised and a bit stunned and more than a bit upset, and surely he saw my face and heard my utter silence. Often I would break the awkward moments when neither of us seemed to have anything to say, but this time it was his turn to do so: "You know what it is?" He knew that I liked us to talk about our work. I said no, I didn't—though in fact the vivid power of his black crayon had come right across to me. "It's that hole we dug in the alley. I made it bigger here. If you fall into it, you can't get out. You die."

He had drawn circles within circles, all of them black, and then a center, also black. He had imposed an X on the center. Nearby, strewn across the circles, were fragments of the human body—two faces, an arm, five legs. And after I had taken the scene in, I could only think to myself that I had been shown "like it is in the alley."

"On the porch I can sit, and my friend Gerry can sit, and we can use our jackknives, and if there's a lot to sweep away, we can just wait until we're all through, and then we do the sweeping. I have a broom, and my mother told me, when my dad gave me the knife, that if I can cut wood I can sweep wood up. So I do. Gerry's mother isn't so good on that score. She says the porch is for sitting and not cutting. That's why we're always here cutting and never there. I can make almost anything, if I can only be patient. I can carve out wood and keep my mother guessing as to what I'm making. First she'll say a boat, maybe, or a little toy for my brother, or an animal, a dog, maybe, but then I come up with a car, you know, or a little pistol for myself, and she has to admit I've fooled her pretty good. If I had a lot of money I'd get a bigger knife. I'd have one with five blades, and I could work a lot faster."

Peter's mother worries about him. She finds herself saying things like this: "He's only nine. He finds his way all over this big, big city. I never thought I'd have a child of mine so smart about a place like this. When we go back to Kentucky I look at him and wonder if he's going to be like a fish out of water back home, back at his own people's home, but he does fine up the creek with his cousins, and funny thing, he's their hero, because he can tell them all the stories about the city. Then we come back to the city, and I do believe the boy turns sad. I think he misses our old place, even if he can't remember living there, because we left when he was three, I believe. That's why I worry about him. I feel he's betwixt and between, you know."

At first glance, and actually for a longer stretch of time than that, Peter seems anything but sad or caught up in the kind of conflict or tension or uncertainty that his mother has several times and in several different ways described to me. He is tall for nine, thin but not bony thin; there are muscles on him. He has long arms, long fingers, long legs, and big feet—and his mother hates the very word shoes, because they are so expensive, and Peter's feet grow so much each year, and in a city he can't run around barefoot and worry only on Sundays about squeezing his feet into a pair of shoes, or about letting his feet swim in another pair. Peter's hair is also long, and blond, and falls over his forehead and comes a little over his ears. He has never been to a barber. His mother cuts his hair. He doesn't like those scissors, though—and so by agreement they hold off until it really *is* time, and then his mother goes easy on the cutting.

The boy's father must once have looked like Peter, but he is a sick man and looks much too old for his thirty-eight years. His name is also Peter, but he is called Pete by his wife, and Peter is Peter to everyone, which means a sister of fourteen, a sister of twelve, a sister of ten, a sister of seven and a brother of five. When the last child was born, the mother nearly died. She bled and bled. The delivery had been done up the hollow that was home, that still is Peter's grandmother's home. The family returned for a "visit," which on that occasion meant a stay at home long enough for the child to be born and the mother to rest and prepare herself for the trip back North to "the building"—her way of combining mention of an apartment house and the city in which the apartment house stands. The child was delivered by a great-aunt of Peter's—his grandmother's sister, his mother's favorite aunt, a woman who radiates self-command and who has delivered many children in her sixty-two years. But after the boy was born there was a near tragedy. An already anemic woman was losing blood fast, had a high fever, was in pain, and had to either see a doctor or die. They drove and drove and got to a hospital, and first had to put their money down, all they could raise from their neighbors and their minister, then the mother was admitted and treated with antibiotics, operated upon, given blood, fed intravenously, and eventually discharged.

Peter's mother talks about such experiences and how they fit in with her life and her husband's life and Peter's life: "We'd only left the creek a year before my youngest child was born. My husband was sick then, and he's sick now. His back was hurt bad in an accident down the mine. His breathing is bad from the coal dust in his lungs. They told him he was no longer good for work, the coal company did, and they gave us one thousand two hundred dollars for Pete's trouble—a payment, they called it, for his injury. We spent it on special treatments at the hospital for his back, and for clothes the children needed. Pete was too honest, that's what our minister told us. Pete was against the coal company, and he was against his own union. He said the union bosses are as bad as the gangsters you see on the television. They'll kill you if you fight them, he used to tell me —and then he'd go to the meetings and argue and argue. I asked him once if he wanted to die. He said no—then he thought and said maybe I was right, maybe we shouldn't stay in Letcher County, Kentucky. That was the night he began to think of going North, and it wasn't a month later that we were up here. We had kin here, and we just came to them.

"Peter was a child of three, and he got over the change easier than the older ones. He even did better than his younger sister. She was very attached to me, and because I was fretful, she became fretful. Peter made friends in the building, and he kept on telling me he was glad we'd come up here. But I wasn't sure then he meant what he said, and I'm still not sure I ought to believe him. He'll *tell* me he's fine up here, but his head starts dropping when we leave Hot Spot, and it never does rise once—not the entire way north on that interstate road. I believe the child half sleeps and half thinks of what he's just been doing up the creek with his cousins.

"Peter's dad tells him all the time that no one's going to help us out in Kentucky. Not the county people. Not the coal-mine owners. Not the union. The county people say they don't have money. The coal-mine people say they don't need too many men, and they gave us the dollars they did, one thousand and two hundred of them, and that's all they can do. The union, they cry poor, and like I said, my husband never was one to wink when he saw a hand in the union till or people fixing up relatives with phony jobs. Up here in the city he's tried to work, and the officials have been good to us. They said we could be on welfare, because he's got a bad back and his breathing isn't the best. So we get by. We're not rich, I'll tell you, and there's a lot we lack, but if we'd have stayed in Kentucky we would have no money, not a cent coming in, and that *is* being poor. Here we're plain poor; back home we'd have been bad, bad, terrible poor. That's what Pete says. And not long ago I heard my boy Peter practically repeating his father's every word to one of his friends. I was going to pull him in and tell him off; but he repeats his father's every word, he likes him so, and I didn't have the heart to punish the boy when all he was doing was being a good talker, like his daddy can be when he wants to."

Peter certainly does admire his father, and he can "go on a bit," to use the expression the father uses when he feels he has talked rather a lot. Peter will even talk about becoming a miner one day; he heard in school about copper-mining in Arizona, and came home and told his parents he might try that. They wondered whether he would want to be so far from Hot Spot, Letcher Country, Kentucky, and when he learned how far off Arizona is, Peter also wondered: "I don't think I'd want to go clear across the country. I like going home. I also like it here, though. In the city you can see a lot of people, and they don't scare you, after you get used to them. My daddy never saw so many people as he did when he first came up here, and he had to go into town, to an office building, and there were elevators going up and down, and they were packed full with people. He took me there, and I was scared. I guess I cried. I don't remember, but he says I did. That was a long time ago. I wouldn't cry now, I know that. I can get home from school four different ways. I've stayed on the bus and gone all the way over the other side of the city, and then come back. I'll bet on a jet plane I could get to Arizona in the time it took me to cross the city. I'll bet I could get halfway around the world in a spaceship in less time. But there are so many people here, and that's why there's a lot of traffic.

"It's not very far to get to a playground. I go there, and we fool around. We do our carving, and there's no worry about cleaning up the pieces of wood. They've got a few trees there, and we mark them up a little with our knives. The man who's in charge gets mad. He says it's a small play-ground, and there aren't many trees in the whole city, and we're ruining it for ourselves. I told him I see a lot of trees when we go home, and I'll bring back a few on one of these trips. The man said we should stop brag-ging about where we *used* to live. He said we're here, and we'll never go back, because we couldn't afford to—we'd starve to death, he said. I asked my daddy, and he says that could be half true. We'd eat what we grow, and people would help us, but it would be close, he'd have to admit it, and up here we get enough money to keep eating, but not much more.

"My mother says we never were meant to live with a lot of money. She tries to hide from my father the cost of everything. After she pays the rent, she says there's barely enough for food. She says she wishes my brother was as big as me, and I was as big as my father, then we could all share the same clothes. She wishes my sisters were all the same size, too. My father wishes he could find work and keep work. He wishes he didn't have the pain he does in his back, and he wishes he could breathe better. He hates to take a penny from the city, but we'd be living on the street and begging for food there on the street if we didn't turn to the city sometimes. We'd go back to Hot Spot, I guess. My folks would like to go back, but they know we're wiser to stay here, Daddy says. I'm glad we go home, and I can see my cousins, but I'm glad to come back here, mostly. Sometimes I wish we'd just stay in Hot Spot, but it's no good that way, Daddy says, and he knows."

So does Peter; he knows exactly why he is living in the city, and why thousands of others like him live in cities north of Kentucky's eastern counties and West Virginia's neighboring mountain counties and North Carolina's western counties and Tennessee's eastern counties. He knows words like "Appalachia" and "poverty" and "disaster area" and "mech-anization of the mines." He has a young teacher who often tells the chil-dren in her class that she is interested in their "special problems." She has yet to go (or be sent) to the mountains, but she has read a lot and has on her classroom walls a lot of pictures and some maps and a list of products and industries and natural resources and state flowers and state mottoes and state capitals. So, Peter comes home and talks about "the

Appalachian region," and how it is an "area," and his father laughs and says this: "Most of the people on one side of Letcher County wouldn't waste their time trying to get to the other side, and why should they? They are settled down where they have lived for a long time—and if they are going to leave and suffer the heartache of moving, then they'd as soon go all the way to California than try another part of the county, or the region, like the teacher calls it. Why she talks about a 'region' I don't know. There are a lot of people in Letcher County who think the county should be divided up, never mind called part of a region."

Peter doesn't want to go back and report to the teacher what his father has said. He senses his father's despair and cynicism and not too friendly amusement, but he also senses that the teacher may be onto something, or those from whom she has drawn her information might be—even if his father may *also* be onto something. I mean to say that the boy gains from his teacher a picture of what a nation must do to help a beleaguered stretch of territory, whose hills and valleys and waterways are beautiful, whose people love what they consider to be almost sacredly theirs; but he also hears from his father the native's just disdain for an outsider's unblinking acceptance of various surveys and studies and analyses that look convincing on paper but ignore things a graph or a chart or a map simply cannot convey. In the words of a nine-year-old boy named Peter, a city boy and a mountaineer's son: "I hear my father talk, and my mother, and when we go home my grandmother and my uncle and aunt, and I have a cousin—his name is Peter, too—and he was in the Air Force, only now he's out. They say there's nothing wrong with where they are, and all they need is work. They say if they're going to be told they should move across the county and halfway across the state to make a living, then they'll move all right, and we'd better find a place in our building for them, because there's no point in halfway moving; you move or you don't, and the bigger the city the better, if it's going to come to that.

"My kin don't want to live in the city, and I know they wouldn't like it in a big city. They might like it better in a town someplace in Letcher County or Harlan County or Perry County. But they say once they're pushed out, they'll quit altogether. My uncle says that he'd like to see anyone come up the creek and try to tell him to move on down some new road they've built to a place over yonder. The man would have some guns trained on him, and no fooling. Like my uncle says: we don't get pushed too easy, no sir, and if they say they're out to help us, let them prove it— because we've heard a lot of that 'help' promised before. That's the way he talks, and I was going to tell our teacher what he says after I came back from the creek a few weeks ago, but I didn't. I think the teacher is a good lady, and I told my daddy, she's always talking about us, about our people. Daddy said that's nice to hear."

Peter and his father do a lot of talking about their people, and they do so on a porch. Not that the porch is what they would like it to be, wide and just above the ground and leading to some rocky pastureland with a vegetable garden and some flowers at the edge to set things off, and then the woods. Not that the porch has a swing on it which goes back and forth, a swing boys like Peter can rush at, jump on, fight for control over, and then exhausted at last, simply lie upon and enjoy. And not that the porch has years and years of initials cut into it and maybe a tire or two and maybe a cabinet or a gun and maybe an old license plate—all just standing there or lying around. No, the porch is a "city porch"—which is what Peter knows to call it. But something is better than nothing, the boy has heard his father say and now reminds me. At least we can sit there, he tells me. Sitting means a lot to Peter's family. Though Peter himself is as active and energetic as other nine-year-old boys are, he does like to sit down on a chair on the porch and talk, rather as his father does. And, like his father, he can whittle away at a piece of wood, even aimlessly whittle the wood down to a mass of chips.

The porch is small and old. The building is four stories tall and is of wood and the porches face a backyard which is all cracked cement and contains barrels and two old and abandoned cars. There are eight apartments in the building, four on one side and four on the other. Open stairs serve the back part of the building and there are two rear doors on each floor. The doors open up on the porch and the porches connect, or it can be said that two families share one porch. The fact is that there used to be wooden fences of sorts to give each tenant family at least a semblance of privacy outdoors, but long ago those partitions were pushed down or collapsed. Indeed, the porches look as if they might collapse; they seem almost to hang loosely from the building proper. For several years the city has been planning to tear down a whole neighborhood of such buildings but has not done so. Peter, who sometimes says he might one day want to be a carpenter, or a builder who puts up "good buildings and skyscrapers, too" can talk about the building he knows best this way: "The man who built this building built a hundred others like it, I think. Every house on the street is the same. The teacher told us a lot of people have come through here before us—all different kinds, she says. A girl asked her if some of the buildings here were built during the American Revolution, when George Washington was President. The teacher thought the girl was being fresh, but she wasn't at all. She told the teacher she was sorry, but she heard her mother say the buildings must have been built hundreds of years ago, and she didn't know if her mother was correct and how long ago they were actually built, so she thought she'd ask the teacher. The teacher said she didn't know either, but it was a long, long time."

The building should indeed be torn down. It is a dangerous building, as the city's fire department has publicly stated. The wiring is old. The coal-burning furnace is old and not always reliable. The radiators are old and often useless. The stoves are old gas ranges that go back thirty or forty years. The hall is unlighted, hence dark, and its stairs are hazardous to climb: a plank is missing here, a section of the banister is gone a little further on. One imagines the things that can happen to small children negotiating their way past those empty spaces to the side of the steps. Since Peter's family has rented an apartment in that building, one child has fallen down, fallen through, properly speaking, and been seriously hurt. Another child did so, but only from half a flight up, and was "only" bruised and frightened. Every day mothers worry about recurrences, but then, as Peter's mother put it: "There's so much to worry about in this world; one thing pushes out another from your mind."

Here are some of the competing worries her mind must contend with: the water that leaks into her apartment from the one above; the cock-roaches and mice and rats that get into the building and try to get into her apartment, however tidy she is; the stench from the basement that comes up a well the height of the building and works its way into each room of the entire house; the mosquitoes and flies that come in during the summer when the windows have to be opened but screens are not available; the flat roof of the building high over the street, to which children have access through an open staircase; garbage, at best irregularly collected, and so always visible from her kitchen window; broken glass all over that neighborhood, on every stretch of sidewalk; the black, sooty smoke that the chimneys emit, the result of old, thoroughly inadequate heating systems. Still, the building is home to her, and I know full well that Peter's mother and father would not like me to recite such a litany of complaints. They make their objections infrequently and one at a time, and not with great bursts of indignation. They pride themselves on their ability to see the bright side of life, even though at heart they feel (and admit to feeling) discouraged.

And Peter—he is their son. He knows that there are other, better places to live; he has traveled enough, within the city and back and forth from Hot Spot, to have a clear idea how it is possible for many Americans to live. Still, his parents live where they do, and he loves them and they love him and that is that—all of which he has his own way of declaring: "I like to sit here on the porch and do my carving and sometimes I bring pebbles up here and see how far I can throw them. My daddy and I have a contest: the one who throws the farthest can throw one more as a bonus, then we throw against each other again and the guy who gets rid of his pebbles first wins. We get the pebbles from the roof—it's covered with them. My mother says she doesn't believe there's anything else on that roof but pebbles, but Daddy and I try to tell her there's black tar and the wood underneath. In the summer the whole building roasts because of the flat roof, and when it rains a big puddle collects in the middle and then it leaks through. I'm not supposed to go up there, and I don't really go anymore. It's no fun going after you've been there a hundred times. You see the same thing from our porch. You see the other buildings. My sister and I count the chimneys. We count the television aerials. We count the skylights, then we count how many are broken and how many have the glass unbroken. My sister said if you imagine hard enough, you can turn all the roof and the chimneys and the aerials into a big forest, and we're here sitting and looking out at the trees, and we rock in Daddy's rocking chair."

That rocking chair was brought up from Hot Spot, from the house up the creek. Peter claims it when his father is not around. Lately, as Peter's young brother has become older and more assertive and more demanding and more fearless and combative, he offers Peter real competition, and their fights over the father's chair go on and on. During warm weather, there are three other chairs on that porch. Often I have sat on one of the three chairs and talked with Peter. On a card table his mother provides we have been able to draw and paint, which the boy says he cannot do well, but enjoys doing. As we have worked he has recalled an uncle, a great-uncle actually, who can draw just about anything, it seems, and who used to draw pictures for Peter when he was three or four—before the family moved away. Peter is not sure of such things—of exactly how old he was when he first started living in the city. He asks me how anyone can be sure. A person can't remember exactly, he tells me, when it's over a year or two in the past that one is going back to, searching for as best he can. Do I agree with that? More or less, I say and hedge. I fumble for a remark that will reassure him and allow my nervous, well-informed mind to relax. Finally, I tell Peter that two or three years back is for him a long, long time; that it's the equivalent in my life of about ten years. He tells me that he sees what I mean, but then I am not sure I do mysef. That is to say, I really don't know whether his forgetfulness is the same as an older person's. His older sister remembers very accurately things that happened to her when she was three or four—so the mother maintains. Peter, on the other hand, was always hazy when it came to remembering details, his mother will say—and then go on to give her explanation of why some people, regardless of age, retain the details of their various experiences right up in the front of their minds, so to speak, while others let almost as much as they can sink into a "background" that we call "distant memory." Very briefly: "The good Lord made us all different. You'll meet people who remember everything and people who remember practically nothing. I believe He has to make sure we don't all turn out the same in our thinking. It would be no good, that way."

I think Peter is inward, likes to think about, to savor, what is on his mind, and therefore he has more and more each year to push back and *not* think about. As a very young child he was called "dreamy" by his mother. Now the boy is described as liking to be "by himself" sometimes, but not all the time by any means. He simply likes to use his slingshot by himself and sit on the porch in his father's chair by himself and, when back home on a visit, go exploring by himself. He has friends. He is quite open and charming with his sisters. He looks up to his father and heeds his mother's words and is considered polite and "responsive" by his teacher—but, again, he likes to be alone upon occasion, and when he talks about such a preference, he does so indirectly but with great candor and simplicity: "When I go back to our family in Hot Spot I ask my daddy if I can take off. He says yes, because I know the woods all right. So I find a path and I'm gone. I whistle and try to fool the birds. I chase a butterfly and let it go. I chase a toad and let it go. The turtles are too slow. They think all they have to do is poke their head inside and they're safe. Then I'll pick them up and they start peeking, just at the wrong time. You can hear the squirrels running out of your way, just ahead of your steps. You can hear the birds warning each other, and even when you stop and don't make a move or a sound for as long as you can stand it, they seem to know you're still there. When I come to a clearing I lie down and I can see the moon sometimes, as well as the sun in the sky if it's clear. There are mosquitoes. There are grasshoppers. There are ants crawling up your leg, but it's no use moving, because they'll follow you. The bees are looking for honey—all of a sudden they smell me! I can see the bigger birds circling; then they land on a tree and look right at me. They're just keeping their eyes open, my daddy says. And suddenly, before you know it, a pheasant takes off into the sky, or a rabbit goes so fast you'd think he was shot out of a gun. My daddy used to take me through the woods, and he'd tell me to soak up everything, so when we left for the city I'd have it all to recollect. Now I go out by myself; like he says, it's a plenty big change from what we have around us in the building."

I mentioned that Peter and I have done some drawing and painting. Peter in general likes to draw animals, animals he has seen in books. He and his classmates were taken by his teacher, to the zoo, and for weeks afterwards I saw Peter's version of an elephant or a lion or a zebra. Sometimes Peter draws a turtle or a rabbit and lets me know the obvious, that no such animals are going to be found around "the building." Sometimes Peter draws his dog, his family's dog, Wally. And through Wally I hear about life in the hills and life in the cities: "My father says he's glad Wally is old. When we came here Wally was four or five. He's a little older than me. They weren't going to take him with us. My mother says my father was near tears at the thought of bringing him and near tears at the thought of leaving him behind. She says she heard my father trying to say good-bye to Wally. He was talking to him. He was saying that we'd be coming back and we'd be seeing him, especially around holidays, when we always try to have something special for Wally. Then he started crying, and my mother says Wally did, too; he just cried the same as Daddy did— and I guess my mother couldn't stand it any more. She says she almost started crying herself, but then she got as mad as she could be, and she came out from hiding and told both of them, my father and Wally, to stop —because Wally was coming up with us to the city and that was all there was to it.

"On the way up, though, Daddy kept changing his mind. He's told me a lot of times how he reasoned things. He figured Wally was no pup, no baby; since he was five or so, he'd lived nearly half his life. He figured Wally would miss us as much as we'd miss him, even if a lot of our kin are still back there, and the house won't be empty, not with my grandmother and aunt and uncle and cousins there, and planning never to leave, come what may. He figured Wally might forget us, and he'd sure be better off running up and down the creek and through the woods and across the meadow over to the rocky part of the hill, where he'd all the time bark and bark at something, and we'd never know what it was. But we'd never forget Wally, and Daddy said Wally was our dog, and we were going to keep him, and we did. I don't remember too much of the first trip we made up here; I was a little kid then. But I can remember Daddy talking with Wally, and I can remember once he stopped the car, and he told Wally to go and have a good run for himself, because the field next to the road might be the last one he'd be running over in a long time. Then he told us kids to go out and do the same, because we weren't any different from Wally, he said—we'd have to get used to the city.

"I think Wally doesn't mind the city too much; he'd rather be back home, but he's old now, and mostly he just lies around the house and sleeps. He doesn't hear very good. He doesn't see very good either. But every time we go back home he turns into a puppy, practically. His tail starts going, the nearer we get to Hot Spot, and then by the time we're at the turnoff from the road and going up the creek, Wally is crying for us please, please to stop the car—just for a second to let him out—even if we have to drive a little further on. We do, and then he's off. Look at him go, my daddy will say, and we all watch. Then he seems to be away so long that we take to worrying; maybe he's forgotten where the cabin is, or maybe the sudden run was too much for him at his age. But he always shows up and then he takes a good long sleep for himself. And you know what? He sleeps better. He doesn't snore so much, and he doesn't have a lot of bad dreams, and he doesn't wake up and cross the room, and fall asleep, and then five minutes later wake up and cross the room—and the same old thing over and over again. He just falls down on that floor near the fireplace, where he used to sleep when he was a puppy, and he's dead to the whole world—except if we get some cooking going. Then his nose wakes him up, and he's after us, staring and begging in the way he looks at you, but not jumping or whining, because we won't let him do that."

Peter worries about Wally's last moments. He wishes the dog would die when they are back home and not in the city, in the building. He feels certain Wally somehow would be happier that way. He sees other dogs, city dogs, who don't at all seem unhappy with their lot—but he knows why: they have never known anything better. As for Peter himself, he is like his father; unlike old Wally, a boy of nine has a lot of curiosity and enthusiasm, and so can find his way all over a neighborhood. He can see men standing in front of houses or sitting on stairs and talking. He can see men going in a bar for a beer or two. He can turn an old abandoned car into a hut, a cave, a hiding place, or he can sit there in that car and hold the steering wheel and imagine himself driving south, south on the interstate, south across the Ohio River, south on the interstate again, and then at last south down the "regular road" to the creek—and now *on* with the gas and *up, up, up* to the cabin. Peter lets it be known in no uncertain terms that one day *he* will do the driving back to the hills. He already knows a good deal about automobiles, and he knows the way back, from the streets he has to take in order to get out of the city itself to the various turnoffs on those interstate highways. He may not have actually driven a car, but his father has taught him what does what and even taught him a lot about motors and how to change oil and where the battery is and what spark plugs are and where the wires from the windshield wiper go. And if I needed proof of Peter's road knowledge, I got it once when I traveled with the family, went "back home," and heard the boy tell his father each turn to make. They were having a fine time, the driver waiting for his in-structions and the boy utterly annoyed by the long, long waits on those interstate highways—until, again, he could let his father know exactly where to go and what to do.

Once Peter told me he'd draw the whole trip for me. I couldn't for the life of me figure out how he was going to do that, but I soon found out. He started with the porch, and I thought he would get completely taken up by that particular "scene," which meant we'd never get out and into the countryside. But he knew what he was going to do—make a road map of sorts. Suddenly he just took us right out and had us on the main highway— and now he could accelerate things, emphasize the crucial twists and turns of direction, and indicate to me not the long distance involved, the miles and miles of the same thing, but the changes of pace he knew so well. And when we did at last arrive, there was no mistaking it: the hills, the trees, water, the grass, the bushes, the birds. Then he had something to tell me. (I often asked him, after he drew, what was going on: if people were being portrayed, I might ask what they were doing, and if an animal or a bird appeared, where they lived or came from.) Did I know, he wondered, where those birds go in the winter? No, I didn't. Well, they go South, perhaps to Texas or even Mexico. Then in the spring they start coming North again, but they stop in Kentucky. Why should they go any farther, after all? Why should they go North to all those cities in Ohio and Illinois and Michigan?

I told Peter what he knew anyway, that birds can be found all over those three states and into Canada, come summer. Yes, that is so, but not in the cities. All he has even seen are pigeons and a few sparrows, and only at the playground and at school, and only there because they're probably on their way to someplace and the peanuts "draw them down." As we talked some more he admitted that birds may live in a big city, some of them, though in nowhere near the numbers a place like Hot Spot attracts. We agreed on that, and then he proceeded to remind me in the course of an afternoon how smart birds are, how many things they can do that we cannot: they can build a home on a thin branch of any tree anyplace; they can fly all over, move around at will; they can seek out the best places, go South, come North, avoid extremes of weather; on the ground they can hop and skip; they can sing enviably, soar into the heavens, and dive down at high speeds; they can find food almost anywhere; they can escape all sorts of predators with a flap of their wings; they can keep good company, cross the country in the most amazing formations, warn one another of impending danger, get up easily and automatically at the first sign of morning, and go to sleep safely and mysteriously in the stillness of early evening. They look so attractive, too; they have bright colors, a fine and decorative set of clothes on them, as it were. They are cheerful, and they inspire cheer in others, maybe envy.

I am not saying that Peter said all of that as I just have done—one, two, three. He has more patience, likes to wander through a conversation, let his ideas slowly emerge, then repeat them, then drop the whole subject, then come back again with a thought, and be surprised himself at what he has said. At the end of that particular afternoon—an afternoon in which I had seen a road map drawn and heard birds acclaimed—the boy brought up Wally's limited future and wondered out loud what his own future held in store for him: "My little brother asked my father the other day if there was anyone luckier than Wally, because all Wally did was eat and sleep and, at least in the city, take a short walk. Daddy said Wally was

Wally, and we're not him. Think of all the things we can do he can't do. He asked us to start mentioning them. So, I said drive, and my brother said ride a bike, and I said carve wood and play music on the guitar and whistle—and then my brother started talking about how he can climb a tree, and Wally can't, and he can pick up a ball and throw it, and all Wally can do is push it with his nose, and then go chasing after it." And before I left we talked for a few minutes about giraffes, and how tall they are, and how they can eat off trees, according to the books Peter has seen in school, but they have trouble bending; and of course with fish, it's great the way they swim, but on land they're dead almost immediately.

So it goes. We can only be what we are. Peter's father has given Peter and his brother that message in many ways and upon many occasions, something all parents have to do—as their children grow up and notice who can do what, and who cannot possibly do what, and who has what and who lacks what, and who goes where and who stays put and who does move around, but only so far. Certainly Peter has no illusions; he knows very well that his father was a coal miner, that he was hurt down in the mines, that he left Kentucky reluctantly, that he looks back upon his life with mixed bitterness and (from the distance of a northern city) a good deal of nostalgia. Peter also knows that his own prospects are better than his father's—maybe. Here is how the boy talks about his future: "I won't work in a mine, I know that. Daddy says to stay in school, and I might get a good job if I go all the way through. I don't know if I will or I won't Sometimes Daddy says he may just drive us all back for keeps, and we'll take our chances from day to day. He says there's no room up here for us; the people don't like a man who's from the mountains, and he's honest, and all he wants is a good job and a fair day's pay. A lot of the older kids on the blocks, they say the best thing is to go into the Army. That way you have good food and good lodgings and good uniforms, and they'll send you all over the world, and otherwise you'd never get to see so many places. My mother says that when the time comes, I'll know what I want to do. Meanwhile, she says I should do the best I can, from the start of the day to the end of the day."

He does just that. He is up early. They live in a four-room flat, so the children are very much together in a room. They are awakened by their mother, who needs no alarm, has no alarm to awaken her. They get dressed, usually in the very same clothes they wore the day before, and help their mother put together breakfast—cereal, hot or cold depending on the time of year, and half milk, half tea, or coffee with less milk, about a quarter of a cup. Eggs and bacon are expensive and served for a Sunday, a birthday, a holiday. The children don't drink orange juice, and their mother can't really stand the sight of it herself, so any thoughts a visitor has about vitamin C and the need the children have for a balanced diet meet up with a family's firm preferences. Then comes school: the approaching bus, the ride, the hours in that classroom, the moments of recess outside in the yard, the time spent in the cafeteria, and soon enough it is time to go home: board the bus, sit and look out at those streets lined by old buildings, most of them wood, some brick, all inhabited by people "from Appalachia," as Peter has heard his teacher mention. Then comes play on the streets, play near the roof, perhaps on it (*that* stoutly denied, if a parent should inquire) and always, every day, a bout of sitting on the front stairs of the buildings or sitting on the porch in the back of the building—and whittling and maybe (in warm weather) listening to the country music which comes out of the windows of various apartments. By six Peter hears his name called, or one of his sisters comes to fetch him and bring him back for supper: a homemade soup, bread, potatoes, beans, gravy and sometimes chicken, sometimes pork. I have heard Peter's father say, upon completion of such a meal: "It's good, eating regular and every day and until you're not hungry any more." Peter hears the words and says yes to himself. Later, he watches television, sees cowboys riding, thinks *that's* good country, too—not like Hot Spot and Letcher County and Kentucky and the "region" called Appalachia, but also not the city, not the place where one eats regularly but dreams of another kind of life. Or, as Peter puts it: "Out West, the cowboys never left the ranches, and they really like their jobs, I think."

In fact the city has been kind to Peter's family, and perhaps as the boy grows up, or certainly as *his* son grows up, the city may seem less a temporary necessity and more a land full of its own pleasures and adventures and promises. I suppose it all depends on what the city itself will become like—on whether our cities ever become anything different for boys like Peter. I sometimes think that Peter's mind is where the changes will have to take place: he will have to give up dreaming of Hot Spot and dig in as one more full-time member of something called a metropolis. That he do so is more "realistic," and "practical," and even a matter of life and death, as the older Peter says often enough, perhaps to justify his day-to-day life, perhaps to squelch any silly, "romantic" thoughts or "fantasies" he may find pressing upon him. In any event, on behalf of both young Peters, the Peter who knows alleys and the Peter who sits on those porches, I hear prayers, the prayers of mothers. I hear the same emphatic, passionate, urgent words, too. I hear: Bless the boy, my God. I hear: Smile upon the boy, dear God. I hear: Find him a life, please do, Lord. I hear: Love him and keep him. And yes—upon many occasions God, the Lord, Christ Almighty are left out, maybe accidentally, or maybe because somewhere in their minds the mothers of such boys know that before the New Jerusalem arrives there is one day after another ahead for a child of nine, one day after another in the cities we now have, in the world we now have.

Perhaps on occasion such women can be too religious to call directly upon any authority, secular or divine, for the kind of help they know their children need, or perhaps they know better than to do so. Perhaps when their calls to God are spoken, they are really calls to themselves, a notice and a warning they give themselves that somehow they will have to struggle along and survive on their own, as has always been the case for people like them.